third edition

Cognitive Development

WITHDRAWN

JOHN H. FLAVELL
Stanford University

PATRICIA H. MILLER
University of Florida

SCOTT A. MILLER
University of Florida

Prentice-Hall International, Inc.

ISBN 0-13-034356-0

To Ellie, Beth, Jim, Ralph, Ben, Catherine, Erica, and Kevin

 © 1993, 1985, 1977 by Prentice-Hall, Inc.
A Simon & Schuster Company
Englewood Cliffs, New Jersey 07632

Printed in the United States of America

10 9 8 7 6 5 4 3 2

ISBN 0-13-034356-0

PRENTICE-HALL INTERNATIONAL (UK) LIMITED, *London*
PRENTICE-HALL OF AUSTRALIA PTY. LIMITED, *Sydney*
PRENTICE-HALL CANADA INC., *Toronto*
PRENTICE-HALL HISPANOAMERICANA, S.A., *Mexico*
PRENTICE-HALL OF INDIA PRIVATE LIMITED, *New Delhi*
PRENTICE-HALL OF JAPAN, INC., *Tokyo*
SIMON & SCHUSTER ASIA PTE. LTD., *Singapore*
EDITORIA PRENTICE-HALL DO BRASIL LTDA., *Rio de Janeiro*
PRENTICE-HALL, *Englewood Cliffs, New Jersey*

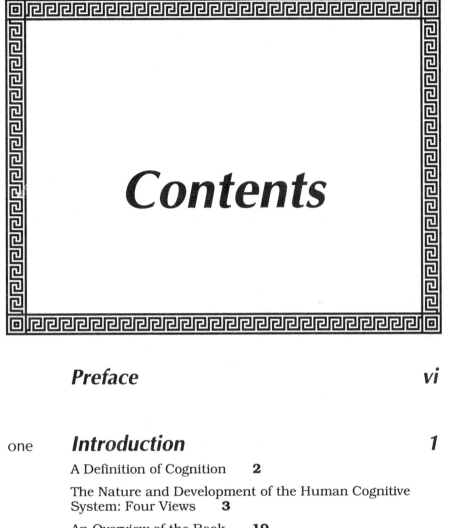

Contents

Preface

The intended audience for this book is anyone who has reason to read about human cognitive development. We hope and expect that it will be comprehensible and interesting to readers with a very wide range of backgrounds: people interested in the topic but with little or no background in psychology; undergraduate and graduate students in general, developmental, cognitive, educational, and perhaps social psychology, various fields of education, and possibly other social sciences; perhaps even postdoctoral professionals in these areas. It certainly should be suitable as a text for either an undergraduate or a graduate course.

Several things were done in hope of making the text useful to a wide variety of readers. Many references are cited in the text, especially secondary sources that would provide quick access to much of the primary research literature in an area. Some readers will find these quite useful; others obviously will not. On the other side, we have explained the meaning of most technical terms used, even those that people with only a little background in psychology might know. We have also tried to make the exposition straightforward and readable, and also perhaps a little lighter and less formal than textbooks sometimes are. We personally do not enjoy reading most textbooks, and therefore would like this one to be, if not actually enjoyable, at least not wholly unenjoyable.

This edition of the book differs from the second edition in a number of ways. Two authors were added—Patricia and Scott Miller. In addition, the text was thoroughly updated. The chapters undergoing the most change were Chapters 1 (Introduction), 2 (Infancy), and 3 (Early Childhood). The introductory chapter now includes an overview of contemporary theories of cognitive development. The enlarged infancy and early-childhood chapters reflect the dramatic surge of research in these areas in recent years. The chapter on infancy now presents a more

A DEFINITION OF COGNITION

The really interesting concepts of this world have the nasty habit of avoiding our most determined attempts to pin them down, to make them say something definite and make them stick to it. Their meanings perversely remain multiple, ambiguous, imprecise, and above all unstable and open—open to argument and disagreement, to sometimes drastic reformulation and redefinition, and to the introduction of new and often unsettling concept instances and examples. It is perhaps not a bad thing that our prize concepts have this kind of complexity and instability (some might call it richness and creativity). In any event, they do seem to have these properties, and therefore we would be wise not to expend too much of our time and energy trying to fix them in formal definition.

So it is with that concept called *cognition*, the development of which is the subject of this book. Obviously, it is important here to communicate some ideas and images about the nature of cognition, but it is neither possible nor desirable to define it and limit its meaning in any precise or inflexible fashion.

The traditional image of cognition tends to restrict it to the fancier, more unequivocally "intelligent" processes and products of the human mind. This image includes such higher-mental-processes types of psychological entities as knowledge, consciousness, intelligence, thinking, imagining, creating, generating plans and strategies, reasoning, inferring, problem solving, conceptualizing, classifying and relating, symbolizing, and perhaps fantasizing and dreaming. Although some of these activities would surely be credited to the psychological repertoires of other animals, they nonetheless have a decidedly human-mind ring to them.

While no contemporary psychologists would want to exclude any of these traditional components from the cognitive domain, they would feel it necessary to add some others. Certain components would have a somewhat humble, less purely cerebral-intellectual cast to them. Organized motor movements (especially in infants) and perception are two such components. As described in Chapter 2, children exhibit intelligent-looking patterns of motor and perceptual behavior before they can operate with symbols at all, let alone engage in syllogistic reasoning. It would seem arbitrary in the extreme to christen children "cognitive" only after they had achieved the ability to engage in the more exalted forms of cerebration. Imagery, memory, attention, and learning are other cases in point. Other components might look more social-psychological than the word *cognition* usually connotes. Instances here would include all varieties of social cognition (that is, cognition directed at the world of human rather than nonhuman objects) and the social-communicative versus private-cognitive uses of language.

Once embarked on this course of broadening and restructuring the domain beyond the classical *higher mental processes*, it is very difficult to decide where to stop. One is finally led to ask, what psychological processes can*not* be described as "cognitive" in some nontrivial sense, or do *not* implicate "cognition" to a significant degree? The answer is that mental processes habitually intrude themselves into virtually *all* human psychological processes and activities, and consequently there is no really principled, nonarbitrary place to stop. To be sure, this book says little about such noncognitive-sounding things as personality, aggression, sex-role development, and so on. There are many *practical* reasons for slighting these and other topics, such as space limitations, lack of an adequate data base in some cases, consideration for teachers' and readers' expectations about what a book with this title should contain, and sheer personal preferences. The point to be underscored,

integrated account of this subject, because much of the previous chapter on perception is incorporated into it. In keeping with recent trends in the field, the book has less emphasis on Piaget and his developmental-stages conception of cognitive growth, and more emphasis on information-processing, contextual, knowledge, theory-change, neo-Piagetian, and constraint approaches. We give special attention to new or rejuvenated areas, such as infants' surprisingly precocious cognitive competencies, toddlers' representational abilities, young children's theories of mind and concepts of natural kinds, the understanding of emotions, and biological or other kinds of constraints on cognitive development.

We want to express our thanks to Brian Ackerman, Psychology Dept., University of Delaware; Carolyn Shantz, Psychology Dept., Wayne State University; and Susan Carey, Brain and Cognitive Sciences, MIT, who offered suggestions for this edition. We also thank Darlene DeMarie-Dreblow, Psychology Dept., Muskingum College, and M. Jeffrey Farrar, Psychology Dept., University of Florida, who read and commented on single chapters. Also, several students at the University of Florida offered helpful suggestions: Derek E. Montgomery, James Probert, Marylynn Pfeiffer, Alison Suffield, and Joseph Beato. We also wish to thank Susan F. Brennan and June Sanns of Prentice-Hall, Inc., for their expert help in turning plans and manuscript into a book.

Introduction

however, is that there is no *principled* justification for excluding them. What you know and think (cognition) obviously interacts in a very substantial and significant way with the type of person you are (personality), to take but one example. Depending only upon the state of existing theory and empirical evidence, a longer or shorter cognitive story could be told about virtually any phenomenon mentioned in an introductory psychology textbook. We only have a single head, after all, and it is firmly attached to the rest of the body.

The need for a broad and complex conception of cognition also lies in the complex interweaving of the various aspects of cognition in the tapestry of actual, real-time cognitive functioning. Each process plays a vital role in the operation and development of each other process, affecting it and being affected by it. This idea of mutual, two-way interactions among cognitive processes is an exceedingly important one. What you know affects and is affected by how you perceive; how you conceptualize or classify things influences the way you reason about them, and vice versa; and so on and on. If we pretend for purposes of psychological analysis that the human mind is a machine or device that carries out a variety of mental operations to achieve a variety of mental products, the present argument would be that the mind is a very highly organized device, one whose numerous "parts" are richly interconnected to one another. It is not a collection or aggregate of unrelated cognitive components, but rather a complexly organized *system* of interacting components. It would be tedious to keep pointing out these interactions throughout the book, but it would be well to bear in mind that they are ubiquitous in cognitive functioning.

THE NATURE AND DEVELOPMENT OF THE HUMAN COGNITIVE SYSTEM: FOUR VIEWS

At present there are four main views of the nature and development of cognition. The most encompassing is that of the great Swiss psychologist Jean Piaget. The others are the information-processing, neo-Piagetian, and contextual approaches. These views are by no means incompatible, and many contemporary psychologists favor some blend of them. Piaget's theory will be described first because much of the research presented in Chapters 2 to 4 flowed from his work or was done in reaction to his work. The information-processing approach stimulated much of the work described in Chapter 6, the chapter on memory, and the neo-Piagetian and contextual approaches emerge from time to time throughout the book.

It is beyond the scope of this text to provide a satisfactory account of these four approaches. Yet, it is important to enter into each chapter with some sense of the general visions that stimulated the research in that chapter. A reasonable compromise is to direct readers to further reading on each approach and to limit the account here to one central aspect of each theory, namely, processes of cognitive change. For general sources that cover several of the approaches see P. H. Miller (in press) and Vasta (1989). Sources specific to each approach will appear in each section.

Each approach addresses the two main questions of cognitive development. First, what does children's thinking look like at various points throughout development (the description question)? Second, how does this development come about (the explanation question)? Because the question of description makes up the bulk of the other chapters, it seems appropriate to focus here on the question of the processes underlying cognitive change (see also Chapter 8). The two questions are not independent, of course. For example, Piaget's search for broad, abstract, complex cognitive structures led him to processes that would keep the entire cognitive system in balance.

Jean Piaget

Jean Piaget's contributions to our knowledge of cognitive development have been nothing short of stupendous, both quantitatively and qualitatively. Moreover, his ideas about cognitive growth are often very complex and difficult to grasp, even when presented as an integrated whole, at length and in full detail. Piaget's ideas are particularly prone to distortion, oversimplification, and general misunderstanding when one tries to integrate brief summaries of them within a more general narrative about the field, such as this book aims to be. That is, the danger of misunderstanding is very great when the ideas are presented briefly and discontinuously, one set of ideas at one point in the narrative and another set at a later point. A reasonable conclusion from these facts is that, unless readers do some supplementary reading (e.g., Beilin, 1989, 1992; Chapman, 1988; Flavell, 1963; Ginsburg & Opper, 1988; P. H. Miller, in press; Piaget, 1970a), they may be destined to mislearn at least some aspects of Piaget's theory in the course of (we hope) learning something interesting and substantive about cognitive development in general.

ASSIMILATION-ACCOMMODATION AS A MODEL OF COGNITIVE FUNCTIONING. Piaget viewed human cognition as a specific form of biological adaptation of a complex organism to a complex environment. The cognitive system he envisaged is, however, an extremely active one. That is, it actively selects and interprets environmental information as it constructs its own knowledge. It does not passively copy the information just as it is presented to the senses. While of course taking account of the structure of the environment during knowledge seeking, the Piagetian mind always reconstrues and reinterprets that environment to make it fit in with its own existing mental framework. Thus, the mind neither copies the world, passively accepting it as a ready-made given, nor does it ignore the world, autistically creating a private mental conception of it out of whole cloth. Rather, the mind builds its knowledge structures by taking external data and interpreting them, transforming them, and reorganizing them. It therefore does indeed meet the environment in the process of constructing its knowledge, and consequently that knowledge is to a degree "realistic" or adaptive for the organism. However, Piaget made much of the idea that the mind meets the environment in an extremely active, self-directed way—meets it more than half way, as it were.

Piaget's conceptions of how the cognitive system interacts with the outside world may become clearer if we examine his concept of *adaptation* more closely. Cognition, like other forms of biological adaptation, always exhibits two simultaneous and complementary aspects, which Piaget called *assimilation* and *accommodation*. While it is convenient to talk about them as if they were distinct and separate cognitive activities, it must be kept in mind that they are two indissociable aspects of the same basic adaptational process—two sides of the same cognitive coin. Assimilation essentially means applying what you already know. You interpret or construe external objects and events in terms of your own presently available and favored ways of thinking about things. The young child who pretends that a chip of wood is a boat is, in Piaget's terms, "assimilating" the wood chip to his mental concept of boat. He incorporates the object within the entire structure of his knowledge of boats. Accommodation roughly means adjusting your knowledge in response to the special characteristics of an object or event. You notice and take cognitive account of the various real properties and relationships among properties of external objects and events. You become aware of the structural attributes of environmental data. The little girl who painstakingly imitates her father's gestures is "accommodating" or adjusting her mental apparatus (and thence, her motor gestures) to the fine detail of her father's behavior. Assimilation, therefore, refers to the process of adapting external stimuli to one's own internal mental structures whereas accommodation refers to the converse or complementary process of adapting these mental structures to the structure of these same stimuli. In the more obviously biological adaptation of ingestion-digestion of food, organisms simultaneously accommodate to the particular structure of the food (chew hard or easy, digest with the help of this enzyme or that, depending upon what the food is) and assimilate the food to their own physical structures (transform its appearance, convert it into energy, etc.). Similarly, in cognitive adaptations we can say that individuals simultaneously accommodate to the particular structures of the objects of their cognitions and assimilate those objects to their own cognitive structures.

Another example may show the extreme interdependence or indissociability of assimilation and accommodation, the sense in which they really are but two aspects of the same cognitive process. Suppose someone shows you a symmetrical blot of ink on a piece of paper, asks you what it reminds you of, and hears you say that it resembles a bat. Piaget's theory would say that you had cognitively accommodated to certain physical features of the blot and had used these as the basis for assimilating the blot to your internal concept of a bat. It is important to recognize that you did not merely accommodate to an external stimulus; that is, you did not just passively and mindlessly scan the blot and "discover" a bat "that was really there." Without a preexisting, well-elaborated conception of bat in your cognitive repertoire you would not have detected and integrated into a whole perceptual structure the particular constellation of blot features that you did. If the perceiver were a 1-year-old baby, with a belfry as yet devoid of bats, the perceiver would not process the structural information contained in the blot as you did and would not see it in the same way that you did because, in a manner of speaking, the perceiver's mind's eye would differ from yours. Thus, the kinds of assimilation that can occur are constrained by what you know. Similarly, in the opposite direction, the kinds of accommodations you can make are limited and constrained by what is there that could be assimilated. Obviously, if there were no bat-compatible physical properties in the blot to be accommodated to, there would be no assimilation of the blot to "bat"—that is, no perception of the blot as resembling that animal. If the inkblot took the form of a thin, straight line, for instance, there would naturally be no temptation to construe it as a bat (except perhaps of the baseball type).

In Piaget's view, therefore, in any cognitive encounter with the environment, assimilation and accommodation are of equal importance and must always occur together in a mutually dependent way. His model of the human cognitive system stresses the constant interaction or collaboration of the internal-cognitive with the external-environmental. Both factors make a vital contribution to the construction and deployment of knowledge. What you know already will greatly shape and constrain what environmental information you can detect and process, just as what you can detect and process will provide essential grist for the activation of present knowledge and the generation of new knowledge. To return to our first two examples, the wood chip likely would never metamorphize into a boat if it could not float and were not vaguely boat shaped, and the father's gestures could not be mimicked if the child could not assimilate them to motor action patterns she already possessed.

ASSIMILATION-ACCOMMODATION AS A MODEL OF COGNITIVE DEVELOPMENT. Thus Piaget's assimilation-accommodation model provides a valuable general conception of how people's cognitive systems might interact with their external environments. However, it also serves as a particularly useful vehicle for thinking about cognitive change—that is, about how the child's cognitive system might gradually evolve with maturation and experience. As we have seen, the model is well set up to give an essentially nondevelopmental, atemporal description of the mind-environment interaction, a description that holds true of any mind interacting with any environment at any given moment of time. The present point, however, is that it is equally well set up to describe how a mind might gradually develop and change its structure and content through repeated interactions with the milieu. Let us reconsider the wood-chip example to illustrate how the model might help us think about cognitive growth as well as about cognitive functioning.

In the situation we are imagining, a young child is playing with his toy boats in the bathtub. He suddenly notices in the corner of the soap dish a tiny fragment of wood from the broken pencil of a professor parent who always keeps a pencil nearby to jot down brilliant ideas. He picks it up, and after some deliberation (he has sailed many a boat, but nary a wood chip), gingerly places it in the water. Upon discovering that it floats, he adds it to his armada and emerges from his bath some time later a wiser as well as a cleaner child. The question is, in what way wiser, and through what sorts of wisdom-building (cognitive-developmental) processes?

Let us credit him, at the beginning of the bath, with a certain organized body of knowledge and certain abilities concerning the concrete, functional properties of the main entities in the situation (toy boats; small, nondescript objects; and water). He knows much about their characteristic look and feel and also something of their characteristic reactions to his actions upon them. We could say that he has already achieved a certain level of cognitive development with respect to this microdomain of his everyday world and, consequently, in Piaget's terms, he assimilates it and accommodates to it in specific ways that faithfully reflect this cognitive-developmental level. As a result of the new things he did and observed during this particular bath, however, that level will have changed ever so slightly, and consequently his future assimilations and accommodations within that microdomain will also have changed ever so slightly.

Let us suppose he has discovered (accommodation) some things he did not know before about what little pieces of wood can and cannot do (float rather than sink, make only a tiny splash when dropped in water, fail to move a big toy boat when they bump into it) and about what one can and cannot do with them (sail them, make them bob to the surface by holding them under water and then letting go, give them rides on top of other toy boats). Additionally, during this process of "minidevelopment," the content and structure of his mind and its capacity to construe and interpret this microdomain (assimilation) has also altered slightly. For example, his functional class of boat-like entities has now generalized to include at least certain small lightweight objects that do not closely resemble the more typical and familiar instances of this class (e.g., his toy boats). Subsequently, this small change in conceptual structure may permit him to construe (assimilate) still other kinds of objects as novel candidates for boat play. Moreover, the category of boat-like things may now be functionally subclassified for him into big, strong ones and small, weak ones, whereas it may previously have been a more or less homogeneous, undifferentiated class.

Thus, in the course of trying to accommodate to some hitherto unknown functional properties of a relatively unfamiliar sort of object, and of trying to assimilate the object and its properties to existing concepts and skills (trying to interpret them, make sense out of them, test out his repertoire of actions upon them), the child's mind has stretched just a little. And this stretching in turn broadens slightly his future assimilatory and accommodatory possibilities. By repeated assimilation of and accommodation to a given milieu, the cognitive system evolves slightly, which makes possible somewhat novel and different assimilations and accommodations. These latter changes then produce further small increments of mental growth. Thus, the dialectical process of development continues in this gradual, leg-over-leg fashion. Mind$_1$ (i.e., at some arbitrary point in its development) makes possible Assimilations$_1$ and Accommodations$_1$ (i.e., assimilations and accommodations of a particular, characteristically Mind$_1$ type), the informational products or feedback from which help to generate Mind$_2$. Mind$_2$ then makes possible Assimilations$_2$ and Accommodations$_2$, which again yield new information to provide some of the developmental raw material for Mind$_3$, and so on. Figure 1–1 illustrates the developmental process just described.

It is clear why such a development would be slow and gradual. Each Mind represents but a small, imperceptible departure from its immediate predecessor; it is rooted in, constrained by, and free to deviate but slightly from that predecessor. It is also clear, however, that a very, very substantial modification in the human cognitive system could emerge from year after year of daily, virtually continuous assimilation of milieu to mind and accommodation of mind to milieu. Thus Piaget's assimilation-accommodation model seems to have the right properties to characterize the childhood evolution of our cognitive system, as well as to characterize the functioning of that system during a particular interchange with the environment. The model makes childhood cognitive growth a logical outcome of repeated cognitive functioning, suggests that it should be slow and gradual, and allows for a considerable amount of total developmental change, given an entire childhood in which to accumulate. These are the very properties we think human cognitive development does in fact possess.

The gradual changes from assimilation and accommodation contribute to stage-like changes during development. Although in his later years Piaget deemphasized stages, much of the research for which he became known focused on the types of thinking that seemed to characterize, more or less, each epoch of development. The *sensorimotor* stage of infancy centers on forming simple sensorimotor representations of motor behaviors directed toward objects; for example,

FIGURE 1–1 An assimilation-accommodation model of cognitive growth. Mind$_1$ (i.e., of some given developmental level) is very gradually transformed into Mind$_2$ (i.e., of some arbitrarily higher level) as a consequence of correspondingly gradual changes in assimilatory and accommodatory possibilities. These changes in turn result from the continuous exercise of these mental functions in the course of adapting to the environment.

$\Rightarrow$ Mind$_1$ $\begin{cases} \text{Assimilation} \quad 1.0 \ldots 1.1 \ldots 1.2 \ldots \\ \text{Accommodation}_{1.0} \ldots 1.1 \ldots 1.2 \ldots \end{cases}$ $\Rightarrow$ Mind$_2$ $\begin{cases} \text{Assimilation} \quad 2.0 \ldots 2.1 \ldots 2.2 \ldots \\ \text{Accommodation}_{2.0} \ldots 2.1 \ldots 2.2 \ldots \end{cases}$ $\Rightarrow$

reaching and sucking. During the age span of approximately 2 to 7, *preoperational* children elaborate symbolic representations to form simple notions of causality and physical reality. The *concrete operational* years (approximately 7 to 11) are marked by more flexible mental manipulations, such as mentally reversing an event in the real world. Finally, *formal operational* thought (ages 11–15) displays the abstract, flexible, logical, scientific thinking found in adults (on good days).

It becomes apparent throughout this book, and from the other approaches described in this chapter, that Piaget's model can be criticized. The question of how the process of cognitive growth is best described and explained is still unsettled, but Piaget's theory has provided a good start. The following approaches do not negate Piaget's theory. Rather, they identify additional important aspects of development and/or provide a more specific account of Piagetian-like changes. In these ways they give us a fuller view of cognitive development. Although we will focus on the mechanisms of developmental change in each approach, it will also be necessary to describe some general aspects of the approaches to show the theoretical contexts in which these mechanisms operate.

Information Processing

The information-processing approach currently is a main strategy for the study of cognitive development. Fuller descriptions of this approach can be found in Siegler (1983b, 1991a), Klahr (1989, in press), P. H. Miller (in press), and Sternberg (1989b). The information-processing approach conceives of the human mind as a complex cognitive system, analogous in some ways to a digital computer. Like a computer, the system manipulates or processes information coming in from the environment or already stored within the system. It processes the information in a variety of ways: encoding, recoding, or decoding it; comparing or combining it with other information; storing it in memory or retrieving it from memory; bringing it into or out of focal attention or conscious awareness, and so on. As Siegler (1991a, p. 59) expresses it, "The quality of children's thinking at any age depends on what information they represent in a particular situation, how they operate on the information to achieve their goal, and how much information they can keep in mind at one time." Because of this heavy emphasis on cognitive processes, including their contribution to cognitive development, the decision in this chapter to focus on processes of cognitive change is particularly apt for this approach.

The information manipulated in the ways described above is of different types and is organized into units of various sizes and levels of complexity or abstraction. As to types, some of the information that is processed is more "declarative" in nature, consisting of knowledge of word meanings, facts, and the like. Other information is more "procedural" in type, consisting of knowledge of how to do various things. As to sizes and levels, some units of information are small and elementary, such as an encoded perceptual distinctive feature that helps the individual recognize a stimulus as a particular letter of the alphabet rather than as some other letter. Other units are organized wholes composed of elementary units and are at higher levels of abstraction, such as the meaning of the written sentence that contains the just-mentioned letter. More interesting higher-order units include the representations or knowledge structures described in Chapter 3—event knowledge, scripts, concepts, categories, and so on—as well as plans, strategies, and rules used in thinking and problem solving. Thus, an episode of information processing may involve retrieving or assembling a complex plan or strategy for solving a problem, attempting to execute that plan or strategy, revising it if it proves inadequate, and so forth. The mind is a well-populated and busy place indeed.

Why does the information-processing approach bother with all these details? It tries to provide an explicit, detailed understanding of what a child's cognitive system actually *does* when dealing with some task or problem, here and now or "on line." It attempts to answer such questions as: What does the system do first, at the onset of the information-processing episode? What is the second thing it does, and the third? Are some of these processing steps carried out simultaneously (*parallel processing*) rather than successively (*serial processing*)? Which ones? An episode of information processing is thus conceived as a kind of odyssey of information flow: Where does the information go first and what happens to it there? What is its next destination and adventure, and so on? The ideal goal of the information-processing approach is to achieve a model of cognitive processing in real time that is so precisely specified, explicit, and detailed that it can actually be run successfully as a working program on the computer. The model should also make specific predictions about how the child (and computer) would behave under specific task conditions or constraints, and in response to specific inputs. Some information-processing psychologists make heavy use of computers to simulate the hypothesized operations of the human cognitive system; they use computer simulation as a tool for testing and revising their information-processing models of thinking and even cognitive change (e.g., Klahr, Langley, & Neches, 1987). Others do not use it much or at all, but still share the information-processing approach's paramount goal of producing an explicit, testable model of here-and-now cognitive functioning and change.

All this data-crunching has its limits, however. There are severe limitations on the number of units of information that can be attended to and processed simultaneously, and cognitive operations such as encoding, comparing, and retrieving information from memory all require time to execute and usually have to be performed serially. It is therefore possible for a task to overload the system—that is, to impose processing demands that exceed its processing capacity. For instance, if a task required a subject to keep five units of information in mind at once and that particular subject was only capable of keeping four in mind, we would have a case of information-processing overload and the subject would likely fail the task (as well as suffer from a tired brain). As we shall see in the fuller discussion of capacity in Chapters 4 and 6, the concept of information-processing limitations is emerging as an important one in our thinking about cognitive development. Some of the most important developmental acquisitions are procedures, such as strategies, for overcoming limited capacity.

The developmental processes identified by the information-processing approach could be illustrated by many different types of information-processing-oriented work (e.g., Klahr & Siegler, 1978; Klahr & Wallace, 1976; Siegler & Jenkins, 1989; Sternberg & Nigro, 1980; Wallace, Klahr, & Bluff, 1987). Some of this work has reanalyzed cognitive-developmental phenomena initially discovered by Piaget, such as conservation and class inclusion, by using concepts and methods from the information-processing tradition (e.g., Klahr & Wallace, 1976). Robert Siegler's investigations of the developmental sequence in which children acquire various rules of reasoning (e.g., 1978, 1981, 1983b) represent a good example of how Piagetian cognitive growth can be studied profitably from an information-processing perspective. In Chapter 4 we will present his work on rules used in the balance-scale task. Other information-processing work has addressed topics given little attention by Piaget, for example, reading and writing (Siegler, 1991a), memory

(Schneider & Pressley, 1989), and individual differences (Bjorklund, 1989; Stern-berg, 1985). We now will use one such topic, strategies for adding, to represent current work from an information-processing point of view, as seen in Siegler's research (e.g., Siegler & Jenkins, 1989). As in much of his work, there are impor-tant implications for formal instruction.

One of the earliest mathematical operations that children acquire is adding. Children ingeniously come up with many ways to perform this simple operation. To add 3 and 5, a child could retrieve the previously memorized fact that the sum of these numbers is 8 or could begin with 1 and count up to 8. Alternatively, she could put up 3 fingers then 5 fingers and recognize them as 8 without counting. Or, in a long-honored tradition among school children, she could simply guess. Finally, an efficient strategy is to begin with the larger number and count up from there (5, 6, 7, 8)—a so-called *min strategy*, which is illustrated in the following protocol:

> E: How much is 6 + 3?
> L: (Long pause) Nine.
> E: OK, how did you know that?
> L: I think I said...I think I said...oops, um...I think he said...8 was 1 and...um...I mean 7 was 1, 8 was 2, 9 was 3.
> E: OK.
> L: Six and three are nine.
> E: How did you know to do that? Why didn't you count '1, 2, 3, 4, 5, 6, 7, 8, 9'? How come you did '6, 7, 8, 9'?
> L: Cause then you have to count all those numbers.
> E: OK, well how did you know you didn't have to count all of those numbers?
> L: Why didn't...well I don't have to if I don't want to (Siegler & Jenkins, 1989, p. 66).

The straight-memorization retrieval strategy is both fast and accurate. Howev-er, children have not memorized more difficult problems and thus must use slower strategies, like the min strategy, that have a high probability of giving the correct answer. When given a series of addition problems to solve, a child is likely to use most or all of these strategies. In fact, a child may use different strategies to solve exactly the same addition problem at different times. Children use multiple strategies not only on other kinds of math tasks, but also on tasks such as causal inference (Shultz, Fisher, Pratt, & Rulf, 1986), referential communication (Kahan & Richards, 1986), memory (McGilly & Siegler, 1989), and reading (Siegler & Campbell, 1989). In Siegler and Jenkins' (1989) view of cognitive change, during development several strategies vie for ascendancy, with the more efficient strategies very gradually becoming more frequent. Although children eventually replace poor strategies, they keep them for a surprisingly long time. And children vary tremendously in how fre-quently they use each type of strategy, how quickly they discover a new strategy, how aware they are of this discovery, and how readily they generalize it to other problems. Interestingly, the discovery of a new strategy does not seem to be stimulat-ed by failure. A child may continue to use a strategy that does not improve perfor-mance or stop using a strategy that does. Siegler and Jenkins suggest that the cogni-tive efficiency (little mental effort required), and even esthetic elegance ("My, what a lovely strategy") or novelty of a new strategy, may encourage children to use it.

Children can be encouraged to use the efficient min strategy more often by giving them "challenge problems" like 23 + 2 or 21 + 1. Surprisingly, they are not likely to continue to use the min strategy regularly right after they discover it. For example, the child who eventually used the min strategy on the highest percentage of trials of any subjects used it on only 7 of the 84 trials following her discovery of it. Siegler and Jenkins (1989) concluded that "discovery of a strategy often is only the first step toward understanding it....understanding often comes only with use" (p. 112). A final intriguing observation is that on the trial before the discovery of a new strategy and on the discovery trial, children exhibit odd behaviors. They take a long time to give the answer, become inarticulate, and verbally contradict their own behavior, as seen in a child who swore he never counted even though he clearly was heard counting. These "hemming and hawing" behaviors at the point of discovery may reflect increased cognitive activity that signals cognitive change (Siegler & Jenkins, 1989).

The procedures for assessing which strategy a child is using are characteristic of the information-processing approach. How long it takes a child to give an answer can provide evidence about how much time a processing step takes. Verbal reports and the types of adding errors made may reveal the plans and strategies the child used. And an analysis of changes in behavior over a large number of trials on a single problem suggests mechanisms of developmental change (Siegler & Crowley, 1991). In other information-processing research, inferences about functioning can be made from the subject's eye movements or from what the child remembers and forgets of the information presented. Other features of the information-processing approach in Siegler's example of research above include the encoding of the problem, procedures for manipulating the numbers, retrieval, capacity limitations, and a sequence of specific processing steps in real time. In essence, the researcher analytically decomposes tasks into their components and tries to infer what the cognitive system must do to deal adequately with each component.

Siegler's research addresses processes of change in children's strategic behavior. It also shows that, for the information-processing approach, changes in one's predominant strategy can stimulate other cognitive change. More specifically, strategy change often involves changes in which perceptual aspects of the task are encoded. An example is the change from encoding only the height of a container filled with a liquid to encoding both height and width when making a judgment of quantity. Cognitive change also can come from new combinations of the knowledge a child already has, as when children varied their strategies during a task in Siegler's research. Other very important processes of change are *automatization*—the "increasingly efficient execution of a procedure that frees mental resources for other purposes" (Siegler, 1991a, p. 337)—and related notions such as increased memory capacity and faster speed of processing a stimulus (e.g., identifying a written word) or applying a rule. Still other processes of change such as greater generalization to other tasks and the acquisition of more complex rules will be illustrated in Siegler's balance-scale problem in Chapter 4. Note that no stages are posited, though the change from one strategy to another or one rule to another is qualitative—a change in one's way of thinking about, or overall approach to, the task at hand.

Neo-Piagetian

The term *neo-Piagetian* refers to a group of researcher-theorists who generally share Piaget's view of development but, in addressing some of the problems with his theory, have adopted many notions from other approaches, particularly the information-processing approach. One such problem is Piaget's characterization of children as being in a particular stage. The problem is that children often do not act as though they belong in that stage. "Conservers" do not always conserve; "formal operational" thinkers often think very concretely. The particular materials, task, social context, and instructions appear to influence children's performance. Although Piaget never claimed that children would automatically apply their cognitive structure to all contexts, he never worked out a systematic account of this variability in behavior (but see Kreitler & Kreitler, 1989). A main goal of the neo-Piagetians is to fill this gap by drawing on processes of change from the information-processing camp. Children express a concept through processes such as attention, memory, and strategies in a particular environment, and children's limited short-term memory capacity constrains this expression. Both the unevenness of children's expression of their knowledge and their progression to more mature thinking reflect processes such as increased capacity, more efficient strategies, and more flexible attention. We will briefly describe the approach of one representative of this "school"—Robbie Case's theory. We will focus on his view of cognitive change, but readers are referred to his writings (e.g., Case, 1985, 1992) for other aspects of his theory such as stages and central conceptual structures. Although we have selected Case's work, we want to emphasize that other neo-Piagetians have also made important contributions (e.g., Demetriou & Efklides, 1987, in press; Fischer, 1980; Halford, in press; Pascual-Leone, 1970, 1987).

Case sees cognitive change as a process of dealing with more and more features of a problem. In a study illustrating this, he places an infant at one end of a wooden balance beam. He demonstrates for her that when the beam is moved down it rings a bell (see Figure 1–2). An infant initially may only be able visually to follow the beam moving down. Later, at 4 to 8 months, she can imitate the experimenter and gleefully make the beam move down and ring the bell, thereby coordinating two actions (visual tracking and hand reaching) rather than simply carrying out one activity in isolation. Stated differently, the infant can simultaneously represent two aspects of the task (movement of beam had an interesting effect, the beam was pushed just before this) and two goals (re-create the ringing, move her hand to the beam). Her coordination represents a qualitative shift to a new structure, much as combining oxygen and hydrogen produces a new product, water. Next, yet another element in the situation is incorporated as the infant, now 8 to 12 months of age, can imitate the experimenter and make the bell ring even when it is moved out of her immediate line of sight to the other end of the apparatus and above the beam. She still makes the bell ring by pushing the same end of the beam down, but must coordinate more information to do so. She may look back and forth between her end of the beam and the bell at the other end. And she may

FIGURE 1–2 Balance beam designed to investigate infant problem solving. Adapted from R. Case (1985), *Intellectual Development: Birth to Adulthood.* New York: Academic Press, p. 83. By permission.

Chapter One

even take a little wind-up before pushing. The next challenge comes from 12 to 18 months when the child has to push the beam up, rather than down, because the bell is beneath, rather than on top of, the opposite end of the beam. The ability to reverse a previous action was absent in younger infants who continued to push the beam down, and became more and more confused and angry at the beam that no longer would behave as it should. Case interprets the older child's success as evidence that the two units, action on the beam and the bell's ringing, are well enough differentiated and coordinated for her to realize their reversible relationship—the beam moves in the reverse direction at one end from the direction it is moved at the other end. Regarding processes of development, this behavior reflects the ability to establish subgoals (push beam) so as to obtain a final goal (ring bell). These types of activities—encompassing more components, differentiation, coordination, setting subgoals—are repeated as the child develops.

Case has tested this model of cognitive change in a variety of content areas, such as (a) judgments about the size of an object's shadow on a screen as a function of the distance and size of the object, (b) the relative happiness of a child at his birthday party as a function of the number of marbles he wanted for a present and how many he received, and (c) the amount of reward deserved as a function of the number of objects made and the number of days worked. In fact, when children aged 4 to 10 engaged in these tasks, performance improved with increasing age but there were no significant differences among the scores on these tasks at any age (Case, 1985). This suggests that these tasks with different content reflect the same underlying structure. Other examples of Case's work include an amazing variety of intellectual skills: manipulating other people's feelings, story telling, eating with utensils in infancy, using vocalizations for social purposes, and judging intelligence in others. Still other examples are concepts of the self, emotions, and concepts of quantity. The crux of the developmental change in all of these domains is the coordination of two units to form a new, higher-order concept.

This tendency to apply a model to a wide variety of domains characterizes other neo-Piagetians as well. One of the most interesting applications of a neo-Piagetian model comes from Fischer and Watson (1981). They hypothesize that the Oedipal complex is a case of a failure to understand the relations inherent in social roles, along with a limited understanding of aging:

> Billy: Mommy, I'm going to marry you.
> Mother: But, Billy, you can't marry me. You're not old enough.
> Billy: Then I'll wait til I grow up, like Daddy.
> Mother: But when you're grown up, I'll be as old as Grandma.
> Billy: Really?
> Mother: Yes, you'll be a young man, and I'll be an old woman.
> Billy: Well, I'll just wait til I'm old as Grandpa. Then I'll marry you. (Fischer & Watson, 1981, p. 84)

If Case's theory of cognitive change has a metaphor, it is child-as-problem-solver. Cognitive development is a sequence of increasingly powerful procedures for solving problems, along with an increasingly powerful set of conceptual knowledge structures. In an attempt to reach their subgoals and goals, children construct new strategies or draw on appropriate preexisting ones. This arsenal of strategies for problem solving becomes more and more impressive as children grow older. Children experiment during attempts to solve problems, drawing on internal and external resources: They explore objects, observe and imitate others, and cooperate with other people in problem solving. Thus, the context of children's cognitive activities is important. If children have the necessary processing capacity, they can use these experiences to construct more advanced cognitive structures for problem solving.

Perhaps Case's main contribution is his emphasis on children's ability to handle more and more information, as seen in the bell-ringing example above. The number of elements (goals, actions, and so on) children can consider is determined by the size of their short-term storage for the particular set of operations involved in that task. Case posits, and presents some evidence for, the view that an increase in capacity is caused by myelinization (insulation of neurons) in the nervous system and practice with operations that are relevant to the task. Regarding the latter, practice gradually makes an activity less effortful (automatization), thereby freeing capacity for other activities (see Chapters 4 and 6). Thus, at first all of short-term memory is needed for just one element, but later it can be spread between two elements, then three and four.

Case (1985) presents various sorts of evidence for the role of capacity in problem solving. First, among children of the same age, the more capacity a child has the more likely she is to profit from instruction on a new concept. Second, the faster a child can count, the greater his or her capacity, as measured on a counting-span task. This span task involves remembering the numbers of objects in several sets. This outcome indicates that when children can perform a mental operation efficiently, their capacity goes further. Moreover, when adults have to count in an unfamiliar language, so that their speed of counting is the same as that of 6-year-olds in their native language, adult and child counting spans (capacity) do not differ (Case, Kurland, & Goldberg, 1982). Then if adults are given training with counting in the unfamiliar language, both their counting speed and counting span return to normal. Again, these results support the link between operating efficiency and short-term store. Finally, although practice increases operational efficiency, there are biological limits: First-grade children given massive practice in counting did not improve in counting speed beyond the level of second-grade children given no practice (Kurland, 1981).

Case proposes a multilevel cognitive system, with levels ranging from the very general to the specific. To illustrate, cognitive change involves the following sequence. An increase in capacity (*general* systemwide change), along with the particular experiences offered by one's culture, leads to a change in the central conceptual structures. These structures are at an *intermediate* level of generality; each is a representational system of a domain of knowledge such as number or space. These structures interpret specific tasks and affect the problem-solving procedures for these tasks (*specific*-level change). By including systems that vary in generality, Case accounts for both the evenness and unevenness of cognitive development.

In summary, Case keeps the spirit of Piaget's theory and the processes of the information-processing approach but adds important new emphases for cognitive change—for example, mental capacity and problem-solving procedures. These elements both constrain and facilitate further development. Case finds cross-domain generality when the requisite underlying cognitive skills and the capacity demands of the tasks are the same, and domain specificity when tasks differ in these two respects.

Contextual

In comparison to the three approaches presented thus far, the contextual approach is a newcomer with respect to its influence on research on current cognitive development. However, its roots go back to the early part of this century, to the work of several Soviet researchers, most notably Lev Vygotsky (1896–1934). An interested reader could examine Vygotsky's works directly (e.g., 1978) or turn to more modern versions of the contextual approach (e.g., Bronfenbrenner, 1979, 1989; Bruner, 1990; R. Cohen & Siegel, 1991; M. Cole, 1988, in press; Greenfield & Childs, 1991; Resnick, Levine, & Teasley, 1991; Rogoff, 1990; Wertsch, 1991).

Although the three approaches discussed thus far assign some role to social influences on cognitive change, only the contextualists have focused on these influences. In particular, the guidance and support of adults is the main process of cognitive development. We said earlier that a child only has a single head and it is firmly attached to the rest of the body. We now will add that this body-with-head has both feet firmly planted in a social environment.

It is important to understand that the contextual approach is not simply proposing the interaction of two separate entities—the child and society. Rather, the *child-in-social context* is a single, irreducible unit of study. Although there are many versions of contextualism, what they have in common is the belief that the social and cognitive realms are inextricably connected; thought is always social, in a sense. Although many levels of the social context exist (e.g., Bronfenbrenner, 1979), they form two general levels. One is distal and molar—the social-cultural-historical moment in which the child exists. This sociocultural legacy includes "technologies such as literacy, number systems, and computers, as well as value systems and scripts and norms for the handling of situations" (Rogoff, 1990, p. 32). Thus, children who happen to be born into a society with computers and television may use these tools to develop their thinking in directions that differ from those of children in a less technologically oriented society (Greenfield, in press). Cognition is not necessarily more advanced in one society than the other; rather, it is simply different. Cultures differ in the kinds of cognitive skills that are valued, and consequently encouraged and developed. For example, a less technologically developed society may nurture the narrative thinking involved in story telling or the cognitive skills underlying pottery making rather than reading processes. Events such as severe economic depressions, the invention of the printing press, wars, and a technological advance with political implications (such as the launching of Sputnik) can change the nature of children's experiences, and thus of their thinking. For example, as a society raises the level of literacy expected of its members, children in that society are given more schooling (Rogoff, 1990). In short, a culture's history and current configuration hand the newborn child a ready-made set of values, beliefs, rules, possibilities, and impossibilities.

The second sociocultural level lies closer to the child's head, in his or her proximal social and physical setting. This level involves the moment-to-moment and day-to-day interactions with parents, siblings, peers, teachers, and other significant figures. To some extent these people are simply "go-betweens"—mediators of the social-cultural-historical forces described above. Parents, for example, encourage independent thinking or obedience to authority, depending on which is needed to succeed in that society (e.g., democratic versus collectivist). Thus, in certain cultures, unlike in the United States, children are discouraged from asking questions (Greenfield & Lave, 1982). Parents in different cultures vary in the value they place on mathematical and scientific studies and homework, as shown in research on Japanese and American children (e.g., Stevenson, Lee, & Stigler, 1986). Parents' beliefs about what children are like, which are shaped to a great extent by what their culture says they are like, also can influence their behavior toward their children (Goodnow & Collins, 1990; S. A. Miller, 1988).

Parents not only are mediators of cultural influences, but also have their own unique contribution. Even within a culture, parents differ in the values and competencies they bring to the child. Simple, everyday parent–child interactions such as reading a book, building a tree house, conversing at mealtime, or feeding an infant have a social overlay of mediated-cultural and direct-parental influences.

More specifically, adults guide, challenge, provide models of to-be-acquired behavior, and arrange and structure the child's participation in activities. In short, adults are "cognitive boosters," cheering children on and directing them so that they will be all that they can be. In this "guided participation," adults arrange the child's activities, regulate the difficulty of the task, direct the child's attention, and provide both explicit and implicit instruction. Parents' guidance can be very simple, as when a parent lightly holds onto a young child who attempts to stand alone. Or, it can be more complex and subtle, as when American adults ask preschoolers "What are you drawing?" This question may encourage children to consider the possibility that their playful scribbles could represent something in the real world and to make up post hoc stories about their drawings (Cole & Cole, 1989).

The contextualists' metaphor for the process of cognitive change is "child as apprentice." A child develops by doing things with more advanced others, observing what they do, responding to their corrective feedback, listening to their instructions and explanations, and learning to use their tools and strategies to solve problems. This instruction can be formal, as in schooling or explicit instruction from parents, but more often is casually interwoven into the fabric of a child's home life. By learning from others how to carry out activities, a child learns how to think: "Apprenticeships provide the beginner with access to both the overt aspects of the skill and the more hidden inner processes of thought" (Rogoff, 1990, p. 40).

It should be noted that children are not passive in this interaction (Rogoff, 1990). They actively make use of the opportunities given them and try out their newly acquired strategies and other cognitive tools. As they become more competent, the division of responsibility for the activity shifts so that they have a greater share and adults have a lesser share.

A final process of cognitive change is perhaps the most important. Rogoff (1990) refers to the process of building bridges between what the child currently knows and new information. Cognitive change involves movement through the *zone of proximal development*, a concept of Vygotsky's. This zone is the area lying between where the child is now, cognitively speaking, and where he or she could be with help. An adult or more advanced peer can guide the child through this zone. Just as the degree of change possible through assimilation and accommodation is constrained in Piaget's theory, so is the zone of proximal development limited. Children have to build on what they already understand and cannot skip over intermediate steps. Thus, cognitive development necessarily proceeds gradually.

As a recent example of the contextual approach, consider a study (Freund, 1990) in which 3- and 5-year-olds helped a puppet move his furniture into his new house. This essentially was a sorting task in which doll house furniture was sorted into rooms. The children were told to put the things into the rooms where they belonged. For instance, a child could place the stove, refrigerator, kitchen sink, table, and chairs into one room and call it a kitchen. They created other rooms in a similar fashion. After the children performed the task on their own (current level of functioning), half of them interacted with their mothers on an easy and hard level of the task. These two versions differed in the number of rooms and items to be sorted. Mothers were told to help their children but not teach them. The other half of the children worked at the same tasks by themselves, but at the end of each task the experimenter corrected any errors as the children watched. Finally, all children performed the task one more time on their own. The children who had interacted with their mothers performed at a more advanced level on the final trial than those who had practiced on their own, even though the latter had been shown the correct solution at the end by the experimenter. Moreover, mothers adjusted their behavior to the cognitive level of the child. They gave more concrete specific content (e.g., "That stove goes in a kitchen") to the 3-year-olds than to the 5-year-olds. The latter received more general help, such as keeping the goal in mind and planning (e.g., "Let's make the bedroom and then the kitchen"). These general prompts were also more likely to be used in the easy version than the hard one, presumably because mothers thought that even 3-year-olds could use them in the easy version. Mothers also did more of the talking in the difficult version. Thus, the results show that mothers gave their children as much responsibility as they thought they could handle, given their age and the task difficulty. Each mother designed the nature of her child's participation in the activity so as to maximize the child's movement through the zone of proximal development. In addition, the mothers sometimes drew on their shared history with their child, as seen in statements such as "Where do we keep our refrigerator at home?"

In summary, these four main views of the process of cognitive development should be kept in mind in the coming chapters. Change comes about through assimilation-accommodation cycles (Piaget); improved procedures for problem solving and increased processing capacity, speed, and efficiency (information-processing and neo-Piagetian); and adult-guided or peer-guided improvement of existing competencies and engagement in progressively more complex tasks and activities (contextual).

Other Approaches

Although these four frameworks are the most influential and well-developed ones, there are other frameworks as well. Two, in particular, have recently risen to prominence. Because an adequate description is beyond the scope of this chapter, we will present only their most salient aspects. One framework, which we will discuss more fully in Chapter 3, is the *theory-based knowledge approach* (e.g., Carey, 1985a; Keil, 1989; Wellman & Gelman, 1988, 1992). The idea here is that developmental differences in thinking primarily reflect differences in children's informal, intuitive "theories," or coherent causal-explanatory frameworks, about the world. Individual concepts are embedded in these larger theories. In infancy (see Chapter 2), these theories are very simple, such as the theory that the world consists of cohesive physical objects with boundaries, substance, and continuity over time and movement (Spelke, 1988b, 1991). Later theories are more complex. Young children may only have a few theories (Carey, 1985a; Wellman & Gelman, 1992), whereas older ones may have theories for various domains. A theory includes a set of beliefs about the entities in a domain and about the relationships among these entities. In particular, theories differ from other types of mental representations in that they are explanatory; they can answer "why" questions. Finally, theories differ from Piagetian conceptual structures in that theories are specific to a particular domain, such as a theory of biology or physics or psychology (Wellman & Gelman, 1992).

Although children's intuitive theories obviously are not as precise and consistent as scientific theories, one of the ways that they are similar is that both undergo continual testing and revision. In fact, cognitive development can be seen as theory change. As one example, consider children's theories of human biology (Carey, 1985a). Preschoolers may believe that people eat because they will it—because they are hungry or want to grow. This is a psychological rather than a biological explanation. By middle childhood, a more truly biological theory identifies the role of eating and other biological functions in supporting life. A main reason for this theory change is that the older child has more factual knowledge about biology—for instance, causal mechanisms such as breaking down the food and absorbing it into the body. This knowledge implies biological mechanisms that make the old theory obsolete and contradictory and spur the construction of a newer, more satisfactory, theory. Knowledge is restructured.

As will become apparent in the presentation on early concepts in Chapter 3, a theory guides and constrains the types of inferences made about an entity. For example, Carey (1985a) showed 4-year-olds a mechanical monkey that looked convincingly like a real monkey. She asked the children whether the mechanical monkey has bones and could eat and have babies like a real monkey. Although the children believed that people and other animals have these properties, they denied that mechanical monkeys had them. Thus, their monkey theories about the biological nature of real monkeys and the mechanical nature of toy monkeys include basic principles about the underlying nature of entities that overrode the perceptual similarity of these two categories. The children saw mechanical monkeys as more like hammers than real animals. More generally, two entities that are both similar and different could be assigned to the same category or different ones, depending on the child's intuitive theories about the world.

A final approach to be mentioned is the nativist *biological-maturational* one. This approach appears under many labels: developmental cognitive neuroscience, cognitive behavioral genetics, cognitive ethology, biological constraints, modularity, and cognitive neuropsychology. In various ways, each version emphasizes the role of genetic endowment and brain maturation in the process of cognitive change. In addition, several other approaches, especially connectionism (e.g., Bates & Elman, 1992; McClelland, 1989), typically are not nativistic, but use neural networks as a model, or analogue, for cognitive change. The best sources for learning about the different varieties of the biological approach are recent volumes edited by Carey and Gelman (1991) and K. R. Gibson and Petersen (1991). Good illustrative experiments include those by Diamond (1991a, 1991b), Fischer (1987), and Shimojo, Bauer, O'Connell, and Held (1986).

Examples of findings from this approach are that maturational changes in the brain are linked to cognitive spurts during childhood (e.g., Fischer, 1987) and to the inhibition of less mature responses (Llamas & Diamond, 1991). One finding, for instance, is that the maturation of the frontal lobe of the brain appears to be necessary for the infant's successful solution of problems related to the notion that objects exist even when out of sight (Diamond, 1991b).

Some of the biologically based investigators believe that the mind is a collection of *mental modules*, highly specialized innate mental abilities directed to very particular kinds of stimulus information (e.g., Fodor, 1983). Examples are processing language, recognizing faces, and concepts of number, physical causality and the mind (Leslie, 1986, 1991). Separate modules are only loosely connected. An example of supporting evidence for modularity comes from the finding that children whose overall level of cognitive functioning is quite low may possess one outstanding cognitive skill. For instance, certain autistic children are outstanding in music, drawing, or mathematical computation. The biological approach, including modularity, will appear again in Chapters 2, 3, and 7 on infancy, early childhood, and language, respectively. A recurring theme will be that the biological make-up of humans both enhances and constrains cognitive development.

These theories or frameworks of cognitive development are useful, for they tell us where to look for clues to children's thinking. However, no one theory provides a satisfactory account. Because the theories focus on different aspects of cognitive development, they are complementary and, as a group, portray the richness and complexity of the child's mind.

AN OVERVIEW OF THE BOOK

We chronicle in Chapters 2 to 4 the major landmarks of general mental growth from birth to adulthood. In these chapters we emphasize work stimulated by Piaget and other research closely associated with a particular age period—infancy, early childhood, or middle childhood and adolescence. After this chronological presentation, later chapters examine particular important content areas in more detail. Chapter 5 describes the development of social cognition, and Chapters 6 and 7 deal with the ontogenesis of memory and language, respectively. Developmental psychologists currently are giving these three topics a good deal of research attention. Finally, in Chapter 8 we discuss some major questions and problems concerning cognitive development.

In the spirit of "truth in packaging," this text has some idiosyncrasies that the reader should know about. It is probably a more "personal" book than most texts. First, we did not feel as constrained as many textbook writers might to cover all the topics in the field. In general, a topic was likelier to get included to the extent that we (1) found it interesting to read, think, and write about; (2) already had a fairly deep, "insider's" acquaintance with it, perhaps because we had previously written or done research in that area; and (3) felt we could write a coherent account of it, in the space available, that a reader unfamiliar with the field of cognitive development could comprehend and remember.

Second, the topics finally selected by these idiosyncratic criteria were also approached in an idiosyncratic fashion. Our approach tends to be somewhat more description oriented and less explanation oriented than that of many developmental psychologists. There is, therefore, considerable emphasis on describing *what* cognitive abilities and knowledge children develop and, if known, the sequential steps involved in their formation. This contrasts with an emphasis on trying to show what factors or variables (e.g., in children's cognitive experiences and environments) generate, facilitate, or impede these developments. Although it is true that there are problems in deciding what constitutes an explanation or a cause of cognitive growth (Chapter 8), this book's emphasis on description would undoubtedly appear excessive to some developmentalists.

Finally, the book contains a fair amount of informed opinion and educated guess where (almost everywhere, it sometimes seems) the facts are not solid.

Those opinions and guesses are mostly our own, and others in the field would undoubtedly disagree with some of them.

SUMMARY

The concept of cognition favored in this text is a broad and inclusive one, covering more than such traditional, more narrowly "intellectual" processes as reasoning and problem solving. The human mind is conceptualized as a complex *system* of interacting processes that generate, code, transform, and otherwise manipulate information of diverse sorts. Four approaches provide useful frameworks for thinking about processes of cognitive development: the *Piagetian, information-processing, neo-Piagetian,* and *contextual* approaches. Piaget's *assimilation-accommodation* model describes how this cognitive system interacts with its environment, and, by means of many such interactions, undergoes developmental change. According to this model, the cognitive system plays a very active role in its cognitive interchanges with the environment. It creates a mental construction of reality in the course of numerous experiences with its milieu, rather than simply making a mental copy of what is experienced. Each cognitive encounter with the world always has two aspects, *assimilation* and *accommodation.* Assimilation essentially means interpreting or construing external data in terms of the individual's existing cognitive system. What is encountered is cognitively transformed to fit what the system knows and how it thinks. Accommodation means changing the cognitive system slightly so as to take account of the structure of the external data. According to Piaget's model, therefore, the cognitive system simultaneously adapts reality to its own structure (assimilation) and adapts itself to the structure of the environment (accommodation). By repeatedly attempting to accommodate to and assimilate novel, previously unassimilated environmental elements, the system itself gradually changes its internal structure—that is, cognitive development takes place (see Figure 1–1).

The information-processing approach takes as its starting point the flow of information through a computer-like system. Humans attend to information, transform it into a mental representation of some sort, compare it with information already in the system, assign meaning to it, and store it. *Automatization* occurs as mental procedures are practiced and are more efficiently executed. These processes, along with an increasing speed of processing and increasing capacity, drive cognitive development. A growing flexibility and completeness in the child's encoding of stimuli and the acquisition of various strategies also appear to be important sources of change. However, limits on how much information can be processed place serious constraints on the child's development. Using either computer simulations or detailed, precise descriptions of behavior, researchers test hypothesized processes of cognitive development.

Neo-Piagetians combine the Piagetian and information-processing approaches. Unlike Piaget, they address the domain-specificity of cognitive skills and developmental increases in mental capacity. For example, Robbie Case emphasizes the role of capacity in cognitive development. Processes leading to cognitive development include processing and coordinating more elements in a situation, differentiating information, and setting subgoals as means to a goal. Activities such as exploring objects, observing and imitating other people, and cooperating with others in problem solving spur on cognitive change.

n, derived from Vygotsky, views the child-in-social context as
...lysis. Global social-cultural-historical influences and proxi-
...ences, particularly parents and other significant adults, are the
...of cognitive change. Adults guide, support, inspire, and correct chil-
...olem solving, thus pulling them through the *zone of proximal develop-*
...y engaging them in guided participation, society helps children reach
... maximal level of cognitive functioning. Children actively learn much as an
apprentice does, by observing more competent others and trying out new skills
under the direction of adults.

Two other approaches are the *theory-based* and *biological-maturational*
approaches. The former argues that children develop a series of coherent, explanatory "theories" of reality. The latter emphasizes how the development of the brain
stimulates and constrains cognitive development.

Together, the various approaches provide a fuller view of how children's
minds gradually become like those of adults. Faced with a barrage of sensory stimulation during infancy and the little challenges of everyday life later on, children
try to make sense of the world and adapt to it by actively constructing notions of
this world. These notions include such phenomena as categories, rules, cognitive
structures, skills, theories, and procedures. This "world" includes physical objects
and events, the self, and other people. This cognitive construction of the world is
both helped by and constrained by their biological endowment; their current cognitive competencies, capacity, and knowledge; and the opportunities provided by
their environment, including the adults who function as "cognitive guidance coun-
selors." The process of construction itself involves assimilation, accommodation,
encoding, and co-construction with adults and peers. The chapters to follow will
describe the various "construction sites" of childhood.

two

Infancy

One hardly needs to read a textbook to recognize that there must be staggering differences between the cognitive system of the very young infant and that of the very young child (0 to 1 versus 18 to 30 months of age, let us say). To the casual observer, these two organisms scarcely seem to belong to the same species, so great are the cognitive as well as the physical differences between them. The newborn—again to our proverbial casual observer—appears to be an intellectual zero, with scarcely any "mind" at all. In contrast, the 2-year-old can represent and communicate information by means of symbols (in speech, gesture, drawing, etc.); can solve a number of concrete, practical problems by the intelligent, planful use of simple tools and other means; possesses a considerable amount of practical knowledge concerning his or her everyday world of people, objects, and events, and much else besides. The 2-year-old, in short, is *like us* in ways that the newborn patently is not.

The brief span from young infancy to young childhood is marked by a momentous transformation of the cognitive system unparalleled by any other period of life. One objective of this chapter is to convey some of the highlights of this transformation. A second objective, however, is to present a more positive picture of the young infant than the casual-observer perspective sketched in the preceding paragraph. Young infants *are* different from the rest of us, but they are far from intellectual zeros. Some of the most exciting contemporary research in cognitive development is devoted to uncovering the previously unsuspected abilities of these seemingly helpless creatures. To those of us in the field—and we hope that this will prove true for you also—the excitement lies not only in the findings but in the process of discovery itself: in the extraordinary ingenuity with which researchers have probed for evidence of competence in this hardest-to-study of all human subjects.

This chapter is divided into two broad sections. We begin with work on infant perception—that is, infants' ability to take in information through the various perceptual senses (sight, hearing, etc.) and to make some sense out of what they have taken in. Perception, in Eleanor Gibson's (1969) words, provides us with "firsthand information" about the world. It is the necessary starting point for higher-level, "secondhand" operations upon the information—reasoning, inferring, problem solving, and the like. And for this reason it provides a sensible starting point for a discussion of infant cognitive development. Before we can ask what else infants do with the multitude of stimuli and events that surround them, we must know what they are capable of perceiving.

The second section of the chapter discusses infant cognition as that term has traditionally been construed. The traditional construal, as we shall see, has been heavily influenced by the pioneering ideas and observations of Piaget, and Piaget's work is therefore one focus for our discussion. As we shall also see, however, recent research has forced some major revisions in this traditional view. Indeed, this recent work is a central part of the "more positive picture" that we wish to present, and it therefore is the focus of the concluding part of the chapter.

INFANT PERCEPTION

In 1962, Hochberg said that it would be highly desirable to study young infants' visual abilities, but that "the human infant displays insufficient behavior coordination to permit its study to give us very much useful information" (Hochberg, 1962, p. 323). Since that time Robert Fantz and other developmental psychologists have devised a variety of ingenious methods for assessing the perceptual abilities and dispositions of infants—even newborns. It is no exaggeration to say that we have witnessed a methodological revolution here in the past 30 years. Thanks to this revolution, infant perception is currently one of the "hottest" research areas in the field. Useful sources from the recent flood of articles and books devoted to infant perception include Aslin (1987b), Granrud (in press), Haith (1990), Salapatek and Cohen (1987), and Yonas (1988).

What has all this recent research taught us about infants' perceptual capabilities? A brief answer is easy to give: The infant is a good deal more perceptually competent than we used to think. The infant is, to be sure, not totally competent; recent years have seen a swinging back from what Marshall Haith (1990, p. 9) dubs the "Gee-whiz, look what baby can do" enthusiasm of the 1970s to a more balanced picture of competencies and limitations. Nevertheless, the conclusion remains: There is more perceptual ability, present earlier in life, than psychologists once believed.

Why did we underestimate the infant's perceptual competence? We think that three reasons may have been important.

1. We made an unwarranted generalization from babies' motor abilities to their perceptual abilities. Young infants have very poor motor skills. They cannot control and coordinate well the movements of their heads, trunks, and, especially, limbs. On the motor side, they fairly radiate behavioral incompetence. What could be more natural, then, than to assume a similar level of incompetence on the perceptual side?

2. Although psychologists in past decades were not able to study infant perception for want of adequate research methods, they could and did study perceptual development in the postinfancy years. These investigations usually found improvements with age in perceptual skills, with young children often performing rather poorly on the particular tasks given. A bit of downward extrapolation from such results easily led to the assumption that infants' perceptual abilities must be very poor indeed.

3. There has been a strong tradition in philosophy and psychology to assume that we begin life with very minimal capabilities and only slowly and gradually, through months and years of experience, construct these capabilities (Gibson & Spelke, 1983). According to this view, we start with next to nothing (virtually a tabula rasa, or blank slate) and build all we have from the ground up, brick by brick. This argument should sound familiar to you, for it represents one answer to the most pervasive and long-standing question in developmental psychology: the heredity-environment or nature-nurture issue. As applied to perception, the heredity-environment debate concerns whether our mature perceptual abilities and perceptual knowledge are provided by initial, inborn biological "nature" (the classic nativist position) or subsequent, postnatal psychological "nurture" (the classic empiricist position). The general answer, as you doubtless realize, must be not one or the other but *both*—recall the favorite cliche of introductory psychology texts: Development is always a matter of heredity *and* environment, never heredity *or* environment. Nevertheless, the general acceptance of this truism has not prevented one or the other position from dominating at particular times for particular topics, and throughout much of the first part of this century theorizing about perception had a decidedly empiricist cast to it. The assumption that the young infant is perceptually incompetent was a natural—indeed necessary—outgrowth of such thinking.

Methods of Studying Infant Perception

Our view of the infant's perceptual abilities has changed as our methods of studying those abilities have changed. The great obstacle to such study, of course, is the fact that infants, unlike older subjects, cannot verbally report on their perceptual activities and experiences. Nor, as we saw, is the young infant capable of much in the way of skilled motor behavior. The key to studying infant perception has proved to be the clever exploitation of what infants *can* do—namely emit various nonverbal (and often minimally motoric) responses that can tell us something about what they are experiencing perceptually. Such nonverbal responses include both behavioral and physiological measures. Here we briefly describe some of the most important and broadly applicable of these measures; we will add some further techniques later in the context of particular issues and studies.

Undoubtedly the most informative behavioral measure in the study of infant perception is looking behavior. It was, in fact, the invention of a looking-based procedure by Robert Fantz (1961) that is generally credited with initiating the revolution in the study of infant perception. In Fantz's "preference method" an experimenter displays two figures simultaneously and measures how long the baby looks at each. Let us suppose that over trials the baby looks systematically longer at one figure than the other—shows a "preference," to use the Fantz terminology. This finding tells us two important things about the infant's perceptual system. First, it tells us that the system can distinguish or discriminate between these two stimuli. Preferences logically imply discriminability: An infant could not systematically attend to one thing rather than another unless he or she could somehow perceptually discriminate one from the other (note, however, that the reverse is definitely not the case—that is, the ability to discriminate does not imply that the infant will necessarily show a preference). Second, preferences tell us about themselves—that is, what the infant is more or less disposed to attend to, and therefore something about the design of the infant's perceptual-attentional system. Comparison of specific stimuli tells us about specific preferences—that this stimulus is more interesting than that. More generally, the very existence of preferences, from birth, tells us something very important about the human infant: Even the newborn is not completely at the mercy of the environment but rather is at least somewhat active and selective in what he or she attends to.

Other measures of looking can also be informative. With modern technology, it is possible to measure not only which of two stimuli is being looked at but exactly where the baby's eyes fixate and how they scan from one part of the stimulus to another. Such eye-movement recording can help to specify the information that the baby uses when discriminating between stimuli. It can also tell us which aspects of a stimulus capture and which maintain the infant's attention.

Infants can do other things besides look. Another behavior that is present from birth is sucking. One way to utilize sucking in the study of perception is the following. The infant is given a pacifier nipple to suck on and his baseline sucking rate is recorded. Then, every time he increases his sucking rate above a certain predetermined level, he is reinforced by the presentation of a particular sound. This reinforcement leads to an increase in sucking rate. Even young babies seem happy to "work" in such ways (increased sucking, head turning, etc.) for purely auditory or visual wages—an important finding in itself, quite apart from its applicability to questions of perception. After repeated presentations of the same sound, however, interest in it begins to wane, as evidenced by a gradual decrease in sucking rate. The experimenter then presents a new and different sound. The infant may signal his recognition of the change and his heightened interest in the new sound by once again increasing his sucking rate. If this occurs, the infant has answered the question to which the paradigm is directed: He can hear a difference between the sounds.

In addition to overt behaviors such as looking and sucking, infants produce physiological responses that can give us clues as to what they are perceiving. Of the many physiological measures that have been used in the study of infant perception, the most informative and widely applicable is change in heart rate. Let us consider how the discrimination-of-sounds problem described in the preceding paragraph might be attacked with heart rate rather than sucking as the dependent variable. The experimenter produces the same sound as before, but this time measures changes in heart rate each time the sound appears. Initially, heart rate slows down in response to the sound, a pattern that seems to reflect an orienting, attentional response. (In contrast, heart-rate *acceleration* would mean startle, upset, etc.) Eventually, however, the sound loses its fascination, and heart rate no longer declines from baseline. At this point the experimenter switches to a new sound. Reappearance of the decelerative response would be clear evidence that the infant can perceive a difference between the two sounds.

The procedure just described illustrates a very general pair of phenomena known as *habituation* and *dishabituation*. Habituation is the first part of the process: a decline in interest as a repeated stimulus becomes familiar. Although our example concerned change in heart rate, other responses (including looking behavior) show the same pattern: an initial strong response when a stimulus is new, much less response when it has become old hat. Dishabituation is the second part of the process: the reemergence of interest when the stimulus is changed and thus becomes new again. Note that this procedure, like the Fantz preference method, tells us about both discrimination and preferences. The particular preference in this case is a preference for the relatively novel over the relatively familiar. And the fact that infants show such a preference allows us to conclude that they can discriminate between the stimuli in question. Note also that habituation of attention implies at least some sort of recognition-type memory capability. If the baby's cognitive system could not somehow code the fact that the repeated stimulus has been perceived before—could not "recognize" it, in some sense, as old or familiar—the system could not habituate to it (see Chapter 6). It is, after all, a physically identical stimulus from one trial to the next. Thus, these research methods can actually give us information about three things rather than just two: (1) infant perceptual-discrimination abilities; (2) infant perceptual preferences; and (3) infant recognition-memory abilities.

Our brief description of current methods has made things sound more simple and straightforward than they really are. The recording and interpretation of looking, sucking, heart rate, and other response patterns are fraught with problems, problems that continue to be the focus of much attention, discussion, and debate among those who do such recording and interpretation for a living (Aslin, Pisoni, & Jusczyk, 1983; Berg & Berg, 1987; N. A. Fox & Fitzgerald, 1990; Gottlieb & Krasnegor, 1985; Haith, 1990). Fortunately, the topic of infant perception—perhaps precisely because it *is* so challenging—has attracted some of the field's most ingenious methodologists, and they have solved enough of the problems to give us some solid conclusions about what babies can do perceptually and when they can do it. In the following synopsis we concentrate on vision and audition, the two most important sensory instruments of human learning and development.

Audition

This summary owes much to reviews by Aslin (1987b), Aslin et al. (1983), and Kuhl (1987). From such reviews it is clear that three issues underlie most research on infant auditory functioning: detection (what sounds can the infant hear?), discrimination (what differences among sounds can the infant perceive?), and localization (how well can the infant localize sounds in space?).

DETECTION. Evidence from fetal recordings and prematurely born infants suggests that the auditory system begins to function at least several weeks prior to the normal term of birth. By the 25th week after conception, changes in brain activity can be demonstrated in response to sound (Parmelee & Sigman, 1983). By the 28th week fetuses clamp their eyelids in response to a loud (110 decibel) vibroacoustic stimulus presented near the mother's abdomen (Birnholz & Benacerraf, 1983). Interestingly, all of the fetuses that failed to respond in this way were later born with hearing problems. Although findings such as these suggest that prenatal hearing is possible, we still know little about how much fetuses hear or how clearly they hear it. Sounds from the outside have to pass through the mother's body tissues and through the fluid of the amniotic sac, a passage that may result in considerable attenuation before they ever reach the fetus's ears. In addition, such sounds may have to compete with a surprisingly noisy intrauterine environment— as high as 85 decibels by some estimates. On the other hand, recent evidence indicates that sounds of frequencies below 1000 Hz may be transmitted with relatively little attenuation through the amniotic sac. The most important frequency range for human speech is from about 500 to 2000 Hz, and thus this finding suggests that some speech sounds may get through. Consistent with this possibility are the results of a study in which a brave mother literally swallowed a (small!) microphone in order to record the sounds within her womb. Although the sounds were muffled, the intonations of the mother's speech were clearly discernible on the recording (Fukuhara, Shimura, & Yamanouchi, 1988).

Whatever the situation may be before birth, infants clearly do hear at birth. Existing estimates suggest that the newborn's auditory threshold is only 10 to 20 decibels higher than the adult's; that is about the magnitude of hearing loss you have when you have a cold. As infants grow older, their auditory sensitivity becomes more and more adult-like. Thresholds do vary with the frequency of the sound, however, and infants approach optimum-level hearing earlier for high-frequency sounds than for low-frequency ones (Trehub & Schneider, 1983).

DISCRIMINATION. Hearing requires not only the ability to detect sounds but also the ability to perceive differences among different sounds. Infants have been shown to discriminate differences along a variety of dimensions of auditory input: intensity, frequency, duration, and timing. In some cases they not only hear differences but respond differentially; the soothing quality of low-frequency sounds is an example familiar to many a parent. Infants' discriminations, to be sure, are not as fine as those of adults, although in some cases they may come close; in one study, for example, 5- to 8-month-old infants discriminated frequency changes on the order of 2 percent, as compared to the 1 percent level achieved by adults (Olsho, Schoon, Sakai, Turpin, & Sperduto, 1982). And discrimination, like detection, becomes better as infants get older. As Aslin (1987b, p. 6) notes, "the most ubiquitous finding in developmental research is that infants show more adult-like performance as they grow older."

LOCALIZATION. On the other hand, infants' ability to localize (i.e., turn toward the source of) sounds shows a surprising, albeit temporary, exception to

Aslin's rule. Infants demonstrate a primitive ability to localize from birth—indeed, in one study, carried out in the delivery room, within 5 minutes of birth (Wertheimer, 1961)! By 2 or 3 months, however, this response has largely disappeared, only to reemerge again by 4 or 5 months (Muir & Clifton, 1985). Localization is one of several behavioral systems that show such a U-shaped developmental curve: a rudimentary form present very early, followed by disappearance of the response, followed by emergence of a more mature level of functioning (Bever, 1982). The usual explanation for such a nonlinear course of development is that early and later forms of response have different underlying bases. The argument in the case of localization is that the neonate's localization is a reflexive, subcortical affair, analogous to other reflexes that are present at birth. Like other reflexes, localization is automatically elicited by particular environmental stimuli, and like many such reflexes, it drops out with biological maturation. The localization of the older infant is different: cortical rather than subcortical, and considerably more exploratory, more skilled, and more attuned to environmental variation. And the localization of the older infant shows the developmental course that we would expect: greater and greater accuracy as the infant grows older (Morrongiello, 1988; Morrongiello, Fenwick, & Chance, 1990).

Our overview of how infants perceive sounds has made no mention of what is undoubtedly the most important source of sounds in the infant's environment: human speech. The story of how babies respond to speech is told in Chapter 7. We will see there that infants' ability to perceive the differences among different speech sounds is perhaps the most impressive of the many impressive things that babies have been shown to do. (We will also see some further evidence that auditory perception, including perception of the mother's speech, may begin before birth.)

Vision

Infant vision has received more research attention than infant audition. This imbalance is reflected in Salapatek and Cohen's (1987) *Handbook of Infant Perception*: seven chapters devoted exclusively to vision, one chapter devoted exclusively to audition. Not surprisingly, the *Handbook* is one of the sources from which the following summary is drawn. Other helpful sources include Aslin (1987b), Banks and Salapatek (1983), and various chapters in Granrud (in press) and Yonas (1988).

In organizing material on infant vision, it is useful to draw a rough distinction between lower-level visual *sensation* and higher-level visual *perception*. Questions of sensation have to do with how well infants of different ages can see. Can their eyes scan, fixate, and focus effectively? How good is their visual acuity or "eyesight"? What about their ability to see colors, forms, patterns, and movement? Questions of perception have to do with what meaningful information about the world infants of different ages can obtain by using these visual capacities. Can they perceive objects as such, for example, or is their perceptual experience instead one of individual parts (edges, angles, surfaces, etc.) independent of the whole? Can they perceive events that occur over time, or are they instead limited to discrete and noncontinuous snapshots? This distinction between lower-level "sensation" and higher-level "perception" is somewhat forced and can lead to conceptual muddles if taken too literally (the same is true, for that matter, for the perception-cognition distinction with which we divide this chapter). Nevertheless, the distinction is—as someone once remarked about such distinctions—good enough for government standards. Above all, it is useful in segmenting this chapter section.

SEEING. A full account of infant vision would have to describe the anatomy and physiology of the various neural systems (retina, lateral geniculate nucleus, visual cortex, superior colliculus) that subserve human visual functioning. For our purposes it is sufficient to cite sources that provide such descriptions (Banks & Salapatek, 1983; Hickey & Peduzzi, 1987), along with some general conclusions about the physiological underpinnings for infant vision. First, none of these relevant systems appears to be fully developed at birth; all seem to be immature to a greater or lesser degree. As a consequence, very little if any of the neonate's visual functioning is of the quality it will be in later infancy. This is not to say that neonates cannot see, because they certainly can, but simply that their visual system has a good deal of developing to do. Second, at least some of this developing appears to take place quite rapidly, for major changes occur across the early months of life. Thus by 6 months the visual system is a good deal more mature and adult-like than it was at birth. Finally, many of the changes that can be observed in the infant's visual performance appear to reflect these biological-maturational changes in the underlying neural systems—perhaps especially changes in the visual cortex.

The neonate's visual system is immature in other ways as well. The quality of our vision depends not only on the functioning of the retina and relevant brain centers but also on various oculomotor mechanisms that serve to bring images into optimal focus on the retina (Aslin, 1987a, 1988). Eye movements of various sorts are necessary to fixate a stimulus in the first place, to scan the parts of a complex field, and to pursue objects as they move through space. If we are to avoid double vision, we must be able to fixate both eyes on the same object simultaneously. Our pupils must be able to dilate and contract in response to changes in illumination. And we must be able to adjust the lens of the eye to bring objects of different distances into focus on the retina (a process labeled *accommodation*). Neonates and young infants are limited in their ability to do all of these things, and these limitations also affect the quality of their vision.

How well, then, does a newborn see, given these various physical limitations? One way to answer this question is in terms of visual acuity. Your visual acuity is defined technically as the highest spatial frequency you can detect. It can be measured, in infant or adult, by presenting patterns of alternating black and white stripes of equal width. The narrower the stripes (= higher the spatial frequency) that can be seen as stripes and not simply a gray field, the better the acuity. Acuity estimates for newborns fall in the range of 20/200 to 20/600 (Dobson & Teller, 1978). This is clearly not very good (at best only one-tenth as good as normal adult 20/20 vision), but it does indicate some ability to see patterning in stimulation. By 6 months, acuity has improved to about 20/70, and by 1 year it is fairly close to adult level.

Another important factor is contrast sensitivity. Your contrast sensitivity refers to your capacity for discriminating differences in light intensity (light-dark differences). Suppose that the stripes in the stimulus were broad rather than narrow, and therefore posed no visual acuity problem. The stimulus would obviously still become harder to see as striped rather than unpatterned as the intensity differences become smaller—that is, as the black and white stripes both change in intensity toward a common gray. Because intensity differences tend to be concentrated at the edges or contours of objects and object parts, they help to tell you where a figure stops and the ground begins, or where this object part ends and that one begins. Like acuity, therefore, contrast sensitivity is critical to your ability to perceive patterning. And like acuity, contrast sensitivity is poor at birth (again, perhaps only about one-tenth as good as adult functioning) but improves rapidly throughout infancy (R. J. Adams & Maurer, 1984).

Thus far we have talked only about the infant's ability to perceive an achromatic world—blacks, whites, and grays. What about color? Assessing infant color vision has long been extremely difficult to do (Teller & Bornstein, 1987). The biggest methodological problem has been to find ways to distinguish cleanly between infant discriminations based on wavelength (what you are after) and infant discriminations based on brightness (a correlated, confounding variable that you want to control for). Although this problem has turned out to be solvable, the solutions all involve running a large number of trials, never an easy task with very young infants. Our knowledge of color perception in the first weeks of life therefore remains limited. Nevertheless, recent evidence suggests that newborns can make some color discriminations: red and green from white in one study (R. J. Adams, Maurer, & Davis, 1986), red and green from each other (although neither from yellow) in another (R. J. Adams, 1989). By 2 months infants can make most of the discriminations that adults with normal color vision make, and by 4 months their color vision appears adult-like in every dimension that has been tested. Hence Teller and Bornstein's (1987) conclusion: "Color vision is in all probability an important component of the child's early mental machinery" (p. 231).

How well babies see is one of the questions that we want to answer when we study infant vision. Another basic question is what infants *like* to see—that is, what preferences they have and why they have them. We have already noted that even newborns show some preferences in what they attend to; indeed, the Fantz preference method is dependent on the fact that infants do not look indiscriminately but rather find some stimuli more interesting than others. The precise description, prediction, and theoretical explanation of infant preferences, however, has turned out to be an exceedingly difficult scientific task. Various possibilities have been proposed over the years: that infants prefer stimuli that are at an optimal level of complexity, or stimuli that are moderately discrepant from what they have experienced before, or stimuli with the right size and number of elements, or stimuli with a high level of contour density. The problem is that each of these models succeeds in explaining some infant preferences but fails to explain others; thus each gives at best a partial account of what infants find interesting. Probably the leading theory at the moment, at least with regard to preferences in the early weeks of life, is the "linear systems analysis" developed by Martin Banks and colleagues (Banks & Ginsburg, 1985; Banks & Salapatek, 1981). This model stresses limitations in the infant's visual capacities—in particular, the young infant's relatively poor contrast-sensitivity capacity. This capacity allows only some of the pattern information present in the stimulus to reach "decision centers" in the baby's central nervous system. Banks and colleagues make their preference predictions on the basis of the information that reaches these centers—roughly speaking, on the basis of what the baby actually sees rather than what the stimulus presents. The mathematical derivation of the predictions is both elegant and complex (see Banks & Ginsburg, 1985, for the details), but at some level the claim is a simple one: "Infants' visual preferences are governed simply by a tendency to look at highly visible patterns" (Banks & Ginsburg, 1985, p. 211). Thus far, the model's predictions of what should be highly visible in early infancy seem to accord well with what young babies tend to look at—edges, angles, areas of high contrast, exterior detail rather than interior, large detail rather than small.

Why do infants show the preferences that they do? More generally, why do infants, from birth, seem to have a positive *hunger* for visual stimulation—a desire to scan the environment and see whatever there is to see? Banks and Ginsburg (1985) suggest two explanations. One possibility (also proposed by Haith, 1980) is that visual stimulation is necessary for normal development of the visual cortex. Exposure to patterned information—not just light, but patterned stimuli—is known to facilitate the development of the cat visual cortex, and the same may be true in humans. By this view, the visual system grows through use, and infants' inborn tendency to exercise their visual abilities is therefore highly adaptive. A second (not necessarily contradictory) possibility is that infants may be biased to attend to the information in the environment that is most important for them to learn about. Faces, for example, are clearly important to learn about, and characteristics of the face correspond nicely to infants' early preferences: a highly patterned stimulus, chock full of contrast, presented at the optimal distance for babies to see it clearly. Obviously, any tendency to attend to psychologically significant information would also be adaptive for the infant's development.

We noted that the linear systems approach works well for preferences in the early weeks of life. Preferences change with development, however, and the preferences shown by the older infant seem to have a different basis from that operative in early infancy. With development, built-in processing biases become less important as determinants of visual preferences, and experience and memory and meaning become more important. Thus a 1-month-old may look at a face because the face presents a package of highly salient stimuli; a 4-month-old, however, looks at a face because of an interest in faces per se—both faces in general and Mommy's face in particular. In general, as infants develop, their attention comes to be directed more and more to aspects of the environment that they are attempting to make sense of—to things that are new, things that are complex, things that are puzzling or surprising. Notice that all of these events are of interest only by virtue of their *relation* to the infant's cognitive system. Properties important in early development, like contrast or movement, can be specified in absolute terms, but a stimulus is never new or complex or surprising in itself; rather, it is new or complex or surprising *to* someone. What infants find new or complex or surprising changes as their cognitive system changes, and thus the specific interests of an 18-month-old will differ from those of a 6-month-old. At both ages, however, it is the fit between new experience and current level that is critical. And at both ages the infant's preferences are, once again, highly adaptive. Indeed, it is hard to imagine a more adaptive motivational system than the one that seems to govern infant attention: Pay most attention to the things that you still need to understand.

PERCEIVING THE WORLD. Our ability to make sense of our perceptual experience eventually extends well beyond the detection and discrimination of specific stimuli. Consider what we see when we gaze at the family cat stretched out before the fireplace. We see a single, solid, three-dimensional object, located in a particular region of space and separate from both the objects it touches (e.g., the rug on which it lies) and the objects it occludes (e.g., in the fireplace behind it). We see an object of a particular size, shape, and color, and do so regardless of the distance between us and cat, the angle of viewing, or the lighting in the room (all factors that change the image on our retina). If an object comes between cat and us, blocking all except head and tail, we do not perceive the cat as being bisected; rather, our perception is still of a continuous, indivisible object. Should the cat meow we correctly perceive the sound as coming from the same object that we are viewing, and should the cat's wet fur emit a certain odor we are quite certain of its source also. If the cat stirs itself and strolls from the room we do not expect its grin or any other part to remain behind; instead, we realize that the parts of an animate object move together in predictable unison. If the movement takes the cat away from us we correctly perceive that it is receding from us (but not changing size, despite changes in the size of the retinal image); on the other hand, if the cat suddenly makes a run for our lap we perceive not only that it is approaching but that its course guarantees contact within a very short time. (Of course, how we feel about such contact depends more on our attitude toward cats than on perception per se.)

The focus of the current section is on whether infants perceive objects, places, and events in the adult-level fashion just described. Much of the work that we discuss was inspired by the theorizing of Eleanor Gibson and James Gibson (E. J. Gibson, 1969, 1988). The Gibsonian emphasis has always been on complex, dynamic, ecologically significant forms of perception. The ability to perceive important invariances such as size and shape certainly fits this description, as does the realization that a visually "looming" stimulus (the cat in midair) signals an impending collision. Methodologically, the Gibsonians stress the need to study perception in situations that approximate the richness and complexity of the natural environment, rather than only through presentation of isolated stimuli in stripped-down laboratory settings. And theoretically, their emphasis is precisely on the richness of information available in the natural environment—on the multitude of cues that specify properties such as size, shape, and movement, and on infants' gradually increasing sensitivity to these cues. Not all of the workers who have followed in this tradition accept all aspects of Gibsonian theory (a fate, as we shall see, that has also befallen Piaget in the realm of infant cognitive development). Nevertheless, the Gibsons (like Piaget) have had a lasting impact on how we think about and study infancy.

Objects. Much of what we know about infants' perception of objects comes from the work of Elizabeth Spelke and colleagues (Spelke, 1982, 1985, 1988a, 1988b, 1990, 1991). Their research has addressed three of the questions about object perception that were sketched in our vignette of the cat: the infant's ability to perceive an object (1) as distinct from the background surfaces behind it (the cat is not connected to the fireplace); (2) as a separate entity from any surfaces that touch it (the cat and the rug are separate objects); and (3) as continuing behind any surfaces that partly hide it from view (the cat remains a single and continuous object even if a footstool cuts off the view of its midsection). The general conclusion that Spelke and colleagues reach, as we shall see, is that the young infant knows a lot but not everything about these characteristics of objects. The story of how these researchers arrive at this conclusion is well worth telling, however, for in a field characterized by ingenious approaches to hard-to-study issues the Spelke research program is among the most ingenious.

Consider first number (1)—the realization that objects are distinct from their backgrounds. Adults can simply report that they perceive cat and fireplace as separate entities. How can we ever figure out what a nonverbal infant perceives? Spelke and Born (Spelke, 1982) decided to see whether infants were surprised when the usual rules of object unity were violated. Three-month-old infants first saw an orange cylinder suspended in front of a flat, blue surface. On some subsequent trials, they saw the cylinder as a whole move forward, toward them, while the background surface remained still. On other trials, the movement broke the object in half; half of the object moved forward in conjunction with an adjacent portion of the background. The investigators "reasoned that if infants perceived the object as unitary and separate from the background, they would be surprised or puzzled when the object broke apart and moved together with part of the background" (Spelke, 1982, p. 412). The infants did in fact exhibit more apparent surprise or puzzlement on the latter trials than on the former ones. Subsequent research showed that infants of this age do not exhibit more surprise or puzzlement on trials of the latter, abnormal-movement kind when object and background are both two-dimensional and initially form part of the same surface, as in a picture, rather than being separated in depth from each other. Spelke (1982) interprets these results as indicating that infants of this age probably do see as unified, bounded wholes objects that are clearly separated in depth from their backgrounds.

Infants' tendency to reach for nearby objects can provide further evidence of their ability to perceive object as separate from background. Hofsten and Spelke (1985) presented 5-month-old infants with two blocklike objects of the same color and texture but of different sizes, with the smaller object in front of the larger one. In one condition the two objects touched and in the other they were separated by a small gap. Infants are known to reach for the closer of two clearly distinct objects (Yonas & Granrud, 1985), and hence the expectation was that the babies would reach for the smaller block if they perceived two blocks rather than one. On the other hand, infants typically reach for single objects by grasping the lateral borders of the object; hence, any infant who perceived but one block was expected to reach for the edges of the larger block (since it provided all the lateral borders in the display). When the objects were separated, infants reached for the smaller block, indicating that they correctly perceived two objects rather than one; when the objects touched, however, the reach was for the larger block, suggesting that the perception was of a single block. Further studies (Kestenbaum, Termine, & Spelke, 1987; Spelke, Hofsten, & Kestenbaum, 1989) demonstrated that infants perceive two back-to-back objects as one even under conditions in which adults clearly see two distinct objects—for example, when the objects differ in color and texture. On the other hand, infants are capable of disentangling the two objects if helpful motion cues are present—for example, if the smaller and larger blocks move at different rates. Motion is a quintessentially Gibsonian cue, for in real-world environments objects or perceiver or both are often moving rather than stationary. And motion, as we shall see, turns out to be a helpful cue with respect to all sorts of aspects of perception.

A full understanding of object boundaries requires not only the ability to perceive object as separate from background but also the ability to perceive two adjacent, touching objects as distinct—that is, ability number (2) in our earlier description. Prather and Spelke (1982) have provided the most directly relevant evidence on this point. They capitalized on the fact that young infants can sometimes become habituated to the number of objects in a display, provided that the number is small—for example, "one" or "two." Some of their 3-month-old subjects were initially habituated to a series of two-object displays and others to a series of one-object displays. The subjects were then shown on some trials two adjacent, touching objects and, on other trials, two clearly separated objects. Subjects acted as though they correctly perceived the latter pair of objects as two objects. That is, if initially habituated to two objects they continued to show habituation when presented with this pair ("two objects again—how boring"), but if initially habituated to one object they showed dishabituation to this pair ("ah, something new"). In contrast, they acted as though the pair of adjacent, touching objects had been perceived as a single entity—as an array of "one" rather than of "two." Objects placed flush up against one another seem to be seen by 3-month-olds as one entity, not two. Notice, however, that the objects in Prather and Spelke's study were static rather than moving. Other work from Spelke's laboratory (Spelke, 1988b) indicates that object movement can help infants to see two adjacent objects as distinct, just as movement helps them to see an object as separate from its background.

Figure 2–1 shows a set of stimuli that were used to test for ability (3): the realization that partially hidden objects are continuous, unitary entities. Shown in the top part of the figure is the original stimulus display: a straight black rod positioned vertically behind a tan block. Adults looking at this array effortlessly and automatically perceive the rod as a single, continuous object located behind another object. Kellman and Spelke (1983) used an habituation-of-looking method to try to ascertain whether 4-month-olds would also perceive the rod as a single object, or, in a more "sensation-like" way, as two rods separated by a space, as the image of this stimulus on one's retina would specify. The infant subjects were first habituated to the sight of the original stimulus display and then saw the two test displays shown in the bottom part of Figure 2–1. If the infants perceived the occluded rod in the original display as a single unitary entity, as adults do, they should look more at the two rods separated by a space than at the complete rod, because the two rods would be perceived as a novel stimulus and the complete rod as a familiar, previously seen one. If, instead, they perceived the occluded rod as two separate objects, they should look more at the complete rod, because that would constitute the novel stimulus for them. Much to the investigators' surprise, the babies did not look more at either test display. They acted as though they had no expectations one way or the other as to what was behind the block. Further studies revealed that this deficit is a general one across a variety of types of objects and methods of

FIGURE 2–1 Habituation and test displays used to assess infants' understanding of partly occluded objects. Adapted from "Perception of Partly Occluded Objects in Infancy" by P. J. Kellman and E. S. Spelke, 1983, *Cognitive Psychology, 15*, p. 489. Copyright © 1983 by Academic Press. Adapted by permission.

HABITUATION DISPLAY

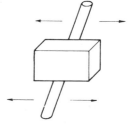

TEST DISPLAYS

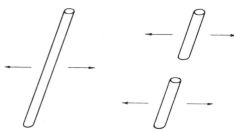

occlusion: Young infants often fail to perceive the unity of objects whose centers are invisible (Spelke, 1988b).

On the other hand (and you haven't been paying attention if you can't guess what's coming next), the young infant's deficiencies are not absolute ones. Failure occurs when the object in question is stationary. If instead the object's visible parts are seen to move in unison—for example, if the rod wiggles back and forth behind the block—then infants, like adults, perceive one continuous object rather than two discontinuous ones. A variety of kinds of movement are sufficient to induce such single-object perception, assuming that the movement honors the Gestalt principle of "common fate"—that is, the parts move in a way that *could* occur if they belonged to the same object (Kellman, Spelke, & Short, (1986). Thus the 4-month-old's perception is in some respects adult-like and in some respects not. In contrast, newborn babies fail to perceive the unity of occluded objects even when the parts move together (Slater, Morison, Somers, Mattock, Brown, & Taylor, 1990). Apparently the ability to use movement as a cue to object unity emerges sometime during the first 4 months of life.

Infants have been shown to be capable of other impressive feats of object perception. Babies 3 to 5 months of age are shown an unfamiliar object that undergoes three sorts of deformation: rotation around the horizontal and vertical axes and zooming through space. Note that all of these deformations are compatible with the sorts of changes that rigid, inflexible objects (sticks, steel bars, etc.) can undergo. Once the babies have habituated to these events, they see a fourth change: either another rigid-object type of deformation or a deformation (squeezing) that implies plasticity rather than rigidity. Infants dishabituate more to the second change than to the first, indicating that they have formed an expectation, based on visual cues alone, about the rigidity of the object (Gibson, Owsley, & Johnston, 1978; Gibson, Owsley, Walker, & Megaw-Nyce, 1979). Gibson et al. (1978) summarize the value of this sort of perceptual competence for the infant's dealings with the environment:

> For an infant to detect this information at an early age would be highly adaptive, since visual recognition of an object as rigid (unyielding to the touch if bumped into or fallen upon, for instance) versus elastic (yielding and potentially soft or even animate) could provide foreknowledge of the consequences of touching or collision. Knowledge of "affordances" given thus is one of the most useful achievements of perceptual development. (p. 408)

An especially important form of motion perception is that directed to the movement of animate objects. One test for such perception is the following. An experimenter attaches luminous dots to the joints of a person, turns off all the lights, brings you into the room, and asks you what you see. If the person is standing motionless you see simply a random array of points. If the person is running in place, however, what you see is no longer simply individual lights but a person running (or walking or dancing or riding a bicycle, depending on the particular movement). This is called the "perception of biological motion," and adults have been found to be very good at it (Johansson, 1973). So, it turns out, are infants. By 3 months of age (although not earlier) babies show more interest in and dishabituate more to patterns that specify biological motion than to either static displays or random arrays of moving points (Bertenthal, Profitt, & Cutting, 1984; Fox & McDaniel, 1982). Whether the babies are seeing a *person* is, of course, not certain, but they clearly are able to extract something of interest when the pattern they view is compatible with human movement. It should be clear to you that such findings fit the leitmotif of the present section: the value of motion cues for specifying the nature and properties of objects.

One very important (and decidedly biological) object that is found in every infant's environment is the human face. Babies are interested in faces from early in life. Exactly when they begin to respond to the face *as a face*, however, and not simply as a collection of interesting parts, has been difficult to determine (M. H. Johnson & Morton, 1992). This question is part of a more general issue: When do infants become capable of perceiving patterns or wholes in stimulation, as opposed to the individual elements (edges, angles, contours, etc.) that are known to drive the very young infant's attention? Like many issues in infant perception, this question does not have a single "correct" answer; rather, what we conclude about pattern perception depends on both the particular patterns in question and the ingenuity with which the experimenter has probed for infant competence. The best current evidence, however, suggests that infants begin to "put together" simple patterns between 1 and 3 months of age, with more complex forms of pattern perception emerging gradually across the first year (Dodwell, Humphrey, & Muir, 1987; Haith, 1990). By about 2 to 3 months infants look longer at a face than at a comparable nonface stimulus (Dannemiller & Stephens, 1988), and by about the same age they show a preference for a familiar face (typically Mommy's) over an unfamiliar one (Barrera & Maurer, 1981). By the second half of the first year they are capable of all sorts of things with regard to face perception—recognizing a face as the same despite variations in expression or side versus frontal orientation (L. Cohen & Strauss, 1979), classifying faces on the basis of sex (Fagan, 1976), differentiating various emotional expressions (Ludemann & Nelson, 1988), even responding differentially to attractive faces compared to unattractive ones (Langlois, Ritter, Roggman, & Vaughn, 1991). Furthermore, it is always possible that research to date has somewhat underestimated the infant's capacities. Many studies have examined response to static, two-dimensional photographs of faces, as opposed to mobile, three-dimensional real faces.

Objects maintain a constant size despite changes in distance from the perceiver (and hence changes in the size of the retinal image), and they maintain a constant shape despite changes in spatial orientation relative to the perceiver (and hence changes in the shape and the orientation of the retinal image). Present evidence suggests that both size and shape constancy become functional during the first half year of life (Day, 1987; Dodwell et al., 1987). The most common method of probing for such competence has been our old friend habituation (e.g., McKenzie, Tootell, & Day, 1980). To study size constancy, for example, we might habituate the infant to an object of a particular size, then test for dishabituation to stimuli of two sorts: objects of the same size but presented at different distances, and objects that vary from the original in both size and distance but that maintain the same-sized retinal image (e.g., an object that is three times larger but also three times farther away). If infants dishabituate (i.e., notice a difference) more for the second sort of stimulus than the first, we would have evidence that they can perceive similarity of real size despite variations in distance and hence in size of the retinal image. Much the same logic underlies a second approach to studying constancy: instrumental conditioning followed by generalization. In this case we first condition the infant to respond to an object of a particular size, and then test for generalization of the response to objects of either the same size or the same retinal image (e.g., Bower, 1966). Studies using these procedures have provided evidence for some degree of shape constancy by about 3 months and some degree of size constancy by about 4 or 5 months. Constancy does not emerge full-blown at these ages, for like many aspects of perception its development is prolonged and gradual, and not an abrupt, absent-to-present transition (Haith, 1990). Nevertheless, there is a fair amount of competence present fairly early—just as is true for other aspects of object perception. Indeed, some recent research, too new as yet for full evaluation, suggests that rudimentary forms of size constancy may be present at birth (Slater, 1991; Slater, Mattock, & Brown, 1990).

Perceptual constancies fit into a larger developmental context that deserves brief mention. The growth of the human mind partly consists of the successive attainment or formation of cognitive *invariants*. As its name suggests, an invariant is something that remains the same while other things in the situation change. Identification of constant features or invariants in the midst of flux and change is an absolutely indispensable cognitive activity for an adaptive organism. Perceptual constancies represent one class of invariants: the realization that the perceivable characteristics of objects (size, shape, color, etc.) remain the same despite variations in viewing conditions and hence retinal image. Further along in our discussion we will encounter more conceptual invariants that are mastered later in development, including two made famous by Piaget: the object concept of infancy and the conservations of middle childhood.

Places. Our mature perceptual capacities allow us to perceive and respond adaptively to numerous aspects of our spatial environment—obstacles, openings, supporting surfaces and drop-offs, left-right and up-down relations, depths and distances. In this section we focus on the development of an especially important type of spatial perception: the ability to perceive three dimensions or depth in stimulation. For more general treatments of spatial perception in infancy, see McKenzie (1987) and Yonas and Owsley (1987).

The perception of depth has been of interest to psychologists for the same general reason that the perceptual constancies have been of interest: namely, that our perception is better than it seems that it should be given the retinal image available to us. In the case of depth, we somehow perceive a world of three dimensions despite the fact that the retinal image is a flat two-dimensional one. The developmental question is how early infants are capable of such three-dimensional perception.

How can we figure out whether babies are perceiving a two-dimensional or a three-dimensional world? Various kinds of evidence are available. We can use the Fantz preference method to determine whether infants can tell the difference between a two-dimensional stimulus, such as a circle, and a three-dimensional stimulus, such as a sphere (Fantz, 1961). We can examine infants' reaching behavior to see whether the probability or the nature of a reach varies appropriately as a function of the distance or solidity of the target object (J. Field, 1977). Or we can measure how infants respond to a "looming" stimulus—that is, to the presentation (typically accomplished with a shadow caster) of an apparently solid object that seems to be rapidly approaching the face (Yonas, 1981). An appropriate defensive response to the loom (blink, head back, arms up) could be argued to show some realization that a solid, three-dimensional object is moving through space. All of these techniques suggest that some ability to perceive three dimensions or depth is present in the early months of life.

A particularly interesting form of depth perception—and the one on which we shall concentrate—is the perception of drop-offs. As adult perceivers, we are capable of making a number of closely related responses when we encounter deep drop-offs. First, our depth-perception mechanisms enable us to see them instantly *as* deep drop-offs—as edges with slopes receding sharply downward to bottoms that are a considerable distance away. Second, we experience fear if we do go off them, or perhaps if even we get too close to them. And third—and quite sensibly and adaptively—we avoid stepping off such fear-arousing drop-offs. Do infants show similar perceptual and behavioral responses to depth?

Eleanor Gibson and Richard Walk invented a device called a "visual cliff" to explore this developmental problem (E. J. Gibson & Walk, 1960). The visual cliff is a large glass-covered table divided by a center board. On one side of the center board the glass rests just above a patterned surface. On the other, deep or "cliff" side, the patterned surface lies a considerable distance beneath the covering glass. Gibson and Walk and other investigators have found that newborn animals of some species (goats, rhesus monkeys, chickens) would readily move from the center board onto the shallow side but would not venture onto the deep side. For these species, clearly, perceptual detection of a drop-off and avoidance of it is innate. On the other hand, the young of some other species (cats, rabbits) do not avoid the deep side initially; they only do so after a few weeks of visual experience (Campos, Hiatt, Ramsay, Henderson, & Svejda, 1978). For these animals, perception and avoidance of drop-offs might be the product of postnatal biological maturation, experience, or some combination of the two.

Young human infants cannot be tested in the usual manner on the visual cliff because, unlike the very young of many other species, they are too immature motorically to be able to locomote. Once they are mature enough to crawl (typically somewhere around 7 months), the method usually used is something like the following (Rader, Bausano, & Richards, 1980): The baby is placed on the center platform facing his or her mother across the deep or the shallow side. The mother calls the baby to cross. (It seems vaguely immoral....) If the baby does not cross within 2 minutes, the mother shows the baby a familiar toy and continues to coax for another 2 minutes. The same procedure is then repeated for the other side. Human infants also show some tendency to avoid the deep side under these testing conditions. Not all infants shun the drop-off (a point to which we will return); most do, however, and the tendency to do so increases with age. Thus the ability to perceive and respond positively to drop-offs appears to be part of human competence by the last third of the first year.

Might the ability to perceive drop-offs be present earlier than can be demonstrated with a crawling-based methodology like the visual cliff? Quite possibly. Many perceptual cues help to specify depth, and the developmental literature on the ages at which infants first become responsive to these cues (Yonas & Granrud, 1985; Yonas & Owsley, 1987) makes the assumption of early competence seem reasonable. (We cannot resist quoting Yonas & Granrud, 1985, p. 45, on the multiplicity of cues for depth: "God must have loved depth cues, for He made so many of them.") There is also more direct evidence on the matter. Campos and his research colleagues have found that prelocomotor (2-month-old) infants show greater heart-rate deceleration when placed on the deep side of the visual cliff than when placed on the shallow side, suggesting that they can perceptually discriminate between the two (Campos et al., 1978). More convincing yet, when slowly lowered toward the glass on the shallow side, prelocomotor babies put their hands out just prior to touchdown; they do not make this placing response just prior to reaching the glass on the deep side, strongly suggesting that they perceive that they still have some distance yet to go (Svejda & Schmid, 1979). Yet babies of this age do not yet show fear in response to drop-offs. If placed over or on the deep side their faces appear calm, they do not cry, and—as just mentioned—they show heart-rate *de*celeration, signifying attentiveness rather than fear. In contrast, older, crawling infants have been found to show heart-rate *ac*celeration in this situation, indicating fear (Campos et al., 1978; Richards & Rader, 1983).

The conclusion to this point is that some ability to perceive drop-offs is probably present in the early months of life but that fear of drop-offs does not emerge until the second half of the first year. This period is also, as we noted, the time during which babies begin to move around on their own. There is, then, at least a rough temporal synchrony between self-produced locomotion and fear of depth. Joseph Campos and Bennett Bertenthal have argued that there is also a causal relation between the two developments (Bertenthal & Campos, 1990; Campos & Bertenthal, 1989; Caplovitz & Campos, 1983). In their view, moving about on one's own contributes to the perception of depth by providing the infant with new information about the spatial environment, as well as forcing increased attention toward and new uses of already available information.

Campos and Bertenthal cite a variety of evidence in support of this claim of a functional role for crawling. We noted earlier that not all babies who have begun to crawl succeed in avoiding the deep side of the visual cliff. The Campos/Bertenthal position predicts that there should be a positive relation between crawling experience and success on the cliff—that is, it should be those babies who have been crawling the longest who are most likely to avoid the drop-off. This, in fact, is exactly what Bertenthal, Campos, and Barrett (1984) found. The Campos/Bertenthal position also predicts that providing babies with increased locomotor experience should hasten the onset of the fear response. Bertenthal and Campos (1990) report an experiment in which prelocomotor infants were given a minimum of 40 hours of experience using infant walkers to get around in the environment. These infants were subsequently more likely to show heart-rate acceleration when lowered over the deep side of the cliff than were matched groups who had not received the extra experience. Finally, Bertenthal and Campos (1990) compared heart-rate responses to the deep side in two groups of 7-month-olds: infants who had begun to crawl and infants who had not yet begun to crawl. They found, as expected, that only the first group showed acceleration to the deep side of the cliff.

Having presented Campos and Bertenthal's argument, we should add that not all of the available evidence supports their position, nor do all investigators agree with their interpretation of the link between crawling and fear of depth (Richards & Rader, 1981, 1983). Nevertheless, that there *is* a link—at the least temporal and quite possibly causal—is clear. And this link, like so much in human development, is highly adaptive: Babies begin to fear depth at just the time that they need such fear—namely when they begin to take control of their own movement.

Relating Information from Different Senses

Objects and events commonly offer information to more than one of our sense modalities. People, for example, do not present themselves to babies as voiceless faces or faceless voices; there is simultaneously a face for the baby to look at and a voice to listen to. Moreover, the face and the voice are unified in space and time: The voice and the face share the same spatial location, and the voice's sounds and the face's mouth movements are temporally synchronized. In addition, certain specific faces always co-occur with certain specific voices; for example, the mother's face with her voice, the father's face with his voice. And, of course, there may be information for the sense of touch as well, both general cues common to humans as complex, three-dimensional objects and more specific cues that identify the particular human object in question (the caress of Mommy's hands, the feel of her hair against the cheek). As adult perceivers, we do not experience such sights, sounds, and touches as completely separate sensations; rather, we experience them as related to one another. We can use information from one sense modality to guide our exploration of another—turn toward the source of a sound, reach out for what we see. Most basically, we can recognize the equivalence or common source of our various sensations—recognize that sight, that sound, and that feel as all originating from one and the same object or event. We are, in short, capable of what is sometimes called *intermodal perception*.

Philosophers and psychologists have presented a variety of views over the centuries concerning the development of intermodal perception (Rose, 1990; Rose & Ruff, 1987; Spelke, 1987). They have seldom disagreed about whether learning and experience play a role in this development. They clearly must play a role. For example, it is obvious that only through experience could a child attain the ability to apprehend, from the sound alone, that the object he or she dimly sees off there in the fog is an ambulance rather than some other kind of vehicle (Spelke, 1987). Theorists have disagreed, however, on whether, or to what extent, or how, the senses might be related innately—prior to experience—versus being largely or wholly dependent upon experience for their coordination. Many theorists, including Piaget, have believed that the major perceptual modalities are entirely uncoordinated at birth and that the infant only gradually learns, through months of sensorimotor experience, to relate information from the different senses. Other theorists, including Gibsonians, believe that we are born with some intermodal perception abilities and/or with aptitudes and predispositions that greatly facilitate the early acquisition of such abilities through experience. Current evidence, as we will see, seems to favor some version of this second position. We discuss the evidence under three headings: infants' abilities to relate (1) sights and sounds, (2) sights and feels, and (3) sights and body movements that imitate what is seen.

Much of the work on infants' perception of sight-sound relations uses the following general methodology (Spelke, 1987). Two visible events are presented successively or simultaneously and a sound specific to one of them is played from a neutral (e.g., central) location. If infants perceive the sound as related to its sound-specified event, they should look more at that event than at the other one. Infants as young as 3 or 4 months do in fact show the ability to link sounds and sights of a variety of sorts. In one experiment (Spelke, 1976), for example, 4-month-old infants were presented with two motion pictures, one depicting a game of peekaboo and the other depicting a percussion musical sequence with baton, tambourine, and wooden block. The sound track for one of the two events was played from a centrally located speaker. Infants looked longer at the film that corresponded to the sounds that they were hearing.

Other studies have explored infants' ability to use common properties of sights and sounds, such as temporal synchrony or pacing, to infer common origin even when the events being presented (unlike peekaboo) are clearly unfamiliar to them. In one such investigation (Spelke, 1979), 4-month-olds were presented with films of two stuffed animals, a kangaroo and a donkey, side by side. Each animal was lifted into the air by puppet strings and dropped to the ground repeatedly, at a steady tempo. Each impact was accompanied by a thump or gong sound, a different sound for each animal. On any given trial, the child saw both of the moving animals but heard the sound of only one of them coming from a central speaker. The critical difference between events lay in the temporal relation between visual information and auditory information. The impacts of one animal were always exactly synchronous and simultaneous with its sounds; for the other animal, impacts and sounds were temporally unrelated. Spelke found that infants tended to look more at the events in which sight and sound were synchronized than at those in which there was a visual/auditory mismatch. Furthermore, Spelke, Born, and Chu (1983) showed that 4-month-olds would tend to perceptually relate a sound and an object whenever the sound occurred simultaneously with an abrupt change in the object's movement, regardless of whether that abrupt change was or was not an impact.

For example, if a puppet animal were raised up by its strings and the sound occurred at the moment that the animal reached its highest point and stopped abruptly (in midair, of course, without touching anything), the babies would relate the sound to that object. Adults shown such nonimpact displays were much less likely to connect sight and sound than in the case in which the abrupt change of movement resulted from an impact. This finding suggests (although of course does not prove, given that the subjects had 4 months of postnatal perceptual experience) that infants may not need experience with sound-producing impacts to link sights and sounds but rather may be born with a tendency to relate sounds to simultaneously occurring changes in object movement. Any such tendency would, of course, facilitate the learning of naturally occurring sight-sound connections, such as the relation between an impact and its ensuing sound.

Some of the most interesting demonstrations of infant intermodal perception concern the topic with which we opened this section: the relation between face and voice. A. S. Walker (1982) presented 5- to 7-month-old infants with two side-by-side films, one of which showed an adult stranger engaging in a "happy" monologue and the other of which showed an adult stranger engaging in an "angry" monologue. As in the kangaroo/donkey study, the sound track from only one of the films was played on any given trial. And as in the kangaroo/donkey study, infants looked longer at the film that corresponded to the sounds they were hearing. They apparently were able to detect the correspondence between visual expression of emotion (via facial expressions and gestures) and auditory expression of emotion (via tone of voice). A study by Walker-Andrews, Bahrick, Raglioni, and Diaz (1991) showed that 4-month-olds can also detect face-voice correspondences on the basis of sex. Infants looked longer at a male face when a male voice was played and longer at a female face when a female voice was played. Given this finding, it is not surprising to learn that infants as young as 3½ months can do the same thing when their own parents provide the faces and voices. Even when the faces are not in fact speaking, infants look longer at mother's face when they hear her voice and longer at father's face when they hear his (Spelke & Owsley, 1979).

Impressive though the ability to match emotion or sex across face and voice may seem, it is not the most impressive of the various feats of intermodal perception that young infants are capable of demonstrating. Spelke and Cortelyou (1981) presented 4-month-olds with the general experimental arrangement with which you are by now familiar: two films shown side by side, with the sound track for one of the films played through a central speaker. In this case each film showed an adult female stranger talking to the baby in a normal, adult-to-baby manner. For only one of the two films, however, did the sounds coming out of the speaker match the movements of the adults' lips. You guessed it: Infants looked longer at the speaker whose mouth movements matched the voice on the sound track. As in the other Spelke studies described earlier, this finding demonstrates the infant's ability to use temporal synchrony to link visual experience with auditory experience. But note how subtle the cues and synchronies are in this case: not just movement or non-movement of the mouth (since both women were talking), but a particular pattern of mouth movements that is or is not compatible with a particular pattern of sounds.

A program of research by Kuhl and Meltzoff (1982, 1984, 1988) takes the story one step further. In their version of the Spelke paradigm, infants see two adult speakers repeatedly pronouncing the same two vowel sounds—for example /a/ (as in *pop*) in the case of one speaker, /i/ (as in *peep*) in the case of the other. By 4 months of age, infants look longer at the speaker whose mouth movements match the sounds they hear. Matching of this sort goes beyond the detection of global synchronies or asynchronies between sounds and movements shown by Spelke and Cortelyou (1981). Instead, Kuhl and Meltzoff's subjects seem to be engaging in a kind of *lip-reading*—recognizing that /a/ sounds go with open mouths, /i/ sounds with retracted lips, /u/ sounds with lips that are protruded and pursed, and so forth. Kuhl and Meltzoff suggest that the ability to detect such visual clues to speech may aid listeners, infant or adult, in the task of accurately perceiving the sounds of speech. As they put it, "there is more to speech than meets the ear" (Kuhl & Meltzoff, 1988, p. 238). And whatever the utility for speech perception, the ability to link specific sounds to specific lip movements is intermodal perception of a very high order indeed.

Some startling results have also been reported in the other two areas of inter-modal perception mentioned: (2) sights and feels, and (3) sights and imitative bodily movements. In the case of (2), Meltzoff and Borton (1979) found in two experi-ments that 1-month-olds are apparently able to recognize which one of two visually perceived shapes matches a shape they previously had explored tactually, in their mouths, but had not previously seen. The experimenter first put special pacifiers in the infants' mouths for 90 seconds: round, smooth ones for half of the infants; round ones with eight hard rubber nubs on them for the other half. The infants then saw two Styrofoam spheres (larger than the pacifiers) for 20 seconds, one visually resembling the smooth pacifier and the other resembling the nubbed pacifier. The investigators found that the infants tended to look more at whichever sphere resem-bled the pacifier they had previously felt in their mouths. Think of what these near-neonates would have had to do to detect a visual-tactile match here:

> (1) tactually discriminate between the shapes presented, (2) visually discriminate between them, (3) store some representation of the tactually perceived shape, and (4) relate a subsequent visual perception to the stored representation of the tactually perceived shape. (Meltzoff & Borton, 1979, p. 404)

Meltzoff and Borton's claims have met a mixed fate in follow-up research to date. Gibson and Walker (1984) obtained congruent results in a study with a similar design (in this case varying object rigidity or plasticity), and Pecheux, Lepecq, and Salzarulo (1988) also reported support; other investigators, however, have been unable to demonstrate such tactile-visual transfer in very young infants (K. W. Brown & Gottfried, 1986; Rose & Ruff, 1987). Conclusions about initial equipment and early competence for this aspect of intermodal perception must therefore be put on hold until some clarifying research is forthcoming. By later in infancy, however, it is clear that infants can bring together tactile and visual information in a number of adaptive ways. We consider one example, a series of studies from Elizabeth Spelke's lab that unite Spelke's interests in intermodal perception with her work on infants' understanding of objects.

Streri and Spelke (1988, 1989) allowed 4-month-old infants to handle (but not to see) a pair of rings that were connected by a rigid rod. In one condition the rings could be moved only as one rigid unit (much like a barbell, for example); in the other condition the rings could be pushed, pulled, and displaced independently. Infants subsequently looked longer at a visual display that was different from the one to which they had habituated tactilely: thus independently moving rings in the first condition, movement of a rigid, barbell-like object in the second condition. Infants thus showed the same ability to transfer information from one modality to another that had been reported by Meltzoff and Borton (1979) and Gibson and Walker (1984). Streri and Spelke's subjects did something more, however. They apparently were able to use information about object movement—in this case, information gained tactilely—to form conclusions about object unity and boundaries. Infants who had felt the rigid display, for example, subsequently looked longer at two separate rings than they did at two rings connected by a bar, a finding that suggests that they experienced the separate rings as novel; infants in the other condition showed the reverse pattern. Note that the infants had touched only the rings and not the bar during the initial phase; hence, either of the two visual displays was compatible with their tactile experience. Apparently, however, the infants used the common movement of the rings in one condition to infer that they were dealing with a single object (hence the novelty of the separate rings), and the independent movement of the rings in the other condition to infer that they were dealing with two objects. Once again, motion cues proved critical to infants' perception of objects—in this case, however, motion cues that were experienced only tactilely and then applied to the interpretation of visual experience.

We come finally to category (3): imitation of bodily movements. The kind of imitation that has been of greatest interest is the ability to imitate actions that one cannot see oneself perform. To illustrate this sort of imitation, suppose that someone makes a strange face, one that you yourself have never made, and asks you to make one exactly like it. You can probably produce a passable imitation of that face, despite its novelty for you and—especially important here—despite the fact that you cannot watch yourself making it or visually compare your facial appearance to the target's when you have finished. Presumably, you accomplish this feat by somehow coordinating and uniting within a single, amodal representation the visual information your eyes provide and the proprioceptive (muscle-sensation) information your facial motor movements provide. In other words, you engage in a form of intermodal perception to do this kind of imitation—namely, that of type (3) in our classification system.

One point that the preceding description is meant to convey is that your ability to imitate facial movements is actually a rather impressive cognitive achievement, requiring as it does the precise translation of purely visual input into the motoric commands necessary to produce a similar, unseen-by-you visual display. It is not the sort of achievement that one would expect to find in young infants. Piaget certainly did not think so—in his studies of infancy this form of imitation was seen as emerging near the end of the first year, and thus only after months of sensorimotor experience and earlier, simpler imitative acts (Piaget, 1962). Yet Meltzoff and Moore (1977, 1983a, 1983b, 1989) reported evidence from a series of studies suggesting that *newborns*, no less, are capable of this sort of imitation—and thus presumably of a very high level of intermodal coordination. As you might expect, the claim of such surprising early competence has sparked a firestorm of research and debate (Anisfeld, 1991; Bjorklund, 1987a; Poulson, Nunes, & Warren, 1989).

How can we test for imitation in neonates? Meltzoff and Moore (1983a) used the following method. The testing was done in a darkened room. The experimenter's face was illuminated by a spotlight to make it perceptually salient to the baby. The baby was seated semiupright in an infant's seat with his or her face positioned about 10 inches from the experimenter's. The experimenter would slowly open and close his mouth four times during a 20-second period, then adopt a passive face for 20 seconds, then slowly stick out and withdraw his tongue four times during a 20-second period, then adopt the passive face again for 20 seconds, and so on, for a total of 12 such alternating periods of mouth opening, passive face, and tongue protrusion; pilot work had shown that interspersing a passive face with the facial gestures helped maintain attention and responsivity. The baby's face was videotaped close up with an infrared-sensitive video camera during all these goings-on. The videotapes were later scored for mouth openings and tongue protrusions by an observer who was uninformed about which gesture had been shown to the infant in any given period. Meltzoff and Moore found that the neonates opened their mouths significantly more often in response to the experimenter's mouth openings than to his tongue protrusions, and also stuck out their tongues significantly more often in response to his tongue protrusions than to his mouth openings. Figure 2–2 shows some examples of the adult models and corresponding infant responses. Quite reasonably, the authors took these findings as evidence that the newborns had selectively imitated each of the two different facial movements. Other studies have reported evidence for newborn imitation of other adult gestures, including head rotation (Meltzoff & Moore, 1989) and lip pursing and widening (Reissland, 1988).

Critical objections to Meltzoff and Moore's claims have been of two sorts. One concerns replicability. Not all investigators who have searched for neonatal imitation have been able to find it. In a recent review of 26 experiments, Anisfeld (1991) concluded that the only gesture for which there was solid, across-study evidence of infant-adult matching was tongue protrusion; data with respect to other gestures were too limited or too contradictory to permit conclusions. The second objection concerns the interpretation of positive results when they do appear. The point at issue here is whether matches between infant gesture and adult gesture really reflect genuine imitation or whether such matches might have some other, simpler basis. One alternative that has been proposed draws on the ethologists' concept of innate releasing mechanisms. Proponents of this position argue that certain adult gestures, such as mouth opening, automatically elicit similar-looking behaviors in neonates, much as a mark on the mother's beak might elicit pecking in baby birds. By this view, the adult's behavior serves as a releaser rather than a model, the infant's behavior is a reflex rather than genuine imitation, and the early "imitations," like many other reflexes, simply wither away with age rather than developing into more mature forms of imitation. Anisfeld's (1991) preferred conclusion is somewhat different, but it also denies genuine imitation in the newborn. Anisfeld suggests that tongue protrusion, which occurs spontaneously with some frequency in neonates, is suppressed during presentation of an adult model, as all of the baby's limited attentional resources are devoted to the task of taking in the interesting facial display. Having been "dammed up" in this fashion, the tongue protrusion response then bursts forth with heightened frequency during the subsequent, postmodel response period. The impression is thus one of imitation, but in fact the correspondence between adult and infant is one of happenstance rather than being causal.

Having noted these criticisms, we should add that Meltzoff and Moore remain convinced of the validity of their conclusions, as indeed do many other students of infancy. Most of the rest of us are still on the fence: fascinated by the possibility that newborns can perform such a remarkable feat, but also—precisely because the feat *is* so remarkable—somewhat skeptical until unequivocal evidence is forthcoming. If Meltzoff and Moore's claims do prove valid, however, they would clearly constitute powerful evidence for an inborn capacity for intermodal perception. They would also stand as one of the most impressive entries in what we will see later in the chapter is a steadily growing list: namely, demonstrations that infants are a good deal more competent than Piaget believed.

FIGURE 2–2   Adult model and infant response in Meltzoff and Moore's study of neonatal imitation. Even very young infants appear to imitate the adult's facial expressions. From "Imitation of Facial and Manual Gestures by Human Neonates" by A. N. Meltzoff and M. K. Moore, 1977, *Science, 198*, p. 75. Copyright © 1977 by the American Association for the Advancement of Science. Reprinted by permission.

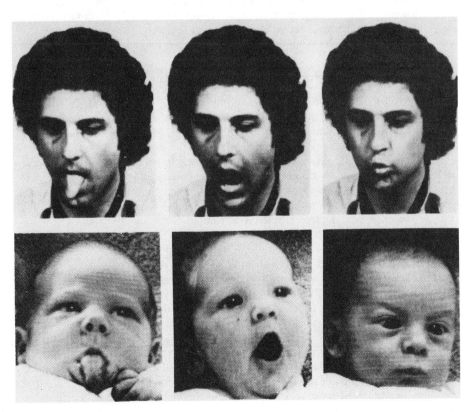

INFANT COGNITION

The writer of a text on cognitive development is faced with a dilemma when the discussion turns to cognition during infancy. On the one hand, it seems obvious that Piaget's work must play a prominent part in any such discussion (as indeed it did in the first two editions of this book). Piaget's studies of his own three infants (Piaget, 1952, 1954, 1962), carried out some 60 years ago, initiated the field of infant intelligence, and they have defined both the empirical phenomena and the theoretical issues that have most intrigued the field ever since. Piaget's theory remains our most comprehensive model of infant cognition, and the descriptive accuracy of much of what he saw in his own babies has been amply confirmed by more rigorous and objective follow-up studies. On the other hand, research efforts in the last dozen or so years—many capitalizing on methodologies not available to Piaget—have raised serious questions about the validity of many of Piaget's claims. These studies indicate that Piaget may have misjudged the nature and developmental course of many of the phenomena he studied. More generally, they suggest that development is not as slow, consistent, and stage-like as Piaget's theory would have it.

Our discussion of infant cognition will therefore be a two-part one. We begin with an overview of the classic Piagetian picture of infancy. This overview includes both the basic six-stage model of sensorimotor intelligence and a focus on an especially important acquisition of infancy: the development of the object concept. As we have just indicated, some parts of the Piagetian picture have held up well, and one goal of the review is to spell out what these enduring conclusions are. A second goal is to identify the Piagetian claims that have proved most controversial and that are the most active foci for current research. The second part of the coverage then summarizes what this recent research has told us.

Infant Cognition as Sensorimotor Intelligence

If the 5-month-old infant can be said to "think" and "know" at all, she certainly does not appear to do so in the usual sense of these terms. In what sense, then? What *does* the infant have or do that permits us to talk meaningfully about the nature and development of "infant cognition"?

According to Piaget, what she demonstrates, in an increasingly clear and unambiguous manner as she grows older, is the capacity for organized, "intelligent-looking" sensory and motor *actions*. That is, she exhibits a wholly practical, perceiving-and-doing, action-bound kind of intellectual functioning; she does not exhibit the more contemplative, reflective, symbol-manipulating kind we usually think of in connection with cognition. The infant "knows" in the sense of recognizing or anticipating familiar, recurring objects and happenings, and "thinks" in the sense of behaving toward them with mouth, hand, eye, and other sensorimotor instruments in predictable, organized, and often adaptive ways. Hers is an entirely unconscious and self-unaware, nonsymbolic and nonsymbolizable (by the infant) type of cognition. It is the kind of noncontemplative intelligence that a dog relies on to make its way in the world. It is also the kind that you yourself exhibit when performing many actions that are characteristically nonsymbolic and unthinking by virtue of being so overlearned and automatized—for example, brushing your teeth, starting the car, mowing the lawn, visually monitoring the grass in front of you for obstacles while doing so, and so on. It is, to repeat, intelligence as inherent and manifest in organized patterns of sensory and motor action, and hence Piaget's description of infant cognition as presymbolic, prerepresentational, and prereflective "sensorimotor intelligence."

Sensorimotor Schemes

In the previous chapter we spoke of the child's assimilating external data to _____ and accommodating _____ to external data, with the blanks variously filled in with "mental framework," "favored ways of thinking about things," "cognitive structure," "conception," "concept," and similar expressions. All of these terms refer to some sort of enduring cognitive organization or knowledge structure within a child's head that does the assimilating and accommodating. When talking specifically about infantile, sensorimotor assimilating and accommodating, as contrasted with developmentally more advanced, symbolic-representational forms, Piaget would fill in the blank with the word *scheme*.

The meaning of *scheme* is easier to convey by example than by formal definition. A scheme generally has to do with a specific, readily labelable class of sensorimotor action sequences that the infant repeatedly and habitually carries out, normally in response to particular classes of objects or situations. The scheme itself is generally thought of as referring to the inner, mental-structural basis for these overt action sequences; it is, in other words, the cognitive capacity that underlies and makes possible such organized behavior patterns. Thus, young infants who automatically suck anything that finds its way into their mouth would be said to possess a "sucking scheme"—that is, they possess an enduring ability and disposition to carry out a specific class of action sequences (organized sucking movements) in response to a particular class of happenings (the insertion of suckable objects). Similarly, one can talk about sensorimotor schemes of looking, listening, grasping, hitting, pushing, kicking, and so on. A scheme is a kind of sensorimotor level counterpart of a symbolic-representational level concept. An older person *represents* (thinks of, verbally characterizes) a given object as an instance of the class, "nipple"; analogously, the baby *acts* or *behaves* toward the same object as though it belonged to the (functional) class, "something to suck."

A very important property of schemes is that they may be combined or coordinated to form larger wholes or units of sensorimotor intelligence. For instance, once an infant has achieved a certain level of cognitive development, he or she is capable of pushing aside ("pushing" being one motor scheme) an obstacle in order to seize (another motor scheme) a desired object. We see a similar integration of sucking and manual prehension schemes once the infant acquires the systematic tendency to bring to the mouth anything the hand chances to grasp. As elementary schemes gradually become generalized, differentiated, and above all intercoordinated and integrated with one another in diverse and complex ways, the infant's behavior begins to look more and more unambiguously "intelligent" and "cognitive."

Cognitive Motivation

Up to this point we have described a cognitive system that is sensorimotor rather than symbolic-representational in type, and one that functions and gradually transforms itself developmentally by simultaneously assimilating data to schemes and accommodating schemes to data. We have said nothing, however, about why the sensorimotor or any subsequent cognitive system should ever operate in the first place, nor about the circumstances under which it would be most likely to operate with maximum intensity and persistence. What needs to be added is an account of cognitive motivation—that is, of the factors and forces that activate or intensify human cognitive processing.

Human beings obviously exercise their knowledge and cognitive skills for a wide variety of reasons to attain a wide variety of goals. Some of these reasons and goals are basically noncognitive in character; they are *extrinsic* rather than *intrinsic* to the cognitive system itself. The infant who grasps and sucks a bottle simply to satisfy his or her hunger rather than to learn about the graspable and suckable potentialities of bottles is clearly activating sensorimotor skills in the service of an extrinsic, noncognitive need or goal. The same is true of the 3-year-old who makes intelligent use of a pair of footstools to obtain an out-of-reach cookie, and of the high school student who studies hard solely for parental approval.

Most interesting, however, is the fact that a very great deal of human mentation, at all developmental levels, is intrinsically rather than extrinsically motivated. That is, the cognitive system is often turned on and kept running by purely cognitive factors, rather than by bodily needs or other motivational sources. The following behavioral episode, brief though it is, illustrates most of the factors of this sort that psychologists have identified:

> Standing by the side of a low table the 12-month-old girl bangs on a pegboard with a block she has been holding; at the far end of the table the lid of an improperly closed coffee pot produces a loud rattle. The little girl freezes; her eyes explore the table top. She hits the pegboard again, and the small movements of the lid attract her attention. She moves over, picks up the lid, and rattles it against the pot; then back to her pegboard and block. She bangs: the lid rattles. The little girl gurgles, a wide smile appears on her face. A glance at her mother—still with that enormous smile—and on with her banging and the pot's rattling, to an accompaniment of gurgles, babblings, and small bounces of delight. (Bronson, 1971, p. 269)

Why does the little girl bang on the pegboard in the first place? While it may sound like circular reasoning to say this, the best answer is that banging things to see, hear, and feel the results represents a common, probably universally acquired sensorimotor scheme, and it is simply in the nature of schemes to exercise themselves repeatedly, especially when first acquired. To ask why the child bangs when provided with a banging scheme and a compliant object to bang with is, for Piaget and many other psychologists, much like asking why she breathes when provided with lungs and air. There exists, in Hunt's words (1969, p. 37), "a system of motivation *inherent in* information processing and action" (italics added). Consistent with this idea is the research discussed earlier which indicates that babies can be operantly conditioned using interesting sights and sounds as the only rewards. That is, babies will "work" (make repeated motor responses) for the sole privilege of viewing pictures, listening to voices, and so on, just as they would "work" for traditional reinforcers such as food.

An intrinsic tendency to be active is part of the motivational story. The other part concerns the stimuli and events that are most likely to engage the infant's interest and activity. The coffee pot vignette provides an example. When the coffee-pot lid makes a loud rattle, the little girl freezes, visually explores the table top, and hits the pegboard again. Certain classes of inputs to the cognitive system tend to turn its operating volume way up. When these kinds of inputs are received, ongoing activities get temporarily suspended, the child becomes somewhat tense and aroused, and a variety of attentional, curiosity, exploratory, and other information-seeking behaviors are likely to ensue. What sorts of inputs have this remarkable quality? According to Piaget, the inputs that are most interesting are those that the infant can almost but not quite understand—that is, those events that are familiar enough to be assimilated by the current schemes but different enough to force some accommodative effort in order for the infant to make sense of them. More specifically, the kinds of events that engage the infant's activity are precisely those that we identified earlier as determinants of infant visual attention: events that—in relation to the infant's cognitive system—are in some way novel, complex, surprising, or puzzling.

Because the earlier discussion concerned vision, it is important to note that such interest-arousing events are not limited to the visual realm; appropriate input to any sensory modality may activate the motivational system (witness the loud rattle in the example). It is important to note as well that response does not necessarily end with increased attention to the interesting event. According to Piaget, the infant will be motivated to continue to act toward the event until she has somehow made sense of it—until what was initially incomprehensible has been made once again comprehensible. This is certainly the case in the example. The little girl explores and experiments until she discovers the cause of the unexpected rattling noise, she shows signs of extreme pleasure and satisfaction when she does discover it, and she then repeats her banging again and again with great gusto. For Piaget, this example illustrates in miniature the nature of cognitive motivation and cognitive change: The infant creates new experiences for herself through her own actions on the environment; some of these experiences prove to be especially interesting because they go optimally beyond what she currently understands; the infant then acts further toward these new experiences, varying her schemes in an effort to arrive at a new understanding; behaviors that serve to reduce uncertainty and lead to new knowledge are especially pleasureful and are likely to be repeated; and in this way—through countless instances of action, uncertainty, and further action—the cognitive system moves to new and better levels of understanding.

One more point about Piaget's motivational model is worth making. The idea that there is motivation intrinsic to the cognitive system (and not, for example, solely from biological drives such as hunger or pain) is today quite widely held. Also quite common, as we have seen, is the idea that there is something especially motivating about events that are novel, discrepant, surprising, and the like. These ideas were by no means common wisdom, however, when Piaget first proposed them 60 years ago; indeed, they were opposed to the models of motivation and of human infancy then extant (e.g., Freudian theory, the behaviorism of John Watson). In this respect, as in many others, Piaget helped to change the ways in which we think about children and about human intelligence.

Piaget's Six Stages of Sensorimotor Development

The sensorimotor period is the first of four general periods into which Piaget's theory divides development (we will encounter the later periods in subsequent chapters). The sensorimotor period is, in turn, divided into six stages.

The age range designated for each of the six stages is meant to be only a very rough average. Individual infants might therefore pass through any of the stages more rapidly or more slowly than these crude age norms would suggest. The *sequence* of stages, however, is believed to be absolutely constant or invariant for children the world over. Thus, Piaget claimed that no earlier stage is ever skipped en route to any later one and no stages are ever navigated in a developmental order other than the one given. Finally, the accomplishments of each stage are said to cumulate—that is, skills achieved in earlier stages are not lost with the advent of later stages.

STAGE 1 (ROUGHLY 0 TO 1 MONTH). The infant comes into the world equipped with a variety of reflexes. Some of them are of no cognitive-developmental interest because they are destined either to remain unchanged with age and never become cognitively relevant (e.g., the sneeze) or to actually disappear entirely (e.g., the Moro response, a specifically infantile type of startle pattern). Others, like sucking, eye movements, and movements of the hand and arm, are destined to undergo significant developmental changes as a function of constant exercise and repeated application to external objects and events. Piaget attributed a great deal of importance to these latter reflexes because he regarded them as the initial, innately provided building blocks of human cognitive growth. He conceived of them, in other words, as the infant's first sensorimotor schemes.

During the initial month of postnatal life, Piaget observed what appeared to be very small but possibly significant alterations in sucking behavior. Although cautious on this point, he felt that these alterations might reflect minimal, beginning changes (consolidation, stabilization, generalization, and differentiation) in the structure of the infant's sucking scheme. Moreover, he believed the changes to be at least partly due to repeated practice and experience with "suckables" of different types—for instance, a soft and milk-producing nipple versus a harder and more arid thumb. Such experience-based changes in the sucking scheme would certainly comprise a humble but genuine instance of that gradual, "leg-over-leg" type of Piagetian developmental process described in Chapter 1.

STAGE 2 (ROUGHLY 1 TO 4 MONTHS). This stage is marked first by the continued evolution of individual sensorimotor schemes, and second by the gradual coordination or integration of one scheme with another. On the first point, individual schemes associated with such processes as sucking, looking, listening, vocalizing, and prehension (grasping objects) receive an enormous amount of spontaneous daily practice—recall our discussion of intrinsic cognitive motivation. As a consequence, each of these schemes undergoes considerable developmental elaboration and refinement during these months. To continue with the Stage 1 example, sucking continues to be perfected as a motor skill. Toward the end of Stage 2 it may even occur anticipatively in response to associated visual or kinesthetic cues—in response, for instance, to the mere sight of the approaching nipple or the mere sensation of being held in the accustomed feeding position.

More interesting than this perfecting of individual, isolated schemes is the progressive coordination or coming-into-relation of one scheme with another. For example, vision and audition begin to become functionally related. Hearing a sound leads the infant to turn his head and eyes in the direction of the sound source. Activation of his listening-hearing schemes with their auditory assimilation-accommodation processes induces a corresponding activation of his looking-seeing schemes with their visual assimilation-accommodation processes.

Two other important scheme-scheme coordinations that get well established in Stage 2 are those of sucking-prehension and vision-prehension. In the case of sucking-prehension, the infant develops the ability (and very strong inclination) to bring to his mouth, and suck, his hand and anything the hand may have grasped, and also to grasp whatever may have found its way into his mouth. The coordination of vision with prehension permits the infant to locate and grasp objects under visual guidance and, reciprocally, to bring before his eyes for visual inspection anything an out-of-sight hand may have touched and grasped. The evolution of vision-prehension coordination is the more noteworthy development of the two, because an ability to coordinate hand and eye will prove to be an extraordinarily important means or instrument for exploring and learning about the child's environment. Recall from our section on Relating Information from Different Senses that recent research has shown that the beginnings of coordination and integration of sensory systems (vision with audition, vision with touch, etc.) are more precocious than Piaget suspected and that, contrary to his belief, some degree of intersensory coordination may even be present from birth.

STAGE 3 (ROUGHLY 4 TO 8 MONTHS). The Stage 2 acquisition of visually guided manual activity helps make possible a new behavior pattern that constitutes the major achievement of Stage 3. The pattern begins when the infant chances to carry out some motor action, often a manual one, that happens to produce some unanticipated but perceptually interesting outcome in the environment. The pattern ends with the child delightedly repeating the action again and again, apparently for the sheer pleasure of reproducing and reexperiencing the environmental outcome. The child might grasp and shake a new toy, for instance, and that new toy might unexpectedly respond with a rattling sound. Whereupon, the child of this stage is likely to pause in wonderment, hesitatingly shake it again, hear the sound once again, more quickly and confidently shake it a third time, and then continue to repeat the action again and again for a considerable period of time.

There are several things to be said about this behavior pattern. First, it is reminiscent of our 12-month-old girl's banging-and-lid-rattling sequence (pp. 48–49). In contrast to the 1-year-old, however, the infant of 4 to 8 months is probably still too immature to have even an implicit, sensorimotor level sense of cause-effect relations, and will accordingly show none of the older child's efforts to explore the cause of the enjoyable perceptual experience. There is reason to doubt whether the younger infant even distinguishes clearly between his motor action and its environmental result, whereas it is certain that the older infant makes this basic distinction.

Second, for the very reason that the action and its environmental result are likely not clearly separated in the Stage 3 infant's experience, Piaget is loath to credit the child with a clear and unambiguous capacity for intentional, deliberate, goal-directed action. It just does not quite seem justified to say of this infant, as it will of the Stage 4 infant, that he kept shaking the toy *in order* to produce the sound—that is, as an intentional, deliberately selected means to a clearly separate, anticipated end.

Finally, despite these limitations, the Stage 3 pattern represents genuine cognitive progress because it possesses one crucial feature. The infant of the two previous stages has been, in a manner of speaking, more preoccupied with his own actions than with the environmental effects these actions might produce. There is a kind of empty, "objectless" quality about the way the younger infant exercises his sensorimotor schemes. He seems to suck for the sake of sucking and grasp for the sake of grasping, evincing relatively little interest in the specific physical and functional properties of the objects sucked and grasped. From Stage 3 on, however, the baby shows an increasing interest in the effects of his actions on objects and events in the outside world and in learning about the real properties of these objects and events by carefully attending to those effects. The baby thus becomes more cognitively as well as more socially "extroverted" in the course of sensorimotor development. He gradually becomes an object explorer rather than a mere scheme exerciser, and the first small signs of this change are manifest in Stage 3.

STAGE 4 (ROUGHLY 8 TO 12 MONTHS). The major novelty of this stage is the appearance of unmistakably intentional, means-ends behavior. The child's actions are now unquestionably purposeful and goal directed, and for this reason look more "intelligent," more "cognitive," than those of previous stages. As in Stage 2, individual sensorimotor schemes become coordinated and integrated. However, the schemes in question are now primarily those outer-directed, environmental-effect-oriented, Stage 3 ones just mentioned, and their integration is more clearly an integration into a means-end action pattern. In Stage 4, the child intentionally exercises one scheme, as means, in order to make possible the exercise of another scheme, as end or goal. He may push your hand (means) in order to get you to continue to produce some interesting sensory effect (end) you had been producing for his benefit. Similarly, he may push aside (one motor scheme) an object in order to grasp (second motor scheme) another object.

There is also a parallel between Stage 2 and Stage 4 regarding the use of signs to anticipate events. It was said of the Stage 2 infant that he sometimes could respond anticipatively to a sign of an impending stimulus rather than having to wait until the stimulation actually occurred; he might occasionally commence sucking movements at the mere sight of the looming nipple, for instance. The Stage 4 infant also does the same thing, of course, and does it much better. In addition, however, the older child can read signs of impending events that are not directly connected, in stimulus-response fashion, with his own behavior. His mother starts to turn toward the door and the Stage 4 child may cry in anticipation of her departure. We might say that the younger infant anticipates the incipient exercise of one of his schemes whereas the older infant anticipates the occurrence of some event in the outside world. This change in how signs are read, in what they are taken to be signs *of*, is obviously in keeping with the aforementioned developmental trend toward cognitive extroversion, toward a heightened concern with the outside world in contrast to one's own purely egocentric, "objectless" actions.

STAGE 5 (ROUGHLY 12 TO 18 MONTHS). Since, according to Piaget, symbolic-representational as distinguished from sensorimotor ways of knowing begin to manifest themselves during Stage 6, Stage 5 could be regarded as the last "pure" sensorimotor stage. Its essence is a very active, purposeful, trial-and-error exploration of the real properties and potentialities of objects, largely through the relentless search for new and different ways to act upon them. Infantile cognitive extroversion is now at its height; the child has a resolutely experimental, exploration-and-discovery oriented approach to the outside world. Present him with a novel object and he will actively try to lay bare its structural and functional properties by trying this, and that, and yet another action pattern on it, often making up new variations on old action patterns in the course of doing so. Similarly, whereas the Stage 4 infant would be apt to carry out a means-end behavior sequence in a more or less fixed, stereotyped way, the Stage 5 child would be likely to vary the means scheme in a deliberate, let's-see-what-would-happen-if sort of attitude; he might, to refer back to a Stage 4 example, remove the offending obstacle this way, then that way, then still another way.

With his strongly accommodative, exploratory bent, the Stage 5 child often discovers wholly new means to familiar ends. For instance, Piaget describes his discovering that an out-of-reach object can be secured by pulling a string attached to it, or a small rug on which it rests. These particular examples are intriguing because they might be early precursors of tool use, an especially important type of human intelligent behavior.

STAGE 6 (ROUGHLY 18 TO 24 MONTHS). "Roughly 18 months on" would be just as accurate a dating for this stage, because its most important achievement remains an essential attribute of cognitive functioning for the rest of the individual's life. That achievement is the ability to represent the objects of one's cognition by means of symbols and to act intelligently with respect to this inner, symbolized reality rather than simply, in sensorimotor fashion, with respect to the outer, unsymbolized reality. The Stage 6 child shows a beginning capacity to produce and comprehend one thing (e.g., a word) as standing for or symbolically representing some other thing (e.g., a class of objects). Moreover, the child becomes capable of mentally differentiating between the symbol and its referent— that is, the thing the symbol stands for. As an example of this differentiation, the symbol could be physically quite different from its referent object and still be treated as a representation of that object. Similarly, the child might spontaneously produce the symbol and think about it even when the referent is not physically present. For the child to name a present object that he *sees* is quite possibly a symbolic act; for the child to name an object that he has just *thought of* is unquestionably a symbolic act. Responding to internal, self-generated objects of cognition is decidedly *not* a sensorimotor activity. Piaget refers to this newly developed, Stage 6 capacity for representation as the *semiotic* (or *symbolic*) function.

As always, the achievements of a new Piagetian stage are clearest when contrasted with the upper limits of the preceding stage. The Stage 5 child discovers new means to attain his behavioral objectives by overt, trial-and-error experimentation; he studiously varies his external behavior and, by doing so, may hit upon an effective procedure for achieving his goal. In contrast, the Stage 6, symbolic child may try out alternative means *internally*, by imagining them or representing them to himself instead of actualizing them in overt behavior. If an effective procedure is found in this fashion, by taking thought rather than by taking overt action, we might think of it more as invention or insight than as trial-and-error discovery. Accordingly, Piaget refers to this aspect of Stage 5 adapted intelligence as "the discovery of new means through active experimentation," whereas its Stage 6 counterpart is called "the invention of new means through mental combinations."

A celebrated example of the latter among Piaget readers was conveniently provided by his daughter Lucienne at the tender age of 16 months. Lucienne wanted to extract a small chain from one of those old-fashioned, sliding-drawer type matchboxes, but the drawer opening was too small for her to reach in and get it. After some unsuccessful, Stage 5 type fumblings she paused, studied the box, slowly opened and closed her mouth a few times, then quickly widened the drawer opening and triumphantly retrieved the chain. It seems reasonable to interpret her mouth movements as a primitive nonverbal, symbolic representation of a possible but as yet untried behavioral means to the desired end. To be sure, her representational response was very similar to its referent physically and was also produced in the same immediate situation. Nonetheless, it would take an unusually tough-minded and skeptical observer to find nothing of the genuinely symbolic and representational in this behavior. Certainly, it is a type of behavior that we are unlikely to see in a younger infant but one that becomes increasingly common by the end of infancy: namely, problem solving based not on overt trial-and-error experimentation but on the generation and manipulation of mental symbols.

Mental problem solving is just one of the Stage 6 accomplishments that leads Piaget to conclude that a general capacity for symbolic functioning has emerged. The child is now capable for the first time of *deferred imitation*, in which actions witnessed but not imitated on a given occasion are spontaneously reproduced in full detail at a later time. One of Piaget's children, for example, watched in mute fascination while another child threw a three-star temper tantrum. She then produced an excellent imitation of it the next day. Presumably, she must have generated some sort of internal representation (possibly a visual image) of the tantrum as a guide for her imitative action, thus making possible her reproduction of a model that was no longer physically present. *Pretend* or *symbolic play* also makes its first appearance in Stage 6. At 18 months, Piaget's daughter Jacqueline said "soap" while pretending to wash her hands by rubbing them together; at 20 months, she pretended to eat bits of paper and other inedibles, saying "very nice." The representational, purely symbolic quality of this kind of play is obvious. Finally, there is the example with which we opened our discussion of Stage 6: the ability to generate a word to stand for an absent object. *Language* is an indubitably symbolic activity, and it is made possible, according to Piaget, by the general capacity for representational functioning that emerges as the culmination of sensorimotor development.

As we noted earlier, sensorimotor intelligence does not disappear with the end of infancy; rather, sensorimotor forms of functioning remain available to us throughout life. Once symbolic ability has emerged, however, the highest and most powerful forms of intelligence occur on a new plane. It is worth taking a moment to reflect on the momentous differences between symbolic-representational thought and sensorimotor intelligence. Sensorimotor actions must proceed slowly, step by step, one action at a time. Symbolic-representational thought can be much faster and more freely mobile in its operation; it can range over a whole series of past, present, and future events in one quick sweep of the mind. The former is by its very nature more oriented toward actions and concrete, practical results, whereas the latter can be more preoccupied with knowledge per se; one focuses more on acts and outcomes, the other more on information and truth. The former is ineluctably concrete and earthbound. The latter is potentially abstract and free to soar, and, in fact, becomes increasingly so as the child matures. Indeed, it can eventually even take itself as its own cognitive object; that is, a relatively mature mind can think about its own thoughts. Finally, the former is necessarily private, idiosyncratic, and uncommunicable to others; each baby is imprisoned in his or her own separate cognitive world. The latter comes to make fluent use of a socially shared symbolic system (natural language) and can thereby communicate with, and gradually become socialized by, other human beings.

Piaget's six-stage model tends to be difficult to learn and remember. Figure 2–3 provides what we hope will be a helpful summary. A sequence of items is generally easiest to remember if each item bears some meaningful relationship to both its predecessor and successor, and Figure 2–3 attempts to point out the relationships of this kind that obtain for Piaget's stages.

The Object Concept

Piaget's *object concept*, or *concept of object permanence*, refers to a set of implicit, commonsensical beliefs we all share about the basic nature and behavior of

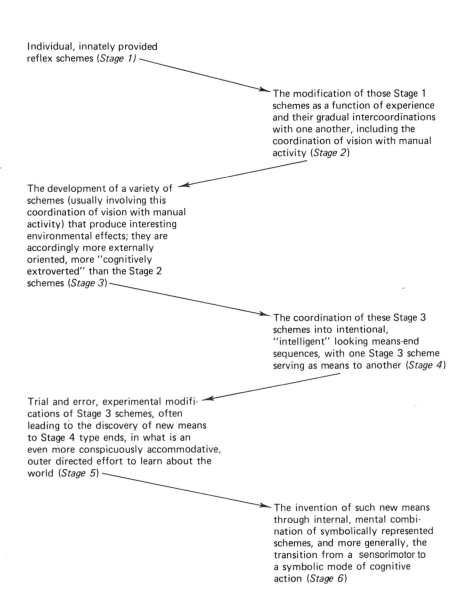

Individual, innately provided reflex schemes (*Stage 1*)

The modification of those Stage 1 schemes as a function of experience and their gradual intercoordinations with one another, including the coordination of vision with manual activity (*Stage 2*)

The development of a variety of schemes (usually involving this coordination of vision with manual activity) that produce interesting environmental effects; they are accordingly more externally oriented, more "cognitively extroverted" than the Stage 2 schemes (*Stage 3*)

The coordination of these Stage 3 schemes into intentional, "intelligent" looking means-end sequences, with one Stage 3 scheme serving as means to another (*Stage 4*)

Trial and error, experimental modifications of Stage 3 schemes, often leading to the discovery of new means to Stage 4 type ends, in what is an even more conspicuously accommodative, outer directed effort to learn about the world (*Stage 5*)

The invention of such new means through internal, mental combination of symbolically represented schemes, and more generally, the transition from a sensorimotor to a symbolic mode of cognitive action (*Stage 6*)

FIGURE 2-3   A mnemonic for recalling the highlights of Piaget's sensorimotor stages regarding adapted intelligence. Each earlier stage can be construed as a reasonable foundation or prerequisite for the one immediately following, and each later stage can be thought of as a plausible next developmental step, once its immediate predecessor is achieved.

objects, including ourselves. We tacitly believe, first of all, that we and all other objects coexist as physically distinct and independent entities within a common, all-enveloping space. We are objects in that space, so are you, and so is this book; we are all more or less equal-status "co-objects" together, each of us with our own individual quantum of space-filling bulk and our own individual potential for movement or displacement within our common spatial habitat. We also implicitly understand that the existence of our fellow objects, animate and inanimate alike, is fundamentally independent of our own interaction or noninteraction with these other objects. When an object disappears from our sight, for example, we do not assume that it has thereby gone out of existence. In other words, we do not confuse our own actions toward another object—our seeing it, hearing, touching it, and so on—with the physical existence of that object, and hence we do not think it automatically becomes annihilated once we lose behavioral contact with it. Finally, we believe that the object's behavior is also independent of our psychological contact with it, just as its existence is. We know that once gone from our sight, for instance, the object could perfectly well move or be moved from one location to another. It may or may not continue to await us at the place where we last saw it; we may or may not have to look elsewhere for it. In summary, we all possess an implicit, unarticulated conception of objects, which asserts that other physical objects and ourselves are equally real and "objective," volume-occupying inhabitants of a common spatial world, and that both the existence and the behavior of other objects are fundamentally independent of our perceptual and motor contact with them.

Piaget made three rather startling claims about the object concept, again based upon observations of the sensorimotor development of his own children. First, he claimed that this utterly basic, "obvious" conception of objects is not inborn but needs to be acquired through experience. Second, its acquisition is a surprisingly protracted one, spanning the entire sensorimotor period of infancy. Finally, this process consists of a universal, fixed sequence of developmental stages or subacquisitions, the infant picking up different aspects or components of the full concept at different stages. Thus, there is a sense in which it could be said that a 1-year-old has "more of," or a "different level of," this concept than a 6-month-old, for instance, although the 1-year-old has not yet achieved the final, complete version of it.

It is inconceivable that anyone writing a textbook on cognitive development nowadays would fail to include something on the evolution of the Piagetian object concept. In the first place, the concept itself is so utterly basic and fundamental. If any concept could be regarded as indispensable to a coherent and rational mental life, this one certainly would be. Imagine what your life would be like if you did not believe that objects continued to exist when they left your field of vision. Worse yet, imagine how things would be if *nobody* believed it. It also happens that Piaget's developmental story here is just plain interesting to most people; it is simply one of the very best tales in the developmentalist's anthology. Moreover, various researchers have attempted to clarify our understanding of just how this development proceeds. Some of this research confirms or extends what Piaget said, and these studies are mentioned in the current section. Some of the research challenges the Piagetian account, and these studies are the subject of the next section.

Piaget assumed that the development of the object concept is intimately linked to sensorimotor development as a whole. He therefore used the same six-stage framework to describe the developmental changes.

STAGES 1 AND 2 (ROUGHLY 0 TO 4 MONTHS). During this early period, the infant characteristically will try to follow a moving object with his or her eyes until it disappears from view—for instance, until it goes behind a screen of some kind. Whereupon, the infant will immediately lose interest and turn away or, at most, continue to stare for a short time at the place where it was last seen. There is as yet no behavior that could be interpreted as visual or manual search for the vanished object, and therefore, Piaget concludes, no positive evidence to suggest that the infant has any knowledge whatever of its continuing existence, once visual contact with it is lost.

STAGE 3 (ROUGHLY 4 TO 8 MONTHS). The infant shows some progress during this stage in differentiating object-as-independent-entity from self's-action-toward-object, but it will become apparent that the differentiation process still has a long way to go. There are several positive accomplishments. By the end of Stage 2, the infant has become quite accomplished at visually tracking objects, pursuing them when they move, and visually fixating them when they stop moving (Bower, 1982). During Stage 3, the infant begins to anticipate their future positions by extrapolating from their present direction of movement. For example, after some experience in watching a toy train repeatedly enter and leave a tunnel on a circular track, babies in this age range begin to anticipate visually the train's reemergence from the tunnel rather than to look toward the exit only when the train actually appears (K. E. Nelson, 1971). The Stage 3 child may also recognize and reach toward a familiar object even if only a part of it is visible, something he could not do earlier. For instance, he might recognize and grasp at his bottle even when all but the nipple end of it is covered by a washcloth.

If this very same bottle is totally covered, however, it is an astonishing fact that the infant will *not* manually search for it. The reaching hand can sometimes be seen even to drop in midflight once the desired object wholly disappears from view. Note that the infant is physically capable of reaching for objects—he will reach if a part of the target is visible, and he will reach if a transparent rather than opaque cover is placed over the object (Bower & Wishart, 1972; P. L. Harris, 1983). Such manual search occurs, however, only if there is some visible evidence of continuing existence. Incredibly, the Stage 3 infant will not retrieve an object *even when he has already grasped it*, if you quickly cover both object and grasping hand with a washcloth (Gratch, 1972; Gratch & Landers, 1971). Instead, he is likely either to continue to hold onto the object and idly look around as though unaware that he has anything in his hand, or else to let go of it, remove his empty hand, and show no further search behavior. Piaget believed that in Stage 3 the object is not yet credited with an enduring life of its own, apart from and independent of the subject's perceptual—especially visual—contact with it.

STAGE 4 (ROUGHLY 8 TO 12 MONTHS). The Stage 4 infant has overcome many of the limitations of Stage 3. In particular, the child will now manually search for and retrieve hidden objects—even when the object is totally hidden and hence no visible clues signal its existence.

There is, however, a most peculiar limitation on this newly developed ability to find hidden objects. The child watches you hide object X under cover A and he gleefully pulls off the cover and grabs it. You repeat the hiding a few times; he repeats the finding each time. Then you very slowly and conspicuously hide X under cover B, located to one side of cover A, making sure that the child watches you do it. Quite often, the Stage 4 child will immediately search under A once again and then abandon the search when he fails to find anything there, thus making what has come to be called the $A\overline{B}$ (i.e., A not B) error. Why on earth would he do such an odd thing? What level of object-concept development might this bizarre-looking behavior reflect?

Piaget believed that the Stage 4 child does not yet have a clear and conscious mental image of X quietly abiding beneath a cover. He may instead have evolved in this situation a little sensorimotor habit or behavioral "rule" that says, in effect, "Search over there, under that, and you'll have an interesting visual-tactile-manipulative experience." The object of the interesting sensorimotor experience (i.e., X) is psychologically embedded in the experience itself and remains secondary to it. According to Piaget's interpretation, the differentiation between self's action and object is not yet complete; X is not yet the genuinely action-independent "object-of-contemplation" it will eventually become.

STAGE 5 (ROUGHLY 12 TO 18 MONTHS). As Stage 4 draws to a close, Piaget believed that the balance begins to shift from previous motoric success to present perceptual evidence, and the Stage 5 child gradually learns to search at whatever place the object was most recently seen to disappear. In the $A\overline{B}$ setup described previously, this, of course, means going directly to B when X is hidden at B, even though X had previously been hidden and found at A. Piaget believed that the Stage 5 child has progressed further than the Stage 4 child in the crucial matter of differentiating the object per se from his actions toward it. The older infant can read the visual evidence of X's present location more or less objectively; he is no longer locked into a rigid dependence on previous patterns of successful action-toward-object.

There is, however, one final limitation to be overcome: The Stage 5 infant cannot imagine or represent any further changes of location the object might have undergone after it disappeared from his view. Let us suppose you put a small object in a felt-lined cup, turn the cup upside down, slide it under a large cloth, silently deposit the object underneath the cloth, and withdraw the empty cup (D. J. Miller, Cohen, & Hill, 1970). The prototypical Stage 5 child is incapable of searching for the object anywhere but in the cup, presumably because the cup rather than the cloth was the place where he saw it disappear. As yet, he cannot represent any unseen but readily (to us) inferable movement of the object when inside the cup. In Piaget's words, the child can cope with *visible displacements* but not yet with *invisible displacements*. More precisely, he can infer X's present location from its most recent visible displacement (as the Stage 4 child could not do, you recall, when under the baleful influence of previous visible displacements), but cannot infer X's invisible displacement on the basis of the visible displacements of its container.

STAGE 6 (ROUGHLY 18 TO 24 MONTHS). The just-mentioned limitation is overcome in this stage, with the child gradually acquiring the knack of using the visual evidence as a basis for imagining or representing X's unseen itineraries and hiding places. The really accomplished Stage 6-er can be very, very good at it. You put X inside your closed fist and move your fist first under cloth A, then under B, then under C, and then open it up, *sans* object (you have actually left it under cloth A). Many a 2-year-old will grin with anticipation and then systematically search each possible hiding place, sometimes in the reverse order from your hiding—that is, first under C, then under B, and finally under A. He may also spontaneously try the same game on you, with his doing the hiding and you doing the finding (and it would be a coldhearted experimenter indeed who would not let him do it). The full-fledged object concept is so clearly "there" in such a child that you feel you can virtually mind-read it. You are *sure* that he is somehow mentally representing that object during its invisible perambulations, and *sure* that he implicitly regards it as an external entity that exists and may move about in complete independence of his own perceptual or motor contact with it. But, of course, he is now in sensorimotor Stage 6, and the essential accomplishment of that stage is precisely that of being able to evoke internal symbolic representations of absent objects and events (recall deferred imitation and symbolic play).

In our discussion of perceptual constancy we noted that one important task for the cognitive system is to figure out what it is that stays the same—remains invariant—when other, usually more obvious, things are changing. The Piagetian object concept is the major such acquisition of infant cognition: the realization that the existence of objects remains invariant despite changes in our perceptual contact with them.

More Recent Research

OBJECT CONCEPT. Far more follow-up research has been done on object-concept development than on any other Piagetian infant acquisition. The object concept is therefore a sensible topic with which to begin our survey of recent research and its implications for Piaget's claims. As we will see, however, the conclusions that emerge from this work are not limited to the object concept but can probably be extended to the sensorimotor theory as a whole.

What are these conclusions? The most general conclusion—and also the one that is least in dispute—is that Piaget underestimated the young infant's competence. Babies know more about objects—and indeed many other things—than Piaget believed. The primary reason for the underestimation is methodological. We noted earlier in the chapter that the young infant is in some respects a rather limited creature, unable to speak, to locomote independently, or to perform much in the way of voluntary and controlled motoric behavior. The young infant just *looks* incompetent to the naked eye, and Piaget—working in the home and without the technological refinements of recent years—was very much dependent on overt behaviors that could be seen with the naked eye.

Consider the case of object permanence. Piaget's conclusions about the infant's knowledge of objects were based largely on the infant's ability to perform active motoric search behaviors—to reach out and remove covers, push aside or peer around screens, and the like. Later studies utilizing similar behaviors have confirmed the accuracy of Piaget's descriptive account: Very young infants tend not to search for objects at all, and when search behaviors do emerge they show the same initial limitations and the same gradual, sequential progress to full mastery reported by Piaget (P. L. Harris, 1989b; Uzguris & Hunt, 1975). But failure to search, in itself, tells us only that the infant is either not able or not disposed to organize an effective search routine. It does not prove that the infant has absolutely no knowledge of the continuing existence of the object.

What *could* a young infant do to demonstrate some knowledge of object permanence? Much of the research of the last 20 years has been based on the same general approach and rationale: See whether the infant somehow responds differently to possible events than to impossible ones—that is, events that in some way violate the rules of object permanence. See, in particular, whether the infant seems to find the latter, never-could-occur events especially interesting, surprising, or intriguing. The infant might signal such a reaction in a number of ways—through increased looking time, for example, or through a change in heart rate, or through a puzzled or perplexed expression. Any adult confronted with a violation of the object concept would certainly show such behaviors. Perhaps we can use similar responses to glean some evidence of understanding in the preverbal, largely premotoric young infant.

The violation-of-expectancy paradigm was first explored in the 1960s and 1970s in some pioneering studies by Thomas Bower and William Charlesworth (e.g., Bower, 1974; Charlesworth, 1966). Its most informative variant has come more recently, however, in an adaptation of the habituation-dishabituation procedure that has proved so valuable in the study of infants' perceptual abilities. A study by Renée Baillargeon (1987a) provides a good example of both the method and the kinds of findings that it yields. Baillargeon's subjects first viewed the event shown in the top part of Figure 2–4, that is, a screen that rotated, like a drawbridge, though a 180° arc. After a series of such trials the infants' looking times decreased, reflecting the fact that they were habituating to the repeated event. At this point a wooden box was placed directly in the path of the screen (see the bottom part of the figure). Note that the infant could see the box at the start of a trial, but that the box disappeared from view when the screen reached its full height. In one experimental condition, labeled the *Possible Event* in Figure 2–4, the screen rotated to the point at which it reached the box and then stopped—as of course it should, given

FIGURE 2–4 The Baillargeon test of object permanence. Infants were first habituated to the event shown in part (a). Response was then measured to either the possible event in part (c), in which the screen rotates to point of contact with the box and stops, or the impossible event in part (b), in which the screen continues to move through the area occupied by the box. Adapted from "Object Permanence in 3½ and 4½-Month-Old Infants" by R. Baillargeon, 1987a, *Developmental Psychology, 23,* p. 656. Copyright © 1987 by the American Psychological Association. Adapted and reprinted by permission of Renée Baillargeon.

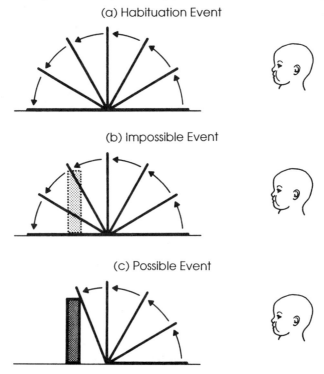

(a) Habituation Event

(b) Impossible Event

(c) Possible Event

the fact that a solid object was in its path. In the other condition, labeled the *Impossible Event*, the screen rotated to the point of contact with the box and then (thanks to a hidden platform that dropped the box out of the way) kept right on going through its full 180° arc! Note that in some respects this second event is less novel than the first: Infants in the Impossible Event condition see a 180° rotation, just as on the habituation trials, whereas infants in the Possible Event condition see only a truncated version of the familiar movement. To anyone with some knowledge of object permanence, however, the second event is decidedly more novel and less expectable, for in this case one solid object seems to pass magically through a second solid object.

Baillargeon found that infants as young as 4½ months (and even some as young as 3½ months) appeared to appreciate the impossibility of the Impossible Event. Looking times remained low when the screen stopped at the point of reaching the box; attention shot up, however, when the screen appeared to pass through the area occupied by the box. It is difficult to think of any explanation for these results other than the explanation offered by Baillargeon (1990, p. 6), namely that the infants

(a) believed that the box continued to exist, as a substantial entity, after it was occluded by the screen; (b) realized that the screen could not rotate through the space occupied by the box; and hence (c) expected the screen to stop and were surprised in the impossible event that it did not.

In further studies Baillargeon has probed the extent of young infants' knowledge about hidden objects. Do infants understand not only that a hidden object still exists but also something about the object's enduring properties? Do they realize, for example, that an occluded object retains its original size, and can they use this knowledge to reason about its possible effects when it is out of sight? The answer is yes. Baillargeon (1987b) presented infants with a screen that rotated through a 165° arc, in the course of which it occluded a box placed in its path. In one condition the box was upright, as in Figure 2–4; in the other condition it was lying flat. The event in the lying-flat condition was therefore a possible one, since the screen stopped just when it should have, at the point of reaching the flattened box; the event in the upright condition, in contrast, was definitely not possible, since it involved the same magical movement of one solid through another as in the first Baillargeon study. Note, however, that to distinguish in this way between the events the infant must retain information about not only the existence but also the size and orientation of the hidden object. Infants looked longer at the first event than at the second, indicating that they were in fact able to remember and to use this information.

Infants know other things about the properties of hidden objects. They realize, for example, that only some kinds of objects hinder the movements of other objects. In another application of the rotating-screen procedure, Baillargeon (1987b) varied the nature of the hidden object: hard and rigid in half the cases, soft and compressible (e.g., a ball of gauze) in the other half. Infants were not surprised by the continued rotation of the screen in the soft-object case, indicating that they were able to retain and use information about the compressibility of the hidden object. Infants can also use information about the location of a hidden object. Baillargeon (1986) first habituated infants to the following event: A toy car rolled down an inclined ramp, passed behind one end of a screen, and exited at the other end. Following habituation, the infants saw a box placed behind the screen. In one condition (possible event) the box was placed behind the tracks on which the car ran; in the other condition (impossible event) the box was placed directly on the tracks. The screen was then set back in place, and the car again made its journey from one side to the other. Infants looked longer at the impossible event than at the possible one, indicating that they knew not only that the box still existed but *where* it was—and that they drew different implications from the different locations.

The studies described here are only a few examples from a rich and ingenious program of research, the consistent finding from which is that infants know quite a bit about hidden objects and their properties (for further details, see Baillargeon 1990, 1991, in press). To be sure, very young infants do not know all there is to know. Many of the studies show age effects; some kinds of knowledge are evident by 3 or 4 months (the youngest ages tested), whereas others may not appear till 6 or 7 months. Baillargeon finds, in particular, that quantitative reasoning about the exact physical properties of objects (just how tall or large must the hidden object be to produce an effect?) is more difficult than purely qualitative reasoning (knowing that the object still exists and could affect another, without having to take into account precise quantities). There is also the suggestion in some recent work from Elizabeth Spelke's lab of a surprising deficit in young infants' understanding of objects. Parts of Spelke's research program confirm Baillargeon's claims about the young infant's competence; in particular, Spelke also reports evidence, very similar to Baillargeon's, that young infants know that hidden objects still exist and realize that one solid object cannot pass through another solid object (Spelke, 1991; Spelke, Breinlinger, Macomber, Turner, & Keller, 1990). Such confirmation by an independent research team is reassuring, given both the importance of Baillargeon's findings and the extent to which they deviate from what had been accepted wisdom. Spelke also reports the following study, however. Four-month-old infants see a hand release a ball, the ball falls behind a screen, and the screen is removed to reveal one of two outcomes: the ball resting on the floor of the apparatus, or the ball suspended in midair. Four-month-olds showed no sign of surprise at the latter outcome, despite its violation of the laws of both gravity (objects do not float in air) and inertia (moving objects do not suddenly stop unless they encounter some resistance). As Spelke herself notes, however, other studies (e.g., Baillargeon & Hanko-Summers, 1990) do find some understanding of gravity and support in young infants; hence, conclusions about this realm of object knowledge are at present not clear.

Despite the qualifications noted in the preceding paragraph, the main message from the Baillargeon and Spelke research programs concerns the hitherto unsuspected competencies of young infants. These studies seem to show clearly that infants possess a basic, Stage 4 knowledge of object permanence months before Piaget believed that such knowledge emerged. Why, then, do babies fail to search for hidden objects? The problem is not simply one of manual dexterity, for infants are physically capable of executing the necessary behaviors (reaching for objects, removing covers, etc.) long before they apply such behaviors to the task of finding hidden objects. Nor is the problem likely to be motivational—a common observation from those who do object-concept research concerns the strong interest that babies often show in the objects used, as well as the evident frustration that ensues when the object cannot be retrieved. But if the infant desires the object, knows that it still exists, and is physically capable of retrieving it, why in the world does he or she not retrieve it?

Both Baillargeon (in press) and Diamond (1991b) have suggested the same general explanation. They note that even young infants *do* sometimes search when doing so requires a single, direct action toward the desired object. Examples include visual search in the area where an object has just disappeared, continuation of an already-begun reach, and reaching for an object that has been "hidden" by the sudden darkening of the room (e.g., B. Hood & Willatts, 1986). Most object-concept searches, however, are more complicated, since they require the coordination of at least two distinct actions into a means-end sequence—for example, reaching for and removing a cover (the means) in order to grasp and play with a hidden toy (the end). But recall that this sort of integration of separate schemes into intentional, means-end sequences is precisely what Piaget has shown infants cannot do prior to Stage 4, and hence prior to about 8 months of age. The suggestion, in other words, is that Piaget is probing for knowledge of object permanence with behaviors that he himself has shown infants are not yet capable of producing.

Although the Baillargeon/Diamond hypothesis seems reasonable, it could be argued simply to transfer the problem of explanation. Granted that infants do not search because they cannot organize means-end sequences. But why are they unable to organize means-end sequences? Although no one knows for sure, some intriguing ideas have been offered. These ideas are best considered after we add a bit more data—specifically, data concerning the A$\overline{\text{B}}$ error of Stage 4.

The A$\overline{\text{B}}$ phenomenon has in fact been the most extensively researched aspect of object-concept development. Recall that the error consists of continuing to search for the hidden object X under cover A, where it has been hidden and found on previous trials, even though the infant clearly sees the experimenter put it under cover B. Of the many surprising, hard-to-believe phenomena reported by Piaget, this bizarre search behavior of the Stage 4 infant has to rank among the most surprising. It is important to note, therefore, that the phenomenon is not somehow idiosyncratic to Piaget's observations but has been replicated in later studies using larger samples and varied techniques of probing for the error (P. L. Harris, 1989b; Wellman, Cross, & Bartsch, 1986). On the other hand, the specific results of these later studies do not always fit comfortably with Piaget's interpretation of the error—namely, that it reflects a kind of sensorimotor minihabit, in which the infant tries to recreate a pleasurable experience by repeating a previously successful action. If Piaget's theory is correct, then presumably the error should be likelier to occur if the infant is given more rather than fewer successful search trials at A prior to the hiding at B. It should also be likelier to occur if the infant does all the object finding at A, rather than just watching the experimenter repeatedly hide and find the object there. Neither of these predictions is consistently supported by follow-up research (P. L. Harris, 1983). Furthermore, factors not considered in Piaget's analysis can affect whether the A$\overline{\text{B}}$ error occurs. The memory demand placed on the infant turns out to be an especially important variable. Infants seldom err when allowed to search immediately at B; confusion occurs when some delay is imposed between disappearance of the object and opportunity to search. Presumably, the short-term memory for the object's disappearance at B is fragile and quickly overpowered by the more solidly established memory of the object being found at A. Diamond (1985) has shown, in fact, that the delay necessary to produce the A$\overline{\text{B}}$ error increases at a rate of about 2 seconds a month across the age span of interest. At 7 months a delay of 2 seconds is sufficient to elicit the error, by 9 months the span has grown to 5 seconds, and by 12 months errors occur only with delays of 10 seconds or more. Indeed, there is even evidence that *adults* with brain damage and consequent memory problems will make the $A\overline{B}$ error (Schacter, Moscovitch, Tulving, McLachlan, & Freedman, 1986).

Are memory problems therefore a sufficient explanation for the $A\overline{B}$ error? Various additional findings tell us that memory cannot be the entire story. Infants may search at A rather than B even when transparent covers are used and they therefore can see both that location A is empty and that X is waiting to be found at location B (Butterworth, 1977)! Whatever the explanation for this strange behavior may be, it must involve something more than memory problems. In addition, Baillargeon and her co-workers (Baillargeon, DeVos, & Graber, 1989, Baillargeon & Graber, 1988) have shown that infants can remember the locations of objects across considerable delays on tasks that do not require active search behaviors. Their approach has involved a variant of Baillargeon's possible event/impossible event paradigm. Infants watch as an object is placed on one of two identical placemats, screens are then slid in front of the placemats, and after a delay a hand reaches behind one of the screens and removes the object. In one condition the reach is to the location where the object had in fact been placed; in the other condition the reach is to the other location. Infants looked longer in the latter, impossible-event condition, indicating that they could remember the location of the object. They did so, moreover, across several trials on which the specific placement of the object varied, thus showing an ability to adjust to changes in location. And they did so across delays as long as 70 seconds.

The $A\overline{B}$ error must therefore reflect not only memory but also some special difficulty that infants have in organizing effective searches when multiple hiding places are involved. Various explanations for this special difficulty have been proposed (Baillargeon, in press; Diamond, 1991b; P. L. Harris, 1989b; Wellman et al., 1986); we here present the one offered by Diamond, with acknowledgment that the other positions may also contribute to whatever the ultimate solution to the $A\overline{B}$ conundrum may be.

Diamond (1991a, 1991b) argues that two abilities are central to successful $A\overline{B}$ performance. One, as we have seen, is memory: the ability to keep alive the information about X residing at B across whatever delay may occur before search is permitted. The other is the ability to inhibit the tendency to reach toward A. Diamond points out that infants often seem to *know* that the object is at B—they may turn immediately to B after a perfunctory search at A; they may even stare at B while reaching out to uncover A. Their problem seems to be that they simply cannot resist the pull toward making the prepotent response, which in this case is search at A. Diamond marshalls evidence, moreover, to show that the difficulty in inhibiting dominant responses is not specific to the $A\overline{B}$ task but rather is a general characteristic of infant behavior during the first year of life. In many situations babies have difficulty not making the most natural, readily available response. Finally, Diamond makes a persuasive case for the proposition that these difficulties in inhibition stem from immaturities in brain development—specifically, from immaturities in the frontal lobe system. The case rests not just on parallels between infant behavior and the developmental course of brain maturation but on several further sources of evidence: the fact that infant monkeys show similar behavioral deficits that correspond to *their* level of frontal lobe development, the fact that experimentally induced lesions in the critical areas of monkeys' brains can produce deficits in behavioral inhibition, and the fact that injuries to the frontal lobes in adult humans are also associated with impaired ability to inhibit behavior.

Diamond does not limit her neuropsychological theorizing to the $A\overline{B}$ error but extends it as well to earlier phases of object-concept development and to the young infant's difficulty in integrating behaviors into means-end sequences. She argues that the ability to coordinate behavioral sequences must also wait upon sufficient maturational development, both of the frontal lobe system and of the earlier maturing supplementary motor area of the frontal cortex. And she notes that young infants' problems in coordinating behavioral sequences, including those necessary for successful search on Stage 4 object concept tasks, may well relate to the general difficulties that they have in inhibiting behavior. In her words:

> It may be that inhibitory control makes possible infants' emerging ability to construct relations. To relate two stimuli to one another, one must fight the tendency to attend only to the more salient stimulus. To relate two movements in a two-directional reach, one must stop the first movement so that the second one can begin. Reasoning and planning require that one inhibit focusing exclusively on one stimulus or idea so that more than one thing can be taken into account and interrelated. (Diamond, 1991b, pp. 104–105)

Diamond is not the only theorist who stresses the importance of inhibition, nor is infancy the only age period for which such arguments have been offered (Dempster, in press; Harnishfeger & Bjorklund, in press). It should be clear that such theorizing fits with what we saw in Chapter 1 to be one of the features of the current Zeitgeist: take seriously the neurological underpinnings of cognitive performance and cognitive change.

What conclusions can be gleaned from all this recent work on the object concept? What this work strongly suggests (but see Fischer & Bidell, 1991, and Montangero, 1991, for cautions) is that young infants probably do have a basic realization that hidden objects still exist—months earlier than Piaget believed and possibly even from birth. Such a conclusion is compatible with other studies of early knowledge of objects, especially the Spelke research discussed in the section on Perception, and more generally with work on what has come to be called "naive physics" in infancy and early childhood (Wellman & Gelman, 1992). Evidence is accumulating that human infants are biologically endowed with a rich set of processing mechanisms that allow them to perceive and to make sense of the physical world. Still unclear is exactly when and why infants become able to "use" this early, possibly innate knowledge. We have discussed various reasons that a young infant's knowledge of object permanence might not be expressed in adaptive search behavior. A mature possessor of the object concept can also think about the object in its absence—for example, form a mental image of mother when she is out of the room. Can a 4-month-old with a Baillargeon-type object concept think about an absent mother? If not, why not—that is, what has to be added to the kind of knowledge that is tapped by the habituation procedure? And how can we ever figure out the answers to these questions?

OTHER INFANT ACHIEVEMENTS. Object concept is just one of the foci for current research on cognitive development in infants. Here we consider three additional and very important aspects of human mental functioning that have their origins in infancy: causal understanding, problem solving, and representation. In each case the starting point for modern work is the traditional Piagetian picture—a picture of slow, gradual, stage-by-stage mastery, critically dependent on the child's own action, marked by partial achievements and surprising gaps in competence, and culminating only at Stage 6 and therefore only at the end of infancy. In each case the more recent work paints a much more positive picture. As with the object concept, competence seems to be present surprisingly early, if we only know how to look for it.

Causal Understanding. If young infants are required to demonstrate their understanding of causality through their own adaptive behaviors they do not perform very impressively, just as Piaget long ago observed. An alternative approach to assessing early understanding of cause-and-effect relations makes use, once again, of the habituation/dishabituation procedure. Leslie (1984; Leslie & Keeble, 1987) showed 6-month-old infants an animated film in which a red brick moved from left to right across the screen until it made contact with a stationary green brick, at which point the red brick stopped and the green brick moved off to the right. Adults watching such a display have a strong experience of causality: The red brick appears to "launch" the green brick into motion (much as one billiard ball launches another). In contrast, events that lack the proper spatial and temporal relations between the elements do not elicit feelings of causality—for example, if the red brick stops short of the green one, or if the green brick moves off only a second or so after the contact is made.

To determine whether infants have a similar experience of causality, Leslie first habituated attention to the launching event and then tested for dishabituation to a variety of changes in spatial or temporal structure. Although infants proved capable of discriminating changes of a number of sorts, they showed the strongest recovery of attention in a condition in which the original film was simply run in reverse. With the film in reverse, the green brick starts in motion from the right side of the screen and continues to the center, where it appears to launch the red brick. This event (unlike the other dishabituation sequences) thus maintains a causal structure, but the causal direction is the reverse of that in the original event. The heightened interest in the case of causal reversal suggests that the infants were encoding not only the individual elements of the experience (particular colors, directions, speeds, etc.) but also the causal relation. What they saw, in other words, was red launching green, and they therefore were quite interested when things somehow changed and green began to launch red. (Just to complicate things, we should add that Oakes and Cohen, 1990, were able to replicate these findings with 10-month-olds—not, however, at the 6-month age tested by Leslie. Oakes and Cohen used real objects rather than animated geometric forms, and hence there may be something about type of object that influences young infants' ability to abstract causal relations.)

By 11 months, infants show a more advanced form of causal perception. Baillargeon and Kotovsky (1991—cited in Baillargeon, 1990) presented the following event: A medium-sized cylinder rolled down an inclined ramp and hit a toy bug, causing the bug to roll to the middle of a horizontal track. Following habituation, the infants were shown a new cylinder, which also rolled down the ramp and struck the bug, in this case sending it all the way to the end of the track, where it was finally stopped only by the wall of the apparatus. In one condition (possible event), the new cylinder was much larger than the original cylinder; in the other condition (impossible event), it was much smaller. Infants looked longer at the impossible event, indicating that they understood not only the basic launch but also something about size and force: A small projectile should not impart greater force than a larger one.

Part of a mature understanding of the causes of movement is the realization that different sorts of movement have different underlying bases. In particular, animate objects are capable of self-propelled movement—can launch themselves, so to speak—whereas inanimate objects require some external force to set them in motion. Exactly when infants begin to appreciate this distinction is not yet agreed upon (cf. Mandler, in press; Poulin-Dubois & Shultz, 1988; Premack, 1990), but it does seem clear that some understanding of the animate-inanimate contrast emerges in the first year or so of life. As we will discuss further in Chapter 3, an understanding of different sorts of movement is relevant not only to concepts of causality but also to concepts of biology: of which things are living and which are not, and of distinctions among different kinds of living things.

These examples of infant competence (and there are others—see Spelke, 1991; Willatts, in press) do not mean, of course, that understanding of causality is complete by 24 months—such is far from the case. But they do indicate a more mature, adult-like parsing of the causal flow than we formerly credited to the young infant. In Leslie's (1986, 1988a) view, much of this early, adaptive response is made possible by a system of perceptual modules (see Chapter 1)—that is, innately provided, highly specialized systems for rapidly analyzing and making sense of particular kinds of perceptual input (such as collisions and launches). These perceptual modules are explicitly *not* equated with a fully mature understanding of cause and effect; rather, they are the starting point upon which a conceptual mastery of causality builds. Perhaps appropriately, Leslie (1986) uses a launching metaphor in speculating about the role of modules. In his words, modules help to "get development off the ground."

Problem Solving.   Our discussion to this point may have given the impression that infants know more than we used to think they know but that they still cannot act on this knowledge to get what they want to get. Thus they realize that hidden objects still exist but are unable to search for them; they appreciate basic cause-and-effect relations but are unable to organize intentional behavioral sequences; and so on. There is some truth to this picture—infants' ability to act adaptively *does* often lag behind their underlying knowledge. But the picture is not totally bleak. Here we consider two examples of important early achievements in problem solving.

Willatts (1989) presented 9-month-old infants with the task of retrieving an attractive toy. The toy was presented within view but beyond the infant's reach, thus preventing the infant from simply reaching out and grasping it. Fortunately for the infant, the toy was resting on an easily reachable cloth, and thus could be brought within range by a pull on the cloth. Unfortunately for the infant, a foam-block barrier prevented a direct reach to the cloth. Solution of the problem thus required several steps: push aside the barrier, and only then reach for and pull the cloth, and only then grasp and play with the toy. As Figure 2–5 illustrates, infants as young as 9 months readily executed this sequence of behaviors and thereby succeeded in retrieving the toy. Their behavior contrasted with that of a control group who were also presented with toy, cloth, and barrier but with the toy sitting next to rather than on the cloth. As Figure 2–5 shows, the control subjects did not bother to pull the cloth (why should they?); rather, they played with the only object available to them, namely the barrier. What Willatts emphasizes is that both groups hit upon the most adaptive behavior in their particular circumstances immediately, on the first trial; they did not need to work through the steps one at a time before determining what the final outcome would be. They thus showed a capacity for the kind of insightful, planful behavior that Piaget saw as emerging only near the end of infancy.

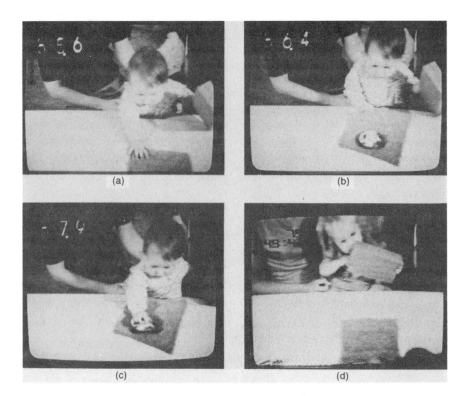

FIGURE 2-5 Problem solving at 9 months of age. The child (a) removes the block of foam, (b) pulls the cloth, and (c) grasps the toy. (d) In contrast, an infant in the control condition ignores the cloth and plays with the block of foam. From Willatts, P., Development of problem-solving in infancy. In A. Slater and G. Bremner (Eds.), *Infant Development* (p. 166). Copyright © 1989 by Lawrence Erlbaum Associates. Reprinted by permission.

Willatts' subjects also demonstrated another precocious accomplishment: the Stage 5 ability to use one object (such as a supporting cloth) to obtain another object. As noted earlier, such behavior can be seen as the earliest form of an extremely important type of intelligent activity: use of tools to achieve a goal. Tool use has been explored more fully in several recent research projects (Bates, Carlson-Luden, & Bretherton, 1980; A. L. Brown, 1989; Connolly & Dagleish, 1989; Uzgiris & Hunt, 1975, 1987). These studies confirm both Piaget's claim that tool use is an emergent achievement of infancy and Willatts' suggestion that simple forms of the skill may emerge earlier than Piaget believed. Success depends on a number of factors. The type of tool can be important. The ability to use a support (such as the cloth in Willatts' study) to retrieve a distant object seems to be mastered by most infants by the end of the first year; in contrast, use of a stick to corral an out-of-reach goal (the other main behavior pattern studied by Piaget) is generally not seen before the 12 to 18 months, Stage 5 time period identified in Piaget's writings (Uzgiris & Hunt, 1975). Perceptual factors can also play a role. Infants are most likely to solve tool-use problems when the tool and the goal are clearly distinct perceptually—for example, different in color or texture (Bates et al., 1980).

Presumably, the perceptual separation of tool and goal helps the infant to realize that there are two distinct objects that must be brought together for problem solution. Not surprisingly, young infants also benefit if there is already some physical contact between the tool and the object to be retrieved. Older infants can not only solve basic tool-use problems but they can also transfer their solutions adaptively to new situations. For example, in a study by Ann Brown (1989), 20-month-old infants first learned to use a long, rounded, candy-cane-painted hook to retrieve a desirable toy. When later tested on a similar task with other would-be tools, the babies ignored the instruments with the greatest perceptual similarity to the original tool (same candy-cane color, same shape, etc.) and zeroed in on the one implement sufficient for the job at hand: a rake with both sufficient length and the requisite pulling head. As Brown notes, much early research on tool use had characterized infants and toddlers as stimulus-bound and noninsightful in their tool-using endeavors. Her work clearly suggests otherwise.

Representation. For Piaget, the crowning achievement of the sensorimotor period was the emergence of representational or symbolic ability at Stage 6. It was this achievement—laboriously prepared for by the whole prior course of sensorimotor development—that was seen as bringing the sensorimotor period to an end and ushering in all higher forms of intellectual functioning.

We have seen that many competencies seem to be present earlier than Piaget believed. Could the same be true of symbolic-representational ability? A positive answer in this case would constitute perhaps the most serious challenge to the Piagetian model of infant intelligence, because it would mean that this intelligence is, at least in part, basically different from what Piaget believed it to be—that it encompasses not just sensorimotor but also symbolic-representational forms of thinking. Infants would become less like a strange, exotic species and more like all the rest of us.

Determining exactly when symbolic-representational competence emerges is an exceedingly difficult task (Mandler, 1983, 1988). Problems of definition and of interpretation abound—what exactly do we mean when we talk about this sort of competence, and what exactly could an infant do to demonstrate to us that he or she possesses it? Piaget's approach to these questions was a conservative one; he was reluctant to credit the infant with symbolic ability prior to the Stage 6 behaviors (deferred imitation, symbolic play, etc.) that announce its presence in unmistakenly clear fashion. Other investigators have been more likely to see a representational underpinning to certain earlier appearing infant achievements. Many would contend, for example, that the basic Stage 4 knowledge that a hidden object still exists implies a capacity to form a mental representation of the object in its absence.

Even if we accept Piaget's criteria for inferring representation, recent work suggests, once again, that he may have placed age of emergence considerably later than is in fact the case. One fascinating example comes from studies of infants learning American Sign Language (Mandler, 1988; Meier & Newport, 1990). Such studies have shown that the first genuine, clearly symbolic signs may appear as early as 6 to 7 months of age—several months earlier than the typical first appearance of words for children learning a spoken language, and long before the expected age for such competence in Piaget's theory.

Work on deferred imitation provides another example. In a study by Meltzoff (1988b), 9-month-old infants watched an adult model perform a series of actions on three novel objects (e.g., pushing a button on a box to produce a beeping sound). Twenty-four hours later the infants were given a chance to play with the same objects, and many reproduced the behaviors they had seen the model perform. Various control conditions served to verify that the babies had not hit upon these behaviors spontaneously but rather were imitating what they had seen a day before. In another study, working with a wider range of objects and more clearly novel behaviors, Meltzoff (1988a) demonstrated imitation across a 1-week delay in 14-month-olds. It is important to point out that in neither study were the babies allowed to reproduce the behaviors immediately after seeing them. This means that the later reproductions were not simply repetitions of the infants' own earlier behaviors; rather, they were genuine deferred imitations. If we agree with Piaget that such imitation requires representation—and it certainly seems reasonable to do so—then Meltzoff has apparently demonstrated that infants as young as 9 months are capable of symbolic representation.

The studies of deferred imitation have implications for our model of infants' memory. Piaget believed that infants were limited to recognition memory; recall, being dependent on the ability to symbolize objects or events in their absence, should not be available to the prerepresentational infant. Imitating a model from the past, however, seems to be a matter of recall and not merely recognition: The infant must store the information about the model's behaviors over time and somehow call it to mind, in the absence of the behaviors themselves, when attempting to perform the same actions. Deferred imitation is just one of several phenomena that suggest that recall memory probably emerges some time during the first year of life (Mandler, 1990). This topic is considered more fully in Chapter 6; here we mention the work on recall simply as further evidence for the general point: The capacity for symbolic, non-sensorimotor forms of representation may well be present considerably earlier than Piaget believed.

Some General Conclusions

It should be clear to you that our picture of infant cognition is considerably richer but also considerably more complicated than it was 10 or 12 years ago. The days when we could comfortably equate infancy with Piaget's sensorimotor period are clearly past. At the same time, it seems fair to say that no completely comprehensive and satisfactory alternative model has yet been proposed, despite a number of intriguing ongoing efforts (e.g., Leslie, 1986; Mandler, 1991; Spelke, 1988a, 1991; Willatts, in press, as well as the various neo-Piagetian theories introduced in Chapter 1). In this final section, therefore, we offer not a grand unifying theory but rather various themes that emerge from recent work on infant cognition.

That infants are more competent than Piaget believed is the theme that has run throughout our discussion. Piaget's emphasis on motor activity led him to underestimate infants' understanding of a number of aspects of their world. To be sure, earlier understanding does not mean complete understanding—there are limitations to be overcome and developmental advances to be made for all of the various topics that we have considered. A very important task for future research is to map out exactly what these limitations and subsequent advances are. In addition, Piaget was correct in his assertion that infants often fail to act adaptively upon the world—to search for hidden objects, to organize means-end sequences, and the like. But he may well have been wrong about the reason why.

The astonishing precocity of many infant capabilities has pushed our conceptions of infant development in a more nativistic direction. Certain competencies emerge so early that it seems they must be largely innate rather than constructed through experience. It is at least roughly accurate to say that, whereas Piaget would think of these abilities as the gradually emerging products of infant development, many present-day infant researchers would instead construe them as the initial cognitive tools that make this development possible. Furthermore, not just initial competence but developmental advances in competence are more likely these days to be seen as having biological-maturational and not solely experiential bases—recall Diamond's work on frontal lobe development and infant search behavior.

Our conceptions of the relative importance of different sorts of experience during infancy have also changed. Not only does motor activity play a less important role than we used to believe, but perceptual activity almost certainly plays a greater role. The Gibsons, as you may recall, have long argued for the importance of perceptual experience, and recent evidence regarding infant abilities and proclivities is certainly compatible with their position. Young infants may be limited in their ability to act motorically upon the world, but their perceptual systems have proved to be surprisingly powerful and mature. Much of the recent work, moreover, has blurred further the already blurry distinction between perception and cognition in infancy. Spelke's research, for example, has shown (contra Piaget) that infants apparently perceive a world of stable, solid, and continuous objects from early in life, and her studies and those of others have demonstrated that the ability to integrate information from the different senses into some more central representation is also available quite early. Exactly how perception feeds into cognition, and exactly how to conceptualize the distinctions and relations between the two systems, are among the questions that most intrigue present-day theorists of infancy (E. J. Gibson, 1988; Leslie, 1988a; Mandler, 1991; Spelke, 1988b, 1991).

A final theme concerns an issue that has long intrigued theorists of any age period, and that is the possibility of stages in development. Piaget's model of infancy, as we have seen, is one of stages: All developments are seen as progressing through the same six-stage sequence, and at any given time all aspects of development are seen as falling within the same stage. There is undoubtedly some very general truth to such a conception. Later acquisitions often do build upon earlier, prerequisite ones, related competencies often do emerge at roughly the same time, and it is important for our theories to recognize and explain these facts. Piaget's theory, however, makes not just general but very strong and specific claims about the stage-tied nature of infant cognition, and these claims have not fared well in recent research. There are simply too many instances of earlier-than-expected competence, too many divergences in level of performance across different tasks, and too many aspects of development that do not seem to depend on the constructive, acting-upon-the-world processes with which Piaget defined his stages. To repeat our earlier point—Piaget's account has enough descriptive accuracy and enough historical importance to merit continued discussion. But the full theory seems unlikely to survive.

SUMMARY

The human perceptual and cognitive systems undergo dramatic changes during the period from birth to the end of infancy. Yet research in recent years has also revealed that newborns and young infants are in some respects much more competent than we used to believe. Some of the most exciting contemporary research in developmental psychology is directed to uncovering exactly what competencies are available at what ages, and therefore exactly what it is that changes across infancy.

Whether our interest is in infant perception or infant cognition, the young infant—nonverbal and only minimally motoric—presents formidable obstacles to study. Advances in our understanding have occurred as investigators have devised increasingly sensitive techniques to probe for early competence. Thus, babies cannot report their perceptual experiences, but researchers can make inferences about their perception from their nonverbal behaviors (sucking, head turning, blinking, reaching, and, especially, looking) and physiological responses (especially heart rate). For example, researchers can measure which of two stimulus patterns an infant tends to look at more. They can also assess whether the infant's visual attention to a pattern *habituates* (wanes) after repeated presentation and *recovers from habituation* or *dishabituates* when a new pattern is presented. Such perceptual "preferences" tell us two important things about the infant's perceptual system: (1) what the system can discriminate perceptually, since a preference implies that a discrimination has been made; (2) what the system is especially sensitive to or selectively attentive to in its perceptual processing.

Although the auditory system appears to be functional at least several weeks before birth, the fetus's ability to hear significant external sounds (e.g., speech) may be hampered by a rather noisy intrauterine environment. Recent evidence suggests, however, that some external sounds probably are perceived in the weeks before birth. At birth, newborns appear to have close to adult-level hearing. Some improvements do occur with development, however, along three dimensions: ability to detect sounds, ability to discriminate sounds, and ability to localize (i.e., turn toward) the source of sounds.

The neural systems that subserve visual functioning are not fully developed at birth in humans. Consequently, the newborn's visual functioning is of poorer quality than it will be in late infancy and early childhood, or even than it will be at 2 or 3 months of age. Newborns have some difficulty in executing the various oculomotor mechanisms necessary to bring images into optimal focus on the retina: fixating a stationary object and pursuing a moving one, converging both eyes on the same visual target, accommodating to objects of different distances. Visual acuity is surprisingly poor at birth—no better than 20/600 by some estimates. Contrast sensitivity (discrimination of light-dark differences) is also poor at birth. Both acuity and contrast sensitivity improve rapidly in the early months of life, however. And recent evidence indicates that another important aspect of human visual competence—perception of colors—is present from very early in life.

The infant visual system is clearly more attracted or sensitive to some visual patterns than to others. It has proved very difficult to characterize and explain such visual preferences, however. The newborn and young infant's attention seems to be governed largely by physical characteristics of the visual surround (e.g., edges, contrast), characteristics that may reflect those aspects of the stimulation that the immature visual system sees most clearly. As infants learn more about specific objects and events in the environment (e.g., people and their actions), memory and meaning begin to supplant such inborn preferences as determinants of what they find interesting. Whatever their specific form and specific bases, the preferences that infants show constitute a highly adaptive motivational system for exploring and learning about the environment.

Researchers in the Gibsonian tradition study the development of higher-order perceptual processing, including the infant's ability to perceive events, objects, and places. Research by Spelke and associates has shown that infants of 3 or 4 months are in many respects similar to adults in their ability to perceive an object as a continuous and unitary entity, distinct from other objects or surfaces that form its background, that touch it, or that partly occlude it. Young infants are more dependent than adults, however, on motion cues that specify object nature. By about 3 months infants can use visual clues to judge the rigidity or plasticity of objects, and they are capable of perceiving biological motion in the systematic movement of an array of lights. By this age infants are beginning to move beyond perception of individual elements to perception of patterns or wholes, including perception of a very important object in any infant's environment: the human face. And by 3 to 5 months, if not earlier, infants show the beginnings of both shape and size constancy.

Various types of evidence suggest that some ability to perceive three dimensions or depth is present in the early weeks of life. Research using the "visual cliff" has shown that most infants exhibit behavioral avoidance of deep drop-offs by about the time that they begin to crawl (typically at around 7 months). Some ability to perceive drop-offs may well be present much earlier in development, but young infants do not yet show fear of drop-offs. The emergence of the fear response seems to be linked—temporally at least and causally perhaps—to the ability to locomote on one's own.

Theorists have disagreed for centuries about whether the senses are related to one another (*intermodal perception*) innately—prior to experience—or whether they only become intercoordinated as a function of experience. Recent evidence seems to support the former position. By 3 or 4 months of age, babies tend to perceive sights and sounds as part of the same event if they are temporally synchronous. They can match particular voices to particular faces, for example; they can even detect the synchrony between particular lip movements and particular sounds. Infants are also capable of visual-tactual intermodal perception; there is evidence, for example, that 1-month-olds can detect equivalences between what something looks like and how it feels in the mouth. Finally, perhaps the most surprising evidence of early intermodal perception comes from demonstrations that newborns may be able to imitate facial movements that they cannot see themselves make. In addition to supporting the nativist view of intermodal capacity, such findings provide one of many challenges to the traditional Piagetian account of infant cognitive development.

Piaget's theory has in fact dominated the study of infant cognition. Piaget saw the cognition of the infant as *sensorimotor* rather than *symbolic-representational* in nature—as an unreflective, practical, perceiving-and-doing sort of intelligence. Such cognition is expressed in the elaboration and intercoordination of cognitive structures called *schemes*: classes or categories of organized, repeatedly exercised action patterns (e.g., sucking, listening, looking, grasping). External data (objects and events) are *assimilated* to the sensorimotor schemes, and schemes simultaneously *accommodate* to these data. The engine or driving force behind the exercise of schemes is a system of motivation intrinsic to the cognitive structures. This motivational system has exactly the properties that we would expect to be most adaptive for an organism that still has much to learn about the world: a tendency to exercise the schemes spontaneously and repeatedly, even when there is no tangible objective to be gained; a disposition to focus attention and activity on events that are in some way novel or surprising and hence still in need of understanding; and a pleasureful sense of competence in achieving and repeatedly reasserting its mastery over such previously unassimilated situations.

Piaget's description of sensorimotor development is divided into six stages. Most of what was said about this sequence of stages is summarized in Figure 2–3, and hence we provide only a brief reminder here. The starting point for infant intelligence consists of various inborn reflexes; the end point is the capacity for symbolic-representational thought—the capacity to represent and act upon the world *internally*, through the use of mental symbols. The developmental sequence that links reflex and symbol is one of the progressive development, elaboration, and integration of various sensorimotor schemes. As infants assimilate new experiences and accommodate to them, they construct progressively more advanced and adaptive means for acting upon and understanding the world.

A particularly important achievement of infancy is mastery of the object concept: the realization that physical objects are distinct and independent entities whose existence does not depend on our actions or our perceptual contact with them. Piaget made the surprising claim that this fundamental and seemingly obvious piece of knowledge requires nearly the whole first 2 years of a person's life to become fully established. In the first two stages of his sensorimotor progression, he saw little evidence for understanding of object concept; at most, the young infant might track a moving object until it disappears or stare briefly at the point of disappearance. By Stage 3, tracking has become more skilled and more clearly anticipatory, and the infant shows some ability to search for partially hidden objects. At this stage, however, there is still no search for an object that is completely hidden. The ability to search for invisible objects emerges at Stage 4 and constitutes a major advance in the infant's mastery of object permanence. There is still a peculiar limitation, however: After a few trials of finding an object under a given cover, the infant continues to search under the same cover even after watching the object disappear in a different place (the A not B error). This limitation is overcome at Stage 5, when the infant becomes capable of handling a series of visible displacements. This achievement, in turn, leads to the final step: the Stage 6, symbolically based ability to solve problems involving *invisible* displacements.

Object concept has been a popular research topic for post-Piaget investigators. Recent research, much of which has employed the habituation/dishabituation paradigm, has demonstrated clearly that young infants know more about objects than Piaget believed. When freed from the demands of motoric search, infants as young as 4 months show knowledge of not only the existence but also some of the properties (e.g., size, location) of hidden objects. Yet infants typically do not search for objects until several months later. The failure to search may reflect a general inability to organize behavioral sequences, an inability that may in turn result from immaturities in brain maturation. Maturational limitations and the resulting difficulty in inhibiting behavior have also been proposed as explanations for infants' problems with the A not B task.

The conclusion that infants are more competent than Piaget believed is not limited to the object concept. Earlier (although not fully mature) competence has been demonstrated for a number of aspects of infant development, including problem solving and causality. Perhaps the broadest challenge to the Piagetian model comes from work (e.g., studies of deferred imitation) that suggests that symbolic-representational ability may emerge during the first year of life. In general, contemporary research on infancy suggests several conclusions in addition to that of greater-than-expected competence: Development may be more strongly biologically-maturationally based than we used to believe; perceptual experience probably plays a greater role and motor experience a lesser role than was once thought; and attempts (à la Piaget) to characterize infant cognition in terms of general stages are at best only roughly accurate, for such attempts fail to explain the many inconsistencies and asynchronies in children's level of development.

three

Early Childhood

The 6-year-old is a much more mature thinker and knower than the 18-month-old. Her cognitive functioning clearly shows a number of positive (i.e., developmentally progressive) attributes when compared with that of a youngster just entering the early-childhood period. On the other hand, the 6-year-old, and even more obviously the 4- and 5-year-old, seems to present cognitive immaturities of her own when compared with the 10- or 14-year-old child. These apparent immaturities led many theorists to describe the mind of the preschooler in primarily negative terms. In Piaget's theory, for example, the 1-year-old is "sensorimotor," the 10-year-old "concrete-operational," and the 15-year-old "formal-operational"—all good, positive-sounding designations. The poor 3-year-old, on the other hand, gets labeled "preoperational" (even at times "preconceptual"), and all too often a description of her thinking has been little more than a dreary litany of her wrong answers to concrete-operational tests. More recent accounts have righted this wrong; they stress the developmental achievements of this period. Just as we underestimated the infant's cognitive capabilities in past years (Chapter 2), so does it appear that we also underestimated the young child's. As in the infant case, the reasons for the underestimation are partly methodological. A child may answer incorrectly on a particular task but still have a partial understanding of the concept being assessed. As researchers probed the young child's mind with new and more sensitive diagnostic tasks, they turned up an impressive number of competencies—often fragile, to be sure, but genuine nonetheless. Some of these preschool competencies are those previously believed by Piaget to develop in the middle-childhood years, while others are cognitive skills not studied by Piaget.

These studies are important because they make us rethink our previous beliefs about childhood cognitive development. If preschoolers have at least the rudiments of abilities previously found only in older children, and are generally more competent than we used to think, then an important question arises: Are middle-childhood minds, and even adolescent and adult ones, as radically and qualitatively different from early-childhood ones as Piaget believed? Thus, our new knowledge presented us with some uncertainties and perplexities about childhood cognitive development that we were spared in the heyday of Piagetian developmental psychology. (Such are the joys of scientific progress!) We now examine some of the most important positive accomplishments of the early-childhood period, deferring to Chapter 4 a consideration of these uncertainties and perplexities. However, we also will report some serious limitations of preschool thought that recently have been discussed. We explore preschoolers' strengths and weaknesses by first examining early symbolic-representational skills, then describing more complex representational knowledge structures. The latter include event knowledge and scripts, concepts and categories, and theory-like knowledge illustrated by children's "theory of mind." A final section focuses on one basic concept acquired during the preschool years that clearly shows unexpected early competencies—the concept of number. All of these early competencies not only are important for preschoolers' functioning in everyday life but also pave the way for later forms of understanding. The relation between early and later forms of understanding is a central issue in cognitive development.

SYMBOLIC-REPRESENTATIONAL SKILLS: PICTURES, MODELS, AND PRETEND PLAY

Being able to make one thing stand for another is one of the grandest achievements of the young thinker. We saw in Chapter 2 that infants can form mental representations, though the exact age is still under debate. They are beginning to use external representations as well. By the end of the second year of life or earlier, children realize that a picture, word, gesture, toy, or other "thing" can stand for a real object or event. These symbolic-representational skills also show a great deal of additional growth during early childhood. The most obvious and important example is the explosive increase in language competence that occurs during this period (Chapter 7). The ability to use numbers to represent quantities is another example that is taken up later in this chapter. Children also begin to acquire skills in drawing and other forms of artistic representation in this period (Freeman, 1980; Gardner, 1973). The ability to engage in *pretend* or *symbolic play* by about 1½ to 2 years of age is a further example, briefly alluded to in Chapter 2. Expressions of this symbolic-representational skill include such acts as pretending to drink out of an empty cup, pretending that a block is a car, and pretending that you are the Mommy and your playmate is the baby. We will focus on three representative representational skills—understanding pictorial representations, using physical models, and engaging in pretend play.

Pictorial Representations

A 2-year-old points to a face in a family photograph and correctly says "Daddy" or looks at a cookie in a picture book then runs to the kitchen in hot pursuit of that goal. No observant parent would doubt that very young children understand that pictures represent real objects. Indeed, even young infants at least perceive the similarity between pictures and the objects they represent (e.g., DeLoache, Strauss, & Maynard, 1979), as well as their differences (e.g., Slater, Rose, & Morison, 1984). However, young children have trouble with certain aspects of pictorial representations. Consider a striking observation by Zaitchik (1990). She showed 3-year-olds an arranged scene—for example, a bathtub and a toy duck on a bed. Then she took a Polaroid picture of the scene. While it was developing, she moved the duck to the bathtub. The children, when asked what the photograph would depict, said that it would show the duck in the tub (as it was now) rather than on the bed (as it was when the photo was taken)! They gave this answer despite the fact that they remembered that the duck was on the bed when the photo was taken. Thus, young children seem to have difficulty accepting a representation that differs from the way they themselves see reality right now. Part of their problem in this particular study, however, may have been their limited knowledge about the imaging process in cameras. When presented with an analogous test with a drawing rather than a photo, 3-year-olds have no trouble declaring that the image is still of the now-absent object rather than its replacement (Lillard & Cho, 1991).

A young child is confused about other aspects of pictorial representation as well. Suppose you show a child a television show involving an inflated balloon and ask, "If I take the top off the TV and then I shake it, would a real balloon come floating out into the room?" The majority of 3-year-olds would say "yes," though when given brief training to emphasize the differences between photos of objects, real objects, and videos of objects, many more can answer correctly (Flavell, Flavell, Green, & Korfmacher, 1990). Flavell and colleagues suggest that 3-year-olds understand that televised objects and events are not real, but tend to encode them as real because their real-world referents are so salient. Consequently, they misconstrue the experimenter's question about the behavior of the image.

The concept of pictorial representations rapidly becomes more complicated once children get beyond the basic idea that a picture stands for, but differs from, a real object. For instance, people have representations of representations of representations, which must be confusing, as seen in the following episode witnessed by one of us. A father and son, about age 3, were viewing a special exhibit of Remington paintings of the Old West at an art museum.

Father: Look, Jason, this picture's in your book at home.
Jason: I know, Dad. I was going to tell you that I don't have to look at it.
Father: But this is the real thing.
Jason: How can it be the real thing? It's a picture, and it's just like in my book.
Father: (Falteringly) Well, um, it just is. It's, well, it's just the real picture.
Jason: Well, I'm *not* going to look at it.

Here we have representations (in the father and son) of a representation (in the book) of a representation (painting) of an object (old-time cowboy) that no longer even exists. No wonder both father and son are struggling.

We have seen that young children readily recognize that pictures of various sorts—drawn, painted, moving, photographed—represent objects and events in the real world. Moreover, they know these representations differ from the real thing. Yet, they have trouble sorting out the exact nature of the relation between reality and its "nonreal" designators. For a discussion of the controversies concerning what types of representations are possible at various ages and which behaviors reflect these types, see Perner (1991).

Models

Consider the following event. An adult shows a young child a doll-house-sized room, a tiny toy dog, and a larger stuffed toy dog. She is told the correspondence between the model and a nearby real room, and between the two dogs: "This is Big Snoopy's big room, and this is Little Snoopy's little room. Look—their rooms are just alike; they both have all the same things in their rooms.... Look—this is Big Snoopy's big couch, and this is Little Snoopy's little couch. They're just the same." As the child watches, the adult places Little Snoopy behind the tiny couch in the model and asks the child to find Big Snoopy "in the same place" in the real room that is identical to the model in their furniture and their locations. DeLoache (1987) found that if this child is 36 months of age or older, she will immediately go to the couch and retrieve Big Snoopy. However, if she is only 6 months younger, she will have no idea where to look for Big Snoopy. She has not simply forgotten where Little Snoopy was hidden, for she can find him immediately when she returns to the model.

DeLoache concludes that 2½-year-olds have great difficulty in detecting the spatial correspondence between models and what they represent. They apparently do not understand that their initial knowledge has any relevance for the second room. They do not use the model to represent the real room. However, quite remarkably, they do much better if a photo or drawing of the large room is used instead of the model (DeLoache, 1991a)! This is surprising because young children generally show more advanced knowledge on cognitive tasks when three-dimensional objects, rather than symbolic materials, such as drawings or photos, are used. DeLoache interprets this facilitation with a drawing as showing that the model's status as a real thing (i.e., a three-dimensional object) distracts young children from its symbolic role. To solve the task, a child must be able to consider a model as two things at once: an object and a symbol of something else. This is easier to do with a picture because its status as a real object is not so overpowering; it has no obvious function of its own.

If using a model as a model depends on detecting its representational aspect, then anything that decreases its thing-in-and-of-itself aspect should improve performance, and anything that increases this aspect should undermine performance. The evidence supports these predictions. Placing the model behind a window in a puppet theater so that the child cannot touch it, which lessens its "objectness," improves performance (DeLoache, 1991b). Conversely, encouraging 3-year-olds to play with the model before being given the standard model task causes poor performance. DeLoache notes that one possible implication of the latter is that giving plastic toy alphabet letters to young children might make it harder, rather than easier, to detect their symbolic aspect. That is, the letters become real entities rather than just squiggles on a page that stand for something else.

Given DeLoache's findings that the use of models is rare until 36 months, it might seem perplexing that a 2-year-old clearly uses a toy car to represent a real car or a doll to represent a baby but cannot grasp the relation between two rooms that are virtually identical except in size. One important difference is that toys refer to a general type of object—for example, cars in general rather than one specific car that exists in reality. It is this specific correspondence to a known referent required by scale models that causes part of the problem. Two-year-olds have trouble grasping the analogy between one specific real thing and a model that simultaneously is a representation and a specific real thing. The 2½-year-old knows that the miniature sofa in the model represents *a* sofa, but not that it represents *the* sofa in the real-life room next door. Another factor that makes using the model difficult for young children is that there is relational (spatial position) information in the model and the room that must be mapped onto each other in order to find the toy. This information may be more complex than that usually involved in play.

To summarize this chapter thus far, we observe that young children acquire three concepts about symbols (DeLoache, 1991b; but see Perner, 1991, for a different view). *Representational insight* involves realizing that something is a symbol that stands for something else. *Dual representation* refers to thinking about one thing in two ways at the same time—as both an object and a symbol. *Representational specificity* is the realization that a symbol can represent a specific real entity.

Pretend Play

Karen: I'm hungry. Wa-a-ah!

Charlotte: Lie down, baby.

Karen: I'm a baby that sits up.

Charlotte: First you lie down and sister covers you and then I make your cereal and *then* you sit up.

Karen: Okay. (Paley, 1984, p. 1)

A 5-year-old, angry at her father, playing with one of her imaginary characters: Zoubab cut off her daddy's head. But she has some very strong glue and partly stuck it on again. But it's not very firm now. (Piaget, 1962, p. 174)

Pretend play is the intentional "layering of a supposed situation over an actual one, in the spirit of fun rather than for survival" (Lillard, 1991, p. 2). For example, when a child pretends that a banana is a telephone he knowingly holds his representation of a telephone over reality—a banana. For the first time, the child himself is constructing a counterfactual representation of the world, for a banana is not really a telephone. Prior to this time, the child's representations were aimed at representing his experience factually. Or, in the case of pictorial representation and models, someone other than the child usually has created the representation. Young children provide us with many clues in their pretend play that they understand that certain entities can represent real objects. They treat props as though they were their real referents, but can tell you that they are not: "That's *real* money, but that's not; those are *playing* money" (Woolley & Wellman, 1990).

IMPORTANCE OF PRETEND PLAY. Several facts about the development of pretend play make it worth discussing in a section on early-childhood cognitive growth. For one thing, it has the unusual property of being largely confined to this particular age period (Fein, 1979a). Children younger than 1 year of age are not capable of pretend play; children older than 6 years or thereabouts have largely given it up in favor of other forms of play (games, sports, hobbies, etc.), though fantasy role-playing games, such as *Dungeons and Dragons*, appeal to some children. Both the ability and disposition to engage in pretend play grow prodigiously in the years between. In fact, much of this growth takes place between 1 and 3 years of age, a period of cognitive development about which we know relatively little. Pretend play is also interesting because the impetus for its development seems to come mainly from within the child. It may be one of those biologically evolved activities that, like language, is spontaneously practiced in all cultures but formally taught in none. Our cousin in evolution, the chimp, also appears to be capable of engaging in pretense (Byrne & Whiten, 1991).

Pretend play is also an intriguing activity because it has family resemblances and possible developmental links to a wide variety of seemingly unrelated phenomena (Fein, 1979a). Consider a prototypical instance mentioned earlier: The young child knows that a block is not a car but deliberately pretends it is. If the child also calls the block a "car," as she might well do, she has created something very like a *metaphor*—that is, she has deliberately used the name of one thing to refer to another thing that resembles it in some way. Mentally transforming object and word meanings in this manner is reminiscent of imagination and creative thinking, and it is possible that pretend play and early metaphor are developmental precursors of these prized cognitive activities. Recall that pretend play can also consist of the child making-believe that she is another person, that a friend is also another person, and that these two fantasied persons are interacting. Such *sociodramatic play*, as social pretend play is sometimes called, could provide valuable practice in differentiating the self from others, in taking the perspective of others, in trying on social roles (e.g., parent, salesperson), and in interacting socially with others. Thus, it could assist social and social-cognitive development as well as cognitive growth in the strict, narrower sense.

Finally, pretend play may be a precursor to understanding the nature of the mind, to be discussed later. Toddlers pretend that dolls are sad, tired, happy, and desiring of food, thereby imbuing them with causal mental states that lead to pretend crying, sleeping, laughing, and eating. Also, pretend play may involve an early understanding that people have mental representations of reality, though the experts disagree on this (for a review of this debate, see Lillard, 1991).

DEVELOPMENT OF PRETEND PLAY.   The development of pretend-play skills during early childhood has been fairly well mapped by Piaget (1962) and Vygotsky (1978), and more recently by Bretherton (1984), Bretherton and Beeghly (1989), Fein (1979a, 1979b), Garvey (1990), Göncü (1989), Leslie (1988a), Lillard (1991), and Nicolich (1977). Our account draws heavily on their ideas.

The development of pretend play consists in part of detaching behavioral routines and objects from their customary, real-life situational and motivational contexts and using them in a playful fashion. The child who really goes to sleep usually does so in bed, at bedtime, and when sleepy. The child who pretends to go to sleep will do so in other places, times, and psychological states; the routine is disconnected from its usual situational and psychological context. Early in development, pretend actions are fleeting and hard to diagnose as such; the child makes a brief eating gesture with an empty spoon, for example. In time, they become decontextualized in another way: The child shows clearly that she *knows* she is pretending. A grin can be suggestive evidence for this knowledge. A verbal declaration ("I'm playing house!") is irrefutable evidence for it. The child also becomes able to step back and forth between play and reality, keeping straight all the while which world she is in. For example, she may tell her playmate what the playmate's next move should be in the play scenario they are acting out together ("Now you're supposed to cry").

What kinds of pretense are possible in young children? In Lillard's (1991) analysis, children can pretend about either the identity or a property of an object, oneself, another person, an event or action, or a situation. Examples are "I am a bear" (self-identity) or "Pretend this water is boiling" (object-property). Pretense often involves object substitutions. Perhaps the best-documented fact about the development of pretend play is that the child becomes progressively less dependent with age upon these concrete and realistic props (e.g., Elder & Pederson, 1978; Fein, 1975; Jackowitz & Watson, 1980; Overton & Jackson, 1973; Ungerer, Zelazo, Kearsley, & O'Leary, 1981; Watson & Fischer, 1977). At first, an object must be present in its familiar form in order to be used in pretend play. For example, the neophyte pretender can only pretend to feed himself if he uses a real spoon or something quite spoon-like in appearance. In contrast, the intermediate-level player can make do with almost any object that can be brought to the mouth in a spoon-like fashion—for example, a little stick—but the child still requires some concrete prop. Finally, the expert player—3 years old, perhaps—can dispense with real objects altogether, using only a spoonless spoon-feeding gesture. There is even additional development at this expert, "Look Ma, no object" level. A 3-year-old is likely to comply with a request to pretend to brush his teeth by extending his index finger and using it as a substitute toothbrush, while an 8-year-old will "hold" an imaginary toothbrush in the usual way and "brush" vigorously with it (Overton & Jackson, 1973).

Another developmental change involves the growing flexibility at using the self and another as either the actor or recipient. At first, the child is both agent and recipient of pretend actions. For instance, he (agent) pretends to feed or wash himself (recipient). Later, other persons and objects can be included in play episodes, first as recipients, then as agents. For example, neo-Piagetian researchers Watson and Fischer (1977) found the following developmental sequence in a study of 14- , 19- , and 24-month-old children's pretend actions: First, the child uses himself as an active agent—for example, he puts his head on a pillow and pretends to go to sleep. At a later age, he uses another object as a passive agent—he places a doll on the pillow and pretends that it goes to sleep. Still later, he uses the other object as an active agent—he has the doll lie down on the pillow and go to sleep, as though the doll itself were actually carrying out the action. These two kinds of substitutions reflect what Werner and Kaplan (1963) called the developing child's progressive "distancing" or differentiation between symbol and referent (object substitutions), and between person and referent (self-other substitutions).

Pretend play becomes increasingly socialized in the course of its development in early childhood. It does so in two respects. First, role-appropriate actions and objects become standardized or conventionalized. In the child's play, "babies drink from bottles, cry, and curl up; adults drink from cups, talk on telephones, make dinner, and wheel baby carriages" (Fein, 1979a, p. 207). Second, solitary pretend play gives way to social sociodramatic play. Even toddlers engage in pretend play with siblings. "I a daddy," says a 2-year-old boy to his older sibling (Dunn & Dale, 1984). By age 2½, a child plays the baby in a baby-and-mother game with her older sibling: She crawls, makes babbling noises, designates a "baby bed," criticizes her sibling's role behavior ("No you not a baby"), pretends to get lost, and acts helpless (Dunn, 1991). The capacity for sociodramatic play increases dramatically in subsequent months and years. "By the age of 5 years, what began as a few simple gestures begins to encompass intricate systems of reciprocal roles, ingenious improvisations of materials, increasingly coherent themes, and weaving plots" (Fein, 1979a, p. 199). This is no simple matter: "Children must become coplaywrights, codirectors, coactors, and vicarious actors, without getting confused about which of their roles they or a playmate are momentarily adopting" (Bretherton, 1989, p. 384). Fein (1979b) points out that, as more young children spend more of their time in group-care settings, the functions of sociodramatic play and techniques for supporting it become increasingly important areas of scientific study.

CHILDREN'S UNDERSTANDING OF PRETENSE. Pretend play presents a puzzle (Lillard, 1991). Two- and 3-year-olds supposedly are perception-bound realists who are reluctant (Markman, 1989) or even unable (Flavell, Green, & Flavell, 1986) to give two different names or descriptions to the same object. At the same age, however, these children readily treat an object as having a second, pretend identity in pretend play. As Leslie (1987, p. 412) asks, "Why does pretending not undermine their representational system and bring it crashing down?" At present there is no clear answer to this question. However, it is likely that unlike most other representations, a critical feature of pretense is that it does not claim that an entity *really* is two different things at the same time. The child intentionally decides to act "as if" a real entity is something other than itself. A 3-year-old might easily pretend that his brother is a fireman but have trouble understanding that his father, who really is a fireman, is both a father and a fireman at the same time.

What do young children think goes on in people's minds when they pretend? Young children must *possess* a mental representation of a telephone when they pretend that a banana is a telephone, but it is not clear whether they *understand* this representational process. They might, for example, think that pretense is action (e.g., talking into a banana) rather than a mental representation that is layered onto reality. Although pretense usually involves action, it does not always. A child could pretend that she is a banana by remaining still and simply thinking banana-like thoughts (the jungle? ripening? banana splits?) without also acting in banana-like ways such as forming a curve or hanging from a tree.

To test whether young children understand that pretending involves a representational state, Lillard (1991) posed situations of the following sort. She showed a troll doll and told the children:

> This is Moe. He's from the land of the trolls. Moe's hopping around, kind of like a rabbit hops. Moe doesn't know that rabbits hop like that; he doesn't know anything about rabbits. But he is hopping like a rabbit. Does he know that rabbits hop like that? Is he hopping like a rabbit? Would you say he is pretending to be a rabbit, or he's not pretending to be a rabbit?

Most of the 4-year-olds and many of the 5-year-olds claimed that Moe was indeed pretending to be a rabbit. They ignored the fact that he could not possibly have a representation of a rabbit, never having seen one. Thus, young children apparently think he can "pretend" even without a mental representation; he merely needs to act like the referent. In further support of this conclusion, Lillard and Flavell (1992) found that children did better on pretense tasks when pretense was accompanied by an action rather than by only a mental representational state. This does not necessarily mean that they do not understand mental representation generally, just that it is not required in their concept of pretense. Still, it is surprising that 4-year-olds appear not to understand the representational nature of pretense. First of all, they have engaged in pretend play for several years. Secondly, as we will see later, they understand that people have representations such as beliefs, preferences, and perceptions. There is much more for developmental psychologists to learn in this area.

In summary, children's pictorial, model, and pretend-play representations show both positive acquisitions and important limitations in young children's thinking. Toddlers know that pictures stand for real things and pretending stands for real things and events but not until later do they fully sort out the differences between the representations (external objects and actions) and reality. A main stumbling block is that an external representation simultaneously is itself (e.g., photo, action, model) and stands for another entity. This is particularly problematic when a child tries to use a model of one specific reality, such as one specific living room rather than living rooms in general. The model as an entity in its own right competes with children perceiving it as a representation as well.

Many of young children's representations seem rather simpleminded. One thing stands for another thing. These representations do not stay simple for very long. During the preschool years they become increasingly organized into structured systems of knowledge. Our examples of sociodramatic play hinted at this complexity. We now will discuss three types of representational knowledge structures—event knowledge and scripts, concepts, and theories.

EVENT KNOWLEDGE AND SCRIPTS

Life is eventful. People and objects in a young child's world do things; children observe these events and enter into them, thus joining the flow of the world around them. They mentally represent these events (*event knowledge*). Some of these event representations are generalized and abstract (*scripts*). This event knowledge, including scripts, of everyday life may be the young child's most powerful mental tool for understanding the world.

Suppose you ask a 20-month-old to give a bath to "Teddy." You demonstrate by removing the Teddy bear's pajamas, putting him in the bath tub, washing him, and drying him. Taking a bath is a familiar sequence to children of this age. Similarly, you ask the child to imitate a sequence that also is causal, but unfamiliar—put a ball in a cup, cover it with another cup, and shake the cups to make a rattle. Finally, the child must imitate an unfamiliar arbitrary sequence—bang a ring on a block, spin the ring on its side, and stack the ring on a stick. When Bauer and Shore (1987) conducted this study, they found that 17½- to 23-month-olds performed quite well in both causal conditions, but not the condition with arbitrary relations. Moreover, they still recalled the causal sequences 6 weeks later. Thus, even toddlers encode order information in their representations of events, even unfamiliar events, if the episode makes sense to them.

In addition to representing a one-time event, a young child also can construct a script—a generalized, temporally and spatially organized, sequence of events about some common routine with a goal. Repeated experience with taking a bath, for example, leads to a script representation of "how people usually take baths." There may be variations from one particular bath to another, such as whether you use "bubble bath," whether you get into the tub before or after you run the water, and whether you play with a rubber ducky or read a book, but certain elements stay the same. For example, normal people, unless very preoccupied, do not take baths without water. Moreover, certain causal relations are never violated. You do not dry off before the bath rather than after. In fact, if you present familiar sequences out of order (dry off, wash, put bear in tub) to 20-month-olds, in their recall they sometimes "correct" the order to the real-life one (Bauer & Thal, 1990). Other common childhood scripts include "going to McDonald's" (ordering food, paying for it, getting it, sitting down, eating) or baking cookies (K. Nelson, 1986).

In addition to studying these naturally occurring scripts, it is possible to create scripts in children, thus condensing experience over months or years into a few hours. One example is Price and Goodman's (1990) novel event, visiting the wizard. A bearded man dressed in a colorful robe led the child through various events, such as a "magic chamber" and "magic goodbye" (a gesture and a slogan). Over a series of visits children aged 2½ to 5 constructed a script for this recurring event—what you usually do when you visit a wizard. However, in some cases a script can be constructed after a single instance (Fivush & Slackman, 1986).

Scripts form general mental templates or molds that tell the child how things are "supposed to go" in such familiar routines. Consequently, scripts provide stability to daily life by allowing children to predict what will happen next, for instance, in their dinner-bathtime-bedtime routine. Violations of this order can be perplexing to a young child. Hudson (1990) reports a 2-year-old who once was given a bath before dinner and became very upset because she thought she would not be fed that evening. Scripts also are important because they provide the foundation of shared social information necessary for successful social interaction in a particular culture. Anyone who has violated the "take a number and wait for your turn" script in our culture knows the social pressure against such sins.

Young children appear to find it easier to organize their experience according to scripts rather than the hierarchical taxonomic categories that we will discuss later in this chapter (e.g., Lucariello & Nelson, 1985). For example, a child more easily recalls items when they fit into a script, for instance, "clothes you put on in the morning"—pants, socks, shirt—than when they form taxonomic categories, for instance, "clothes"—pants, coat, pajamas. Script organization is temporal-spatial, and often causal, whereas taxonomic organization is hierarchical (e.g., clothes, types of clothes). Perhaps children's active personal involvement in events and their rehearsal of scripts in pretend play enhance this form of representation. In fact, in their pretend play children often seem deliberately to manipulate and transform scripts in imaginative ways. Also, scripted events often function to satisfy the child's desires—eating freshly baked cookies or beloved fast food, having fun at a birthday party or movie, and so on. The power of motivation and personal involvement should never be ignored.

Our final comments about scripts are, naturally, developmental ones. First, scripts not only emerge earlier than taxonomic concepts, but may also facilitate their development (K. Nelson, 1986). For example, "eat cereal for breakfast" and "eat a sandwich for lunch" become joined into a taxonomic category of "food." Second, scripts increase in complexity during the preschool and grade-school years, but even preschoolers produce well-organized, coherent accounts of familiar events. In a later chapter on memory (Chapter 6) we will pursue further the effects of developmental changes in scripts. Good sources on children's construction of scripts are K. Nelson (1986), K. Nelson and Hudson (1988), and Fivush and Hudson (1990).

Closely related to event and script knowledge is narrative thinking, or story telling, for all involve a coherent set of occurrences over time and space. Even a simple, garden-variety story has a complex underlying structure that is relatively fixed (Mandler, 1983). Stories have an underlying structure consisting of a setting component in which the protagonist and background information are introduced. Next are episodes that construct the plot. Each episode has a beginning event to which a protagonist reacts, often by formulating a goal. The protagonist next attempts to attain the goal. The success or failure of that attempt draws the story to a close. The ending may refer to the long-range consequences of the episode, responses of the characters to the events, or simply "They lived happily ever after." Because young children have script representations they can use to assimilate these stories, they can comprehend stories at an early age. In fact, they can infer important information that is not explicitly stated. They also can produce simple, but understandable, narratives about personally experienced events (e.g., Hudson & Shapiro, 1991).

The development of event and script representations probably is related to two other types of knowledge—representations of scenes and physical causal relations. A central feature of event, script, and narrative thinking is their spatial component. The actions in an event occur in different parts of the restaurant, kitchen, or zoo. Children's representations of spatial scenes seem to parallel event, script, and narrative representations. They tend to organize furniture into meaningful, event-related units—for example, chair, footstool, and table with lamp. Thus, they have more difficulty recalling scenes with randomly organized furniture (Mandler, 1983). Even 2-year-olds possess this kind of knowledge about space and objects (Ratner & Myers, 1981).

Moreover, like their elders, young children usually represent the locations of objects in familiar surroundings objectively, in spatial relation to one another or the entire room or area, rather than (or in addition to) subjectively, in relation solely to their own bodies (L. P. Acredolo, 1990; Mandler, 1983; Newcomb, 1989). Thus, they too tend to use a spatial code or frame of reference that is external rather than only self-defined, or *egocentric*. For instance, they are apt to represent and remember that the coffee table and rocking chair are located in the living room and right next to each other, rather than merely that the table is on their right as they come into the room (egocentric spatial coding). In contrast, there is some evidence to suggest that young infants tend to rely on an egocentric representation, especially in less familiar environments (e.g., L. P. Acredolo, 1979). However, this tendency to fall back on an egocentric frame of reference when in an unfamiliar environment probably remains with us all our lives (Mandler, 1983).

Because young children are sensitive to the order of events it is not surprising that they also appear to have at least a rudimentary representation of causal relations—one that goes beyond that of infants described in Chapter 2. For example, Bullock and Gelman (1979) have shown that preschool children know that physical causes precede rather than follow their effects. Their 3- to 5-year-old subjects saw the following sequence of events: One hand puppet dropped a ball onto a runway; the ball rolled down the runway and into a hole; a jack-in-the-box popped up and another hand puppet simultaneously dropped a ball on another runway; that ball traversed its runway and dropped into another hole. The two holes were at equal distances from where the jack appeared, so spatial proximity was not a cue to the causal source. The younger subjects often and the older subjects almost always identified the first, prior-to-effect event rather than the second, subsequent-to-effect event as the cause of the jack's jumping up. For instance, when asked to make the jack jump up themselves, most of the children elected to drop the ball down the first hole rather than the second. Bullock and Gelman (1979) also showed that children of this age seem not to expect physical causes to act at a distance—that is, without any kind of direct or indirect physical contact with their effects. For a useful review of young children's causal processing, see White (1988).

A study by A. L. Brown (1989) described in Chapter 2 points out one reason why early causal understanding is critical for early cognition. Young children use principles of causality to guide their learning and generalization. If two situations share the same underlying causal principle, children ignore perceptual similarity in favor of causal similarity, and generalization then occurs easily. Children aged 20 months of age were given experience with retrieving a toy out of reach with a long rigid hook. On a transfer trial with new potential tools, they ignored tools of the same color or pattern and chose instead objects of the correct length, rigidity, and hookedness of end. Only the latter attributes are relevant to the causal principle of "first make contact and then pull toward you." This research suggests that young children are not necessarily perception bound if they detect a causal structure that is relevant to their goal.

In summary, young children's representations of objects, events, and scenes reveal that they have many abilities previously thought to be beyond them. These knowledge structures incorporate temporal order and logical relations, and even permit children to tell coherent stories about real or make-believe other people or even about their own lives. For more details about the various representations described in this section, see K. Nelson (1986), Mandler (1983), Fivush and Hudson (1990), and Newcomb (1989).

CONCEPTS AND CATEGORIES

Children develop representational knowledge structures of many sorts. Just as scripts serve to organize the events and scenes of the world, so do concepts serve to organize the types of entities that populate that world.

One of us once referred to the task of defining the term *concept* as "a lexicographer's nightmare" (Flavell, 1970a, p. 983). Despite numerous attempts to pin down what we mean when we speak of concepts, the notion continues to defy a single, agreed-upon, applicable-to-all instances definition. Rather than get bogged down in such definitional matters, we settle here for a rough characterization that will be sufficient to get our discussion started, with elaborations and qualifications to be picked up as we go. A rough definition is that a concept is a mental grouping of different entities into a single category on the basis of some underlying similarity—some way in which all the entities are alike, some common core that makes them all, in some sense, the "same thing." All of us, for example, have a concept of *dog* that unites the numerous and diverse exemplars that share the properties of dogness; we also have a concept of animal that brings together the even more variegated members of this category. Concepts serve to cut the world into useful categories—to identify pockets of similarity in the midst of what would otherwise be unmanageable diversity. The interesting developmental questions then have to do with how children cut up their worlds. What bases do they use when they think about things as being similar—and how do these bases change as their cognitive abilities develop?

Natural Kinds and Other Kinds

A study by Susan Gelman and Ellen Markman (1986) is a good starting point, for it is typical—in issues examined, methods used, and results obtained—of much recent work in early concept development. Gelman and Markman first taught their 4-year-old subjects some new information about pairs of pictured objects. The children were told, for example, that "This fish [experimenter presents a picture of a tropical fish] stays underwater to breathe," but that "This dolphin pops above the water to breathe." Similarly, the children heard that "This bird's [picture of flamingo] legs get cold at night," whereas "This bat's legs stay warm at night." Following each pair, the experimenter presented a third picture that closely resembled one member of the original pair but received the same label as the other member—thus in the first example a shark (quite perceptually similar to the dolphin) that was labeled a "fish," and in the second example a blackbird (close in looks to the bat) that was labeled a "bird." The child's task then was to infer which of the contrasting properties applied to the new object. Would the shark breathe like a fish or breathe like a dolphin? Would the blackbird's legs get cold at night or stay warm? The contrasting bases for response should be evident. Judgments on the basis of common label and category membership would result in one set of inferences; judgments on the basis of perceptual similarity would result in a quite different set of inferences.

A considerable body of theorizing and research prior to Gelman and Markman's study would lead us to predict that 4-year-olds' inferences will be governed by perceptual similarity. Young children have been quite widely characterized as perceptually oriented. Such a characterization is certainly part of the Piagetian notion of a preoperational period, and Piaget's research documented numerous situations in which young children tend to be misled by an overreliance on perceptual features. As we will see later in the chapter, recent research has shown that young children often have difficulty in distinguishing appearance and reality—that is, in penetrating beyond immediate perceptual appearance to get at the true nature of things. Studies of so-called concept formation, in which the subject must discover some experimenter-defined criterion for correct response (e.g., pick the middle-sized stimulus, or the one on the left, or the one not chosen last time), present a similar picture of the perception-bound young child. So too do studies of free-sorting behavior in which children are asked to group objects on the basis of which ones "go together." Presented, for example, with a fire engine, car, and apple, most 3- and 4-year-olds group fire engine and apple—the two red things—rather than fire engine and car—the two vehicles (B. Tversky, 1985).

Given all this evidence of the perception-dominated 4-year-old, you have probably guessed by now that the interest of Gelman and Markman's results lies in the fact that their 4-year-olds did *not* respond perceptually. Faced with a choice between category membership and perceptual appearance, most children opted for the former as a determinant of the generalization of properties. They decided, therefore, that the shark would breathe like a tropical fish rather than a dolphin, despite its much greater resemblance to the dolphin, and that the blackbird would probably have cold legs at night, despite its resemblance to the warm-legged bat. A follow-up study demonstrated that these properties were not things that the children already knew about sharks or blackbirds; rather, their choices were dependent on the inferences drawn from category membership. A further follow-up showed that the use of a common label (e.g., dubbing both tropical fish and shark as "fish") was not necessary for good performance; similar findings emerged when synonyms (e.g., "rock-stone," "puppy-baby dog") were given rather than identical labels. Indeed, in a later publication, Gelman and Markman (1987) demonstrated that young children have some ability to recognize and to use category membership from pictures alone, in the absence of any labels. Finally, yet another study showed that the children were properly selective in the inferences they drew. When attributes such as weight or visibility at night were at issue, the usual reliance on category membership gave way to judgments based on perceptual similarity. When told, for example, that a tropical fish weighs 20 pounds and a dolphin 100 pounds, children picked the latter as the more likely weight for a shark.

Whenever some sort of competence is demonstrated at a surprisingly early age, developmentalists tend to wonder whether age of emergence can be pushed even younger. Gelman and Markman (1986) showed that 4-year-olds are unexpectedly adult-like in their inference patterns. What about younger children? Gelman and Markman (1987), using a somewhat simplified methodology, obtained similar results for 3-year-olds. S. A. Gelman and Coley (1990), using still simpler techniques, found that even 2½-year-olds have some ability to overlook perceptual appearance in favor of category membership when appropriate. At present, 2½ is the youngest age at which the Gelman and Markman procedure has been attempted. Research with other methods, however, makes clear that categorization begins well before the preschool period. Toddlers (e.g., Mandler, Bauer, & McDonough, 1991) and even infants (e.g., Ross, 1980; Younger, 1990) have been shown to organize their experiences into simple concepts.

The message from the Gelman and Markman research—as well as from many similar studies in recent years (for reviews, see A. L. Brown, 1989; Wellman & Gelman, 1988, 1992)—is that young children's concepts are not simply collections of perceptual features. Rather, children's concepts, like adults' concepts, emphasize basic, often nonobvious similarities among exemplars, similarities that permit powerful generalizations from one category member to another. Yet the older research literature cannot be totally in error; in many situations young children *do* respond on the basis of immediate perceptual appearance. Why, then, the more positive conclusions from the Gelman and Markman line of research? Wellman and Gelman (1988) point out two important differences between most earlier studies of children's concepts and the more recent work. One difference concerns response measures. Much of the earlier work used the free-sorting ("which ones go together?") methodology. Although the ability to group members is certainly part of what is meant by having a concept, grouping alone cannot capture all of the knowledge that underlies concepts. *Why* do certain things belong together, and what functions do concepts serve? In contrast, the *induction technique* utilized by Gelman and Markman speaks directly to the essential nature of concepts. One important role that concepts play is to permit inferences or inductions about category members, even those that have never been encountered before. If told, for example, that we are about to meet a new breed of dog called a malamute, we have some definite expectations about what we will encounter, even though we have never seen a malamute before. Furthermore, the inductions that we make help to reveal the nature of our concept of dog. We are likely, for example, to draw inferences concerning such dog-defining matters as internal organs, diet, and general behavior patterns. In contrast, we are unlikely to have any expectations with regard to such nonessential features as age, place of birth, or exact size.

The second difference identified by Wellman and Gelman (1988) concerns the nature of the concept. In some studies the concepts examined have been arbitrary ones created on the spot for the purposes of the research—for example, the category of blue circles in a study of sorting behavior. Naturally occurring concepts are not arbitrary, however; rather, they reflect important commonalities among real-world entities, commonalities that children extract from their everyday experiences. Among the many concepts that children naturally form, a particularly interesting subset has to do with what philosophers call *natural kinds* (Schwartz, 1977). Natural kinds are categories that occur in nature—classes of things whose existence and nature are not dependent on human activity. Animals are natural kinds; so too are plants and minerals. The underlying structure of natural kinds makes them a particularly rich source for inductive inferences. The concentration on natural kinds in the Gelman and Markman research may well have contributed to the children's impressive performance.

Of course, natural kinds are not the only sorts of concepts with which children or any of us must deal. Keil (1989) discusses two other general categories. *Nominal kinds* are categories defined more by human convention than by nature; examples cited by Keil include circle, odd number, island, uncle, and princess. Unlike natural kinds, nominal kinds tend to have clearly defining features and dictionary-like definitions—an island is a body of land surrounded by water, an uncle is your parent's brother, and so on. The third category is *artifacts*: objects created by humans. Examples here include cups, tables, chairs, cars, and computers.

All of us possess numerous specific concepts within each of these three general categories. But all of us also know quite a bit about differences among the categories. We know, for example, that cups are dependent on a human creator but that turtles, oaks, and grains of sand are not. We realize that a table can be transformed into a bookcase or a glass into a vase, but that neither science nor magic can turn lead into gold or a lion into a lamb. Do young children understand these basic differences among categories? The answer turns out to be "in part but not fully." Here we consider two lines of research, one initiated by Susan Gelman and the other by Frank Keil.

The Gelman and Markman (1986, 1987) studies demonstrated that even 4-year-olds use knowledge of category membership to draw a wide range of inferences. But not all categories are as conducive to inferences as are the natural kinds examined by Gelman and Markman. Children need to be able not only to make inferences but to *constrain* their inferences—that is, avoid generalizing too broadly from one category member to another. If we learn, for example, that a particular rabbit has an omentum inside, we are likely to be quite confident that all rabbits have omentums (omenta?) inside and reasonably certain that all animals have them as well. Learning, however, that a particular chair has urethane inside gives us little basis for predicting to other chairs, let alone to furniture in general. Natural kinds typically have insides that are essential to their nature and common across category members; artifacts typically do not (though modern artifacts—the computer most notably—do blur the distinction). S. A. Gelman (1988) tested for this and related sorts of understanding and reported a developmental progression between ages 4 and 7, with the older children generally more likely than the younger ones to make appropriate, adult-like distinctions among categories. Young children, to be sure, are not totally lacking a natural kind-artifact distinction. Gelman found, for example, that even 4-year-olds can answer direct questions about which sorts of things are human-made and which are not, and other studies have elicited other sorts of evidence for some early appreciation of the distinction (S. A. Gelman & Kremer, 1991; S. A. Gelman & O'Reilly, 1988; S. A. Gelman & Wellman, 1991). Nevertheless, one safe generalization in this area is that a full understanding of the differences among different sorts of concepts is a gradual developmental achievement.

This same conclusion emerges from Keil's research (Keil, 1979, 1989, 1991). Keil has devised a number of ingenious techniques to probe understanding of kinds and concepts; here we concentrate on his *transformations* procedure. Consider the vignettes in Table 3–1. As you can see, the idea of the transformations procedure is that an object starts out as indubitably one thing and ends up with the characteristic appearance (looks, smells, behaviors, functions) of something quite

TABLE 3-1 Examples of Keil's Transformations Procedure

NATURAL KIND: RACCOON/SKUNK

The doctors took a raccoon (show picture of raccoon) and shaved away some of its fur. They dyed what was left all black. Then they bleached a single strip all white down the center of its back. Then, with surgery (explained to child in preamble), they put in its body a sac of super smelly odor, just like a skunk has (with younger children "odor" was replaced with "super smelly yucky stuff"). When they were all done, the animal looked like this (show picture of skunk). After the operation was this a skunk or a raccoon? (Both pictures were present at the time of the final question.)

ARTIFACT: COFFEEPOT/BIRDFEEDER

The doctors took a coffeepot that looked like this (show picture of coffeepot). They sawed off the handle, sealed the top, took off the top knob, sealed closed the spout, and sawed it off. They also sawed off the base and attached a flat piece of metal. They attached a little stick, cut a window in it, and filled the metal container with birdfood. When they were done it looked like this (show picture of birdfeeder). After the operation was this a coffeepot or a birdfeeder? (Both pictures were present the time of the final question.)

Note: From *Concepts, Kinds, and Cognitive Development* (p. 184) by F. C. Keil, 1989, Cambridge, MA: MIT Press. Copyright © 1989 by MIT Press. Reprinted by permission.

different. Some of the transformations involve natural kinds: tiger into lion, diamond into pearl, grapefruit into orange. Others involve artifacts: tire into boot, garbage into chair, tie into shoelace. The critical question in each case concerns what the transformed object really is—really a skunk, for example, or just a strange-looking, bad-smelling raccoon? Children at all ages accept the transformations of the artifacts, as indeed do most adults—if a former coffeepot looks like a birdfeeder and functions as a birdfeeder, why not consider it a birdfeeder? Four-year-olds, however, are also likely to believe that one natural kind can be turned into another. They do not, it is true, accept just any sort of transformation (putting a costume on is not sufficient), and they are reluctant to admit changes that cross fundamental category boundaries—in particular, any change from animate to inanimate or vice versa. Nevertheless, their grasp of the natural kind-artifact distinction is still somewhat shaky, as the following protocol vividly illustrates.

E: Well, which do you think the animal really is? Do you think it's really a raccoon or do you think it's really a skunk?

C: A raccoon!

E: Can it be a…

C: (Interrupting) It's a skunk.

E: Which do you really mean?

C: A skunk.

E: Can it be a skunk if its mommies and daddies were raccoons?

C: Yes.

E: Can it be a skunk if its babies were raccoons?

C: Yes.

E: (Repeats entire story) Which do you think it really was?

C: A skunk. Because it looks like a skunk, it smells like a skunk, it acts like a skunk and it sounds like a skunk. (The child was not told this.)

E: So it can be a skunk even though its babies are raccoons?

C: Yes! (Keil, 1989, p. 188)

Levels and Hierarchies

Concepts differ not only in the kinds of entities to which they are directed but also in the level of abstraction at which any particular entity is represented. A particular dog, for example, can be conceptualized not only as dog but also (among other possibilities) as animal and as poodle. In general, almost any concept can be placed within a taxonomic hierarchy in which it stands simultaneously in a subordinate relation to the more general categories that contain it (as does dog to animal) and a superordinate relation to the more specific categories that it itself contains (as does dog to poodle). Much theorizing and research have been directed to the question of how children come to understand such taxonomic classification. With even more than our usual selectivity (these are large literatures!), we briefly discuss two kinds of research, one stemming from some theorizing by Eleanor Rosch and the other stemming from Piaget. Further discussion can be found in Blewitt (1989), Markman (1989), Markman and Callanan (1983), and Neisser (1987).

Rosch and colleagues (Mervis & Rosch, 1981; Rosch, Mervis, Gray, Johnson, & Boyes-Braem, 1976) have argued that there is a *basic-level* at which concepts are most naturally and readily represented. Basic-level representations are those that offer an optimal blend of within-category similarity and between-category dissimilarity; the members of the category are similar enough to permit easy mental grouping (less true at the superordinate level) but also distinct enough from nonmembers to permit ready separation of categories (less true at the subordinate level). "Dog" is thus basic-level, whereas "animal" and "poodle" are not. "Chair" is basic-level, whereas "furniture" and "rocking chair" are not. The main developmental prediction has been that basic-level categories, being most natural, should be the first ones that children form.

The evidence with regard to this prediction is mixed. Support comes from the finding (discussed more fully in Chapter 7) that children's first words tend to be at the basic-level (Anglin, 1977). Studies of sorting behavior are also supportive: Young children group objects more readily at the basic-level (e.g., all the dogs) than at the superordinate level (e.g., all the animals) (Rosch et al., 1976). On the other hand, tests of the supposed primacy of the basic-level have been complicated by difficulties in defining exactly what is basic, as well as by the possibility that there may be a "child-basic-level" (Mervis, 1987) that, at least for a while, is different from adult-basic-level. In addition, Mandler and Bauer (1988; Mandler et al., 1991) report evidence that 18-month-olds distinguish and group objects more readily on the basis of global categories (e.g., animals vs. vehicles) than on the basis of basic-level distinctions within such categories. They suggest that the primacy of basic-level by age 3 (the lower age bound for most sorting studies) may mask an earlier reliance on more global categories.

Whether the basic-level is primary from the start or only becomes so with development, its ascendancy by age 3 has implications for how children draw inferences from their knowledge of category membership. Susan Gelman (1988; Gelman & O'Reilly, 1988) has shown that children who are taught a new fact about an object are more likely to generalize to objects at the same basic-level than to objects that share only the same superordinate level with the original. This strategy makes sense: The basic-level, by definition, *is* more homogeneous and thus more conducive to inferences than is the superordinate level.

Piaget's interest in classes centered on children's understanding of the hierarchical structure of classes and the inclusion relation that holds between superordinate and subordinate. Because a subclass (such as dogs) is subsumed within a superordinate (such as animals), there can never be more members in the subclass than there are in the superordinate. Inhelder and Piaget (1964) demonstrated—and later studies (Winer, 1980) have confirmed—that even middle-childhood subjects often have great difficulty correctly answering quantitative class-inclusion questions that probe for such knowledge. For example, after the experimenter establishes with an 8-year-old that, say, a bunch of 16 flowers consisting of 10 red ones and 6 blue ones are "all flowers," this child is asked,"Are there more red flowers or more flowers?" A child of this age is likely to compare the red flowers with the blue flowers, rather than with the entire bunch, and incorrectly reply "More red flowers." Markman (1978) found that even children who pass this test may view the greater numbers of superordinate (e.g., flowers) than subordinate (e.g., red flowers) class members as an empirical fact rather than as a logically necessary truth. For example, they may say "yes" when asked questions like, "Could you make it so that there will be more spoons than silverware on the table?" Similarly, S. A. Miller (1986a) found that many children who passed the standard task were still quite willing to draw a picture that showed more cats than animals.

On the other hand, children's failures on some versions of the class-inclusion problem do not imply a total inability to construct taxonomic hierarchies or to reason about inclusion relations. Even more than is true for most Piagetian concepts, different forms of class inclusion vary greatly in difficulty, and the surprising failure of older children (and even college students—see Rabinowitz, Howe, & Lawrence, 1989) on some versions must be set against the precocious success of much younger children on other versions. A striking demonstration in the latter category has been reported by C. L. Smith (1979), who showed that 4-year-olds can sometimes make valid inferences based on class-inclusion representations. For instance, most of her subjects correctly said yes to questions such as "A pug is a kind of dog, but not a German shepherd. Is a pug an animal?" and no to questions such as "A yam is a kind of food, but not meat. Is a yam a hamburger?" Some subjects even justified their answers in ways that strongly suggest some class-inclusion knowledge: for the German shepherd question, for example, justifications like "Yes, you said it was a dog" and "Yes, dogs are animals."

Earlier-than-expected success is also the theme of a series of interesting studies by Markman (1981b, 1989). Markman's research contrasts children's abilities to deal with *classes* versus *collections*. Those tall things that squirrels climb constitute the class "trees," but when a number of them cluster together they also constitute the collection "forest." In general, collections are labeled by collective nouns ("family," "army," "pile," etc.), and their elements enter into part-whole relations rather than subclass-superordinate class relations. An oak, for example, is a kind of tree but a part of the forest, just as a private is a kind of soldier but a part of the army. Markman has shown that children tend to find it easier to operate conceptually on collection structures than on class structures. For instance, they are surer that one would necessarily have more wood if one chopped down the _____ than if one chopped down the oaks, when the blank is filled with the word "forest" (collection term) than when it is filled with the word "tree" (class term). That is, children can grasp the logic of the inclusion relation more easily when the including whole is described as a collection rather than as a class.

The message from this discussion is that class inclusion is not the sort of knowledge that a child either "has" or "does not have." Rather, there clearly are different senses and different degrees of "having," depending on the task and the response measure in question. Studies such as C. L. Smith's (1979) suggest that even young children possess some representations of class-inclusion relations that are, in most important respects, not qualitatively different from those of older people. That is, their basic conceptual organization is probably not radically different from that of adults. Other research on early concepts, both work already discussed and work still to be discussed, is certainly compatible with this conclusion of early competence. On the other hand, young children probably have less explicit and general or abstract knowledge about these representations, and consequently are less able to talk or reason about class hierarchies and class-inclusion relations than older people are. They solve a narrower range of experimental tasks, and they may not use their knowledge in everyday thinking as much or as fully as older children and adults do. And their approach to class-inclusion problems may at first be primarily empirical, without a full appreciation of the logical necessity of the subclass-superordinate class relation.

Some Specific Examples: Concepts of Biology

So far we have said quite a bit about Concepts in general but little about concepts in the particular—that is, interesting forms of knowledge that are developing during the early childhood years. Biological concepts certainly qualify as interesting forms of knowledge. Questions of life—of living versus nonliving, of animate versus inanimate, of origins and of growth—have fascinated children for as long as they have fascinated scientists. Such questions were among the topics that Piaget explored in his earliest work (Piaget, 1929), and they have recently reemerged, after a somewhat fallow period, as the focus of a good deal of exciting contemporary research. A consideration of some of this research will both reinforce points already made and lead to some further conclusions about the nature of children's concepts.

We noted that biological categories fall under the general heading of natural kinds. Most research on natural kinds has in fact concentrated on animals and plants, and hence studies already reviewed have told us quite a bit about what children know about living things and how they use their knowledge to draw inferences. But biological categories are a subset of natural kinds in general, and they share certain properties not found either in other natural kinds or in human-produced artifacts. Furthermore, animals share a further subset of properties not found in plants. Young children, it turns out, understand some but not all of the ways in which living things differ from nonliving and one kind of living thing differs from another. We consider research on biological understanding with regard to three properties: growth, inheritance, and self-produced movement.

The capacity for growth is one distinguishing characteristic of life. All living things grow, and only living things grow. Biological growth, moreover, is lawful and predictable. Organisms may increase in size as they get older but with rare exceptions (e.g., tadpole into frog) they do not decrease. They may change greatly in appearance but they do not change their basic identity; the wizened octogenarian is the same individual as the squirming newborn, just as the strappling tree is continuous with the tiny seedling. Although environmental factors (nutrition, sunlight) may be essential to growth, they do not provide its basic motor; the impetus, rather, is internal—something that organisms are born to do. None of these characteristics apply to the changes that occur in nonliving things. An artifact such as a car may change appearance over time as a result of human intervention (a new paint job) or environmental elements (sun and rain); such changes, however, do not constitute growth. Nor, despite our everyday use of the term "grow," do the increases in size that nonliving things (an expanding balloon, rising bread) may occasionally undergo.

Children as young as 3 or 4 have some appreciation of these distinctions. They are reasonably (although not perfectly) accurate in answering questions about which things grow and which do not (Inagaki & Sugiyama, 1988); they also show some understanding of the inevitability of growth, indicating, for example, that a small and cute baby rabbit cannot be kept small and cute forever just because the owner wishes it so (Inagaki & Hatano, 1987). Even preschoolers recognize the directionality of growth, judging that living things but not artifacts grow larger as they grow older (Rosengren, Gelman, Kalish, & McCormick, 1991). This understanding is, to be sure, somewhat incomplete, for young children are less willing than older ones to accept the possibility of large increases in size or dramatic changes of the caterpillar-to-butterfly sort. They are also somewhat doubtful that really small things (butterflies, worms) can be said to grow (R. Gelman, 1990). Nevertheless, the main message from this work is of fairly good understanding from fairly early on of which kinds of things grow and how they grow. As Rosengren et al. note, there is an interesting contrast between their work and that of Keil (1989) on changes in natural kinds. Recall that Keil found that many young children were willing to believe that one animal could be so altered by surgical techniques or other interventions that it would actually become a different species. Keil's studies, however, involved distinctly nonnatural transformations that never in fact occur. Children's understanding of change is more impressive when the focus is on the natural changes that come with growth.

Living things are distinguished not only by growth but by origins. Living things come from other living things, and they inherit properties both of the species in general and of their own parents in particular. Recent research (Gelman & Wellman, 1991; Springer & Keil, 1989, 1991) has shown that young children have some definite ideas about inheritance. Even preschoolers realize that like beget like—that dogs have baby dogs, and cats have baby cats. Children adhere to this principle even in the face of countervailing environmental forces, judging, for example, that a rabbit raised by monkeys will prefer carrots to bananas, just as a cow raised by pigs will say "moo" rather than "oink." By age 4, children posit different mechanisms of transmission for biological properties than for nonbiological ones. The color of a flower or dog is assumed to be inherited from the parent through natural, lawful means (even though children may not yet understand the means); the color of a can, in contrast, is attributed to mechanical, human-engineered processes. Within biological kinds, some properties are assumed to be more heritable than others. Children are most likely to expect parent-to-child transmission when the property in question is one with functional consequences—for example, a pink heart that is described as helping the animal stay healthy, as opposed to a pink heart that receives no further description. Interestingly, the youngest children in these studies evidence a Lamarkian strain of reasoning, in that they do not seem to care whether the property in question is inborn or acquired from experience. By age 6 or 7 a preference for inborn qualities as the stuff of inheritance has begun to emerge.

Whereas growth and inheritance are common to all life, independent movement is unique to animals. That children are attentive to movement has been clear ever since Piaget's (1929) examinations of children's beliefs about what it means to be "alive." Piaget claimed that young children were often *animistic*—that is, attributed life to nonliving things—and that movement cues were one source of their confusion. Thus clouds, bikes, and watches might all be judged to be alive because they are seen to move. Later studies have verified that young children do sometimes have difficulty in drawing the border between living and nonliving; the confusion, however, is both less pervasive and less persistent than Piaget believed (Carey, 1985a; R. Gelman, Spelke, & Meck, 1983). In addition, recent work has demonstrated that young children are surprisingly sensitive to the different types of movement that different sorts of objects can undergo. An impressive example of such sensitivity is provided by Massey and Gelman (1988), who presented their 3- and 4-year-old subjects with photographs of the sort shown in Figure 3–1. The basic question with regard to each object was whether it could move up and down a hill by itself. The children proved quite good both at answering this question and at justifying their answers, despite the unfamiliarity of the objects and despite the limitation to pictorial cues. Note that we have here another example of the young child's ability to overlook on-the-surface perceptual appearance in favor of some deeper underlying essence. The statue certainly looks more like the self-propelling objects with which the child is familiar than does the echidna (spiny anteater), yet only the latter is judged as capable of navigating a hill by itself. In Rochel Gelman's (1990) view, children's ability to make such distinctions is made possible by a set of innate processing mechanisms that direct attention, from very early in life, to the cues that differentiate self-propelled movements from externally generated ones (recall our discussion of movement and causality in Chapter 2). The child's understanding of animacy then builds upon this sensitivity to the causes of movement: Animate objects are things that can move themselves—things that have, in Gelman's phrase, "causal innards."

Some General Conclusions

Having sampled some particular concepts from the realm of biology, we return to Concepts in general and to some general conclusions to be taken away from recent work on how young children conceptualize the world. We offer three conclusions that are suggested by the research just reviewed, followed by a return to the general question of what it means to have a concept.

1. One conclusion concerns the level of maturity of young children's concepts. It should be clear that research on conceptual development provides a prime example of the theme with which we opened the chapter: Preschoolers are smarter than we used to think. Rather than being perceptually dominated, inconsistent, and illogical, the young child's concepts turn out, at least sometimes, to be surprisingly adult-like and powerful. Because our emphasis has been on this early competence, we should add that 4-year-olds' concepts are not fully equivalent to those of 8- or 10-year-olds, let alone adults. We have already noted some limitations and corresponding developmental improvements—in the ability to distinguish natural kinds and artifacts, for example. In studies of the S. A. Gelman and Markman (1986) genre, the preference for category membership over perceptual appearance, although sometimes found, is less solidly established in younger children than in older (Farrar & Boyer, 1991; Farrar, Raney, &

FIGURE 3–1 Stimuli used in the Massey and Gelman study of preschoolers' understanding of movement: echidna (top left), sloth (top right), and statue of quadruped (bottom). From "Preschooler's Ability to Decide Whether a Photographed Unfamiliar Object Can Move Itself" by C. M. Massey and R. Gelman, 1988, *Developmental Psychology, 24,* p. 309. Copyright © 1988 by American Psychological Association. Reprinted by permission of Christine M. Massey. The echidna photograph by J. A. L. Cooke is reprinted with permission of Oxford Scientific Films Ltd. (Picture No. 36991). It and the photograph of the sloth are from *Life on Earth* (p. 206 and P. 250, respectively) by David Attenborough (1979), Boston, MA, Little, Brown. The quadraped statue photograph is reprinted courtesy of the Freer Gallery of Art, Smithsonian Institute, Washington, DC (Acc. 40, 23).

Boyer, in press). In the domain of biology, Carey (1985a) has shown that young children are overly dependent on analogy from humans in reasoning about biology, tending to attribute biological properties (e.g., heart, blood) only to species that resemble humans. Siegler (1989a) summarizes other limitations in preschoolers' biological knowledge. The moral to be taken away here has to do with balance and the avoidance of overstatement in either direction. At any age period, including adulthood, the cognitive system has both strengths and weaknesses. It is important that our models capture both.

2. Despite the cautions just expressed, a clear leitmotif of recent work on concepts is that young cognitive systems are not as qualitatively different from older ones as we used to believe. Young children often seem to be thinking in the same way as older children—just not as often, not as fully, or not as consistently. Often, their problem seems to be that they simply do not know enough about the content area in question. The importance of content-specific knowledge has emerged as a major emphasis in recent research and thinking, both with regard to concepts in particular (Farrar et al., in press; Kalish & Gelman, 1991) and with regard to cognitive functioning more generally (A. L. Brown, 1989; Flavell, 1984a). It is (as befits a pervasive emphasis) a notion that we will encounter again—in the discussion of problem solving in middle childhood and adolescence, for example (Chapter 4), and in the treatment of memory and developmental changes therein (Chapter 6).

3. A third conclusion is related. If content-specific knowledge is an important component of children's concepts, then there is little reason to expect that all of a child's conceptual thinking will be at the same level of maturity and effectiveness. In fact, children's concepts are not all at the same level. Keil (1979; Keil & Batterman, 1984) provides an example with regard to understanding of nominal kinds. He shows that there is a shift with development from an emphasis on characteristic features (e.g., an uncle is someone who gives presents) to an emphasis on defining features (e.g., an uncle is your parent's brother); the shift, however, is not across the board but rather occurs at different times for different concepts. Note that there *is* a general development change here: Less mature ways of thinking take one characteristic form, and more mature ways take a different characteristic form. Achievement of the mature form, however, requires not only general cognitive advance but also content-specific knowledge. The domain-specific nature of much of cognitive functioning and cognitive change will be another recurring theme in chapters to come.

So far we have said some things about what concepts are not. They are not simply bundles of perceptual features, for example. In the case of natural kinds, they probably are not explicable solely in terms of defining features (what are the defining features for tiger? for gold?) or probabilistic representations of characteristic elements. But what *are* concepts?

The most popular answer to this question at present is provided by the theory-based approach to knowledge introduced in Chapter 1. In this view (e.g., Keil, 1989; Medin, 1989), concepts are theories that help us make sense of the world. No one believes, of course, that a concept has all the properties of a formal scientific theory. But concepts—perhaps especially those of the natural-kind ilk—do seem to function in some ways like mini-theories ("theorettes," as Forguson, 1989, calls them) for particular aspects of reality. Consider our earlier example of the concept of dog. The set of beliefs that make up our concept of dog shares a number of features with scientific theories. Like a theory, a concept involves fundamental distinctions, such as natural-kind versus nonnatural, living versus nonliving, animal versus plant, and domesticated versus wild. As in a theory, the beliefs that make up a concept are not isolated but rather cohere into a tightly interconnected, mutually supportive system. Our beliefs concerning a dog's behavior patterns, for example, are related both to our general knowledge of its status as pet and more specific knowledge concerning what kind of dog it is (watchdog, hunting dog, etc.). Similarly, our beliefs concerning behavior are in accord with beliefs concerning the physical attributes (e.g., teeth, claws, sense of smell) that make the behavior possible. As in a theory, causal relations among elements, such as the relation between behavior and requisite physical structure, play an especially important role in concepts. And like a theory, a concept serves to explain current experience and predict future experience. Such explanation and prediction, in fact, are at the core of the S. A. Gelman and Markman (1986) induction technique for studying concepts. It is our theory of what it means to be a dog that allows us to override perceptual factors to categorize Chihuahua and St. Bernard together and to use our knowledge of one to predict to the other. In the same way, children as young as 3 use their theories, incomplete or erroneous though they may sometimes be, to understand what they have already encountered and to make inferences about what is still to come.

As a number of commentators (e.g., Keil, 1989; Siegler, 1991a) have noted, the term "theory" has been used with different degrees of breadth and scope by workers in the knowledge-as-theory camp. Its most specific use is the one just discussed: Every concept is a theory, and hence children develop many specific theories. At the other extreme, the term "theory" has been used to refer to broad domains of reality for which children eventually develop quite broad and multifaceted theories, theories that have a number of specific concepts, or mini-theories, embedded within. In a recent review, Wellman and Gelman (1992) identify three grand theories of this sort that may subsume much of early cognitive development: a theory of the physical world, or naive physics; a theory of living things, or naive biology; and a theory of behavior and mental functioning, or naive psychology. The previous section sampled some of the research directed to children's theory of biology, and much of the work covered in Chapter 2 (e.g., Spelke's studies of knowledge of objects, Leslie's studies of causality) and in a section on scientific thinking in Chapter 4 can be grouped under the heading of naive physics. We turn next to what is probably the most active current arena for research and theorizing from the theory perspective: studies directed to the development of naive psychology, or what has come to be called "theory of mind."

THEORY OF MIND: CHILDREN AS MIND READERS

Minds are a main difference between people and other entities. Children cannot make much progress toward understanding everyday events involving people until they have some understanding of the mind. For example, a little girl makes sense of her friend's behavior of purposefully rummaging through his toy box by assuming that he *wants* a particular toy, *believes* it can be found there (is *looking* for it), *intends* to play with it, will *feel* sad if he does not find it, and so on. This common-sense understanding, or "folk psychology" (Churchland, 1984), about how the mind works brings order to the social events around her. It provides explanations of others' behavior and allows her to predict others' actions by referring to their beliefs, desires, perceptions, thoughts, emotions, and intentions. Researchers have dubbed these implicit notions about the psychological realm children's *theory of mind* (Bretherton & Beeghly, 1982; Premack & Woodruff, 1978; Wellman, 1979). Investigators use this term in both a loose and a restricted way. It can refer loosely to any knowledge about the mind—any naive psychology—the beginnings of which can be seen in infants. Or the term can be used more strictly, as it is in the theory-based approach described above and in Chapter 1. This more restricted definition refers to an abstract, coherent, causal-explanatory system that allows the child to explain and predict behavior by referring to unobservable mental states such as beliefs and desires. In this view, which philosophers call a "theory theory," children do not merely have a set of unconnected facts about the mind and behavior. Rather, their concepts of emotions, desires, beliefs, and perceptions are all interrelated, as shown in the toy box example above. And minds are clearly distinguished from non-minds. Researchers disagree regarding the extent to which young children have a theory of mind in this stricter sense (e.g., Chandler, 1988; Hobson, 1991; C. N. Johnson, 1988; Wellman, 1990).

Because theories have postulates, we will summarize what children appear to learn about the mind by positing five postulates of this knowledge: the mind (1) exists, (2) has connections to the physical world, (3) is separate from and differs from the physical world, (4) can represent objects and events accurately or inaccurately, and (5) actively mediates the interpretation of reality and the emotion experienced. The evidence we have thus far suggests that some minimal understanding of each postulate might be necessary before the next one can begin to be acquired, but development continues within each postulate even after the later ones have emerged. Postulates 1–3 probably emerge in quick succession, for they are very closely related concepts having to do with the differentiation of, and relations between, the mind and the external world. In fact, the developmental ordering of Postulates 2 and 3 is unclear at this point. The step from Postulate 3 to 4, which is the most drastic change in the conception of the mind, probably comes more slowly. Postulate 5, which is an elaborated implication of Postulate 4, would emerge still later.

The following account of the developing knowledge of the mind is our view of this phenomenon. Although there is general agreement among theorists of theory of mind about the general pattern of development, there is disagreement as to the details—for example, the age of attainment of a particular concept. For other views, see Astington and Gopnik (1991), Chandler (1988), Hobson (1991), Leslie (1988b, 1991), Perner (1991), and Wellman (1990). Good recent collections of papers on this topic are plentiful as well (Astington, Harris, & Olson, 1988; Butterworth, Harris, Leslie, & Wellman, 1991; Frye & Moore, 1991).

Postulate 1: The Mind Exists

The obvious first developmental acquisition is knowing that there is such a thing as a mind—that human beings are sentient, cognizing subjects. Our discussion of social cognition in infancy in Chapter 5 will suggest many precursors of this knowledge. One is looking at a parent's face for an interpretation of a potentially fearful event. Another is responding differently to people versus things, particularly in differentiating what people versus objects can do, such as when an infant intentionally tries to communicate with others and influence them to approach, comfort, and entertain. Infants obviously are not imputing truly mental states to others, but they probably understand that people possess "something"— perhaps agency (self-initiated movement) and influenceability—that non-people entities do not. Moreover, they may dimly perceive that others, and perhaps the self, are experiencers (Wellman & Gelman, 1992). Perhaps most importantly, infants and toddlers learn they can predict others' behavior and even affect the psychological-emotional states of others by comforting, hurting, or teasing. These predictions may lead to a rudimentary notion that people have "dispositions to behave" in certain ways.

Another important precursor emerges around 18 to 24 months when children begin to use external symbols, in which one object represents another, as in the pretend play described earlier. When a child talks into a banana as though it were a telephone, he or she can consider it as a banana and a telephone at the same time, but knows it really is a banana. This differentiation between the real thing (a real telephone) and another thing that represents it (a banana that the child pretends is a phone) foreshadows the full understanding of the distinction between an object and its *mental* representation. Interestingly, toddlers pretend that dolls have self-initiated behavior such as walking and talking, which, as we shall see in our discussion of intentions in Chapter 5, is a notion acquired with respect to real people several months earlier.

Even toddlers spontaneously refer to mental states. Two-year-olds mention emotional states and even participate with a sibling in pretend games in which they take on a pretend internal state themselves, assign it to the sibling, or share it with the sibling (Dunn, Bretherton, & Munn, 1987). They also discuss the causes of the feeling states, and sometimes use these states to try to influence behavior, as illustrated in the following exchange between a mother and a 24-month-old who spots a chocolate cake (Dunn et al., 1987, p. 136).

> Child sees chocolate cake on table.
> Child: Bibby on.
> Mother: You don't want your bibby on. You're not eating.
> Child: Chocolate cake. Chocolate cake.
> Mother: You're not having any more chocolate cake either.
> Child: Why? [whines] Tired.
> Mother: You tired? Ooh!
> Child: Chocolate cake.
> Mother: No chance.

By age 2 or 3, children more clearly refer to needs, emotions, and other mental states: "My baby needs me," "Don't feel bad, Bob," and "I forgot my pacifier" (Bretherton & Beeghly, 1982). They also use intentional action or desire words, for example, "wants to" (Bartsch, 1990; Huttenlocher & Smiley, 1990). Cognitive terms such as know, remember, and think generally come after perceptual and emotional terms, but are in place before age 3. Later, children will make finer distinctions in their language among mental phenomena, such as guessing versus knowing, believing versus fantasizing, and intending versus "not on purpose." This awareness of mental states continues to develop throughout childhood, as seen in children's changing conceptions of themselves and others and of the psychological causes of behavior (see Chapter 5).

Of course, it is not clear to what extent these early references to mental states actually involve psychological states rather than behaviors or internal physical states. Moreover, even if young children can conceptualize a mental state they may be referring to people's "attitudes" toward objects and events in the situation, for instance, desiring and hoping, rather than more abstract mental entities (C. F. Feldman, 1988). A 3-year-old and a 9-year-old who say "think," "nice," and "want" undoubtedly have different degrees of sophistication in their concepts. Older children's more advanced ability to infer a wider range of mental states, including abstract stable traits during person perception, will be described in Chapter 5.

Postulate 2: The Mind Has Connections to the Physical World

Psychology has a long tradition of characterizing the mind as a black box that intervenes between environmental stimuli and behavior. Certain stimuli lead to certain mental states, these mental states lead to behavior, and the mental state can be inferred from these stimulus-behavior links. The mental state can include emotions, motives, intentions, attitudes, beliefs, knowledge, or personality traits. The first postulate describes the awareness that this black box with unobservable events exists; the second postulate refers to a rudimentary understanding of the input and output relations between the mental events in the black box and physical phenomena such as behavior, objects, and events. One way to characterize this phase at age 2 or 3 is to view children as knowing that people can be "cognitively connected" (Flavell, 1988) to objects and events in the external world in various ways: see them, hear them, like them, want them, fear them, and so on. Three-year-olds have some understanding that cognitive connections can change over time, as when a person sees something now but did not a minute ago. They also appreciate the relative independence of these connections, for example, hearing something without seeing it. Finally, in a show of nonegocentrism, they have some understanding that their connections are inner, subjective experiences that are independent of those of others. They can have a dream that someone else does not. By their awareness of the connections among (a) stimuli, (b) mental states, and (c) behavior, they possess a "rudimentary but coherent mentalistic theory of human action" (Wellman, 1988, pp. 87–88). Children are like amateur psychologists in that they come to know the effect of stimuli on the mental state, to predict behavior from the mental state, and to make use of behavior and other observable events to infer unobservable events in the black box.

This knowledge about connections between the mind and stimuli and behavior is quite crude in 2-year-olds, but becomes somewhat more impressive in 3-year-olds. On the input side, some of the perceptual perspective taking to be described in Chapter 5 is relevant here. A 2-year-old can manipulate stimuli to bring about a certain perceptual state when he or she hides objects so that another person cannot see them (Flavell, Shipstead, & Croft, 1978) or ensures perception by bringing a small picture on the bottom of a box near a person's eyes (Lempers, Flavell, & Flavell, 1977). By age 3, children more clearly are aware of the influence of perception on knowledge. For example, they know that if an object is hidden in a container, someone who has looked in the container knows what is in there, whereas someone who has not looked does not know (Pillow, 1989; Pratt & Bryant, 1990; Woolley, 1991; but see Wimmer, Hogrefe, & Perner, 1988, and Ruffman & Olson, 1989, for a more conservative conclusion). Not until age 4, however, does a child remember the source of the knowledge, for example, how he or she found out the contents of a drawer—by looking or being told (Gopnik & Graf, 1988). Thus, young children have a rudimentary, but rapidly developing, understanding that exposure to external stimuli brings about a particular mental state.

Although 3-year-olds know that information comes from the world, they do not appreciate the complexity of this process. Knowing that access to information is a prerequisite for knowing something becomes more differentiated during the school years. For example, 3- and 4-year-olds have a very limited understanding of the modality-specific nature of knowledge. In one study they were likely to claim that they needed to feel an out-of-view football to find out what color it is and even proceeded to feel it (O'Neill, Astington, & Flavell, 1992). One 3-year-old felt the football, looked at the experimenter with a blank expression, was silent for a few seconds, then said, emphatically, "Red! I can tell it's red," and (lucky guess) triumphantly pulled the red football into view! Thus, young children appear to overestimate what can be learned from one modality. In a follow-up study, O'Neill and colleagues outfitted Ernie and Bert puppets with blindfolds to keep them from seeing an object. They asked children a series of questions about finding out the properties of an object by looking or feeling—for example, whether blindfolded Ernie could best find out whether a sponge is wet or dry by feeling it or looking at it. Again, 3-year-olds had a great deal of difficulty with the concept that specific aspects of knowledge, such as a texture and color, are the products of specific sensory experiences.

On the output (mind-to-behavior) side, older 2-year-olds can predict action and emotional expression based on desires, as when understanding that a child wants a cookie, tries to get one, and is happy if he is successful. However, they apparently cannot predict action based on beliefs (Wellman & Woolley, 1990). For example, if Sam wants to find his rabbit but does not find it in one location, children predict that he would be sad and would look for it somewhere else. But they do not know that Sam's *beliefs* about possible locations influence where he will look. More generally, Wellman (1990, in press) proposes that during ages 2 to 3 or 4, a *desire psychology*, which includes knowledge about desires, perception, and certain emotions, develops into a *belief-desire psychology*. Both of these psychologies provide their child theorists with an explanatory framework for other people's behavior. Desires and beliefs are different in important ways, however. A desire is an internal experience or disposition (longing, leaning) toward an object or state; a desire can be satisfied or not satisfied. In contrast, a belief is a conviction about reality; it is true or false. Moreover, young children need not consider a desire to be a representation. In support of Wellman's view, toddlers spontaneously talk about wanting before they talk about thinking or knowing (Bretherton & Beeghly, 1982). The same is true of conversations between mothers and toddlers (Brown & Dunn, 1991). In a transitional period a child can predict a person's actions based on what the person believes to be true, if this belief does not conflict with what the child knows to be true (Wellman & Bartsch, 1988). Older children can do this even when this conflict exists (see Postulate 4).

In addition to inferring connections from stimuli to a mental state, or from a mental state to a behavior or emotion, 3-year-olds also tend to infer mental states from behavior or other outcomes. In their spontaneous language they invoke mental causes of an action—for example, a 3-year-old who explains that he has paint on his hands "because I thought my hands are paper" (Wellman, 1988), giving new meaning to the phrase "finger painting"! As we will describe in Chapter 5, sometimes 3-year-olds can use a person's behavior to infer whether certain acts are intentional or unintentional (Shultz, 1980), as when mistakes when repeating a tongue twister are considered unintentional. Also, as mentioned above, older 2-year-olds (Wellman, 1990, chap. 8) infer that people are happy when behaviors fulfill their desires and sad when they do not. By age 4 or 5, children can differentiate the internal emotional states of desire and belief caused by an external event. They predict that obtaining a desired piece of bubble gum leads to happiness, and being proven wrong when expecting that some unidentified juice is orange juice leads to surprise (Wellman, 1990, but see Ruffman & Keenan, 1991, for a more conservative conclusion).

Thus, children acquire knowledge about the links among stimuli, mental states, and behavior fairly early. These links gradually become more clearly causal as children grow older. We will focus on some of these changes in causal knowledge about percepts, feelings, thoughts, intentions, and personality in Chapter 5.

Postulate 3: The Mind Is Separate from and Differs from the Physical World

The previous postulates describe a theory of mind in which the mind connects with the physical world. However, a child still might confuse the nature of the two, as seen in Piaget's (1929) observations that preschoolers confused the mind with the observable head or mouth (speech), or claimed that thoughts are smoke. In contrast, Wellman and Estes (1986) report convincing evidence that even very young children know that mental representations are not physical things. They know that the mind is different from rocks, roller skates, and even the head. As one example, a 3-year-old who is told that one boy has a cookie and another boy is thinking about a cookie knows which cookie can be seen by others, touched, eaten, shared, and saved for later. By the second postulate, a child would know that seeing a cookie could cause a thought about a cookie, but only in the third postulate would the child know that the two are quite different sorts of entities. Moreover, young children spontaneously make explicit contrasts between mental states and reality: "The people thought Dracula was mean, but he was nice" (Shatz, Wellman, & Silber, 1983). Thus, just as they earlier grasped that an external representation such as a picture is not the same as the real object (see earlier in this chapter), they now realize that the same is true of an internal mental representation. They also are able to distinguish thinking, a purely mental activity, from other activities with which it might be confused (Flavell, 1992). For example, they realize that a person can be thinking about an object even though not at that moment seeing the object, contacting it physically, or talking about it.

Young children also know that because thoughts are not external entities, they are not public. Other people cannot directly know our thoughts. Children's explanations for these judgments give the flavor of their understanding (Wellman, 1990): You cannot see an image because "People can't see my imagination." You cannot touch an image, for "How can you reach inside your head; besides it's not even there," and "Imaginations is imaginations." You also can mentally transform an image: "I have dream-hands" and "Your mind is for moving things and looking at things when there's not a movie or a TV around." The children knew that, in contrast, you cannot transform a real cup hidden in a box just by thinking.

Finally, 3-year-olds know they can fantasize things that do not even exist, such as Martians, ghosts, dragons, or a spoon that sings (Wellman & Estes, 1986). Thus, children know that the mind can soar, can transcend reality, can have flights of fantasy. If young children know that monsters and things that go bump in the night are not real, does this mean that they do not really fear them? Obviously, they do fear them. DiLalla and Watson (1988) observed a young child pretend to be a monster in order to frighten other children, then burst into tears himself when his pretense seemed too real. For a more experimental analysis, we can consult a series of studies (P. L. Harris, Brown, Marriott, Whittall, & Harmer, 1991) in which 4- and 6-year-olds asserted that an imagined monster was not real, even when they imagined it chasing after them. Yet, they showed signs they were not totally convinced that an imaginary creature could never wander across the barrier between fantasy and reality: When they pretended that an empty box contained a monster, although they said it was not real they avoided that box in favor of a box with an imaginary puppy and preferred to poke a finger into the puppy box and a stick into the monster box, rather than the reverse! These behaviors did not appear to be mere pretend play; almost half of the 4-year-olds spontaneously suggested that the monster had disappeared before they had a chance to see it, perhaps escaping, as one child suggested, "to that University place where they put the skeletons" (the museum?). Most interesting was the behavior of the children in an experiment with the monster box and a rabbit box when the experimenter said he needed to leave the room to get something. Several of the 4-year-olds in the condition with the monster box asked the experimenter not to leave, even after they had checked that the box was empty. Overall, nearly all of the children thought the monster was pretend rather than real, but only about half were sure it was not in the box (see also Woolley, 1991). It appears that something scary can be not real, and yet, in a sense, very real. And, of course, even adults have been known to scream at horror movies.

Postulate 4: The Mind Can Represent Objects and Events Accurately or Inaccurately

Infants have mental representations, toddlers can generate alternative mental and external representations in their pretend play, and many 3-year-olds know that a mental representation is not the real thing. Moreover, 2- and 3-year-olds talk about mental states and understand that desires can cause behavior. However, they probably do not reflect on mental representations—have representations of representations. That is, they do not engage in metarepresentation—both representing the belief and representing it as a belief. Postulate 4 describes the major shift in children's knowledge about the mind, for they now understand that a mental state can be a representation, which is the essence of the human mind. In particular, they understand that because an object or event is different from its mental representation (Postulate 3) there may not be a single, accurate representation. Rather, a specific real-world thing can be mentally represented in different ways, some of which may be false. Younger children, who believe that an object or event can be represented mentally in only one way, have a theory of mind that is qualitatively very different from that of 4-year-olds. Stated differently, the stimulus-mind-behavior connections of Postulate 2 are transformed to a higher level in that a 4-year-old now knows these connections may be inaccurate; the world (stimulus)-representation link may be false.

Consider the following story acted out for children with dolls. A boy puts some chocolate in a blue cupboard and goes out to play. In his absence, his mother moves the chocolate to a green cupboard. When the boy returns and wants his chocolate, the subject is asked where the boy will look for it. Three-year-olds generally say "the green cupboard," where the chocolate actually is, even though the boy had no way of knowing that the chocolate was moved (Wimmer & Perner, 1983). Thus, 3-year-olds do not understand that a person acts on the basis of what he or she believes to be true rather than what they themselves know to be true in reality. They also do not understand that a person's access to information determines his or her knowledge and beliefs. The boy's absence during the moving of the chocolate prevents his knowledge of the new hiding place. In contrast 4- and 5-year-olds usually understand false beliefs. They know why a belief can be false (i.e., it is only one of many possible representations) and know that one's belief, rather than reality, guides one's behavior. That is, they know what sort of thing a belief is and know how it is causally related to behavior. People's behavior usually is determined not by reality directly but by beliefs about reality. The false belief test has been called the "litmus test" (Wellman, 1988) of the child's "belief-desire psychology" of Postulate 4, because it assesses the understanding that representations are just that—representations—and therefore may be true or false but still affect behavior.

On the false belief task, 3-year-olds may not even be helped much by massive assistance, including making the cues for false belief very salient and redundant. Moses and Flavell (1990) showed a story similar to the above in a film and made the disconfirmation of the belief very salient by having the actor appear surprised when she looks in the old place and finds a different object there. Even probing questions about why the actor looked in the original place and why she was surprised elicited little awareness of a false belief (but see Wellman, 1990, for evidence of greater awareness under questioning among older 3-year-olds). Memory checks and linguistic pretesting ruled out the possibility that children's poor performance merely reflected forgetting and misunderstanding. Remarkably, in another study, when 3-year-old subjects knew there was a blue cup behind a barrier, even when a confederate *said* that she thought there was a white cup behind the barrier, they said that she thought there was a blue cup there (Flavell, Flavell, Green, & Moses, 1990).

The concept of false beliefs also is expressed in the understanding of representational change. Suppose someone showed you a candy box and asked you what you think is inside the box. Unless you thought this was an experiment conducted by psychologists and suspected deception, you would say that you think that candy is inside the box. If you then opened the box and found pencils, you would be aware that you had had a false belief and that you had changed your mind about the contents of the box. When Gopnik and Astington (1988) presented these events to children, they found that 3-year-olds, after opening the candy box and finding pencils, claimed not only that a naive other child would believe there were pencils in the box, but also that they had initially believed that themselves! In contrast, 4-year-olds, after finding pencils in the candy box, giggled and appreciated the trick when they had to predict what another child would think was in the candy box; they also realized, of course, that they too had had a false belief initially. Thus, they understood that representations can be wrong and can change, as theirs did, even when the reality that the representation is about did not change.

Across a variety of tasks, understanding of false beliefs generally appears in 4- or 5-year-olds but usually not 3-year-olds. Interestingly, deviant moral and social-conventional beliefs seem to be as hard as false beliefs for 3-year-olds to understand. Flavell, Mumme, Green, and Flavell (in press) told children stories in which a child thought it was "okay" to do a particular act, such as bite a child on the leg (deviant moral belief) or wear pajamas to school (deviant conventional belief). Although 3-year-olds were repeatedly told that the child in the story thought it was okay to do the deed, a number of them simply refused to attribute this deviant belief to the child. Even more striking, some of them could not comprehend that a girl could think a toothbrush was hers, whereas a boy thought it was his, and that, consequently, she would think it was okay for her to take it home but he would think she should not.

Several recent clever studies have shown that there are some circumstances in which even 3-year-olds may possess at least a shaky understanding of false beliefs. For instance, some studies show that 3-year-olds can create a false belief in another person in a simple situation involving deception (Chandler, Fritz, & Hala, 1989; Hala, Chandler, & Fritz, 1991). Children used a puppet, who left washable purple footprints as she walked, to hide a treasure in one of several table-top containers. They were told to hide the treasure so the seeker, momentarily absent, would not be able to find it. Most of the 2-year-olds and 3-year-olds erased the footprints to the real hiding place, made small footprints to the wrong box, or lied about the treasure's location, in an attempt to deceive the seeker. (However, work by Sodian, Taylor, Harris, & Perner, 1991, questions whether 3-year-olds actually understand the effect of deceptive ploys.)

A second way to elicit an early understanding of false belief is to decrease children's certainty about the real state of affairs (Zaitchik, 1991). Big Bird *told* children that he'll tell Frog that a toy plane is in the closet though it really is in the toy box. Three-year-olds inferred Frog's false belief in this condition but not in a similar condition in which they were *shown* the plane in the toy box. Their poor performance when they did see the true location suggests that they cannot ignore their own visual experience; seeing is believing. As we will see in Chapter 4, preschoolers have trouble decentering from a salient physical stimulus.

A third procedure that may help 3-year-olds is to clarify the temporal reference of false-belief questions asked. It sometimes helps to use the word "before" (instead of "when") and to place the temporal clause at the end of the questions: "What did you think was in the box before I took the top off?" (Lewis & Osborne, 1990). Similarly, it may help to ask them where the child will look "first," as in "Where will Jane look first for her kitten?" (Siegal & Beattie, 1991). Given this set of results, it probably would not surprise you to know that a main point of disagreement among theory-of-mind researchers is whether the understanding of false beliefs emerges at age 3 or 4 and, if it does emerge at age 3, what are the critical conditions for eliciting it.

This awareness of the possible discrepancy between the mental and physical, or a belief and the true state, revealed on the false-belief task, may be related to four other distinctions that emerge at about the same time. Three are discussed in other sections. First, consider perceptual perspective taking, to be discussed in Chapter 5. Just as two different people can have different beliefs about reality, so can they have different visual perceptions of the world, as when a child in his backyard has a different view of his house from his sister in the front yard. As described in the second postulate, by age 2 or 3 children grasp the connection between objects and perception. For example, they know that a person can see a present object, but not an absent one. However, they are limited to thinking about *whether* something is seen, but not exactly *how* something appears to the viewer. The latter requires the Postulate 4 understanding of representations—namely, the particular representation (e.g., view of the house) that each person has. Two people's representations (views) often conflict. Second, the domain of emotions, to be discussed in Chapter 5, also illustrates the discrepancy between two representations. When a child sees a friend smile after falling off his bike and cutting his knee, she is faced with two conflicting representations of the friend's emotion: happy because the child is smiling, sad because of the physical evidence of pain. Perhaps the other child really and truly feels sad, but deliberately feigns feeling happy to hide his pain. Only a child who understands the representational process will not be confused by these conflicting representations. Knowing that a single reality can be represented in two conflicting ways also is relevant for understanding that a single situation may elicit different emotions in different people. For instance, whereas one child may feel happy when given a dog, another could feel apprehensive (Gove & Keating, 1979). Third, the notion that an experience can be ambiguous implies that two conflicting representations can be imagined. Four-year-olds are beginning to understand, for example, that the identity of an animal cannot be inferred from seeing only its color through a small hole in a box if two kinds of animals are the same color (Ruffman, Olson, & Astington, 1991). For example, seeing gray through the hole could lead to a representation of a gray elephant or a gray rabbit.

A fourth acquisition implied by Postulate 4 is the *appearance-reality distinction*, which we will describe in some detail. Just as a child knows that a wax apple that looks remarkably like (appearance) a real apple is not a real apple (reality), so may he know that someone might falsely believe that it is a real apple. And just as two different people can have different representations (beliefs about or perspectives) of the world, so can a single person represent an object in two different ways—the way it appears at the present moment and the way it really is (Flavell, 1986). Similarly, just as someone can feel sad but appear to be happy, an object can appear one way but really be another way.

Children who cannot make this appearance-reality distinction do not understand that something can look different from what it really is. They do not understand that people have mental representations or experiences of objects that may differ from the way things really are. Knowing that what you see may not be what you get has adaptive significance. Young children need to know not to eat plastic food or walk through glass patio doors that appear to be an open passage. Even adults need to be aware of misleading appearances. What we take to be a star turns out to be a plane flying toward us; what we think to be a Picasso proves to be a forgery; what looks like an innocent conversation from a distance is actually a robbery in progress. Finally, all theory and research in all fields of scholarship amounts to an effort to find new realities hidden beneath new and old appearances (Carey, 1985a). The need for erasers in this world has no limits. The discovery and understanding of appearance-reality contrasts in domain after domain is undoubtedly among the child's most important cognitive-developmental odysseys.

With few exceptions (Flavell, Green, & Flavell, 1989; Flavell, Green, Wahl, & Flavell, 1987) 3-year-olds tend to perform poorly on appearance-reality tasks, even when the distinction is made clear to them during pretraining. The following child-friendly procedure (Flavell, Flavell, & Green, 1983) is a typical one: First the experimenter shows the children a Charlie Brown puppet inside a ghost costume. She then explains and demonstrates that Charlie Brown "*looks like* a ghost to your eyes right now" but is "*really and truly* Charlie Brown," and that "sometimes things look like one thing to your eyes when they are really and truly something else." For the test she then presents various illusory situations and asks several questions about their appearance ("looks like") and reality ("really and truly is"). For example, if 3-year-olds see a red filter wrapped around a glass of white milk they say that the milk looks red and it "really and truly" is red (Flavell et al., 1986). Remarkably, there are informal observations that they say the same about their own hands under a filter. In these cases, children's perception distorts their knowledge about the real state of affairs. Children sometimes make the opposite error as well; they let their knowledge of what something is override their perceptual judgments. For instance,

Flavell, Flavell, and Green (1983) presented preschoolers with an extremely realistic fake egg. After the children found out that it actually was a painted stone, many then claimed that it looked like a stone! It is an eerie experience to see a 3-year-old peer at an imitation egg that would fool the most discerning hen and solemnly indicate that it *looks* like a stone to his eyes right now. Three-year-olds also show appearance-reality confusions with other modalities as well, for example, when smelling a peanut butter-scented sock (smells like peanut butter, really is a sock), and when hearing a cow-like sound produced by turning over a small can (sounds like a cow, really is a can).

The absence of the appearance-reality distinction in 3-year-olds may reflect something universal about the 3-year-old mind. Chinese 3-year-olds perform exactly like American ones on these tasks, despite differences in culture and language (Flavell, Zhang, Zou, Dong, & Qi, 1983). This outcome also suggests that the results with American children do not simply reflect experimenters' poor choice of words that might lead to misunderstanding what was being asked. Moreover, attempts to teach 3-year-olds the appearance-reality distinction have been unsuccessful (e.g., Flavell, Green, & Flavell, 1986; M. Taylor & Hort, 1990). Everyday observations also attest to this confusion of appearance and reality, as when one unsuccessfully tries to convince a 3-year-old that a scary, cackling Halloween witch actually is a benign neighbor. This bias toward believing appearances suggests that it might be difficult for parents to instill in their 3-year-olds a healthy wariness of pleasant-appearing adults who might want to harm them. Still, 2- and 3-year-olds have some inkling of the true nature of an object. When asked, for example, to choose something to keep a piece of paper from blowing away in the wind, they choose a real rock over a realistic sponge rock (Gauvain & Greene, 1991).

Because 3-year-olds do not fully understand the nature of representation, "they do not clearly understand that even though something may be only one way out there in the world, it can be more than one way up here in our heads, in our mental representations of it" (Flavell, 1988, p. 246). When 3-year-olds consider what an object "is," they do not consider that an object may have more than one "is." They believe that each object or event has only one nature—one "way that it is at this moment"—and cannot be two different, contradictory things at the same time, such as red (looks red) and white (really is white). Thus, the experimenter's two questions, "looks like?" and "really and truly is?" may appear to be essentially the same question to the 3-year-old mind, and the child gives the same answer. Because children do not realize that their perception of the object's appearance is *just* a representation that can be changed, they find this perception a very compelling characterization of what that object *is* right now. Consequently, they encode the object in a particular way and stick with that: When the white paper under the red filter looks red they believe it "looks red" and "really and truly is red."

A fragile understanding of the appearance-reality distinction emerges during ages 4 to 6 when children understand the nature of representation. However, they are not very sensitive to the distinction so may tend to encode an object in a single way. Eventually children easily represent both the way the object appears in their perception of it and what the object actually is, despite their conflicting nature. Furthermore, they can "mentally tag each representation for the cognitive perspective or stance that gave rise to it, for its epistemic credentials, so to speak" (Flavell, 1988, p. 247). Thus, children tag one representation as "what it looks like it is" and the other as "what it really is."

To summarize our story thus far, Postulate 4 implies that reality can be represented in different ways. Thus, a representation can be false with respect to a real object or event (in false beliefs and ambiguous visual displays), behavior can be false with respect to a mental state (as when a sad person smiles), physical appearance can be false with respect to an object's identity or property (appearance-reality distinction), and two people's perceptual views or beliefs can differ (perspective taking). These concepts appear to emerge in a child at about the same time and are positively correlated with one another within subjects (Flavell et al., 1986; Friend & Davis, 1991; Gopnik & Astington, 1988; Moore, Pure, & Furrow, 1990).

We can point to still other possible instantiations of a representational concept of mind: understanding the nature of lies or other false statements, jokes, metaphors, sarcasm, and ambiguous statements. Also, in self-presentation (e.g., Aloise, 1991) people deliberately try to appear, for example, more competent than they really are. People, like fake eggs, present external appearances that may differ from their underlying realities. People may not really be, think, feel, want, and so on, what surface appearances suggest. They may intentionally or unintentionally deceive others about almost anything imaginable. They also deceive themselves and are deceived by other people, objects, and events. In one investigation (Flavell, Lindberg, Green, & Flavell, in press), preschoolers heard a story about a child's behavior (mean or nice) while seeing a photograph of that child with a neutral expression. A second photograph showed the same child "after an operation" that temporarily gave the child the expression opposite to his behavior. As in nonsocial appearance-reality tasks, 3-year-olds had a great deal of difficulty differentiating appearance and reality. The manipulation of how one appears to others may be perfected to an art among actors and politicians. For Postulate 4, we also might include the understanding of displaced aggression (e.g., P. H. Miller & DeMarie-Dreblow, 1990). Person A aggresses against Person B when angry at Person C. The overt behavior does not reflect the person's true feelings. More generally, people may have different thoughts, motives, and intentions from those that they appear to have. In all of these realms, things are not always as they seem.

Children younger than age 4 have trouble understanding dual representation in other domains as well. In early word learning, children often are reluctant to accept a second name for an object; if they know an animal as "kitty" they may reject "cat" (E. V. Clark, 1987; Markman, 1989). They also have trouble with hypothetical statements that refer to how things might have been at some other time (Kuczaj, 1981). Perhaps an earlier, less sophisticated, version of dual representation appears around 36 months when children can use the hiding place of an object in a small-scale model of a room to locate an object hidden in the real room (DeLoache, 1991b), as we described earlier. DeLoache (1991b) argues that they have to understand that one can represent the model as both a real, three-dimensional array and as a symbol for the room (but see Perner, 1991).

In summary, young children, drawing on postulates 1, 2, and 3, know that mental states exist, and are connected to the physical world, but are different from the physical world. Only when they come to understand that these connections involve internal mental representations that can change over time, can be true or false, can be converging or contradictory, and so on, do they understand the essence of human thought—its active, constructive nature. The latter leads to the next postulate.

Postulate 5: The Mind Actively Mediates the Interpretation of Reality and the Emotion Experienced

The understanding of the nature of representation expressed in Postulate 4 implies some understanding that the mind mediates the experience of reality. If it mediates, then it potentially could select, organize, or transform information from the environment and therefore distort or enrich reality. Although the notion of an active mind does not really become apparent until after age 6 or so, the germs of this notion can be found in the understanding of false belief and false appearance. In these "false" tasks the mind's belief or perception distorts reality.

Chandler and Boyes (1982) have proposed that there is a developmental shift from a copy theory of knowledge to a constructivistic one (see also Pillow, 1988a, & Wellman, 1988), from a Lockian mind that passively takes in information to a Piagetian mind that actively constructs and interprets, from an entity notion of mind to a process one (Wellman, 1990). In the early years, as Chandler and Boyes (1982) colorfully put it,

> Children seem to proceed as though they believe objects to transmit, in a direct-line-of-sight fashion, faint copies of themselves, which actively assault and impress themselves upon anyone who happens in the path of such "objective" knowledge. Within such a view, projectile firings from things themselves bombard and actively victimize individuals who function as passive recorders and simply bear the scars of information which has been embossed upon them. (p. 391)

This "copy-container" mind is considered a passive receptacle that takes in information automatically, accurately, and without modification. In Postulate 2 thinking, for example, perceptual contact is necessary for, and determines, knowledge. Before age 6, children have little conception of mental processes that may act on the content received to produce false beliefs, illusions, biased judgments, inferences, or concepts elaborated with prior knowledge.

In the perceptual realm, preschoolers tend not to understand that what information a person acquires through perception is influenced by what he or she already knows. Suppose you show a child a picture of a giraffe, then place a card with a small hole on top of it and show that to another person who can see so little of the giraffe through the hole that he or she cannot identify it. Preschoolers believe that the person can see that it is a giraffe, but 6-year-olds are beginning to understand that whether you know it is a giraffe beforehand influences whether or not you see it as one (M. Taylor, 1988). Similarly, 3-year-olds incorrectly think that a tiny picture of a cup, which they earlier saw up close, looks like a cup rather than a spot when viewed from afar (Flavell, Flavell, & Green, 1983). In both cases young children fail to comprehend that prior knowledge can bias current knowledge or perception. In addition, children increasingly understand that there is a difference between the auditory information available and what a person actually listens to and processes because humans are limited in how much information they can process at once (Pillow, 1988b). Finally, children have difficulty comprehending the fact that the capabilities of the mind affect what one can know through verbal messages (Taylor, Cartwright, & Bowden, 1991). Montgomery (1991), for example, found that even 8-year-olds think that a preverbal baby will understand a verbal message that would be understood by an adult (e.g., "The poster is in the bottom drawer"). They make this claim even though they understand that babies cannot talk and do not even know the meaning of the words in the message.

Theory-of-mind research suggests a new interpretation of *egocentrism*—a young child's assumption that others think, feel, perceive, and know the same as he or she does. Egocentric behaviors actually may indicate a lack of understanding that people know, understand, and interpret on the basis of the source of their knowledge, specifically, their experiences and perceptual perspective (Perner, 1991). This lack of understanding can be seen in the following study by Mossler, Marvin, and Greenberg (1976). Children of 2 to 6 years of age individually viewed a videotape in which much of the information about what was happening was carried by the audio portion. Each child's mother was absent from the room during this initial showing of the film. Each mother then returned and watched the film with her child, but with the audio portion conspicuously turned off (the child's attention was explicitly drawn to this fact). The child was asked questions about the mother's knowledge of various film happenings—for example, "Does your Mommy know whose house the boy went into?" The oldest children inferred correctly and nonegocentrically what the mother did and did not know on the basis of her restricted perceptual experience with the film. In contrast, most of the youngest children blithely asserted—probably without any sort of social-cognitive inference at all—that the mother knew everything that happened in the film. They showed no evidence of attributing any differentiated, individuated knowledge or cognition to her at all. Other studies have also shown a striking improvement during the preschool years in conceptual role or perspective taking of this simple and elementary, "privileged-information" type (e.g., Abrahams, 1979; Brandt, 1978; Selman, 1980; Shantz, 1983).

More generally, preschoolers have a lot of trouble tracking the flow of information—from the world to the mind (e.g., perceptual access), within the mind (e.g., inferences), and from one mind to another mind (e.g., communication). They have difficulty sorting out the contributions of reality and the mind in this process. Although 3-year-olds know that knowledge comes from being exposed to something in reality, not until age 4 or 5 do they know that information leads to a representation and that different kinds of information lead to different kinds of representations. Moreover, they now are beginning to understand how they know what they know, for example, from seeing, feeling, or being told something (O'Neill & Gopnik, 1991). Not until age 6 or later do children know that knowledge can also come from the contributions of the mind, in the form of inferences. For a recent review of research on children's theories of knowing, see Montgomery (in press).

The shift from viewing the mind as passive to viewing it as active also appears in children's knowledge that prior experiences affect current mental states, which in turn affect emotions and social inferences. During the elementary school years, children change from viewing emotions as determined by external events without any mediation by internal states, to viewing emotional reactions to an external event as influenced by a prior emotional state, experience, or expectations (Gnepp, 1989; Harris & Olthof, 1982). For instance, 6-year-olds do not understand that a child would be sad or scared when her friends suggest they ride bikes if that child previously was nearly hit by a car when she could not stop her bike because her legs were too short. Regarding social inferences, Pillow (1991) told children stories in which an observer would have a biased interpretation of a person's behavior. In one story, for example, Mike dislikes Tom because he thinks he is mean, starts fights, and gets into trouble a lot. One day Tom bumps into Mike's desk at school, knocking Mike's special airplane he built onto the floor where it breaks into pieces. Second graders realized that Mike, because of his negative beliefs about Tom, would think that Tom knocked off the plane on purpose. Kindergartners also had some understanding of such social biases in which the same event can be interpreted differently by observers who vary in their prior mental states. Social processing biases show the workings of an active, interpretive mind.

Conclusions and Issues

The young of our species clearly show a great deal of curiosity and contemplation about one of our defining characteristics—thinking. They are turning their thoughts toward thought, even as that process is developing in them. By age 3, children possess a cognitive-connections (Postulates 1–3) knowledge about the mind. They understand that they and others have internal experiences (mental states) that connect humans cognitively to external objects and events. Later, when they understand mental representations (Postulate 4), they develop the understanding that the same object or event can be seriously (other than in pretense) mentally represented in different ways. People actively construct simultaneous, and sometimes conflicting, representations of belief and reality, overt expression and covert feeling, appearance and real identity, and motive and behavior. The guileless, trusting preschooler becomes the more suspicious, "street smart" older child and adolescent. More generally, children understand that a particular experience provides access to certain information, which causes a particular representation and even a particular interpretation (Postulate 5), which in turn causes a particular behavior.

A main issue for cognitive development is how these early competencies are related to later forms of understanding. In the current case, preschoolers' theory of mind provides a solid foundation for the many social-cognitive abilities (see Chapter 5) that school-age children need to make their way among peers, parents, siblings, and strangers. Their knowledge about the mind allows them to operate much like a research psychologist: They observe stimuli and behavior, make attributions about behavioral tendencies, mental states, or psychological traits, and predict future behavior. The social world around them becomes somewhat predictable and they can make intelligent guesses as to what ripples their own behavior will make in the world. Their awareness of conflicting mental representations gives meaning to the concepts of opinion, prejudice, belief, deception, dispute, impression, irony, sarcasm, illusion, and interpretation. They know that they may hold false beliefs, and so are open to the possibility that they might be wrong about something. It is not surprising, then, that many developmental psychologists consider knowledge about the mind to be one of the most significant aspects of all human cognitive development. And no wonder this area currently is one of the most active areas of research in cognitive development.

Now that we have described developmental changes in theories of mind, the next question is what causes these changes (Astington & Gopnik, 1991; Flavell, Green, & Flavell, 1989; Wellman, 1990). Researchers have proposed both experiential and biological causes. Regarding experiences, some are universal and some culture specific. As for universal experiences, children everywhere have environments providing experiences that would stimulate the awareness of cognitive connections, and of the mental world in general. These experiences often would reflect the independence of different mental connections, as when a child simultaneously hears and sees an object, then closes his eyes and discovers that he continues to hear it but no longer to see it. Also, subjective experiences and objective reality sometimes do not match: A flower in a vase turns out to be plastic and a favorite toy is not where a child thinks he left it. In addition, parents often point out their children's false beliefs to them—"You think it's not bedtime, but it really is." Moreover, cooperative interactions with siblings apparently encourage an understanding of representations (Dunn, Brown, Slomkowski, Tesla, & Youngblade, 1991). Another apparently universal experience is pretend play, which could help sensitize children to the distinction between the way things are and the way they are made to seem. Given these universal experiences, it is not surprising that studies in about a dozen countries suggest that the development of certain knowledge about the mind is the same everywhere in its essentials (e.g., Avis & Harris, 1991; Flavell, Zhang, Zou, et al., 1983).

Harris (1989a) has proposed that children's understanding of others' mental states arises in part from their pretend play. Between ages 2 and 2½, children begin to use their imagination to endow dolls with desires, emotions, and sensations. They say that a doll wants to eat, feels happy, and feels cold. This capacity for make-believe allows them to conjure up possible mental states in both dolls and people, based perhaps on their awareness of their own mental states and their ability to imagine being in various mental states. Because a child can imagine herself wanting a pizza and also imagine being happy if a pizza is obtained, she may be able to simulate these mental states in others. Once children can construct the other person's desires, they can anticipate that person's behavior intended to achieve the goal and then the emotion that results from satisfaction, or lack of satisfaction, of the desire. Thus, through a sort of "phenomenological bootstrapping," young children could use awareness of their own feelings, desires, and other mental states to infer others' mental states and to construct during development more general theory-like concepts of mind.

Despite the overall similarity in children's concepts of the mind across cultures, the developmental work of the contextualists and the fact that adults' folk models of the mind differ somewhat across cultures (e.g., D'Andrade, 1987) predict diversity among children as well. A culture's set of beliefs about the human mind and behavior would be passed on to each generation. For example, cultural differences in beliefs about dreams may be reflected in children. The Atayal adults of Formosa generally believe that the soul leaves the body during a dream and experiences things in other places, and children develop this belief during adolescence (Kohlberg, 1966). Another example is that Americans are more likely than Hindus to attribute behavior to psychological, rather than contextual, causes (J. G. Miller, 1984). These cultural differences suggest that some of children's psychologizings may simply reflect a set of social and cultural practices and conventions. In this view, "children would learn how to psychologize appropriately in the way that they learn how to dress properly or eat politely" (Astington & Gopnik, 1991, pp. 19–20). In this case, some knowledge might not be a "theory" in the strict sense.

Regarding biological causes, Leslie (1988b, 1991) has proposed an innate theory-of-mind module, an example of the mental modules approach mentioned in Chapter 1. He points to the meager understanding of the mind in older autistic children (Baron-Cohen, 1991a, 1991b; Leslie & Frith, 1988), who are believed to have an inborn neurological deficit. They fail to distinguish between mental and physical entities, and between appearance and reality, and do not understand false belief, but do understand desires and their connections to sad and happy. This deficit appears to be rather specific, because autistic children have a rudimentary understanding of other social concepts, such as reciprocity between people and personal relationships (Baron-Cohen, 1991b), and of physical causality (Baron-Cohen, Leslie, & Frith,

1986). Because retarded children of the same or lower mental age do not show this deficit, general retardation does not seem to account for these results with autistic children. These findings are consistent with the fact that autistic children can be rather intelligent but still have great difficulty with social interaction.

Another interesting question is whether we are the only species having anything like a theory of mind. There is considerable controversy about this issue. Chimpanzees appear to engage in both pretense and elementary mind-reading activities. They have been seen to pull an imaginary pull toy, carefully disentangling the imaginary string (Hayes, 1951), and to pretend to eat imaginary food, even spitting out a bad bite and communicating "bad" on keyboard symbols (Savage-Rumbaugh & McDonald, 1988). Judge for yourself whether mind-reading activities are displayed in the following episode reported by Byrne and Whiten (1988): A chimp observed a second chimp acting as though no food were available at a feeding hopper. There in fact was food. The first chimp appeared to depart, but actually hid behind a nearby tree and watched until the other chimp took the food. At this point the first chimp emerged and snatched the food! For a fascinating comparison of chimpanzee versus child mind-reading prowess under controlled laboratory conditions, see Povinelli and deBlois (in press).

A main unanswered question concerns the relations between a child's theory of mind and his or her social behavior (Chandler, Lalonde, Fritz, & Hala, 1991). Does awareness of the possibility of false belief cause the child to communicate more clearly with others in anticipation of their lack of access to relevant knowledge? Does the lack of awareness of the active nature of the mind lead to intolerance of the opposing opinion of another person with a different cultural heritage whose views are influenced by this heritage? How does social experience stimulate the development of a theory of mind? Such cognitive-behavioral links may be the next frontier in theory-of-mind research.

Finally, are there important changes in the theory of mind occurring during late childhood and adolescence or even later that have been slighted because of the focus of research on preschoolers? Chandler (1988) in fact argues that a mature constructivist view of mind may not appear until adolescence. One such promising area is metacognition. For example, it seems likely that knowing that one needs to be actively strategic while memorizing requires a view of the mind as active (Wellman, 1990). The various cognitive changes of middle childhood and adolescence described in Chapters 4 and 5 surely have implications for a theory of mind. Yet, with few exceptions (Fabricius, Schwanenflugel, Kyllonen, Barclay, & Denton, 1989; P. H. Miller & Aloise, 1989; Pillow, 1991; Yuill, in press), little attempt has been made to explore these implications.

BASIC NUMERICAL ABILITIES

Children's theory of mind is a very recent area of research on young children's concepts. In contrast, work on concepts of number has a long history.

The development of basic numerical abilities is an absorbing subject of study for several reasons. People spend years and years in school improving and building upon these basic skills, and years and years after they leave school putting them to practical use in everyday life. Numerical abilities are surely core, "ecologically significant" cognitive acquisitions if any abilities are. As a consequence, they are of concern not only to psychologists but also to educators, parents, and others. Furthermore, numerical abilities are of additional interest to the student of cognitive development because some of these concepts and skills are also informally picked up and extensively practiced on the child's own initiative prior to formal schooling, during the period of early childhood. For these reasons, numerical understanding has long been a popular topic for researchers of development, and some of our most informative forays into the preschool mind have been attempts to determine what young children do and do not know about numbers.

Much of the early, ground-breaking research on the development of basic numerical abilities was done by Piaget and his co-workers (Piaget & Szeminska, 1952; see also Flavell, 1963, pp. 309–316). This research was carried out within the framework of Piaget's general stage theory, and the youngest participants (children between about 3 and 6) were therefore seen as falling within the preoperational stage of development. Piaget, as we noted earlier in the chapter, painted a predominantly negative picture of preoperational competence, and the work on number was no exception. Most of what Piaget had to say about young children's dealings with numbers concerned confusions and deficits in understanding. Nowhere were the confusions more evident than with respect to the aspect of numerical understanding that Piaget regarded as most important: the ability to conserve number in the face of a perceptual change. As with conservation tasks in general, a conservation-of-number task pits immediate perceptual appearance against inferable conceptual reality. For example, the experimenter might initially set two rows of 10 buttons each in visual one-to-one correspondence, with one of the two equal-length rows placed directly above the other. After the child agrees that the two rows contain the same number of buttons, the experimenter lengthens one of the rows. To conserve number, the child must maintain that the two rows are still numerically equal despite the difference in appearance. And this, Piaget found, is precisely what children younger than about 5 or 6 cannot do. Instead, the young child tends to be fooled by the misleading perceptual appearance, judging (usually) that the longer row now contains more.

That young children often fail not only conservation of number but other forms of the conservation task has been amply confirmed in hundreds (count them) of follow-up studies (Ginsburg & Opper, 1988; Modgil & Modgil, 1976). Yet the preschooler's understanding of number, although doubtless incomplete, is by no means as barren as the classic conservation literature suggests. Recent studies have convincingly demonstrated that preschoolers possess a good deal more knowledge and skill in the domain of number than we used to believe. The work of Rochel Gelman and her collaborators has been central in teaching us all about the competencies of young children, and we consequently begin with some of their findings.

What types of numerical knowledge and skills might be acquired during early childhood? R. Gelman and Gallistel (1978) have identified two major types: number-abstraction abilities and numerical-reasoning principles. Number-abstraction abilities refer to processes by which the child abstracts and represents the numerical value or numerosity of an array of objects. For instance, the child could count the array and thereby achieve the representation that it contains "four" objects. Numerical-reasoning principles include those that allow the child to infer the numerical outcomes of operating on or transforming sets in various ways. For example, these principles will allow the child to infer that the numerical value of a set of objects is not changed by merely spreading the objects out (the Piagetian conservation problem), but is changed—more specifically, increased in value—by adding one or more objects to the set. Thus, spreading out is a number-irrelevant transformation, whereas adding is a number-relevant transformation. In brief, the abstraction abilities help children establish numerical values and the reasoning principles help them make inferences about, and operate further upon, the numerical values thus established.

Counting Principles

Gelman has paid special attention to the number-abstraction process of counting. Her studies suggest that young children use counting as their principal method for obtaining representations of numerosity. She also shows that their counting activity comes to be governed and defined by five counting principles. The first three principles tell the child how to count properly, the fourth principle tells the child what can be counted, and the fifth principle involves a combination of features of the first four.

1. **THE ONE-ONE PRINCIPLE.** According to this principle, a counter must successively assign one and only one distinctive number name to each and every item to be counted. The first item attended to is ticked off as "one," the next as "two," and so on through the entire set of countables. The person counting should not skip any items that should be counted, should not count any item more than once, should not use the same number name more than once, and should stop the counting sequence precisely when the last item has been enumerated. Thought of in this way, it is clear that accurate counting is a surprisingly complex and demanding process of precisely coordinating the sequential production of number names with the sequential designation of items to be counted. As the process unfurls in this carefully coordinated fashion, both number names and items are progressively "used up" and cannot be reused during that counting act. Although preschoolers do make counting errors that violate the one-one principle, especially when trying to enumerate larger sets of items, there is good evidence that even 2½- to 3-year-olds are likely to have at least some implicit grasp of the one-one principle. For example, R. Gelman (1982) reports that young children will notice and correct their own violations of the principle and also detect violations of it deliberately made by another (e.g., the experimenter's puppet). Thus, their violations seem to reflect performance problems more than lack of tacit knowledge of the one-one principle.

2. **THE STABLE-ORDER PRINCIPLE.** When counting out a set of items, one should always recite the number names in the same order. For instance, one should not count out a three-item set "one, two, three" sometimes and "three, one, two" other times. Gelman found that young children usually honor this principle, despite other—and often amusing—limitations in their counting abilities. For example, a 2-year-old might enumerate a set of two objects by saying "two, six," or even "A, B," but would still use that same stable order of counting tags the next time he counted two objects. Older preschoolers sometimes produce longer idiosyncratic but stably ordered strings, such as "one, two, three, four, eight, ten, *eleben*." A more advanced acquaintance of ours produced the following string: "...nine, ten, infinity, infinity + 1, infinity + 2..."

3. **THE CARDINAL PRINCIPLE.** This principle simply asserts that the final number name uttered at the end of a counting sequence gives the cardinal-

number value of the set. For example, we would use it this way in totaling up the number of counting principles described so far: "one, two, three—*three*." Gelman's research indicates that, as with the one-one principle: (1) Young children often do act as though they are following the cardinal principle when counting out sets of items, especially small sets, when they have good command of the relevant number words; (2) the information-processing demands of counting may sometimes interfere with the use of the principle, and thereby lead us to underestimate the young child's grasp of it. For example, the child may not succeed in counting to n and then correctly indicating that there are n things there. On the other hand, he or she may well spot a puppet's mistake when the puppet counts up to n and then says there are $n + 1$ things there.

4. THE ABSTRACTION PRINCIPLE. The three principles just discussed are how-to-count principles. This one is a what-to-count principle. It stipulates that anything is a potential countable; we may enumerate events, inanimate objects, animate objects, intangible and abstract objects (minds, Gelmanian counting principles)—any sort of entity whatever. Although no 4-year-old has yet been observed to enumerate the Gelmanian counting principles, children of this age do not seem to actively exclude any particular type of entity from the potentially countables. Likewise, they are willing to try to count up all the objects in a room without worrying about their heterogeneity (e.g., animates lumped together with inanimates), treating them as though they were all identical, featureless "things" for purposes of counting.

5. THE ORDER-IRRELEVANCE PRINCIPLE. This principle states that it does not matter in what order you enumerate the objects you are counting. For example, in counting out a set consisting of a dog, a cat, and a mouse, you will end up with the same numerical value whether you begin with the dog and call it "one" or end with the dog and call it "three." Recall that the stable-order principle says that the order of the *number names does* matter; it must always be "one," "two," "three," and so on. In contrast, the order-irrelevance principle says the order of the *items* to which this stably ordered enumeration process is applied does *not* matter; the items can be counted out in any order you please. Clever studies by Gelman and colleagues (R. Gelman, 1982; R. Gelman & Gallistel, 1978) have shown that 5-year-olds have fairly explicit knowledge of the order-irrelevance principle and that even 3-year-olds may well understand it implicitly. In one test, for example, the child was asked to repeatedly count a small set of objects, beginning sometimes with the leftmost object, sometimes with the one second from the left, and so on. The children proved generally able to count successfully regardless of the starting point or order of counting; they were also unfazed by the fact that the same label (e.g., "one") might be applied at different times to different objects. In marked contrast, they stoutly objected to moving around nonnumerical, *object* names in this fashion—for example, calling a baby "baby" on one occasion and "doggie" on another. They clearly thought one should not play musical chairs with objects and object names but seemed to assume it was all right to do so with objects and number names.

The Gelman research program has inspired a number of related efforts in recent years (e.g., Briars & Siegler, 1984; Frye, Braisby, Lowe, Maroudas, & Nicholls, 1989; Fuson, 1988; Fuson & Hall, 1983; Sophian, 1988a, 1988b; Wynn, 1990). In general outline, these studies support two of Gelman's most important conclusions: that even quite young children use counting as a means of estimating number, and that even quite young children show some knowledge and some skill in their counting endeavors. At a more specific level, disagreements have arisen concerning just how early in development children should be credited with knowledge of the various counting principles. In Gelman's "principle-first" model, the principles are assumed to be available—albeit only in implicit, unverbalizable form—from quite early on and to guide even the 3-year-old's counting efforts. Gelman acknowledges, as we saw, that these early efforts sometimes go astray; the young child's problems, however, are attributed to various performance limitations that obscure the underlying knowledge about counting, not to a lack of knowledge per se (R. Gelman, Meck, & Merkin, 1986; Greeno, Riley, & Gelman, 1984). Other investigators are less certain that it makes sense to credit children with knowledge of the counting principles when their performance is so variable and so error-prone. Siegler (1991b) has proposed a contrasting "skills-first" hypothesis: that children first develop some degree of skill at counting, prior to any knowledge of the general principles, and that experience in counting then leads to the gradual abstraction of the underlying principles. Children might come to realize, for example, that they always arrive at the same value no matter what order they count (the order-irrelevance principle), but that they get quite different values if they are not careful to count each item once and only once (the one-one principle). It may be, of course, that both positions have some truth to them: that the principles (or at least some subset of them) are indeed present in nascent form from early in life, but that they become more solidly established and more accessible with age and experience. In any case, however we conceptualize initial competence and developmental change, it is important not to lose track of the fact that improvements do occur across the preschool years. Three-year-olds may be more skilled at estimating numbers than we used to believe; they will be more skilled by age 4, however, and still more skilled at 5 or 6.

Numerical-Reasoning Principles

Children acquire numerical-reasoning principles as well as number-abstraction abilities during the early-childhood period. By the end of this period they are likely to have learned that merely changing the color or the identity of a set of items is not a transformation that alters the number of items in the set. They are also likely to have learned that, contrariwise, adding items increases the set's numerical value, subtracting items decreases it, and first adding one item and then subtracting one item leaves the numerical value unchanged. They can also determine the numerical equality and inequality relations between two sets—that is, they can infer that set A and B contain the same number of items and that set C contains more items than set D. They are apt to rely heavily on counting to determine these relations and, as with number abstraction, are generally better at numerical reasoning when the sets involved are small, easily countable ones.

What about Piagetian conservation—the realization that changes in spatial arrangement do not alter number? We have already seen that preschoolers tend to fail the standard form of the conservation problem. Such failures, however, need not imply a total inability to reason about the invariance of number in the face of a perceptual change. In simpler, more child-friendly situations, even 3-year-olds show some ability to separate number from appearance. One of Gelman's so-called magic studies (R. Gelman, 1972) provides perhaps the most striking evidence for this conclusion.

Gelman's subjects ranged in age from 3 to 6½ years. Each subject saw two plates, each plate with a row of toy mice on it. There were three mice in one row and two in the other. For some subjects, the lengths of the rows were identical, with the two-mouse row naturally being less dense than the three-mouse one (since the middle mouse was missing). For others, the densities or spaces between the mice were identical, with the three-mouse row consequently being longer than the two-mouse row. The child's initial task was simply to learn which plate was the "winner" (always the one containing three mice) and which the "loser" (always the two-mouse plate). Notice that the child could learn to identify winners and losers in this task without paying the slightest attention to number and number differences. In the first group, the winner row was denser as well as more numerous; in the second group, it was longer as well as more numerous. The child was reinforced for correctly identifying winner and loser plates but was never told why a given choice was correct.

After a series of such trials, the experimenter surreptitiously ("magically") made a change in the winner row before exposing the plates to the child. For some subjects in each group, the experimenter removed one mouse from the center or end of that row, thereby making the two rows numerically equal. For others, the experimenter shortened or lengthened the winner row. Surprise reactions were noted, and the children were subsequently asked various questions about what happened. Gelman found that even her 3- and 4-year-old subjects conceptualized the winner and loser rows in terms of number rather than length or density. For example, 29 out of 32 three-year-olds gave number descriptions of the rows at some point in the experimental proceedings, often using the terms "three" and "two"; in contrast, not one ever referred to differences in length or density. Reactions following the experimenter's surreptitious change in the winner row also clearly showed that number, not length or density, was what the children were attending to. When length of row was changed (and number not changed), the children showed little surprise and continued to identify the three-mouse row as a winner, even when it had been made shorter than the two-mouse row. When a mouse was removed from the three-mouse row, on the other hand, subjects registered surprise, were uncertain as to which row was now the winner, asked where the missing mouse was or searched for it, and offered various explanations for the disappearance (our favorite: "Jesus took it"). In both situations, therefore, the children showed some ability to disentangle number from the countervailing cues of length or density.

Later Acquisitions

Children's numerical abilities continue to improve and expand during the middle-childhood and adolescent years, partly as a direct consequence of formal teaching in school and partly through a continuation of the spontaneous and informal learning about numbers that begins early in life. Skills that were rudimentary and situation-specific in early childhood become more powerful and more broadly applicable as children develop. Three-year-olds may recognize the invariance of number in certain simple situations, such as Gelman's magic task; 6- or 7-year-olds can handle any conservation-of-number task that might come along. Children's knowledge about how to abstract and reason about numbers also becomes more explicit with development. Whereas younger children can sometimes detect errors in counting or numerical reasoning, older children can go on to reflect on them and explicitly indicate why they are errors, what effects they have on the outcome, and the like. It is not hard to imagine carrying on a meaningful and articulate dialogue about Gelman's five counting principles with a child of 10, say. In contrast, we surely could not do this with a child of 3, even though the 3-year-old might also abide by these principles when actually engaged in counting small sets.

Not surprisingly, much of the work on understanding of number in the middle-childhood years has concentrated on numerical skills that are important in school—adding, subtracting, multiplying, dividing. We introduced one particularly informative example of such work in Chapter 1: Siegler's studies of the strategies that children use to solve simple arithmetic problems (Siegler, 1988; Siegler & Jenkins, 1989; Siegler & Shipley, in press). As we saw there, Siegler's goal has been to move beyond simply documenting correct or incorrect answers to such problems to specify *how* children arrive at their solutions. Perhaps the main message from the research concerns the variety of methods of how—that is, the diversity of strategies that children develop to cope with the task of addition: counting up from one, counting up from the larger addend (the "min" strategy), relating the problem to similar problems, retrieving the answer from memory, guessing. Quite typically, children use not just one but several strategies at any point in development. A main determinant of successful problem solving is the ability to select the most appropriate and efficient strategy for the task at hand. And a main determinant of developmental change is the gradual replacement, through a kind of survival of the fittest, of less efficient strategies by more efficient strategies. These conclusions apply, we should note, not just to addition but to other basic arithmetical operations that are mastered (at least in part!) during the middle-childhood years: subtraction, multiplication, division. More broadly, the emphasis on strategies and strategy change is one distinctive characteristic of the information-processing approach to children's thinking.

Earlier Foundations

That 3- and 4-year-olds are as competent in dealing with numbers as they have proved to be came as a surprise to many of us. Even more surprising is recent evidence suggesting that *infants* are sensitive to the dimension of number and may even—more mind-boggling still—spontaneously engage in some sort of nonverbal "counting" activity when presented with sets of two to four stimuli.

How might infants show a sensitivity to number? An experiment by Starkey, Spelke, and Gelman (1980) capitalized on the fact that even young infants are capable of showing habituation and dishabituation of attention—that is, of decreasing their attention to a repeatedly presented and therefore familiar stimulus and of increasing attention when they detect a change in the stimulus (see Chapter 2). Starkey and colleagues showed 6- to 9-month-old infants a series of slides of three-item displays until the infants habituated to them. The items shown were common household objects such as a memo pad, a comb, and a scraper. The three objects on any one slide were different from the three on any other slide and also differed in their spatial arrangement; it appears, therefore, that the only thing the object arrays had in common was their numerical value—their "threeness." After the infants had habituated to these slides they were presented with an alternating sequence of three-item and two-item slides. These slides also contained new household objects in varying spatial configurations. Starkey et al. found that the infants looked longer at the slides that showed the new numerical value (the two-item slides) than at those showing the old one (the three-item slides). That is, they appeared to exhibit continued habituation of attention to displays of three things but dishabituation to displays of two things. This in turn suggests that they must have perceptually discriminated between the two types of displays. Other infants of the same age who were first presented with two-item slides and then with two- and three-item slides in alternation showed the same psychological pattern: They subsequently looked longer at the novel, three-item slides.

In view of the surprising and counterintuitive nature of these findings, it is important to note that similar studies with similar results have now been carried out in a number of laboratories (Antell & Keating, 1983; R. G. Cooper, 1984; M. S. Strauss & Curtis, 1981; Trehub, Thorpe, & Cohen, 1991; Treiber & Wilcox, 1984; van Loosbroek & Smitsman, 1990). There is nothing like successful independent replication to render hard-to-believe results believable. These further studies, moreover, have added in various ways to our picture of numerical sensitivity in infants. Some ability to discriminate very small-sized sets has been shown even in neonates (Antell & Keating, 1983). By 4 months of age infants have been shown to be capable of discriminating between sets as large as four and five elements (Treiber & Wilcox, 1984); no one, however, has yet shown successful performance on sets larger than this in infancy. Discrimination of number is not limited to the visual realm; comparable results have been obtained with auditory patterns that vary in the number of tones (Trehub et al., 1991). Finally, all of the studies have attempted in various ways to control for the worrisome possibility that the babies might be responding to some aspect of the arrays other than number—differences in density, for example, or in overall configuration. Perhaps the most ingenious control comes in a study by van Loosbroek and Smitsman (1990), in which the stimuli to be compared were in constant, random motion. With the elements continually swirling around, there are no static pattern cues to mediate response; rather, infants must be responding to individual units and thus to number per se.

Starkey, Spelke, and Gelman (1983; see also Starkey, Spelke, & Gelman, 1990) reported results that are perhaps even more startling. Their experiment examined not habituation-dishabituation but rather intermodal perception. It capitalized on the fact—as has much of Spelke's research on intermodal abilities—that infants given a choice of two visual stimuli tend to look at the one that corresponds to whatever they are listening to at the moment. As we saw in Chapter 2, infants tested with this methodology have proved capable of some quite impressive feats of auditory-visual matching; they can match faces and voices, for example, on the basis of emotional expression, or sex, or patterns of lip movements. In the study by Starkey and associates, the critical dimension was number. On each of a series of trials, infants of 6 to 8 months were presented with two visual displays side by side, one containing two household objects and the other three. The nature and spatial arrangement of the objects differed from one display to the next. On some trials the infants heard a sequence of two drumbeats while viewing the displays, on others a sequence of three drumbeats. Over the course of the 32 trials, the infants developed a weak but statistically significant tendency to look longer at the three-item display than at the two-item display when three drumbeats sounded, and to look longer at the two-item display when two drumbeats sounded. That is, they acted as though they came to detect some sort of abstract, sense-modality-independent equivalence between sets of stimuli as physically dissimilar as visual displays and auditory sequences. Starkey et al. (1983, 1990) attained essentially the same results in several similar experiments. It is difficult to imagine what the abstract equivalence could be other than numerical equivalence. It is also difficult to imagine how that equivalence could be detected except by some neurological process akin to nonverbal counting.

Basic Numerical Skills: Natural Human Abilities?

The infant studies are taken by Rochel Gelman (1982, 1990, 1991; R. Gelman & Meck, in press) as evidence for her belief that basic numerical skills may constitute natural and universal abilities for members of our species. Number, Gelman believes, is like language in this regard: a species-wide set of abilities that *Homo sapiens* has evolved a special aptitude and disposition to acquire. As with objects (Chapter 2) and language (Chapter 7), the development of numerical competence builds upon a skeleton of innately given, domain-specific principles, principles that are not themselves learned but rather serve as the starting point that makes learning possible.

Various lines of argument support this position. First, as we have just seen, human beings appear to be both able and disposed to process numerical information from early in infancy—well before language, well before formal tuition, well before relevant experience of any obvious sort. Second, young children show both high motivation and high aptitude to acquire basic numerical knowledge and skills on their own, without adult pressure or tutelage. In young children, Gelman's counting principles function very like a Piagetian scheme. Like a sucking or prehension scheme, they spontaneously and voraciously assimilate countable objects and new number words to their own structures. Young children seem to go around counting things and learning new numbers for the sheer pleasure of it. Furthermore, some form of counting procedure seems to be found in every human culture, including those in which there is no formal schooling. Such universality is clearly compatible with the idea that numerical processing, like speech, is something that humans are born to do. Finally, the plausibility of Gelman's position is bolstered by its congruence with the current Zeitgeist. As we will discuss more fully in Chapter 8, the field is much more favorably disposed now than formerly to the notion that some degree of innate, domain-specific pretuning guides many aspects of development (see Wellman & Gelman, 1992). Gelman's work on number both prefigured and contributed to these modern emphases.

Basic Numeral Skills: Social Contributors

Whatever the innate bases may be, no one, least of all Gelman, believes that numerical development results solely from the unfolding of biologically programmed abilities in the absence of any experience. Such is obviously not the case. Children, as we have seen, exercise their numerical skills frequently and spontaneously, and they clearly benefit from these experiences. Numerical concepts of various sorts are also the focus of thousands of hours of explicit tuition in school. The lives of both children and teachers would be much easier if all numerical knowledge were somehow programmed in from birth.

In recent years the development of numerical competence has also been a fruitful topic area for applications of the Vygotsky-inspired contextual approach to cognitive development. As we saw in Chapter 1, the emphasis of the contextual approach is on the social context within which cognitive development takes place, both the distal context provided by the general culture and the more proximal context of interactions with significant others, especially the child's parents. Cognition is assumed to be inextricably embedded within the social world and critically dependent on the kinds of information and assistance that social interaction provides. Researchers in this tradition who are interested in number therefore focus on the ways in which different cultures symbolize and transmit numerical knowledge, as well as the forms of guidance that more knowledgeable members of the culture provide to the growing child who is attempting to master this knowledge.

A monograph by Saxe, Guberman, and Gearhart (1987) provides an example. Subjects for the research were 2- and 4-year-olds and their mothers. Mother and child were videotaped as they worked together on several simple numerical tasks—counting the number of objects in a small array, for example, or matching the number of objects in one array with the number in a second array. Of interest were the kinds of help that the mothers provided to their children and the children's ability to benefit from the help. Saxe and co-workers found that mothers adjusted the level of their help to the level of the child; 2-year-olds received more explicit guidance than did 4-year-olds, and less numerically competent children within an age group (as assessed by independent tests) received more guidance than more competent children. Mothers also showed an ability to make on-the-spot adjustments to the level of their child's performance. When a child succeeded at some step toward task solution, the mother's next instruction was typically at a less explicit, more on-your-own level; conversely, when a child failed at some step, mothers tended to up the level of their help, spelling out procedures that had been only implicit before. This sort of flexible, child-sensitive method of teaching has come to be known as "scaffolding" in the Vygotskian literature (Wood, 1980), and it certainly appears to be a sensible way to help children learn. Finally, Saxe and colleagues found that the children were often able to accomplish a task with maternal help that they had been unable to perform on their own. You may recall that such actualization of potential level of performance through appropriate assistance is the essence of the Vygotskian notion of the zone of proximal development.

Two more points can be made about the Saxe et al. (1987) research. The finding that maternal teaching is helpful on laboratory tasks would not mean much without evidence that mothers and children do in fact work together in situations involving number—naturally and spontaneously and not just when some experimenter sets them a task to complete. Through interviews with the mothers, Saxe and colleagues provide some evidence for such ecological validity: At least in their sample, the children dealt frequently with numbers, mothers and children engaged frequently in number games and activities of various sorts, and the complexity of the games and activities increased as the children developed. The second point is that the boost in performance in response to maternal help would be of limited significance if the gains did not transfer to the child's later, independent problem-solving efforts. Our interest, after all, is not just in what children can do with help but in what they take away from the help and make their own. Although Saxe and colleagues did not include such independent measures, other studies in the contextual tradition (e.g., the Freund, 1990, study discussed in Chapter 1) have, and they typically report improved independent performance following social interaction. Nevertheless, our knowledge on this important point is rather limited. We still have much to learn about exactly what sorts of adult assistance promote exactly what degrees of independent mastery, in number and in other domains—and about whether anything adults do is really *necessary* for mastery (as opposed to being merely helpful). This is an issue that we will encounter again in Chapter 7 when we tackle the difficult question of how children learn language.

Researchers in the contextual tradition have also provided some fascinating data with regard to the more distal level of cultural systems of number and cultural supports for numerical development. Here we briefly mention three findings. First, although basic principles of mathematics are of course universal (1 + 1 = 2 in every culture), the symbolic systems through which numbers are expressed and dealt with may vary greatly across cultures. In parts of New Guinea, for example, a body-parts system of counting is used (see Figure 3–2); the count begins with the thumb on one hand and progresses through 29 distinct locations before reaching the far side of the other hand (Saxe, 1981). Second, the ways in which a culture symbolizes numbers can affect the speed with which numerical operations are mastered during development and the ease with which they are executed in maturity. Saxe (1981, 1982) found, for example, that both number-abstraction and numerical-reasoning skills tended to be slower to develop among New Guinea children dependent on the body-parts method of counting than among Western children. Similarly, K. Miller and Stigler (1987) reported that Chinese children were superior to American children in some aspects of counting, apparently because the Chinese language symbolizes the relevant terms in a more consistent, accessible fashion than does English (the "teen" numbers, like the "teen" years, are especially problematical). Finally, cultural experiences beyond simply the number system itself can either nurture or hinder the development of numerical skills. A striking example comes from Saxe's (1988, 1991) studies of child candy vendors on the streets of Brazil. Faced with a multitude of numerical tasks, all of which must be performed quickly and accurately under highly competitive circumstances

FIGURE 3–2   A body-parts system of counting used in parts of New Guinea. From "Body Parts as Numerals: A Developmental Analysis of Numeration among the Oksapmin in Papua New Guinea" by G. B. Saxe, 1981, *Child Development, 52,* p. 307. Copyright © 1981 by the Society for Research in Child Development. Reprinted by permission.

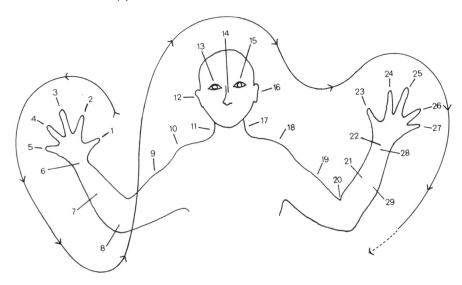

(purchasing the candy, setting the sale price, making change, adjusting for infla-tion), these children develop a mathematical facility that most of us, shorn of our pocket calculators, would be hard-put to match.

SUMMARY

The developmental psychologist's portrait of cognition during the period of early childhood (roughly 1½ to 6 years of age) used to be rather negative and unflatter-ing. For example, preschool children's thinking was often characterized as "preop-erational," or even "preconceptual." However, recent research has shown that an impressive number of fragile but nonetheless genuine competencies have been acquired by the end of this period. It seems that we had underestimated the young child's abilities, just as we had underestimated the infant's (Chapter 2).

Symbolic-representational skills undergo a great deal of growth during early childhood. Young children not only form both mental representations and physical representations (e.g., pretend play), but also begin to understand the nature of these representations. The ability to form representations emerges in infancy and is fol-lowed by three more advanced abilities: understanding pictorial representations, using models, and engaging in pretend play. Infants know the real entities to which pictures refer and also know that the two are not exactly the same. However, they have trouble sorting out certain differences between the two. For example, even 3-year-olds do not seem to understand that a change in reality does not necessarily cause a change in the representation of that reality, such as an earlier photograph. They also are unsure of the boundary conditions between television images and their real-life counterparts. Three-dimensional scale models cannot be used until about 36 months. At this age the majority of children can locate an object hidden in one physical layout based on its hiding place in a larger or smaller layout. The req-uisite concept may be that an entity can be both itself and a representation of some-thing else.

There is a marked increase in children's abilities to engage in *pretend* or *sym-bolic play*. Pretend play tends to be decontextualized and involves pretense about properties or identities of objects. One object often is substituted for another, and the role of the self and another person or object can be readily reversed. Pretend play also becomes socialized in that it becomes more conventional and incorporates more complex social roles and themes. Although very young children engage in pretend play and know they are pretending, they do not fully understand that pre-tense primarily is a mental state—a representation—rather than simply an action.

The simple representations of infancy become much more complex knowl-edge structures over the preschool years. These representations greatly assist chil-dren in predicting and making sense of their everyday worlds. For example, event representations, including *scripts*, can be thought of as mental forms, molds, or templates that help us assimilate and accommodate to environmental inputs. Chil-dren begin to acquire such mental templates for the structure of simple stories dur-ing this age period and to use these structures when comprehending and recalling stories. They construct scripts for representing and anticipating the usual sequence of events in preschool, at bedtime, and during other familiar routines. Young chil-dren have acquired at least a rudimentary knowledge structure for causal rela-tions—for instance, they are likely to know that physical causes precede rather than follow their effects. Like older people, they are capable of representing the locations of objects by means of an objective external, object-referenced spatial frame of reference, as well as by means of an *egocentric* (self-referenced) one.

Preschoolers also form *concepts* that organize the world into meaningful categories. In contrast to traditional views of the perception-bound young child, these early concepts do not depend solely on perceptual appearance but often reflect deeper, less obvious relations among the members of a category. For example, young children can use their knowledge that blackbird and flamingo belong to the same category, and that blackbird and bat do not, to infer that the former pair are more likely to share fundamental properties than are the latter. Such inferences reflect a primary cognitive function that concepts serve: They help us to abstract basic similarities in the face of obvious dissimilarities, and to use our knowledge of familiar examplars to predict to unfamiliar ones. Productive inferences based on underlying similarity are especially likely for the type of concept known as *natural kinds*: categories that occur in nature, such as animals and plants. Although their grasp of the distinction is somewhat shaky, even preschoolers show some appreciation of the ways in which natural kinds differ from other sorts of concepts.

An important aspect of conceptual development involves understanding the hierarchically organized levels within which entities can be represented. Research inspired by Rosch has examined the prediction that representations at the *basic-level* (e.g., dog, chair) are psychologically most natural and hence should emerge earlier in development than representations at either the superordinate (e.g., animal, furniture) or subordinate (e.g., poodle, rocker) levels. This prediction has received mixed support in research to date. Research inspired by Piaget has examined children's understanding of the hierarchical structure of classes, with a particular focus on the principle of *class inclusion*: the knowledge that a subclass cannot be larger than the superordinate class that contains it. The difficulty of class inclusion turns out to vary greatly across different forms of the problem and different response measures; even preschoolers show some understanding of the principle, but full mastery may not come until many years later.

Studies of children's understanding of biological phenomena (growth, inheritance, movement) provide an interesting content area in which to examine particular childhood concepts. Such studies also serve to illustrate several general conclusions about young children's concepts. Preschoolers' understanding of biology is more advanced than we used to believe—a conclusion in keeping with much recent research on this age period. This understanding is not complete, however, and developmental improvements are evident for each of the biological concepts examined. Often, differences between younger and older children seem to reflect differences in content-specific knowledge; young children have limited knowledge in many domains, and this lack of knowledge constrains the level of their concepts and reasoning. The importance of content-specific knowledge suggests that children's concepts will not all be at the same level of maturity, and research indicates that in fact they are not. Finally, the most popular way at present to characterize the nature of concepts is to think of them as implicit *theories*. Like theories, concepts consist of a set of interrelated causal-explanatory principles, and, like theories, they help us to understand and predict experience.

The theory-based approach is clearly illustrated in recent research on young children's *theory of mind*. Such a theory helps a child explain and predict others' behaviors by referring to their desires, beliefs, emotions, and so on. Shortly before age 2, children's spontaneous speech refers to mental states, suggesting a rudimentary awareness of other people's minds (Postulate 1: the mind exists). Two- and 3-

year-olds realize that the mind has connections with the physical world (Postulate 2) via seeing and hearing objects, wanting them, and so on. They know the effect of stimuli on a mental state, can predict behavior from the mental state, and use behavior and events to infer mental states. They also may have a sort of *desire psychology*, a causal-explanatory theory of mind that attributes desires to other people and predicts their behavior based on these desires. However, they also learn that the mind is separate from, and differs from, the physical world (Postulate 3). For example, a 3-year-old knows that a person could see, touch, and eat a real cookie, but not a thought-about cookie. However, imagined monsters can still be scary.

Around age 4 a *belief-desire* psychology emerges, primarily because of a new and fuller understanding of mental representations (Postulate 4). Four- and 5-year-olds have representations about representations. In this understanding, beliefs (a) are representations, (b) can differ among people and change within a person, (c) may be accurate or inaccurate (*false beliefs* about reality), depending on one's experience, and (d) cause behavior. Younger children may show glimmerings of understanding of false beliefs under certain task circumstances. Postulate 4 also may be expressed in a variety of other skills such as perspective taking, understanding that one's facial expression may mask one's real emotion, understanding ambiguity, and distinguishing between appearance and reality. The *appearance-reality distinction* is acquired gradually during early childhood. It seems to hinge on the notion that a property or object can be represented simultaneously as it really is and as it appears perceptually. Preschoolers often err on appearance-reality tasks and resist attempts to teach them the concept. Understanding lies, jokes, metaphors, and false presentation of self may involve the appearance-reality distinction as well.

Finally, Postulate 5 refers to the fact that the mind actively contributes to what is known. Prior knowledge, expectations, and psychological limitations can distort or embellish reality. The mind does not simply copy reality. These five postulates chart representational changes that lead to children's growing awareness of representations in themselves and others.

We still know very little about the causes of theory-of-mind development. Universal and culture-specific experiences must play some role; interactions with parents and siblings and pretend play with dolls may be particularly important. Certain cultural differences in theory of mind emerge as well. In addition, specific theory-of-mind deficits in autistic children suggest biological causes.

The acquisition of basic numerical abilities is of compelling interest for several reasons, not the least of which is their great ecological significance. A great deal of exciting research on this topic has been carried out in recent years by Rochel Gelman and others. Gelman distinguishes between *number-abstraction abilities* and *numerical-reasoning principles*. Prominent among the number-abstraction abilities is the preschooler's developing command of five *counting principles*: (1) assign one and only one number name to each and every item to be counted (*one-one principle*); (2) always recite the number names in the same order (*stable-order principle*); (3) the final number name uttered denotes the total number of items counted (*cardinal principle*); (4) any sort of entity may be counted (*abstraction principle*); (5) the order in which the objects are enumerated does not matter (*order-irrelevance principle*). An important numerical-reasoning principle that children gradually acquire is the number-conservation rule first studied by Piaget: the knowledge that merely spreading a set of objects does not change the number of objects in the set.

It is not surprising to learn that children's numerical abilities continue to develop in various ways after early childhood. Nor is it surprising to learn that aspects of the social context, such as parental teaching, can contribute to these developments. However, it certainly *is* surprising to learn that numerical abilities may begin their development *before* the early-childhood period. Recent research suggests that infants are sensitive to the dimension of number and, incredible although it sounds, may even engage spontaneously in some sort of nonverbal "counting" when presented with small-sized sets. These astonishing findings raise the possibility that basic numerical processes may—like walking and talking—be activities we humans are predisposed through evolution to learn and do.

The picture of preschoolers emerging from this chapter is that they can and do make more inferences about the unobservable, the covert, and the mental than developmental psychologists once thought. In particular, they seem to prefer causal-explanatory representations that go beneath surface appearances to a deeper reality, although—like the rest of us—they sometimes are distracted by these perceptual features and have trouble integrating them with the underlying features. Much of their knowledge is acquired informally as they construct an intuitive understanding of natural domains—objects, events, and people. Overall, children possess surprising cognitive strengths in their pretend play, scripts, basic categories of reality, desire psychology, and intuitive grasp of number. At the same time, they still have much to learn about the more subtle aspects of mental representation, about biology, and about quantity.

four

Middle Childhood and Adolescence

Exactly how do the minds of older children, adolescents, and adults differ from those of young children? Despite the existence of thousands of research studies comparing the cognitive performance of early-childhood and older subjects, we still lack a wholly satisfactory answer to this basic question. It is not that these studies fail to show marked age differences in cognitive performance; they almost always do. Rather, the problem is to know how best to describe and explain the age differences found. We first will present Piaget's view of the main developmental trends during the middle childhood and adolescent years, then identify important cognitive changes in addition to those described by Piaget. Finally, these various changes will be illustrated by examples of children's scientific thinking.

PIAGET'S VIEW OF MIDDLE CHILDHOOD AND ADOLESCENCE

Piaget's theory postulates the following sequence of major stages or periods of cognitive development: (1) the sensorimotor period of infancy; (2) the preoperational period of early childhood, conceived as a period of preparation for concrete operations; (3) the concrete-operational period of middle childhood; (4) the formal-operational period of adolescence. In this sequence (see Table 4–1), the child moves from a physical action to a symbolic to a mental action form of representation. Although infants are more competent than Piaget believed (see Chapter 2), we think a good case could be made for Piaget's claim that infants (at least younger ones) have cognitive systems that are fundamentally different in some ways from those of older humans, including very young children. In particular, a cognitive system that uses symbols just seems on that account alone to be radically, drastically, qualitatively different from one that does not and cannot. So great is the difference that the transformation of one system into the other during the first year or two of life still seems nothing short of miraculous to us, no matter how much we learn about it. Are subsequent changes that basic, that fundamental? Do they also seem nothing short of miraculous, or do they rather seem something short of miraculous, although no doubt still considerable? Piaget thought they were very fundamental indeed, as did other major developmental theorists like Vygotsky and Werner. Mental actions (operations) are applied first to concrete, present objects and events and later to mental operations themselves, the thoughts about thoughts of formal operations.

However, two kinds of recent findings challenge the notion of dramatic across-the-child changes in Piagetian stages or anyone's stages for that matter. First, a child's cognitive performance is somewhat uneven across different domains (see Chapters 1 and 3). Second, it appears that young children are more competent (see Chapters 2 and 3) and older children less competent than Piaget thought. Consequently, the cognitive changes across childhood may be less stagelike and dramatic than Piaget imagined. Still, Piaget does seem to have captured important developmental *trends* that ring true. We will organize these trends into two sets of contrasts: (1) contrasts between early-childhood and middle-childhood cognition; (2) contrasts between middle-childhood and adolescent-adult cognition. However, these should be thought of as rough age trends, not as sharp and clear contrasts among three entirely different and discontinuous mentalities. Also note that what follows is not a review of the vast research literature on concrete- and formal-operational thinking. Reviews of some of this literature

TABLE 4-1 Piaget's Periods of Cognitive Development

PERIOD	APPROXIMATE AGES (YRS)	DESCRIPTION
Sensorimotor	0–2	Infants understand the world by overtly acting on it. Their motor actions reflect sensorimotor schemes—generalized action patterns for understanding the world, such as a sucking scheme. Schemes gradually become more differentiated and integrated, and at the end of the period infants can form mental representations of reality.
Preoperational	2–7	Children can use representations (mental images, drawings, words, gestures) rather than just motor actions to think about objects and events. Thinking now is faster, more flexible and efficient, and more socially shared. Thinking is limited by egocentrism, a focus on perceptual states, reliance on appearances rather than underlying realities, and rigidity (lack of reversibility).
Concrete-operational	7–11	Children acquire operations—systems of internal mental actions that underlie logical thinking. These reversible, organized operations allow children to overcome the limitations of preoperational thought. Conservation, class-inclusion, perspective taking, and other concepts are acquired. Operations can be applied only to concrete objects—present or mentally represented.
Formal-operational	11–15	Mental operations can be applied to the possible and hypothetical as well as the real, to the future as well as the present, and to purely verbal or logical statements. Adolescents acquire scientific thinking, with its hypothetico-deductive reasoning, and logical reasoning with its interpropositional reasoning. They can understand highly abstract concepts.

can be found in C. Acredelo (1982), Braine and Rumain (1983), Byrnes (1988a), Chapman (1988), Flavell (1963, 1970a), R. Gelman and Baillargeon (1983), Ginsburg and Opper (1988), R. Gold (1987), Gray (1990), Halford (1989), Keating (1990), Kuhn (1979), and Moshman and Franks (1989).

Contrasts between Early-Childhood and Middle-Childhood Cognition

PERCEIVED APPEARANCES VERSUS INFERRED REALITY. We will illustrate the contrasts with Piaget's hallmark task, the conservation task. However, these trends also apply to other physical concepts and to social concepts such as role taking and person perception (see Chapter 5) as well.

Piaget's test for conservation of liquid quantity illustrates the meaning of this and the other contrasts: (1) The child first agrees that two identical glasses contain identical amounts of water; (2) the experimenter pours the water from one glass into a third, taller and thinner glass, with the child watching; (3) the experimenter then asks the child whether the two amounts of water are still identical, or whether one glass now contains more water than the other. The typical preschool nonconserver is apt to conclude, after the liquid has been poured, that the taller and thinner glass now has more water in it than the other glass. Why? One reason is that it *looks* like it has more, and the preschooler is more given than the older child to make judgments about reality on the basis of the immediate, perceived *appearances* of things. More than their school-age counterparts, preschool-age children are prone to accept things as they seem to be.

The middle-childhood conserver, on the other hand, may also think that the tall glass *looks* like it contains more water because the liquid column is higher, but this child goes beyond mere appearances to *infer* from the available evidence that the two quantities *are really* still the same. That is, the child makes an inference about underlying reality rather than merely translating perceived appearances into a quantity judgment. More generally, the older child seems to be more sensitive to the basic distinction between what seems to be and what really is—between the phenomenal or apparent and the real or true (see the appearance-reality distinction in Chapter 3). Of course, this is not to suggest that young children never make inferences about unperceived states of affairs or that older children never base conclusions on superficial appearances. Indeed, some of young children's concepts discussed in Chapter 3, especially their "theories," clearly go beyond the perceptual information given. Still, the tendency to do so (a) increases across this broad segment of childhood, and (b) becomes less limited to particular aspects of reality—for example, may include not only the identity and nature of an entity but also its quantity.

CENTRATION VERSUS DECENTRATION. The foregoing contrast emphasizes younger children's heavy reliance on perceptual input when dealing with conceptual problems like Piaget's conservation-of-liquid-quantity task. But of course older children also are carefully attending to the perceptual input throughout that task, even though they recognize that the task ultimately calls for a conceptual rather than a perceptual judgment. Moreover, they are apt to be distributing that attention in a more flexible, balanced, and generally task-adaptive way than younger children are. Preschoolers are more prone to concentrate or *center* (hence, *centration*) their attention exclusively on some single feature or limited portion of the stimulus array that is particularly salient and interesting to them, thereby neglecting other task-relevant features. In the present example, the difference in the heights of the two liquid columns is what captures most of the child's attention (and "capture" often does seem the apposite word), with little note given to the compensatory difference in column widths.

In contrast, older children are likelier to achieve a more balanced, "decentered" (hence, *decentration*) perceptual analysis of the entire display. While, of course, attending to the conspicuous height differences, just as younger children do, older children also carefully note the correlative differences in container width. They therefore attain a broader and more inclusive purview of the stimulus field. They are likelier to notice and take due account of *all* the relevant perceptual data—in this case, the lesser width as well as the greater height of the new liquid column. Piaget (e.g., 1970b) believed that the younger child's centration tendency often takes the form of relying heavily on *order* or *ordinal* information in making quantitative judgments. If one of two identical pencils is slid ahead of the other, for example, it is apt to be judged as longer than the first (nonconservation of length). Ordinal relationships like "ahead of," "first," "out in front," "X has passed Y," and so on are very salient for the preoperational child and are often used inappropriately as the sole basis for quantitative comparison.

O'Bryan and Boersma (1971) have captured "live" ongoing patterns of centration and decentration by filming the eye movements of nonconservers and conservers. Nonconservers centrate on the dominant part of the visual display, such as the water level. Transitional conservers display a sort of dual centration, shifting occasionally between two dominant features such as water height and width. Conservers shift their gaze frequently over many parts of the display. Thus, attention can be a window to the child's mind.

STATES VERSUS TRANSFORMATIONS. The test of conservation of liquid quantity can be thought of as comprising two *states*, one initial and one final, plus a *transformation* or process of change that links these two states. In the initial state, two identical glasses of water contain identical amounts of water. In the final state, two dissimilar glasses contain identical amounts of water (identical in "reality," if not in "appearance"). The transformation that links them is, of course, the process of pouring water from one glass to another. The act of pouring is a dynamic event that changes, in the course of a brief time period, one static situation into another static situation; it is a transformational process that produces or creates a later state out of an earlier state.

Piaget made the profound observation that younger children, to a greater degree than older ones, tend to focus their attention and conceptual energies on states rather than on state-producing transformations, and also on present states more than on past or future ones. When solving problems of all sorts they are less likely to call to mind or keep in mind relevant previous states of the problem, or to anticipate pertinent future or potential ones. In particular, Piaget argued they are both undisposed and relatively unable to represent the actual, detailed processes of transition or transformation from one state to another. Thus, they exhibit a kind of "temporal centration" analogous to the spatial one just discussed. They center their attention on the present spatial field or stimulus state to the exclusion of other relevant states and state-linking transformations in the "temporal field," which consists of the recent past, the immediate present, and the near future. They do this just as, within the present spatial field itself, they center their attention on a single, privileged segment of that field. To put it more briefly and concretely, the preoperational subject tries to solve the conservation problem by attending only to the present stimulus field ("temporal centration") and, within it, only to selected, highly salient stimulus features ("spatial centration").

In contrast, conservers are likely to make spontaneous reference to initial state and intervening transformation when asked to justify their conservation judgment. They might say that the two quantities had, after all, been identical at the outset (initial state), or that the experimenter had merely poured the water from one container to the other, and without spilling any or adding any (intervening transformation). They might even say that the continuing equality of amounts could be proved by pouring the liquid back into its original container (future or potential transformation, yielding new state equal to initial state). The conservation task is a conceptual problem rather than a perceptual one precisely *because* of the real or potential existence of such nonpresent states and transformations of states. Older children are more attuned to these background, not-now-perceptible factors and uses them in producing a conceptual solution to this problem and other, similar conceptual problems.

IRREVERSIBILITY VERSUS REVERSIBILITY. According to Piaget middle-childhood subjects possess *reversible intellectual operations* (hence the term "concrete *operational* period"); their thought is said to exhibit the property of *reversibility*. Contrariwise, preschool children's mental operations are *irreversible*, and their thought is said to show *irreversibility*. In the particular conservation problem we have been using as an example, older children can exhibit reversibility of thought or reversible mental operations in two distinct ways.

On the one hand, children may recognize that the effect of the initial pouring of the water into the tall, thin glass can be exactly and completely undone or negated by the inverse action of pouring the water back into its original container. Older children readily sense the possible existence of such an inverse, wholly nullifying action that changes everything back to its original state, and they may cite this possibility as a justification for their conservation judgment. A middle-childhood mind is more sensitive than an early-childhood one to the fact that many mental and physical operations have opposites that exactly—in a rigorous, precise, quantitative way—negate them, and thereby reset the entire situation to zero, so to speak.

On the other hand, older children similarly recognize that something equivalent to situation zero can also be achieved by an action that compensates for or counterbalances the effects of another action, rather than one that literally undoes it in the manner of the inverse or opposite action just described. For example, children might justify their belief in conservation by pointing out that the increase in height of the liquid column, which results from the pouring transformation, is exactly offset or compensated for by the accompanying decrease in column width. According to this kind of reversible thinking, the column loses in width what it gains in height, and hence the quantity must remain the same. The width decrease obviously does not literally wipe out or annul the height increase, as actual repouring would. It has the same effect and cognitive significance (i.e., it provides a rational justification for a conservation verdict), but it does so by virtue of constituting an indirect compensation rather than a direct, literal negation. As with direct negation, older children are more attuned than younger ones to the potential existence of such indirectly countervailing, compensation-type factors, and they better understand the utility of these factors in making rigorous quantitative inferences.

Other examples of these two forms of reversible thinking abound in Piagetiana. Recall that conservation of length can be assessed by first placing two identical pencils (sticks, rods) side by side so that their ends exactly coincide and then, after the child agrees that they are equal in length, sliding one a bit to the right, so that its end leads or is ahead of the other's end on that side. The younger child focuses "irreversibly" on this "transformation"-produced, immediately perceptible "state" of the sticks ("temporal centration") and, within that state, equally irreversibly "centers" his or her attention on the right-hand portions of the sticks ("spatial centration"); mistaking "appearances" for "reality," the child concludes that the rightmost stick is now longer than its companion. (Whereby it is demonstrated that all four of the early-childhood-middle–childhood contrasts just discussed can be insinuated into a single sentence, although the use of the semicolon does admittedly represent a bit of fudging on our part.) In the same situation, the older conserver may exhibit reversible thinking, either by appealing to the results of the inverse, directly negating act of realignment of the pencils, or by suggesting that the length gained by the displaced stick at its right end is exactly compensated for by the length lost at its left end. These two types of concrete-operational reversibility are often referred to by Piagetians as *inversion* and *compensation*, respectively. Both are mental operations that make up the concrete operational mind and underlie conservation, according to Piaget. However, evidence that these operations are necessary for conservation is rather shaky (e.g., R. Gelman & Weinberg, 1972).

QUALITATIVE VERSUS QUANTITATIVE THINKING. As we saw in Chapter 3, children do acquire some basic numerical skills during the preschool period. Furthermore, a series of studies by Bryant and Kopytynska (1976) has shown that children of 5 to 6 years are even capable of simple measurement operations under some task conditions. Asked to find out which of two holes was deeper, their young subjects spontaneously used a stick as a measuring device. Nevertheless, most of what people come to know about mathematics and measurement is acquired after early childhood. A research example is Siegler's information-processing work on mathematical strategies described in Chapters 1 and 3. Older children have a more quantitative, measurement-oriented approach to many tasks and problems than do younger children. The younger child's approach appears to have a more global, qualitative cast to it. The older child seems to understand better than the younger one that certain problems have precise, specific, potentially quantifiable solutions, and that these solutions may be attained by reasoning in conjunction with well-defined measurement operations. The younger child often lacks the cognitive equipment to do other than guess or make simple perceptual estimates. In contrast, the older child has come to understand that wholes are potentially divisible into unit parts of arbitrary size, and that these parts can serve as units of measurement in making a quantitative judgment about the whole.

Once again, Piaget's conservation problems are useful in illustrating this difference between a qualitative, "guestimate"-minded approach and a quantitative, measurement-minded one. Six wooden matches are placed end-to-end but nonlinearly, so that they form a jagged, angular "road" on the table. An objectively shorter (e.g., only "five matches long") but perfectly straight stick representing a second road is placed directly above the first. Because it is straight, the crow's-flight distance between its end points is actually longer than the distance between the end points of the other, crooked road. Who makes the longest trip, the experimenter asks, the person who drives the entire length of the crooked road or the person who drives the entire length of the straight road? The second person, says the nursery school child, centering only on the end points. The first person, says the fourth grader, carefully attending to what lies *between* the end points. Unlike the younger subject, this child recognizes that total lengths (distances, areas, volumes, etc.) are composed of, and are conceptually divisible into, subparts of any arbitrary desired magnitude. He understands that whole lengths are potentially fractionable into so-and-so many length segments of such-and-such size, or alternatively, into some different number of segments of any other, arbitrarily selected size. If asked to prove that the crooked road was actually longer than the straight road, appearances notwithstanding, the child might, of course, simply straighten it out, align the two, and point to the difference. He might instead, however, use one of the matches as a convenient, preformed unit measure, and prove that the crooked road was "one match longer" than the straight one. Equivalently, he could use a ruler, or a meter stick, or a hairpin, or anything else that would allow him to arrive at a rigorous, exact, quantitative solution to the problem. Such a child, we would say, has a metric, genuinely quantitative conception of length. He possesses what Bearison (1969) has termed a "quantitative set," and it allows him to envision exact solutions to a variety of quantitative problems.

Quantification and measurement (e.g., K. F. Miller, 1989) obviously do not apply only to one or a few specific knowledge domains. They are, as Carey (1985b) nicely puts it, "tools of wide application" to a range of situations. The ability to read is another such tool. Acquisition of these mental tools must indelibly color one's cognitive life (Flavell, 1982a).

Contrasts between Middle-Childhood and Adolescent-Adult Cognition

An experimenter and a subject face one another across a table strewn with poker chips of various solid colors (Osherson & Markman, 1975). The experimenter explains that he is going to say things about the chips and that the subject is to indicate whether what the experimenter *says* (i.e., his *statements*) is true, false, or uncertain ("can't tell"). He then conceals a chips in his hand and says, "Either the chip in my hand is green or it is not green," or alternatively, "The chip in my hand is green and it is not green." On other trials, he holds up either a green chip or a red chip so that the subject can see it and then makes exactly the same statements.

Middle-childhood subjects are very likely to try to assess the truth value of these two assertions solely on the basis of the visual evidence. They focus on the concrete, empirical evidence concerning poker chips *themselves* rather than on the nonempirical, purely logical properties of the experimenter's *statements* about the poker chips. Consequently, they say they "can't tell" on the trials in which the chip is hidden from view. When the chip is visible, both statements are judged to be true if the chip is green and false if it is red. In other words, if the color (green) mentioned in the statement matches the color of the visible chip, the statement is said to be true; if there is a mismatch, it is judged false; and if the chip cannot be seen its truth status is uncertain. What middle-childhood subjects fail to appreciate is that such "either-or" statements are always true and such "and" statements always false, regardless of the empirical evidence (see also Moshman & Franks, 1986; Russell & Haworth, 1987). Logicians call the former a *tautology* and the latter a *contradiction*, and they are true and false, respectively, solely by virtue of their formal properties as propositions.

Adolescent and adult subjects, on the other hand, are likelier to focus on the verbal assertions themselves, and to evaluate their internal validity as formal propositions. They appear to have a better intuition than do younger subjects of the distinction between abstract, purely logical relations and empirical relations. These more mature thinkers recognize that one can sometimes reason about propositions as such, instead of always "seeing right through them" to the entities and states of affairs to which they refer. Thus, Osherson and Markman's data hint at some of the important changes in the nature and quality of thought during the adolescent years proposed by Piaget (Inhelder & Piaget, 1958).

REAL VERSUS POSSIBLE. Piaget argued that adolescents and adults tend to differ from children in the way they conceive of the relation between the real and the possible. The elementary school child's characteristic approach to many conceptual problems is to burrow right into the problem data as quickly as possible, using various concrete-operational skills to order and interrelate whatever properties or features of the situation he can detect. His is an earthbound, concrete, practical-minded sort of problem-solving approach, one that persistently fixates on the perceptible and inferable reality right there in front of him. His conceptual approach is definitely not unintelligent and it certainly generates solution attempts that are far more rational and task-relevant than anything the preoperational child ever produces. It does, however, hug the ground of detected empirical reality rather closely, and speculations about other possibilities—that is, about other potential, as yet undetected realities—occur only with difficulty and as a last resort. An ivory-tower theorist the elementary school child is not.

Adolescents or adults are likelier than are elementary school children to approach problems quite the other way around, at least when operating at the top of their capacity. The child usually begins with reality and moves reluctantly, if at all, to possibility; in contrast, the adolescent or adult is more apt to begin with possibility and only subsequently proceed to reality. The latter may examine the problem situation carefully to try to determine what all the *possible* solutions or states of affairs might be, and then systematically try to discover which of these is, in fact, the *real* one in the present case. For the concrete-operational thinker, the realm of abstract possibility is seen as an uncertain and only occasional extension of the safer and surer realm of palpable reality. For the formal-operational thinker, on the other hand, reality is seen as that particular portion of the much wider world of possibility that happens to exist or hold true in a given problem situation. Possibility is subordinated to reality in the former case.

EMPIRICO-INDUCTIVE VERSUS HYPOTHETICO-DEDUCTIVE. This subordination of the real to the possible expresses itself in a characteristic method of solving problems. The formal-operational thinker inspects the problem data, *hypothesizes* that such and such a theory or explanation might be the correct one, *deduces* from it that so-and-so empirical phenomena ought logically to occur or not occur in reality, and then tests her theory by seeing whether these predicted phenomena do in fact occur. More informally put, the formal-operational thinker makes up a plausible story about what might be going on; figures out what would logically have to happen out there in reality if her story were the right one; checks or does experiments out there to see what does, in fact, happen; and then accepts, rejects, or revises her story accordingly. If you think you have just heard a description of textbook scientific reasoning, you are absolutely right. Because of its heavy trade in hypotheses and logical deductions from hypotheses, it is also called *hypothetico-deductive* reasoning, and it contrasts sharply with the much more nontheoretical and nonspeculative *empirico-inductive* reasoning of concrete-operational thinkers.

Notice that this type of thinking begins with the possible rather than the real in two senses. First, the subject's initial theory is only one of a number of possible ones that she might have concocted. It is itself a possibility rather than a reality, and it is also only one possibility among many. Second, the "empirical reality" predicted by or deduced from her initial theory is itself only a possibility, and also only one possibility among many. Actual, concrete reality only enters the scene when the subject tries to verify her theory by looking for the "reality" it has predicted. If it is not found, new theories and new theory-derived realities will be invented, and thus the sampling of possibilities continues. It is important to emphasize that these theories and theory-derived realities are purely conceptual entities, not physical ones. They are complex objects of thought constructed by a mature, abstract reasoner on the basis of a careful analysis of the problem situation; they are not mere representations of the perceived situation itself.

What would really good, vintage hypothetico-deductive thinking sound like were it verbalized aloud? Following are two made-up examples:

> Well, what I have just seen gives me the idea that W and *only W might* have the power to cause or produce Z, that the presence of X *might* prevent W from causing Z, and that Y *might* prove to be wholly irrelevant to the occurrence of Z. Now if this idea is right, then Z should occur *only* when W is present and X is absent, whether or not Y is also present. Let's see if these are, in fact, the only conditions under which Z does occur.... Oh no, that idea is shot down because I've just found that Z also occurs sometimes when neither W nor X is present. I wonder why. Hey, I have another idea....

> I am a college student of extremely modest means. Some crazy psychologist interested in something called "formal-operational thinking" has just promised to pay me $20 if I can make a coherent logical argument for the proposition that the federal government should under no circumstances ever give or lend money to impecunious college students. Now what could a nonperson who believed *that* possibly say by way of supporting argument? Well, I suppose he *could* offer this line of reasoning....

INTRAPROPOSITIONAL VERSUS INTERPROPOSITIONAL. Children of elementary school age can construct mental, symbolic representations of concrete reality and can also evaluate their empirical validity under many circumstances. They might, for example, quite explicitly formulate the proposition that there is still the same number of objects in the two rows after one has been spread out (number conservation test), and then might prove it to you by counting the objects in each row. Thus, middle-childhood subjects can produce, comprehend, and verify propositions. There is, nonetheless, an important difference between them and formal-operational subjects in the way they deal with propositions. The child considers them singly, in isolation from one another, testing each in its turn against the relevant empirical data. Since what is confirmed or inferred in each case is but a single claim about the external world, Piaget calls concrete-operational thinking *intrapropositional*—that is, thinking within the confines of a single proposition. Although a formal-operational thinker also naturally tests individual propositions against reality, she does something more that lends a very special quality to her reasoning. She reasons about the logical relations that hold *among* two or more propositions, a more subtle and abstract form of reasoning that Piaget terms *interpropositional*. The less mature mind looks only to the *factual* relation between one proposition and the empirical reality to which it refers; the more mature mind looks also or instead to the *logical* relation between one proposition and another.

The first of the two examples of hypothetico-deductive reasoning given in the previous section illustrates interpropositional reasoning particularly well. The individual's initial theory asserts ("proposes") that the logical relation called *conjunction* holds among three propositions: W is the sole cause of Z *and* (conjunction relation) X neutralizes W's causal effect *and* (conjunction relation) Y is not causally related to Z at all. Conjunction is also used to interconnect a set of hypothetical propositions or predictions about external reality: The conjunction of W present and X absent produces ("conjoins with") the presence of Z, and none of the other logically possible conjunctions involving the presence or absence of W and X will yield Z. Moreover, the conjunction of Y's presence or absence with the foregoing changes nothing. There are other logical relations that our imaginary subject might also apply to various combinations of these propositions, although she would not necessarily use the logician's terminology in describing them. For instance, she would understand that, within her theory, the presence of Z (one proposition) *implies* (logical relation) the presence of W (another proposition), whereas the reverse implication, W implies Z, does not hold, owing to the *incompatibility* (logical relation) between X and Z. Above all, the "if...then" phrasing in her second sentence shows that she knows that the entire complex of conjoined propositions constituting her theory logically *implies* the entire complex of conjoined propositions which constitutes her predicted reality. That is, she establishes a logical relation between two *sets* of propositions, the constituent propositions of each of which she has already knitted together by logical connectives. This is certainly "interpropositional" thinking in the fullest sense.

It should now be clear why this type of reasoning is also called *formal*. To reason that one proposition "logically implies" ("contradicts," etc.) another is fundamentally to reason about the relation between a pair of *statements*, not about any *empirical phenomena* to which these statements might refer. The statements in question may not be factually correct assertions about the real objects and events to which they refer; they may not refer to real objects and events in the first place; indeed, they may not even refer to anything at all, real or imaginary. Consider the following bit of formal reasoning: If A is true in all cases where B is true, then B will be false in all cases where A is false (or equivalently, if B implies A, then not A implies not B). This is logically valid reasoning, but its validity has to do with the way the statements are related, not with the referential meaning of A and B (they have been given none). It is now apparent why the Osherson and Markman (1975) questions might differentiate a formal reasoner from a concrete one. The formal reasoner knows that the experimenter is asking about the logical truth or falsity of pairs of statements as a joint function of what they state (affirmation, negation) and how they are logically linked (conjunction, disjunction); this person knows that the experimenter is not really asking anything about the color of chips. As Piaget put it, whereas concrete operations are "first degree" operations that deal with real objects and events, formal operations are "second degree" operations that deal with the propositions or statements produced by the first degree, concrete ones (Inhelder & Piaget, 1958, p. 254).

The second of the two hypothetical hypothetico-deductive reasoners described in the previous section illustrates a closely related insight—namely, that one does not have to believe something is either true or just in order to argue for it (although it sure helps). Formal-operational thinkers understand that logical arguments have a disembodied and passionless life of their own, at least in principle. Concrete-operational thinkers have enough trouble seeing what logically follows from credible premises, let alone from premises that actually contradict one's knowledge, beliefs, or values.

Researchers are still clarifying the nature of formal operational thinking. For a useful discussion of various issues in this area, see a volume by Overton (1990) and an exchange between Byrnes (1988a, 1988b) and Keating (1988).

OTHER DEVELOPMENTAL TRENDS DURING MIDDLE CHILDHOOD AND ADOLESCENCE

Although Piaget's pioneering work mapped out much of the cognitive change beyond early childhood, more recent research by other investigators has identified additional developmental trends that must be incorporated into a satisfactory account of cognitive development. The following trends seem to us to be the most important.

Increase in Domain-Specific Knowledge (Expertise)

Continuing a theme of Chapter 3, we observe that as children grow older and accumulate learning experiences they gradually acquire a great deal of knowledge and skill in many specific areas or domains. It may seem puzzling to you that this trite-sounding view could be regarded as either new or interesting. Surely the idea that cognitive development might consist largely of the accumulation of knowledge would not surprise many psychologists past or present; anyone with experience with children would not exactly be bowled over by it either. It just sounds like commonsensical, layperson-type developmental theory, if anything does. However, there is a good reason why the present incarnation of this old developmental saw deserves our serious attention. The reason is that its proponents are doing more than just affirming it as a possible alternative to Piagetian-type stage theories. They are also painstakingly trying to build up, through careful research, a precise and detailed picture of exactly what the acquisition of expertise in a domain does to and for our heads—that is, they are trying to discover all of the powerful and pervasive effects of the acquisition of domain-specific knowledge on our problem-solving and other information-processing activities in that domain (Carey, 1985a; Chi, Glaser, & Farr, 1988; Chi, Hutchinson, & Robin, 1989).

Chi and Glaser (1980) make a rough distinction between two components of human information processing relevant to expertise: (1) a knowledge structure or content component that can be conceptualized as a network of concepts and relations; and (2) a set of processes or strategies for performing a sequence of cognitive actions on the content. Chi and Glaser identify several novice-expert differences within the knowledge structure or content component in the domain of elementary physics, a richly structured area of knowledge.

First and most obvious, the physics expert simply knows more different domain-specific concepts than does the novice. Whereas the novice might be able to define and recognize a few concepts such as mass, density, and acceleration, the expert also commands many others (e.g., force, momentum, coefficient of friction). Moreover, a physics expert can represent physics problems at a deeper, more abstract, and causal level. The expert may, for example, categorize together problems on the basis of a physics principle, such as the conservation of energy, rather than a surface similarity, such as the presence of coiled springs. In addition, the expert's stored representation of each concept is apt to be richer than the novice's, in that it contains more conceptual relations and features. For the novice, mass may only be represented as related to the concepts of weight and density. In contrast, the expert's mental representation of mass may additionally include acceleration, force, and other related concepts. This means that each of the expert's concepts is closely connected in long-term memory with many other concepts. As a consequence, there are multiple routes from each concept to each other concept in the expert's stored conceptual network; we might say that each concept is multiply cross-referenced in the expert's mental dictionary of physics concepts. These multiple interconnections make it likely that thinking of any one concept will cue the retrieval from memory of related concepts and concept features. Consistent with this claim is Larkin's (1979) finding that an expert in physics is more likely than a novice to recall small groups of conceptually related equations in rapid bursts, with pauses in between groups, as if related equations were stored together as chunks in the expert's long-term memory.

Chi and Glaser (1980; Glaser & Chi, 1988) also describe differences between novices and experts in the cognitive processes or strategies they use in solving problems (component 2 earlier). For example, experts are apt to be more planful. They are more likely to analyze and categorize a problem before attempting to solve it. This initial processing may then provide the expert with an effective plan of action to execute in the actual solution of the problem. Here also, the expert's vast and richly organized memory store of knowledge affords him or her many advantages over the novice. For instance, a very effective way to solve a new problem is to notice its similarity to some other problem that one already knows how to solve. The noticing is a matter of memory (recognition memory) and so is the knowing how to solve it (stored procedural knowledge). Obviously, this "memory method" of solving problems can be used much more often by the expert than by the novice because the expert has traces of many more previously solved problems stored in long-term memory.

This example illustrates a significant point about how experts differ from novices. We usually think of the expert as the more able reasoner of the two, as the one who is more capable of extended chains of complex inferences or judgments (within his or her area of expertise). Although this is undoubtedly true, it is also true that experts often solve problems by quick and easy remembering that novices must try to solve by slow and laborious reasoning. In such instances, experts appear more cognitively mature and sophisticated than the novice because their mental processing is so fast, effortless, and effective. In reality, however, this processing may have been more "mnemonic" than "rational" in nature, more a matter of recognition and recall memory than of complex reasoning and fancy mental computation. And, of course, the experts' processing was not fast, effortless, and effective *despite* the fact that it involved "mere remembering" rather than "sophisticated ratiocination." Rather, it had these qualities precisely *because* of this fact— that is, because it involves the relatively automatic processes of detecting familiar problem patterns and executing overlearned solution procedures. It normally takes many years for a person to become expert in any complex domain. During that extended period the person may gradually acquire the ability to recognize and respond adaptively to a surprisingly large number of domain-relevant problem patterns. For example, the work of Herbert Simon and his colleagues suggests that chess experts have learned to recognize and react appropriately to some 50,000 chessboard patterns (Anderson, 1980). Thus, if one benefit of expertise is the ability to think better in the area of one's expertise, another is the ability to solve many problems in that area without having to think much at all.

Expert knowledge appears to facilitate cognition not only by supplying ready-made solutions or strategies but also by freeing mental capacity. When concepts, technical terms, problem patterns, and other domain-specific data are highly familiar, they require less time and mental energy to process. This in turn means that more of them can be attended to or held in working memory at one time, effectively increasing the person's attentional or short-term-memory capacity. This increase in capacity has at least two beneficial effects. First, since more units of information can be held in focal attention or working memory at the same time, more of them can be compared and related to one another. Complex tasks often demand the active interrelating of a number of dimensions or other pieces of information. Second, this functional increase in information-processing capacity creates some unused mental work space or mental energy that can be devoted to higher-level, "executive," or "metacognitive," processing. The person has some capacity left over for selecting problem-solving strategies, for regulating their activity, for monitoring their effectiveness, and for other vital managerial activities.

In what domains are children and adolescents likely to build up complex knowledge structures through years of experience and learning? The physics example makes us think first of those domains in which they receive extensive formal schooling. In this vein, Carey (1985a) has shown that major changes in the content and structure of children's biological knowledge take place between the ages of 4 and 10 years (see also Chapter 3). Piaget and others had observed that young children tend to attribute the properties of life and consciousness to certain nonliving things, especially things that are capable of autonomous movement (e.g., Flavell, 1963). For example, children might say that a fire is "alive." Piaget referred to this tendency as *animism* and believed that it reflected an early developmental stage of thinking. However, Carey (1985a) argued that young children's animistic responses reflect a lack of domain-specific (i.e., biological) knowledge rather than a more general, stage-type level of cognitive ability.

Many other candidate domains are less closely associated with formal education. As examples, children gradually build up elaborate knowledge structures through countless hours of experience and practice with various sports, games, hobbies, all sorts of cultural artifacts and institutions, and numerous forms of social interaction and exchange. For instance, 10- to 13-year old tennis novices and experts show many of the knowledge differences found with adults in the domain of physics (McPherson & Thomas, 1989). And a 4-year-old's expert knowledge about dinosaurs exhibits the characteristics of experts in general (Gobbo & Chi, 1986). In later years people similarly build up knowledge structures in the occupational domains they enter. The above reference to social interaction implies that the development of social as well as nonsocial cognition can be conceptualized in terms of domain-specific knowledge acquisition. For example, young children appear to be experts at using deception, teasing, pretense, and language to manipulate and cooperate with others within the familiar domain of family—siblings and parents (Dunn, 1988). As in the domains of physics, chess, and so on, a vast store of organized social knowledge allows us to recognize and respond appropriately to a very large number of specific patterns of input from our everyday "social chessboard." This memory-based pattern-recognition process often allows us to behave reasonably in many complex social situations without benefit of much, if any, complex social reasoning (Higgins, 1981; Shantz, 1983).

For children, expertise is particularly important because their more abstract knowledge allows them to generate causal explanations about that domain. These causal explanations in turn constrain the inferences they generate about novel instances. For example, 4- to 7-year-old experts on dinosaurs used their causal understanding of categories of dinosaurs to constrain their inferences about novel dinosaurs: "It's a meat-eater because it has sharp teeth" (Chi et al., 1989). Novices had to use animals in general as a source for inferences, so they often drew on information about the novel dinosaur that was irrelevant to assigning it to a family of dinosaurs: "Could walk real fast cause he has giant legs." In other words, the experts sought out critical features in the novel dinosaur that allowed them to assign it to a category of dinosaurs, then generated additional inferences on the basis of this initial classification (e.g., "he's pretty dangerous"). Thus, the experts were reasoning deductively in this domain at an age not known for such a skill.

The evidence is beginning to suggest, then, that having a great deal of knowledge and experience in an area has all sorts of positive, beneficial effects on the quality of one's cognitive functioning in that area. Unlike the novice, the expert attends to and keeps in mind all the right features of the problem situation, selects the right problem strategies and uses them in the right ways, and generally engages in sustained feats of reasoning that appear highly logical in quality. In short, the expert looks very, very smart—very, very "cognitively mature"—when functioning in his or her area of expertise.

If, as is often the case (A. L. Brown & DeLoache, 1978), the novice in any given domain is a young child and the expert is an older child or adult, what may we be led to conclude? We may think we are witnessing a fundamental developmental shift of the infancy-postinfancy variety. It may appear that the younger novice and the older expert are in qualitatively different stages of intellectual development and that we are dealing with two very different cognitive machines. However, several considerations may lead us to temper that judgment. The older person may appear to be a much less mature and logical thinker when operating in domains in which he or she lacks expertise. Both everyday observation and a good deal of research (E. E. Jones, 1990; Nisbett & Ross, 1980; Shaklee, 1979) attest to the fact that even highly intelligent and well-educated adults often fail to process information adequately and to think rationally and logically. In fact, adults even resort to sensorimotor-like thinking when encountering a highly novel robot whose movements they try to control (Granott, 1991). Finally, even if it is in the person's area of expertise, a particularly complex and difficult problem might at least temporarily overtax the information-processing system and thus greatly diminish the quality of reasoning and problem-solving activity on that problem.

Conversely, a young child may show cognition of distinctly better quality in those few domains in which he has already achieved some expertise. Even in domains in which he is a relative novice, he may at least show glimmerings of good thinking, especially on very easy problems. We can usually make a problem easier for a young child by (1) stripping away all but the most essential elements of the problem; and (2) making the problem setting and problem elements as familiar and meaningful as possible to the child (Brown, Bransford, Ferrara, & Campione, 1983). Both procedures either reduce the information-processing demands the problem makes on the child or, which amounts to the same thing, they increase the child's capacity to process information effectively. Recall from Chapter 3 that recent research has demonstrated unexpected competencies in young children. These competencies have usually surfaced only in task situations made easier by these procedures.

If the cognitive differences between young children and their elders proved to be largely due to differences in knowledge, we would hesitate to speak of qualitatively different "stages" of cognitive development. First, a "difference in knowledge" has more of a quantitative than qualitative sound to it. It suggests one kind of mind with two different amounts of accumulated knowledge rather than two basically different kinds of mind. It does not suggest a fundamentally different intellectual modus operandi, as is at least arguably the case for the young infant as contrasted with the child and adult. Second, neither younger children nor their elders would be completely and consistently "in" any single stage, in the strong sense of always functioning cognitively in the general manner and at the general level specified by that stage (Flavell, 1982a, 1982b). In domains in which they have considerable knowledge, both age groups would perform above their usual levels. In domains in which their knowledge is skimpy or nonexistent, they would perform below those levels—sometimes well below. Neither group would be consistently enough like itself, nor consistently enough unlike the other group, to warrant a sharp division into two different "stages." The recent trend in the field has been to highlight the cognitive competencies of young children (see Chapter 3), the cognitive shortcomings of adults, and the cognitive inconsistencies of both, effectively pushing from both ends of childhood toward the middle and blurring the difference between the two groups.

Does this view of development as a number of novice-to-expert shifts rather than as general Piagetian cognitive changes mean that postinfancy cognitive development is primarily the acquisition of knowledge in many specific domains? Many cognitive developmentalists are currently pondering this issue, and it is far from settled (see Carey, 1985b, for a thought-provoking discussion of this question). Our own intuitions are that the acquisition-of-expertise model will *not* account for all of cognitive growth. As Markman (1979) points out, when adults are in a novel situation they know a great deal more than do children about how to move quickly from novice to expert status. They are experts at becoming experts. They quickly detect what it is they do not understand, have more potential solutions in their cognitive bank from which to draw, and more easily see similarities between the current situations and other previously encountered situations. Experts know how to acquire new relevant information, and to hone their new skills.

A final question about knowledge remains: Is the child's mind simply "a collection of different and unrelated mindlets" (Flavell, in press) or are there systemwide cognitive frameworks? The current thinking about whether cognitive development involves domain-general structures or domain-specific knowledge is as follows (Case, 1992; Siegler, 1989b; Sternberg, 1989a). Rather than debate the two positions it is more useful to try to identify in what ways representation and processing are domain-general and in what ways they are domain-specific, and how the two types of knowledge develop together during childhood and interact during problem solving. For example, Siegler (1989b) suggests that children tend to use backup strategies (strategies other than simply retrieving the answer) in all domains when they are unsure of the correct answer. However, the particular backup strategies they choose (e.g., counting on the fingers), and the efficiency with which they use them, are specific to each domain (reading, addition, subtraction). For further discussion of various issues regarding domain-specific cognition in children and adolescents, see the special issue of *Merrill-Palmer Quarterly* ("Children's Cognitive...," 1989) devoted to this topic. We return to this question in Chapter 8.

Greater Information-Processing Capacity

Suppose someone were to read aloud to you a random sequence of numbers at the rate of one per second. Your task is to reproduce the sequence exactly, right after you hear it. The experimenter might begin, for instance, with "3-4-5-9," and you immediately respond "3459." She then tries a 5-digit series, then a 6-digit one, and continues making them longer and longer until you reach your limit, sometimes referred to as your *memory span* for this kind of input. Your memory span provides an estimate of your processing capacity. A main legacy from the information-processing approach (Chapter 1) is evidence that the human cognitive system has significant limitations on its information-processing capacity: Each processing step requires a certain amount of time and cognitive resources for its execution; only a small number of units or "chunks" of information can be kept active in working memory at once. These limitations are more severe in children than adults. For example, digit, letter, and word spans increase from 4 or 5 for 5-year-olds, to 6 for 9-year-olds, to 7 for adults (Dempster, 1981, but see Halford, Maybery, & Bain, 1988, for lower estimates).

The gradual increase with age in capacity makes possible more complex and higher-order forms of cognition as well as greater recall (Chapter 6). This argument has been presented and critically examined in many publications (e.g., Brainerd & Reyna, 1988; Case, 1985, 1992; Chapman, 1987; Chi & Rees, 1983; Dempster, 1981, 1985; Flavell, 1982a; Halford, in press; McLaughlin, 1963; Pascual-Leone, 1970; Rabinowitz et al., 1989). The general idea is that below a certain age children may find it difficult or impossible to engage in certain types of mental activity, acquire concepts of a certain level of complexity, and the like; the reason is that doing so would require them to attend to and cognitively interrelate more pieces of information than their working-memory capacities can handle. As capacity gradually increases with increasing age, such interrelating of information becomes possible and cognitive growth can occur. The neo-Piagetian approaches described in Chapter 1 provide many examples of this argument, particularly the idea that increases in capacity allow children to move to the next stage. Stage-like changes are especially likely if the increased capacity is accompanied by relevant experience and knowledge.

Capacity demands contribute not only to developmental differences but also to domain or task differences. Neo-Piagetian Robbie Case (1985) has argued that one cause of inconsistent performance across domains is that the tasks associated with these domains differ in difficulty, especially in the complexity of their required mental operations. If solving a task in domain A requires more capacity (e.g., requires a consideration of more features) because of its complexity than solving a task in domain B, then cognition will appear to be domain specific rather than domain general. If the difficulty of the tasks is equated, then cognition appears to be more domain general. For example, when Marini and Case (1989) controlled the complexity of a balance beam task and an understanding-of-emotions task, the sequence and rate of development were similar across the two domains. In addition, other investigators have demonstrated that the more capacity required to solve a task the poorer the child's performance on those tasks, ranging from role taking (Lapsley & Quintana, 1989) to class inclusion (Halford & Leitch, 1989; Rabinowitz et al., 1989).

What is it, exactly, that determines a person's capacity? Speed of processing seems to be the main contributor (Case et al., 1982; Dempster, 1985; Henry & Millar, 1991; Hitch, Halliday, & Littler, 1989; Kail, 1991a). How fast a child can identify a number, read a word aloud, or decide if a toy standing upside down is identical to a toy standing right side up influences that child's capacity. The faster the processing, the greater the amount of information that can be handled at any one time. This would amount to an increase in *functional*, or available, capacity because it would allow the child to keep more items or processes "alive" or "on stage" at once in active, working memory.

The main tool for assessing speed of processing is reaction time, mentioned in Chapter 1 as a measure often used by information-processing researchers. Reaction time is the latency between the presentation of a stimulus and the person's response (pressing a button, saying a word). Studies of reaction time (Hale, 1990; Kail, 1986, 1991b, 1991c) support the above argument that differences in speed of processing, believed to underlie differences in capacity, cause differences in performance across tasks and across ages.

First, it is clear that children have faster reaction times on some tasks than on others. For example, in one study (Hale, 1990) four tasks given to 10- , 12- , and 15-year-olds and adults differed in speed (from fastest to slowest) as follows: (1) choice reaction time (pressing the left response button if the stimulus was an arrow pointing to the left and the right response button if the arrow pointed to the right), (2) letter matching (pressing the left button if two letters are different letters of the alphabet and pressing the right button if they are the same letters, even if one is uppercase and the other is lowercase), (3) mental rotation (pressing one of two buttons to indicate whether two flags, which may be in different spatial orientations, have stars in the upper left-hand corner or upper right-hand corner), and (4) abstract matching (pressing one of two buttons to indicate whether the set of letters on the left or the right was most like the set at the bottom of the screen; sets could vary in their letters, the number of letters, or their orientation). The tasks with slower processing seem to be more complex, and presumably involve cognitive processes more than simple motor responses to a stimulus.

Second, speed of processing on all tasks increases with age. However, the most important outcome from these experiments was that the rate and pattern of the developmental improvement was the same on all tasks. This became clear when researchers compared the children's and adults' latencies on a given task (e.g., Hale, 1990; Kail, 1986, 1991a, 1991b). On the four tasks described above, Hale (1990) found that on *all* tasks the 10-year-olds were approximately 1.8 times slower than college students, 12-year-olds were 1.6 times slower, and 15-year-olds were as fast as college students. That is, children executed all processes more slowly than adults by the same constant multiplier. In addition, the pattern of all tasks was a steady increase in speed during early and middle childhood and less change during adolescence. Kail's (1991b) analysis of 72 studies involving diverse ages and tasks strengthens the conclusion that, at least from age 4 on, there is a general, systemwide developmental change in processing speed that indicates some coherence and domain-generality in the processing system. This developmental across-the-board increase in processing speed could increase the available capacity during development, which in turn would permit more advanced cognition in the way suggested by the neo-Piagetians. This systemwide developmental change in speed of processing is believed to reflect a maturational, "hard wired," neurological change.

Does experience play any role? Consider a rough analogy to physical capacity, such as muscular strength. Obviously, two people could differ in "raw muscle power" as evidenced, for example, by how hard they could push or squeeze something. We could say that the individual with more raw muscular strength had more physical-strength capacity than the other person. More specifically, his absolute quantity of resources is greater. However, two people with identical *structural* physical-strength capacities might nevertheless differ considerably in their *functional* (usable, actual, effective) capacities in specific physical tasks. That is, they would differ in how well they can do with what they have despite the quantitative similarity of their physical, maturation-based resources. Experts at karate, boxing, wrestling, shotputting, weightlifting, golf, and the like can deploy and exploit their structural, raw-muscle-power capacities far more fully and effectively in their areas of skill than can physically identical nonexperts. They know how to deliver the maximum force possible at precisely the right moment and place and can thereby get considerably more mileage (total functional capacity) than nonexperts can out of a fixed and limited physical potential (the structural contribution to functional capacity).

Turning this analogy to mental activity, during development "raw mental muscle power" or structural processing capacity increases because neurological maturation permits faster processing. Full functional capacity appears to reflect not only this maturational change but also various experience-based changes in the use of resources. For example, older children and adults may be more likely than younger children to use their world knowledge and activities such as rehearsal or organizational strategies (see Chapter 6). In the digit span task described earlier, older children may be able to remember 149217761918 because it can be chunked into 1492, 1776, and 1918, important dates in history (Lachman, Lachman, & Butterfield, 1979).

Similarly helpful are external aids, such as pencil and paper, libraries, computers, and other people's minds. The skillful use of such external aids or "mental prostheses" can greatly increase the amount of information and information processing an individual can manage per unit time. There is a physical-capacity analogue here also, although it is a bit absurd: An athlete could lift much heavier weights than his structural capacity permits by enlisting the aid of his friends or, better still, by using a crane. Another type of experience-based difference in efficiency is that people of various ages use similar mental activities, such as recognizing an item, but these activities are more difficult, and therefore take more effort, for younger children. Consequently, younger children use up more of their capacity when performing these activities, leaving little capacity for other activities. Many operations undoubtedly become faster or otherwise less capacity-consuming in the course of years of practice, experience, and accumulation of knowledge. Highly practiced operations in a particular domain or task can be performed more automatically and thus less effortfully in that domain. Indeed, the ever-present possibility that these factors may be at work in any task situation makes it difficult to assess the contribution of maturation-based structural capacity to total functional capacity. On any given task in which older children behave as though they command more information-processing capacity than younger children, it is hard to be sure that experientially based factors like strategy use and faster processing due to practice are not the sole causes. Whatever the relative contribution of structural and nonstructural causes, however, the age increase in children's effective, usable information-processing capacities appears to constitute a very important "core" developmental trend during the postinfancy years.

Advances in Metacognition

Preschool and elementary school subjects were instructed to study a small set of items until they were sure they could recall them all (Flavell, Friedrichs, & Hoyt, 1970). Older children studied them for a while, judged that they were ready, and usually were: They then usually went on to recall every single item correctly. Younger children studied them for a while, judged that they were ready, and usually were not: They usually failed to recall some of the items. It seems that the preschoolers could not monitor and evaluate their current memory capabilities as accurately as the older children could. Monitoring and evaluating one's current memory capabilities is an example of *metacognition*, and this study is only one of many showing marked developmental advances in metacognitive skills during middle childhood and adolescence.

What is metacognition? It has usually been broadly and rather loosely defined as any knowledge or cognitive activity that takes as its object, or regulates, any aspect of any cognitive enterprise (e.g., Flavell, 1981a). It is called *meta*cognition because its core meaning is "cognition about cognition." Metacognitive skills are believed to play an important role in many types of cognitive activity, including oral communication of information, oral persuasion, oral comprehension, reading comprehension, writing, language acquisition, perception, attention, memory, problem solving, logical reasoning, social cognition, and various forms of self-instruction and self-control. Because of its broad applicability, the concept is reintroduced several times in subsequent chapters; for example, metamemory in Chapter 6 and metacommunication in Chapter 7. Also, the idea that knowledge and cognition can take cognitive as well as noncognitive objects appears in our discussion of theory of mind (Chapter 3) and social cognition (Chapter 5). Metacognition is closely related to children's theory of mind in that both examine concepts about thinking. However, research on theory of mind focuses more on younger children, on everyday activities often social-emotional in nature rather than "cold cognition" and academic tasks (P. L. Harris, 1990), and on the general nature of the mind, especially understanding sources of knowledge and the nature of representations. It also could be argued that Piagetian formal-operational thinking is metacognitive in nature because it involves thinking about propositions, hypotheses, and imagined possibilities—cognitive objects all. The "sense of the game" described in the next section is also clearly a form of metacognition; it is given a section of its own only because we want to highlight it. Metacognition or related concepts (e.g., executive processes) have also seen service in the fields of cognitive psychology, intelligence, artificial intelligence, human abilities, social-learning theory, cognitive behavior modification, personality development, gerontology, and education. For example, metacomponents, a close cousin of metacognition, play a central role in Sternberg's (1985) theory of intelligence.

Different theorists have conceptualized and classified the domain of metacognition in somewhat different ways. Following are some of the sources that contain useful discussions of the concept: Borkowski & Turner, 1990; A. L. Brown et al., 1983; Chi, 1987; Flavell, 1981a, 1981b, 1987; Forrest-Pressley, MacKinnon, & Waller, 1985; Kluwe, 1987; Kurtz, 1990; Weinert & Kluwe, 1987; Wellman, 1985b; and Yussen, 1985. As we see it, most of what is considered metacognition refers to *metacognitive knowledge* and *metacognitive monitoring and self-regulation*.

METACOGNITIVE KNOWLEDGE. This refers to the segment of your acquired world knowledge that has to do with cognitive matters. It is the knowledge and beliefs you have accumulated through experience and stored in long-term memory that concern not politics or football or electronics or needlepoint or some other domain, but the human mind and its doings. Metacognitive knowledge can be roughly subdivided into knowledge about *persons*, *tasks*, and *strategies*.

The person category includes any knowledge and beliefs you might acquire concerning what human beings are like as cognitive processors. It can be further subcategorized into knowledge and beliefs about cognitive differences within people, cognitive differences between people, and cognitive similarities among all people—that is, about universal properties of human cognition. Examples of the within-people subcategory might be your knowledge that you are better at psychology than physics or your belief that your friend learns better by reading than by listening. An example of the between-people category could be your belief that your parents are more sensitive to the needs and feelings of others than many of their neighbors are (a belief about others' social-cognitive skills). The cognitive-universals subcategory is the most interesting of the three. It refers to what you have come to know or believe about what the human mind in general is like—any person's mind, from Shakespeare to Hitler to your next door neighbor to your own. For instance, you did not have to read this book to sense that everyone's short-term memory is of limited capacity and highly fallible. Similarly, you are aware of the important fact that sometimes people understand, sometimes they do not understand, and sometimes they understand incorrectly, or *mis*understand. You also know that what you cannot recall now you may be able to recall later. More generally, you have learned that the human mind is a somewhat unpredictable and unreliable cognitive device, although still a remarkable one. We believe that people the world over must acquire considerable metaknowledge of this subcategory and also must make important use of it in managing their lives. Try this thought experiment to convince yourself of its usefulness: Imagine how you would fare as an adult in any human society if you were incorrigibly ignorant of the fact that you and other people sometimes misunderstand or forget things.

The task category has two subcategories. One subcategory has to do with the nature of the information you encounter and deal with in any cognitive task. You have learned that the nature of this information has important effects on how you will manage it. For example, you know from experience that complex and unfamiliar information is liable to be difficult and time-consuming for you to comprehend and remember. You have also learned that having only skimpy and unreliable information at your disposal implies that judgments and conclusions based on this information are apt to be wrong. The other subcategory concerns the nature of the task demands. Even given the exact same information to work with, you have learned that some tasks are more difficult and demanding than others. For instance, you know that it is easier to recall the gist of a story than its exact wording. You also know that it is generally easier to recognize something when you see it than to recall it outright; recognition memory is usually better than recall memory.

As for the strategy category, there is much you might have learned about what means or strategies are likely to succeed in achieving what cognitive goals—in comprehending *X*, remembering *Y*, solving problem *Z*, and so on. For instance, if someone asks you what a person might do to memorize a phone number you could no doubt say that the person might try rehearsing it. You also probably have knowledge of more sophisticated cognitive strategies, such as the strategy of spending more time studying more important or less well-learned material than less important or better-learned material. Moreover, if you are a metacognitively "intelligent novice" (A. L. Brown & Palinscar, 1985), you know you do not have the background knowledge needed in some domain about which you are reading, such as twelfth-century Japanese poetry, but you know how to go about getting that knowledge by stopping occasionally to summarize or to rehearse important points. You know that such activities are not necessary in your area of expertise.

Finally, the bulk of your metacognitive knowledge actually concerns combinations of, or interactions among, two or three of these three categories. To illustrate knowledge of an interaction between strategy and task, you would undoubtedly select a different preparation strategy if your task were to give a talk on some topic than if you only needed to follow a talk on that topic given by someone else.

The mind is a rich and varied instrument. It comprises different, but related, mental activities such as comprehending, remembering, attending, and inferring. Do children appreciate the differentiation and integration of the mind? For example, most children memorize the Pledge of Allegiance long before they understand it. And they sometimes even distort the words of a memorized song because of their lack of comprehension, and encode "Gladly, the Cross-Eyed Bear" instead of "Gladly the Cross I'd Bear." Are they aware of such discrepancies between memorizing and comprehending? These two mental activities are an interesting case in point, for they are highly interconnected in many cognitive tasks, yet differ in important ways. One important difference is that some strategies that help us remember (e.g., rehearsal) provide little help in understanding. Conversely, some strategies that help our comprehension (e.g., looking up unfamiliar words in a dictionary) are of little help in remembering. Another difference is that although almost any type of material can be memorized, only organized material such as words, sentences, paragraphs, and stories can be said to be understood (Markman, 1981a). Finally, certain task variables have a large impact on one process, but little impact on the other. For example, the amount of material typically affects memorization much more than comprehension. Failure to understand the difference between memorizing and understanding can cause serious processing errors, as when a child fails to realize that rotely memorizing material does not ensure understanding.

To examine this issue, Lovett and Flavell (1990) showed first graders, third graders, and undergraduates three tasks—a list of words to be rotely memorized (memorization but not necessarily comprehension), a list of words to match up to a picture (comprehension but not necessarily memorization), and a list of words to both memorize and match. The experimenter asked the subjects to decide which of three strategies was the best way to prepare for each task. The strategies, uniquely suited to the above three tasks respectively, were rehearsal, word definition, which provided a verbal description of unfamiliar words, and a combination of the two. Lovett and Flavell also tested for subjects' knowledge about how different task variables differentially affect comprehension and memory tasks. They asked them which of two lists of words would be easier to learn for a memory test and which would be easier to learn for a comprehension test. The lists differed with respect to length, length and word familiarity (i.e., a short list of unfamiliar words vs. a long list of familiar words), and whether they formed a category (e.g., kinds of fruit).

Only the third graders and undergraduates showed some understanding that rehearsal would help memorization, and word definitions would help comprehension, but that each strategy would not help the other task appreciably. The variables task proved to be even more difficult. Only the undergraduates understood their differential effects. The pattern of errors suggests that the children understood memory better than they understood comprehension. In fact, they seemed to treat comprehension tasks as though they were memory tasks, as when they chose a rehearsal strategy for the comprehension task.

Further evidence that children increasingly see memory pervading the mind comes from research on their view of the conceptual structure of the mind (Fabricius et al., 1989; Schwanenflugel, Fabricius, & Alexander, 1991, 1992). Fabricius and co-workers (1989) asked 8- and 10-year-olds and undergraduates to rate the similarity of how the mind is used in various common activities. Each activity involved mainly comprehension (e.g., learning a new board game from the instructions on the box), inference (e.g., seeing a puddle on the ground and realizing it must have rained last night), memory, or attention. Techniques for assessing conceptual structures showed that children of both ages failed to differentiate memory from comprehension and attention, although they could differentiate it from inference. Interestingly, 10-year-olds and undergraduates tended to see the mind as organized around memory. That is, even though undergraduates differentiated among all four mental processes, they saw the most important relation among the various mental activities to be the degree to which they involved memory. In contrast, 8-year-olds organized mental activities primarily into the categories of conceptual (memory, listening, comprehension, inference) versus perceptual (attention, reading comprehension) activity. Thus, sorting out the various functions of the mind appears to be one of the latest metacognitive concepts to develop. Although young children can make simple differentiations among certain types of mental activities (e.g., Yussen, 1985), more subtle distinctions are not fully understood until adolescence.

Its exotic and high-sounding name may suggest to you that "metacognitive" knowledge must be qualitatively different from other kinds—perhaps a different species of knowledge altogether. However, there is no good reason to think it actually is fundamentally different. Like much other knowledge, metacognitive knowledge is acquired gradually and is somewhat domain-specific. Also, much as the chess expert automatically recognizes a familiar chessboard situation and automatically retrieves from memory a set of possible responses, so too may you recognize and respond appropriately to a familiar type of cognitive situation. You may categorize and respond to it as a situation that is going to be very difficult and time-consuming to get through, as one that is basically easy but needs careful attention to detail, as one that you will not be able to solve without outside help, as one that needs clearer specification, and so on. Finally, just like your knowledge about other things, your knowledge about cognitive enterprises can have various shortcomings. A given segment of your metacognitive knowledge may be insufficient, inaccurate, not reliable retrieved and used when appropriate, or otherwise flawed. Thus, although metacognitive knowledge is an important kind of knowledge, it is not a mysterious, qualitatively different kind.

METACOGNITIVE MONITORING AND SELF-REGULATION. A high school student settles down at her desk to do her homework. She may plan in what order to do the assignments, test herself on a few of the vocabulary items on tomorrow's test to see how much she has to study, check whether the vocabulary flash cards actually are helping her, and switch to a strategy of using each word in a sentence. These are monitoring and self-regulation activities. They develop hand in hand with metacognitive knowledge. Her metacognitive knowledge that she often makes careless adding errors leads her to double-check her solutions to some problem. In the opposite direction, her metacognitive monitoring and self-regulation can lead to new metacognitive knowledge, as when she learns that her own memory for word meanings is helped more by a meaning-based strategy than rote memorization.

These metacognitive strategies involved in monitoring and self-regulation can be roughly distinguished from straightforward cognitive strategies. The main function of a cognitive strategy is to help you achieve the goal of whatever cognitive enterprise you are engaged in. In contrast, the main function of a metacognitive strategy is to provide you with information about the enterprise or your progress in it. We might say that cognitive strategies are invoked to *make* cognitive progress, metacognitive strategies to *monitor* it. Other metacognitive monitoring and self-regulation activities are less strategy-like, as when the children in the study by Flavell and his colleagues (1970) described earlier decided when their recall was ready to be tested.

Metacognitive monitoring sometimes involves *metacognitive experiences*, which are cognitive or affective experiences that pertain to a cognitive enterprise. Examples include the feeling of puzzlement you may have after reading a section of instruction in your federal income tax form, or the thrilling "aha" you feel when you finally think of an interesting new angle for organizing a term paper that has stumped you for days. Metacognitive experiences can be brief or lengthy, simple or complex in content. For instance, you may sense only a momentary flicker of uncertainty or bafflement, or you may obsess at considerable length about whether you *really* understand what your friend is like, "deep down."

Metacognitive experiences can serve a variety of useful functions in ongoing cognitive enterprises. For instance, the sudden realization that you are not understanding what you have just been reading may instigate any of several adaptive actions: As examples, you may reread the passage, rethink what you already understand (or *thought* you understood), read ahead to see whether something further on clarifies the muddle, enlist someone else's help, or try to modify your task objective in such a way as to reduce the importance of the problem (Collins & Smith, 1982).

ISSUES AND APPLICATIONS. Metacognition clearly refers to many different phenomena. In fact, Ann Brown and her colleagues (1983) argue that the phenomena typically included in this broad domain may be collectively just too heterogeneous, just too different in both nature and developmental course, to warrant the use of any single cover term, such as *metacognition*. They think we might be better off retiring the term, or else restricting its use to stable and statable knowledge about cognition, and then studying various forms of cognitive regulation (monitoring, self-directing, etc.) as separate executive processes. Although metacognition may be a messy area to study, it is a particularly important one for two reasons. First, metacognition is a "tool of wide application." Metacognitive knowledge and experiences serve us well when we play chess, or solve physics problems, or engage in mental activity in any other knowledge domain. A great deal of metacognition can be usefully employed in any domain—for example, the metacognitive strategy of double-checking one's cognitive procedures and products. However, we will *not* further metastasize "metas" by labeling this a "metadomain." Second, metacognition has important applications in the field of education (e.g., Baker & Brown, 1984; A. L. Brown et al., 1983; A. L. Brown & Campione, 1990; Flavell, 1981a; Garner, 1990; Graham & Harris, 1989; Paris, 1988; Schneider & Pressley, 1989, chap. 7). Consider the cognitive activity of reading, for example. Baker (1982) cites research evidence that younger/poorer readers may show metacognitive or metacognitive-like deficits in no fewer than nine areas: (1) understanding the purposes of reading; (2) modifying reading strategies for different purposes; (3) identifying the important information in a passage; (4) recognizing the logical structure inherent in a passage; (5) considering how new information relates to what is already known;

(6) attending to syntactic and semantic constraints—for example, spontaneously correcting errors in the text; (7) evaluating text for clarity, completeness, and consistency; (8) dealing with failures to understand; (9) deciding how well the material has been understood. More recently, Garner (1990) has added the importance of children attributing their successful comprehension to their strategies.

As an example of area (2), there is some evidence that older/better readers are more likely than younger/poorer ones to expend additional effort on more demanding reading assignments, such as the assignment to study a text versus that of only skimming through it to find one specific piece of information (Forrest & Waller, 1979). Younger/poorer readers thus appear less sensitive to the need to tailor their reading activities to the specific demands and objectives of the reading task (A. L. Brown et al., 1983). More generally, they are less likely to allocate and reallocate their efforts and attention in an efficient, task-adaptive fashion over time. For instance, they do not concentrate most of their study efforts on those segments of the material that are currently most difficult or least well learned and hence currently most in need of study, and then strategically reallocate their study efforts to other, still-unmastered segments when those segments are mastered (A. L. Brown et al., 1983; Dufresne & Kobasigawa, 1989). The ability to deploy and redeploy one's cognitive forces intelligently over time in accord with changing needs and circumstances seems an essential one for adapting successfully to the complex and changeable life situations most of us face—both in school and out.

If metacognitive skills are useful in school learning and if students, especially younger ones, are deficient in them, an intriguing possibility arises: Perhaps these skills could and should be directly taught to children, as an integral part of the school curriculum. Ann Brown, Joseph Campione, Scott Paris, and others are currently investigating this possibility with respect to metacognitive skills in reading comprehension (A. L. Brown et al., 1983; A. L. Brown & Campione, 1990; Paris, 1988). It appears that these skills can be successfully taught, and that learning them improves children's reading comprehension markedly.

Development of a Sense of the Game

This putative developmental trend is based more on intuition than on solid research evidence and, consequently, you should be appropriately skeptical about it. As children develop, they gradually learn more and more about what "the game of thinking" is like and about how it is supposed to be played (Flavell, 1977, 1982a). We have seen (Chapter 3) that young children acquire schemas and scripts for "how things are supposed to go" in stories, daily routines, and the like. It seems likely that as they grow older they also build knowledge structures concerning "how things are supposed to go" in cognitive enterprises.

They might learn the following things, and doubtless many more. Tasks and problems usually have solutions. One normally has to engage in some sort of cognitive activity in order to solve them—that is, cognitive activity is the usual means to achieving ("scoring") goals in cognitive games. Some cognitive outcomes or end products are of better quality than others. They are likely to be of better quality (more true, more adaptive, more in accordance with the rules of the cognitive game) if they were arrived at by plausible or logically valid reasoning, if they can be justified or explained by appeal to sound evidence or compelling arguments, if they are not incoherent or self-contradictory, and the like. One is not playing by the rules of the cognitive game if one just picks an answer or solution at random, reasons illogically, ignores crucial evidence, tolerates contradictions or inconsistencies, and so on. Cognitive games do not have to have real-world meaning or significance to be playable (Donaldson, 1978). They are legitimate cognitive games even if they have no ecological significance or practical value. A cognitive game may be as decontextualized and unrelated to "real life" as a conundrum in a bridge or chess column, a problem in a logic test, a question on an intelligence test, and a cognitive task in a psychological experiment.

Good cognitive game players nearly always have a plan. For example, an older child is more apt than a younger one to search for information in a systematic and methodical fashion (A. L. Brown & DeLoache, 1978). Vurpillot (1968) gave children of different ages the task of comparing pairs of houses to determine whether they were identical. Some were, in fact, identical, whereas others showed differences in one or more pairs of corresponding windows. For instance, the top-left window of one house might have a different appearance from the top-left window of the other. Older children proved likelier than younger ones to approximate the ideal perceptual-attentional strategy for this task: Scan corresponding windows pair by pair in some systematic fashion that ensures that none will be missed—for example, scan column by column. If a difference is detected, stop—the houses are nonidentical. If no difference is detected after all pairs have been compared, stop—the houses are identical. The perceptual search of the young child is often, as here, incomplete and unsystematic in relation to what the task demands. It is, in a real sense, less "intelligent" than that of the older child in its lack of planning.

The fact that one has acquired a sense of the cognitive game does not imply that one will play it well. Although older children, adolescents, and adults usually do engage in higher-quality cognitive play than young children do, it is nevertheless true that the quality of their play is often not very high. As mentioned earlier in this chapter, even very bright and well-educated adults often fail to process information adequately and reason intelligently (Braine & Rumain, 1983; Kuhn, 1990; Nisbett & Ross, 1980; Shaklee, 1979; Winer, Hemphill, & Craig, 1988). In fact, adult cognition is frequently of poor quality—sometimes of surprisingly, even shockingly poor quality. Examples include the use of false analogies, preference for positive instances, neglect of alternative hypotheses, overreliance on familiar content, and the tendency to delete, change, or add premises (G. A. Miller & Cantor, 1982).

Yet, the fact that most of us can understand and appreciate the force of these claims—namely, that we often play the thinking game quite poorly—suggests to us that we *have* acquired a fair sense of what the game is about and how it *should* be played. We do not think that preschool children possess this sense. They have not yet learned about explanation, justification, evidence, hypotheses, proof, logical necessity, contradiction, and other intellectual creatures that figure importantly in the game (Bullock, Gelman, & Baillargeon, 1982; Carey, 1985b).

Improvement in Existing Competencies

When we think of cognitive development we naturally think of the acquisition of new knowledge and skills. However, cognitive development also consists of the further growth of knowledge and skills that already exist in the child's repertoire but only in rudimentary or immature form. We saw in Chapter 3 that preschoolers have more knowledge and skills than we used to think they had. However, virtually all of these competencies are still quite immature at this age and will undergo considerable further development during middle childhood and adolescence (A. L. Brown et al., 1983; Gelman & Baillargeon, 1983; Wellman, 1982). Similarly, competencies that first appear during middle childhood continue to develop in subsequent years (Danner, 1989). In fact, the period of time between first budding and final blooming of a cognitive acquisition can sometimes be surprisingly long (Flavell, 1971c). Thus, the final developmental trend discussed here is the prosaic but important one of further developing what one has already acquired.

In the course of development a cognitive competence can be improved or perfected in a number of closely related ways (A. L. Brown et al., 1983; Chandler & Chapman, 1991; Flavell, 1972, 1982b; Siegler, 1981; Wellman, 1982). As it develops, a competency may become more reliably accessed and used in any given task that calls for it. In fact, much of development seems to involve learning to use what one already has, rather than acquiring new "haves." When the competency first emerges it may be activated and properly used on one presentation of a task but not on the next presentation of that very same task. On an appearance-reality problem (see Chapter 3), for example, it is possible that a young child would correctly say that the fake egg *looks* like an egg but *really and truly* is a stone on one presentation of the fake egg but then fail to access his or her fragile and precarious grasp of the distinction on a subsequent presentation of the same fake object. Embryonic competencies tend to have this unreliable "now-you-see-them-now-you-don't" quality.

They also tend to be highly restricted and limited in their range of application, often seeming tightly bound or "welded" (A. L. Brown et al., 1983) to a few specific task situations. Here are two examples: (1) Preschoolers might at first be able to make an appearance-reality distinction in only a few familiar task situations; (2) preschoolers may be able to apply some of their number knowledge (see Chapter 3) only to small sets—for example, sets of two to four objects (Siegler, 1981). Thus, as a competency develops it not only becomes more reliably and dependably applied in any single appropriate situation, but it also extends its range of application to more and more appropriate situations (Fischer & Farrar, 1987). In addition to this extension of range, or generalization, there may also be some restriction of range, or differentiation. That is, children may initially apply a competency to some situations in which it should not be employed and then later restrict its use to appropriate situations only.

A competency may also further develop by changes in the relative weighting given by the child to different problem-solving rules or procedures and to different stimulus information in the task environment. For example, a younger child might possess two competing procedures for dealing with appearance-reality problems. If asked to report what the object really is or, alternatively, how it appears, the child may either: (1) use his or her budding understanding of the appearance-reality distinction to attend to and report correctly whichever of the two is requested; or (2) simply report whichever happens to be uppermost in consciousness when the question is asked—that is, whichever of the two is more cognitively salient to the child at that particular moment. For the young child, these competing strategies might have roughly equal weights, on average, and whichever wins out on a given task may depend on specific stimulus features or other properties of that task. As knowledge about the appearance-reality distinction improves, however, strategy (1) above would become increasingly dominant. A similar change in rule weightings seems to occur in Siegler's mathematical strategies described in Chapters 1 and 3. A child uses a variety of strategies for addition problems, but gradually learns that certain ones are most efficient for particular types of problems. It is apparent that such developmental changes in dominance relations among rules or strategies are closely related to the other changes described earlier. For instance, as the "correct" task-appropriate strategy becomes increasingly dominant over its competitors, it will be more reliably accessed and used on any given relevant task and also will be applied to an increasing number of such tasks.

Still other changes in existing competencies are related to these changes and to one another. For instance, competencies may become linked with other competencies to form larger systems of interrelated knowledge and skills. Competencies may also become more accessible to conscious reflection and verbal expression. Such changes may constitute or engender further development of these competencies. For example, once we become able to reflect on and deliberate about the distinction between appearance and reality, we may become capable of generating new ideas about the distinction and of identifying new and more subtle instances of it (Flavell et al., 1983).

Finally, concomitant with or in consequence of the just-mentioned changes, acquisitions that were fragile and unstable in early or middle childhood may become consolidated and solidified in adolescence or adulthood. Consider, for example, the Piagetian concepts of conservation of weight and transitivity of weight. To assess these competencies, the experimenter takes two identical balls of clay and puts one on each pan of a balance scale. The two pans remain horizontal—that is, in equilibrium—and the subject agrees that the two balls weigh the same. The balls are then removed from the scale and one of them is deformed in some way—for example, flattened into a pancake or rolled into a sausage shape. The subject would fail to evidence a belief in conservation of weight by denying that the two pieces of clay would necessarily still weigh the same and still depress the two scale pans equally. A nonconserver of weight is therefore someone who does not understand that object weight remains unchanged when object shape is changed. An individual would fail to show a recognition of the transitivity property of weight if, having established by using the balance that object A weighs the same as object B and that object B weighs the same as object C, he or she denied that A had to weigh the same as C. The same would be true if "less than" or "more than" were substituted for "the same as" in the foregoing sentence. Hence, subjects are said to recognize the transitive nature of weight relations if they understand that, for any weights A, B, and C; $A = B$ and $B = C$ always implies $A = C$; that $A < B$ and $B < C$ always implies $A < C$; and that $A > B$ and $B > C$ always implies $A > C$.

There is evidence that subjects' beliefs in both conservation and transitivity of weight, initially acquired during middle childhood, may become firmer as they move into adolescence and adulthood (S. A. Miller, 1973; S. A. Miller & Lipps, 1973; S. A. Miller, Schwartz, & Stewart, 1973). Recall from Chapter 2 that infants' tacit beliefs in the permanence of objects have been assessed by presenting them with "impossible" conditions that apparently violate the object-permanence rule and observing their surprise. Miller and his colleagues have similarly put older subjects' beliefs in weight conservation and transitivity to very severe tests by similar machinations. Their trick was to rig the scale balance with electromagnets so that it gave false weight information on any trial the experimenter chose. What does a subject who has previously demonstrated both beliefs say when confronted with, for example, a flattened ball that now inexplicably appears to weigh more than what had just been its exact duplicate, or a series of pairwise weighings of three objects that yields the startling information $A = B$, $B = C$, and $A < C$? In the case of the conservation belief, only a minority of elementary school subjects who had initially been diagnosed as weight conservers continued to maintain this belief in the face of such apparently disconfirming evidence. College students, on the other hand, showed considerably more fidelity to the conservation concept, although some of them did succumb. Transitivity of weight proved to be a sturdier concept. A minority rather than a majority of Miller's younger elementary school subjects abandoned it when given false feedback, and a significantly smaller proportion of his older elementary subjects abandoned it. Miller (1973) concluded that even after a child is usually considered to "have" a concept there may be developmental increases in the certainty with which the concept is held. Concepts become more consolidated and solidified during middle childhood and adolescence. (Because such research involves deception, we should add that the subjects *were* debriefed at the end of the experiment—that is, shown the trick and reassured that their original answer was correct.)

How do children improve their existing competencies? One obvious way is through using them, thus strengthening them and discovering the many situations in which they can be applied. Contextualists would note that the child does not have to do this alone. Children's many cognitive apprenticeships not only impart new competencies but also provide opportunities for perfecting those competencies. Adults can use hints to help the child access a relevant cognitive skill in a range of appropriate situations; by referring explicitly to a concept or strategy, adults may make it more conscious to the child. Much more than in the preschool period, middle childhood and adolescence offers an exciting range of possible adults and older peers outside of the home who can provide contexts for learning.

In this chapter we have identified some very important and substantial changes in thinking and knowledge that typically occur during the middle childhood and adolescent years. Let us now return to the question with which we began the chapter. Does the foregoing set of trends mean that cognitive development in the postinfancy years is not general-stage-like in any meaningful sense? There is no clear answer at this point. It is true that the concept of stage in general and Piaget's stages in particular have come under heavy fire (e.g., Brainerd, 1978a, 1978b; Flavell, 1971c, 1982b). Nevertheless, the issue remains controversial and some, particularly many of the neo-Piagetians, still continue to believe that a viable stage theory of cognitive growth may yet be possible (Case, 1985, 1992; Fischer, 1980; Flavell, 1982a; Halford, in press). Furthermore, it is very far from certain at present that all important postinfancy developmental changes can be explained by appeal to age increases in domain-specific knowledge, capacity, and accessibility (Markman, 1979). It simply is the case that the conservative term *trends* seems to be a more realistic descriptor than the more radical term *stages*, at least until some future Piaget can convince us that postinfancy developmental changes in the cognitive system are as truly fundamental and deep-lying as those that take place between early infancy and early childhood.

SCIENTIFIC THINKING

One important cognitive advance of middle childhood and adolescence is scientific thinking. This topic also happens to illustrate many of the trends presented in this chapter.

Scientific Concepts

An 11-month-old looks longer at the impossible event of a small cylinder making a toy bug roll farther than does a large cylinder (Chapter 2). A 17-month-old intentionally varies the manner in which she drops a toy, and attends with interest to the outcome (Chapter 2). A 4-year-old knows that a rabbit raised by monkeys will still prefer carrots to bananas (Chapter 3). A 5-year-old claims that simply pouring a glass of juice into a taller, thinner glass can result in more juice, whereas a 7-year-old does not (Chapter 4). All five children seem to have implicit, intuitive notions about the nature of objects and substances and how they typically behave. More generally, as discussed in Chapter 3, children appear to have naive theories in at least three areas—physics, biology, and psychology (Wellman & Gelman, 1992).

The metaphor of child-as-intuitive-scientist currently is one of the most pervasive in the field of cognitive development. This view derives from Piaget's theory, the theory-based approach, and the information-processing approach (Chapter 1). According to this metaphor, cognitive development is a progression toward "better" thinking, with the "better" defined as "like a scientist." In this view, children try to make sense of their physical environments by constructing mental models (some developmentalists would say causal-explanatory "theories" [Chapter 3]) of some sort that account for the everyday physical events they observe. Like a scientist "wannabe" they revise these mental models as new evidence arises and substitute new theories for old ones.

Developmental change in scientific theories can be placed along a continuum from weak to strong restructuring (Carey, 1991). At one end children simply enrich their theory; they may create new relations among its components or make new differentiations but the theory maintains its core assumptions. An example from biology (Chapter 3) is that a 10-year-old sees more relations among processes such as growing, eating, dying, and having babies than does a 4-year-old (Carey, 1985a). At the other end of the continuum in strong restructuring, children change the core concepts or assumptions of the theory so that the old and new theories are *incommensurate* (i.e., incompatible). The new theory cannot be directly translated into the old theory. The new theory does not just revise the earlier theory but truly replaces it, similar to the historical change from phlogiston to oxygen theories of burning. In fact, Carey (1985a) and others have argued that parallels exist between developmental changes in intuitive scientific theories and historical changes in the field of science. A biological example of strong theory change is Carey's (1985a) proposal that a preschooler's theory of biological functioning based on wants and beliefs—actually a psychological theory—is transformed into a school-age child's more truly biological theory.

We find children's naive intuitive scientific theories intriguing, especially in the realm of physics, because infants are surprisingly knowledgeable and older children and adults are surprisingly unknowledgeable. Work by Spelke and others in Chapter 2 showed that infants know a great deal about the physical integrity and behavior of objects, yet older children and adults hold many blatantly wrong theories of physics. Here are some examples: (1) The majority of sixth graders think that when a person sees an object, energy or rays go out from the eyes à la Superman (Winer & Cottrell, 1991). (2) Grade-school children often predict that a ball exiting from a curved tube will continue in a curved path based on a persistence-of-motion theory, whereas preschool children correctly predict a straight line (Kaiser, McCloskey, & Proffitt, 1986). (3) Children and even college students believe that when a race car travels around an oval track both car doors move at the same speed, ignoring the fact that the outer door is covering more distance in the same time (Levin, Siegler, & Druyan, 1990). (4) Both 11-year-olds and a sizable minority of college students erroneously believe that an object dropped from a moving train falls straight downward from its release point, rather than in front of it (Kaiser, Proffitt, & McCloskey, 1985). These intuitive scientists seem to overextend their everyday theories of physics. For instance, in the third example above, children hold the "single-object/single-motion" theory that all parts of a single object must move at the same speed. This theory is accurate in many situations, such as movement in a straight line, but does not hold in certain other situations, such as the one described above.

It is important for educators to realize that students come to the classroom with *mis*conceptions of science, as opposed to no conceptions. These misconceptions can be remarkably resistant to instruction. Instruction often is not just a matter of teaching new information; it also involves correcting old beliefs—often by showing that the child's beliefs work in some situations but not others—or removing old beliefs and replacing them with new ones (e.g., Chi, 1992). The latter is an example of Carey's strong restructuring described above. An entire theoretical system of interconnected beliefs must be replaced.

Process of Scientific Thinking

Although it may be useful to use the metaphor of children and lay adults as intuitive scientists with "theories" of reality to depict their understanding of scientific phenomena, the metaphor may be misleading with respect to the *process* of scientific thinking (Kuhn, 1989). Regarding the process of theory testing, children and many lay adults do not appear to think like scientists. The essence of scientific thinking is the coordination of theories and evidence: Evidence supports or refutes a theory; a theory organizes and interprets evidence. Similar thinking operates in other areas such as medical diagnosis and legal practice (Kuhn, 1989). It is this process of revising theories in response to encounters with new evidence that leads to theory revision—the heart of cognitive development. Is this process of relating evidence and theories the same in children of various ages, the lay adult, and the scientist?

Based on work by Kuhn (1989; Kuhn, Amsel, & O'Loughlin, 1988), Klahr and Dunbar (1988; Dunbar & Klahr, 1989), and Karmiloff-Smith (1988), children and even lay adults appear to be flawed scientific thinkers in three main ways. First, they tend to be *theory bound*. Unlike scientists, children and lay adults often either ignore discrepant evidence or attend to it in a selective, distorting way. They sometimes adjust evidence to fit their theories; the processing of evidence is biased toward a favored theory. This occurred in a study (Kuhn et al., 1988) in which subjects were given evidence that there was no correlation between the kind of candy bar or the type of relish children eat and how likely they are to catch colds. Of subjects who entered the study with the notion that kind of relish was causal and kind of candy bar was not, many interpreted the identical pattern of evidence (no correlation) as supporting their theories—correctly in the case of candy bars and incorrectly in the case of relish (e.g., they thought the evidence showed that mustard co-occurred with colds). These subjects focused on positive instances and ignored the cases in which mustard co-occurred with no colds.

Another way that people are theory bound is that they hold their theories with certainty. Half of the adolescents and adults in one study (Kuhn, 1990) believed that complex questions such as why prisoners become repeat offenders can be answered with complete certainty. Others (e.g., C. Acredolo & O'Connor, 1991; Byrnes & Beilin, 1991; S. A. Miller, 1986a; Scholnick & Wing, 1988) have shown that although even 6-year-olds can appreciate the distinction between logically necessary Piagetian concepts and empirically true statements, school-age children have a surprising amount of difficulty with the notion that many problems have uncertain answers, or are unresolvable, or can have more than one answer because of the nature of the available evidence. Scholnick and Wing (1988) presented a fantasy game in which the goal was to rescue a unicorn from a castle by traveling through various locales and collecting various necessary materials such as magical objects. In one game situation, for example, children were shown two large houses and told that "Dwarfs can live in large or small houses." This presented children with an undecidable situation—either house could contain the dwarf with the magical object, so there was no basis for choosing a house. Because children had been told to pay a bridge toll to enter a house only if they were certain which dwarf had the magical object, the proper decision was to leave, rather than guess and risk receiving no gain from the toll. Eight- and 9-year-olds had a great deal of trouble detecting when an answer was undecidable (finding the dwarf as above) versus decidable. An example of the latter is finding a giant when there is one large and one small house, and "Giants can only live in big houses." The older children were more aware of logical uncertainties and thus did not guess when the answer was undecidable.

Kuhn (1989) argues that children and often even lay adults do not adequately differentiate evidence and a theory; they have trouble setting aside their own theory and viewing the evidence as separate from any theory. They have trouble understanding what it means to test an idea and even have trouble thinking of what kind of evidence would refute their theories. As a result, when subjects are asked to generate evidence to show that their theory is correct or incorrect, they simply restate their theory or give illustrations of the theory rather than refer to existing or potential evidence that stands alone from the theory and could test it. They misinterpret the task of hypothesis testing as generating an effect predicted by the theory. And when evidence and theory are in fact compatible, they blend into a single representation of "the way things are." People must learn to separate data and theory before they can coordinate them.

This poor differentiation of theory and evidence seems to occur mainly when the child or adult already has a favored theory and when several potential causes exist. Again, we hear echoes from a recurring theme of this book that prior knowledge constrains thought. When children have no preconceived notions, for instance, when they must decide whether a mouse in a dwelling is large or small, even first and second graders can differentiate the evidence from a hypothesis (Sodian, Zaitchik, & Carey, 1991). One need not be a Sherlock Holmes to draw the proper conclusion about the size of the mouse when you use a mouse food box with a small hole and note the disappearance of the food overnight. One other feature of this study may have facilitated hypothesis testing as well. A single conclusive comparison, rather than a pattern of covariation, which entails greater complexity, could test the hypothesis.

A second blatant flaw is that children and many lay adults tend to be *data bound.* Young children are able to construct a theory to explain the most recent result, but tend to ignore the entire earlier set of discrepant and congruent results. Older children and adults attempt to construct a more comprehensive theory, but then become welded to it, unable to abandon it when new evidence arises, and even manufacture observations to support it. They may even appear to regress, for they have become less accurate observers.

Third, children and adults appear to *need theories*, and perhaps even require them. When contradictory evidence mounts and can no longer be ignored, they will finally acknowledge contradictory evidence only after they can generate an alternate theory to explain it (e.g., some plausible way that certain types of relishes could increase resistance to cold germs). As argued above, they do not seem to be able to deal with evidence independently of a theory. They need a plausible causal link between a factor and its results before they can accept the data.

A study by Schauble (1991) illustrates these three conclusions. She presented 9- to 11-year-olds with a computer microworld in which they were to determine the effect, if any, of five factors on the speed of racing cars. Initially children believed that a large engine, large wheels, and the presence of a muffler increase speed. They discounted tailfins or the color of the car. The microworld was set up so that a large engine and medium-sized wheels increased speed, muffler and color were irrelevant, and absence of tailfins increased speed only when the engine was large. Over eight sessions the children could learn about the cars by putting whatever features they wished on different vehicles and seeing how fast they went. Pristine scientific procedure would dictate holding all variables constant except for one, and repeating this method for each factor. Not surprisingly, given Piaget's work on concrete operational thinking, the children often failed to follow this procedure, frequently varying several factors at once. More interesting was the fact that even when children performed valid experiments they often drew conclusions from the results that were inconsistent with the results but consistent with their initial beliefs. Moreover, even after correctly predicting the effect of a factor and seeing the prediction confirmed, they were reluctant to abandon their previous beliefs until they could generate an alternative theory that could account for the unexpected observation. Finally, in their research journals not a single subject recorded covariation information (i.e., features and speed), the most essential information. Some recorded only features and others recorded only outcomes and some recorded neither. Thus, the children did not even seem to know what they needed to know to solve the problem. On the more positive side, the children showed some improvement in their thinking over the sessions.

Although these nonscientific ways of thinking become less prevalent during the grade-school years, they show little change after about age 15 and are common even in adults. College students do, however, think more scientifically than other young adults (Kuhn, 1989). The developmental change involves a restructuring of the way children relate theory and data.

In Kuhn's view, people must possess a metacognitive awareness of their own thought processes before they can gain control over the interaction between theory and evidence in their thinking. She argues that people must think *about* their theories rather than just *with* them (see also, Moshman, 1979, 1990). If people are not aware that their theories are just theories, they are unlikely to monitor carefully how well these theories are supported by evidence. For scientific reasoning, it is necessary to develop a metacognitive understanding of the nature of logic and its limits, and of why some mental strategies are better than others and what their range of application is. In other words, scientific thinkers understand, monitor, and direct their own higher-order reasoning.

If we dare act as though we are scientists rather than lay adults, and thus claim immunity to the above pitfalls, we would use all the above facts to come to the following conclusions. It appears that thinking about a phenomenon in one way often precludes thinking about it in any other way. Just as 3-year-olds have trouble understanding false beliefs because they would have to entertain two different representations of the same reality (Chapter 3), so do much older children (and adults in many situations) have trouble constructing or even entertaining two contradictory theories of the same reality. Carrying the parallel further, we propose that they have trouble seeing that their pet theory might actually be a false belief.

Our focus on recent research on the theory-based account of scientific concepts and the fallacious scientific reasoning of children and adults should not overshadow the enormous impact of Piaget's work. His account of scientific concepts such as time, speed, distance, conservation, physical causality, density, and space is still being examined and refined today. Examples include C. Acredolo (1989), Levin (1989), Marini (1992), Newcomb (1989), Siegler (1981, and see below), and Winer, Hemphill, and Craig (1988).

Siegler's Information-Processing Approach

We now turn to a program of research with a different point of view. Siegler, as an information-processing researcher, believes that much of cognitive growth can be usefully characterized as the sequential acquisition of increasingly powerful rules or strategies (see Chapter 1) for solving problems (Siegler, 1991a). In his *rule-assessment* approach, Siegler begins his study of cognitive growth within a particular conceptual domain by predicting the different problem-solving rules that children of different developmental levels might use. These hypotheses about the developmental ordering or sequence of rules are usually based, in part at least, on prior research findings by Piaget. It is in this sense that Siegler's work can be said to build on and extend Piaget's. Siegler's next step is to administer a special, very carefully selected set of problems in that domain to subjects of different ages. A subject's pattern of responses across this set of problems may then help to determine which of Siegler's hypothesized rules, if any, the subject is using. One response pattern might suggest that rule *A* had been used, another that rule *B* had been used, and so on. More fine-grained analyses usually follow. For example, Siegler might go on to determine that two subjects who use the same problem-solving rule may nonetheless differ in how adequately they attend to or encode the critical features of the problem situation. He might then be able to show that the subject who encoded these features better will progress more quickly and easily to the next higher problem-solving rule in the sequence. He might then further show that the other subject will similarly progress once taught to encode more adequately. Siegler's immediate goal in each study is to gain more precise and solid information about how development proceeds in the specific scientific conceptual domain investigated. His ultimate and more ambitious goal is to use his research findings from a variety of domains to draw general conclusions about the nature and development of the human cognitive system.

Let us now examine Siegler's rule-assessment approach more concretely and specifically. In one series of investigations, children of different ages were presented with a simple balance scale that had four equally spaced pegs on each side of the fulcrum (Siegler, 1976, 1978), a device similar to one used by Inhelder and Piaget (1958) in a study of formal operational thinking. The arm of the scale could fall down to the left or right, or remain horizontal and balanced, depending on the number of equal-sized weights that were placed on the pegs and their distance from the fulcrum. Weights were never placed on more than one peg on a side on each trial, to simplify the problem. The subjects' task was to predict which, if either, of the two sides would go down if a lever that kept the scale from moving were released.

Siegler hypothesized that the knowledge that children of different ages would have about the balance scale could be represented as four developmentally ordered, increasingly complex rules. The simplest and earliest-acquired rule, Rule I, takes into account only the number of weights (thus, the total weight) on each side of the fulcrum. If the number of weights is the same on both sides, Rule I users always predict that the scale will balance; and if the number of weights is greater on one side, that side is always predicted to go down. Rule I subjects completely ignore the distances the weights are from the fulcrum on each side. Subjects who follow Rule II also predict solely on the basis of which side has the greater number of weights, except when the number is equal on both sides. When that happens, and only then, the distances from the fulcrum are correctly taken into account. That is, Rule II subjects predict balance if the two distances are equal. If they are not equal, they predict the descent of whichever arm has its weight located farther from the fulcrum.

In contrast, subjects who follow Rule III always try to consider both weight and distance equally in making their decisions. If both dimensions are equal on both sides, balance is predicted. If one dimension is equal and the other not, the decision is based on that other dimension. For instance, if the weights are equal but the distances are not, the subject predicts that the side with the weights farther out will go down. And, of course, if both are unequal and favor the descent of the same side, that side will be predicted to go down; thus, if one side both has more weights than the other and also has them placed on a peg that is farther from the fulcrum, that side will be judged to go down. However, if both dimensions are unequal but favor the descent of different sides, Rule III subjects have no recourse but to guess. For example, Rule III subjects do not know what to predict if the left side has three weights situated two pegs out from the fulcrum and the right side has two weights situated four pegs out. They just have to guess—"muddle through," as Siegler puts it. Finally, Rule IV subjects know how to compute the torques on each side. That is, they multiply the distance (expressed as the number of pegs out from fulcrum) by the number of weights placed at that distance, and correctly predict that the side with greater product (torque) will tip down. In the problem just mentioned, for instance, they would correctly predict that the right side would go down ($2 \times 4 = 8$) and the left side would go up ($3 \times 2 = 6$).

Siegler tested for the presence of these four rules in subjects' thinking by presenting them with the following six types of problems:

1. Balance problems, with the same configuration of weights on pegs on each side of the fulcrum.
2. Weight problems, with unequal amounts of weight equidistant from the fulcrum.
3. Distance problems, with equal amounts of weight different distances from the fulcrum.
4. Conflict-weight problems, with more weight on one side and more "distance" (i.e., occupied pegs farther from the fulcrum) on the other, and the configuration arranged so that the side with more weight goes down.
5. Conflict-distance problems, similar to conflict-weight except that the side with greater distance goes down.
6. Conflict-balance problems, like other conflict problems, except that the scale remains balanced (Siegler, 1978, p. 114).

Table 4–2 shows how a user of each rule would be predicted to behave on each of the six types of tasks. For example, it shows that Rule I children should be correct only on problems for which attending to weight alone happens to yield the right answer—namely, those problems in which weights and torques always correspond (balance, weight, and conflict-weight problems). In contrast, users of Rule III should be correct on all problems in which the weights and distances do not conflict or suggest different answers but they should be reduced to chance responding (33 percent) on all problems in which they do conflict. Notice that inferences about rule use are based on the subject's *pattern* of responding over the entire *set* of problem types, rather than on how any single problem is handled, because it is only the pattern as a whole that discriminates among the four rules. Notice also that Siegler's model predicts that more cognitively advanced (Rule III) subjects will actually do worse than less advanced (Rules I and II) subjects on conflict-weight problems—not the usual "older-children-do-better" developmental prediction.

How well does the rule model fit subjects' response patterns across this set of different scale-balance problems? Very well indeed, it turns out. In one of Siegler's studies (1976), 120 children of ages 5, 9, 13, and 17 years were given the just-described set of problems. Of these 120, fully 107 (89 percent) consistently responded in accord with one of the four rules: 29 used Rule I, 22 Rule II, 48 Rule III, and 8 Rule IV. Children's verbal descriptions of how they solved the problems were also highly consistent with their response patterns, and thus provided additional corroborating evidence that they were using Siegler's rules. All the 5-year-olds who could be classified as rule users employed Rule I. Most of the older children used one of the other three rules; among these older subjects there was also a slight increase with age in the tendency to use more advanced Rules III and IV. In a similar study using 3- to 5-year-olds, Siegler (1978) found that almost all of the 5-year-olds used Rule I, about half the 4-year-olds did, and almost none of the 3-year-olds did. Moreover, the younger children who did not employ Rule I did not seem to be using any consistent rule at all.

TABLE 4–2 Predictions for Percentage of Correct Answers and Error Patterns for Subjects Using Different Rules

	RULE				COMMENT
Problem Type	I	II	III	IV	
Balance	100	100	100	100	
Weight	100	100	100	100	
Distance	0	100	100	100	Rule I predicts "balance"
Conflict-Weight	100	100	33	100	Rule III performance at chance (33%)
Conflict-Distance	0	0	33	100	Rules I and II fail to take into account greater effect of distance than weight; Rule III performance at chance
Conflict-Balance	0	0	33	100	Same comments as Conflict-Distance

Note: From Sternberg, R. J., & Powell, J. S. The development of intelligence. In J. H. Flavell & E. M. Markman (Eds.), P. H. Mussen (Series Ed.), *Handbook of Child Psychology: Cognitive Development* (Vol. 3, p. 387). Copyright © 1983 by John Wiley & Sons, Inc. Reprinted by permission of John Wiley & Sons, Inc.

Chapter Four

Siegler (1978, 1981) has applied his rule-assessment approach to a wide variety of other Piagetian problem-solving tasks, with generally similar results. That is, a small set of rules closely analogous to those just described models nicely the performance of children of age 5 and older on many tasks; 3-year-olds typically show no evidence of consistent rule use on any task. These results led Siegler to the interesting hypothesis that the development of scientific reasoning in children may be roughly divisible into two phases: one prior to about age 5, during which children develop from nonrule-governed to rule-governed approaches to problems, and the other from about age 5 to adulthood, during which increasingly sophisticated rules are employed (Siegler, 1978). Other researchers have found similar sequences of rules for other types of problems such as the ways in which two variables affect happiness and fairness (Case, Marini, McKeough, Dennis, & Goldberg, 1986) or the force of an object sliding down a ramp (Zelazo & Shultz, 1989).

Siegler (1976) has also shown that children who use the same rule in a problem area may still differ cognitively from one another in ways that affect their subsequent learning and development in that area. For example, Siegler found that groups of 5-year-olds and 8-year-olds, both of whom consistently used Rule I on scale-balance problems at the beginning of the experiment, nevertheless differed in how much they profited from additional experience with conflict-distance and conflict-weight problems. The 8-year-olds advanced to the use of Rules II or III following this additional experience, whereas the 5-year-olds continued to use Rule I. Subsequent research suggested an explanation for this age difference in responsiveness to a learning opportunity: The younger children were encoding the distance dimension less adequately than were the older ones; the younger ones were not attending to it and storing it in memory as well. For instance, Siegler showed that younger subjects were less likely than older ones to notice and remember how far out on each side the weights were placed on any given problem. Once 5-year-olds had been trained to encode the distance dimension adequately, they too advanced in rule use following additional experience with conflict problems—that is, once their encoding problems were remedied, they benefited from the same learning experience that had previously benefited only 8-year-olds. This strongly suggests that inadequate encoding had been at least the proximate cause of their inability to learn. Siegler has also found a similar close relation between encoding adequacy and ability to learn at other developmental levels and on other kinds of problems. For example, 4-year-olds spontaneously encode weight more adequately than do 3-year-olds. Similarly, they acquire Rule I when given appropriate experience, whereas 3-year-olds do not. However, 3-year-olds can also learn Rule I if first trained to encode weight adequately (Siegler, 1978).

As was stated earlier, Siegler's ultimate objective is to use the specific research findings generated by his rule-assessment approach as a basis for making broader generalizations about the nature and development of both scientific thinking and the entire cognitive system. The following outline illustrates the sorts of generalizations Siegler's research has suggested so far (Siegler, 1978, 1981, 1983a, 1983b).

1. Children's cognitive performance on a variety of tasks and at a variety of age levels appears to follow rule-like patterns. Their grasp of many concepts progresses through a sequence of qualitatively distinct rules, such as the four described previously in connection with the scale-balance task.

2. For any given concept, later-developing rules are more likely to predict correct answers than are earlier-developing rules over the whole range of tasks testing for that concept. A rule that more often makes the same prediction that the most advanced rule does will be acquired later than one that makes the same prediction less often. In the case of scale-balance problems, for instance, later-developing Rule III will lead to the same prediction as Rule IV more often than earlier-developing Rule I will, over the entire range of these problems.

3. Relevant to the issue of domain specificity, reasoning across concepts may be more similar when children (or adults) have relatively little knowledge about the concepts than when they have more. When they have little knowledge, they may rely on more general, all-purpose rules. On the balance-scale problem, for example, 5-year-olds act as though they are following a general rule that says one should reason and predict only on the basis of the most salient or important-seeming dimension present—in this case, the weight dimension. Siegler and others have found that children of this age also tend to respond in a similarly "unidimensional" manner in other conceptual areas where they lack sufficient knowledge, such as Piagetian conservation tasks (Siegler, 1981, 1983b). When their knowledge increases, however, the rules they evolve will increasingly conform to the structure and demands of the conceptual area and therefore are likely to be different for different areas. Expressed in Piaget's terminology, Siegler's argument seems to be that when children know little about a concept area they will assimilate it to very general, all-purpose rules. As they learn more about its particularities their rules will increasingly accommodate to these particularities. As mentioned earlier, Siegler further believes that very young children may not even use these general rules when dealing with many problems—that is, the very tendency to approach problems in any sort of consistent, systematic, rule-governed fashion is itself an important product of development, what we earlier called "a sense of the game."

4. Limited encoding can be an important obstacle to developmental progress. As we have seen in the case of the scale-balance problem, children who do not adequately encode a relevant stimulus dimension may not profit from experiences designed to help them acquire more advanced rules that properly take that dimension into account. Improved encoding leads to improved ability to learn and thus could be considered a mechanism of cognitive development.

Like all theoretical approaches, Siegler's has its problems and limitations and is subject to criticism (Ferretti & Butterfield, 1986; Kerkman & Wright, 1988; Siegler, 1983b; Strauss & Levin, 1981; Wilkening & Anderson, 1982). Perhaps the most important question about it is how much of a person's knowledge and thinking can be adequately expressed or captured in rules, whether of the type Siegler posits or of any other type. Whatever the final verdict will be on his rule-assessment method and the generalizations about intellectual development it has spawned, Siegler's work represents an interesting and well-articulated example of recent information-processing approaches to the growth of scientific reasoning and strategies of mathematical computation (Chapter 1).

The developmental trends of middle childhood and adolescent cognition described earlier are expressed in a variety of domains, including scientific thinking. Piaget's work on many scientific concepts, but particularly conservation, illustrates trends toward inferred reality, decentration, attention to transformations, reversible thinking, and quantitative thinking. His work on formal operational thought highlights a growing ability to address the logical properties of statements, to generate possible outcomes, and to engage in hypothetico-deductive and interpropositional reasoning. In more recent research programs, intuitive theories of physics and biology demonstrate that children ignore observable appearance in favor of inferred reality in a variety of domains. Studies of the process of scientific thinking by Kuhn and others reveal the role of metacognition and a sense of the game in regulating one's logical reasoning about data. A person's prior knowledge in a particular domain can facilitate scientific thinking, but also can bias it toward particular theories based on preconceptions. Moreover, a person must overcome the tendency to center temporally on the most recent result. Siegler's balance-scale task shows the trends of decentration away from a single attribute such as number of weights, a more quantitative orientation when calculating the exact torque, and a sense of the game when moving from a nonsystematic to a rule-based approach. Siegler also documents the contributions of a growing information-processing capacity and domain-specific knowledge. The latter determines whether the child uses rules specific to the domain or must rely on general, all-purpose rules.

SUMMARY

Piaget believed that the cognitive systems of early-childhood (*preoperational*), middle-childhood (*concrete operational*), and adolescent-adult (*formal operational*) thinkers are qualitatively different from one another. However, there is growing doubt in the field that these differences are that radical and stage-like. Specifically, a child's cognitive performance is somewhat uneven across different domains. Moreover, young children are more competent and older children less competent than Piaget thought, thus making age differences less dramatic. Still, many of the developmental trends Piaget described seem very insightful and largely on the mark even today. Development from early to middle childhood exhibits the following closely related trends. In conservation and other tasks, younger children often base their judgments on *perceived appearances*, older ones on *inferences* that go beyond surface appearances to the underlying *reality*. Younger children are prone to *center* their attention on a single, highly salient task element (*centration*), older ones to *decenter* their attention and distribute it more equitably across all important task elements (*decentration*). Younger children focus on problem *states*, especially the current state, whereas older ones also take note of the *transformations* that link one state with another. Younger children's thinking tends to be *irreversible*; older children's thinking is more *reversible*, showing an understanding of *inversion* and *compensation*. Finally, younger children are more likely to approach problems in a *qualitative* way, older children in a more *quantitative* measurement-oriented way.

Development from middle childhood to adolescence and adulthood also shows a set of trends closely linked to one another. In scientific-reasoning problems, especially, the elementary school child begins with the *real* and moves reluctantly, if at all, to the *possible*; the adolescent may begin by trying to imagine all that is possible in the present situation and then try to find out which of these possibilities actually obtains in this situation. Therefore, the child's approach is more *empirico-inductive* in nature, whereas the adolescent's is more *hypothetico-deductive*. The child considers propositions singly, in isolation from one another (*intrapropositional* thinking); the adolescent reasons, in addition, about the logical relations (e.g., logical implication) that hold among two or more propositions (*interpropositional* thinking).

Piaget's trends, however, do not capture all of the important cognitive changes during middle childhood and adolescence. Five additional ones seem particularly important.

1. Increase in Domain-Specific Knowledge (Expertise). Older children have accumulated more knowledge in various knowledge domains than younger ones have, and this greater expertise makes for better cognitive performance in these domains. We now know a number of specific ways that the possession of expertise in a domain can dramatically improve the quality of one's cognitive functioning within that domain. For example, experts possess a more abstract, complex, causal knowledge structure for a particular domain. They also plan more carefully and are cognitively efficient during problem solving. In addition, possession of expertise permits us to solve many problems more by memory processes than by complex reasoning processes—that is, by recognizing familiar problem patterns and responding to them with overlearned solution procedures. The domains of knowledge in which the growing child gains expertise include those taught in school plus many others, such as social-cognitive domains.

Just how much of postinfancy cognitive development can ultimately be accounted for by the acquisition of domain-specific knowledge is currently one of the "hot issues" in the field. We would hesitate to say that older minds truly are qualitatively different from younger ones—constitute distinct and different cognitive systems—if disparities in domain-specific expertise were largely responsible for the appearance of qualitative difference. For one thing, the older mind might look almost as immature as the younger one when operating in domains in which it, too, is an utter novice. More generally, both child and adult minds can vary considerably over domains and occasions in the quality of their cognitive performance. At present, therefore, it is difficult to identify really clear-cut, stage-like "cognitive metamorphoses" during the childhood and adolescent years. A main question is how domain-specific and domain-general knowledge are related.

2. Greater Information-Processing Capacity. There appears to be a maturation-based increase with age in information-processing capacity (*structural capacity*). This "hard-wired," neurologically based processing capability might be interpreted as the number of "slots" in our short-term or working memory "box," or as the total amount of attentional energy we can expend during any brief span of time. Evidence includes systemwide increases in speed of processing, which are tied to age. *Functional capacity* refers to the processing we are actually able to carry out in specific task situations, by using our basic structural capacities plus whatever other resources we may command, such as greater processing speed due to well-practiced operations or familiar stimuli, internal information-processing strategies, and external attentional and mnemonic aids. There is widespread agreement that older children and adolescents have more functional information-processing capacities in more task situations than do younger children, and also that this greater capacity may be at least partly responsible for their frequently superior cognitive performance. Capacity demands also may account for uneven performance across tasks that appear to tap the same concept. Neo-Piagetians have argued that apparent domain-specific knowledge may reflect the varying capacity demands of different tasks. The large demands on capacity in one task may prevent a child from fully applying his or her knowledge to that task.

3. Advances in Metacognition. *Metacognition* ("cognition about cognition") includes any knowledge or cognitive activity that takes as its object, or regulates, any aspect of any cognitive enterprise. Metacognitive abilities undergo considerable development during middle childhood and adolescence. A distinction can be made between *metacognitive knowledge* and *metacognitive monitoring and self-regulation.* The former refers to one's accumulated knowledge concerning cognitive matters, and it can be divided into three categories: *person, task,* and *strategy.* The person category includes knowledge and beliefs about people as cognitive processors. The task category refers to knowledge about the cognitive-processing implications of task information and task demands. The strategy category includes knowledge about various strategies. Its high-sounding name notwithstanding, metacognitive knowledge is assumed to be similar in important respects to the other classes of knowledge that children acquire. Children gradually understand the differences among various mental activities, such as memorizing and comprehension. Metacognitive monitoring and self-regulation involve activities driven by metacognitive knowledge that provide information about one's progress in some cognitive enterprise. This information sometimes comes from metacognitive experiences—cognitive or affective experiences that pertain to a cognitive enterprise, such as the sudden feeling that you do not understand something you just read. Metacognitive knowledge and monitoring and self-regulation are assumed to interact with one another as they influence our cognitive activities. There is reason to believe that metacognitive skills play important roles in reading and other areas of school learning, and therefore there is reason to try teaching them directly to children. Metacognition is a cognitive tool with very broad applicability.

4. Development of a Sense of the Game.   As children develop, they may gradually increase their knowledge about what "the game of thinking" is like and about how it should be played. This does not imply that they will always play the game well, even when they reach cognitive maturity; on the contrary, considerable research evidence suggests that adult cognition is frequently of poor quality. Unlike the young child, however, older individuals have some sense of what it means to think well versus poorly, and that sense seems like an important cognitive attainment in its own right.

5. Improvement in Existing Competencies.   An important part of cognitive growth is the further development of recently acquired, immature competencies. A competency may be improved in the course of development by becoming more reliably invoked and used on any one task, more generalized and differentiated in its use across tasks, more dominant over competing, inappropriate approaches, more integrated with other competencies, more accessible to conscious reflection and verbal expression, and more consolidated and solidified.

Many of these developmental trends are seen in children's scientific concepts and processes of scientific reasoning. Children of all ages appear to possess intuitive concepts of this kind. During development these concepts may undergo either weak restructuring—an elaboration of the same "theory"—or strong restructuring—the replacement of one theory by another. Although many of these concepts are accurate, a startling number are not—even in adults. These misconceptions can interfere with scientific instruction at school.

Similarly, although Piaget has documented that the process of scientific reasoning becomes formal operational during adolescence, more recent research has identified important inadequacies in this process. Work by Kuhn and others reveals that children and many lay adults do not clearly understand the difference between a hypothesis and evidence and their respective roles. This is especially true when they already have a theory that they try to apply to the problem at hand. Several problems result. First, they tend to be theory bound. They often ignore evidence that does not support their theory or distort it so that it does. They have unreasonable certainty about their theories in situations where there are no certain answers. Second, children and lay adults tend to be data bound; they focus on the most recent result, ignoring earlier results. Third, they find it difficult to deal with evidence independently of a theory. They are reluctant to abandon a failed theory until they have a plausible new theory to explain the discrepant result. Metacognition about one's own thinking processes may be essential in overcoming these problems.

Robert Siegler's *rule-assessment approach* provides an apt contemporary example of how the development of scientific thinking can be investigated within an information-processing perspective. Siegler argues that much of cognitive development consists of the sequential acquisition of increasingly powerful rules for solving problems. He begins his investigation of any given problem area by predicting the different problem-solving rules that children of different developmental levels would use in that area. The next step is to administer to subjects of different ages a very carefully designed set of problems. The specific pattern of responses each subject produces across the entire set of problems then suggests which of Siegler's hypothesized rules, if any, that particular subject used to try to solve these problems. Siegler has been quite successful in his efforts to predict and find orderly and plausible-looking developmental sequences of rule acquisitions in several problem areas, most notably in his work with a scale-balance problem involving the concept of torque. In addition, he has shown that the more adequately subjects attend to and store in memory the task information pertinent to a rule they have not yet acquired, the more easily they can learn that rule. Finally, Siegler's rule-assessment research has also led him to other intriguing conclusions about the nature and development of the human cognitive system.

five

Social Cognition

Up to this point our story of cognitive development has the plot of "child-in-the-physical world." The child seems headed toward becoming a scientist. But even scientists, whether age 4 or 40, are feeling people with social needs and goals. Indeed, hints of this second story plot emerged in previous chapters: contextual theory (Chapter 1), attention to faces (Chapter 2), social script knowledge, concepts of animacy, and theory of mind (Chapter 3), and metacognition (Chapter 4). We now will flesh out the story of "the other cognitive development."

Social cognition takes humans and human affairs as its subjects; it means cognition about people and their doings. Machines, mathematics, and moral judgments are all objects and products of human cognition, for instance, but only the latter would be considered a topic within human *social* cognition. Social cognition deals with the strictly social world, not the physical and logical-mathematical ones, even though all three worlds obviously have people's fingerprints all over them. The scientific investigation of this kind of cognition currently is of great interest to psychologists, but its actual practice has undoubtedly been of even greater interest to practically everyone since the dawn of the species. Numerous motives, ranging from self-preservation to idle curiosity, must continually impel people the world over to try to make sense out of themselves, other people, interpersonal relations, social customs and institutions, and other interesting objects of thought within the social world. And psychologists well ought to be interested in the nature and development of processes that are that significant in everyday mental life.

Social-cognitive development has received a good deal of scientific study, especially in recent years. General sources on this topic include Dunn (1988), P. H. Miller and Aloise (1989), Pryor and Day (1985), and Shantz (1983).

The theme of this chapter pertains to a main goal of human social development: to separate oneself from others and to achieve a solid sense of self independent from others, while at the same time establishing emotional-social connections to others. We will look at the cognitive substrate that permits, and is enriched by, this dual movement away from others and toward others. We first present three frameworks that psychologists have used to study the development of social cognition. Next we describe the general nature of social cognition and compare and contrast it with nonsocial cognition. Our story starts with the beginnings of separation and connection in infancy. We then turn to children's understanding of emotions and percepts. Subsequent sections discuss children's knowledge about the personal attributes of others and the self, and about the causes of behavior, and their understanding of social relationships. These sections describe how children cognitively differentiate themselves from others, but also discern their cognitive commonalities with others and understand reciprocal relationships such as friendship and caring. The mind turns itself to both intrapersonal content such as intentions, emotions, traits, perceptions, memories, desires, and beliefs, and interpersonal content such as love, conflict, and power. At the broadest level, children also form concepts of social groups, structures, or situations, such as minority groups, the government, poverty, and discrimination. Except under unfortunate circumstances, the developmental story has a happy ending—an adult with a realistic, confident self-concept in a meaningful social network. Finally, we will raise some unresolved issues in these areas.

THE NATURE OF SOCIAL COGNITION: THREE MODELS

Self, Other, Social Relationships

We find three models particularly useful for thinking about social cognition. In one, schematized in Figure 5–1, S means the self and O means another person or group of persons. The dashed arrows represent acts and products of social cognition. They mainly include a person's inferences, beliefs, or conceptions about the inner psychological processes or attributes of human beings, and are therefore represented in Figure 5–1 as penetrating into the interior of their targets. The solid arrows represent overt social acts rather than covert mental ones, and consequently they cannot "penetrate" their objects in quite this sense. For instance, a person may be able to infer what is going on inside your head if given enough clues (social

FIGURE 5–1 A representation of social cognition

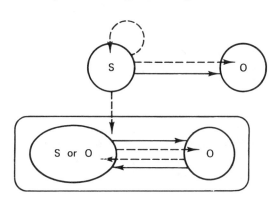

cognition), but can affectionately pat only the outside of it (social act). The top part of Figure 5–1 shows that the self can have all manner of cognitions about the self as well as about another person or group of persons. The bottom part shows that social cognition can also encompass various relationships and interactions among individuals or groups. It further shows that the self can be one of the interacting individuals the self is mentally representing, and that the interactions represented can themselves include covert social cognitions (Flavell, 1981b) as well as overt social acts. Thus, a person may think about himself or herself in isolation, about you in isolation, and also about the social acts and social cognitions each may carry out with respect to the other.

Existence, Need, Inference

A second model for characterizing social cognition indicates some very general preconditions for the successful execution of any specific act of social thinking (Flavell, 1974; Flavell, Botkin, Fry, Wright, & Jarvis, 1968/1975). There are at least three such preconditions: *Existence, Need,* and *Inference.*

Existence refers to the person's basic knowledge that a particular fact or phenomenon of the social world exists as one of life's possibilities. In order to think about something in the social world, one obviously first has to be aware of its very existence as a possible object of social cognition. If young children have not yet become aware that people even *have* such psychological goings on as percepts, thoughts, and motives, for instance, they manifestly cannot try to infer their presence and detailed characteristics within particular people and on particular occasions. The point is a most unprofound one: There scarcely can be any thinking about social-cognitive phenomena if the very existence of such phenomena is not yet represented by the thinker. In Chapter 3 we indicated that even young children have some awareness of the existence of mental activity or states.

Need refers to the disposition or sensed need to attempt an act of social cognition. A person may know perfectly well that she and other people have experiences called feelings (Existence), and yet she may not even try to diagnose them when opportunities arise (Need). She may not think to, may not want to, or may not see any point to making such an effort. One of the great truths about child cognition is that children often do not make use of the knowledge and cognitive skills they possess.

Inference concerns the skill or capacity to carry off a given form of social thinking successfully. The thinking need not involve "inference" strictly defined—any social-cognitive process qualifies (Flavell, 1974). Someone may know of the existence of the type of thought or feeling you are currently having (Existence), and may very much want to figure out what you are presently experiencing (Need), and yet may simply not have the ability to identify it on the basis of the evidence provided (Inference). He can infer, perhaps, that you are feeling something unpleasant, and knowing even that much, of course, requires some Inference ability. However, lack of sufficient evidence, his general inadequacies as a people reader, or both, may prevent his obtaining a more detailed and precise understanding of exactly what sort of unpleasant affect you are experiencing.

The distinction between Existence and Inference is especially clear in the area of cognitions about visual percepts. Suppose your friend sits on one side of a random arrangement of complex objects (e.g., four vases of different shapes and colors, each containing a variety of different flowers) and you sit on the other. His task is to select, from a large number of different photographs of the array taken from different positions, that photograph which shows exactly how the array looks to you, from your vantage point. He is not allowed to walk around and look; he must figure out what you see from where he sits. The problem of computing (Inference) another person's visual perspective in such tasks can range from the trivially easy to the near impossible, depending upon the complexity of the array, the set of photographs used, and so on. Even in the most difficult of these tasks, however, he knows perfectly well that you have *some* visual experience of the array, just as he does (Existence). He also knows some other things that require little or no on-the-spot computation, and therefore seem more Existence-like than Inference-like. For instance, he knows at the onset that you have one and only one view of the array and that, whatever that view is, it is different from his own; consequently, only one photograph in the set can possibly be the right one, and any photograph depicting his own view can automatically be excluded (Flavell, Omanson, & Latham, 1978; Salatas & Flavell, 1976).

To characterize the general nature of social cognition in this way is implicitly to indicate what the child's developmental task is—what social-cognitive development is the development of. It is the developing awareness and general knowledge (Existence) of the enormous variety of possible social-cognitive objects alluded to earlier in this chapter and in Chapter 3. It is also a developing awareness (Need) of when and why one might or should try to take readings of such objects. Finally, it is the development of a wide variety of cognitive skills (Inference) with which to take these readings.

Dodge's Information-Processing Model

A third model analyzes the processing of social information during social interaction, and it comes from the information-processing approach described in Chapter 1. This approach emphasizes the inference component discussed above. Kenneth Dodge (1986) provides the most well-developed model of this type. In his model, depicted in Figure 5–2, children process and use social information much as they do physical information. To illustrate the model, imagine a playground episode in which a child is hit with a ball from behind. Most children would see this as an ambiguous event; the act could have been an intentional act of aggression or an accident. However, highly aggressive boys interpret such an act against them as intentional (Dodge, Murphy, & Buchsbaum, 1984). Let us examine this in terms of the model. The child comes to the situation with a set of relevant biologically determined capabilities and predispositions, such as motor skills or temperament, and a data base of remembered similar past experiences. There are social cues, such as peers' facial expressions, the events leading up to the act, and the reactions of observers. During encoding and representation, the child attends to, and interprets, certain cues. As a child develops, he must learn how to attend to relevant cues, integrate them with previous knowledge, and interpret them accurately. Note that a feedback loop in Figure 5–2 allows the child to search for more information to test his interpretation; a nonaggressive child may notice that the children's ball throws are not very accurate, so conclude that the "aggressor" may actually have unintentionally overthrown the ball. Next the child searches his repertoire for possible responses, perhaps thinks through the consequences of each, selects a response, and carries it out. If a child believes he has been the victim of an intentional aggressive act, he is likely to retaliate, and not consider more pacifist solutions. Children differ in how many responses they have

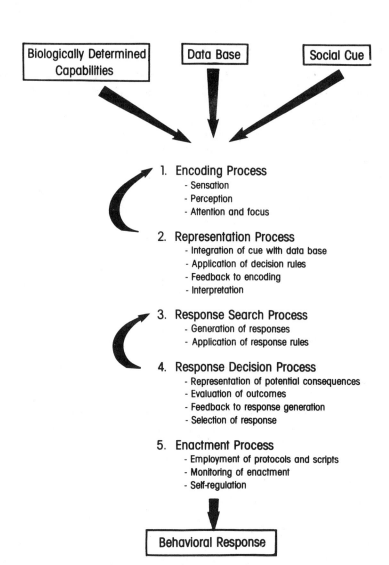

FIGURE 5–2 A social information-processing model of competence. Reprinted from K. A. Dodge, A social information-processing model of social competence in children. In M. Perlmutter (Ed.), (1986), *Minnesota Symposia on Child Psychology: Vol. 18. Cognitive perspectives on children's social and behavioral development.* Hillsdale, NJ: Erlbaum, p. 84. By permission.

available and how likely they are to use each one. A highly aggressive child may, for example, conduct a biased search and consider only deviant responses. Similarly, maltreated children are less able to withhold attention from distracting aggressive stimuli than are nonmaltreated children (Rieder & Cicchetti, 1989). Dodge (1991) recently has added emotions to his model. The child's emotional state affects, and is affected by, each stage of the model. For example, an upset child may attend to a narrow range of social cues, and this new information increases arousal, which in turn stimulates the child to choose an aggressive response very quickly.

This model has several important features. One is that socially inappropriate behavior can have many different causes, ranging from biased encoding to faulty translation of a decision into behavior. A second is that a child's lack of social competence may be restricted to certain situations. A child may be skilled at entering a play group but unable to deal with aggressive situations. For these reasons, we would expect to see some inconsistency (1) between social cognitive measures and actual child behavior, and (2) among situations. Third, each processing step has a developmental history. Thus, there are many sources of developmental change. Finally, the child's thinking described in the model often is nonconscious. Conscious processing is most likely to occur when a novel response is necessary or when children are asked to think before they act or to justify their behavior.

The three models we have described are complementary. They emphasize different facets of social cognition and behavior more than they present three opposing views. It is a useful exercise to think about each of the areas of social cognition we discuss in terms of these models.

SIMILARITIES AND DIFFERENCES BETWEEN SOCIAL AND NONSOCIAL COGNITION

In what respects are social and nonsocial cognition similar to one another? How might they be different, and why? What about possible similarities and differences in their developmental courses? A number of psychologists have wrestled with these important questions and the following discussion owes much to their ideas (e.g., Butterworth, 1982; Damon, 1981; Flavell & Ross, 1981; Gelman & Spelke, 1981; Higgins, 1981; Hoffman, 1981; Shantz, 1983; Shweder, 1980).

Similarities

A little reflection should convince you that there have to be many similarities between social and nonsocial cognition. In the first place, the head that thinks about the social world is the selfsame head that thinks about the nonsocial world. All of the basic mental tools described in previous chapters (knowledge structures, symbolic abilities, information-processing capacities, etc.) can be used to categorize, remember, reason about, and otherwise manipulate social data as well as nonsocial data. Thanks to these tools, both the social and nonsocial world come to be experienced as "structured, stable, and meaningful" (D. J. Schneider, Hastorf, & Ellsworth, 1979, p. 10). As with nonsocial cognition, some of our social cognition involves complex reasoning (e.g., elaborate perspective taking) and some of it involves only the recognition of familiar input patterns and the automatic running off of overlearned responses to these patterns.

In addition, social and nonsocial inputs are similar in certain fundamental respects. Things are physical objects in space and so are people. Things participate in events that take place over time and so do people. Things relate to and interact with one another in numerous ways and so do people. Nonsocial concepts can be concrete ("ball") or abstract ("entropy") and so can social ones ("girl," "friendship"). Not surprisingly, therefore, many of the trends in the development of nonsocial cognition described in previous chapters can also be seen in the area of social-cognitive development. Following are the most salient examples.

SURFACE TO DEPTH. We have seen that cognition about nonsocial phenomena often begins with surface appearances alone and only later gets beneath the surface to construct an inferred underlying reality. Social-cognitive development also tends to proceed from surface to depth. Infants begin by reading only the most external, immediately perceptible attributes of themselves, other people, social interactions, and other social-cognitive objects. They pay attention to people's appearances and overt behaviors, but they initially do not use these or other kinds of evidence to make inferences about the covert-social-psychological processes, meanings, and causes which underlie them. The dashed arrows in Figure 5–1 initially stop at the boundaries of those circles and ellipses, and only gradually penetrate into the interior. However, this penetration now is believed to begin during the second year of life.

THE PULL OF SALIENT FEATURES. The social cognition of younger children also shows vulnerability to salient physical features of the here-and-now. They are prone to attend only to the most obvious and highly salient features of a social object in the present situation, neglecting subtler but possibly more important features (see Figure 5–2, encoding process). For example, young children can read the big, obvious signs of gaiety in another, but will require additional social-cognitive growth before they can also pick up the little, nonobvious signs that indicate that this individual's gaiety is forced and false. Seeing through social facades is not the long suit of young children, any more than seeing through Piagetian-task nonconservation facades is. The same applies to temporal salience. Younger children are likely to hew closely to the immediately present social situation. It is only later that they will spontaneously infer its likely past antecedents and future consequences—for example, what prior social experiences, motives, intentions, and so on, led the people to act as they are now acting, and what will be the likely next steps in the episode. Children only gradually learn to integrate over time and events, to interlink states and transformations, and this is as true in the social domain as in the nonsocial one.

INVARIANT FORMATION. Another parallel is that there is a good deal of invariant formation in both worlds. Children gradually come to think of themselves and others as stable human beings who conserve, over time and circumstances, their personhoods, personalities, social and sexual roles and identities, and many other attributes. Day-to-day changes in one's own or another's mood and behavior come to be construed as variations on an enduring theme, rather than as a succession of unrelated melodies. The cognitive construction of these social invariants can, of course, reflect a breaking away from the pull of the salient present as the child identifies important personal continuities that persist over time.

ABSTRACT AND HYPOTHETICAL THINKING. Similarly, the sometimes abstract and hypothetical quality of mature thinking is also visible when its cognitive objects are social. People become capable of thinking about groups, institutions, and people in general (concepts of "human nature," etc.) as well as about specific individuals. Moreover, specific individuals, both self and others, become endowed with more general, enduring traits and dispositions as well as more spe-

Chapter Five

cific and transient processes. Likewise, mature thinkers may think about all manner of abstract ideas and ideals in such areas as morality, religion, and politics. Finally, their hypotheses in a science experiment have their social-cognitive counterparts in their speculations about their personal future (e.g., Elkind, 1967).

COGNITIVE SHORTCOMINGS. We have seen that even mature thinkers are vulnerable to all sorts of errors and fallacies when reasoning about impersonal phenomena. The same is true for social reasoning. Social psychologists and personality theorists (e.g., Mischel & Peake, 1982; Nisbett & Ross, 1980; D. J. Schneider et al., 1979; Skowronski & Carlston, 1989) have shown that our inferences about ourselves and other people are subject to numerous biases and distortions. For example, laypeople and psychologists alike tend to overestimate the degree to which a person's negative or neutral behavior is consistent over situations—that is, the degree to which the behavior is governed by stable and general internal traits and dispositions versus variable, external circumstances (e.g., Mischel & Peake, 1982). This is especially true when trying to explain another's behavior rather than our own (Jones, 1990; W. Mischel, 1973; D. J. Schneider et al., 1979): You tripped because you are clumsy (a stable trait) whereas I tripped because it was dark (a variable circumstance). Children show the same bias (Abramovitch & Freedman, 1981; Curtis & Schildhaus, 1980).

An ailment that particularly bedevils social cognition, however, is what Piaget called *egocentrism* (see Chapter 3)—the failure to differentiate or distinguish clearly between one's own point of view and another's. For instance, a person's assessment of your opinions and feelings about something is egocentric to the degree that she has unwittingly misattributed her own opinions and feelings to you. Poor perspective taking is often assumed to be very prevalent in early childhood, though certainly not inevitable (Wellman, 1990). It is also often assumed that egocentrism declines thereafter, much like logical errors in nonsocial cognition. However, we believe that most people are "at risk" (almost in the medical sense) for egocentric thinking all of their lives, just as they are for certain logical errors. The reason lies in our psychological designs in relation to the jobs to be done. We experience our own points of view more or less directly, whereas we must always attain the other person's view in more indirect ways. Our own points of view are usually more cognitively "available" to us than another person's views (Tversky & Kahneman, 1973). Furthermore, we are usually unable to turn our own viewpoints off completely when trying to infer another's viewpoints. Our own perspectives produce clear signals that are much louder to us than the other's, and they usually continue to ring in our ears while we try to decode someone else's perspectives. It may take considerable skill and effort to represent another's point of view accurately through this kind of noise, and the possibility of egocentric distortion is ever-present. For example, the fact that you thoroughly understand calculus constitutes an obstacle to your continuously keeping in mind a friend's ignorance of it while trying to explain it to him; you may momentarily realize how hard it is for him, but that realization may quietly slip away once you get immersed in your explanation. Interestingly, the "other" can be oneself in another time and condition, rather than a different person (Flavell, 1981b). For example, it can be hard to imagine yourself feeling well and happy next week if you feel terribly ill or unhappy today. Taking the perspective of yourself, when that perspective is different from your current one, can sometimes be as hard as taking the perspective of another person. Thus, we can no more "cure" ourselves of our susceptibility to egocentrism than we can cure ourselves, say, of our difficulties in understanding two simultaneously presented messages. Both cases represent a human information-processing limitation with respect to a certain class of cognitive task.

A SENSE OF THE GAME. Unlike young children, mature thinkers know that others have a mental life that they may hide, that their own perspective may interfere with their representation of others' perspectives, that people try to influence other people and other Existence-type truths about social cognition. Therein lies a final parallel with nonsocial cognition. Grown-ups the world around surely have developed some "sense of the game" of people reading, just as they have in the case of impersonal thinking games.

Differences

People are different from most other objects in a number of ways. Moreover, our relations with people differ in key respects from our relations with most other objects. These two sets of differences together make for some differences in what we think about and how we think about it in social versus nonsocial cognition. Our social cognition acquires certain characteristic and distinctive qualities from the fact that the objects of this cognition and our relation to them are somewhat distinctive. As Shweder put it, "What one thinks about has some influence on how one thinks" (1980, p. 270).

How are people different from most nonsocial objects? They are sentient creatures who can act spontaneously and deliberately. They can perceive, represent, know, believe, think, mean, intend, want, emote, and learn. They are causal agents who can, within limits, freely and intentionally generate their own mental and physical acts and hence can be held responsible for these acts. Their behavior is often difficult to predict because they respond to internal as well as external events, and also to their own representations and interpretations of external stimuli rather than to the "raw stimuli" themselves. They can deliberately reveal and conceal critical information about themselves, and this adds to their unpredictability.

Our relations with people are typically very different from our relations with other objects. There is first of all the static relation of similarity. We are very similar to the objects of our social cognition (indeed, we *are* those objects in the case of social cognition about the self). This similarity makes possible the use of cognitive processes that are distinctively social-cognitive. In contrast, toys are *not* us. There are also the dynamic relations that include all the special ways we respond to social objects and they to us. Our interactions with other people are often intricately coordinated, mutual, reciprocal affairs, interactions quite unlike those we have with nonsocial objects. Our thoughts and behaviors concerning another person are apt to be importantly guided by our cognitive representations of the social roles, relations, and behaviors in play between us. Our thoughts and behaviors may also be guided by our representations of the other person's thoughts and intentions concerning us, even including the other person's possible representations of these representations of ours (e.g., "I think she knows I like her ideas"). Thus, the social cognitions of two people can overlap and include one another in complex and changing ways over the course of a social interaction between them (see Figure 5–1).

In addition to these differences in type of cognitive object and in relations between self and social or nonsocial object are differences in content. Examples of distinctively social-cognitive content include our mental representations of (1) other people's thoughts and attitudes about us and our behavior; and (2) their and our own moral or social-conventional obligations and responsibilities. Obviously, when trying to solve a problem in, say, mechanics, our mental contents do not include inferences about the attitudes and moral responsibilities of the various masses and forces involved.

Possible examples of uniquely or at least predominantly social-cognitive processes have not been very precisely specified as yet by students of social cognition. In general, however, it can be said that we use information about ourselves and our own reactions more often and in a different way when engaged in social cognition than when engaged in nonsocial cognition (Hoffman, 1981). For example, we may either deliberately or nondeliberately (i.e., egocentrically) assume that the other person will think, feel, and act in his or her present situation as we would if we were in that same situation. If we would feel upset in that situation, for example, we might assume that the other person would too. Furthermore, because people often do respond to the same situation in much the same way, such an assumption will often be correct. Alternatively, if we know or believe that the other person is very different from us in certain respects, we might assume for that reason that the person will respond differently from how we would—and we may again be right. Of course, both of our assumptions might turn out to be wrong instead, but that is beside the point. The point is that in both instances the social-cognitive process that was employed made heavy and special use of the self as a point of reference and basis for judgment.

Similarly, in *empathy* affective arousal in another person automatically and involuntarily elicits affective arousal in ourselves (Hoffman, 1981). It seems unlikely that empathic-type mechanisms see much service in our cognition of nonsocial content. Even when empathic processes are not involved, it is possible that affect plays a more important and varied role in social than in nonsocial cognition. Moreover, it would not be surprising if it turned out that our species has evolved at least some distinctive, "domain-specific" cognitive tools for gaining information about social objects (Leslie, 1991), just as it probably has for acquiring natural language (Chapter 7). For example, the posterior region of the right hemisphere of the brain mediates recognition of facial expressions (C. A. Nelson, 1987).

It would be unwise to exaggerate the role of special, domain-specific processes here, however. Most of the basic processes and operations used in social cognition are probably also used in nonsocial cognition. Although what one thinks about probably does influence how one thinks, we should also remember that it is the same human mind that does the thinking.

SOCIAL-COGNITIVE DEVELOPMENT DURING INFANCY

Stephanie (7 months) developed a very shrill shriek which her parents saw her as using primarily in situations when she was getting no attention; for example in a supermarket her mother would hear the shriek and turn around in a hurry with some alarm, to find Stephanie sitting in her trolley grinning at her. (Reddy, 1991, p. 145)

Such behaviors show that even babies are beginning to develop notions about other people, themselves, and the relation between the self and others. It should not be surprising that babies possess the ability to forge these social cognitions early in life, for they are members of a species that is dependent on other people for survival during infancy. Cognitive equipment that helps infants attract the attention of adults, keep them nearby, and predict and control their behavior clearly helps them adapt to their environment. The social utility of infants' abilities described in Chapter 2 will now become apparent. Early preferences for attending to voices, faces, and biological motion; intermodal perception (for example, matching mouth movements and speech patterns); imitations; and the concept of object permanence are put to good use as the baby becomes a social thinker.

Infant Social-Cognitive Development as a Process of Separation-Differentiation and Connection

Part of infant social-cognitive development can be characterized as a process of *differentiation*—differentiation of self from nonself, of human objects from nonhuman objects, and of one human object from another. In the case of the self, the child has as one of her major developmental tasks in this area the gradual evolution of a sense of herself as a distinct and separate entity, clearly differentiated from all the other entities, human and nonhuman, that populate her everyday world. She must acquire some conception of herself both as a physical object and as a person among persons. This process of articulation and definition of self begins in early infancy, but has not progressed very far by the end of infancy. We will discuss this process further in the later section on the self.

Infants learn fairly early that human beings are very special objects with which they can interact in very special ways. Human objects gradually become distinguished from nonhuman ones in ways such as the following. Infants as young as 2 months of age may become upset if a person faces them in an impassive manner, without moving or speaking. This distress probably reflects the learned expectation that people, unlike most other objects, will spontaneously interact and communicate with them. A baby quickly discovers that people, but not objects, are responsive to her signals. She learns that when she wants a ball no matter how much she shouts at it or smiles at it, the ball does not roll to her.

A baby becomes aware that other people's behavior is predictable and can even be contingent on her own behavior. She acts and the other person reacts appropriately. If her action is a request, the other person will function as a means to her goal without her making physical contact with him—that is, he will behave as an active, communicative agent in the service of her needs and wants (her personal slave) rather than as a passive, uncommunicative tool or instrument that she must physically manipulate. She senses both her personal active initiatives, or *agency* (e.g., "I can make Mommy come by crying"), and the agency inherent in others (e.g., "Mommy can feed me"). Thus, infants come to see other people as influenceable "compliant agents" who honor requests for help in obtaining goals. That is, other agents can be influenced by the infant's intentional communications and consequently can make good things happen.

Babies learn that contingency proceeds in the opposite direction as well. The other person acts and the baby reacts appropriately. Eventually, the baby expands her awareness to reciprocal contingencies. She learns how to manage an alternating sequence of reciprocal actions with another person: She takes her turn in a simple social game like peek-a-boo or in a baby-style "conversation" of prelinguistic utterances, then she waits for him to take his turn, then she takes another turn, and so on. Consider the following example of a sequence of contingent social interchanges between an infant and her father:

Shamini (9 months) within a chatting session following some showing-off with eye-crinkling, etc., and following a few pleasant give and take exchanges, offers objects to F saying "ta" and waving her fingers with it as an additional call, looking at F's face intently; F stretches hand out to take it, as F's hand comes closer, Shamini with eyes intently on F's face begins to smile, then withdraws object with smile broadening and turns away, then looks back, F laughs, and says in a voice acknowledging being teased "You, gimme, gimme, gimme" stretching his hand closer to her face; Shamini makes briefly as if to run, but is caught by the high chair she is in, then turns around again, by which time F has withdrawn his hand. She repeats offer saying "ta, ta" with her face this time less intent and with a slight smile, F holds out hand again, Shamini repeats withdrawal with smile broadening as F's hand approaches and as she turns rapidly away. (Reddy, 1991, p. 146)

One cannot imagine a baby trying to engage in such behavior with her blocks or blanket.

There are three implications of this account thus far. One is that the infant has separated herself cognitively from others, but at the same time has built up connections with them through her expectations about their reciprocal interactions. Second, as a baby succeeds in making other people treat her like a person, this may thereby help her become one. Her cute expressive face, responsive smile, and appropriate signals, such as calls and gestures, make caretakers feel as though she is a real person with a mind and personality. Their imbuing her with a mind may cause them to give her even more exposure to the psychological world in the form of conversations, turn-taking games, and mental verbs. Third, if a parent is unresponsive to an infant's overtures, then she learns less about human modes of interaction and constructs a quite different view of others and herself. For example, clinically depressed mothers, who may not synchronize well with their infants' behaviors, present such an environment (e.g., T. Field, Healy, Goldstein, & Guthertz, 1990). Similarly, the erratic behaviors of an alcoholic or drug dependent mother may disrupt a baby's attempts to predict her behavior.

An interfacing of minds also is suggested by several other infant behaviors besides a sequence of reciprocal behaviors. By 9 months, babies reliably and easily follow their mother's line of sight (Scaife & Bruner, 1975) and begin to follow her pointing gestures (Murphy & Messer, 1977), an ability that we will discuss more fully later. The result is shared attention to some object or event of mutual interest. The infant's early attempts to communicate, described in Chapter 7, also are attempts to connect with another person. Infants also gradually become more responsive to other people's facial and gestural expressions of emotion. They eventually even learn to use these expressions as guides to prudent actions, a behavior called *social referencing*. For example, when a 12- or 18-month-old is introduced to a novel and somewhat frightening toy in the company of his mother, he is likely to consult her facial expression before making his next move. If her expression is happy, he will approach the toy; if it is fearful, he will approach her instead (e.g., Klinnert, Campos, Sorce, Emde, & Svejda, 1983). Imagine, if you can, an infant "consulting" a nonsocial object in this way. All of these behaviors suggest that by the end of the first year infants at least dimly realize that inner experiences, which adults would call desires, emotions, and intentions, exist (the Existence category). Furthermore, these inner states can be shared with another person, a "meeting of minds," through signals (Bretherton, 1990). An infant points to her open toy box and says "ga!" Her mother picks up a toy and says, "You want this one?" Typically, of course, the mother has to repeat the question for a dozen toys, under a barrage of progressively louder "ga"s, before guessing the desired toy.

Clearly, some grasp of the person-nonperson distinction and the unique features of human beings is achieved by the end of infancy. Needless to say, a more detailed and penetrating knowledge of the psychological characteristics of personhood (e.g., that people act out of inner motives or may not mean what they say) is still a thing of the distant future for a child of this age.

Cognitive-Developmental Basis of Social Attachment

The pinnacle of connecting to others during infancy is *social attachment* (Bowlby, 1969), the development of affect-laden bonds to certain people, such as one's mother and father. Social attachment is always a two-way process of social interaction, necessarily involving the feelings and behaviors of both parent and infant, though we concentrate on the infant's half of the interaction. Infants express their attachment by protesting when the parent leaves and smiling and approaching when the parent returns. Depending on their age, infants do some things that bring or keep them satisfactorily close to the attachment figure (clinging, sucking, crawling after), and other things that tend to bring or keep the person near to them (smiling, crying, calling). Most babies show these unmistakable signs of having begun to form specific social attachments sometime during the third quarter of their first year.

Attachment serves as an apt example of how cognitive development and social development are intimately intertwined during development. Each constrains and facilitates the other. Regarding the social-to-cognitive direction, infants' social interactions and emotional relations with their caretakers must constitute a nearly indispensable crucible for the formation and development of cognitive processes. It is difficult to conceive how there could be any significant cognitive development at all if the amount and quality of the infant's social relations with other human beings fell below some unknown minimum. Human beings are intrinsically social beings, and human cognitive development requires human social relations.

A little thought will indicate that something like the reverse also has to be true. Social behavior is always partly managed and mediated by cognitive processes, and the developmental level or quality of social behavior that an individual is capable of showing must be at least partly dependent on the developmental level or quality of that individual's cognitive abilities. The latter is conceived as a necessary but definitely not sufficient condition for the former—that is, having achieved a certain general level of cognitive development does not *ensure* the occurrence of a particular kind of social behavior, or a particular kind of social cognition either, for that matter; it only makes it *possible*. For example, a person cannot cooperate with another person in some common endeavor (social behavior) unless he or she has the wherewithal upstairs (cognitive processes) to integrate and coordinate responses with the other person's responses in such a way as to merit the term *cooperative behavior*. At the same time, the mere possession of the necessary penthouse equipment obviously does not *oblige* the person to be cooperative. For want of sufficient cognitive skill, young babies *cannot* cooperate; for want of sufficient motivation rather than sufficient cognitive skill, old misanthropes *can* cooperate but *will not*.

How might the course of infant attachment development reflect or be partly mediated by the course of infant cognitive development, in the necessary-but-not-sufficient-condition sense just described? One very plausible cognitive prerequisite for the formation of social attachment to a specific person is developing infants' increasing ability to make fine visual discriminations (Yarrow & Pederson, 1972). Until infants are perceptually capable of discriminating one looming face with a silly grin from another (no mean achievement, when you think about it), they obviously cannot recognize or identify particular faces as special, recurrent, and familiar ones; and until they can do the latter, they can hardly form social-emotional bonds to particular individuals. More generally, the parent constitutes a complex bundle of sights, sounds, feelings, and smells, and this bundle has to become quickly and easily distinguishable from other, quite similar bundles before the infant can become differentially attached to it.

Fortunately, human infants, like the young of many other species, are well equipped cognitively by evolution to begin the developmental process of becoming attached to conspecifics. Consider first their visual abilities and preferences. As indicated in Chapter 2, babies tend to be especially visually attentive to large objects that move, have edges and contours that exhibit high light-dark contrast, and are brightly colored or shiny. And what objects in the baby's environment have those properties in spades? You guessed it—looming and animated human faces displaying high-contrast hairlines and prominent, shining eyes. People are goods with flashy packaging for the infant consumer. Better yet, these animated faces also make noise. As described in other chapters, babies seem to be pretuned to process human speech sounds, prefer them over other stimuli, and appreciate the synchrony of a voice and its proper face. These predispositions ensure that babies attend often and long to the people they see most often—usually the parents. This repeated experience allows them to discriminate specific people to whom they eventually will become attached.

Another cognitive prerequisite for attachment is the cognitive ability to construct expectations about reciprocal interactions with an adult, described earlier. Moreover, infants may generalize similar routine interaction sequences with a caretaker into generalized episodes, much like the scripts described in Chapter 3. Infants register "a small but coherent chunk of lived experiences," consisting of "sensations, perceptions, actions, thoughts, affects, and goals, which occur in some temporal, physical, and causal relationship so that they constitute a coherent episode of experience" (Stern, 1985, p. 81). Psychologists call this representation of the self, a significant other, and the relationship between the two an "internal working model" (Bowlby, 1969; Bretherton, 1991), which connotes the relationship's dynamic, changing nature during development as people and life circumstances change. Infants use these internal working models to interpret events and predict what will happen in the future. If a mother has consistently responded to the baby's signals, the child will develop the expectation that the mother will do so in the future.

Another cognitive prerequisite for attachment that would be on everyone's list is infants' knowledge about objects, particularly their permanence. If an infant were too cognitively immature to differentiate external objects from his own actions and to conceive of them as independent entities that continue to exist when perceptually absent, he could scarcely either yearn for or search for an absent mother (attachment figure), since she is, of course, also an external object. As long as "out of sight, out of mind" applies to his mother as well as to other objects, one could hardly say that a baby's attachment to her had progressed very far. Conversely, once the object concept is established, he can bridge her physical absences by symbolic-representational means and thereby sustain an enduring affective link to her that we can comfortably refer to as genuine social attachment. Moreover, Piaget and others have suggested that the mothering figure might well become the very *first* of the infant's permanent objects, a most plausible idea in view of her general emotional and attentional salience for him, and in view of the frequency with which he must see her disappear and reappear every day. Unfortunately, this very plausible parallel between the development of the object concept and attachment has been difficult to capture experimentally (e.g., Campos & Stenberg, 1981). The problem may be that, as we saw in Chapter 2, researchers cannot agree on the age at which infants can be said to "have" the concept of object permanence; indeed, recent research suggests that infants may never wholly lack it.

Still another cognitive skill that draws babies and parents together is babies' early competence regarding imitation. As described in Chapter 2, possibly from very early in life babies can imitate certain facial expressions of adults. Besides reinforcing adults, this behavior often sets in motion a series of imitative sequences. Surely this encourages a feeling of "us." Moreover, babies apparently somehow know when they are being imitated and prefer to attend to adults who do so. Meltzoff (1990a) showed this in an experiment in which a 14-month-old baby faced two adults across a table. All three had the same toy. Whenever the baby moved or otherwise manipulated the toy, both adults responded immediately. One imitated the baby's actions, while the other performed some other action with the toy (i.e., those of the previous subject). The babies smiled and looked longer at the imitated adult. We would not conclude that babies, like adults, know that imitation is the sincerest form of flattery, but we would conclude that they detected behaviors that matched their own and were interested in adults (usually parents in real life) who tend to imitate them.

In summary, by the end of infancy a child has a fragile sense of an autonomous agentic self that is physically and psychologically separate from other autonomous agentic creatures. At the same time, the child knows that he or she connects with these separate social objects in many ways, such as shared imitations, the turn-taking of games and vocalizations, and the satisfaction of desires by compliant others. The biggest prize, of course, is one or more caretakers with whom the child has cognitive and emotional bonds. Babies and their parents share a history that allows the development of mental models of parents. These include parents' consistent behaviors, which allow babies to predict parental behaviors, especially those that will satisfy babies' desires.

Infants' emerging concepts of others, the self, and social relations may reflect a beginning awareness of the mind (the Existence category), which blossoms into a theory of mind during the preschool years (see Chapter 3). Specifically, infants' observations of others' present actions eventually lead to predictions of their future actions and to attributions of "dispositions to behave" and intentions. The awareness of these dispositions may even be central to a desire psychology in 2- and 3-year-olds—their belief that a person's desires lead to certain behaviors that satisfy that desire. Preschoolers' knowledge about desires, beliefs, thoughts, and the like in turn provides a conceptual foundation for their reasoning about the social world. Another set of knowledge basic to social cognition concerns the realm of emotions, to which we now turn.

UNDERSTANDING EMOTIONS

Emotions are not only felt experiences but also objects of people's thinking. It is difficult to imagine a socially competent human who did not possess an understanding of emotions and their relation to cognition and behavior. Children must acquire this knowledge to do effective "social work," such as identifying the feelings of other people toward them, anticipating whether their parents will be angry or pleased about their behavior, and hiding their socially inappropriate feelings. Such knowledge surely promotes positive relationships with others, effective self-presentation, and the attainment of rewards or interpersonal advantage. Perhaps reflecting the importance of this topic, research in the area has boomed in the last several years. Recent useful sources are available (Gross & Ballif, 1991; P. L. Harris, 1989a; Saarni & Harris, 1989). Also, several neo-Piagetian accounts are promising (e.g., Case, Hayward, Lewis, & Hurst, 1988; Fischer, Shaver, & Carnochan, 1989).

Inferring Emotions

In Chapter 2 and earlier in this chapter we described precursors to the understanding of emotions. For example, by about 12 months infants use their mother's face as a social barometer and approach or avoid objects depending on her smile or frown. Infants of course also express a variety of emotions themselves—often long and loud.

If you observed children during their second and third year of life, you would be struck by their rapidly increasing skill at differentiating among emotions. They must, of course, have this ability in order to refer appropriately to an emotion in themselves or others. By 20 months, they may use the words "happy," "sad," "mad," and "scared" (Bretherton, McNew, & Beeghly-Smith, 1981) and, by 28 months, "have fun" and "love" (Bretherton & Beeghly, 1982). By 2½ they even talk about the causes and consequences of these emotions in themselves and others (Beeghly, Bretherton, & Mervis, 1986). For example, "Santa will be happy if I pee in the potty" and "Bees everywhere. Scared me" (Bretherton & Beeghly, 1982). Note that these causal statements can refer to the past or the future, and imagined circumstances, as well as the present. Concepts of emotion evolve from a global "feels good" and "feels bad" to a range of differentiated emotions, for example, "mean" and "excited" by age 3 (Ridgeway, Waters, & Kuczaj, 1985), "proud," "jealous," and "worried" by age 7, and "relieved" and "disappointed" by preadolescence (P. L. Harris, Olthof, Meerum Terwogt, & Hardman, 1987). A similar development during the preschool years from simple to complex, subtle emotions emerges in children's ability to point to the appropriate facial expression for an emotion word or for a character in a story.

To a great extent these early inferences of emotions may rely on seeing happy, sad, or angry faces. However, life presents many situations when facial expressions cannot be used as cues—the face is not visible, the emotion in question is a subtle one not easily linked to a facial expression, or the true emotion is masked by a different facial display. In these cases how are emotions inferred? More generally, what cognitive skills could young children have that would help them organize certain events as sadness-producing and others as happiness-producing? After all, very different kinds of events can produce sadness—for example, breaking a favorite toy, being called "stupid," having to eat spinach, and seeing a parent leave. What general principle organizes these together into a single category of sadness?

One proposal (P. L. Harris, 1989a) is that children draw on their own social experiences to identify the critical aspects of the situation. There may be a cognitive simulation of sorts, as children imagine, based on their own experience, the mental state that someone would have in that situation (see also Smiley & Huttenlocher, 1989). Another proposal (Stein & Levine, 1989) is that children define an emotion in terms of whether a goal is satisfied, rather than just the overt situation such as a birthday party or a smile. Recall that the theory of mind work discussed in Chapter 3 shows that preschoolers come to grasp the causal relations among desires, beliefs, and emotions (Hadwin & Perner, 1991; P. L. Harris, 1989a; Wellman, 1990). Even young 3-year-olds understand that if Joey wants hot oatmeal for breakfast he will be happy if that desire (goal) is satisfied and sad if he gets cold spaghetti instead (Banerjee & Wellman, 1990). Because people differ in their beliefs and desires, their emotional reaction to the same situation may vary. A person who dislikes oatmeal would not be happy upon receiving it and would not be sad if he or she does not. This realization that a situation can cause different emotional reactions in different people is explicit in children's speech by about their third birthday, as seen in the following conversation (Banerjee & Wellman, 1991, p. 7):

Father: Okay, I'll stop. Marky's mad at your daddy.
Ross: But I'm happy at my daddy. (2 years, 10 months)

Thus, even preschoolers to some extent view emotions as mediated by a mental state. The unfulfillment of a desire leads to sadness, whereas the disconfirmation of a belief leads to a more cognitive emotion—surprise. The latter concept appears to be a later acquisition. Three- and 4-year-olds do not think a protagonist will be surprised when, for example, he goes to collect eggs from a goose and finds that she has laid an apple (Hadwin & Perner, 1991). However, see Banerjee and Wellman (1990) for evidence of earlier acquisition.

With increasing age, children become more aware of various sources of information for inferring emotions. Suppose that at nursery school a child is trying to decide whether to ask Jimmy, who has a desirable toy, to share that toy, and is attempting to gauge his mood. She could draw on cues such as his facial expression, the context, the disposition of the person, or normative information about a group to which the person belongs (e.g., Gnepp, 1989). Specifically, she could consider that he is smiling, that there were several fun events at school that day, and that Jimmy is generally a happy child, but also that boys at that school tend to become angry when asked to share. This sounds rather complicated for a young child to sort out, and in fact, she may be limited in several ways. First, the ability to infer emotions from information about the person such as his group membership (e.g., gender, age, race) and specific personal experiences such as encountering a person who earlier treated you badly, comes rather late—during grade school and preadolescence (Gnepp, 1989). On the other hand, as mentioned earlier, even preschoolers understand the impact of personal likes and desires on emotions. Second, when there are several cues, a child younger than about 6 is likely to be able to use only one cue to infer Jimmy's emotional state, perhaps because of capacity limitations. Third, preschoolers have trouble dealing with conflicting cues, such as when one cue suggests sadness and another suggests happiness.

Chapter Five

Understanding Facial Display Rules and Mixed Emotions

One of the most difficult cases of cue conflict is when a person's facial expression conflicts with his or her true emotion. A good example is when a preschooler knows that another child wants a computer game for his birthday, and sees him receive socks instead, but smile nevertheless. She is unlikely to make the inference that the child just appears happy but really is sad. Preschoolers rarely go beneath the surface and ignore the apparent emotion in favor of the real emotion. The notion of hiding one's emotions is foreign to them. This is a fairly complex concept, for the child must mentally represent two contradictory states: the felt emotion and the socially appropriate one. We will examine this concept in some detail because it is an important one, permitting new and adaptive ways of interacting with others—ways that prevent negative reactions from others. A child learns very quickly that expressing certain emotions leads to taunts of "scaredy-cat," "party-pooper," "wimp," or "crybaby" from peers.

Let us consider two experimental examples of children's understanding of *display rules*—putting on a false face or saying something one does not really believe so as to hide the way one really feels. In one (Gnepp & Hess, 1986), children aged 6, 8, 10, and 15 listened to stories and decided which facial expression the child in the story would display and what he would say. In one story, for example, a child lost a talent contest and saw everyone applaud the winner. Children's understanding of facial displays—for example, that the child would smile to hide his disappointment—increased during this age span, though it leveled off after age 10. Interestingly, children understood verbal displays (for example, "I didn't really want to win anyway") better than facial displays. Parents may socialize display rules mainly by stressing verbal behaviors such as, "Tell Aunt Grace how much you like the nice shirt she gave you."

Our other experimental example of display rules assessed display behaviors rather than reactions to stories. It is likely that these behaviors draw on the knowledge that feelings can be masked by engineering an appropriate facial expression. Saarni (1984) first built up an expectation among 6- to 10-year-olds that they would receive desirable presents, by giving them a good present for helping with a task. However, a final present was an undesirable one, a drab and unimaginative baby toy. Many of the 10-year-olds, but few of the 6-year-olds, smiled or said "thank you" enthusiastically after opening the present. This finding is consistent with the everyday observation that adults can read young children's faces "like a book." Many of the children, in a transitional phase, gave an interesting in-between reaction—smiling slightly and mumbling their thanks. Because producing an appropriate display rule requires skill and motivation, as well as understanding, these behaviors are not a pure assessment of the relevant cognition. Still, the application of knowledge to social behavior is a central issue for the study of cognitive development.

Although little knowledge of display rules seems to emerge until age 6 (P. L. Harris, Donnelly, Guz, & Pitt-Watson, 1986) or later (Gnepp & Hess, 1986), one study challenges the above age norms by finding that even preschoolers can produce facial displays to some degree. Pamela Cole (1986) observed 3- and 4-year-old girls opening a disappointing gift either alone or in the presence of the experimenter. Motivation to hide negative feelings should be higher in the latter condition. The children concealed their disappointment with at least a half smile when the experimenter was present but not when they were alone. However, they were not able to verbalize the use of display rules. They either have the concept but are not aware of it or do not possess it and simply are following a "politeness rule" (P. L. Harris, 1989a)

Although school-age children are well aware of the value of hiding one's feelings in certain situations, they also know that it is maladaptive to carry this to the extreme of rarely expressing one's real feelings to others. The majority of children aged 6 to 13 believe that such a child would be disliked and perceived as maladjusted, and would be difficult to get to know (Saarni, 1988). One psychodynamically oriented 13-year-old girl predicted that "if she kept everything inside her all the time, she'd consume all her anger, jealousy, whatever, and then one day she'd explode, commit suicide, and get emotionally disturbed" (p. 289).

Do emotionally disturbed children even use facial display rules? Paul Harris and his colleagues (Adlam-Hill & Harris, 1988; M. Taylor & Harris, 1984) studied emotionally disturbed boys aged 7 to 11 who had a variety of problems such as anxiety, depression, explosive behavior, cruelty to others, or extreme uncooperativeness. They presented these boys, and a sample matched for verbal intelligence and family background, with hypothetical situations. In situations in which facial displays would avoid hurting someone else's feelings, the normal boys were more likely than the disturbed boys to say that what they said would not reflect how they really felt. The groups did not differ in self-protective situations, such as hiding embarrassment at having to wear a red velvet suit with a lace collar. The normal boys also were more likely to mention the thoughts or feelings of other people. Thus, emotionally disturbed children may have less awareness of others' emotional life or may be less motivated to spare the feelings of others. Harris concluded that they "are less attuned to the emotional dialogue that takes place between people, whereby the expression of emotion of one person arouses thoughts and hence feelings in another" (P. L. Harris, 1989a, p. 145).

It is interesting to note that with display rules children in a sense unlearn what they had learned earlier. Preschoolers gradually learn that physical evidence, such as behaviors, facial expressions, and speech, provide clues to the contents of the mind. But then they learn that such evidence may not only be unreliable or inaccurate but may even be a red herring, designed by other people to deceive. This surely is a major developmental step regarding social cognition.

In addition to the case of conflicting cues when there is only one true emotion is the case when people actually do have two or more conflicting emotions—for example, feeling happy about going on a long summer vacation while feeling sad about leaving friends. Although even toddlers behave ambivalently, as when they both approach and avoid an interesting but strange event, such as a department store Santa, they cannot conceptualize this emotional state until many years later. If you suggest the possibility of having two simultaneously conflicting emotions to young children, they will be confused or amused. Young children explain that it is impossible to feel happy and sad at the same time because, for example, "You can't make your mouth go up and down at the same time" (Harter & Buddin, 1987) and "You haven't got two heads—you haven't got enough brains" (P. L. Harris, 1989a). Before 6 or 7 years of age, children generally are limited to describing situations eliciting two successive emotions: "If you were in a haunted house you'd be scared but then you'd be happy after you got out of it" (Harter, 1982). Later they accept two concurrent emotions, but only if they are of the same valence, such as mad and sad, and directed toward a single target—for example, "If your brother hit you, you would be both mad and sad" (Harter & Buddin, 1987). Not until approximately age

10 (but see Stein & Trabasso, 1989, for evidence of earlier competence) do children understand that two opposite-valenced emotions, such as happy and sad, can be experienced simultaneously: "I was mad at my brother for hitting me, but at the same time I was really happy that my father gave me permission to hit him back" (Harter & Buddin, 1987). The conceptual difficulty posed by all of the dual, conflicting representations presented in this chapter is consistent with the work on representation in children's understanding of the mind (Chapter 3).

Other major advances in concepts of emotions also emerge with increasing age (e.g., Flapan, 1968; Rothenberg, 1970; Savitsky & Izard, 1970). Older children and adolescents are more likely than younger children to try to infer feelings spontaneously, without explicitly being asked to (a development in the Need category). They become increasingly accurate at diagnosing emotional states, and they need fewer obvious clues to do it. In addition, they know that a person's emotional reaction to a current situation may be colored by a previous emotional experience (see Postulate 5 in Chapter 3). For example, they recognize that a person might continue to brood about an earlier unhappy experience and that this mediating mental event could serve to dampen a person's positive feelings about a present happy event. In contrast, younger children tend to take into account only the immediate, present situation in predicting the person's feelings. Older children also are more disposed and able to explain the feelings they have diagnosed (Hughes, Tingle, & Sawin, 1981). Furthermore, their explanations increasingly will include the actions and feelings of others as causes (e.g., "He is unhappy because she doesn't love him") as well as impersonal causes (e.g., "He is unhappy because he lost his watch"). Predictably, their affect inferences can also be more complex, abstract, and broad-ranging. For instance, an adolescent may represent and sympathize with the chronic, silent plight of some distant group as well as the temporary, noisy distress of a familiar individual (Hoffman, 1978). Altogether children's increasingly mentalistic concept of emotions makes for profound and pervasive changes in their social cognition in this area.

Are there certain circumstances in which normal children who understand a good deal about emotions cease to use this knowledge? This question was examined in a group of 6- and 10-year-olds hospitalized for a variety of ailments, ranging in severity from an ingrown toenail to serious conditions such as multiple burns (P. L. Harris & Lipian, 1985; Lipian, 1985). In comparison to healthy children, these children doubted that emotions could be masked or changed, or could be mixed, and were pessimistic about successfully tempering their illness in any way by directing their emotions (i.e., psychosomatic effects). Thus, they saw emotions as visible and beyond strategic control. These differences did not simply reflect the ill children's inability to deal with their own emotions effectively, due to considerable stress. They conceptualized others' emotions in the same way, for example, when discussing a hypothetical child with a minor illness or when they were dubious that their parents might use display rules and act more cheerful than they really felt. Healthy children, in contrast, believed that cognitive control of emotions is possible. For example, one healthy 10-year-old believed in the power of positive thinking: "Yeah, think like, 'I'm gonna be better tomorrow'—and three days later, you *are* better. It's like hair conditioner, or soap—you think that it's gonna work, so it *does* work" (P. L. Harris, 1989a, p. 184). Harris attributes these differences to ill children being engulfed in the patient role and thus having trouble stepping outside their current passive role to consider other situations in which they can be more active cognitively or can experience more positive emotions.

Cultural and Social Influences

Although we have sketched the developmental milestones in concepts of emotions, we have not yet addressed the cultural and individual differences that would be expected by the contextualists. Cultural differences sometimes lead to variations in the cognitive structuring of emotions. For example, Japanese and American children and Japanese mothers believe that a child lost in a store would experience sadness, whereas American mothers believe the emotion would be fear (Lewis, 1989). Some cultures protect children from observing certain emotions, such as grief or lust, in other people, or discourage them from expressing these emotions. Many cultures discourage the awareness of, and expression of, sadness and fear among boys more than girls. Thus, the culture encourages boys' use of display rules for these emotions though, interestingly, boys generally are less likely to use display rules to hide disappointment than are girls (Davis, 1992; Saarni, 1984).

A culture's language is a powerful influence on concepts of emotions. For example, Samoans do not verbally distinguish between hate and disgust (Gerber, 1975) and the Utku of Canada distinguish fear of physical calamity, *ighi*, from fear of being treated unkindly, *ilira* (Briggs, 1970). When a child experiences an emotion and the parent gives it a label, this naming makes the emotion salient and influences how a child interprets the feeling. For example, Ifaluk parents in Micronesia sensitize their children to the emotion *metagu*, roughly translated as "social fear and anxiety," by frequently, and approvingly, labeling children's reactions as *metagu* in the presence of strangers, in large groups, and in other appropriate settings (Lutz, 1983). The important point here is that to some extent emotion concepts are social constructs. The culture teaches the child what to feel and when to feel it. Children learn to define, categorize, and label emotions differently in different cultures. Cultural beliefs, values, and socialization serve to direct and organize conceptions of emotion. These cultural factors encourage certain emotions, or their expression. They also impart social scripts (see Chapter 3), which inform children of what emotions to anticipate in the self and others, what emotions to express, and how to express them in particular settings, such as funerals, birthday parties, movies, and encounters with bullies (e.g., Lewis, 1989; Russell, 1989).

With respect to social influences causing individual differences within a culture, certain maternal behaviors seem particularly important. Mothers who have many talks with their young children about emotions, and about their causes and consequences, tend to have children who talk more about these topics later on (Dunn et al., 1987) and, at age 6, these children are better able to infer and explain the feelings of others (Dunn, Brown, & Beardsall, 1991). These discussions in the context of family conflicts are especially beneficial, as is frequent cooperation with an older sibling (Dunn, Brown, Slomkowski et al., 1991). Perhaps positive interactions with someone near the child's level of feelings, thoughts, and interests help the child gain insights into the emotional life of another. Moreover, mothers who had been highly responsive and affectionate *with the sibling* had children who possessed a superior affective perspective-taking ability. Thus, children are, after all, members of a family, and they carefully observe and try to understand what happens between other family members in emotion-laden contexts. Discipline practices matter as well. Mothers who tend to talk about their own emotions with their child and endorse control of children through inducing guilt tend to have children with a good understanding of the causes of emotion (Denham & Zoller, 1990).

This suggests that martyr-mothers made famous in Woody Allen films are very effective for teaching about the causes of emotions.

An interesting gender difference has emerged in several studies. Mothers talk more about emotions with their daughters than with their sons, and this difference is paralleled in their children's language (Dunn et al., 1987). Overall, mothers discuss anger more often with their sons than with their daughters, and sadness or positive emotions more often with daughters than with sons (Fivush, 1990). Importantly, mothers cognize about anger differently to their sons and daughters, as seen in the following two conversations (Fivush, 1990, pp. 13, 17):

> Mother: Does it make you sad when mommy and daddy tell you that you can't do something?
> Son: No.
> Mother: No?
> Son: No, you make me mad.
> Mother: I make you mad? Oh, ok.
>
> (Mother and daughter are discussing a time when a sister took the child's crayon)
> Mother: How did you feel?
> Daughter: ummmm, FINE.
> Mother: You cried?
> Daughter: NO! FINE!
> Mother: Oh, fine (laughs). You felt fine. Were you upset when Catherine took your crayon?
> Daughter: Yeah.
> Mother: Umm-hmmm. What did you say to her?
> Daughter: To not take it!
> Mother: Right. Don't you take it. That's my crayon. Do you love Catherine?
> Daughter: Ummm, let's see…YEAH!
> Mother: Good, I'm glad you said that. Good answer.

The first mother accepts anger in her son. In contrast, the second mother, even in a situation in which anger in her daughter would be a reasonable response, directs the conversation toward keeping the relationship with the sister intact, despite the sister's inappropriate behavior toward the child. Given these experiences, it is not surprising that both girls and women are poorer than males at identifying anger (or more reluctant to identify anger) in characters in videotaped episodes (Riess & Cunningham, 1989). They performed equivalently for other emotions. As Fivush (1990, p. 2) concludes, these findings suggest "that the way in which emotions are talked about early in development has an impact on the individual's developing understanding of emotions and the way in which emotions are integrated into one's self-concept, gender-concept and interpersonal behavior."

Effects on Behavior: Prosocial Acts and Self-Control over Emotions

Our discussion of the development of the understanding of feelings is incomplete because it has only hinted at the connection with the child's own emotions and the child's behavior toward others and the self. Regarding other people, a child who infers another's distress may be more likely to engage in prosocial behavior such as comforting and helping, especially if he or she empathically feels distress as well. Even toddlers occasionally appear to try to change other people's emotions. In the second year of life they begin to comfort younger siblings in distress by patting, hugging, or kissing them, and may even bring a security blanket to an adult in pain (Wolf, 1982). Their attempts to cheer up others sometimes take unexpected forms. Dunn and Kendrick (1982a) describe a plump 15-month-old who often amused his parents by pulling up his shirt to reveal an impressive stomach. One day, upon observing his 3-year-old brother crying after a fall, he approached him, pulled up his shirt to show off his stomach, and looked expectantly at him! This new power to change emotions, however, is a force for evil as well as good. As parents stretched to the limits of their patience know, young children sometimes tease or otherwise annoy siblings, hoping to elicit frustration and anger. These episodes usually involve destroying a favorite possession or taunting, but occasionally are more subtle, as when one 24-month-old child teased her sister by pretending to be her imaginary friend (Dunn & Munn, 1985). Such behaviors, positive or negative, are revealing, for they suggest that children are beginning to identify the conditions that elicit or change emotional states.

Notice that both comforting others and producing facial or verbal displays, discussed earlier, are behaviors that attempt to manipulate the mental state of someone else. The mental state is an emotion in the former case and a belief in the latter. Children also learn how to control their own emotions. For example, boys at an English boarding school acquired the understanding that they could distract themselves from feelings of homesickness with a situational strategy—immersing themselves in games or other activities (Harris & Guz, 1986; P. L. Harris & Lipian, 1989). Later, by age 10 or so, they offered mentalistic explanations for why this strategy works. In other settings, children use other mentalistic strategies such as controlling their desire for something they must wait for by changing their cognitive state, as when a desired marshmallow is imagined as a puffy cloud or a "yucky" tasting object, or as filled with an evil spell (H. N. Mischel & Mischel, 1983). Children learn many ways to put Satan behind them. When all else fails, one strategy that works is leaving the situation. One grade-school child who suddenly felt like giggling at a funeral suggested: "I'd walk over away from Mom, like walk over to a tree, turn away, and then giggle if I really had to" (Saarni, 1989). These examples suggest some important links between cognition and behavior.

These concepts of emotions may be part of children's general theory of mind discussed in Chapter 3. By age 3, children realize that emotions exist (Postulate 1), and connect to events in the world and behaviors (Postulate 2), but are different from those events and behaviors (Postulate 3). Understanding facial displays is an expression of Postulate 4—understanding that a single reality can lead to two mental representations. A late acquisition includes understanding that an emotional state can be controlled by creating cognitive distractions or transformations (Postulate 5, an active mind).

UNDERSTANDING PERCEPTS

A second basic social concept concerns what other people are experiencing perceptually. Knowing what goes into the mind through the senses (e.g., "She sees a candy bar") surely influences one's knowledge of what another person desires

("She wants it") and believes ("She thinks she can reach it if she stands on her tiptoes on a chair"). A young child's concept of percepts sometimes shows *egocentrism*, the belief that other people hold the child's own perspective on the world. However, from early on, children have many direct opportunities to learn that their own perceptions differ from situation to situation and that their perception can differ from that of others. They see in the light but not in the dark or when their eyes are closed. A sibling on the other side of a book one is holding says that he cannot see the picture in the book. Children gradually understand that other people also see objects, and that the nature of another person's visual experience at a given moment can often be inferred from various clues (e.g., the apparent direction of the person's gaze or the spatial relation between the person and what he or she is looking at). A recent review by Newcomb (1989) provides a comprehensive account of perspective taking and related spatial knowledge.

Level 1 and Level 2 Knowledge

There appear to be at least two roughly distinguishable developmental levels or stages of Existence-type knowledge about visual percepts (Flavell, 1974, 1978a; Flavell, Everett, Croft, & Flavell, 1981; Hughes & Donaldson, 1979; Masangkay, McCluskey, McIntyre, Sims-Knight, Vaughn, & Flavell, 1974; Shantz, 1983). At the higher one, called Level 2, the child has a symbolic-representational (i.e., not merely sensorimotor) understanding that an object or array of objects presents different appearances when viewed from different spatial locations. The child is aware that even though she and another person both see the very same object, they nonetheless see it differently—have different visual experiences of it—if located at different observation points. She knows that, consequently, they form different representations of that object (see Postulate 4 in Chapter 3).

The younger, Level 1 child has acquired the very fundamental and important insight that another person need not always see the same object that she herself currently sees. For instance, she is likely to realize that, if a picture of an object is held vertically so that the picture's face is toward her and its back toward another person seated opposite her, she sees the depicted object but the other person does not. Similarly, she probably would be aware that, if she placed an object on the other person's side of an upright opaque screen, the other person would see it even though she herself no longer could. What she fails as yet to represent, however, is the Level 2 idea that an object which is currently seen by both is seen differently from different spatial perspectives. What is addressed at Level 1 is the global, all-or-none question of *whether* someone does or does not see something; *how* that something looks from here versus there, assuming that it is visible from both positions, is probably not yet a meaningful question. The Level 1 child thinks about *viewing objects*, according to this theory, but not yet about *views of objects*. The presence of an object causes a single representation. In Level 2, the child realizes that two people can have two conflicting representations of one object.

Masangkay and colleagues (1974) found that 2- to 3-year-olds can usually solve very simple Level 1-type problems, such as the vertical-picture problem just mentioned. It is not until 4 to 5 years of age, however, that children get to be equally facile with very simple Level 2-type problems, such as the following. Child and experimenter sit facing one another and a sideview picture of a turtle is placed flat on a small table between them. The experimenter first shows the child repeatedly that the turtle appears "right side up" (i.e., standing on its feet) to him when the picture is placed in one horizontal orientation, and "upside down" (i.e., lying on its back) when the picture is rotated 180° from that orientation. He then asks the child which of these two perspectives of the turtle he and the experimenter see in each of a series of these 180° picture rotations. Only 9 out of 24 3-year-olds were consistently correct in attributing the upside-down view to the experimenter when they saw the right-side-up view, and vice versa, although all 24 children were always accurate in describing their own views. In contrast, 35 out of 36 subjects aged 4 to 5½ years old were consistently accurate in their inferences about how the turtle looked to the experimenter (see also Flavell, Everett, Croft, & Flavell, 1981). As indicated earlier in our example of the flowers-and-vases perspective task, however, it is one thing to know in general that object appearance covaries with observer position (Level 2 Existence knowledge) and quite another to construct an accurate, detailed representation of exactly how something appears from a position other than one's own (Inference skills). The turtles task was the easiest, least-taxing perspective problem Masangkay and colleagues could think up. Even though it may indeed have required some genuinely Level 2 Existence knowledge for its solution, as intended, it certainly required next to no Inference skill. Numerous other studies (see Newcomb, 1989; Shantz, 1983) have shown how very much more Inference-skill acquisition 4-year-olds have ahead of them before they reach their zenith as visual perspective takers.

Where does this knowledge about percepts begin? Lempers and colleagues (1977) gave a large battery of simple tasks to 12- to 36-month-old children in their homes with the help of their mothers. They designed the tasks to assess various skills within each of three major categories of Level 1 ability: (1) *percept production* or provision, where the child causes another person to have a visual percept of an object that the other person did not previously have—for example, by showing the person an object picture or pointing to an object; (2) *percept deprivation* or prevention, where the child hides an object or otherwise prevents the other from seeing it; (3) *percept diagnosis*, where the child infers what object the other is visually attending to by interpreting the other's eye or finger orientation, as indicated by the child looking where the other looks or points, rather than simply staring at the person's eyes or outstretched finger.

A number of interesting results emerged. The favored method of showing pictures at 18 months seems to be to share the percept—for example, holding the picture flat or while standing directly beside the other. This method gives way at 24 months to the adult-like procedure of holding the picture vertically, turning it around, and thrusting its face toward the other so that only the other sees it. If the other holds his hands over his eyes at the time, the 18-month-old may, and the 24-month-old will, uncover the eyes before showing the picture. The latter child can also solve showing problems with which she has presumably had little experience in everyday life, such as showing a picture that is glued to the inside bottom of a hollow cube. Children acquire percept-deprivation skills (e.g., hiding objects) later than they do percept-production ones, but both seem well developed by age 3 (see also Flavell, Shipstead, & Croft, 1978). In general, the results of these studies suggest that at least some elementary forms of cognition about visual percepts may develop toward the beginning of the early-childhood period.

Levels 1 and 2 are related to the distinction between pre-Postulate 4 and Postulate 4 (understanding representations) knowledge in children's theory of mind. This can be illustrated in a study by Flavell, Green, and Flavell (1990). Children viewed objects under a variety of perceptual conditions. Three-year-olds accurately said that they saw an object but did not hear it, that they heard an object but did not see it, and that they neither saw an object nor heard it. They also knew that an object was still there even though it was not visible nor audible, and that another person could see an object when they could not and vice versa. Thus, they understood the Postulate 2 connections-level versions of perspective-taking tasks; you perceive something only if you are exposed to it. This is Level 1 percept knowledge. Note that it is an impressive show of nonegocentrism that they could deny that another person sees something that is compellingly visible to them. However, they did poorly on the Postulate 4 representations-level counterparts of the first set of tasks, which corresponds to Level 2 percept knowledge. Three-year-olds could not say, for example, that a toy bear who was behind a large elephant mask and meowed, looked like an elephant, sounded like a cat, and really was a toy bear—even though the experimenter had just told them what it looked like, sounded like, and really was. Remarkably, they had the same problem when an adult they knew well put on, while they watched, a dog mask but talked in her normal voice. Thus, they had problems discriminating between what an object looked like it was from its visual appearance and what it sounded like it was from the noise it made, and discriminating between these appearances and what the object really was. This set involves conflicting representations of an object: its visually given apparent identity, its auditorily given apparent identity, and its real identity. In other words, 3-year-olds understand conflicting cognitive connections on a variety of tasks, but not conflicting representations on analogous tasks. Expressions like "It looks like an A from here," "It looks like a B from where you are," "It sounds like it is a C," and "I (you) believe it is a D" are meaningful to a 4-or 5-year-old, but tend to be terra incognita for 3-year-olds. This poor understanding astonishes the adult mind, particularly given that the stimulus sometimes was a real person, and that the experimenter even had told the children the correct responses.

Understanding Line of Sight

Let us examine in more depth one basic concept about others' percepts, namely, what falls within a person's line of sight. The contextual approach views the ability to interpret parental gaze as an important part of attention-directing activities in "apprenticeship" settings with young children. Also, this knowledge enhances joint visual attention with adults, which creates shared experiences believed to support language acquisition. How early do children consider others' line of sight?

Consider what one mother reports about her 8-month-old:

> He likes the curtains—to try and close them, he doesn't like to be told off for that; he usually waits to go for the curtains when I'm in the kitchen, when I'm around here he doesn't tend to go that much because he knows he's not really allowed to do it, because if I just go into the kitchen and get something, he thinks I'm not looking and makes a beeline for the curtain. Makes a dash for it, you can see him looking over his shoulder to see if I'm watching him, and if I tell him from the kitchen "no"—he stops and looks at you and grins for a while and if I sort of say no really loudly—not loudly it's actually more deep—he lets go and gives a start and whimpers a bit. As soon as I've turned my back he makes another move for it—tends not to do it if I'm actually watching. (Reddy, 1991, p. 146)

Thus, very early in life children may have some rudimentary sense of Level 1 knowing about what someone else can or cannot see, though this 8-month-old may only require that the person be in the room, or that he be able to see the person, before inferring that the person can see him. As mentioned earlier, around this age infants follow their mothers' line of sight and look at where she points.

The concept of line of sight actually is more complex than it seems. For example, one might ask whether young children know that lines of sight are always straight, that is, cannot curve around visual barriers. It seems plausible that they would have learned from experience that they cannot see around corners without moving their heads. Flavell, Green, Herrera, and Flavell (1991) asked 3- to 5-year-olds to predict whether they would be able to see, by looking into a tube, an object inside that was toward the far end of the tube. All children correctly said "yes" when the tube was straight (180°). However, when the experimenter curved the tube to angles of 140° (like a smile), 90° (like a bigger smile), or 0° (like a candy cane), most of the 3-year-olds, and many of the 5-year-olds, continued to predict that they still would be able to see the object. The 3-year-olds were remarkably firm about this belief. Even after they looked into curved tubes and found out that they could not see the object, they still believed that they would be able to see the object in a curved tube! Moreover, they held the same belief about other people's lines-of-sight as about their own. Presumably they would see nothing humorous in a cartoon of an astronomer with a curved telescope! In fact, the only situation in which 3-year-olds seemed to understand that someone could not see an object, in this case outside the tube, along a curved-looking path was when a salient barrier occluded the line of sight.

We conclude that, by age 3, children know that to see something an observer's eyes must be (a) open, and (b) aimed in the general direction of the target. They also will usually infer that (c) an observer cannot see the target if there is a salient and familiar barrier between observer and target. However, they apparently do not yet know that (d) an observer *always and necessarily* sees targets via straight-line-looking paths. Understanding of eye line may require attending to *how* seeing is accomplished, which looks like a Level 2-type of awareness of perceptual process rather than perceptual product (whether a viewer sees the object or not, as in Level 1). Young children also may be confused by their experiences with the power to change the direction of their gaze and to see objects via peripheral vision. This knowledge may interfere with their efforts to sort out which aspects of line of sight can be changed and which cannot.

A final central fact about vision is that you can be looking right at something and not really see it, as when you frantically look all over your house for your car keys, only to find them finally in the place you looked first. P. H. Miller and Bigi (1977) asked children to select objects to surround the target in a visual search task so as to make the search for the target, a red triangle, harder (or easier). Younger children had the simple notion of adding a lot of objects, regardless of color or shape, so that the game player would have to look through many objects. By age 8 or 9, children began to realize, in addition, that surrounding the target with objects identical to the target in shape and color (other red triangles of various sizes) would make the target blend into its background and not be seen immediately even though it was "right in front of his eyes."

We know much less about children's knowledge about sensory modalities other than vision. In the auditory modality, research has focused on attention, specifically on the distracting aspects of noise or on the failure to attend to verbal messages. P. H. Miller and Bigi (1979) found that when talking about attention, young children usually assert that unless the situation is noisy, a person will hear and comprehend what someone says to him. The disruptive effect of noise was vividly described by an 8-year-old: "When it's noisy, I can't read; it seems as though everything around me is moving around and dropping on the floor and breaking or something, so when I'm reading I just can't stand it." By about age 8, children begin to realize that the mind controls the attentional process to some extent (the Postulate 5 knowledge of Chapter 3). They also know that a lack of interest in what someone is saying (usually a teacher!) makes a person shut out the message, even if the room is quiet. Similarly, strong interest in an activity reduces attention to other sounds. One child thought that she would not hear her mother calling her if she were engrossed in reading because "when I'm really getting into something everything just stops and I can't hear anything except what I'm doing." Higher forms of knowledge about attention also would include the ability to detect feigned attention ("You're not *really* listening, Mommy!") and inattention ("You're just *pretending* not to notice, Mommy!").

This awareness of the contribution of psychological states to the attention process is solidly in place by the late grade-school years. However, older preschoolers show this knowledge if they merely have to indicate which of two or three situations is most conducive to attending to the task at hand (P. H. Miller & Bigi, 1979; P. H. Miller & Shannon, 1984; P. H. Miller & Zalenski, 1982; Pillow, 1988a, 1989).

Thus, children gradually realize that perception of sights and sounds involves more than just open, correctly oriented eyes, unobstructed ears, the absence of barriers, and sounds loud enough not to be drowned out by other noise. Sounds must be attended to. Objects must be attended to and in one's straight line of sight. Even objects "right in plain sight" (or "right in plain hearing") may not be perceived fully, in the case of selective attention, or immediately in the case of target-background similarity.

KNOWLEDGE ABOUT PERSONAL ATTRIBUTES

Children acquire an understanding of minds in general—for example, that minds are responsive receptacles of desires, beliefs, emotions, and percepts. These general concepts about thought also will help children construct concepts about particular other people, especially regarding their unique personal attributes such as behavioral dispositions and personality traits. Moreover, children develop concepts about one very special familiar person—the self. No discussion of social cognitive differentiation and connection would be complete without a look at concepts of other people and the self.

Others

The counterpart of this section in Shantz's (1975) review of social-cognitive growth has a homely but apt title: "What is the other like?" How, in other words, do children of different ages construe and characterize the personal characteristics of other people? What are the salient developmental changes in the way they describe human personalities? Excellent reviews of this topic can be found in Rholes, Newman, and Ruble (1990), Hill and Palmquist (1978), Livesley and Bromley (1973), and Shantz (1975, 1983). The Livesley and Bromley text also contains an extensive and insightfully discussed empirical investigation that serves to illustrate the way research is commonly done in this area. The subjects in their principal study were 320 English boys and girls, 40 at each of eight age levels between 7 and 15 years.

Over a series of sessions the children wrote descriptions of themselves and other people they knew well. They were very carefully and repeatedly instructed to indicate what sort of person the individual is, what he or she is like and what they think of him or her, and *not* to describe the person's physical appearance, clothing, and so on. Although such free-description procedures have their problems (Berndt & Heller, 1985; Shantz, 1975), they illustrate some of the most pervasive developmental trends in the social-cognitive literature. The following developmental sketch is a synthesis of their findings and those of other studies (e.g., Barenboim, 1977, 1981; Flapan, 1968; Peevers & Secord, 1973; Rosenbach, Crockett, & Wapner, 1973).

The child of 6 to 7 years or younger is very prone to describe the other person's general identity, appearance, family, possessions, environment, and so on, despite the experimenter's explicit instruction to the contrary. Almost 50 percent of Livesley and Bromley's (1973) 7-year-olds failed to mention even a single psychological quality. If any personal traits do get mentioned they are apt to be global, stereotyped, and highly evaluative ("He is very bad"). Children of this age are also likely to describe the other in rather egocentric, self-referential terms ("She gives me things"). This excerpt from a 7-year-old's description of a woman she likes illustrates some of these properties:

> She is very nice because she gives my friends and me toffee. She lives by the main road. She has fair hair and glasses.... She sometimes gives us flowers.... (Livesley & Bromley, 1973, p. 214)

During middle childhood, children cognitively penetrate beneath the skin, and their descriptions become more focused on traits and dispositions. Their trait vocabulary increases considerably and the trait-descriptive terms they select seem less global and stereotyped, more abstract, and more precise in meaning than before ("nice" gives way to "considerate," "helpful," etc.). They often endow the other person with attitudes, interests, abilities, and other psychological qualities seldom found in younger children's descriptions. The more external types of attributions (possessions, etc.) also occur, however, and will continue to do so into adulthood. (Peevers and Secord [1973] make the interesting observation that nonpsychological descriptors do sometimes seem to help create a vivid impression of the essence of an individual.) The middle-childhood subject's character sketch is still likely to be rather poorly organized, however, with different attributions just strung together in a more or less random sequence. In the same vein, young children have trouble perceiving a person as possessing simultaneously both positive and negative traits. For example, a liar who becomes a good baseball player is no longer considered a liar (Saltz & Medow, 1971). More generally, there is not apt to be much explanation and integration in their descriptions. Two 10-year-olds' descriptions illustrate these points:

> She is quite a kind girl.... Her behaviour is quite good most of the time but sometimes she is quite naughty and silly most of the time.... (Livesley & Bromley, 1973, p. 218)

> He smells very much and is very nasty. He has no sense of humour and is very dull. He is always fighting and he is cruel. He does silly things and is very stupid. He has brown hair and cruel eyes. He is sulky and 11 years old and has lots of sisters. I think he is the most horrible boy in the class. He has a croaky voice and always chews his pencil and picks his teeth and I think he is disgusting. (Livesley & Bromley, 1973, p. 217)

Some interesting novelties become increasingly prominent during the adolescent years. The subject flexibly and methodically selects ideas from a wide range of possibilities, and carefully shapes them into an organized, integrated portrait of the other. He knows that his impression of the person is only *his* impression, and may therefore be inaccurate or different from other people's. He is sensitive to the presence of seemingly contradictory traits and of different levels of depths within the individual's personality; the individual may be both this and that, or may appear to be this and really be that "underneath." For example, a 13-year-old acquaintance of one of us began his written character sketch of a friend this way (it was an English class assignment, and was therefore judged to require fancy vocabulary—this too represents a bit of social cognition): "He may appear a joker in class because of his unique style of eloquence, but in reality he feels a deep responsibility toward the advancement of his own personal knowledge." The adolescent also feels that a human personality represents a unique blend of qualities and therefore deserves an idiosyncratic, nonstereotypic characterization. Because he is aware of these considerations, he tries to explain and justify, not merely describe, and he tries to particularize and qualify, not just baldly assert. Since there are apparent contradictions within or between levels of an individual's personality, he knows that one must appeal to dispositions, motives, personal history, environmental factors and forces, or other internal and external causes to explain and reconcile them. And since each individual is believed to have a unique personality, he feels one should search out (and explain) unexpected combinations of traits, unusual blends of feelings, and so on. The best examples of these higher forms of personality description are, of course, to be found in great literature, not in Livesley and Bromley (1973). Nonetheless, Livesley and Bromley and other investigators have obtained some fairly impressive specimens from lesser mortals: "She is curious about people but naive, and this leads her to ask too many questions so that people become irritated with her and withhold information, although she is not sensitive enough to notice it" (Livesley & Bromley, 1973, p. 225).

We find Shantz's (1983) précis of developmental changes in the child's "implicit personality theory" both apt and easy to remember:

> If one were to view the "child as a psychologist" who subscribes to certain positions or theories, the developmental changes, broadly put, suggest the following: prior to 7 or 8 years of age, the child conceives of persons largely as one who is both a demographer and a behaviorist would, defining the person in terms of her environmental circumstances and observable behavior; during the middle childhood, persons are conceived more as a trait-personality theorist would, ascribing unqualified constancies to persons; and by the onset of adolescence, a more interactionist position emerges in which people and their behavior are often seen as a joint function of personal characteristics and situational factors. (p. 506)

Much debate centers on the age at which this transition from external to internal attributes occurs (Rholes et al., 1990). Recent studies using assessments other than free descriptions (e.g., Eder, 1989) report a rudimentary awareness of traits, or at least behavioral consistencies or enduring internal states, in preschoolers. Of course, at any age a number of motivational and situational factors affect whether a child will focus on psychological or physical attributes. For example, 5- and 6-year-olds who expected to interact later with a child they viewed on a videotape showed an increased tendency to describe the child in psychological terms, including traits, up to the level normally found in much older children (Feldman &

Ruble, 1988). Psychological attributes are of more concern to children when they think they will be personally involved. Thus, motivation affects children's cognition about other people.

We end this section by simply mentioning two active areas of research on person perception. One documents that perceptions of other people are influenced by various preexisting ideas, or "stereotypes," as to what females, males, minorities, heavy people, redheads, teachers, old people, and so on "usually are like." Social categories enrich, but can also distort, children's perceptions of others' personal attributes. Good sources for this literature on children are Biernat (1991), Katz (1982), and Ruble and Stangor (1986). The second area examines parents' perceptions of their children's attributes and abilities (e.g., Goodnow & Collins, 1990; S. A. Miller, 1986b, 1988; S. A. Miller & Davis, in press). Research to date provides some support for the guiding ideas behind this line of inquiry: that children are important targets for most parents' social-cognitive efforts, and that the perceptions parents form can influence their behavior toward their children and hence the children's development.

Self

We can use the concept of differentiation to help us organize the course of development of the self concept—the mind's "I." Recall our organizing theme that a central task for the child is to acquire the sense that she is a distinct and separate entity, clearly differentiated from all others, but also socially and emotionally connected to others. The reciprocal interactions with others, described earlier, serve as a training ground for an infant's primitive sense of self. She learns that she is a physical object that occupies a particular location in space, is physically detached and separate from other objects, and has her own distinctive physical properties (physical appearance, voice quality, etc.). She begins to see herself as a psychological being (a person, a self) as well as a physical one, again to be distinguished from all of her fellow psychological beings; she has her own unique selfhood and others have theirs. Moreover, this self eventually will be conceived as somehow retaining its own singular, unique identity ("me-ness") over time and the physical and psychological changes that time brings.

Later, she may make further differentiations between her own conception of herself and the various conceptions of her that she thinks various other people have. There are also many other self-other and within-self differentiations that will follow this development. She will learn that she is a female rather than a male, a differentiation that will have profound implications for her conception of what and who she is, and will engender many other differentiations. Within the self, but achieved through comparisons with others, she will distinguish between attributes (personality traits, intellectual competencies, moral qualities, etc.) she thinks she has and those she thinks she lacks. She will build up a differentiated psychological profile of herself. These differentiations will in time lead to a greater or lesser differentiation between the self she thinks she is stuck with (actual self) and the one she wishes she owned instead (ideal self). Thinking of the development of self-conceptions as an extended process of making many differentiations will not take us the whole way in understanding this development, but it definitely helps. For other aspects of this development, see Kopp and Brownell (1991), Damon and Hart (1988), Gunnar and Sroufe (1991), and Cicchetti and Beeghly (1990).

Our story of the development of the self-concept, which began with our earlier discussion of infant social cognition, now moves to toddlerhood. One of the earliest researched questions was whether toddlers can recognize themselves visually. This question was stimulated by an observation by Gallup (1977) that, after a few days of experience with a mirror, chimpanzees began to use the mirror to examine and experiment with visually inaccessible parts of their bodies. For example, Gallup saw them grooming parts of their bodies that they could not see, making faces at the mirror, and picking bits of food out of their teeth. Instead of treating the image in the mirror as though it were another creature, as other animals have been observed to do and as they themselves did at first, the chimps seemed to construe it as a *self*-image. That is, they acted for all the world as though they recognized themselves in the mirror, and recognized themselves *as* themselves—that is, they knew that the familiar-looking objects they saw were their own bodies.

To test this possibility more rigorously, Gallup anesthetized the chimps and, while they were asleep, applied a bright red, odorless, nonirritating dye to parts of their faces that they could not see without a mirror. After recovery from the anesthesia they were observed in front of the mirror. The chimps did not reach out and touch the directly visible red marks on the surface of the mirror, as they might well have done; instead, they touched the "invisible" red marks on the surfaces of their faces. Significantly, they also examined and smelled their fingers after touching their faces, in an apparent attempt to find out what had gotten onto their faces.

Can other animals recognize themselves as themselves, as assessed by Gallup's mark-on-the-face method? The orangutan, another great ape, definitely can (Gallup, 1977), gorillas probably can (Patterson, 1979), but gibbons, baboons, and monkeys apparently cannot. Gallup believes that these startling findings may testify to the presence of some form of self-concept and self-awareness in the great apes, a capability that had previously been thought unique to human beings. Apes who have been taught to use nonvocal, language-like symbol systems can use them to refer to themselves (e.g., Premack, 1976), a finding that also seems to support Gallup's contention.

What would happen if a procedure similar to Gallup's were used with human infants of different ages? Several studies of this kind have now been done and their results are in quite close agreement; see Brooks-Gunn and Lewis (1984) for reviews of these studies. A study by M. Lewis and Brooks-Gunn (1979) illustrates the method and typical results. Infants aged 9 to 24 months were first observed, unmarked, in front of a large mirror to get baseline data. Their mothers surreptitiously applied rouge to their noses with a cloth, under the pretense of wiping dirt off their noses, after which they were again placed in front of the mirror. Only 2 infants touched their noses during the baseline period, whereas 30 did after the rouge was applied. No child younger than 15 months of age showed this mark-directed behavior, and there was an increase in age from 15 to 24 months in the number of children showing the behavior. This understanding of the physical self may be necessary before a child can feel self-conscious. Infants who act embarrassed in the mirror test nearly always touch their noses (Lewis, Sullivan, Stanger, & Weiss, 1989). Interestingly, young children's behavior before mirrors does not depend on having experience with mirrors. Infants from a nomadic desert culture in Israel, who had no prior experience with mirrors or other reflective surfaces, showed the same self-recognition behavior as infants in a nearby city (Priel & de Schonen, 1986).

These studies and others provide ample evidence of the self-recognition prowess of older infants (circa 1½ to 2 years of age). In addition to touching their noses they will also say "nose," show clear nonverbal signs of recognizing themselves in videotape replay and still photographs as well as in mirrors, and use their own names to refer to the external image of themselves that they see. Children of this age also show other signs of a developing sense of self, such as a growing sense of how things are supposed to be and a tendency to want to perform tasks by oneself and to express elation upon completing a task independently (Bullock & Lütkenhaus, 1990; Kagan, 1981).

The onset of language affords us more information about self-concepts. If you were to ask a preschooler to describe himself, as did Harter (1988), he might, if unusually articulate, give you something like the following:

> I am a boy, my name is Jason. I live with my mother and father in a big house. I have a kitty that's orange and a sister named Lisa and a television that's in my *own* room. I'm four years old and I know all my A,B,C's. Listen to me say them, A, B, C, D, E, F, G, H, J, L, K, O, M, P, R, Q, X, Z. I can run faster than anyone. I like pizza and I have a nice teacher. I can count up to 100, want to hear me? I love my dog, Skipper. I can climb to the top of the jungle gym. I have brown hair and I go to preschool. I'm really strong. I can lift this chair, watch me! (Harter, 1988, p. 47)

Jason's self-portrait, besides leaving us breathless, illustrates several characteristics of the preschool "me," a portrait that is similar to preschoolers' perceptions of other people described earlier. He gives specific examples rather than generalizations, telling us about his cat and dog rather than his love for animals. He refers to physical, concrete, observable behaviors, skills, possessions, and characteristics rather than inferred stable traits such as being smart or good at sports. Finally, Jason's knowledge of the alphabet makes us question the accuracy of his self-assessment, though not his pride in his achievement! Young children's overly rosy view of their abilities pervades the literature (for example, their overestimations of their memory abilities described in Chapter 6). Perhaps children are confusing the *wish* to be competent with reality (Harter, 1988). Or, they may lack a mature concept of ability and do not yet use the performance of other children to determine how hard a task is and how much ability they have if they succeed on the task (Stipek & MacIver, 1989). This Pollyanna view may be desirable for optimal development, for this view may encourage children to try tasks that they would be discouraged from trying had they a more realistic self-appraisal (Bjorklund & Green, 1992). Indeed, by age 11 or 12 when children clearly differentiate ability and effort, both their enthusiasm and their optimism are dampened, for they now realize that they have inherent limitations in certain areas that cannot be overcome simply by trying harder (Skinner, 1991). It is interesting that a slightly overly positive perception of one's competence is associated with mental well-being in adults (S. E. Taylor, 1989).

By middle childhood, these self-descriptions change drastically. They are the opposite of those of preschoolers: general dispositions (often bolstered with examples) that are fairly accurate. Moreover, now that children do more comparing of themselves with other children, they include comparative information: "I'd like to be an actress when I grow up but nobody thinks I am pretty enough. Jennifer, my older sister, is really pretty, but I'm smarter than she is" (Harter, 1988, p. 49). Also, as children approach preadolescence, their self-descriptions become increasingly based on their relationships with others, the "connectedness" aspect described earlier: "I'm pretty popular. That's because I'm nice and helpful, the other girls in my class say that I am. I have two girlfriends who are really close friends, and I'm good at keeping their secrets. Most of the boys are pretty yucky"

(Harter, 1988, p. 49). At this age children also refer to how they feel about what they are like. Expressions of shame and pride are particularly revealing of children's *evaluation* of their perceived self.

The grade-school years also bring the realization that the self "resides" in the brain, a developmental change supported by a series of studies of children's judgments about the consequences of hypothetical transplants of various body parts (C. N. Johnson, 1990). Kindergartners realized that after a Frankenstein-like operation a pig with a human brain would still look like a pig, but they had little understanding that behavior, feelings, and thoughts would change. By age 7, children generally understood the consequences of transplanting their own brain into a character of categorically different status, such as a pig or baby. For example, they thought the pig would still look like a pig but now would "like to get tucked in all cozy in bed at night" rather than "love sleeping in the sloppy mud," and would have memories of being a child rather than a pig. By age 9 or 10, they believed that transplants of the mouth, face, or heart have a much more limited effect, though they believed that giving one's own heart to a mean 2-year-old would (like the Tin Woodsman?) increase his kindness! Several concepts probably contribute to this developmental trend: biological knowledge, categories of living things, and a theory of mind.

This description of development probably underestimates preschoolers' knowledge about the self in at least one way, namely, in depicting it as concrete and specific, as opposed to being trait-like—abstract and general. As we have seen so many times before, different methods elicit different levels of knowledge from young children. In this case, if instead of asking a 4-year-old to describe himself, you were to ask him a general trait question (e.g., "Tell me how you are at school when you're with friends"), he would give you general trait answers, such as "I usually am good" (Eder, Gerlach, & Perlmutter, 1987). As Eder and colleagues point out, it should not be surprising that preschoolers have at least a rudimentary notion about what they usually are like or usually do, because similar notions appear in their scripted knowledge (see Chapter 3)—abstract concepts of what usually happens in certain events. "What I usually am like at school" and "what usually happens at school" both call forth general, abstract information. Still, it is important to note that the differing results with the open-ended method and the more directed methods suggest that global descriptions of the self are not as accessible to the young child as are specific, concrete descriptions.

Do these global descriptions of the self provide any evidence in young children for a "theory of self," in the sense of an organized, coherent set of concepts characteristic of the theory-based approach (see Chapter 3)? Eder (1990) used pairs of puppets to present dispositional statements, for example, "I get mad a lot" and "I don't usually get mad." Three-year-olds were asked to choose the puppet who was more like them. Their choices of dispositional self descriptions formed psychologically meaningful groups and were somewhat stable over one month. For example, if a child chose the high end of the bipolar dimension for one "aggression" item he tended to do the same for other aggression items. He also tended to be low on a larger "self-control" factor: He would say he feels like hitting people when he is angry, tries to push in front of people in line, gets grouchy a lot, thinks it would be fun to hang upside down on a jungle gym, and disobeys his mother or teachers. Thus, even preschoolers seem to possess general, organized knowledge about the self, rather than just a set of concrete, independent descriptions of specific behaviors.

In addition to the developmental trends described above, some critical individual differences in self-concepts emerge that affect children's academic progress.

A particularly interesting one is differences in boys' and girls' attributions about their academic success or failure (e.g., Dweck & Reppucci, 1973). In general, when a boy performs poorly, such as when receiving a poor grade on a test, he tends to attribute it to not trying hard (i.e., not studying much for the test). In contrast, girls tend to attribute failure to poor ability ("I'm just not good at math"). You can see the cause for concern here if you predict their behavior before the next exam or when they must choose courses for the next year. A boy would assume that he could do better if he were to study more, whereas a girl might assume that this would have little payoff, given her limited ability. She also might not be likely to select advanced math courses. Fortunately, intervention can change these attributions, with the expected changes in behavior (Dweck, 1975).

Now that we have described the development of the self-concept and mentioned some individual differences, the next question might be "So what?" "What is the function of the self-concept?" Brownell and Kopp (1991, p. 297) suggest that from early in life "the function of self might be said to be the location of or imposition of order in the world from a simple consistent vantage point, and the definition of the world from that vantage point." Just as an infant uses the self to bring stability to a complex, changing world, so older children may achieve this by actively constructing rules about themselves and their social world (Ruble, 1987). Ruble argues that these self-based organizing rules influence children's behavior and, consequently, how others respond to them. Thus, children play an active role in their own socialization. More specifically, children actively seek information about themselves (for example, through social comparison) and interpret this information in light of their beliefs about themselves. For instance, at around age 7 children begin to switch from seeking information about other children's appearance or behavior to seeking information about others' levels of performance. Particularly important is the child's heightened interest in, or susceptibility to, relevant information at particular developmental periods. Information about the behaviors or preferences of one's own gender may have little influence at one age but considerable influence at another when children are preoccupied with that aspect of their self-definition. The kind of information supplied at this sensitive period is critical because it guides subsequent information processing in self-perpetuating ways. Ruble suggests that once children have labeled themselves as incompetent, they may interpret feedback in a way that perpetuates that belief, such as attributing failure to lack of ability.

One hard-to-resolve issue is the relation between social-cognitive development regarding the self and others. One may pull the other along, they may pull each other along, or both may emerge from a more general cognitive structure. The evidence is contradictory at this point. This issue is very important, because school-age children construct self-concepts in part from comparisons with their peers.

KNOWLEDGE ABOUT THE CAUSES OF BEHAVIOR

People construct not only concepts of themselves and other people, but also plausible theories (see Chapter 3) about why people do the things they do. The "person-on-the-street" (or "child-on-the-playground") makes causal attributions about everyday behavior. From the theory of mind research (Chapter 3) it is clear that even young children are beginning to explain behavior by appealing to desires, beliefs, emotions, and percepts, but much more develops in this area. We will address three questions. First, what is the developmental course of what is perhaps the most basic causal notion—that human behavior can be, and usually is, intended (caused by human volition)? Second, how early do children understand and detect specific psychological causes? Third, do children tend to use external-physical or internal-psychological causes to explain behavior and does this change developmentally?

Understanding Intentions

Acquiring the concept of intentionality is a highly significant development for children for at least two reasons. First, it helps them understand how people differ from other objects. Unlike the behavior of other objects, much of the behavior of human beings is caused by their intentions. Certain of their actions are voluntary or willed—instigated and impelled by their own inner intentions, motives, and plans. The second reason is that knowledge about intentions is indispensable for understanding responsibility and morality (Astington, 1991). Children must learn that people deserve to be praised or credited, blamed, or judged to be blameless, depending in part upon whether what they did was intentional or unintentional, and whether the effects of what they did were intended or not intended. Good sources on the childhood development of knowledge about intentions include Astington (1991), Karniol (1978), Shantz (1983), Shultz (1991), Shultz and Wells (1985), and M. C. Smith (1978).

One concept acquired during infancy and toddlerhood that may set the stage for the concept of intentionality is that of *agency* (Shultz, 1991). This notion is that a being moves or behaves of its own accord without an external cause and can carry out some activity. Most physical objects do not have this characteristic. Near the end of the first year of life, an infant seems to have a rudimentary notion that people are agentic when she tries to communicate with people, but not objects, to get them to do things for her. At about the same time she also realizes that only people have autonomous movement. In a study by Poulin-Dubois and Shultz (1988), infants saw a ball "spontaneously" roll and hit a second ball, which struck a wobbling doll. The 13-month-olds did not significantly decrease their attention (habituate) to this ball-as-agent condition over the 10 trials. In contrast, they did habituate to a person-as-agent condition, a person pushing a ball, which is a less interesting event if you believe that people but not objects are agentic. Thus, fairly early in life babies seem to have a rudimentary notion of human agency that may serve as a building block for the concept of intentionality. This concept of agency later may be linked to preschoolers' concept of animism (see Chapter 3). The concept of intentionality goes beyond that of agency and animacy by inferring an internal mental state that guides behavior. A person not only *can* act; she in fact wants and tries to act.

Most of the research on postinfancy concepts of intentionality has focused on children's use of intention information in making moral judgments, rather than on their knowledge about intentions per se. Research on moral reasoning in children grew out of Piaget's (1932) seminal studies on this topic. One of his many findings, subsequently confirmed by others, was that there is a developmental tendency during middle childhood for blameworthiness to be based on intentions rather than amount of damage done. For example, children were asked which child is naughtier—a child who clumsily breaks one cup in the course of doing something he should not do, or one who, through a completely unavoidable accident, breaks 15 cups in the course of doing what his mother told him to do. Children of 6 to 7 years of age were apt to say that the second child was naughtier because his action resulted in more damage. In contrast, children of 9 to 10 years were likelier to assert that the first child was naughtier because of his bad intentions.

For a long time researchers tended to interpret the results of these studies as suggesting that children below 8 or 9 years are either unaware of intentions or do not see their relevance to judgments of moral responsibility (Shultz, 1980). However, it gradually became clear that these studies have serious methodological flaws that preclude the drawing of such conclusions. To illustrate, since *both* children in Piaget's story did their damage accidentally rather than intentionally, we have no way of knowing whether the younger "damage-responsibility" subjects are or are not cognizant of the intentional-unintentional distinction. Similarly, we could only conclude that they did or did not see the relevance of intentions to culpability if we changed the research procedure so that key variables would not be experimentally confounded. For example, we could use a story in which both children do the same amount of damage. In fact, several investigators have used such methods and have found that children even younger than 7 to 8 years are able to recognize that the one who did the damage intentionally is more blameworthy (Shultz, 1980).

More recently, researchers have studied children's understanding of intentionality more directly, rather than inferred it from research on moral judgments. Some clever studies by Shultz (1980) suggest that 3-year-olds may have some ability to distinguish intended actions from such nonintentional behaviors as mistakes and reflexes. In one of his tests for the distinction between intentional and mistaken behavior, he asked the child to repeat tongue twisters (e.g., "She sells sea shells by the sea shore"). Of course, the child was likely to make mistakes. Then he would ask either that child, or another 3-year-old bystander who had previously experienced the task, or one who had not, "Did you (he/she) mean to say it like that?" Shultz found that his 3-year-old subjects could usually answer that question correctly, and about equally so whether in the role of speaker, experienced bystander, or inexperienced bystander. That means that even a child who had not yet tried to repeat a tongue twister knew that another child who repeated it incorrectly did not "mean to say it like that." Less clear was whether 3-year-olds understood that a knee jerk reflex was not done "on purpose." Shultz (1980) also reported some naturalistic observations of 3-year-olds using the "not on purpose" argument. For instance, one child accidentally hurt another and was asked to apologize to the crying victim. The child refused, indignantly claiming that he had not done it "on purpose."

Do all these correct uses of "mean to" and "on purpose" by 3-year-olds reflect a genuine grasp of the intentional-unintentional distinction, or is there a simpler concept underlying them? One possibility is that children may simply have formed an association between these phrases and certain preceding events (e.g., errors) or outcomes. Perhaps children associate errors with "not on purpose," and also associate the latter with avoiding punishment for a misdeed.

For another interpretation, consider the following pair of stories read to children (Astington, 1991). In one story a girl takes some bread outside, throws crumbs to the birds, and the birds eat them. In the other story another girl's mother gives her some bread, which she takes outside to eat. Some crumbs happen to drop behind her and the birds eat them. The stories had the same outcome, in both cases resulting from the actor's behavior, but only the first story involved intentionality. When asked which girl meant for the birds to eat the crumbs, 4- and 5-year-olds correctly chose the first girl, but the 3-year-olds chose each girl equally often. The latter were not sensitive to intentionality. Astington proposed that Shultz's 3-year-olds inferred intentionality only when a person's desire is fulfilled. When a desire and the outcome did not match, as when wanting to say a tongue twister correctly but making an error, children concluded that the behavior was not intended. If outcomes are the same and desires are not explicitly stated, as in the bread crumbs study, 3-year-olds cannot distinguish between the two girls in terms of who meant to achieve the outcome. This indicates that they do not fully understand intentionality. They do not understand that an intention might not be fulfilled, and a desired outcome could come about fortuitously, not caused by the child's intention. Their "desire theory of mind" (Chapter 3) leads them to confuse desire and intent, possibly because each is either fulfilled or not fulfilled by an outcome. What the children understand by age 4 or 5, in a true concept of intention, is that intent is a mental state that exists regardless of the outcome. Intention is a prior state, a mental representation, that plays a mediating causal role between desires and actions. Thus, an adequate concept of intent involves two components: (a) a nonaccidental behavior related to desires and differentiated from outcomes; and (b) a prior mental state of thinking about and planning a future action.

What causes this developmental progression? Certain experiences may facilitate the understanding of intentionality. Adults may respond to unintended and intended actions differently—for example, telling the child that her harmful action had been done on purpose, and punishing her for it. Children might work out various rules of thumb for making the distinction. As examples, they might come to assume that an outcome is likely to be intended if it matches the agent's stated intention, if the agent looked as though he was trying to achieve it, and if he does not look disappointed, surprised, or puzzled when it occurs. Also, in the case of one's own behavior, intended and unintended actions and outcomes engender very different thoughts and feelings in oneself—very different "metacognitive experiences," to use a concept from the previous chapter.

Although intentionality usually is well understood by grade-school-age children, some interesting exceptions exist. As described in Chapter 1 in the context of Dodge's information-processing model, highly aggressive boys tend to interpret violence toward themselves as intended in situations in which normal boys would consider the intent ambiguous; the violence could have been intentional or accidental. Further evidence that deviant social perceptions can cause aggression comes from programs that attempt to change social cognition in order to change behavior. For example, a group of adolescents incarcerated for aggression offenses participated in such a program that encouraged attending to relevant nonhostile cues, seeking additional information, and generating nonviolent responses (Guerra & Slaby, 1990). Participants showed increased social problem solving, decreased endorsement of beliefs supporting aggression, and decreased aggression.

In summary, infants have some notion of people as agents. By age 3 children often can distinguish intentional behavior from mistakes or accidents, but children probably do not understand intent as a prior causal mental state that is independent of the outcome of actions until age 4 or so. This ability to infer intentions accurately continues to develop throughout childhood as more and more subtle cues can be used to make the inference. Some children fail to develop this skill adequately and are at risk for developing various problematic social behaviors, such as social aggression.

Understanding Specific Psychological Causes

An intent is a very general psychological cause of behavior. Thus a second issue posed by young children's reasoning about the causes of behavior is how early they can understand and detect *specific* psychological causes and how their ability to do so improves in the course of development. Plenty of examples from earlier in the chapter (e.g., talk about emotions) and from theory-of-mind research (Chapter 3) come to mind to suggest that even toddlers are beginning to detect specific psychological causes. Their spontaneous speech refers to psychological states, for example, "I left it [TV] open because I wanna watch it" (L. Hood & Bloom, 1979, p. 6). However, we must be careful not to attribute too much competence to these utterances. They could merely reflect toddlers' awareness of a temporal link—"because" may equal "happens after." This issue is difficult to resolve because much causal reasoning at any age is derived from temporal and spatial contiguities (Shultz, 1982).

It is interesting that nearly all of children's early causal utterances refer to the social world rather than the physical world (Bloom & Capatides, 1987b; Hood & Bloom, 1979). Perhaps 2-year-olds have more need to communicate with others about their own needs and desires than about the physical world. Or, perhaps young children know more about possible psychological mechanisms, such as desires, than they do about physical causal mechanisms (P. H. Miller & Aloise, 1989), as would be predicted by their desire theory of mind.

During the preschool years children broaden the range of causes they can detect. As described in other sections, they can predict the effect of a variety of emotions, abilities, perceptual perspectives, beliefs, and motives on a person's behavior. Also, they are acquiring event or script knowledge that allows them to see how psychological states fit into event sequences, as when a person buys a ticket to enter a movie house because he wants to see a movie and buys popcorn because he believes he will crave it once the movie starts and he smells other people's popcorn. Not until middle or late childhood do children fully differentiate closely related causes, such as ability and effort (e.g., Skinner, 1990; Stipek & MacIver, 1989), and become aware of more subtle psychological causes. One example of the latter is "distant" indirect causes such as influential events in the person's past or his or her personality traits (Gnepp & Gould, 1985), to be discussed below. Still other psychological causes are not fully understood until early adolescence. For example, P. H. Miller and DeMarie-Dreblow (1990) showed videotaped vignettes of children displaying displaced aggression, such as a girl knocking over a younger sister's tower of blocks after an older sister forgot to buy ice cream as promised. Although the 5-year-olds understood that the aggression was redirected from its intended target, they did not understand the underlying motivation for this redirection or the unconscious psychological process at work. The 10-year-olds were beginning to acquire these concepts (see also Chandler, Paget, & Koch, 1978; Weiss & Miller, 1983; and Whiteman, 1967).

One efficient type of internal causal explanation is a trait that causes the person to behave in a consistent way over time and situations. A "mean" peer can be counted on to steal the candy bar from your school lunch, distract you in the middle of an intense video game, and push you down in the park. If he did these things last month, last week, and today, you can sadly assume he will do them, or something equally mean, tomorrow. How early in life do children explain and predict behaviors on the basis that "he is just that kind of person"? Earlier we reported that preschoolers may occasionally include traits in their description of a person. However, they may have specific behaviors rather than general dispositions in mind (Rholes et al., 1990). Also, they rarely draw on traits as causes of behavior. Age 5 to 7 appears to be a transitional period, with some studies (e.g., Gnepp & Chilamkurti, 1988; Heller & Berndt, 1981; Ruble, Newman, Rholes, & Altshuler, 1988) revealing appropriate predictions of behaviors based on traits and other studies (e.g., Rholes & Ruble, 1984; Stipek & Daniels, 1990) finding serious limitations. For example, children of this age overpredict that a person with a positive trait would do well in unrelated domains—for instance, predicting that a "nice" classmate would jump over higher hurdles than classmates labeled not nice (Stipek & Daniels, 1990). On the other hand, they underpredict in that they have only a shaky understanding that a trait can be expressed in different, but related, behavior (Rholes & Ruble, 1984). Thus, young children detect behavioral regularities, give them a trait label, and sometimes treat them as causes, but may not see the trait as a stable, abiding, differentiated internal cause until age 8 to 10. For excellent reviews of this research see Rholes et al. (1990) and Yuill (in press).

The lesser tendency of young children to infer similar behavior across situations may reflect their belief that situations control behavior, so behavior may change from one situation to another. Some behaviorists, such as B. F. Skinner, might argue that social-cognitive development should stop right there! Another explanation is that young children do not yet have the cognitive ability to fully differentiate attributes of people from the contexts in which these attributes are expressed. This issue of differentiating situational and psychological causes leads us to our final question about causes: Do children of various ages prefer external or internal causes?

Tendency to Use External or Internal Causes

Suppose a 3-year-old sees his friend walking down the street holding his mother's hand as a Great Dane approaches them. He could encode this event as "He's holding his mommy's hand" or "He's scared of the dog"—a more informative and satisfying account for someone trying to understand human behavior. Thus, like psychologists, young children could be considered either "behaviorists" or "mentalists" in their portrayals of human behavior. Ten years ago young children were considered behaviorists, tending to describe events in observable, physical terms and to attribute behavior to external causes. This chapter has provided plenty of examples of such behaviorist tendencies to focus on external aspects of a situation: Young children tend to describe others in terms of their appearance, behavior, and possessions. They also rely on facial expressions for cues to emotions and associate intentionality with desirable outcomes. Moreover, they tend to judge the wrongness of a behavior in terms of the amount of damage done, rather than the person's intentions. Given this external stance, it is not surprising that when young children are asked to explain the behavior of a child in an oral or videotaped story they tend to refer to external rather than internal phenomena. For example, they often simply refer to events in the story (Flapan, 1968).

Recently, this apparent developmental change from external to internal attributions has been challenged (e.g., Lillard & Flavell, 1990; P. H. Miller & Aloise, 1989) on several grounds. First, as we have discussed, toddlers and preschoolers actually do have some awareness of mental states and may even have a coherent "theory of mind." Second, Piaget's (1929) observations of preschoolers' animistic thinking (Chapter 3) suggest a tendency to refer to human-like desires and intentions in inanimate objects. They impute psychological causality freely—in this case where it does not belong. Third, when assessments are made less verbally demanding or when internal states are made more salient, young children can use psychological states to describe or explain human action, and often even prefer to do so. Two studies illustrate this latter conclusion. Both reduced verbal demands and equated the salience and accessibility of mental and physical features by using a forced choice procedure. Because mental states by their nature cannot be observed directly, whereas external features can, there ordinarily is an imbalance in their salience. Consequently, young children in real life may be satisfied with the more salient and accessible external description or causal explanation and thus appear to prefer external causal explanations.

Lillard and Flavell (1990) examined 3-year-olds' preferred way of describing events. They showed them three differently colored copies of the same picture. The experimenter described the first picture in terms of the mental state of the person in the picture, and the second picture in terms of the person's behavior, or vice versa. Then the experimenter presented the third copy and the child was asked to tell a puppet about the picture. In this way, the child could choose between the mental and behavioral description. The pictures did not supply cues to either the behavior or the mental state. For example, in one picture a child was sitting on the floor crouched over a glass of spilled milk; neither his face nor his behavior (wiping up the milk) was visible (see Figure 5–3). Therefore, the two possible descriptions offered ("He's feeling sad about his spilled milk" and "He's wiping up his spilled milk") were equally plausible. Other vignettes depicted choices such as being happy with the puppy versus patting the puppy, wanting to get a cupcake versus standing on tiptoes by the cupcakes, and wondering what game to play versus standing still. The children tended to choose mentalistic descriptions. This was true even in a second study (See Figure 5–3) when pictures were biased toward behavioristic descriptions as follows: (a) the behavior was made fully visible—for example, one could see the boy's hand holding a sponge over the spilled milk, and (b) mental states were not even suggested by the picture—for example, a boy sitting in a corner had the mental description of, "He's hoping his teacher will read him a story." Thus, when mentalistic accounts of behavior are available, children prefer to use them, even when a behavioristic description is more salient.

This preference for mental descriptions carries over into mental causes by age 4. P. H. Miller (1985) presented a series of vignettes, illustrated with small dolls, depicting two children engaging in the same activity. One child was described in terms of an internal variable (interest, motivation, psychological effort, or intellectual ability) and the other child in terms of an external variable (parental pressure,

FIGURE 5–3 Illustration depicting boy wiping up/feeling sad about his spilled milk. Picture on left is from Study 1 (wiping behavior is not visible); picture on right is from Study 2. From Lilliard, A. S., and Flavell, J. H. *Child Development, 61*, p. 733. Copyright © 1990 by The Society for Research in Child Development, Inc. Reprinted by permission.

noise level, visual distractions, or external reward). The child was then asked which of the children would do the "most" of the activity. As a group, 3-year-olds preferred no external causes and preferred only one internal cause—intellectual ability. However, 4-year-olds favored three of the internal causes—interest, intellectual ability, and motivation—and none of the external causes. Thus, the 4-year-olds preferred internal psychological causes over external ones.

It certainly should not be concluded that young children always prefer psychological causes. Several studies (e.g., Higgins & Bryant, 1982) have found a preference for nonpsychological causes—causes outside of the person—in the preschool years. Indeed, as was noted earlier, adults often prefer to attribute behavior to external causes, especially when explaining their own behavior rather than that of others (e.g., Nisbett, Caputo, Legant, & Marcek, 1973). Overall, it appears that preschoolers prefer psychological causes unless the relevant information for making this inference is too complex or subtle (P. H. Miller & Aloise, 1989). This problem occurs when children are asked open-ended questions about filmed stories, especially if these stories involve social knowledge not possessed by young children. For example, in one such story (Flapan, 1968) an overly harsh father has somewhat unjustly punished his daughter. He feels guilty and tries to make it up to her by taking her to the circus. Not surprisingly, 5-year-olds do not detect this rather subtle psychological cause of his behavior. The cause preferred also appears to depend on the type of event being explained (e.g., choosing a game vs. a friend), the target of the attribution (self vs. others), and the valence (positive or negative) of the behavior (P. H. Miller & Aloise, 1989).

It seems likely that the degree of experience with the type of event in question and cultural influences may affect the child's attributions. As an example of the former, consider a situation in which a child is told about two children at play. Child A has a coloring book and a puzzle and he chooses the puzzle to play with. Child B has the same choice, but his mother tells him that if he plays with the puzzle he can have a piece of cake. The subject is asked which child really wanted to play with the puzzle. Numerous studies have shown that after age 7 or 8 children typically choose the child not offered the contingency (e.g., Karniol & Ross, 1976, 1979), reasoning that the mother is using the contingency to manipulate the child into choosing the puzzle, which suggests that he does not really want it. Younger children believe the opposite, namely, that the offer of the cake as a reward enhances intrinsic interest in the toy, so they choose the child offered the contingency.

Contrast this behavior with that when the story character is changed from a mother to a "big mean brother" (Aloise & Miller, 1991). If one assumes that young children are more familiar with not-very-subtle manipulations at the hands of an older peer or sibling and also have a rosy view of their mother, then they might be more likely to detect the manipulative intent of the mean brother. This attribution would lead them to discount the intrinsic motivation of the child offered the contingency. This was the case. Even 3-year-olds thought that the child not offered the contingency was more interested in the puzzle than was the other child. Interestingly, using a "big mean mother" or simply a "big brother" did not produce this effect, suggesting that both role and valence are important. Thus, children's knowledge, based on their real-world experience, influences their choice of psychological or external causes (see P. H. Miller & Aloise, 1990, for a review addressing this issue).

The role of cultural influences, emphasized by the contextualists, can be illustrated in research by J. G. Miller (1986) comparing the types of causes used by children (ages 8, 11, and 15) and adults in India and the United States, all from the middle class. Subjects had to explain why a person performed a particular prosocial or deviant behavior that was described. In both cultures the youngest children tended to refer to events and visible aspects of the social/spatial/temporal context. For example, the actor bandaged a hurt face because "his face was cut and she was his friend" and went for help when a child's pants stuck in a bike chain because "there was no one else around and she had her bike also." These causes do not refer to internal dispositions. What is of interest is that referring to contextual causes increased during development among the Hindus but not the Americans. That is, Hindus referred to the duties of one's social position, mutual interdependence between people, sensitivity to the needs of society, and one's social relationship with other people. Americans, in contrast to Hindus, tended to show a developmental increase in references to traits (J. G. Miller, 1987). This pattern is consistent with the belief of American and other Western cultures that people are individualistic and autonomous, whereas many non-Western cultures, including India, emphasize social contextual factors. The latter believe a person to be an inherent part of the social system rather than an entity with rights and desires that conflict with that system.

Thus, a general lesson from this line of research is that social-cognitive development involves both universally developing cognitive abilities (as seen in the similar causal reasoning of the 8-year-olds in the two cultures) and culturally specific belief systems acquired during socialization (also see Markus and Kitayama, 1991, for an interesting review comparing Eastern and Western self-concepts).

UNDERSTANDING SOCIAL RELATIONSHIPS

Much of children's social cognition discussed thus far has to do with their distancing themselves from other people by treating them as objects of their cognition, albeit interesting objects full of psychological equipment. What of the complementary component of understanding connections between the self and others and between other people? As the contextualists reminded us in Chapter 1, a thinking child is always part of a social network, and we dare not ignore his or her concepts about this network. An understanding of this network begins early, as seen in our earlier discussion of infants' working models of attachment.

For development during childhood, we have chosen several representative topics. They are recursive thinking, Robert Selman's theory of the development of interpersonal understanding, children's concepts of friendship, and work on moral judgments.

Recursive Thinking

We can illustrate one cognitive precursor to a mature understanding of relationships with a study by Flavell and colleagues (1968). Subjects of 7 to 17 years played a game of strategy that allowed for sophisticated cognition about thoughts. In this game, the subject saw two cups placed upside down on a table. One had a nickel glued to its upturned bottom to show that it concealed a nickel inside; the other was similarly marked to show that it contained two nickels. The subject was told that another person would shortly enter the room, select one or the other of the two cups, and get to keep any money that might be hidden under it (two nickels had not yet inflated to the status of play money when this study was done).

The subject's task was to fool the person by taking the money out of one cup, whichever one she thought the person would select. She was also told that the person knew full well that she was going to try to fool him in this way. She was encouraged to think hard, pick a cup, and explain why she thought the person would choose that one.

A few of the older subjects showed some bravura displays of social cognition on this task. For example, one subject first reasoned that the other person would probably select the one-nickel cup because he (the other person) would anticipate that the subject would think he would choose the two-nickel cup (because it contained more money), and hence he would try to fool the subject by selecting the one-nickel cup. (Clear so far?) However, the subject then went on to reason that the other person would anticipate this whole line of reasoning on the subject's part and therefore would switch back to the two-nickel cup in a master stroke of double duplicity. We experimenters could empathize with the subject's struggle to put all this complex thinking about thinking about thinking...into words:

> ...he might feel that we, that we know that he thinks that we're going to pick this cup so therefore I think we should pick the dime cup, because I think he thinks, he thinks that we're going to pick the nickel cup, but then he knows that we, that we'll assume that he knows that we, that we'll assume that he knows that, so we should pick the opposite cup. (Flavell et al., 1968, p. 47)

Complex, wheels-within-wheels social cognition of this genre really occurs in life and literature as well as in the laboratory. Here is our favorite example from literature:

> "Does he know I know?" I asked. "No, he doesn't. Does he know you know? Who can tell?"
> "Does he know I know you know they know she knows you know?" Steven asked. (Francis, 1978, p. 206)

Children cannot easily think about human relationships until they realize that people can think about each others' thoughts. One of the most intriguing and distinctive properties of thought or mental representation is its potentially *recursive* nature. An action or process is said to be recursive if it can repeatedly (i.e., recursively) operate upon itself or its own output, thereby creating increasingly longer and more complex self-embedded structures. People's motor and perceptual actions and experiences with respect to themselves and others are not recursive in the way that their conceptual or representational actions and experiences are. For instance, someone's visual experience cannot literally include your visual experience nor can yours include his or a third person's. It therefore follows that more complex recursive structures like "his visual experience of [your visual experience of (his visual experience...)]" make no sense. In contrast, "his mental representation of [your mental representation of (his mental representation...")]—for example, "He thinks that you think that he thinks..."—and innumerable other structures of the same type are both possible and psychologically real.

These mind-boggling displays of social cognition illustrate not only an awareness of the active (overactive?) nature of mind, but also a highly sophisticated understanding of representation. This thinking seems to require "an ability to create and manipulate a mental model of two individuals' belief states about each other" (Bretherton, 1991, p. 29). In fact, understanding recursive thought would

be a good candidate for a sixth postulate for a theory of mind in late childhood or early adolescence.

The development of children's understanding of the recursive nature of thinking has been the subject of several research investigations (Barenboim, 1978; Flavell et al., 1968/1975; Landry & Lyons-Ruth, 1980; P. H. Miller, Kessel, & Flavell, 1970; Oppenheimer, 1986; Perner & Wimmer, 1985; see also Selman, 1980, and Shantz, 1983). Although there is evidence for some understanding of it during middle childhood, perhaps even earlier (Oppenheimer, 1986), it is clear that this understanding continues to improve during adolescence. Miller, Kessel, and Flavell (1970) found that even some of their oldest subjects (11- to 12-year-olds) failed to show a full understanding of "one-loop" recursions (e.g., "the boy is thinking that the girl is thinking of him"), and that still more of them had difficul-

Chapter Five

ties with "two-loop" recursions (e.g., "The boy is thinking that the girl is thinking of him thinking of her").

One could hardly be said to have acquired a mature, adult level of knowledge about human relationships if one did not know that thoughts can recursively take other thoughts as cognitive objects. A surprising amount of the ordinary, everyday social thought and communication of adolescents and adults seems to presuppose this knowledge. Consider, for example, the sorts of things two people often say to each other when analyzing and clearing up a previous misunderstanding between them: "Oh, you thought I meant X," "I thought you already knew about Y," and even "I didn't realize you thought I really meant it when I said that." Statements like these, which are fairly commonplace in adult conversations, surely reflect a tacit assumption on the speaker's part that mental representations can recursively include other mental representations. Moreover, as Shultz speculates, recursive thinking "is one of those few distinctly human characteristics, serving to make our social interactions not only truly interactive but also essentially human" (1980, p. 156). All things considered, the acquisition of this insight about thinking seems like a cognitive-developmental milestone, and one that would well repay further scientific study.

Selman's Theory

Robert Selman (Selman, 1980; Selman & Schultz, 1990) has proposed an interesting theory showing that several of the developmental acquisitions described in this chapter lead the child to an eventual understanding of social relationships. Selman describes four developmentally ordered levels (0 to 3) of the coordination of social perspectives that correspond to ways of interacting with others (see Table 5–1). The age range given for each level is approximate and is meant only as a very rough guide. Selman identifies children's level of social perspective coordination from their answers to stories. The most commonly used story concerns a boy who is trying to decide whether to give a new puppy as a birthday present to his friend whose puppy ran away and never returned. This story assesses children's ability to take the perspective of others, to infer complex emotions, and to understand relationships.

Selman recently has used his theory to try to understand the normal development of skills for forming peer relationships and to develop skill-training therapies for children who have failed to acquire these skills. All children use their knowledge of other people to try to play or work with them in relative harmony. A clash of desires is inevitable in any human relationship, but is especially apparent when children play with each other. Simultaneously wanting the same toy, disagreeing about what to play or how to do a particular activity, and jealousy or envy are part of normal peer play. What changes developmentally is how children resolve these interpersonal dilemmas, in part because of the social-cognitive concepts underlying *negotiation strategies* at each developmental level. These strategies are ways that children try to meet their needs in a situation in which this goal is blocked by another person.

Consider a situation in which Jeff and Greg are each building a spaceship with small plastic construction blocks (Selman & Shultz, 1990). Jeff finishes a few moments ahead of Greg and puts the only astronaut into his ship. Greg finishes his ship, looks for an astronaut, and realizes that Jeff has the only one. At this point various violent or nonviolent events could occur. Table 5–1 describes the typical

TABLE 5-1 Selman's Levels of Social Perspective Coordination and Associated Shared Experiences and Negotiation Strategies

INTIMACY FUNCTION (SHARING EXPERIENCE)	CORE DEVELOPMENTAL LEVELS IN CAPACITY TO COORDINATE SOCIAL PERSPECTIVES	AUTONOMY FUNCTION (NEGOTIATING INTERPERSONAL CONFLICT)
Shared experience through unreflective (contagious) imitation	Egocentric Impulsive Level 0 Ages 3–6	Negotiation through unreflective physical strategies (impulsive fight or flight)
Shared experience through expressive enthusiasm without concern for reciprocity	Unilateral One-Way Level 1 Ages 5–9	Negotiation through one-way commands/orders or through automatic obedience strategies
Shared experience through joint reflection on similar perceptions or experiences	Reciprocal Reflective Level 2 Ages 7–12	Negotiation through cooperative strategies in a persuasive or deferential orientation
Shared experience through collaborative empathic reflective processes	Mutual Third-Person Level 3 Ages 10–15	Negotiation through collaborative strategies oriented toward integrating needs of self and others

Sourcenote: Adapted from R. L. Selman, & L. H. Schultz, *Making a Friend in Youth,* p. 29. Copyright © 1990 by University of Chicago Press. Reprinted by permission of University of Chicago Press.

negotiation strategy expressed by each of Selman's levels of interpersonal functioning, and its associated type of shared experience. If Greg acts in the impulsive, unreflective, physical way characteristic of Level 0, his egocentric social perspective precludes a consideration of Jeff's mental state. In fact, he cannot clearly differentiate Jeff's mental and physical characteristics or behaviors. He simply tries to get the toy or removes himself physically or psychologically from the situation. Preschoolers typically operate at this level. At Level 1, Greg considers Jeff's mental state, but tries to change Jeff's behavior, rather than his mental state, through threats or by acting victimized. He shows no reciprocity yet, for he can think about personal influence in only one direction at a time—self to others or others to self. At Level 2, Greg realizes that he has the power to change Jeff's mental state, so he tries to manipulate Jeff psychologically through persuasion: "Your ship is probably so good that it can fly without an astronaut." Or, he at least brings his own feelings or desires into the discussion in some way: "You can have the astronaut this time, but next time we play I get to have it." Here we see the beginnings of true reciprocity. More generally, Greg can step outside of himself and take a "second-person" perspective on his own thoughts. At level 3, Greg can reflect on both his own feelings and those of Jeff and come up with a compromise that is mutually satisfying. They "work through" their conflict, perhaps by deciding to link their ships and have one astronaut control both. Greg, by taking a "third-person" perspective, can see both himself and Jeff as actors and objects and thus can coordinate their perspectives. He sees a relationship that is above and beyond the sum of its parts (the two people involved). Thus, with each advance in children's understanding of the mind come new possibilities for handling conflict with peers. In particular, children first learn that the self and the other have separate mental states and then learn to coordinate these two sets of feelings, desires, and thoughts. They also focus more and more on their relationship rather than simply toys and games.

Concepts of Friendship

Selman's work on peer interaction leads us into a discussion of children's concepts of friendship. There is currently a lively and growing research interest in the child's developing thought and understanding concerning friendship (e.g., Asher & Coie, 1990; Berndt, 1988; W. Furman & Bierman, 1983; Rubin, 1980; Selman, 1981). These investigators agree that friendship is obviously very important in the lives of children. Children discover that their fortunes with regard to friendship can powerfully affect their present happiness. Developmental psychologists, parents, and other concerned adults know that children's fortunes here can also powerfully affect their future development. It seems likely that children's cognitive and social skills in this area would be related, though not all studies find this relation, and even those that do often report modest effects (Dodge & Feldman, 1990).

Most of our knowledge about the development of friendship concepts derives from interview studies with children. Children are questioned about why children they have named as their best friends are their best friends, what they expect of a friend, how they know if another child is their friend, how one becomes a friend, how friendships end, and the like. This work shows that cognition about friendship changes with age in a manner that is consistent with and partly predictable from the course of social-cognitive development in general. If you can remember the latter you can largely reconstruct the former. The typical course of development is roughly as follows (Berndt, 1988; Damon, 1977; Shantz, 1983).

During the late preschool and early school years, children tend to conceive of friends as peers who are nice and are fun to be with, and with whom one plays and shares material goods. They tend to regard friendships as transient affairs, quickly and easily formed and quickly and easily terminated. There is no sense of either liking or disliking particular stable and distinctive personal traits in the other children. Thus, they conceive of neither the friends' personal characteristics nor the friendship relations themselves as having an individualized and enduring quality.

During middle and late childhood, friends come to be represented as people who help and trust one another. Reciprocal helping and mutual trust become defining elements of friendship. Children also begin to conceive of friendship as a subjective as well as an objective state of affairs. They no longer represent friends only as agreeable others with whom one plays, but also as individual persons who have specific traits and dispositions that one likes.

Finally, during adolescence, intimate disclosures increase (Jones & Dembo, 1989). Friends become conceptualized as

> persons who understand one another, share their innermost thoughts and feelings (including secrets), help each other with psychological problems, and avoid causing each other problems. Compatibility of interests and personality are the bases for selecting one as a friend, and the termination of friendship is viewed likely if one

shows bad faith to a friend. Adolescents' reasoning also emphasizes communication as critical to friendship, both as an end in itself and as a means to share and assist one another. (Shantz, 1983, p. 531)

It should be apparent that these age changes in children's conceptions of the friendship relations between people reflect developmental changes in their conceptions of people considered as individuals. For example, the "surface to depth" developmental trend for conceptions of people is clearly evident in the case of friendship. There is a change "from defining friendship as a concrete, behavioral, surface relationship of playing together and giving goods to more abstract, internal dispositional relationships in adolescence of caring for one another, sharing one's thoughts and feelings, and comforting each other" (Shantz, 1983, p. 531). To illustrate more concretely how adolescents may conceive of friendship, consider this answer by a 13-year-old to the question "How do you know who to become friends with and who not to?"

> Well, you don't really pick your friends, it just grows on you. You find out that you can talk to someone, you can tell them your problems, when you understand each other. (Damon, 1977, pp. 163–164)

One can scarcely imagine a 5-year-old, say, thinking about friendship in this deep "psychological" way.

Finally, there is exciting research on a most unusual educational venture—teaching rejected or socially isolated children social skills that will help them achieve the acceptance and friendship of their peers (Asher & Coie, 1990; Rubin & Krasnor, 1986; Selman & Schultz, 1990; Shantz, 1983). Many rejected or socially isolated children simply do not know how to make friends or maintain friendships (Rubin & Krasnor, 1986). In one study (Oden & Asher, 1977), the subjects were third- and fourth-grade children who were identified by sociometric measures as the least popular children in their classes. These children were given five sessions of instruction and actual practice (with other peers) in the nature and use of such social skills as cooperation (e.g., taking turns, sharing materials) and communication (e.g., talking with and listening to a would-be playmate). Results indicated that this coaching program helped the subjects become better accepted by their classmates. More impressive yet, a follow-up assessment one year after coaching showed that the subjects had made still further gains in peer acceptance. One wishes that schools would provide "friendship coaches" to increase the peer acceptance of unpopular children, just as they provide athletic coaches.

Researchers believe that these training programs, as well as Selman's pair therapy, are effective because they change peer interaction, which then increases the understanding of peer relations, which in turn enhances peer interaction, and so on in a continual back-and-forth process. Similarly, in natural settings, peer interaction and conceptions of friendship influence each other during development. As peer interaction becomes more complex, it challenges children to try to take the perspective of the other person and to conceptualize the notions of reciprocity and negotiation that underlie this overt interaction. And, as they more fully understand these covert feelings and thoughts, they can develop more advanced forms of friendships based on trust and intimacy. Even in infancy one can find examples of cognitive change engendering interaction with baby peers. Brownell (1986) finds two cognitive skills of particular importance in this respect: the growing ability to integrate behaviors into larger combinations and the capacity to separate oneself from the environment à la Piagetian decentration. Language learning and the concept of object permanence play a role as well.

More generally, peers are an important source of developmental change. Piaget (1932) and Kohlberg (1969) were aware of this in their accounts of how cooperation and conflict with peers force a child to consider different perspectives and thus progress to a higher, more relativistic level of moral reasoning. A more recent example is peer tutoring, in which children teach other children in a school setting (e.g., Gerber & Kauffman, 1981).

Moral Judgments

Development of moral reasoning is a fascinating and important area of research, but unfortunately too large and complex to be covered adequately in a book of this size. Fortunately, insightful recent accounts are plentiful (e.g., Damon, 1988; Hoffman, 1989; Kurtines & Gewirtz, 1989; Schrader, 1990; Walker, 1988). We will simply highlight one recent issue that focuses on social relationships. Work on moral judgments by Piaget (1932), Kohlberg (1969), and others describes how children use issues of justice, equality, and competing rights to guide moral judgments. This approach views the autonomous individual as the fundamental moral unit. In contrast, Carol Gilligan (1982; Gilligan, Lyons, & Hanmer, 1989) argues that this approach has ignored moral reasoning that is based on relationships, a type of reasoning that she found in her female subjects. Caring, responsiveness, commitment, and conflicting responsibilities often affect one's moral decisions. Thus, aggression could be considered wrong because it infringes on the rights of others (Piaget, Kohlberg) or because it damages human relationships (Gilligan).

Similarly, others (e.g., Markus & Kitayama, 1991; Shweder, Mahapahtra, & Miller, 1987) have argued that many non-Western cultures also tend to consider social relationships, along with the social obligations and collectivist and cooperative ideals they entail, when making moral judgments. For example, a moral duty to care for elderly parents may be given priority over justice considerations. Markus and Kitayama (1991) contrast the American view of the autonomous self with the Japanese emphasis on an interdependent self that attends to others and fits in with others in a harmonious, connected relationship. They liken the two concepts to the beliefs that "the squeaky wheel gets the grease" versus "the nail that stands out gets pounded down." These different conceptions of the self in relation to others lead to different systems of moral beliefs. As the contextualists argue, the values of a culture guide the child's social cognition. This attention to cultural-related and gender-related diversity promises to broaden the future study of the development of moral judgments. And the main message of such work is that the growing understanding of social relations has implications for moral judgments. Understanding friendship, the parent-child relationship, or membership in a larger social unit includes understanding the caring behaviors that maintain that relationship and are dictated by it.

SUMMARY

Social cognition is cognition about people and what they do and ought to do. It includes thinking and knowledge about the self and others as individuals, about social relations among people, and about social customs, groups, and institutions.

Social cognition helps us differentiate, and thereby separate, ourselves from others, but also understand and develop emotional connections with others. Figure 5–1 is one representation of what social cognition entails. Another model emphasizes three preconditions for successfully identifying any social-cognition object (e.g., another person's feeling state): knowing that such states can exist in people (*Existence*); being motivated or disposed to identify them (*Need*); being able actually to identify them on the basis of the available evidence (*Inference*). A third model (Figure 5–2) describes how children process social information and select a behavior.

Both similarities and differences exist between social and nonsocial cognition. Inevitable similarities stem from the fact that it is the selfsame head that does both social and nonsocial cognition and from the fact that social objects and concepts are similar in some respects to nonsocial ones. As a consequence of these similarities, many of the developmental trends in nonsocial cognition described in previous chapters can also be seen in social cognition. Like its nonsocial counterparts, social-cognitive growth tends to proceed from *surface* (people's appearance and behavior) to *depth* (their inner thoughts, feelings, etc.), and also shows *invariant formation*; immature social thinking is plagued by the *pull of salient features* of people and events; mature social thinking is *abstract* and *hypothetical*, has characteristic cognitive shortcomings (e.g., *egocentrism*), but clearly has a *sense of the game* of people reading.

People differ from most other objects in several ways. Unlike other objects, they are sentient beings who can intentionally behave and reveal/conceal information about themselves. Our relations with people usually differ from our relations with other objects. As examples, we are similar to other people and our relations with them entail mutual and reciprocal coordination of actions, communication, and perspective taking. There are also some distinctively social-cognitive processes, such as empathy and using information about ourselves to make inferences about others.

We can characterize part of infant social-cognitive development as a process of *differentiation*—of self from nonself, of human from nonhuman objects, and of one human object from another. One important thing infants gradually learn about people is that their own behavior and that of others are often predictably *contingent* on one another. The best-researched aspect of infant social development is the growth of *social attachment*, which involves *connecting with others*. For instance, the baby engages in certain behaviors (crying, crawling, etc.) that tend to maintain a desired level of physical proximity to the object of her attachment—her father, say—and exhibits certain feelings (pleasure, fear, etc.) when that level of proximity is achieved or lost. Attachment illustrates how social behavior mediates cognitive growth, and cognitive skills mediate social development. As examples of the latter, babies are born with or soon develop precisely the sorts of perceptual skills and preferences that could help mediate the development of social attachment. An infant forms a "working model" of herself, her caretaker, and their relationship. This model results from and leads to expectations about behavior.

One important social-cognitive development during the postinfancy years is the understanding of *emotions* and *percepts*, as well as other mental states described in Chapter 3. Preschool children can correctly attribute global positive and negative feelings to another person on the basis of his facial expression or his immediately prior experience (e.g., someone just gave the person a present). Children's spontaneous speech also refers to a variety of emotional states. Even preschoolers have some understanding that mental states mediate between the

Chapter Five

emotion-eliciting event and the affected person's behavioral or expressive behavior. For example, they know that satisfying or not satisfying a mentally represented goal leads to different emotions. Thus, understanding and inferring others' desires is essential for understanding and predicting their emotions. During middle childhood children learn to monitor and shape their own affective expression (e.g., consciously feign a certain emotion), as well as to detect such behaviors in others. They eventually understand more complex emotional states, such as *multiple conflicting emotions*. Both cultural-specific beliefs about emotions and the extent to which mothers talk about emotions with their young children influence the course of the developing understanding of emotions. Children try to change not only their own emotions, through strategies of emotion regulation, but also those of others. The latter can be expressed negatively, as in teasing and other annoying behaviors, or positively, in comforting, helping, and other prosocial behaviors.

At least two developmental levels of cognition concerning visual percepts exist: At Level 1, the young child represents *whether* another person sees a given object; at Level 2 the child represents *how* an object that the person sees looks to that person from his or her particular spatial perspective. Some Level 1 understanding seems to be present in 2- and 3-year-olds, some Level 2 understanding by age 4 and 5. Interestingly, the understanding that one's line of sight is necessarily straight, never curved, seems to come surprisingly late—after age 5 for many children. Young children also have trouble understanding visual and auditory selective attention.

In addition to learning about mental states, children form *conceptions of the personal attributes of other people and themselves*. There are striking ontogenetic changes in the way children conceptualize and describe another individual's personality. Up to 6 to 7 years or thereabouts, a child often characterizes another person in terms of "surface" rather than "depth"—the person's appearance, possessions, overt behavior (especially toward the self), and so on, rather than the person's inner, psychological qualities. During middle childhood, children emphasize these internal aspects and acquire a larger and more differentiated set of trait-descriptive terms. Personality descriptions become increasingly well organized and integrated during adolescence. Children mention the other's seemingly conflicting and idiosyncratic combinations of traits and attempt to explain, justify, and qualify what they say about the person.

The development of knowledge and cognition concerning the self closely parallels and overlaps the development of knowledge about other people. For example, conceptions of both self and others become more differentiated, "psychological," and trait-like with increasing age. In fact, much of the development of self-conceptions consists of making key differentiations—for instance, between one's self and other objects and selves, and between one's real or actual self and one's ideal self. Research has shown that both apes and older human infants recognize their images in a mirror as images of their own bodies, suggesting that they possess at least a rudimentary form of *self-concept* or self-awareness. Later, individual differences in attributions about the self affect behavior. A general conclusion is that children play an active role in forming their self concepts, for instance, by seeking information about themselves from others, organizing information in terms of the self, and interpreting information in light of their beliefs about themselves.

Changes in knowledge about the causes of behavior involve understanding *intentions* and more *specific psychological causes*, and *choosing between psychological or situational causes*. Infants learn that people are self-initiating agents, and 3-year-olds believe that desirable outcomes are usually intended, whereas undesirable outcomes usually are not. Also, 3-year-olds may have some ability to distinguish intended actions from such nonintentional behaviors as mistakes and reflexes. Children acquire true understanding of intent in the late preschool years with the emerging notion that intent is a mental state that plans a subsequent behavior but is independent of the outcome.

Evidence of some understanding of specific psychological causes appears in 2-year-olds' spontaneous speech. Subsequently, script knowledge and greater awareness of, and differentiation of, mental states allow children to infer increasingly subtle psychological causes. After about age 6 or 7, these inferred causes often are *traits*. Preschoolers seem to prefer psychological causes over behavioral descriptions or situational causes, if the psychological cause is made explicit. Otherwise young children usually refer to external causes. Finally, cultures vary in their tendency to emphasize internal or external causes.

Social-cognitive growth includes the development of children's knowledge about between-person *social relations* as well as about the within-person processes already discussed (percepts, feelings, thoughts, etc.). One cognitive acquisition underlying the understanding of social relations is the recognition that thought is potentially *recursive*—that is, one thought can subsume or take as its object another thought, which in turn can simultaneously include yet another, and so on, to create complex and extended chains of inference: "I think that you think that he thinks..." Selman's theory of *social perspective taking* and *peer negotiation skills* provides a description of important social-cognitive changes during childhood. Recent investigations have shown that the ontogenesis of *friendship* conceptions, like that of self-conceptions, is consistent with and partly predictable from the course of social-cognitive growth in general. For instance, as they mature cognitively, children increasingly come to conceive of friendship as a subjective, "psychological" affair entailing mutual assistance, trust, and intimate communication. It appears possible to increase the popularity of unpopular children simply by coaching them in social skills that are useful in making friends. Children's *moral judgments* usually involve evaluations of social interactions. Concepts of justice, rights, and equality, as well as perhaps caring for others and commitments to others, generate these judgments.

A chronological summary may help integrate the various components of social cognition in this chapter. An infant's perceptual predispositions encourage interactions with other people. The infant eventually detects that other people (1) act as agents, (2) have predictable behaviors, (3) are compliant ("influenceable") to the infant's own desires, and, perhaps (4) possess unseen internal states (e.g., dispositions to behave, desires). By age 3, children know that a person tries to achieve desired situations, and that successfully achieving them reflects her intent to do so and pleases her (Perner, 1991). In time, the concept of internal states more clearly refers to mental states and, eventually, to representations such as beliefs and intentions. Similarly, two concepts especially important for social cognition—emotions and percepts—become increasingly mental, representational, differentiated, and complex (e.g., multiple simultaneous emotions). One outcome of the understanding that emotions are represented mental events is realizing that they can be changed, and thus controlled. Thus, children are increasingly likely to produce facial displays, strategies for controlling one's own emotions, and behaviors such as comforting or teasing designed to change others' emotional states. This growing awareness of the *existence* of mental states, coupled with social experience revealing the *need* to engage in social cognition, stimulates children to make *inferences* about the mental states. Children become increasingly sophisticated at inferring traits and psychological causes of behavior, engaging in recursive thinking, using various simple and complex mental events or states as psychological causes of behavior, and engaging in social perspective taking. These developing social-cognitive skills are applied to concepts of the self, specific others, and of social relationships, thus continuing the process of separation and connection begun in infancy.

Memory

In *The Man Who Mistook His Wife for a Hat*, Oliver Sacks describes a man with a neurological impairment that left him with almost no memory for recent events:

> He is...isolated in a single moment of being, with a moat or lacuna of forgetting all round him.... He is man without past (or future), stuck in a constantly changing, meaningless moment....a man without roots, or rooted only in the remote past. (1985, p. 29)

This tragic situation illustrates how central memory is to our sense of self and to our ability to conceptualize constancy and change in the world around us. For children, memory does all of this and more. Children could not develop even basic concepts of reality without somehow representing the past in order to interpret the present.

Children have a mixed reputation regarding their memory ability. On the one hand they recall poorly, compared to adults, with lists of words or pictures presented in laboratory studies or on IQ tests. On the other hand, the accuracy of their recall of certain everyday events, such as a story or television show, may be startling. Moreover, as intelligent adults who have been humiliated in a game of "Concentration" by a 5-year-old know, children perform as well as, or better than, adults on this memory-for-locations game (Baker-Ward & Ornstein, 1988).

Children's memory is probably the most advanced area of research on cognitive development, at least in terms of sheer amount of research. Most of the work falls within the information-processing approach described in Chapter 1. This research shows that if we feed younger and older memory machines the same amount of information, the older machines can usually give more of it back to us than the younger ones can. But *why* can they? Possibly because the older ones were thinking and doing something different or better than the younger ones were in the period between the beginning of our input to them and the conclusion of their memory output to us. Our focus in this chapter reflects that of current memory research: What kinds of cognitive processes and knowledge might underlie and account for these more superficial age differences in sheer memory output? Fine secondary sources on memory development include Bjorklund, Muir-Broaddus, and Schneider (1990), Fivush and Hudson (1990), Folds, Footo, Guttentag, and Ornstein (1990), Howe and O'Sullivan (1990), Kail (1989), Schneider and Pressley (1989), and Weinert and Perlmutter (1989).

In a very broad sense, everything we have told you about cognition so far is memory, in that children store their acquired knowledge about the world. They "remember" that hairy four-legged creatures that bark are called dogs, that there are many kinds of dogs, and that these creatures continue to exist even when they are out of sight. However, most research examines memory in a narrower sense, such as remembering a list of items or remembering a specific event occurring at a particular time and place. A child may remember that yesterday she tried to give her own hairy, barking, four-legged creature a bath and he ran away. We do not mean to suggest that memory in the broad and narrow sense are independent. In fact, as we will describe later, each is heavily influenced by the other. Also, the distinction sometimes is blurry, as when "I remember that my dog usually runs away when I try to give him a bath."

SOME CONCEPTS AND DISTINCTIONS

Let us begin with some concepts and distinctions that are useful in thinking about memory and its development. Students of memory distinguish between *storage* and *retrieval* activities. As their names suggest, storage activities put information into memory while retrieval activities recover information from memory. When you store a set of definitions in preparation for an exam, you attend to, encode, study, and memorize them: "Learning" is sometimes a good synonym. Your retrieving means recognizing, recalling, and reconstructing them—the "remembering" of what had previously been stored. These storage and retrieval activities not only occur between your ears but also take place in the external world when you take notes, use a tape recorder, store your thoughts on a computer, or ask others to help you remember something. In real life, most retrieval scenarios involve a sequential, back-and-forth movement between internal and external memory stores. For example, you remember (internal) that you made a note on your calendar and so you go look at it; it explicitly spells out (external) certain information, which in turn reminds you (internal) of yet other information not contained in the note. Storage and retrieval are closely interdependent in practice. For instance, how information is organized when initially stored in memory determines in what manner (e.g., via what retrieval cues) and how successfully it will be retrieved subsequently.

There are a few other concepts to mention on the retrieval side of memory. Two kinds of retrieval are commonly distinguished: *recognition* and *recall*. You may recognize as familiar something that is presently perceived or thought about— that is, you may identify it as identical to, similar to, or reminiscent of something previously experienced. After studying a list of words you could pick them out of a larger list of words because you have created some sort of enduring representation of the earlier words in memory that is somehow contacted in the course of your experiencing the present words. This contact somehow gives rise to the feeling of recognition. For recall, on the other hand, the words you studied are not in front of you; the familiar something is not initially present in conscious thought or perception. Rather, *recall* is the term we use for the very process of retrieving a representation of it from memory. In recognition, the thing that is recognized is already there to serve as its own "cue" for retrieval. In recall, the subjects have to do more of the retrieval job on their own (but not all of it, because it is usually assumed that there must be some sort of retrieval cue present to lend a hand). Recall-like processes are often involved in recognition activities, and recognition-like processes are often involved in recall activities. For example, after recognizing something as familiar we commonly go on to recall additional information about it, such as where we were and who we were with when we first encountered it. Similarly, when trying to recall someone's name, for instance, we will test for recognition any name that comes to mind—that is, we see if we can recognize it as being the name we are after.

Models of memory often make a distinction between a *sensory register*, *short-term memory* (also called "working memory"), and *long-term memory* (e.g., Atkinson & Shiffrin, 1968). Stimulation exists very briefly in the sensory register before moving on to short-term memory, a system of limited capacity. Unless a person does something quickly to the information, such as rehearse it, the information is lost forever. If the material is kept alive in short-term memory and transferred to long-term memory, it joins the person's permanent memory and knowledge. Long-term memory possesses a large capacity and includes memory both in the broad and narrow sense. Other models of memory follow a *levels-of-processing* approach (Craik & Lockhart, 1972). In this approach, the more deeply people process information by assimilating it into their knowledge system, the better their memory for the material. For example, children often remember words better when their task is to pick out the "odd" word in a difficult set, such as fly-beetle-moth, than an easy set, candy-beetle-gum (Ackerman, Spiker, & Bailey, 1989). The harder set requires deeper processing in the search for ways in which the objects are the same and different.

With these distinctions in mind, we turn to the research on children's memory. Our discussion is divided into two parts: an initial section on memory in infancy, followed by a longer section on memory in childhood and adolescence.

INFANT MEMORY

The first question to ask about infant memory is whether babies have any sort of memory capability. Both logical considerations and a great deal of research evidence clearly indicate that they do (Moscovitch, 1984; G. M. Olson & Sherman, 1983; Rovee-Collier, 1987). Infants do many things that logically imply the existence of a memory system. The following are a few examples. As indicated in Chapter 2, habituation of attention presupposes some sort of recognition-type memory ability. If the baby could not somehow retain the fact that the repeatedly presented stimulus has been experienced previously, the baby could not habituate to it—that is, treat it as "old" or familiar. Infants also come to recognize familiar people, objects, and events (e.g., daily routines). Imitation and search for hidden objects (object permanence) likewise require memory for previous events. So too do classical and operant conditioning, both of which can be demonstrated from very early in infancy.

Not only does memory exist from early in life, but experiments have shown that infants have quite good information-retention abilities. In an experiment by Fagan (1973), 5-month-olds exposed to a photograph of a face for only a couple of minutes gave evidence of recognizing it as long as 2 weeks later. In studies by Rovee-Collier and colleagues (Rovee-Collier, 1990; Rovee-Collier & Hayne, 1987), infants have been operantly conditioned to kick their feet when they see a mobile. By 3 months of age infants can retain this learned association between the sight of the mobile and the kicking response for a period of 2 weeks. Memory is even more durable if the infant is given a reminder of the association in the interim between initial learning and memory test—for example, if the experimenter jiggles the mobile in a familiar way (Rovee-Collier, Sullivan, Enright, Lucas, & Fagen, 1980). Rovee-Collier and Hayne (1987) argue that naturally occurring instances of such *reactivation*—that is, reencounters with at least some aspect of the to-be-remembered situation—may act to ensure that many memories remain intact for considerable periods of time. And certainly there can be little doubt, for this and for other reasons, that memory for often-presented and important stimuli, such as Mommy's face, must extend for considerably longer than 2 weeks.

Although memory may be operative and effective from early in life, it is not at full strength from the start. Various improvements occur across the span of infancy. Older babies can typically retain information for longer periods of time than can younger babies. They also require less initial exposure, or less "study time," to place some stimulus or event into memory. With development, infants come to encode more and more of the information from any particular experience; they also, as their cognitive abilities grow, become sensitive to, and thus likelier to remember, increasingly subtle and increasingly complex aspects of the world around them. Furthermore, an act of recognition in an older infant or young child undoubtedly includes processes not found in the young baby. Older individuals are likely to be conscious and explicitly aware of the fact that the object or event they have recognized is familiar and has been experienced before. Moreover, recognizing it may stimulate additional retrieval activity. This activity could even include, in older children, deliberate and effortful attempts to recall further information concerning the recognized stimulus. In contrast, recognition in the neonate and young infant is probably of the unelaborated, "bare-bones" variety that we associate with recognition processes in lower organisms. The very young infant may respond differently to familiar stimuli than to unfamiliar stimuli, but probably has no "I-have-seen-that-before" type feelings or cognitions.

Recognition, then, changes across infancy. What about recall? Are there developmental changes here as well? Piaget certainly thought so. As we saw in Chapter 2, in Piaget's view the infant is capable of recognition memory but not of recall memory, because recall requires symbolic-representational abilities that the infant lacks. Like many aspects of Piagetian theory, the claim that recall is impossible prior to about 18 months has come under attack in recent years. Work on deferred imitation provides one major challenge. Remember from Chapter 2 that Meltzoff (1988b) has demonstrated that infants as young as 9 months can imitate a model that was viewed 24 hours earlier, a behavior that would seem to require recall of previous experience and not merely recognition of something that is perceptually present. In itself, this finding might seem to shift the Piagetian age norms downward but to leave the basic developmental picture unchanged: an initial period in development during which recall is not yet possible, followed (at about 9 rather than 18 months) by the emergence of a new form of memory. Remember as well, however, that Meltzoff and Moore (1983a, 1983b) have provided evidence that *newborns* can imitate facial movements that they cannot see themselves make. In one of their experiments (Meltzoff & Moore, 1977), the infants had pacifiers in their mouths while the to-be-imitated movement was being produced, and they were thereby prevented from imitating the movement until after it was no longer perceptually present. The imitations observed were therefore "deferred," albeit across a much briefer time delay than is typically at issue in studies of deferred imitation. Might such early imitations indicate a nascent, available-from-birth capacity for representing and recalling information? Meltzoff (1990b) thinks so, and is currently conducting studies to determine whether newborns can tolerate more extended delays between presentation of model and opportunity to imitate. Certainly, the longer the delay between model and imitation, the more likely all of us would be to credit the baby with some capacity for representation and recall.

Imitation as a guide to recall has also been explored in studies by Mandler, Bauer, and associates (Bauer & Mandler, 1989, 1990; Mandler, 1990). We saw in Chapter 3 that even toddlers can form event representations, or scripts, for meaningful sequences of actions (e.g., giving a Teddy bear a bath). The Mandler-Bauer research has probed for the possible emergence of such representations in infancy, using the infant's ability to imitate a sequence of modeled actions as evidence. By 11 months babies can reproduce very simple sequences within the experimental session itself, and by 20 months they show memory for sequences across a 2-week delay. One of the studies, moreover, provides intriguing evidence that some memories may persist for considerably longer than 2 weeks. McDonough and Mandler (1989) retested a subset of their initially 11-month-old subjects a year after exposure to the modeled actions. The now 23-month-olds showed some above-chance ability to reproduce actions that they had seen modeled a full year earlier. Even longer-term memory has been demonstrated in research by Perris, Myers, and Clifton (1990). In their study 6½-month-old infants learned to reach in the dark for a sounding object. Some of the children showed memory for this one-time experience when placed in the same setting a full 2 years later!

Deferred imitation is not the only indication that a capacity for recall may emerge earlier than Piaget believed. The infant's search for vanished objects provides another source of evidence. In Chapter 2 we argued from the research evidence on object permanence that infants can represent the continued existence of an absent object by about 9 months of age, and quite possibly even earlier (recall Baillargeon's research). Whether success on such tasks requires a capacity for conscious recall—given the behaviors and the time spans involved—is debatable, but some researchers (e.g., Mandler, 1990) believe that it does. Recall is more clearly implicated in the infant's ability to remember the typical locations for familiar objects across extended periods of time—for example, to crawl to the cupboard where a favorite cereal is kept, even though the cereal has not been seen for several days. Most babies show such long-term memory for familiar locations by the end of the first year (Ashmead & Perlmutter, 1980). Indeed, the heroine of the following vignette was only 7 months old:

> Trying to change Anne's diaper and dress in a.m. on changing table. She immediately turns over and crawls to top edge of table and reaches over edge several times. Today

I had picked up the pink lotion so it wasn't where she expected it to be. Anne paused, looked back and forth and looked at me puzzled. Her eyes brightened when she saw the bottle—immediately took it from me. (Ashmead & Perlmutter, 1980, p. 11)

It appears, then, that infants are capable of recalling infant experiences. Are they also capable of recalling infant experiences later, as children and adults? It has long been believed that they are totally incapable of recalling such early experiences—a puzzling memory limitation that Freud (1905/1953) called *infantile amnesia*. Although we still do not understand this curious phenomenon very well, the recent studies by McDonough and Mandler (1989) and Perris and colleagues (1990) suggest that the amnesia may not be as total as previously believed.

Having presented the evidence for recall during infancy, we should add that students of infancy are by no means agreed on how to interpret this evidence. Exactly what sorts of mnemonic capacity are necessary to explain certain behaviors is still very much a topic of debate (a graphic example of this point is provided by the discussions that follow the papers on infant memory by Mandler, 1990, and Meltzoff, 1990b). Furthermore, whatever recall-like processes may be operative during infancy, they are certainly not fully equivalent to the recall of the older children or adult. Just as recognition has primitive as well as advanced forms, so too—and even more obviously—does recall. But then more advanced forms of recall are the subject matter of most of the remainder of this chapter.

One more finding from infancy research is worth mentioning before we turn to older children. Studies of recognition memory, as we saw, have often used the habituation paradigm, in which infants' recognition of a stimulus is inferred from their decreased interest as the stimulus is repeatedly presented. In such studies, some infants habituate more quickly than do others. Some investigators of infant habituation have followed their subjects up in later childhood to see whether rapid or slow habituation in infancy is predictive of any aspect of later intellectual functioning. It turns out that infant habituation *is* predictive, and of a kind of intellectual performance that has received considerable attention: namely, scores on IQ tests. On the average, children who were relatively rapid habituators as infants do well on childhood IQ tests; so too do children who showed an especially strong interest in novelty when tested in a Fantz-type paired-comparison paradigm as infants (Bornstein & Sigman, 1986; Fagan, Shepherd, & Knevel, 1991; McCall, 1990). This was a surprising finding, because psychologists previously could find no infant predictors of later cognitive ability. We hasten to add that the infant measures are far from perfectly predictive of later IQ—and that IQ, in any case, is a far from complete measure of cognitive development. Still, this research does provide tantalizing evidence for some continuity in intellectual functioning from infancy to childhood—continuity previously thought to be lacking. And the fact that an early interest in novelty is predictive of later intelligence fits with the model of cognitive motivation that we presented in Chapter 2: Infants who make sense of events quickly and seek out new experiences are most likely to benefit from their experiences and to make cognitive progress.

We turn now to memory in older children. As noted, our concern is not just in documenting the memory improvements that come with age but in explaining *why* these improvements occur. Four categories of phenomena will be useful in this attempt. The first is a special class of storage and retrieval activities termed memory *strategies*. Deliberately rehearsing someone's name in order to memorize it would be an example of a memory strategy. The second, *knowledge*, refers to the more or less automatic effects of what you have to come to know on what you will store and retrieve—roughly, the effects of memory in the broader sense on memory in the narrower sense. The third category is called *metamemory*, and it refers to an individual's knowledge or cognition about anything pertaining to memory (e.g., that certain kinds of information are harder to learn and remember than others). Metamemory is metacognition (Chapter 4) concerning anything having to do with memory. The fourth category, memory *capacity*, involves one's total "amount" of mental resources available for mnemonic activities, including the above three. We now will describe the nature and course of memory development by considering each of these four categories in turn.

STRATEGIES

Suppose an experimenter showed you a card with these 12 words printed on it, arranged as shown here:

apple	bicycle	house	bear
cheese	lion	apartment	tiger
carrot	car	hotel	bus

Your task is to memorize them well enough to be able to recall them all, in any order, when the card is removed. You, as a sophisticated memorizer, probably would think of preparing yourself for this free-recall test with one or more of the following activities: Rehearsing the list by saying the words over and over to yourself. Organizing the list by studying together words that are closely related semantically. This means mentally rearranging it so that, for instance, "lion" is moved over with the other two animals and "bus" with the other two vehicles. Elaborating the list by creating meaningful connections among the words; for instance, by making up a story or imaging a scene that includes these objects. Testing yourself for readiness to recall all the words before you are tested. And when you are tested, checking to be sure you have recalled all three objects from each of the four categories (food, vehicles, dwellings, animals) before you say you are finished. All of these activities are memory strategies that keep the words alive in short-term memory and encourage transfer to long-term memory.

The category of memory strategies encompasses the large and diverse range of potentially conscious activities a person may voluntarily carry out as means to various mnemonic ends. Verbally rehearsing a telephone number during the brief interval between looking it up in the phone book and going to the phone to dial it is an everyday, nonlaboratory example of a mnemonic strategy. Others include (1) taking notes in class; (2) underlining key expressions in a textbook; (3) noting tomorrow's dentist appointment on your calendar; (4) trying to reconstruct your day's events step-by-step in hopes of recalling where you may have left that missing watch; and (5) attempting to remember someone's name by trying to recall people and events associated with that person.

The distinction between strategies and other aspects of memory may be more apparent if we consider memory in animals (Flavell & Wellman, 1977). An adult horse surely has basic memory processes—for example, mechanisms of recognition memory. It has also certainly acquired much practical knowledge of its world from years of experience that enormously influences what it will learn and remember.

And it has enough memory capacity for simple horse-like memories. We doubt, however, if many psychologists would want to argue for the existence of intentional and planful equine memory strategies, let alone equine metamemory.

The childhood acquisition of memory strategies has been the subject of a great deal of research. In fact, it was mainly the discovery of memory strategies as fruitful objects of developmental investigation in the 1960s that launched memory development as a popular area of scientific inquiry. You know from other chapters in this book that there currently is great interest in unearthing the earliest possible competencies or "protocompetencies" in all areas of cognitive development. The recent surge of interest in infant memory, described earlier, is one symptom. The recent search for evidence of memory strategies in the postinfancy years is another (e.g., Wellman, 1989).

Strategic Behaviors in Very Young Children

Toddlers and preschoolers do very poorly with lists of the type presented to you, and they show little evidence of any strategies. However, strategic-looking behaviors arise in the recall of the locations of objects fairly early in life. In one study (DeLoache, Cassidy, & Brown, 1985), children aged 18 to 24 months watched the experimenter hide a toy, such as a Big Bird stuffed animal, under a pillow (or some other location) in a living room or laboratory playroom. The children were told that they should remember Big Bird's location so they could find him later. Although they then were distracted with attractive toys for 4 minutes, they frequently interrupted their activities to talk about Big Bird or his hiding place ("Big Bird chair"), point at the hiding place, look at it, hover near the hiding place, or attempt to retrieve the toy. These seemed to be attempts to remember the location rather than just incidental comments about Big Bird. To ensure that these behaviors actually were mnemonic strategies, two control conditions were included: Big Bird was simply put on top of the pillow ("get Big Bird after he's taken a nap"), so that no memory was required for retrieval, or the experimenter rather than the child was to retrieve the toy. In these conditions the above activities occurred much less frequently. The activities resemble, and thus may be precursors of, the mature strategies for keeping the material alive in short-term memory that we mentioned earlier.

Researchers (Baker-Ward, Ornstein, & Holden, 1984) have observed similar strategic-looking behaviors in 4-year-olds during a free-recall task, which is more similar than the hidden-object task to memory assessments traditionally used with grade-school children. Children in the memory condition were told that they could play with a set of toys, but should try to remember a specified subsample of the toys. Children in control conditions were simply told that they could play with the toys; no later recall was mentioned. Children in the memory condition not only played less than the controls, but also named the to-be-remembered objects and looked at them intensely. Thus, 4-year-olds approach a memory task with behaviors that may reflect deliberate attempts to remember. These behaviors can be considered rudimentary strategies.

Although it generally is believed that preschoolers do not spontaneously and deliberately group items into categories when trying to memorize them, there is recent evidence that grouping occurs when the categories are spatial rather than meaning based, such as "animals" or "transportation." DeLoache and Todd (1988) had preschoolers watch an experimenter hide either candies or small wooden pegs inside a variety of small opaque containers. The experimenter told the children that they should remember which of the 12 containers held the candies. The children took each container as it was handed to them and placed it on the table. By age 5, children spontaneously separated into two groups the containers holding candies and small wooden pegs. This behavior appears to be strategic because they did not do this grouping in a control condition in which no recall was required. Informal observations also suggested the intentional use of a strategy. One child who put the containers with the candies together close to her and the containers with the pegs far away gleefully announced, "I know how to keep the pegs out!" In a subsequent study, when the two categories of containers were made perceptually distinctive (e.g., paper-clip boxes held candies and film canisters held pegs), children aged 2 to 4 were also able to use the spatial categorization used by the 5-year-olds in the first study. DeLoache and Todd concluded that the younger children used the perceptual differentiation already present in the two sets to form categories, but 5-year-olds in addition could construct categories based on an internal representation. The overall lesson here is that when young children are given the chance to organize materials in a manner consistent with their knowledge base, in this case spatial rather than meaning-based categories, they can be strategic.

Young children clearly change their behavior in certain mnemonic situations, and probably do so deliberately. These behaviors most likely are precursors of the more complex, generalizable, and effective strategies of older children, to which we now turn.

Rehearsal

We will use the most commonly studied strategy, verbal rehearsal, as a vehicle within which to present some general conclusions about the development of memory strategies in children. Numerous studies have shown that spontaneous rehearsal becomes more common throughout the grade-school years (e.g., Flavell, Beach, & Chinsky, 1966). What causes this increased strategic competence? Keeney, Cannizzo, and Flavell (1967) administered the following task to first graders, a transitional age at which some children would be expected to have developed a tendency to rehearse and some would not. On each of several trials, seven pictures of common objects were displayed and an experimenter slowly pointed in turn to, say, three of them. The child understood that his task subsequently would be to point, after a 15-second delay, to those same three pictures in exactly the same serial order that the experimenter had. The child wore a toy space helmet with a translucent visor. The visor was pulled down over the child's eyes during the delay interval, so the child could see neither pictures nor experimenters. One of the experimenters had been trained to lip-read semicovert verbalization of these particular object names and carefully recorded whatever spontaneous verbal rehearsal he could detect. There were four major findings. First, children who spontaneously rehearsed the picture names, according to the lip-reading evidence, recalled the sequences of pictures better than those who did not. Second, the nonrehearsers were quite capable of rehearsing and could be gotten to do so with only minimal instruction and demonstration by the experimenter. Third, once induced to rehearse, their recall rose to the level of that of the spontaneous rehearsers. Fourth, when subsequently given the option on later trials of rehearsing or not rehearsing, more than half of them abandoned the strategy, thereby reverting to their original, preexperimental status as nonrehearsers.

This study typifies the research literature on memory-strategy development in two respects. First, it dealt primarily with strategies initiated during the storage rather than the retrieval phase of a memory problem. Rehearsal is something you start doing now, at storage, in hope that starting it now will facilitate performance later, at retrieval. You know in advance you will have to remember something later, so you try to prepare for the recall test by rehearsing. Second, the task materials used were discrete, rote-type "items," as contrasted with the highly meaningful, connected discourse more typical of everyday life. Similarly, they presented the children with traditional, in-the-head storage and retrieval problems. The children could not use the strategy of writing down the object names, for example, or of asking someone else to help them remember the names. In short, the tasks were definitely of the traditional laboratory-memory-experiment genre and, as such, were not wholly representative of the information storage and retrieval enterprises that children and adults undertake in the real world.

Table 6–1 presents a simplified overview of how memory strategies such as verbal rehearsal usually seem to develop (A. L. Brown et al., 1983; Flavell, 1970b). Initially (left column), the component skills and skill integrations that make up an act of verbal rehearsal are largely or wholly absent from the child's repertoire. These components might include the ability to recognize and subvocalize stimulus names quickly and accurately; the ability to repeat (rehearse) words or word sequences to yourself in a fluent, rapid, well-controlled fashion; and the ability to keep constant track of where you have been and where you are going in the execution of your rehearsal plan. When you stop to think about it, it is apparent that verbal rehearsal entails a rather complex coordination and integration of skills. Needless to say, if children are unable to rehearse at all, it follows that they will show no spontaneous rehearsal in a memory-task context. We also assume, to simplify matters, that no significant amount of mnemonically useful rehearsal can be elicited from children in this earliest period, even with strenuous efforts at rehearsal training.

The second period in Table 6–1 (middle column) is much more interesting because it is a transitional period. The experiment by Keeney and colleagues (1967) described previously is only one of a large number that testify to the existence of this curious transitional stage. Recall that some of their first-grade subjects did little or no spontaneous, deliberate rehearsing in that particular memory-task setting. Nevertheless, these children proved to have good ability to rehearse,

TABLE 6–1 Typical Course of Development of a Memory Strategy

	MAJOR PERIODS IN STRATEGY DEVELOPMENT		
	Strategy Not Available	Production Deficiency	Mature Strategy
Basic abilty to execute strategy	Absent to poor	Fair to good	Good to excellent
Spontaneous strategy use	Absent	Absent	Present
Attempts to elicit strategy use	Ineffective	Effective	Unnecessary
Effects of strategy use on retrieval	—	Positive	Positive

rehearsal was easily elicited by the experimenter, and its elicitation did help their subsequent retrieval. A distinction frequently is made in the trade between a *production deficiency* and a *mediational deficiency* (Flavell, 1970b). A child is said to have a production deficiency for a particular strategy if he fails to produce it on his own for reasons other than the sheer lack of ability or skill to enact it properly. A child is said to have a mediational deficiency if his execution of the strategy, whether spontaneous or elicited, does not facilitate his recall. The transitional pattern usually observed in research studies is the one shown in Keeney et al. (1967) and in Table 6–1—namely, a marked production deficiency coupled with no apparent mediational deficiency.

Why would a child exhibit a production deficiency? If he is equipped with the strategy and if its production would benefit his memory performance, why on earth would he fail to produce it spontaneously? To say that he does not produce it because it does not occur to him to produce it sounds like a gross evasion of the question. Nevertheless, thinking about production deficiencies this way may point us toward some deeper explanations.

Several possible reasons exist why it might not occur to him to produce it. One possibility is that he does not yet fully grasp the implicit demands of this or perhaps any storage-memorization task (Bem, 1970). It may not be as obvious to the child as it would be to you that he ought to do *something* special with those pictures now so as to enhance his memory of them later. He may not achieve or maintain, at storage time, a clear image of what is going to happen later, at retrieval time. In short, he may be insufficiently planful, foresighted, or goal oriented, at least in this particular memory-task situation (Paris, 1978).

Another possibility is that, although he can produce certain strategies, he cannot spontaneously invoke and use this particular strategy—for example, verbal rehearsal specifically—again, either in this particular task situation or more generally. One reason for this might be that the task situation tends to call forth some other mnemonic strategy instead. Another strategy might win out over rehearsal because it has been in the child's repertoire longer, is less difficult and effortful to execute, or for some other psychologically sensible reason. Such a strategy would, therefore, generally be an earlier-developing, more elementary-looking one than rehearsal. Examples from the Keeney et al. (1967) task might be simple one-time naming, or careful visual inspection of each object as the experimenter points to it, but without any appreciable cognitive processing of the items during the 15-second delay period that follows. Such a child may be behaving more or less methodically and strategically with respect to the eventual mnemonic goal, unlike the possibility described in the previous paragraph, but the plan or strategy the child has selected happens not to be rehearsal.

There may be yet other reasons why it "happens not to be rehearsal," however. A rather banal one is that this child simply has not yet learned that rehearsal can benefit recall, and indeed, there are circumstances in which some kinds of rehearsal do not (Skeen & Rogoff, 1987). In fact, many studies have shown that young children are likelier to use a memory strategy spontaneously once they have learned that using it aids their recall (e.g., Borkowski, Levers, & Gruenenfelder, 1976; Fabricius & Cavalier, 1989; Fabricius & Hagen, 1984; Lodico, Ghatala, Levin, Pressley, & Bell, 1983).

A less banal reason is that a skill must be fairly well developed in its own right before it can be effectively deployed as a strategic means to a memory goal. A behavior pattern like verbal rehearsal is still rather effortful, challenging, and attention demanding as an act in itself for a young child (e.g. Guttentag, 1984). Thus, the child may have trouble incorporating it as a subroutine within a larger cognitive program such as a memorization problem. The child's trouble could take the form of not readily thinking to use it that way in the first place, or of failing to maintain and continue its use without outside prompting. Recall that the Keeney et al. (1967) first-grade nonrehearsers showed both kinds of trouble. Needless to say, such problems are likely to be more severe as we move leftward in Table 6–1— that is, as the child we are considering has a fair rather than good or a poor rather than fair ability to execute the strategy. The child's production deficiency may be then coupled with a marked *production inefficiency*—that is, an actual inability to carry out the strategy skillfully and efficiently (Flavell, 1970b). This large effort required to execute the strategy increases the probability of a production deficiency. In summary, then, there are many reasons why a child might exhibit a production deficiency for a given strategy.

The rightmost column of Table 6–1 is almost self-explanatory. Production of the strategy can now occur spontaneously, without the experimenter's assistance. As already suggested, this spontaneity may be explainable partly by the child's increased ease and fluency in executing the strategy. There may now be enough space in his cognitive operating room to rehearse efficiently, *and* to monitor the progress of his memorization, *and* to keep the upcoming retrieval task firmly in mind—*and* perhaps even to worry about how well he will perform on it.

The course of strategy development shown in Table 6–1 could be illustrated experimentally in the following way: Subjects of, say, three age levels are divided into two groups. One group at each age level is simply given the memory task. The second group is additionally provided with some sort of aid in using a certain strategy—for example, instruction or training in using it, or task conditions that favor its employment. Then the experiment would show that providing such aid greatly increases strategy use, but only in the intermediate (production-deficient) age group. It would not significantly increase strategy use in either the youngest or the oldest groups because the former is unable to profit from it and the latter is already using the strategy spontaneously.

As usual, we have made things seem more straightforward than they really are. For example, recent evidence suggests a curious transitional phase preceding mature strategy use, a so-called *utilization deficiency* (P. H. Miller, 1990). This deficiency refers to a developmental phase when children first begin to spontaneously produce the strategy but accrue no benefit, little benefit, or less benefit than do older children. For instance, when a younger and older child are executing the strategy to the same extent, their recall is not equivalent (DeMarie-Dreblow & Miller, 1988; P. H. Miller, 1990). Older children somehow can more fully exploit the strategy. The reason for this remains an issue. One plausible candidate is that strategy production is very effortful for novice strategy producers (P. H. Miller, 1990; P. H. Miller, Seier, Probert, & Aloise, 1991). If producing and executing the strategy require most of the young child's information-processing capacity, then little remains for mnemonic processing per se. Older children, who can rather automatically execute the strategy, do not have this problem. As evidence, young children recall more when the capacity required for a strategy is decreased (P. H. Miller, Woody-Ramsey, & Aloise, 1991) and when children possess greater than average capacity (Pressley, Cariglia-Bull, Deane, & Schneider, 1987; Woody-Ramsey, 1989). A utilization deficiency differs from a mediational deficiency in that the former refers only to *spontaneously* produced strategies. Also, in a utilization deficiency a child is unable to profit from the strategy only under certain conditions, such as when the strategy requires a great deal of effort to execute.

A second wrinkle in our tidy classification system is that the concept of production deficiency, while useful, is flawed by our inability to define "spontaneous production" unambiguously. People "spontaneously" rehearse only in the context of some memory-task environment. But this environment always contains stronger or weaker cues, more or less subtle prompts, as possible facilitators or elicitors of rehearsal activity. After reviewing the relevant literature regarding rehearsal and other memory strategies, Folds and co-workers (1990) concluded that the conditions that facilitate successful strategy use include the following: (1) The goal of remembering is explicit, (2) the materials to be remembered encourage strategy use (e.g., are highly associated in the case of grouping items into categories), (3) the instructions and other task procedures encourage the use of strategies (e.g., the items are kept in view in the case of multi-item rehearsal), (4) the information-processing demands of the task are low (e.g., little memory capacity is required), and (5) the child has considerable knowledge about the materials. We will return to some of these dimensions later in the chapter. These conditions are more important for younger children than for older ones, because older children usually do not need these supports. All of these variations in performance are interesting because they help us identify factors that may underlie the development of the memory system.

An important implication of all of this is that one cannot speak of *the* age when the child changes from being production deficient to spontaneously productive for a particular strategy because that age is likely to vary considerably within a single individual as a function of the exact task conditions in which strategy use-nonuse is assessed. The strategic-looking behaviors of 2- and 3-year-olds, described in an earlier section, testify to this conclusion. When—or even whether—a particular memory strategy comes to be used spontaneously in a particular task setting also depends on other factors, such as culture, schooling, and intelligence (e.g., Rogoff, 1990; Wagner, 1981).

Ages of transition are also relative rather than absolute in other ways. In the first place, many possible types and patterns of rehearsal or rehearsal-like activity exist (Ornstein, Naus, & Liberty, 1975), and there is reason to believe that each may have its own developmental timetable. Suppose, for example, you are to memorize, in order, a list of words presented one at a time for several seconds each. One rehearsal strategy would be to say each word over and over again during its presentation period. A more advanced, more active, rehearsal strategy would be to repeat several words rather than just one—for example, to rehearse the first, second, and third words rather than just the third word alone during the third word's presentation interval. The second strategy, cumulative rehearsal, appears to yield better recall than the first. The first is more likely to be elected by younger subjects, the second by older subjects (Cuvo, 1975; Naus & Ornstein, 1983; Ornstein et al., 1975), but any given child from about age 5 to 8 uses both types (McGilly & Siegler, 1989). Young children may have difficulty with cumulative rehearsal because the previous items are no longer present, so somehow must be maintained internally. Leaving previously presented items visible increases spontaneous cumulative rehearsal in 8-year-olds (Guttentag, Ornstein, & Siemens, 1987). Do we say that a child "has" rehearsal when she repeats single items or only when she uses cumulative rehearsal?

As children become older and more experienced, they become more active in initiating strategy use in a variety of situations, including those that do not so strongly encourage optimal processing or strategy use—that is, children show strategy generalization to even nonsupportive contexts. Ironically, progress in the use of one strategy can actually hinder recall when it is applied inappropriately to another situation. Skeen and Rogoff (1987) illustrated this misapplication in a study of children's memory for spatial relationships. Children explored a laboratory fun house under three conditions. One group was told to remember the locations of the rooms—the fire-truck room, Mickey Mouse room, turtle room, Sesame Street room, fuzz-ball room, and so on—then given a tour, and allowed to explore on their own. (Not surprisingly, at the end a few children had to be reminded that their time in the fun house was up! Most laboratory research is not this much fun.) A second group was not told to remember, but interacted fully with the information by unrolling a ribbon through all rooms of the fun house. Much previous research suggests that, by about age 7, children attempt to remember lists through linear strategies such as rehearsal. Such a strategy would be inappropriate for a complex nonlinear spatial memory task and could even interfere with remembering spatial relations. Consistent with this possibility, the 7-year-olds recalled room locations more poorly when told to remember them than when simply involved with the rooms with no instructions to remember. They often organized their retrieval linearly, by drawing the rooms in a line or naming them in a list rather than by describing their central or peripheral location. These behaviors suggest that they misapplied a linear rehearsal strategy to the situation. In contrast, the 5-year-olds' performance in the two conditions did not differ because they did not try to rehearse. Thus, children must not only learn to use particular strategies but also learn when not to use them.

Just as there are many rehearsal strategies, so also are there many memory strategies besides rehearsal. Even though it can be quite complex and sophisticated, rehearsal is fundamentally a rather prosaic memory strategy. It is, after all, only a form of imitation or mimicry. Items are presented and rehearsers simply parrot them over and over, quite possibly adding little or nothing conceptual to the process. In particular, they may not be trying, as they rehearse, to discover or create meaningful relationships among the items that might cause groups of items to clump together at retrieval. Other memory strategies do go beyond the bare bones of the input by adding relationships.

Organizational Strategies

One of the most frequently studied of these meaning-based strategies is organizing items into categories. In your list earlier in the chapter you probably automatically noticed that there were a few animals and some things to eat and perhaps would rehearse them by category. During the retrieval you would recall the animals together, foods together, and so on. Such *clustering* need not be and often would not be complete, as in the following sequence from your list: carrot, lion, tiger, house, bear, bus, car, bicycle.

The developmental story for organizational strategies is much the same as for rehearsal. First, if allowed to manipulate a randomly arranged but potentially categorizable set of object pictures during a study period, older subjects are likelier than younger ones to adopt the strategy of physically segregating the pictures into groups by category and then studying same-category items together (e.g., Moely, Olson, Halwes, & Flavell, 1969; Neimark, Slotnick, & Ulrich, 1971). Second, such clustering increases their recall. Third, younger subjects exhibit the usual transitional production-deficiency pattern with respect to this strategy (see Table 6–1). Fourth, although preschoolers typically do not spontaneously group items, under certain conditions they can do so; the strategy helps their recall, and they generalize it to new stimuli (Lange, Pierce, & Schedler, 1989).

When overt grouping is not possible prior to testing, as when the items cannot be moved, mental grouping is still possible. In these cases, clustering during recall is the only behavior that could reflect an organizational strategy. However, the mere presence of clustering in a subject's recall does not prove that he or she had consciously and intentionally used a clustering strategy when storing and retrieving those items (Lange, 1978). To illustrate, Goldberg, Perlmutter, and Myers (1974) found that recall of one item can cue the recall of a semantically related item even in 2-year-olds. Two-year-olds may have some impressive mnemonic talents but conscious, intentional use of a clustering strategy is surely not one of them (N. A. Myers & Perlmutter, 1978). Also, children who use clustering at recall do not necessarily use it during the study phase (Lange, Guttentag, & Nida, 1990), which questions whether both reflect an underlying organizational strategy. Bjorklund (1987b) has argued that the clustering during recall of even school-age children often is of an automatic, nonstrategic sort, with closely associated words in the same category simply triggering each other. When a child says "dog," she is reminded automatically of "cat." Bjorklund argues that clustering may not be a strategy until early adolescence when it is intentional and leads to high recall. However, he proposes that the early automatic association-based clustering can provide experiences that eventually lead to the later organizational strategy. When monitoring their recall, children may notice some of the category relations among items they have clustered together and begin to use this information in a more deliberate way.

It is likely that organizational behaviors at input and output sometimes reflect the same process and sometimes do not. The older the child the more likely that both reflect deliberate strategies. In any case, virtually all memory researchers agree that both strategic and nonstrategic aspects of meaning-based organization contribute to memory development. This will become clearer later when we examine the knowledge category.

Elaboration

Another, closely related type of strategy is called *elaboration* (see Schneider & Pressley, 1989, for a review). Children identify or construct some sort of shared meaning or other link between two or more things to be remembered. Elaboration strategies are usually studied in the context of a paired-associate learning task. In such tasks, subjects have to learn pairs of items so that when one word (e.g., "elephant") is presented, they can recall the other (e.g., "pin"). You would be using an elaboration strategy here if you deliberately generated an absurd or otherwise memorable visual image linking the two members of the pair. You might, for example, create an image of an elephant delicately balanced on the head of a pin, demurely acknowledging the applause of the audience. Another elaboration strategy would be to think of a sentence that describes an event involving the two—for example, "The elephant picked up the pin with his trunk." Much research shows that elaboration can be a very effective method of cementing items together in memory. Just try forgetting what object was paired with "elephant" in the preceding example. As a real-world application, the use of elaboration techniques can be helpful in learning the meaning of words in a foreign language (Pressley, Levin, & Bryant, 1983).

Most of the developmental improvement in learning paired associates comes from an increase in the use of elaboration strategies (Beuhring & Kee, 1987). Older children are more likely than younger ones not only to construct elaborations without outside help (Rohwer, 1973) but also to retrieve them to help recall (Pressley & MacFadyen, 1983) and to transfer them to another task (Pressley & Dennis-Rounds, 1980). This developmental pattern should sound very familiar to you by now.

Both organizational strategies and elaboration are later-developing strategies than at least the simpler forms of rehearsal (Pressley et al., 1983; Schneider & Pressley, 1989). It also is probably true that most forms of conscious and deliberate elaboration are apt to appear later in ontogenesis—and less certainly, less universally—than most forms of conscious and deliberate organization (Pressley, 1982; Schneider & Pressley, 1989). Still, even 5-year-olds have increased recall when instructed to use elaboration if there is external support—for example, if part of the image is shown in pictures (Ryan, Ledger, & Weed, 1987).

Allocation of Cognitive Resources

In the experiments described thus far, the experimenter presents the material to be recalled. However, in many or even most natural settings, children themselves must select certain material to process and commit to memory. It is appropriate to remember only a subset of the material when only part of it is relevant or when the child has only enough capacity to remember the most important material. P. H. Miller (e.g., Miller, 1990; Miller, Haynes, DeMarie-Dreblow, & Woody-Ramsey, 1986; Miller & Weiss, 1981) devised a procedure for directly observing the child's choice of information to process. The 12 items that can be selected for viewing are behind a 2 × 6 matrix of small doors. Only six items are relevant—for example, the child is told to remember where each of six animals is hidden. The other doors conceal household items. The type of item concealed is indicated by a drawing of a cage or a house on each door. Children have a study period, typically 30 seconds, for opening whichever doors they wish, as many times as they wish. The most efficient strategy is to be selective, that is, to open only the relevant doors. Older children tend to use this strategy. Preschoolers, however, typically are not selective. Instead, they simply follow the spatial layout of the apparatus, usually opening first one row (some animals and some household objects) and then the other. During a transitional period children are partially selective.

Interestingly, preschoolers are more selective when the task is embedded in a familiar script—putting toy animals or household objects away in toy boxes at nursery school and finding them later (Woody-Ramsey & Miller, 1988). This outcome foreshadows the interaction of knowledge and strategies discussed later. More generally, older children are more flexible in the allocation of their attention, adjusting their pattern of door-openings to the goal of the task (P. H. Miller et al., 1986). This method of observing the allocation of cognitive resources has been extended to other tasks (e.g., P. H. Miller & Harris, 1988) and to another culture (P. H. Miller & Jordan, 1982). Selectivity also has been related to individual difference variables such as temperament (McManis & Miller, 1992), cognitive capacity (Woody-Ramsey, 1989), and cognitive style (Haynes & Miller, 1987).

A second example of a growing ability to allocate resources efficiently during memory tasks comes from work by Kobasigawa and colleagues (e.g., Dufresne & Kobasigawa, 1989). They find that young grade-school children generally do not devote more study time to memorizing difficult items than easy items. They become selective only if the differential difficulty is made very obvious.

Thus, as children develop they become more flexible and efficient in how they invest their resources—processing all available information when that is necessary, or processing only a part when that strategy is appropriate. This developmental trend applies not only to memory tasks but also to many other cognitive tasks. Our own mental image of a cognitively mature information processor is that of a conductor who directs an ensemble of musicians (attentional processes and resources)—now calling forth one instrument, now another, now a blended combination of several or all, depending upon the effect desired. We think we do not so much "pay attention" as "play our attentional system"—that is, we intentionally exploit and deploy it in a flexible, situation-contingent, adaptive fashion (cf. Lane, 1979).

Retrieval Strategies

Children's attempts at retrieval have been likened to finding a particular book in a badly organized library (Sechenov, 1935). So far we have discussed mainly storage strategies—that is, the kinds of mnemonically oriented data processing individuals do now because they know they will have to retrieve those data later. As indicated earlier, retrieval strategies refer to the resourceful moves that individuals may make when actually trying to recover things from memory storage, whether or not they had previously known they would now be doing that. Like storage strategies, retrieval strategies vary greatly in complexity and sophistication. A less sophisticated one is not to give up one's memory search immediately just because the sought-for item does not come to mind immediately (Flavell, 1978d). Sticking with the problem a little longer does not always pay off, of course, but it certainly qualifies as an elementary retrieval strategy. More sophisticated, later-developing strategies often involve knowledge about what retrieval cues are and how to use them effectively, knowledge noticeably lacking in young children (Beal, 1983; Fabricius & Wellman, 1983; Flavell, 1978b; Gordon & Flavell, 1977; Kreutzer, Leonard, & Flavell, 1975; Ritter, 1978). Even more advanced strategies involve a complex interplay among specific memory fragments, general knowledge of the world, and reasoning or inference: " I remember hearing the sound of waves outside [memory fragment], so it probably happened near an ocean [inference, general knowledge]; but I've only been to the ocean once, in 1969 [memory fragment], so it must have been that summer, during vacation [inference]." At their most sophisticated levels:

> The individual's retrieval strategies have something of the quality of a Sherlock Holmes tour de force.... When he realizes that X [the retrieval target] probably will not come to mind by just sitting and waiting...he deliberately searches his memory for related data, in hopes that something recalled will bring him closer to X. In the most elaborate cases of this sort of intelligent, highly indirect and circumlocutious retrieving, the process is virtually one of rational reconstruction of "what must have been," in the light of remembered data, general knowledge, and logical reasoning. (Flavell & Wellman, 1977, p. 20)

A study by Keniston and Flavell (1979) illustrates some of the developmental changes that have been observed in this area (see also Flammer & Luthi, 1988). Subjects were in grades one, three, seven, and college. The experimenter named a letter of the alphabet, the subject wrote it on a small card, the experimenter removed the card and named another letter, the subject wrote that letter on a new small card, and so on, until a random sequence of 20 different letters had been written on the cards. Unexpectedly, subjects had to recall these letters. A very effective retrieval strategy in such a situation is to go through the entire alphabet in your mind and write down each letter that you recognize as having just recently been seen and written out. This strategy deftly transforms a very difficult free-recall task into a very easy recognition task. It is easy for the experimenter to tell when a subject has used this strategy: The target letters are retrieved in alphabetical order. Younger subjects in the Keniston and Flavell (1979) study could use the recognition strategy both skillfully and effectively (i.e., it improved their recall) when merely *told* to use it; no training or practice was needed. If not told to use the strategy, however, it did not occur to most of them to use it, and their recall suffered accordingly. Thus, they showed the familiar production-deficiency pattern of being quite capable of using the strategy effectively when told to use it but of not being able to think of it on their own.

Based on the results of this and other studies (Flavell, 1978b; Kobasigawa, 1977; Salatas & Flavell, 1976), Keniston and Flavell (1979) proposed that, with age and experience, children gradually acquire at least two important pieces of strategy knowledge about how to retrieve information effectively. First, they know that, when possible, it is useful to take a stroll down memory lane—a systematic, exhaustive mental walk through a relevant section of the internal world, such as the alphabet in the Keniston and Flavell (1979) study. "Trying to remember something" and "searching one's memory for something" are roughly synonymous. Much of what develops in the area of memory retrieval consists of the ability and propensity to search the internal world intelligently: efficiently, flexibly, systematically, exhaustively, selectively, indirectly—whatever the retrieval problem at hand demands (Flavell, 1978b; Keniston & Flavell, 1979). With few exceptions (Schneider & Sodian, 1988), the available evidence indicates that this ability develops relatively late in ontogenesis—during middle childhood and adolescence rather than during infancy and early childhood. Second, children learn that when the entire potential set is not known, it is useful to use an indirect, circumlocutious retrieval strategy. Retrieving nontarget items may trigger other items, some of which may be target items. Not surprisingly, this indirect strategy is used mainly by older children who are more likely to know that one thing can remind us of another (Beal, 1983; Gordon & Flavell, 1977) and that a recognition task is generally easier than a recall task (Speer & Flavell, 1979).

In marked contrast, there is considerable growth during infancy and early childhood in the ability to search the *external* world (Wellman, 1985a). Even infants show some ability to search the external world when they seek and find hidden objects in Piaget's object-permanence tasks (Chapter 2). By 3 or 4 years of age, young children are quite accomplished searchers (e.g., Sophian & Somerville, 1988). If, from available evidence, a hidden object could logically be in any one of the hiding places present, children of this age will conduct a systematic, exhaustive search of all these places—analogous to what older subjects do in the internal world when faced with certain memory-retrieval tasks (Keniston & Flavell, 1979). On the contrary, if the evidence indicates that the missing object must be located in a particular subset of the available hiding places—that logically it could not be in other available hiding places—then children will selectively focus their search on this logically possible subset. A study by Haake, Somerville, and Wellman (1980) showed this quite clearly. In this study, an experimenter took each preschool subject's picture with a camera at locations 1, 2, 3 of an itinerary that included stops at eight locations. When experimenter and child reached location 7 they discovered that the camera was missing. Thus, location 3 was the locus of last-known possession of the camera and location 7 was the locus of first-known nonpossession, making locations 4 to 6 the critical subset. Much as a grown-up would do, these young children tended to concentrate their search at locations 4, 5, and 6, and—impressively—to avoid searching at 1, 2, and 3, the only locations that had actually been associated with the camera in their experience. Older individuals are similarly selective in their search of the internal world, often concentrating their search in areas of remembered past experience that are likely to contain the retrieval target (Keniston & Flavell, 1979; Williams & Hollan, 1981).

It is interesting to speculate about possible developmental relationships between these outer-world search skills and inner-world (memory) search skills. Perhaps the principles of intelligent, task-adaptive external search that are gradually worked out during late infancy and early childhood (Somerville & Haake, 1985) subsequently become generalized and applied to formally similar problems of internal search. As argued earlier in this chapter, mnemonic scenarios in everyday life frequently entail a sequential, back-and-forth movement between internal and external memory stores. Similarly, we often search our memory stores to aid us in finding things in the external world and often search the external world for retrieval cues that will jog our memories. It would be surprising if such formally similar and functionally interconnected skills were not also developmentally related.

Strategies for Learning and Remembering Complex Material

We mentioned earlier that most studies of strategy development have used, as the material to be remembered, discrete, rote-type "items" (words, depicted objects) rather than semantically rich information structures. However, it is both feasible and adaptive to apply voluntary, deliberate strategies to the understanding, storage, and retrieval of complex, meaningful, and organized information as well as simple word lists and paired associates (A. L. Brown et al., 1983; A. L. Brown & Palincsar, 1985; Pressley, Forrest-Pressley, & Elliott-Faust, 1988). Learning to study effectively in school settings is a familiar and very important example of developing useful storage strategies for comprehending and retaining complex, meaningful information. Just idly reading a passage about the complex and interrelated causes of World War II probably will yield some understanding and memory. But reading it very actively and "intelligently," taking really good notes, deliberately searching for relationships that are only implicit in the text—these are strategies that can yield much better understanding and memory. For this kind of material, the best memory strategy is, ultimately, to strive for a really rich and deep understanding. The same is true on the retrieval side. The previously mentioned sophisticated retrieval strategies, which interweave specific memories, general knowledge, and inferences, are equally applicable to highly meaningful material of various types. They can be used to reconstruct the causes of World War II as well as to reconstruct that single, isolated experience by the ocean mentioned earlier. It is obvious that a better understanding of the nature and development of these types of storage and retrieval strategies, and especially about how they might be solidly and permanently instilled through systematic training and instruction, would have considerable educational significance.

Ann Brown and other developmental psychologists have studied the developmental acquisition of a variety of such strategies. Although strategies for learning and remembering complex meaningful material tend to be acquired later than some of the rote-recall ones considered earlier (e.g., rehearsal), their developmental course seems to be quite familiar: a production deficiency, sporadic spontaneous production, and increased stability, generalization, and effectiveness. Strategies investigated include identifying, selectively attending to, underlining, and summarizing the main ideas in a segment of meaningful text; asking oneself questions about the text and other methods of fostering and monitoring one's comprehension and memory of it; and judicious, task-adaptive allocation of study effort and retrieval effort (A. L. Brown et al., 1983; Pressley et al., 1988). A study by A. L. Brown, Smiley, and Lawton (1978) will serve to illustrate this line of strategy development research. Students from grades 5 to 12 and college students first read a story and then selected those idea units from it that they would prefer to have by them if they were asked to remember the story. In effect, their task was to select the most useful retrieval cues for recalling a body of organized, meaningful information. Half of each age group (naive students) selected idea units before they were given practice studying and recalling the passage; the other half (experienced students) selected them after having had this study and recall experience. Naive students at all ages tended to select as their retrieval cues the most important, central ideas of the story. So did the experienced students—except for the college students, who selected idea units of intermediate importance. Why? The college students said they realized from their recent recall experience that they would probably remember the main ideas without further effort on the next trial, whereas those of intermediate importance had been and probably still would be harder to remember; ergo, to maximize overall recall, select the latter rather than the former as retrieval aids next time. As Brown and colleagues (1978) make clear, this memory strategy is a rather high-level, complex one—so much so that even their high school seniors did not discover it.

In ending this section, we emphasize that the acme of development is not the mere ability to invoke this or that strategy spontaneously. Rather, it is the ability to select the most effective strategy or strategies for the memory problem at hand, and then to modify or replace those strategies appropriately as the mnemonic situation changes—for example, as one's learning progresses, or when changes appear in the nature of the information that has to be memorized (A. L. Brown et al., 1983; Lodico et al., 1983; Pressley, Borkowski, & Schneider, 1987).

KNOWLEDGE

People's acquired knowledge powerfully influences what they store and what they retrieve from storage. You already know one good example—using one's knowledge of categories to form subgroups of items to be recalled. As another example, master chess players and amateurs show an interesting pattern of similarities and differences in their ability to reconstruct from memory the positions of chess pieces on a chessboard (Chase & Simon, 1973). If the pieces are arranged randomly, both groups perform equally poorly. If the arrangement of pieces is one that could legitimately occur in an actual chess game, the masters' abilities to remember the positions are far better than the amateurs'. Similarly, inputs that have little meaning for individuals—that do not fit readily into their acquired knowledge structure, that cannot easily be assimilated into their existing cognitive schemes, and so on—tend to be hard to store and retrieve. The effect of knowledge on memory is domain-specific; knowledge about chess affects memory for chessboards but not memory for the names of contemporary rock bands. This fact is consistent with the domain-specific nature of our knowledge structures, as discussed in Chapters 3 and 4.

This powerful effect of knowledge suggests an interesting hypothesis: Children might actually be able to perform *better* than adults on a memory task if, in contrast to the usual case, they were more knowledgeable than the adults about the content to be remembered. Chi (1978) conducted a clever experiment to test this hypothesis. She tested expert and novice chess players on their ability to remember legitimate chessboard arrangements and found, as Chase and Simon (1973) had, that the experts remembered them better. No surprise so far. In Chi's experiment, however, the novices were adults and the experts were children (mean age = 10.5 years) recruited from a local chess tournament (see also Chi & Koeske, 1983). The superior recall of the child experts was limited to the domain of chess. Their digit span was not larger than that of adult novices. Similarly, Lindberg (1980) found that third graders outperformed college students on a free-recall test that contained items that were highly salient and familiar to the third graders (e.g., cartoon characters). Except for these occasional age reversals, however, adults generally know more than do children and consequently tend to remember better. Children are "universal novices" (A. L. Brown & DeLoache, 1978).

Research on the influence of knowledge on memory development has taken two main directions. One examines how a person's content knowledge, particularly semantic knowledge about relations between words or concepts, influences memory in a particular domain (for a recent review see Bjorklund et al., 1990). This approach focuses on the organization of knowledge, and is closely associated with the work on organizational strategies discussed earlier. The second area, constructive memory (see Fivush & Hudson, 1990), illustrates our tendency to make our experiences richer and more coherent by filling in with what we know or believe about that input.

Content Knowledge

A child's content knowledge often is a sort of mental dictionary of objects and the relations among these objects (Bjorklund, 1987b; Chi, 1985). The organization sometimes is taxonomic—a hierarchical arrangement of superordinate (e.g., animal) and subordinate (e.g., house, farm, and jungle animals) classes. Each item has associations not only with other items but also with features that characterize it (e.g., has stripes, eats other animals). In this view, the mind is like a road map with highways connecting major cities.

Content knowledge can help a child's recall during development in three main ways (Bjorklund, 1987b). First, it can make specific items more accessible, perhaps because they are more richly represented (e.g., have more features) and therefore are more vivid. For example, for most children "pizza" is a more elaborated representation than "casserole." An experimental example is that when the meaningfulness of words on a list is equated for younger and older children, age differences in recall are eliminated (Ghatala, 1984). Second, a well-developed knowledge system facilitates recall by activating relations (associations) among sets of items in a relatively effortless, automatic way. These associations contribute to the clustering described earlier. The nature of the associations changes during development. Seeing Mickey Mouse may cause a child to look for Donald Duck at age 4, but not age 2. The older child's more elaborate semantic knowledge has more associations and stronger associations among items. Thus, he or she is more likely to be able to access items because they can be triggered by more stimuli; there are alternate retrieval routes.

Third, well-developed content knowledge can support strategies, metacognitive processes, and the processing of material at a more abstract categorical level, which in turn help recall. Bjorklund (1987b; Bjorklund & Harnishfeger, 1990) hypothesizes that capacity is freed for these activities in older children because familiar items with many associations are processed with little effort. Content knowledge can also facilitate strategies by providing the conceptual foundation for an organizational strategy. Children obviously cannot organize items to be recalled into categories until they possess the relevant categorical structure.

What is some of the evidence for the influence of content knowledge on recall and on the use of strategies? Researchers have demonstrated the domain-specific superior recall of child experts not only in the domains of chess and cartoons mentioned earlier, but also of dinosaurs (Chi & Koeske, 1983), soccer (Schneider, Korkel, & Weinert, 1989), and baseball (Recht & Leslie, 1988). For example, in one study (Chi & Koeske, 1983), a 4-year-old dinosaur expert remembered a familiar list of dinosaur names better than a less familiar list, even one year later. In a less esoteric domain, all children have expert knowledge about their classmates, and recall is high for their names (Bjorklund & Zeman, 1982) and for the frequency with which their faces are seen in a set of faces (J. F. Harris, Durso, Mergler, & Jones, 1990). Furthermore, cross-cultural and social-class differences in recall can be eliminated when each cultural group is tested with materials that correspond to its structures of knowledge (Lancy & Strathern, 1981; Simmons, 1985). As a final, living example, consider yourself as an experiment in the making. If we have done our job, by the time you finish reading this book we will have filled your head with concepts and associations, transforming you into a memory expert regarding cognitive development.

A child's expertise in a particular domain can sometimes influence his or her memory even more than does the child's general learning ability. Schneider and colleagues (1989) presented a story about a soccer game to children in grades 3, 5, and 7 who were classified as soccer experts or novices and as poor or good learners. As expected, the experts recalled the story better than did the novices and made more story-consistent inferences. More interestingly, expertise predicted performance better than did general learning ability. Experts who were poor learners even outperformed novices who were good learners. The implication for education is that low-ability children can recall new material fairly well if it is introduced to them in the context of a domain about which they are knowledgeable. This was also demonstrated by Bjorklund and Bernholtz (1986) when differences in the free-recall and strategy use of good and poor readers were eliminated when the items for each child were chosen on the basis of that child's ratings of how typical the items were for the categories, thus equating the lists on this measure across subjects.

Most of the research presented so far has focused on a direct, automatic effect of knowledge on memory due to the representational richness of items and the number and strength of the connections among items or categories (Bjork-lund's first and second type of facilitation described earlier). In addition, can there be an indirect effect, an effect on recall mediated by a strategy (Bjorklund's third type of facilitation)? The answer appears to be yes. Giving 8-year-olds familiar materials—words that elicit many associations—increases the number of items rehearsed as a group and the level of recall to that found among 11-year-olds (Tarkin, Myers, & Ornstein, cited in Ornstein & Naus, 1985). In addition, soccer knowledge predicts the use of organizational strategies and the amount of recall in adults (Naus & Ornstein, cited in Ornstein & Naus, 1985). In another study (Best & Ornstein, 1986), third graders told to sort so the groups will help them remember could do so on the basis of meaning when presented with high-associated items, but not low-associated ones. Thus, if the material fits into the child's knowledge base, the child tends to use a strategy.

These demonstrations of content knowledge effects on memory per se and on memory strategies are quite striking. However, we offer two cautions. One is that it is not clear which aspect or aspects of knowledge underlie the effect. Experts and novices differ in many ways, including the number of facts known, the degree of hierarchical structure (superordinate and subordinate categories), the number of category members, and the familiarity and meaningfulness of the items. These variables need to be teased apart. In addition, knowledge usually is confounded with interest in the materials (Saarnio, 1986). It is safe to assume that a child chess expert is quite interested in chess.

A second caution is that virtually all of the research has examined preex-isting knowledge and has tested experts and novices rather than people along the entire spectrum of knowledge: Experts, who already have a well-developed knowledge base in a particular domain, have better memory for items and events in that domain than do novices. However, more convincing evidence that knowledge affects recall would be a demonstration that experimentally manipu-lating this variable by helping children with various degrees of knowledge con-struct new knowledge leads to better recall. Using such a design, DeMarie-Dreblow (1991) assessed 8- to 11-year-olds' knowledge about birds and then showed them five instructional videotapes about birds over a week's time. Also, college students viewed the tapes in a single session. She replicated previous studies' finding that preexisting knowledge correlates with recall. However, contrary to expectation, the amount of new knowledge acquired was not related to increases in recall. The training created new associations between birds and their categories but recall did not improve. Thus, the relation between knowl-edge and memory may be quite complex. It is interesting that college students with high levels of initial knowledge increased their recall as a result of the instruction, suggesting that a certain amount of knowledge may be required before a person can use additional experience to help recall. DeMarie-Dreblow concluded that knowledge may need to be in a particular form in order to become accessible or to become useful for recall (Chi, 1985). For example, knowledge may need to be at a very high level and become hierarchically orga-nized (birds–talking birds–parrot) before it can facilitate the recall of items that form such categories. In this case, associations both among category members and between each member and the superordinate category would need to be strong so that a person would spontaneously generate category labels and use them to generate category members. This would be true of adults in many domains or child experts in one domain, but not of people at other points on the knowledge continuum. In sum, not only what you know but also the form in which you know it affects your recall.

Constructive Memory

Students of constructive memory share with the Piagetians the view that memory is "applied cognition" (Flavell, 1971b, p. 273)—that is, the application to mnemonic problems of whatever intellectual weaponry the individual has so far developed. Most of the things we remember in everyday life, say the proponents of constructive memory, are meaningful, organized events or bodies of structured information. They are not the isolated, largely meaningless "items" of the classical laboratory study of rote learning. Pairs of nonsense syllables, random sequences of digits, or lists of unrelated words are not usually the objects of everyday, extralaboratory learning and remembering. Moreover, these meaningful, structured inputs are not just copied or printed into memory at storage time and equally literally and faithfully recopied or reproduced at retrieval time. Rather, the act of comprehending and encoding into memory is a Piagetian assimilation-type process of *construction* of an internal conceptual representation of the input (hence, "constructive memory"). What is usually constructed and stored in memory could variously be described as a sensible (to the subject) interpretation of what he or she has perceived, an integrated rendering of it, or an organized representation of its gist. The mnemonic construction disregards some features of the input, highlights others, integrates or reorganizes still others, and even adds information not actually present in the input.

Similarly, retrieval also is an active and assimilatory process of *reconstruction*, rather than a passive, unedited copying out of what is stored in memory. It is somewhat akin to the archaeological reconstruction of an ancient civilization based upon building fragments, bits of pottery, and other artifacts, plus a lot of logical inference, conceptual integration, and just plain guessing on the archaeologist's part. These constructions and reconstructions, which are so ubiquitous in everyday, meaningful memory, are usually more automatic, involuntary, and unconscious than we have made them sound here, although they certainly can be, and sometimes are, very conscious and intentional (very "strategic," very "metamnemonic"). The point is that, automatic or deliberate, the memory machine is nothing at all like a tape recorder or camera. We most emphatically do *not* simply take mental photographs of inputs at storage and then simply develop them at retrieval.

It is time for an example. The following story certainly qualifies as a meaningful input to memory:

> Linda was playing with her new doll in front of her big red house. Suddenly she heard a strange sound coming from under the porch. It was the flapping of wings. Linda wanted to help so much, but she did not know what to do. She ran inside the house and grabbed a shoe box from the closet. Then Linda looked inside her desk until she found eight sheets of yellow paper. She cut up the paper into little pieces and put them in the bottom of the box. Linda gently picked up the helpless creature and took it with her. Her teacher knew what to do. (Paris, 1975)

A person could not really understand Linda's adventure, let alone recall it, without doing a lot more than simply copying its constituent sentences into memory. Consider the eight memory questions Paris (1975) asked his subjects after reading them the story.

1. Was Linda's doll new?
2. Did Linda grab a match box?
3. Was the strange sound coming from under the porch?
4. Was Linda playing behind her house?
5. Did Linda like to take care of animals?
6. Did Linda take what she found to the police station?
7. Did Linda find a frog?
8. Did Linda use a pair of scissors?

You may have noticed a difference between questions 1 to 4 and questions 5 to 8. The first four could be answered by a tape-recorder-type of memory machine, since the answers are literally "there" in the surface structure of the story. In sharp contrast, questions 5 to 8 can only be answered by a human type of memory machine, since they require the subject to draw inferences from what is on the surface. The ability to make those inferences clearly depends, in turn, upon stored knowledge about the world (e.g., that birds have wings but frogs do not) and reasoning abilities (e.g., a person who would do what Linda did probably likes to take care of animals).

The constructivists' argument is that we are constantly making spontaneous inferences and interpretations of this sort in processing, storing, and retrieving information. Such additions and elaborations are the rule rather than the exception, and they are believed to be of the very essence of cognition and memory. The argument is buttressed by the fact that we may not even be able to distinguish on a later memory test what we have constructed or elaborated from what had actually been initially presented (Bransford & Franks, 1971). For instance, after hearing sentences like "The box is to the right of the tree" and "The chair is on top of the box" subjects may falsely believe that "The chair is to the right of the tree" was one of the presented sentences, because it is semantically consistent with the mental representation of the input they have constructed (Paris & Mahoney, 1974). A similar but nonconsistent sentence like "The chair is to the left of the tree" will likely be identified as nonpresented, on the other hand. Under some circumstances, subjects actually may be even *more* confident that they remember hearing a semantically consistent but never-presented proposition than one that was presented (e.g., Bransford & Franks, 1971).

Children, like adults, have a constructive memory. Studies by Paris and others (Paris, 1975; Paris & Lindauer, 1977; Paris & Mahoney, 1974) have found that grade-school children show the sorts of constructive-memory phenomena just described. They are apt to believe that Linda found a bird, used scissors, and so on. Similarly, they are likely to think they previously had heard semantically consistent but not presented sentences, while correctly denying that they heard nonpresented sentences that were not consistent with their semantic integration of the input. As Hagen, Jongeward, and Kail (1975) point out, children could scarcely carry on everyday conversations if they could not make the kinds of spontaneous inference, integrations, elaborations, and reorganizations we have been talking about. A great deal has to be assumed, presupposed, or otherwise added by a listener in understanding and remembering what a speaker says; a surprising amount of what gets said in an ordinary conversation is inexplicit and elliptical. As children grow older, they generally seem more prone and able to make the sorts of inferences that allow for a full, integrated, and meaningful memory representation of what they experience.

Probably the most important developmental changes in constructive memory are changes in what knowledge structures the child has with which to constructively remember. As children acquire story and scene schemas, scripts for everyday routines, category knowledge, and innumerable other "mental templates" (Chapter 3), they automatically use these templates to constructively process inputs at storage and to reconstruct them at retrieval (Hudson, 1986). Because scripts are a knowledge structure that seems to be a particularly potent organizer of memory for preschool children, they deserve extra attention here. As described in Chapter 3, a script refers to knowledge about real-life routine events, such as attending a day-care center, baking cookies, or going to a fast-food restaurant. It involves a causal-temporal sequence of events that is constant across its occurrences. By age 3 children's descriptions of such events are ordered, conventionalized, and abstract—all characteristics of a script (K. Nelson, 1986). In general, scripts perform good memory work. Just as the semantic memory structure facilitates grouping and then recall, so does a script, scene, or story schema facilitate the storage of material that can easily be assimilated into it (e.g., Mistry & Lange, 1985). And when presented with stories about scripted events, but with the acts out of sequence, children's recall will repair the stories. For example, they will state that children took presents (party favors) home at the end of a birthday party story in place of the misordered act at the end, "children brought presents" (K. Nelson & Hudson, 1988).

Although scripts usually help recall, they sometimes hinder it because an episode that fits a script may be quickly fused with it, causing any one episodic event to lose its distinctiveness. A 5-year-old, trying to remember a particular trip to the zoo after several visits, recalled:

> I remember only a time that I went to the Israel one. There was a wolf there. I think.... No, that was another zoo. There was no wolf.... There was a duck. There wasn't no zebras.... I think there was zebras, but I'm not sure. (Hudson, 1986, p. 114)

Children as young as 2½ years tend to recall the mundane, script-like features, rather than any one specific episode or distinctive features of events, even novel, unusual ones (Fivush & Hamond, 1990). Farrar and Goodman (1990) argue that such confusions are especially true for young children when they are faced with a complex event that is difficult to organize. Their explanation of this developmental phenomenon assumes that schema-based processing of information involves two phases. First, in a schema-confirmation phase, children attempt to use a schema (e.g., a going-to-the-zoo script) to understand an event. If they have a well-developed schema, they focus cognitive resources on information expected by the schema (e.g., zebras, tigers), thereby confirming the schema. If the schema is confirmed, the second phase can begin.

In the schema-deployment phase, children process script-inconsistent information (e.g., a magic show at the zoo). The latter process forms an episodic memory for a single event, distinct from the scripted memory. Older children and adults, because of their large repertoire of strong scripts that permit rapid processing, quickly process schema-consistent information and then concentrate on processing schema-inconsistent information unless they face a situation not covered by a strong script. In contrast, young children may remember only the script-consistent information or confuse the episodic and script memories because the first phase, schema confirmation, was so effortful for them that they have no remaining capacity for the second phase. They may not recall the magic show. In support of this model, Farrar and Goodman (1992) found that, when given equal amounts of experience with events, 4-year-olds have more difficulty than do 7-year-olds with keeping separate, in memory, script-consistent and script-deviant events. This outcome suggests that the younger children are still forming the script, so they cannot both confirm it and encode unexpected events separately from the script.

To summarize this section on knowledge, we conclude that the increasing content and organization of the knowledge system can account for much of the developmental improvement in memory by making material more familiar, meaningful, and coherent. In short, what the head knows has an enormous effect on what the head learns and remembers. But what the head knows changes enormously in the course of development, and these changes consequently make for changes in memory behavior.

METAMEMORY

The subjects of one investigation, an extensive interview study of children's metamemory, or knowledge about memory (Kreutzer et al., 1975), were kindergartners, first graders, third graders, and fifth graders. In one of the interview items, the experimenter said to each child:

> Jim and Bill are in grade ___ (S's own grade). The teacher wanted them to learn the names of all the kinds of birds they might find in their city. Jim had learned them last year and then forgot them. Bill had never learned them before. Do you think one of these boys would find it easier to learn the names of all the birds? Which one? Why? (Kreutzer et al., 1975, p. 8)

Although this task tests children's knowledge that is relevant to memory, it differs from the tasks in the previous section on knowledge, which assessed how content knowledge affects memory for objects, events, or places in the world. Both the above task and the present section examine knowledge about memory, or metamemory. More specifically, the above task probes the child's intuitions about a specific memory phenomenon—namely the advantage or "savings" involved in relearning something previously learned versus learning something for the first time.

Many of Kreutzer and colleagues' subjects, even at the kindergarten and first-grade levels, did, in fact, seem to intuit that the relearner would have the advantage. Moreover, a number of them gave reasonable justifications for their choice—for example, "Because as soon as he heard the names, they would probably all come back to him" (an allusion to the process of recognition memory). That answer clearly testifies to some metamemory. This third grader's answer clearly testifies to even more: The new learner would actually do better than the relearner, the subject said, "because the kid who learned them might think he knew them, and then he would get them wrong, but the kid who didn't learn them last year might study more than the kid who *thought* he knew them" (Kreutzer et al., 1975, p. 9).

Metamemory is one type of metacognition, defined in Chapter 4 as any knowledge or cognitive activity that takes as its object, or regulates, any aspect of any cognitive enterprise. Useful reviews and critiques of work on metamemory include Borkowski, Milstead, and Hale (1988), Forrest-Pressley, MacKinnon, and Waller (1985), Schneider and Pressley (1989), Schneider and Weinert (1990), Weinert and Kluwe (1987), and Wellman (1985b). Following the conceptualization given in Chapter 4, we can roughly distinguish between *metacognitive knowledge concerning memory* and *metacognitive self-monitoring and regulation*, with the former further divisible into knowledge about mnemonic *persons, tasks,* and *strategies.* Before discussing metamemory development, however, a quick test of *your* metamemory: Do you think you can recall everything said about metacognition in Chapter 4? If you cannot (and our own knowledge about memory assures us that you couldn't possibly), we suggest that you review it before reading on.

Metacognitive Knowledge Concerning Memory

PERSONS.   This category refers to what children could come to know about themselves and others as mnemonic beings. Probably the most basic acquisition in this category is the ability to recognize and identify experiences of remembering and forgetting when they occur, conceptually differentiating these experiences from such others as thinking, dreaming, and perceiving. There is evidence that primitive concepts of remembering and forgetting begin to be formed during the early preschool years, as part of the development of the child's implicit "theory of mind" discussed in Chapter 3. Once the child has acquired some sense of what it is to remember and forget:

> There is...much to learn about the capacities, limitations, and idiosyncrasies of the human memory system. The growing person could discover that immediate memory is of small span and limited duration, and that additional processing may be needed to optimize subsequent retrieval. He could also induce from experience the related, sad fact that one cannot always count on retrieving later what was stored earlier, plus the happy fact that what cannot be remembered right now will often be remembered eventually. There is the further knowledge that the memory system can be untrustworthy as well as porous: It is possible to remember what did not happen and to misremember what did, in addition to outright forgetting. (Flavell & Wellman, 1977, p. 11)

As regards the first of Flavell and Wellman's proposed "acquirables," there is evidence that older children tend to have a more realistic and accurate picture of their own memory abilities and limitations than do younger ones (Flavell & Wellman, 1977; Schneider, 1985). In one study (Flavell et al., 1970), the experimenter briefly exposed a strip of pictures of common objects, with the number increasing on each trial until the child said the series had gotten too long to remember the objects in order. Kindergarteners greatly overestimated their memory span. In fact, over half of the kindergarteners thought they would remember all ten items, when they actually could remember only about four. Such wild inaccuracies might seem maladaptive. However, Bjorklund and Green (1992) suggest that overestimations actually are beneficial because they keep children optimistic and eager to try tasks that in reality are beyond their current abilities. If young children were more realistic about their abilities, and their reach did not exceed their grasp, they might make less cognitive progress.

With increasing age the predicted and actual span come closer together; the predicted span realistically decreases to meet an increasing actual span. Even at younger ages, when the span-prediction task is presented in a context that is more familiar and meaningful (a board game or a simulated shopping situation), children's span estimations tend to be more realistic (Schneider, 1985). In addition, kindergarteners' estimates are more accurate if they have to stop an audio tape of a list of words when they hear as many words as they think they can recall, rather than make a prospective verbal prediction (Cunningham & Weaver,

1989). Interestingly, underestimations appear as well. Young elementary school children underestimate their recall of categorizable lists (Worden & Sladewski-Awig, 1982), presumably because they do not understand the effects of categorizing on memory.

TASKS.   There is a great deal for the developing child to learn about what makes some memory tasks more difficult than others. First, a memory task can be harder or easier because of the amount and kind of information to be learned and remembered. Second, for any given amount and kind of stored information, some retrieval demands or requirements are more severe and taxing than others. As already mentioned, for example, the requirement merely to recognize, as previously encountered, something experienced earlier is usually much easier than the requirement to recall it from memory—that is, without its being perceptually present. Therefore, task difficulty is a joint function of two things: what has to be stored and the nature of subsequent retrieval demands.

Even young children know that increasing the sheer number of individual items to be remembered makes a memory task harder (Kreutzer et al., 1975; Wellman, 1977; Yussen & Bird, 1979). As implied in the earlier discussion of organization and elaboration strategies, items also become easier to remember if the learner discovers or creates meaningful connections among them. Studies have documented the growing child's increasing awareness of the mnemonic value of various kinds of interitem relationships (Flavell, 1978b; Flavell & Wellman, 1977). For example, when asked to think of three words that would be very easy to remember along with the word "blue," older elementary school children are much likelier than younger ones to think of three more color words (Tenney, 1975).

Kreutzer and colleagues (1975) found the same age trends with respect to two insights concerning retrieval demands. First, their older subjects sensed that it may become harder to recall one set of words if, before the recall test, one also had to learn a second set of words easily confused with the first set; as you may know, students of memory call this phenomenon *retroactive interference.* Second, older subjects knew that it is easier to retell a story in one's own words than in the exact words it was heard—that is, memory for the semantic gist of a story is better than memory for its exact linguistic form (see also Myers & Paris, 1978).

STRATEGIES.   Because this topic has been discussed at length in an earlier section we only mention a few examples in which the metamemory component is especially prominent—that is, in which the emphasis is on verbalizable knowledge about strategies as distinguished from actual "on-line" strategy use in memory situations.

Preschoolers have only rudimentary concepts regarding strategies. For example, when asked to choose between two strategies demonstrated on videotapes, 4-year-olds know that they can better help themselves remember where Cookie Monster is hidden by marking his hiding place with a colored chip rather than by looking away when the stimulus array is rotated (Justice, 1989). By age 5, they also know that touching the hiding place or looking at it is better than looking away. In contrast, they know little about the value of organizational strategies for recall. Older children are quicker to recognize the values of organizational strategies. Best and Ornstein (1986) asked third and sixth graders to tutor a first grader in a memory task, specifically, to tell the younger child what they had done to help themselves remember the pictures. The children who earlier had been exposed to categorized materials incorporated organizational principles into their instructions more than did control subjects who had not.

When discussing retrieval strategies in a previous section we mentioned that young children have much to learn about the nature and use of memory-retrieval cues. F. R. Gordon and Flavell (1977) and Beal (1985) have proposed that the core acquisition here is the concept of *cognitive cueing*. Cognitive cueing refers to the fact that thinking about one thing can lead you to think about another thing—that one mental event tends to trigger or cue others. It can be argued that this "obvious" fact about how our minds work is an exceptionally important piece of metamemory for children to acquire, a key component of their developing "theory of mind" or "naive cognitive psychology" (Beal, 1985; F. R. Gordon & Flavell, 1977). In a simple cueing situation, placing a police car in front of a police officer's house is a better cue than a lamp when remembering in which of the identical houses the officer lives (Schneider & Sodian, 1988). However, many young children do not understand the basic notion that reminders should be placed where they will be seen, before they are needed. In a study by Beal (1985), children were to remember the location of a penny hidden inside one of four identical opaque cups with lids. Almost 40 percent of the 4- and 5-year-olds thought that hiding a paper clip marker inside the cup with the penny would be an effective reminder!

In several of Kreutzer and colleagues' (1975) interview items, subjects were presented with hypothetical storage (preparation for future retrieval) and retrieval problems and asked how they would solve them. In one storage problem, for instance, children were asked how many things they could think of to do to make sure they would not forget to take their ice skates to school with them the next morning. Older subjects were able to think of more different things to do than younger ones, and generally seemed more strategic and planful in their approach to this real-world-type memory problem. Nonetheless, a number of kindergarten and first-grade subjects were able to describe appropriate strategies. Interestingly, for them as for the third and fifth graders, the most commonly mentioned strategies were not of the familiar, in-the-head variety, such as thinking again and again about bringing the skates (rehearsal). Rather, they involved external actions and the use of outside reminders, such as putting the skates where they would be sure to see them the next morning. One child wanted to guarantee retrieval by sleeping with his skates on—a heroic but exceptionally powerful retrieval cue! Other external strategies included asking their mothers to remind them and writing themselves a note. The fact that they could not write failed to deter a number of the subjects from proposing the note-writing strategy. This tendency to think of external versus internal mnemonic aids was also noted in children's responses to other interview items in the same study (see also Neisser, 1982, Part VI).

Some of Kreutzer and co-workers' (1975) subjects gave strategy descriptions that attested to some unexpectedly sophisticated intuitions about the nature of memory. The following is our favorite example. The question was: "What do you do when you want to remember a phone number?" A third-grade girl replied:

> Say the number is 633-8854. Then what I'd do is—say that my number is 633, so I won't have to remember that, really. And then I would think now I've got to remember 88. Now I'm 8 years old, so I can remember, say, my age two times. Then I say how old my brother is, and how old he was last year. And that's how I'd usually remember that phone number. [Is that how you would most often remember a phone number?] Well, usually I write it down. (Kreutzer et al., 1975, p. 11)

Self-Monitoring and Self-Regulation

A good way to see metacognition in action is to look at how children use their metacognitive knowledge to monitor their own memory status and regulate their mnemonic activities. Self-monitoring involves knowing where you are with respect to your goal of understanding and remembering the material. Self-regulation includes planning, directing, and evaluating your behavior. Metacognitively sophisticated children or adults are like busy executives, analyzing new problems, judging how far they are from the goal, allocating attention, selecting a strategy, attempting a solution, monitoring the success or failure of current performance, and deciding whether to change to a different strategy.

A recent, comprehensive account of how children actually use their metacognitive knowledge is the Good Strategy User Model developed by Pressley, Borkowski, and their colleagues (e.g., Borkowski & Turner, 1990; Pressley, Borkowski, & Schneider, 1987). Not surprisingly, good strategy users possess *strategies*. In addition, they possess *general strategy knowledge*—general concepts about strategy functioning such as knowing that mental effort is necessary to execute most strategies or that switching strategies sometimes is necessary. Also important is their *specific strategy knowledge,* knowledge about particular strategies (e.g., rehearsal, elaboration) and when and where to use them. A novel feature of this model is a mechanism for acquiring new metacognitive knowledge, the *metacognitive acquisition procedures,* which select strategies, fill in the gaps when certain components of strategies have not been acquired, and evaluate the relative effectiveness of strategies. This evaluation could involve, for example, testing whether you can recall the material. *Relational strategy knowledge* involves an awareness of similarities and differences among strategies. Also important are children's *knowledge base, beliefs about their competencies*, and *cognitive style* (i.e., reflective rather than impulsive); all of these components interact and thereby increase both metacognitive knowledge and the effective use of this knowledge. For example, if a child finds that staring hard at the items or squinting his eyes in concentration (a strategy plus specific strategy knowledge) does not cause good recall (metacognitive acquisition procedure) he may consider other strategies such as verbal rehearsal. In this case the child's specific strategy knowledge has been refined. A main goal of this model is to identify ways to train children to generalize their strategies to various situations. Generalization has been the main stumbling block for all attempts to teach strategies.

Children have several ways of acquiring information about how, when, and where to use a particular strategy (Pressley, Borkowski, & O'Sullivan, 1984). They sometimes can discover the information on their own, perhaps by trying out various strategies and observing the results. Alternatively, another person—a teacher, parent, or peer—can directly or indirectly convey this information (e.g., Verdonik, 1988). At Disney World's immense parking lot a father may say, "I want someone in this family to write down that we're in the Goofy lot or we'll never find our car again." At school, children may be given casual occasional instruction in monitoring their strategy use. However, this instruction rarely is systematic and intensive. Finally, children can learn about using specific strategies if they are taught the metacognitive acquisition procedures described above. In particular, they can be taught to monitor their use of strategies (e.g., Ghatala, Levin, Pressley, & Goodwin, 1986). For discussions of various strategy self-monitoring training programs for normal, hyperactive, learning disabled, and retarded children see Schneider and

Pressley (1989, chap. 7), Pressley et al. (1988), Graham and Harris (1989), and Campione (1987). Typically, these programs teach children to assess their performance when using different types of strategies and to attribute their relative performance to these various strategies. Training often involves group discussion and modeling of strategies. The following is an example of what a trainer might say:

> Today we're going to talk about some ways that we can use our minds better. There are two parts to remembering things. First, we have to fasten things in our minds, then we have to take out the things we put in. Today we're going to talk about things we can do to help us both put things in our minds and take them out. (Kurtz & Borkowski, 1984, p. 341)

Self-monitoring sometimes involves "metacognitive experiences." An example of an illusory, misleading metacognitive experience is when a college student, perplexed at a low grade on a test, exclaims, "But I felt really confident that I knew the material!" A more accurate and useful metacognitive experience would be correctly perceiving that someone's name is on the threshold of recall (that tantalizing "tip of the tongue" feeling) and feeling optimistic about retrieving the name with a little more effort. You would not have this feeling of optimism if you had never been introduced to the person. Finally, as you skim through next week's reading assignment you may get the buoyant feeling that the material will be very easy to remember—or the sinking feeling that it will be almost impossible to remember (e.g., because you just cannot understand it). You then react accordingly: Study lightly in the former case; study hard, get help from others, or give up in despair in the latter case.

Through years of experience as a rememberer (and forgetter!), you have learned to recognize and respond adaptively to numerous "patterns" (Chapter 4) of memory-relevant material and feelings. You recognize a zillion situations as situations in which you should try to store the material well, because you will surely need to retrieve it later. Someone's telling you the address of a future rendezvous is an instance of this class of situations: You respond automatically, without thinking, by trying to store that address effectively. In contrast, you recognize a zillion other situations as ones in which you should deliberately search memory, because they call for sustained retrieval efforts. For instance, you suddenly discover that you have lost your keys, and automatically respond by trying to remember where they might be. Furthermore, you readily discriminate these two zillion situations from zillions of others, some of them quite similar to these, in which neither preparation-for-retrieval nor retrieval efforts are needed. A person who has acquired a great deal of knowledge about memory could be thought of as an excellent pattern recognizer in mnemonic situations, much as the physicist and the chess expert are excellent pattern recognizers in their domains of expertise (Chapter 4; cf. Chi, 1987).

Preschoolers show some minimal competencies regarding metacognitive experiences. DeLoache and Brown (1984) found "feelings of knowing" in 2-year-olds in a vanishing toy situation. Children saw a toy hidden, then searched at that spot after the experimenter had surreptitiously removed the toy. The children kept searching the hiding spot or nearby or related areas as though they felt sure the toy had been hidden there. One child exclaimed, "Darn! Somebody taked him!" By age 4, children are aware of tip-of-the tongue states (Cultice, Somerville, & Wellman, 1983). Still, most developmental changes are yet to come: Kindergarteners are likelier to keep trying to recall items they feel they once knew than items they feel they never knew (Wellman, 1983); "items that feel known" may have become for them a recognized "pattern" that automatically triggers further retrieval efforts. Elementary-school-age children are better able than preschoolers to sense when a set of items has been memorized sufficiently to ensure perfect recall (Flavell et al., 1970). Older children are more aware than younger ones that items they have just failed to recall on a test are more in need of further study than ones they have just succeeded in recalling (Masur, McIntyre, & Flavell, 1973).

Metamemory-Memory Relations

Developmental psychologists study metacognition for two reasons. One is that it is of interest in its own right as one aspect of children's cognitions about the world. Just as children think about the wind, toys, and airplanes, they also think about human thought (see Chapter 3). The second reason is that metacognition may stimulate the use of strategies and other activities relevant to thinking. Thus, we turn our attention briefly to the question of the relation between metamemory and strategies or memory performance. The bad news is that the evidence is inconsistent; some studies find a relation, whereas others do not. The good news is that we have a much clearer idea than we did several years ago about how to think about the metamemory-memory question and where to look for answers to it.

It should not surprise you that children often do not use their knowledge about memory. Certainly one of the lessons from research across many areas of cognition is that children often do not use their available knowledge (true also of adults, alas). Our earlier discussion of production deficiencies suggests several reasons why children might not use their available metamemory to help their memory. A child might know that rehearsal is a good strategy for remembering a list of chores to be done, but not rehearse because he or she lacks time, energy, capacity, or motivation to exert the effort. Or the child may perceive the list as too short or too long to make the strategy worthwhile or believe that some other strategy, such as simply trying hard, is sufficient. Thus, in general only a moderate-to-good correlation between metamemory and memory performance would be expected. And this is what is generally found. An analysis of 60 studies (with 7097 subjects) produced an average correlation of .41 (Schneider & Pressley, 1989). Thus, children's metamemory makes a modest contribution to their memory performance. After reviewing the relevant literature, Schneider and Pressley (1989) concluded that the size of the correlation between the two appears to depend on several factors such as the type of task (e.g., memory monitoring or organizational strategies), age of the subjects, task difficulty, and presentation of the metamemory assessment before or after the memory task. For example, the relation appears to be stronger among older children than among younger ones, and after experience with a memory task rather than before.

At this point the most promising places to look for answers are suggested by the following recent studies. Several studies (e.g., Hasselhorn, cited in Schneider & Pressley, 1989; Weinert, Schneider, & Knopf, 1988) have used sophisticated statistical techniques to examine the causal relationships among several variables—metamemory, strategies, intelligence, and recall. They find that metamemory sometimes has an indirect effect on recall, as when knowledge about organizational strategies affects grouping during study, which in turn affects clustering during recall and produces good recall. Schneider and Pressley (1989) concluded from these studies that there often are stronger relations between metamemory concerning a strategy and use of a strategy than between metamemory and memory itself, because many other forces such as knowledge and capacity are acting on memory.

Another promising line of research examines children's causal explanations of their memory performance. For example, children trained to use a strategy were more likely to maintain and generalize that strategy if they attributed success on a task to their own effort rather than to the nature of the task, luck, or ability (Kurtz & Borkowski, 1984). In another study (Fabricius & Cavalier, 1989), children aged 4 to 6 who attributed their good recall to their use of a labeling strategy were more likely to spontaneously use the strategy at a later time if they understood the psychological basis for the effect of the strategy. These children said that labeling worked because it kept them thinking about the pictures after they said the names, gave them pictures in their mind, or made them say the words in their minds. Most of these child amateur cognitive psychologists also were aware that their thinking was disrupted on a trial in which they had to count rather than label. As one 6-year-old expressed it, "I couldn't say the names in my mind when I said the number. It disturbed my mind" (Fabricius & Cavalier, 1989, p. 303). Unlike these psychological explanations, explanations that referred to perceptual or behavioral activities such as looking longer at the pictures were not associated with later spontaneous labeling. Thus, it is not enough to know that a particular strategy helps recall; children are more likely to use a strategy if they have plausible psychological explanations of how it works.

A third promising avenue is the training approach described earlier. Incorporating metamemory instruction into strategy training enhances the effectiveness of this training (e.g., Gruelich & Baker-Ward, 1989; Paris, Newman, & McVey, 1982). In fact, it has been claimed that evidence for the link between knowledge about strategies and strategy use is stronger in these studies than those that assess preexisting metamemory and spontaneous strategy use (Folds et al., 1990).

CAPACITY

The most straightforward explanation of memory development might be that memory capacity simply increases, perhaps because of neurological maturation. Yet, this chapter is filled with talk of knowledge, strategies and metamemory. Where did memory capacity per se go? This section will address the important issue of memory capacity and show how it interacts with these other aspects of the cognitive system.

The notion of capacity was introduced in Chapter 1, as part of the legacy of the information-processing approach, and discussed further in Chapter 4 as a developmental trend of middle childhood and adolescence. Applying the latter analysis to memory, memory development could reflect an increase in biologically based *structural* capacity. In this container model, children have small boxes in their heads and adults have bigger boxes (Brown & DeLoache, 1978). Or perhaps the *functional* (total actual usable) capacity of memory increases as children learn to handle information more efficiently, perhaps by processing information more rapidly.

Robbie Case (1985), a neo-Piagetian described in Chapter 1, proposes a model of the relation between capacity and memory. In his model, short-term memory consists of two components, a *storage space* and an *operating space*. Storage space refers to the amount of space available for the short-term storage of information; operating space refers to the amount of space available for executing intellectual operations, such as adding two numbers or performing strategies. Together they make up the total processing space. It is assumed that this total processing space does not change during development, but the proportions allocated to the storage and operating spaces do change as follows.

During development, there is increased speed, and thus increased efficiency, in performing the processing operations. This increased efficiency is due to greater automatization of basic processing and strategies as a result of practice, and also, probably, neurological changes associated with increasing age (Kail, 1991a). When operations can be performed more rapidly, then more can be executed per unit time. Thus more can be "on stage" at once in one's cognitive workspace, which amounts to an increase in one's functional information-processing capacity. Moreover, storage and operating spaces have a reciprocal relationship, such that the developmental decrease in the capacity needed for operating releases capacity for storage. Hence, more can be stored with increasing use. An example of the kind of evidence supporting Case's model is that by giving adults unfamiliar nonsense words (e.g., loats, zarch) and 6-year-olds familiar words to identify quickly, one can equate their processing speed and make their memory spans nearly identical (e.g., Case et al., 1982). A familiar item has been processed many times in the past and is securely in semantic memory (Bjorklund, 1987b), so it can be processed quickly.

The implications of both empirical and theoretical work regarding young children's limited capacity are clear: Although the child memory machine has wondrous memory aids such as knowledge, strategies, and metamemory, capacity constrains their use. Only a limited number of mental items (to-be-recalled items, knowledge about strategies, factual knowledge, concepts, etc.) can be activated at any one time and kept alive. Thus, a child may be unable to make full use of these memory-relevant abilities because of capacity limitations (Case, 1985). If the obligatory information processing, such as identifying stimuli, nearly exhausts the child's capacity, then he or she may be unable, or reluctant, to conduct additional activities, such as executing a strategy.

Children also may be reluctant to use a strategy if it requires a lot of effort. This is nicely illustrated in a series of experiments that used the so-called dual-task paradigm to assess the capacity required to execute a strategy. This paradigm is based on the notion that if performing one task uses most of one's capacity, then performing a capacity-demanding second task will draw capacity away from the first task. If you foolishly volunteered for this study, you first would be asked to push a button (or perhaps tap a key) rapidly, certainly a familiar activity for a generation that is growing up with joysticks and computer games. The experimenter then would compare this baseline rate of the number of finger taps per second on this task alone with the rate when you were told to perform simultaneously a second task, such as cumulatively rehearsing a set of items to be recalled. Your decrease in finger tapping from the one-task to the two-task situation provides a rough measure of the capacity you need to execute the rehearsal strategy. When testing children, instructing all ages to use the strategy of cumulative rehearsal ensures that strategy performance on that task is equated across ages. Seven- and 8-year-olds slow their finger tapping more than do 11-year-olds (Guttentag, 1984), indicating that the strategy is more capacity-demanding for the younger children. Furthermore, the less capacity required to produce the strategy when children are instructed to rehearse, the larger the number of items in their cumulative rehearsal set when they spontaneously (without instruction) rehearse. In addition, an easy strategy (rehearsing one word at a time) is less effortful than a more difficult strategy (cumulative rehearsal) for the younger children. Finally, when older and younger children use an equal amount of capacity for the strategy, older children rehearse more and recall more than the younger. All these outcomes indicate that a strategy "costs more" in capacity for younger children than for older ones. Similar results with other ages, strategies, and tasks are reported by Bjorklund and Harnishfeger (1987), Kee and Davies (1988), Kee and Howell (1988), and P. H. Miller, Seier, Probert, and Aloise (1991).

This pattern of results suggests that as children acquire experience with using a strategy during development, this strategy becomes more automatic and demands less capacity (for a different interpretation see Brainerd & Reyna, 1989, and Howe & Rabinowitz, 1989). A skill must be developed in its own right before it can be used effectively for memory. Thus, young children may exhibit a production deficiency in part because they are reluctant to try to produce an effortful strategy (Guttentag, 1984). Moreover, even when children spontaneously produce the strategy, if they must devote most of their capacity to executing it they may have little capacity remaining to perform other aspects of the task efficiently and consequently to fully utilize the strategy in the service of recall (P. H. Miller, 1990). This *utilization deficiency* described earlier, in which a strategy provides little or no help for recall, disappears in older children, perhaps because the freed capacity may make the strategy fully effective for recall.

In the dual-task approach, investigators increase demands on capacity and measure the degree of interference. An opposite approach would be to eliminate the capacity requirement of a strategy and observe any facilitation of recall. This can be done on a task described earlier in which the strategy involves opening certain doors that reveal objects to be memorized and not opening other doors that hide irrelevant objects. When children execute this strategy it is effortful. When an adult performs this selective memory strategy for children, they do not need to devote any capacity to the strategy. This reduction of capacity demands eliminates age differences in recall of the relevant items (DeMarie-Dreblow & Miller, 1988). Moreover, having the experimenter rather than the child do the door opening increases the recall of 5- and 6-year-olds who already were spontaneously producing this selective memory strategy (P. H. Miller, Woody-Ramsey, & Aloise, 1991). These results suggest that when children first begin to produce a strategy, they cannot fully utilize it for recall because it greatly drains their capacity.

Another approach to studying the effect of capacity on recall is a very direct one: See if children's memory span predicts their use of a strategy (e.g., Cariglia-Bull & Pressley, 1990). In one study (Pressley, Cariglia-Bull, Deane, & Schneider, 1987) children had to remember sentences, such as "The tiny alligator moved fast on his red scooter." Children with larger memory spans were able to benefit in their recall from training in a strategy of forming an image of the sentence more than children with smaller memory spans, even when age and verbal competence were controlled for statistically. A larger memory span permits the simultaneous comprehension of the sentence and construction of mental images.

In summary, children's memory capacity, ability to use strategies, and knowledge have a reciprocal relation. We humans have a limited capacity, due at least in part to our biological endowment, but we develop strategies and knowledge that help us expand our memory capabilities. This limited capacity may hinder our initial attempts to access and use these strategies and knowledge. As processing speed increases during development, as seen in faster rates of identifying items, capacity is freed. Consequently, children find it easier to apply strategies to these items and ensure their encoding and retrieval.

CURRENT ISSUES IN MEMORY DEVELOPMENT

What issues, questions, and research problems most preoccupy students of memory development these days? Oddly enough, given the large amount of research on strategies over the last 20 years, one current controversy concerns the very definition of a strategy (Bjorklund & Harnishfeger, 1990; Howe & O'Sullivan, 1990). Although behaviors that look like strategies appear by age 2 or earlier, they may or may not be considered strategic, depending on the way this issue of defining strategies is resolved. One critical question is whether strategies must be intentional (conscious, deliberate, planful, controllable, goal-directed) or can also refer to automatic, unconscious, effortless processes such as activating associations automatically and looking at the materials to be remembered. A middle-of-the-road view is that strategies are *potentially* conscious and controllable activities (Pressley, Forrest-Pressley, Elliott-Faust, & Miller, 1985), though this definition is not without its problems (Howe & O'Sullivan, 1990). By this definition, you might not be aware that you were grouping items from the same category together, but could be if you reflect on your learning activities. We are not convinced that the intentional-automatic dichotomy is a fruitful one. We agree with Howe and O'Sullivan (1990) that there most likely is a continuum, with intentionality-effortfulness a matter of degree. Many activities may be predominantly automatic or predominantly controlled, but contain elements of both. Moreover, during development, an activity may gradually move from one point on the continuum to another. For example, as Bjorklund (e.g., 1987b) suggests, clustering may at first be predominantly automatic because it is based on associations, then predominantly deliberate when children actively look for categories. Clustering may finally become predominantly automatic again as it becomes a highly practiced, and therefore effortless, skill. This developmental sequence would involve transitional phases during which the clustering could not easily fit into a dichotomy of intentional or nonintentional.

Definitional issues also continue to plague work on metamemory. That this is a knotty issue is attested to by the definitional and conceptual finessing we have done on previous pages of this chapter. For instance, how and to what extent do the processes or phenomena subsumable under "strategies" and "metamemory," especially memory self-monitoring and regulation, really differ? You may have noticed that we did not tell you that. Any attempt to separate them conceptually is muddied by their close connections both developmentally and nondevelopmentally. A plausible developmental scenario is that some strategy use (however instigated) leads to some dim knowledge of the strategy's usefulness, which in turn mediates more strategy use. This experience may then lead to more and better knowledge of its usefulness, and so on, in this reciprocally mediative fashion through developmental time. These various fuzzy boundaries in work on children's memory may be inevitable, for they may reflect the nature of memory. Memory skills may not dichotomize themselves neatly for our convenience in studying them.

Another main issue concerns the role of experience in the development of strategies or procedures for remembering. Where do strategies come from? Do they emanate from the child's early semistrategic behaviors such as looking or naming, automatic processes such as associative clustering, or rudimentary metamemory? Do parents, siblings, peers, and teachers provide models or direct instruction in strategy use or other procedures for remembering? The contextual approach described in Chapter 1 reminds us that memory is embedded in a larger social context (Hudson & Fivush, 1990). Recent research suggests that children, in adult-guided conversations, learn how to remember and to recount in a coherent narrative form personally experienced events in the distant past (Fivush, in press; Hudson, 1990). With their prompts and questions, adults provide the structure for retrieval that is lacking in the child, then gradually withdraw it as it no longer is needed. Thus, remembering in young children often is a jointly constructed activity. These memory conversations may even teach children how to conduct their own memory search (Hudson, 1990).

Cultures or subcultures vary in the extent to which they encourage and support particular types of memory or particular mnemonic activities (e.g., Kurtz, 1990; Rogoff & Mistry, 1990). For example, schooled Western children recall better on list-learning tasks, which require rehearsal or organizational strategies, than do unschooled children in less industrialized societies (e.g., Cole & Scribner, 1977). In contrast, this superiority does not appear in memory for stories or visual scenes. Kearins (1981) found that Australian aboriginal children are better at remembering locations of objects in an array than are Anglo-Australian children. Similarly, Dube (1982) reported better recall of stories in African junior high or unschooled adolescents than American junior high students.

Children in all cultures have considerable exposure to oral stories and spatial arrays, and may even excel in memory on these tasks if their culture has a strong tradition of oral story telling or requires strong visual-spatial skills for survival. An example of the latter is an ability to orient oneself spatially in a relatively unvaried terrain. A difference even among Western cultures is that German third graders spontaneously use an organizational strategy considerably more than do American third graders (Schneider, Borkowski, Kurtz, & Kerwin, 1986). Interview data show that German teachers and parents spend more time teaching and explaining memory strategies to children than do their American counterparts (Carr, Kurtz, Schneider, Turner, & Borkowski, 1989). Thus, consistent with the contextual approach described in Chapter 1, different social-cultural contexts create different memory-relevant learning environments and consequently enhance different skills (Rogoff, 1990).

Schooling appears to underlie some of the cultural influences on memory (Wagner, 1978). In a clever design, Morrison (1987; see also L. K. Smith, 1989) compared two groups of similarly aged children whose birthdays clustered around the cutoff date used for permitting entry into school. That is, the "old kindergarteners" just missed the cutoff date for the first grade and the "young first graders" barely made that date. The latter group, which had an extra year of school but was only a few days older, was superior in recall and strategy use, as well as various other cognitive tasks.

It no longer is an issue whether strategies, knowledge, metamemory, and capacity influence recall. They clearly do. This issue has been replaced by two further issues. First, what is the relative impact of these various processes? Second, how do these processes interact? Regarding the first issue, few studies have included more than one or two influences, so the information is meager. In a major exception, Hasselhorn (cited in Schneider & Pressley, 1989) found that metamemory, processing speed, the knowledge base, and strategy use contributed independently to predicting the recall of 176 fourth graders. Interestingly, the knowledge base was by far the most powerful predictor. Similar studies with grades 3, 5, and 7, as well as elderly adults (Schneider, Korkel, & Weinert, 1989; Weinert, Knopf, Korkel, Schneider, Vogel, & Wetzel, 1984, as reported in Schneider and Weinert, 1989), generally produced the same pattern. It should be kept in mind, however, that the relative impact of the influences may vary from age to age and task to task. Thus, similar studies should be performed on younger children and in other tasks.

The issue of how these various processes interact is no easier. We were tempted to end this chapter with a section titled "Putting it all together." Though our hubris failed, we want to express our view that memory research is on the verge of revealing the interplay among strategies, knowledge, metamemory, and capacity (see, for example, a model by Bjorklund et al., 1990). Recent tantalizing results suggest, for example, that a well-developed knowledge base or experience with a strategy frees capacity that can be used for other mnemonic activities. Also, whether strategy training leads to improved recall depends on children's metamemory, particularly their attributions about the mechanisms by which a strategy has its effect. Many loose ends obviously still remain to be tied. In particular, the mechanisms underlying some of the observed relations are frustratingly unclear.

Throughout this chapter we blithely have made general statements about memory at various developmental levels (e.g., "Preschoolers can..."; "By age 9, children..."). However, we do not want to give the impression that the developmental milestones in memory are universal in time of emergence, or perhaps even sequence. One of the most recent issues to capture interest is that of individual differences in memory (Bjorklund, 1989; Schneider & Weinert, 1989). Individual differences can exist in any of the aspects of memory we have discussed—strategies, knowledge, metamemory, or capacity. Individual differences in metacognitive knowledge predict strategy use and recall better than does a traditional intelligence test (Kurtz & Weinert, 1989), and as described earlier (Schneider et al., 1989), knowledge about soccer facilitated recall of a soccer story more than did a good learning ability. Another individual difference, type of attributions about one's performance, is seen when gifted children attribute their successful recall to ability, whereas average children attribute it to effort (Schneider et al., 1987). Differences in motivation also are important. Preschoolers' recall for names of objects was related to their mastery motivation, specifically, their inclination to seek out and master challenging tasks (Lange, MacKinnon, & Nida, 1989). This study also identified another important individual difference—cognitive style. Being attentive and reflective rather than impulsive was correlated with the use of memory strategies (see also Haynes & Miller, 1987, and McManis & Miller, 1992). It seems plausible that a child who tends to consider options and to plan before acting should be more likely to engage in strategies than a child who tends to "jump into" a task.

One very socially relevant individual difference is that grade-school children who hold rigid, traditional gender stereotypes are more likely than children with less rigid stereotypes to distort their recall of items inconsistent with those stereotypes. More specifically, a child holding a rigid gender stereotype regarding occupations may view a female doctor but later incorrectly remember viewing a female nurse or a male doctor (Signorella & Liben, 1984). Similarly, preschool children had poorer memories for story characters acting in ways that are inconsistent with racial stereotypes than for stereotype-consistent characters (Bigler & Liben, 1989). This was especially true for children with more stereotyped attitudes and those who spontaneously sorted people by race rather than by age. These results carry the rather sobering message that simply presenting instances that are counter to gender and racial stereotyped concepts may not change these stereotypes. More intensive cognitive training, however, increases memory for counterstereotypic information (Bigler & Liben, in press).

A final issue given much attention recently is an applied one—children's eyewitness testimony. The increase in crimes, particularly sexual abuse, involving children has raised important questions concerning children's competence to testify about events they have experienced or witnessed. Often the child is the only witness to the crime. In our society, "a child who reports a sexual assault may be seen as an innocent, truthful victim or a creature of uncontrolled sexual fantasy" (Goodman, 1984, p. 11). The difficulty of this issue is illustrated in a recent case in which young children described sexual abuse from their babysitter and her husband—later corroborated by the sitter's confession—but also fantasized that they later were eaten for dinner by the couple (Goodman, Aman, & Hirschman, 1987).

Several questions about children's memory are particularly relevant to the issue of child testimony. Are children susceptible to misinformation or misleading information given during repeated questioning, so that they "remember" the false postevent information given to them by others rather than what they actually experienced? Do children's emotional states at the time of the event affect their recall of the event? Is retrieval affected by the types of questions asked during interrogation? How well do children of various ages remember faces? In the typical case in which at least 6 months elapse between the initial event and the trial, can a 3- and 4-year-old be counted on to maintain the original memory trace?

Basic research, including some that we already have presented, addresses some of these questions. In fact, you can test how much you learned from this chapter by trying to answer some of these questions. In general, we know that young children recall accurate information about personally experienced events over rather long periods of time, especially if the event is salient. Four-year-olds accurately report events occurring before age 2½ (Fivush & Hamond, 1990) and by age 5 children can store an event for up to 6 years later (Hudson & Fivush, 1991). And when a young child simply has to reenact events of several weeks ago rather than describe them, even 2-year-olds provide good evidence of remembering (Fivush & Hamond, 1989). Consistent with the contextualist view, young children are more likely to recall distant events if there is social support, such as a mother asking specific questions or giving prompts (for reviews see Fivush, in press, and Pillemer & White, 1989). On the negative side, as we described earlier, children, like adults, have a constructive memory that embellishes encoded information in a schema-consistent way. Accurately reporting one abusive event when many similar abusive events have occurred over time, as in a "child abuse script," should be difficult for young children. But this problem of constructive memory exists with adult eyewitness testimony as well. In fact, adults may be more likely to make errors of plausible inference than are children (Goodman et al., 1987).

In addition to these examples of basic research, investigations more directed to eyewitness testimony are beginning to provide valuable information to the legal system (for useful reviews see Ceci, Ross, & Toglia, 1989; Ceci, Toglia, & Ross, 1987; Doris, 1991; and Ornstein, Larus, & Clubb, in press). Many legal professionals and laypeople perceive children as unreliable witnesses (Goodman, Golding, & Haith, 1984), largely because children are considered more suggestible than adults. The attitude is that during the course of questioning children can be made to believe that events occurred that did not or that the events were different from what they really were. Children's lack of credibility obviously affects the impact of their testimony. This suggestibility has been demonstrated in children with certain types of assessments (Ceci, Ross, & Toglia, 1987). Children aged 3 to 12 were told a story about a little girl named Loren who, on the first day of school, ate her eggs too quickly and got a stomachache. The next day, half of the children were given misinformation, namely, that Loren ate her cereal too fast and got a headache. The other half received neutral information—that Loren ate her breakfast too fast and got sick. Two days later the children had to choose between eggs and cereal for what Loren ate and between stomachache and headache for how she felt. The youngest children were most susceptible to the misinformation. Not all assessments, however, reveal such susceptibility in children (Zaragoza & Wilson, 1989). It should be noted that suggestibility also occurs in adults (see Zaragoza, 1987, for a review) and it is not clear that children actually are more susceptible than adults (Duncan, Whitney, & Kunen, 1982). More generally, although children often report less information than adults, what they report may be equally accurate, at least from age 5 on (Goodman et al., 1987). Even if leading questions initially elicit agreement, these distortions nearly always are absent in the child's later free recall. And perhaps most importantly, children almost never make up sexual incidents, even in experimental studies in which anatomically correct dolls are used (Goodman & Aman, 1990) or an adult touches the child's body, for example, when lifting her onto a table (Goodman, Rudy, Bottoms, & Aman, 1990; Rudy & Goodman, 1991).

One way in which a crime is different from nearly all the experiences in laboratory studies of memory is that the former usually involves intense fear and sometimes pain, whereas the latter never do. There are few studies on the effects of negative mood on memory in children, and even these incorporate only mildly negative emotions, for ethical reasons. One way around this ethical dilemma is to study children's memories for a personally significant, fear-arousing experience that they would have to endure in the normal course of events. One such experience for many children is a visit to the dentist or doctor, which may involve a physical examination, having blood drawn, or receiving shots. Drawing on this analogue, Goodman and colleagues (1987) examined 3- to 6-year-olds' memory, several days later, for receiving inoculations. Children's recall generally was quite good. They were more willing to accept erroneous information about peripheral details, such as characteristics of the room, than central information, such as the actions that took place or the physical characteristics of the "criminal" (the nurse giving the shot). Moreover, older children resisted misleading information more than did younger ones. However, children never made up false stories of abuse even when asked questions that might encourage such reports.

Although this area of research cannot yet provide definitive answers about the reliability of children's testimony, it does identify the sensitive spots where children's memories are particularly vulnerable. For example, adults who question children need to be careful to separate a specific event from general scripted knowledge and to provide retrieval cues that can trigger recall, but do not mislead the child. Adults also need to establish good rapport and to avoid social demand characteristics—making children feel that they must agree with answers suggested by the adults' questioning. Preschool children are particularly vulnerable to misinformation, especially regarding peripheral details of events in stressful situations. Even young children, however, do not appear to make up memories that would wrongfully condemn a defendant in a child-abuse case.

SUMMARY

Memory development became a popular field of inquiry when researchers turned their attention from the overt products of the child's memory to the underlying cognitive processes that generate these products. Several concepts are useful in analyzing memory development. Getting things into memory is called *storage*; getting them out again, *retrieval*. Retrieval may consist of: *recognition* of something that is already present in perception or thought; *recall* of something that is not present (often with the help of reminders or *retrieval cues*); blends and mixtures of the two. Two types of models describe memory: a *short term–long term* dichotomy, or a continuum of superficial to deep processing in the *depth-of-processing* models.

Many interesting developmental questions about memory concern the period of infancy. First, do infants show any sort of memory capability? Clearly they do, as evidenced by such memory-mediated processes as habituation of attention; recognition of familiar people, objects, and events; imitation; search for hidden objects; and classical and operant conditioning. Second, are there developmental changes in basic memory processes during infancy? Again, the answer is yes, although we still have much to learn about the exact nature of these changes. At least some primitive form of recognition memory appears to be operative very early on. Likewise, the presence of conditioning and imitation capabilities suggests the presence of some sort of recall or recall-like processes in early infancy. Toward the end of the first year, however, recall appears to become a more conscious experience, as one in which some kind of mental representation of the past object or event is present in focal awareness.

It is convenient to discuss memory development under four headings: *strategies, knowledge, metamemory,* and *capacity. Strategies* are potentially conscious activities that a person may use to facilitate memory. Rudimentary versions of many memory strategies emerge in the postinfancy period. Looking, pointing, naming, and talking about items to be remembered keep the information alive over a period of time. We used *rehearsal* to describe the typical course of development of memory strategies. Initially, the child is unable to execute the potentially strategic activity at all, even under experimenter instruction or tuition. Subsequently, the child is likely to exhibit a pattern of *production deficiency* with respect to the strategy. That is, she can and will use it if explicitly directed to do so, and using it benefits her memory in the expected fashion, but she does not use the strategy spontaneously on her own initiative. The causes of production deficiencies are not well understood, but some possible ones were suggested: (1) The child may not have the foresight to use any special cognitive activity now, in order to facilitate retrieval later; (2) the task situation may trigger the use of some other, better-developed strategy than the one under study; and (3) the target strategy may not yet be well-enough mastered—qua cognitive activity, as an end in itself—to be brought into service as a means to a mnemonic goal. In the final period such obstacles are no longer in force, and the child employs the strategy spontaneously.

Several factors make this simple picture of strategy development more complex. First, strategies become increasingly effective during development, as children overcome a *utilization deficiency* and accrue greater "payoff" for recall. Second, many contextual variables influence whether children produce a strategy already in their repertoire. Older children need less contextual support than do younger ones. The focus has shifted from simply identifying production-deficient children to identifying task and situational factors that influence strategy production and recall. Third, strategies become more complex, flexible, and tailored to the task at hand.

Other storage strategies are more sophisticated and sometimes more mnemonically effective than rehearsal. Learners would be using an *organizational* strategy if they studied conceptually related items together, in groups by category membership, and then tended to *cluster* same-category items together in recall. A current controversy is whether clustering in school-age children reflects a strategic process or an automatic process such as associations between items. *Elaboration* strategies also add meaning to what is presented. An example of elaboration would be the construction of a vivid visual image linking two normally unrelated objects that are supposed to be remembered together, as in a paired-associate learning task. Strategies for the efficient *allocation of cognitive resources* develop as well. The ontogenetic pattern shown in Table 6–1 also appears to apply to these types of strategies.

The developing child acquires *retrieval strategies* as well as *storage strategies.* Development here consists largely of an increasing ability and propensity to search memory intelligently: efficiently, flexibly, systematically, exhaustively, selectively, indirectly—in whatever manner the specific retrieval problem at hand requires.

Investigators have begun to study the development of effective strategies for storing and retrieving complex, meaningful, organized material—for example, the sorts of strategies that would be useful in studying for and subsequently taking an essay exam in a history course. Although these strategies are acquired later than some of the rote-recall ones already discussed (e.g., rehearsal), the course of their acquisition appears to be quite similar.

In the *Knowledge* section, the argument was made that what people know greatly influences what they learn and remember. The power of knowledge is illustrated when child chess experts can remember chessboard arrangements better than adults who are less knowledgeable about chess. Developmental changes in the knowledge structures should lead to developmental changes in what is stored and retrieved. Well-developed *content* knowledge helps recall in at least three ways. First, its vivid, rich representations can be accessed quickly. Second, the organized connections automatically activate the associations among items. Third, it supports the use of strategies, perhaps by freeing capacity for that purpose. We raised several issues and limitations to the research on content knowledge.

Most students of memory share Piaget's view that storage is construction and retrieval is *reconstruction.* According to this view, we do not simply make a copy of information presented at storage and then simply reprint that copy when we retrieve. Rather, both storage and retrieval involve a great deal of active conceptual organization and reorganization, much gap filling and inference, as the individual tries to achieve a meaningful representation of the information. Considerable evidence shows that children as well as adults use constructive and reconstructive processes when they remember. *Constructive* memory is spurred by the acquisition of the knowledge structures or "mental templates" (schemas, scripts, etc.) described in Chapter 3. Scripts, in particular, appear to be a powerful shaper of young children's memories, toward both increased and decreased accuracy.

Metamemory means knowledge or cognitive activity bearing on anything mnemonic; it is, therefore, metacognition (Chapter 4) that takes memory enterprises as its object. Two major categories of metamemory were distinguished: *metacognitive knowledge concerning memory* and *self-monitoring and regulation.* The former is further divisible into knowledge about mnemonic *persons, tasks,* and *strategies.* In the *person* case, children learn, among other things, to identify experiences of remembering and forgetting as such and to distinguish them from other mental experiences. They also come to recognize the capacities, limitations, and idiosyncrasies of the human memory system. Regarding *tasks*, children discover that a set of items will be easier to recall if the items are few in number, familiar, and meaningfully related to one another—for example, categorizable. Similarly, they come to appreciate the fact that some retrieval-test requirements are more taxing than others. As an example, it is a more demanding test of memory to repeat a story word for word than to retell it in your own words. Children also become better able to think of and articulate plausible storage and retrieval *strategies* in response to hypothetical memory problems. For instance, they acquire the concept of *cognitive cueing* and knowledge about the nature and use of retrieval cues.

The other major category of metamemory, *self-monitoring and regulation*, can be considered applied metacognitive knowledge concerning memory. Children learn to assess their current memory state, select a strategy, evaluate their progress toward their goal, and so on. Some of the most successful programs to train strategies in laboratory or academic settings involve teaching knowledge about strategies and self-monitoring and regulation. An important component of self-monitoring is *metacognitive experiences* concerning memory, which include judgments or feelings ("mnemonic sensations") about how difficult or time-consuming something will likely be to store or retrieve, about whether the present situation is one that tacitly calls for storage or retrieval efforts, and the like. It is likely that years of experience in remembering and forgetting have made most adults sensitive to innumerable "patterns" of internal and external stimulation that have implications for the conduct and probable success/failure of their memory enterprises. The relationship between metamemory and strategic behavior or recall is far from clear, but in general there is a moderately positive correlation. We discussed several promising new approaches in this area: relations with other cognitive processes, causal attributions concerning good recall, and metamemory training.

Memory capacity refers to the total mental workspace available for basic mental processes during encoding, retrieval, or strategy use. As basic mental processes, such as identifying words, become more practiced they become faster and less effortful. The freed capacity can be devoted to strategies or to storing more items. Similarly, executing a strategy becomes less effortful with increasing age, thus freeing capacity for other mnemonic activities.

A number of issues, questions, and research problems currently preoccupy students of memory development. Must a definition of a strategy include intentionality? How does metamemory concerning strategies differ from strategies per se? What is the role of experience in the development of strategies? How do strategies, knowledge, metamemory, and capacity interact and affect recall? Which individual differences are the most powerful predictors of memory? Can children accurately recall real-life highly stressful events, such as abuse? These questions will occupy researchers for some time to come.

Language

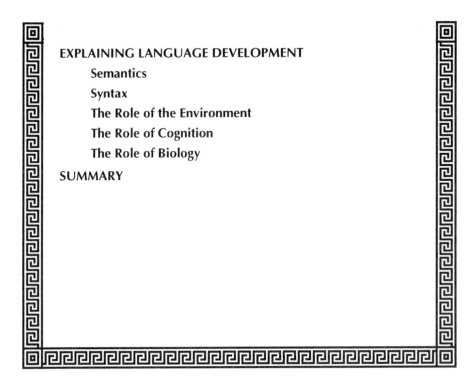

EXPLAINING LANGUAGE DEVELOPMENT
    Semantics
    Syntax
    The Role of the Environment
    The Role of Cognition
    The Role of Biology
SUMMARY

> Father, making up a story to help his little girl settle down for the night: "…and then Trina [the canine heroine of his impromptu narrative] was chased by another dog. I wonder what happened next." Girl: "I know—the dog catched her!"

What tacit knowledge about language can we reasonably attribute to this little girl on the basis of this brief interchange? First, she has clearly acquired a lot of expertise in both producing and understanding the speech sounds of English. Thanks to her considerable *phonological* development, she effortless segmented and interpreted her father's rapid and unbroken burst of sound ("anthentrinawuz…," roughly) as the English word string "…and then Trina was…." Imagine what it would have sounded like to a person who knew no English; he or she would likely not even be able to make out the individual vowels and consonants, let alone know where one word ended and the next began. Similarly, the "accentless," native-speaker-like word pronunciation and intonation pattern of the child's reply would be the envy and despair of most adults trying to learn English as a second language. A little probing would undoubtedly also show that her knowledge of English phonology is a productive, generative, rule-governed affair, like the rest of her linguistic knowledge. For instance, "Trina" undoubtedly sounds like a proper word to her, although she has never heard it before. In contrast, "Zdrina"—which does not follow English phonological rules for word construction—would probably just not sound right.

Second, there is also evidence of substantial *semantic* development, or acquisition of linguistic meaning. The girl knows how a great many concepts and relationships among concepts can be expressed in English words and word combination (phrases, sentences). She probably knows by now which creatures are called "dogs" and which are not almost as well as her father does. She has also acquired more subtle semantic knowledge: She knows that "chase" implies more than just "run" but is not synonymous with "catch." And she knows that the "I" her father utters does not refer to the same person as the "I" she utters. She also knows how semantic relations like agent-action-object (e.g., one animal chasing another) can be expressed in English—that is, by the left-to-right order of words.

Third, the little girl's tacit knowledge of English syntax is likewise noteworthy. She knows how word order and word formation, such as the addition of inflections, are used as clues to sentence meaning. For instance, she tacitly knows that "another dog" is the logical subject and "Trina" is the logical object of the verb "chase" in her father's passive sentence. A younger, less grammatically advanced child would not have learned to interpret sequences like "was-verb-ed-by" as clues that the normal subject-object order is reversed; in fact, the younger child would undoubtedly interpret the sentence as a declarative and think that it was Trina rather than the other dog that did the chasing. Even the childish expression "catched" attests to an important grammatical attainment. Her addition of the inflection or grammatical morpheme "-ed" to "catch" proves that she has productive, generative command of the grammatical rule for forming the simple past tense in English. What she has not yet learned is the much more trivial fact that the past tense of a few common verbs (irregular verbs like "catch") is not generated by this rule.

Finally, the little girl has learned much about the *pragmatic* or *communicative* side of language. She knows how to produce and comprehend *speech acts*, such as assertions, requests, and questions, and to engage in linguistic discourse with others. For example, she knows that her father's second utterance is not the simple assertion a purely syntactical analysis of it would indicate. Rather, it is really an indirect question or request that invites the child to participate in the story-construction process. That is the kind of speech act the father intended to produce and that is the kind of speech act the child interpreted it to be. Similarly, the child seems to have acquired the rule of discourse according to which (roughly stated) one refers to something by an indefinite article (*a* dog, *a*nother dog) and only subsequently by the definite article (*the* dog). It is a good bet that she would have used "a" rather than "the" if the unnamed chaser of Trina had not already been introduced into the story when she referred to it.

This interchange hints at the many and diverse sorts of accomplishments that mark the miraculous-seeming accomplishment that is human language acquisition. The field of language development has undergone a striking metamorphosis in the past 25 years. For those of us who are old enough to remember, it used to be a dull field. What facts we had seemed colorless and pedestrian. The main reason they seemed so was that there were no interesting theoretical perspectives to organize and enliven them. We lacked an adequate, theoretically informed conception of all the many and marvelous things a person knows and can do when he or she has acquired a native language. Because we had an impoverished vision of what people end up having inside their heads when language has been fully acquired, we had a correspondingly impoverished vision of the developmental steps, sequences, and processes or mechanisms that describe and explain the course of that acquisition.

Thanks to the work of Noam Chomsky, George Miller, Roger Brown, and many other scientists, both visions are far richer now. As a consequence, language development has become one of the most stimulating and challenging areas in all of developmental psychology. It also has the frustrating property of being more stimulating and challenging the more one knows about it; frustrating, because that means an introductory chapter like this just cannot communicate all the excitement that is really there. For instance, it may be necessary to know a fair amount of linguistic theory to appreciate fully the staggering amount of complexly organized grammatical knowledge a native speaker of any language tacitly has. The excitement comes from trying to imagine how on earth a person could possibly have acquired all that as a young child.

PREVERBAL DEVELOPMENTS

Important developments in infancy help prepare children to acquire their first words. Phonological skills, both innate and acquired, help children discriminate and produce the speech sounds that compose these words. Communicative skills allow them to exchange meanings and intentions with other people even before the onset of words. Furthermore, these early, preverbal interchanges provide the framework within which words and the first genuinely linguistic communications eventually emerge.

Phonological Development in Infancy

PERCEPTION OF SPEECH SOUNDS.   Questions about infants' perception of speech are of two sorts. One sort concerns preferences: what infants like to listen to. The other sort concerns abilities: what they hear when they so listen.

A general answer to the first question is clear enough: Infants like to listen to speech. From birth, the human infant seems to be biologically pretuned and predisposed to process speech sounds, and human speech is in fact the infant's favorite auditory diet. De Villiers and de Villiers (1979) summarize some of the evidence for this conclusion.

> Within a matter of days after birth, they are highly responsive to speech or other sounds of similar pitch to the human voice. In fact, speech seems to be rewarding to the infant in a way that other sounds are not. Newborns will learn to suck on an artificial nipple hooked to a switch that turns on a brief portion of recorded speech or vocal music, but they will not suck as readily in order to hear instrumental music or other rhythmical sound. In the first few months of life, speech elicits greater electrical activity in the left half of the child's brain and music elicits greater activity in the right half of the brain, as is the case with adults. This suggests that at a very early age the two hemispheres of the brain are already specialized for dealing with the different kinds of sound. So from the beginning of infancy children are able to discriminate speech from nonspeech, and they seem to pay particular attention to speech. (p. 16)

Infants' preferences extend beyond simply speech versus nonspeech. From early in life they show a preference for the form of speech known as "motherese." Motherese (as we will discuss more fully later) is the label for the type of speech that mothers typically direct to babies and young children; among its features are a slow tempo, high pitch, and greatly exaggerated intonation (Fernald & Simon, 1984; Grieser & Kuhl, 1988). It is, in short, the kind of speech that tells you that there must be a baby nearby. Among its attributes, motherese has a strongly "up and down" quality that might be expected to attract an infant's attention. Fernald (1985) was the first to show that babies do in fact find motherese interesting; she found that by 4 months of age infants would rather listen to tape-recorded motherese than to tape-recorded adult-to-adult talk. Subsequent work has shown that a preference for motherese is evident even in the first few days of life (R. P. Cooper & Aslin, 1990). Such preferences emerge even when the voice is that of a female stranger rather than the child's mother. They emerge for male speakers as well as female speakers (Werker & McLeod, 1989). Interestingly, 4-month-olds (although not 1-month-olds) even show a preference for *nonspeech* sounds that have expanded pitch contours in comparison to nonspeech sounds that do not (R. P. Cooper & Piston, 1991; Fernald & Kuhl, 1987).

Infants also prefer their own mother's voice over those of other speakers. Mehler, Bertoncini, Barriere, and Jassik-Gerschenfeld (1978) have demonstrated such preferences as early as 1 month—only, however, when the speech was of the normal, mother-to-baby, motherese sort. When both voices took the form of nonintonated monotones the infants showed no ability to discriminate mother and stranger. Early as it seems, 1 month is not the lower bound for such own-mother preferences. DeCasper and Fifer (1980) tape-recorded mothers as they read a Dr. Seuss children's story. These recordings served as the auditory stimuli for subsequent testing of the mothers' 3-day-old infants. In three experiments it was found that the newborns tended to suck in such a way as to produce the sounds of their own mothers' voices in preference to that of another mother. The authors concluded that "within the first 3 days of postnatal development, newborns prefer the human voice, discriminate between speakers, and demonstrate a preference for their mothers' voices with only limited maternal exposure" (DeCasper & Fifer, 1980, p. 1176).

How could infants so young have learned to recognize and prefer a specific voice? The exposure to the mother for DeCasper and Fifer's subjects was indeed "limited": a total of 12 or fewer hours of contact prior to the testing. These infants had, however, spent 9 months in close proximity to the mother prior to birth. In Chapter 2 we reviewed evidence suggesting that the auditory system is functional for at least the last several weeks before birth. Perhaps, reasoned DeCasper and Fifer, it was the prenatal exposure to maternal speech that led to the postnatal preference for mother over stranger.

A subsequent experiment—often dubbed "The Cat in the Hat study"—was designed to test the hypothesis that infants could remember specific events that had been experienced only in utero. DeCasper and Spence (1986) asked pregnant women to read aloud twice a day for the last 6 weeks of pregnancy. Each mother was assigned one of three children's books (one of which was Dr. Seuss's *The Cat in the Hat*), and it was this story that she faithfully recited during the daily reading sessions with her fetus. Two days after birth the infants were tested in the same sort of differential-sucking paradigm utilized by DeCasper and Fifer. In this case, however, the auditory stimuli being compared were not different voices but different stories: either the story that the mother had read during pregnancy or one of the other two stories. The infants sucked more diligently to produce the story to which they had been exposed prenatally—and did so even when the voice reciting the story was that of a stranger. Thus the infants had clearly processed and remembered something specific about their prenatal auditory experience. Needless to say, no one thinks that this something has anything to do with the content of the story; presumably, it was aspects of rhythm or pacing to which the infants were sensitive. Nevertheless, the infants were somehow retaining much more about their prenatal experience than most of us would have thought possible prior to DeCasper and Spence's work.

The Cat in the Hat study suggests some remarkable conclusions about the young infant's response to speech, and it is worth taking a moment to spell out what these conclusions are. First, the study adds another preference to the list of early preferences: a preference not just for a familiar voice but for a familiar auditory stimulus. Furthermore, the study suggests that a number of early preferences may have a common basis: namely, exposure to the mother's voice during the prenatal period. This early exposure may contribute to (but not necessarily fully account for) the preference for speech over nonspeech, for the mother's voice over a stranger's voice, and for a familiar speech stimulus over an unfamiliar one (R. P. Cooper & Aslin, 1989). All of these preferences would seem adaptive not just for the task of learning language but for the equally important task of getting attached to the mother. Finally, the study necessarily tells us something not only about preferences but about our second general question: the infant's ability to process speech sounds. Clearly, infants can be affected by prenatal speech input only if they are able to hear prenatally. And they can show the specific effects demonstrated by DeCasper and associates only if they possess sufficient perceptual ability to process particular aspects of the prenatal input and sufficient cognitive/mnemonic ability to store the processed information over time.

Interest in speech is an important part of language learning, but it is far from the whole story. To understand words the child must be able to perceive the phonological contrasts that make up words—must be able to tell the difference between a "pa" sound and a "ba" sound, for example. It is to this aspect of speech perception that much of the research of the last 20 years has been devoted, and the conclusions that it has produced can only be described as astonishing. Once again, the young infant has proved to be much more competent than we once believed.

It is necessary to say something about the nature of speech perception in adults before the infant findings can be understood and appreciated. Someone once remarked that there are only two levels of understanding of the field of international trade and finance: One takes about five minutes to achieve and the other about five years. The same is true of speech perception. We try only for the five-minute variety here; you are referred to Kuhl (1987) and the sources she cites if you want to get started on the five-year course.

The purely physical, acoustic difference between an auditory stimulus that sounds like "ba" and one that sounds like "pa" is a completely quantitative, continuous one. The acoustic dimension involved is a continuum, just like length or weight. Suppose we were to vary the auditory stimulus on that dimension. We start on the "ba" end of the dimension and gradually, continuously change the stimulus until we get to the "pa" end, much as we might gradually, continuously lengthen a line by slowly moving our pencils along a straightedge. What would we expect to happen perceptually? The "ba" should come to sound more and more "pa"-like, and there should be a broad zone in the middle of the dimension where the listeners cannot easily say which of the two consonants the sound most resembles. They might be inconsistent in their choice from trial to trial within this broad zone, or report hearing blends of "ba" and "pa."

A major discovery of speech-perception research is that adults do not perceive certain speech sounds in this expected, continuous fashion. What happens instead is that suddenly, abruptly—almost at a single point on that continuous dimension—the stimulus is heard as "pa" instead of "ba." As the stimulus continuously varies, the listener discontinuously reports…"ba," "ba," "ba," "pa," "pa," "pa".... Thus consonant perception tends to be discontinuous or "categorical" rather than continuous, in marked contrast to most other forms of perception. For instance, our pencil line will not suddenly and thereafter be perceived as "long" rather than "short" when it reaches, say, 8.23 inches.

What the research of the last 20 years has shown (beginning with a study by Eimas, Siqueland, Jusczyk, & Vigorito, 1971) is that infants as young as 1 month also exhibit categorical perception of consonantal sounds (Eimas, Miller, & Jusczyk, 1987; Kuhl, 1987—but see Burnham, Earnshaw, & Quinn, 1987, for a partially dissenting view). To illustrate the nature of the evidence, let us suppose that our "ba"-"pa" acoustic dimension was arbitrarily marked off into equal physical segments, like this: 1-2-3-4-5-6. Let us further suppose that adults hear stimuli 1, 2, and 3 as "ba" and stimuli 4, 5, and 6 as "pa," since the dimension's small transition zone lies between stimuli 3 and 4. Even though sounds 1 and 3 are no more different from each other from the physicist's standpoint than sounds 3 and 5 are from each other, a listener hears the members of the first pair as the same sound ("ba") and the members of the second pair as two different sounds ("ba" and "pa"). This is a clear instance of categorical speech perception. If a young infant is exposed to sound 1 until she habituates to it, she will continue to show habituation if 1 is replaced by 3. In contrast, if initially habituated to 3 and then presented with 5, she shows dishabituation. In other words, the baby acts as if she does not hear the difference between sounds 1 and 3, just as adults do not, but as if she does hear the difference between sounds 3 and 5, just as adults do.

It used to be believed that infants learned to discriminate speech sounds only gradually, through months of experience listening to their own babbling and the speech of others. However, there is now a great deal of evidence showing that they are capable of perceptually discriminating between many acoustically similar speech sounds during early infancy and that such perceptions are categorical rather than continuous. Infants make such discriminations, moreover, not just for syllables in isolation (such as "pa" vs. "ba") but for contrasts embedded in multisyllable utterances (e.g., "marana" vs. "malana"). Language does not typically occur in single-syllable chunks, and hence this ability to process more complex input is clearly important. It is interesting to note, however, that infants are best able to make such discriminations when the speech is of the highly intonated, motherese sort (Karzon, 1985). Thus adults' usual ways of talking to babies may in fact aid speech perception.

Could the early ability to make these discriminations possibly be the result of perceptual learning—that is, could it be acquired by infants through experience listening to the speech they hear around them? There are several reasons why that cannot be the case (Aslin et al., 1983). First, the ability to make at least some of these contrasts is present as early as one can test for it (1 month of age). This suggests that it may well be present at birth, and thus prior to any speech-perception experience. Second, young babies who live in different speech communities and consequently hear different languages are nevertheless very similar to one another in the phonetic contrasts they can discriminate perceptually. They also tend to make discontinuous categorical discriminations at about the same points on the various acoustic continua. In the example given earlier, that is tantamount to saying that young babies would discriminate between sounds 3 and 5 but not between sounds 1 and 3, even if the language they heard did not make use of that particular contrast. If a language does not use a phonetic contrast, the adult speakers of that language may not be able to hear that contrast, at least not without some training and practice. We would expect, therefore, that young babies might be able to hear some speech contrasts that their parents could not easily hear. In fact, the research evidence indicates that this is precisely what happens. To illustrate, Trehub (1976) tested the ability of young infants from English-speaking homes to discriminate a phonetic contrast that occurs in Czech but not in English. The infants showed clear evidence of being able to make the distinction. A group of English-speaking adults, on the other hand, had considerable difficulty hearing the contrast.

Findings such as Trehub's raise a natural next question: At what point in development is the facility at making certain discriminations lost? Werker (1989; Werker & Pegg, in press) reports a series of studies directed to this question, working with contrasts from both Hindi and Inslekapmx (a North American Indian language) that do not occur in English. Werker notes that the initial assumption behind such research was that the decline would occur around puberty, a time when language flexibility in general was believed to decrease (Lenneberg, 1967). Her first study, however (Werker & Tees, 1983), found that 12-year-old English-speaking children were no better than English-speaking adults at discriminating Hindi contrasts; not only that, but 8- and even 4-year-olds were also no better. Subsequent studies therefore pushed the age back even earlier, and they led to a clear conclusion: The decline in sensitivity occurs between 6 and 12 *months* of age. Werker emphasizes that the decline is a matter of degree and not absolute loss, for older subjects *can* still make distinctions. Without supportive experience, however, discriminations that were once made with ease become more and more effortful. One further finding from her research suggests how little experience may be necessary to maintain facility: Adults who had been exposed to Hindi during the first 2 years of life, but never again thereafter, were virtually as skilled as native Hindi speakers in making Hindi contrasts (Tees & Werker, 1984).

Categorical perception ensures that infants will be able to hear the contrasts that are important in the language that they are learning (along, for a while, with many other contrasts as well). But categorical perception is not the only important component of speech perception; such skills must be complemented by the ability that Kuhl (1987) labels *equivalence classification*. Equivalence classification refers to the realization that acoustically distinct stimuli belong to the same phonological category—that all of those various "pa's," for example, are simply variants of the same basic sound. In part, of course, such equivalence is guaranteed by the limits of discrimination; as we have seen, we often have difficulty hearing the differences among various forms of "pa." In some cases, however, the differences are quite discriminable—most obviously when the "pa's" came from different speakers. The infant who was unable to perceive a basic similarity between Mommy's "pa" and Daddy's (in some ways quite different) "pa" would have a difficult task indeed in learning language. Fortunately, Kuhl's research indicates that by 6 months of age infants are quite skilled at identifying such basic similarities in the face of irrelevant differences. Note that this ability is central not only to perception of speech but also to the eventual ability to imitate speech. The 1-year-old whose goal was to match her Daddy's "bye-bye" in every respect would be doomed to failure. Children, however, seem able from the start to recognize the equivalence of their sounds and those of their parents.

The impressive competencies that we have described have led to a quite natural hypothesis about the special nature of speech perception. This hypothesis is that we are equipped from birth with a highly specialized mode of perception, a so-called speech mode, designed solely and specifically to help us acquire and use the phonological distinctions found in human natural languages. This hypothesis suggests two predictions: (1) Since only humans acquire human speech, only humans should show categorical, speech-mode-like auditory discriminations; (2) since it is a "speech mode," humans should use this capacity only when perceiving speech sounds.

Experimental tests of these two quite reasonable-looking predictions yielded a very surprising outcome, however: The evidence ran counter to *both* predictions (Kuhl, 1987). The first prediction was initially disconfirmed in a particularly shocking fashion: *Chinchillas*, of all creatures, turn out to show categorical perception of human speech sounds (Kuhl & Miller, 1975). Subsequently, macaque monkeys were also found to do the same (Kuhl & Padden, 1983). In addition, even the absolute location of the category boundaries along the acoustic continua tested proved quite similar for chinchillas, macaques, and humans. The second prediction was disconfirmed by the finding that certain nonspeech-like sounds are also perceived categorically rather than continuously, both by adults and (probably—the evidence is not totally clear) by infants (Kuhl, 1987). For that matter, categorical perception turns out not even to be specific to the auditory realm, for it also occurs in the domain of color perception (Bornstein, 1981). Thus present evidence suggests that categorical auditory perception is—contrary to what many used to think—neither species-specific nor speech-specific.

If the capacity for categorical auditory perception is neither species-specific nor speech-specific, what are we to make of it? One highly speculative line of reasoning is the following (Kuhl, 1987): It is a general auditory capacity (thus, not restricted to speech perception) that other mammals also share (thus, not restricted to humans). Because other mammals also possess it, it may have been acquired quite early in our evolutionary history—earlier than the capacity for human oral speech. More speculative yet, perhaps the sound structure of human language then evolved to fit the particular processing characteristics (e.g., proclivity for categorical perception) of this general auditory capacity. To put it another way, it is at least conceivable that human speech sounds are as they are partly (probably *only* partly) because our mammalian auditory system is so constructed that it can easily discriminate and categorize them. If all this were true, we would expect that infants as well as adults would possess this capacity, because it will help them discriminate and eventually learn human speech sounds, and we should not be surprised to discover that other mammals also possess it, because it evolved so early, in the eons when we were mammalian but not yet human.

PRODUCTION OF SPEECH SOUNDS. Language involves production as well as reception, and the productive side of the enterprise also gets started in infancy, well before the appearance of the first words. Between 4 and 6 months of age, roughly, infants begin to *babble*—that is, to make vocalizations that sound quite speech-like. Vintage babbling, complete with complex intonation patterns, sounds for all the world like fluent speech in a language you do not happen to know. Infants will usually continue to do some babbling even after they start producing words, at about 1 to 1½ years. There are good reasons to believe that at least the onset and early course of babbling are largely controlled by maturational factors rather than inputs from the external environment (Locke, 1983). First, babies the world over begin to babble at about the same age, and their initial babbling sounds much alike from one speech community to another. Second, Lenneberg, Rebelsky, and Nichols (1965) have shown that infants doggedly begin to make the usual babbling sounds even if those around them cannot hear and respond (deaf parents), and even if they cannot hear themselves babble (deaf infants). Finally, there seems to be no evidence that one can change the kinds of sounds young babblers produce by modeling or selective reinforcement (de Villiers & de Villiers, 1978).

On the other hand, the course of babbling is not entirely maturational, for experience can also exert effects. Deaf infants may babble, but their productions begin later, end sooner, and are less varied in form than those of hearing infants (Oller & Eilers, 1988; Oller, Eilers, Bull, & Carney, 1985). Experiences of a different sort can be examined in the case of tracheostomized infants, that is, infants who have been prevented from uttering any sounds because respiratory problems have forced them to undergo tracheostomies (insertion of a breathing tube in the throat). In one particularly detailed case study, Locke and Pearson (1990) examined the first vocalizations of a 20-month-old girl in the weeks following the removal of the breathing tube. They found that her vocalizations were markedly restricted in both quantity and variety, showing closer resemblance to those of very young infants or deaf infants than to those typical for her age. These data suggest that neither maturation nor the experience of hearing others' speech is sufficient to ensure normal babbling; rather, infants must have an opportunity to practice and to hear their own sounds. Finally, studies of babbling across different languages suggest that the initial equivalence of babbles ("all babies sound the same") has disappeared by about 10 months; French babies babble somewhat differently from Chinese babies who in turn babble somewhat differently from Arabic babies (Boysson-Bardies, Halle, Sagart, & Durand, 1989). As Boysson-Bardies and colleagues note, there is an interesting temporal convergence between their findings and those of Werker (1989): Infants' babbling begins to show effects of the surrounding speech environment at about the same time that their perception of speech becomes less sensitive for sounds not represented in that environment. We should add, however, that the cross-language differences in babbling are not large: Babies around the world still sound much more alike than different.

Much of the interest in babbling—for both psychologist and parent—lies in possible links to first words and to language. Is babbling a preparatory period for language, a phase during which infants practice and perfect the sounds that they will need when they begin to produce words? Such a speculation seems reasonable, and it has in fact been embraced, in somewhat different forms, by theorists of a variety of stripes. Finding clear evidence in support of such a "continuity hypothesis," however, has proved surprisingly difficult. We know, for example, that babbling of the normal sort cannot be *necessary* for language acquisition, because children who are unable to babble can nevertheless learn language (Locke and Pearson's tracheostomized child, for example, eventually developed excellent language). We know also that babbling of specific sounds is not necessary for those sounds to appear later in language. Infants do not (in contrast to what was once believed) babble all or even close to all of the world's speech sounds. This naturally implies that there will be sounds in the language they learn that they have never practiced during the babbling period, yet they master these sounds when words require them.

Despite these caveats, most contemporary opinion seems to favor some form of continuity hypothesis (Blake & Fink, 1987; Eilers & Oller, 1988; Locke, 1989; Vihman & Miller, 1988). It is simply hard to believe that there could exist a universal and extended period of babbling if it did not serve *some* role in the development of language. Continuity does in fact seem to hold with respect to phonological form: For the most part, the sounds that make up children's first words are the same sounds that occur in their contemporaneous babbles. As Locke (1983) puts it, the beginning talker "reaches—as it were—into his collection of readily available articulations. The available articulations, at this point, are the segments of his babbling repertoire" (p. 83). Similarly, Messick (1984) has shown experimentally that children learn and use new words most readily when those words contain sounds that they already babble. Continuity may also hold with respect to the functions served by babbling and by first words. Many of the important functions of language—requesting, asserting, negating—emerge first in infancy, prior to the appearance of language. Infants recruit a number of their available behaviors, both vocal and non-vocal, to achieve these functions, and babbling is among the behaviors so recruited. We consider such preverbal communications more fully in the next section.

Communicative Development in Infancy

Children have already acquired some communicative skills by the time they start learning to talk, and these skills continue to serve them when their interchanges with others become linguistic (Feagans, Garvey, & Golinkoff, 1984; Golinkoff, 1983b; Shatz, 1983). It has been argued, in fact, that preverbal communicative experiences may play an important role in the child's mastery of the syntactic and semantic rules of the language (Bruner, 1975; Zukow, Reilly, & Greenfield, 1982). This claim is controversial, however, as we will see in the later "Explaining Language Development" section.

Preverbal infants can send and receive messages in a variety of ways. They can engage and direct other people's attention by vocal and manual actions, such as crying or pointing or simply staring at an object of interest. Conversely, they become able to respond to other people's attention-directing actions—for example, to look where someone else is looking or pointing. They can initiate and maintain interactions with others by making eye contact with them—a behavior of enormous reinforcement value to parents. They can also terminate interactions by averting their gaze from the other person.

At first, infants' message-bearing behaviors do not constitute intentional communications—that is, the behaviors are not produced with the goal of instilling a particular understanding in another or eliciting a particular response from the other. The cry of the hungry newborn sends a message, but this message is not an intentional communication. The question of when and how intentional communication emerges has been a topic of much interest among researchers of infancy (e.g., Harding, 1984; Scoville, 1984; Wetherby & Prizant, 1989). Decisions at the extremes are clear enough—the cry of the hungry newborn, the determined pointing of the 18-month-old—but there is a long in-between period during which interpretation may be doubtful. Did the infant point at the out-of-reach toy in an attempt to elicit help from her mother, or simply because of general interest and excitement? There is always the danger of reading more into the child's communicative act than is there, or even of misreading it entirely. As is shown later, the same problem arises at all levels of language acquisition: Should our interpretations of the child's language competence be "lean" or "rich" (R. Brown, 1973)? For example, should we interpret the young child's one-word utterances as having the force and meaning of full sentences? Similarly, are we justified in reading grammatical structure into the child's two-word utterances? A sobering caution with respect to our present topic—preverbal communication—is the fact that other cultures may be much less likely to see intentional messages in infant behavior than is our own (Schieffelin & Ochs, 1983). Indeed, Rochel Gelman (1983) notes that, "ours seems to be a culture which is quick to assign intentions to babies" (p. 277).

With this caution in mind, we can note that most researchers of the topic (who, to be sure, are members of our culture) agree that children are capable of intentional communication by 1 year of age (Bretherton, 1988; Sachs, 1989). By this age parents begin to see behaviors in their children that seem (again, to us Westerners) to cry out for such an interpretation. Bates (1976), for example, describes the following sequence of behaviors from a thirsty 13-month-old:

> C. is seated in a corridor in front of the kitchen door. She looks toward her mother and calls with an acute sound *ha*. Mother comes over to her, and C. looks toward the kitchen, twisting her shoulders and upper body to do so. Mother carries her into the kitchen, and C. points toward the sink. Mother gives her a glass of water, and C. drinks it eagerly. (p. 55)

This sequence illustrates many of the characteristics that have been proposed as criteria for intentionality, including the use of multiple means to achieve the goal (vocalizing, gazing, pointing) and the persistence when the first signals proved insufficient. Indeed, the ability to correct "failed messages" has been argued to be both a clear indication of intentionality and a major developmental achievement of infancy (Golinkoff, 1983a).

Infants' preverbal communications embody early forms of two basic speech acts: *requesting* and *asserting* (Bates, 1976; Bruner, 1975). Requests for objects that are out of reach may be made by urgent and insistent open-handed reaching out toward the objects, often accompanied by heart-rending calls or whines and beseeching looks at the would-be adult "tools." If you have ever been the recipient of this communicative package you know that it has REQUEST! written all over it. The example from Bates clearly falls in this category. The nonverbal precursors of verbal assertions look quite different. Infants see objects that interest them and they touch them, hold them up and show them, or point to them. In the clearest, easiest-to-interpret cases, the touching is a one-finger pointing-like affair that is not followed by picking up, the object showing is not followed by object giving, and the pointing is done with hand closed and index finger extended, not at all like the open-handed request. In addition, the manual gestures are accompanied by looks at the other people, perhaps to make sure that they also see the interesting objects.

In addition to learning how to send and receive specific messages, infants learn something about how to behave in a continuing nonverbal dialogue, involving an alternating sequence of communicative sending and receiving. For instance, they are likely to have learned how to take turns in peek-a-boo games or other ritualized interactional routines. This skill will serve them well later, when they begin to engage in verbal conversations.

We can note finally that the various communicative competencies that we have described do not arise in a vacuum; rather, such competencies clearly relate to other skills that the infant is in the process of mastering. The question of when intentional communication emerges is part of the more general question of when infants become capable of intentional behavior of any sort (see Chapter 2). Emergence of symbolic forms of communication during the second year, including nonverbal symbols such as ritualized gestures, can be linked to a more general capacity for representational functioning (L. P. Acredolo & Goodwyn, 1988, 1990). Finally, the infant's ability to use another as the means to an end can be seen as evidence for a beginning theory of mind—that is, a primitive realization that others have mental states and that one's own behavior can influence those states (Bretherton, 1988—see Chapter 3).

ONE-WORD UTTERANCES

Children usually begin to produce their first words at about 10 to 13 months of age. They typically understand at least a few words prior to the first productions of their own, and most children continue to understand more words than they can say (Ingram, 1989). This pattern, in fact, is a general one that holds for an extended period and across a variety of aspects of language: Children often comprehend more than they produce.

Vocabulary growth proceeds slowly at first for most children. At roughly 18 months, however, many children show a spurt in word learning that has been labeled the *naming explosion* (Bloom, Lifter, & Broughton, 1985; Markman, 1991). The naming explosion is a phenomenon that may be all too familiar to the parents of a toddler: The child has discovered that things have names, and now—tirelessly, incessantly—demands to know what the names are. In one well-documented case a 16-month-old learned 44 words in a single week (Dromi, 1987)!

The Nature and Meaning of Children's First Words

What sorts of words are children learning during the one-word stage? Not surprisingly, children's first words often refer to things that the children themselves can act on, and more generally to objects and events that are salient, familiar, and important to them (K. Nelson, 1973). In our society, at least, first words often denote family members (e.g., "Mama"), animals ("dog"), vehicles ("car"), toys ("ball"), edibles ("juice"), salient body parts ("eye"), items of clothing ("hat"), and household implements ("cup"). Although names are common in most early vocabularies, children also learn greetings ("hi"), action words ("up"), relational words ("more"), and locational terms ("there") (Gopnik & Meltzoff, 1986b). There appear to be individual differences in the sorts of early vocabularies that children construct (McCabe, 1989; K. Nelson, 1981). Some children, dubbed "referential," acquire a preponderance of object names that allow them to talk about the inanimate world ("milk," "blocks," "shoes," etc.); others, dubbed "expressive," seem to concentrate less on names than on personal-social terms that can be used in social interaction ("want," "please," "yes," "no," "stop it"). Such differences, however, are matters of degree rather than of absolute kind, for all children learn words of both sorts (Goldfield & Snow, 1989).

Both the words that make up children's early vocabularies and the meanings assigned to those words may differ from the words and meanings of the adult lexicon. When children first learn names for objects or events they tend to learn labels that are at an intermediate level of abstraction or generality—labels that correspond to what is called the "basic-level" of categorization (see Chapter 3). This means, for example, that "dog" will be learned before "spaniel" (less general) and "animal" (more general), just as "flower" will be learned before either "rose" or "plant." Presumably, intermediate-level labels are learned first because they reflect the level of abstraction that is functionally most useful for children in their early dealings with the world (Anglin, 1977; R. Brown, 1958). It is more important, for instance, for the child to distinguish dogs from other animals than spaniels from other dogs. The early labels that children learn also clearly relate to parents' labeling practices, which in turn may reflect parental beliefs about the distinctions that the child needs to make (Mervis & Mervis, 1982). A mother of a 1-year-old is unlikely to point down the street and say "There goes the spaniel."

When first learning a new word, the child may not use it to refer to exactly the same objects or events an adult would (e.g., Clark, 1983; Ingram, 1989). A common and easily observed referential error is *overextension*. For example, a child might initially overextend "cat" by applying it not only to cats but also to dogs and squirrels. Words are often overextended to objects that are perceptually similar to the words' correct referents, and sometimes also to objects that are functionally similar—for example, those that can be acted on in the same way (Clark, 1983). One examination of the first 75 words learned by a sample of 1-year-olds found that 33 percent of the words were overextended (Rescorla, 1980).

Children's early meanings for words may show other deviations from the adult language. Sometimes children *underextend* word meanings instead of overextending them. For instance, a child may initially apply "cat" only to the family pet, or only to cats seen out the window, rather than to cats in general. Underextensions are harder to detect than overextensions, because they involve absence of a correct response (e.g., failing to call a particular cat "cat") rather than production of an incorrect response (e.g., calling a dog "cat"); careful studies reveal, however, that they too occur frequently (Kay & Anglin, 1982). Whereas the child who overextends must eventually narrow the scope of reference (attaching "cat" to cats only and not all small animals), the child who underextends must broaden the scope to encompass all the exemplars (small cats, large cats, striped cats, fat cats, etc.) that adult usage entails.

The meanings that children are attempting to convey with their one-word utterances may also be less stable and consistent than the meanings that the words hold in the adult language. With *complexive* meanings the child seems to shift from one feature or set of features to another when using the same word in different situations, with there being no single feature that all objects named by that word have in common (Bowerman, 1978). As a striking example (de Villiers & de Villiers, 1979), the de Villiers' son Nicholas successively applied the family dog's name to other dogs, to all animals and birds, to various other furry or cuddly objects, and even to a salad with black and shiny pitted olives reminiscent of the dog's nose! With *holophrases* the child uses the single word not simply as a label but rather to convey a meaning akin to an entire sentence, with the particular meaning varying from one context to another. Thus, "ball" might mean not simply "That's a ball" but "I want the ball," "I threw the ball," or "The ball hit me." We should add, however, that this sort of "rich" interpretation of one-word speech is controversial. It is in fact very difficult to know how much sentence-like meaning to credit children with when they are limited to producing one word at a time (Barrett, 1982; Ingram, 1989).

Children's deviations from adult usage are not limited to words from the adult lexicon. Many children invent words of their own when faced with the challenge of talking about something for which they do not yet know an adult word. Clark (1982) and Becker (1992) document a number of charming instances: "fix-man" for mechanic, "scale it" for weigh something, "nose-beard" for mustache, "many talls" for height. This phenomenon is not limited, by the way, to children learning oral language; creative coinages are even more striking in the gestures that many deaf children invent in order to communicate (Goldin-Meadow, 1979). The spontaneous, child-initiated nature of such inventions has implications for models of language acquisition, and we consequently return to this work later in the chapter.

So far we have concentrated on the child's production of words. Language requires comprehension as well as production, and it is therefore important to ask whether children make the same sorts of errors in understanding others as they do when speaking. For instance, does the child whose own use of "cat" extends to all small, furry animals have a similarly broad interpretation when she hears others use the word? Studies of comprehension reveal that overextensions *do* occur in comprehension, but that they are far less frequent than in the child's own speech (Hoek, Ingram, & Gibson, 1986; Thompson & Chapman, 1977). Thus, the same child who calls all small, furry animals "cat" may have no trouble at all correctly picking out the cat from an array of similar-looking animals when told to "find the cat." If the child knows the word as well as this comprehension test suggests, why does she overextend it in production? There are various possible explanations (E. V. Clark, 1983; P. L. Harris, 1983; M. D. Smith, 1988). The child may have learned that the small animal that climbs trees in the back yard is called "squirrel" but, unable to recall that word on a particular occasion, she produces a word that she *is* able to recall: "cat." Alternatively, the child may not yet have learned "squirrel" at all; however, trying to find some name to apply to this interesting object, she comes up with the most appropriate name she can think of: again, "cat." Yet a third possibility is that the child is perfectly aware that squirrels are not cats but is commenting, metaphorically, on the similarity—saying, in effect, that the squirrel is like a cat. Each of these explanations suggests that overextensions, at least sometimes, should be thought of less as errors than as the child's attempt to fill gaps in the lexicon or to comment upon the world. And each also suggests—as studies of comprehension often do—that children know more about language than their own speech reveals.

Ties to Emotions

One essential function of language is to express feelings and desires. Babies certainly have feelings and desires, and they find ways, from early in life, to convey these emotions to those around them. In this section we consider how the expression of emotions fits into the child's emerging language.

The question of emotion-language links is an intriguing one because different regions of the brain are specialized for emotional expression (predominantly the right hemisphere) and language (the left hemisphere), even in infants (e.g., C. Best, 1988). This separation might make it difficult to integrate the two functions. There is an interesting finding that young children who more frequently express emotions are slower to reach the early language milestones such as first words, a vocabulary spurt, and multiword utterances (Bloom & Capatides, 1987a). One explanation is Bloom's (e.g., Bloom & Beckwith, 1989) proposal that these two mental activities, speech and emotional expression, compete for cognitive resources in infants and toddlers, making it difficult to express emotions in speech. As the development of language brings automaticity of speech production, these two forms of expression become integrated. Support for this hypothesis comes from Bloom's observations of mothers and their infants playing with toys and eating a snack (Bloom & Beckwith, 1989). First, the children at the beginning of the single-word period (mean age of 14 months) tended to say something at *about* the time they displayed an emotion (e.g., whining, laughing, facial expression, body tension). This suggests that they were beginning to express their feelings even though they were not using emotion words. In fact, it suggests that children first use language for expression more than for getting things done in the world (Bloom & Beckwith, 1988). Most revealing, however, was that the children's emotional expression decreased about 5 seconds before an utterance and peaked immediately after the utterance, with a neutral expression during it. The child seems to put emotions on hold and concentrate on achieving *le mot juste*. This pattern suggests that infants cannot talk and express feeling at the same time, perhaps because these simultaneous cognitive activities are beyond the child's cognitive capacity. Perhaps the lesson here for parents trying to calm down an emotionally aroused infant is to try to keep the child talking! By about 20 months, when the children reached their vocabulary-spurt period, they were speaking and expressing emotion at the same time.

Another interesting outcome was that when babies in their vocabulary-spurt phase expressed emotion and speech together, the valence was usually positive rather than negative. Negative emotions may require more cognitive work because they typically disrupt behavior and involve the construction of an alternate plan to reach a goal, whereas positive emotions do not (Kinsbourne, 1988; Stein & Jewett, 1987). Thus, there is more strain on cognitive resources for the expression of negative emotions than for positive ones. Also, infants have more left-hemisphere activity associated with positive emotional expressions and more right-hemisphere activity with negative expressions (e.g., Davidson & Fox, 1982). Because speech and positive emotions are being processed in the same hemisphere, they may be more likely to be integrated than are speech and negative emotions. Further support for the resources hypothesis was the finding that the co-occurrence of words and emotional expression was greatest with the most frequent and earliest learned words, and with low intensity emotional expression, perhaps because these require less cognitive work. Eventually the child is able to produce emotion words rather than just any types of words at times of emotional arousal, and such words provide clues as to which emotions the child is experiencing.

TWO-WORD UTTERANCES

At about 18 months of age, children's single-word utterances begin to be joined by two-word and sometimes even longer expressions. Parents start to hear the likes of "put book," "mommy sock," and "more milk." Just before genuine two-word utterances appear, parents may hear two one-word utterances produced close together in time—for instance, "more" (pause) "milk" (Bloom, 1973). Both the intonation pattern and the evident semantic link between the words suggest that the child is struggling to produce a longer utterance but is not quite able to get all the parts together. This situation is in fact a common one throughout language development: parts in isolation first, and only later in larger combinations (Scollon, 1976).

Utterances of young children the world over have a "telegraphic speech" quality (R. Brown, 1973). Much like telegrams, they tend to omit the small and communicatively less essential words, such as articles (e.g., "the"), conjunctions ("and"), auxiliary verbs ("can," "will"), and prepositions ("on"). Two-word utterances, at least in English, also seldom contain any morphological inflections (e.g., progressive "ing," as in "going," past tense "-ed"). Gleitman and Wanner (1988) suggest one contributor to this early selectivity: Children tend to reproduce those aspects of speech that receive the strongest intonational stress (typically nouns, verbs, and adjectives) and leave out those that are less heavily stressed.

Despite the commonalities just noted, not all children go about forming their initial sentences in exactly the same way. The individual differences that we discussed at the one-word level have parallels in children's earliest word combinations. Some children, for example, build sentences primarily from combinations of content words ("mommy sock," "daddy sit," etc.), a natural continuation of the early referential style; others show higher proportions of pronouns, function words, and person-oriented expressive forms (Bates, Bretherton, & Snyder, 1988). As you might expect, differences are even more marked when we move beyond the bounds of a single language to compare different languages (Slobin, 1985). Such variations do not negate the simultaneous presence of important similarities among children, a point to which we return later. Researchers of early language are much more aware than they used to be, however, that children do not follow a single, invariant path to language mastery.

A striking and important characteristic of children's speech even at the two-word phase is its creativity. From the start of their sentence-generating careers, children produce utterances that could not possibly be imitations of the adult models around them. Examples of such creative constructions abound; two of our favorites are "More up" (produced by a child who wants his daddy to continue tossing him in the air) and "Allgone sticky" (produced, triumphantly, by a child who has just succeeded in washing his hands). The originality of children's utterances tells us that they are not simply mimicking what they have heard but rather are generating sentences based on some sort of rule system. Exactly what these early rules are, however, has been the subject of much debate.

Semantics

One possibility is that children's early language is organized in terms of semantics or meanings. There do appear, in fact, to be characteristic meanings that young children try to express in their two-word utterances. Roger Brown (1973) carefully reviewed developmental data from a number of languages and suggested that the majority of two-word utterances seem to express any of eight semantic relations: *agent-action* (e.g., "mommy kiss"); *action-object* ("hit ball"); *agent-object* ("mommy doll," when the child wants her mother to do something with the doll); *action-locative* ("sit chair"); *entity-locative* ("cup table"); *possessor-possession* ("daddy car"); *entity-attribute* ("big car"); and *demonstrative-entity* ("that car"). Two-word utterances also seem to express meanings like *recurrence* ("more milk") and *nonexistence* ("allgone milk"). These meanings, moreover, are likely to be very similar in different languages the world over. "If you ignore word order and read through transcriptions of two word utterances in the various languages we have studied, the utterances read like direct translations of one another" (Slobin, 1970, p. 177).

That children are expressing meaning relations in their speech is therefore much clearer than was the case during the one-word utterance period. Two things remain unclear, however (Braine, 1976; C. J. Howe, 1976; Ingram, 1989; Maratsos, 1983). One is whether these early semantic relations are really as abstract and adult-like as suggested in Brown's analysis. To claim, for example, that the child has mastered *possessor-possessed* is to claim that the child has formed a general class of things that can be possessors and another general class of things that can be possessed, knows something about which members of one class can go with which members of the other, and knows something about how to link the classes in language. Some researchers have suggested that the child's initial knowledge might be a good deal more limited and specific than this. Perhaps all the child really knows, for example, is that the big person he calls "daddy" is frequently seen inside the interesting object he calls "car"; hence, "daddy car" expresses this familiar association and not true possession. Or perhaps the child knows that he and his older sister both have things they will not let others take away from them ("*my doll!*"), but his concept of possession is at first limited to this primitive notion of "*mine!*" *Possessor-possessed*, although undoubtedly eventually a part of linguistic competence, may be too rich an interpretation of what the young child knows and is trying to express.

The second uncertainty about two-word speech is whether the underlying semantic knowledge, whatever it might be, is *all* that the child should be credited with or whether some knowledge of grammar or syntax must also be assumed. It is this issue to which we turn next.

Syntax

What sort of evidence would indicate that there is a syntactic basis to children's two-word utterances? The most obvious possibility is word order. If a child consistently said "pat daddy" when she was patting her father and "daddy pat" when he was doing the patting, and did the same for all other action-object and agent-action expressions, we might credit her with some syntactic knowledge: She would be exploiting the purely syntactic device of differential word ordering to signal differences in intended meaning. The words are the same in both utterances; only the word order discriminates them. Most young children do seem to make use of word order in their two-word utterances. Likewise, during this period children can often use word order as a clue to meaning when listening to the speech of others (Tager-Flusberg, 1989). Indeed, children as young as 17 months, whose own productions are still at the one-word level, show some ability to infer meaning from word order—another demonstration of comprehension in advance of production (Golinkoff, Hirsh-Pasek, Cauley, & Gordon, 1987). It is interesting to note that this sensitivity to word order is one characteristic that differentiates children's language from that of chimpanzees who are being taught human language (Gleason, 1989).

Should we conclude, then, that some knowledge of syntax underlies early child language? The matter is still not resolved. The problem is that the systematicity that is evident in early speech might be accounted for solely on semantic and not syntactic grounds—by the tendency for agents to come before actions, actions before objects, and so forth. A purely syntactic category such as *noun* is defined not by semantic criteria (dog, lightning, and truth are all nouns) but by the way in which nouns work within sentences and interact with other units (e.g., all can be preceded by "the"). Similarly, the syntactic *subject* of a sentence may but need not be the actor or agent; subjects can also be the object of the action ("The door was opened") or the instrument with which the action was performed ("The key opened the door"). Early child language does not provide clear evidence for such abstract syntactic categories that transcend specific semantic relations. It is possible, with a sufficiently rich interpretation, to read such knowledge into the child's early utterances. But it is also possible to remain skeptical (Ingram, 1989; Maratsos, 1983; Ninio, 1988).

LATER DEVELOPMENTS

Syntax

As the child's sentences grow longer, the evidence for syntactic knowledge becomes clearer. The use of word order becomes more definitely syntactic, as links are established between grammatical and not merely meaning-based classes. Morphological inflections begin to be added to words—the "-s" for plural, the "-ed" for past tense, and so forth. The child's sentences also begin to exhibit the hierarchical grammatical structure so characteristic of human language. In the four-word child sentence "Big dog run home," for instance, "Big dog" is one main sentence constituent (called a *noun phrase*), "run home" is another (*verb phrase*), and the syntax of English demands that the two be produced in that order. However, each of these main constituents also has lower-level constituents nested within it (hence, "hierarchical") that must also be produced in the order given: "Big" before "dog," "run" before "home." As in the passage from one-word utterances to two-word ones, transitional forms are sometimes seen. For instance, the child might say "Go nursery" and then immediately afterwards crank it up to "Lucy go nursery" (Maratsos, 1976, p. 9).

THE ORDERED DEVELOPMENT OF GRAMMATICAL MORPHEMES. The acquisition of what Roger Brown (1973) calls "grammatical morphemes" makes an interesting and informative developmental story. These morphemes consist of the little function words and inflections that "tune" or "modulate" the meanings associated with the major content words like nouns, verbs, and adjectives. For example, adding the grammatical morpheme "-ed" on the end of "push" to make "pushed" modulates or qualifies the verb's meaning by indicating that the pushing action (the main meaning expressed) occurred in the past (modulation of that main meaning). The presence of these morphemes in the child's sentence makes the sentences seem more adult-like, less telegraphic. Brown (1973) made an intensive developmental study of 14 grammatical morphemes. They included three "-s" inflections: the plural ("dogs"), the possessive ("dog's"), and the third-person singular verb ending ("runs"). They also included the present progressive ("-ing") and past ("-ed") inflections, the prepositions "in" and "on," the articles "the" and "a," various forms of "be," both when used as an auxiliary verb ("I *was* going home") and as a main verb ("I *was* home"), plus several other morphemes. The reason the developmental story here is interesting is the remarkable finding (R. Brown, 1973; de Villiers & de Villiers, 1973) that all young children tend to master these 14 morphemes in the same fixed sequence. For example, although the three "-s" inflections are identical phonologically, children almost always acquire the plural earliest, the possessive later, and the verb inflection later still.

Why a constant order of development, and why the particular constant order found? Perhaps how often children hear these morphemes in the parents' speech explains the order of their acquisition. Morphemes frequently modeled by parents offer more learning opportunities for the child and therefore might be acquired first. Although this explanation seems reasonable, the available evidence suggests that it is wrong: The frequency of occurrence of these morphemes in parental speech to children and their order of appearance in children's speech seem to be essentially uncorrelated (R. Brown, 1973). Rather than frequency per se, what seems to be important is the semantic or syntactic complexity of the form. An example involving semantic complexity shows how this explanation works (de Villiers & de Villiers, 1978). To use "was" correctly the child has to take into account the person of the subject ("I" and "he/she" can precede "was" but "you" cannot), the number of the subject (e.g., singular "I" but not plural "we"), and when the event happened (in the past rather than in the present or future). In contrast, to use the verb ending "-ed" correctly the child has to take into account only one of these three factors—when the event happened. The correct use of "was" can therefore be interpreted as a more complex cognitive achievement than the correct use of "-ed," because the user must keep track not only of time of occurrence, but also person and number. Accordingly, "-ed" should be mastered before "was" and other forms of "be," and it is. Similar analyses of either semantic or syntactic complexity lead to correct developmental-order predictions of the other grammatical morphemes. Unfortunately, in many cases semantic and syntactic complexity are confounded; hence, it is often impossible to know which if either is the primary determinant of difficulty (Tager-Flusberg, 1989).

THE CHILD AS HYPOTHESIS TESTER AND RULE LEARNER: ACQUISITION OF INFLECTIONS. Imagine yourself a subject in perhaps the most famous experiment in psycholinguistics (Berko, 1958). The experimenter shows you a picture of a man swinging an object and informs you, "This is a man who knows how to rick. He is ricking. He did the same thing yesterday. What did he do yesterday? Yesterday he _____." You confidently finish the sentence: "Yesterday he ricked." In similar fashion you are able to indicate that a man who knows how to spow must have spowed yesterday and that one who likes to naz every day probably nazzed yesterday as well. You could supply these forms despite the fact that you had never heard the words "rick," "spow," or "naz" before. You could do so because your knowledge of English past tense is based not on rote memorization but on rule: Form the past tense by adding "-ed" to the end of the verb.

It is a striking fact about human languages that they are strongly rule governed. To master the grammatical structure of one's native language is to acquire a rich network of implicit, functional rules. What is even more striking is that young children seem to expect language to be strongly rule governed. They are constantly on the *qui vive* for rules and regularities in every corner of language—in syntax, phonology, semantics, and pragmatics or communication. They act as though they are constantly forming and testing hypotheses about the lawful and systematic properties of their language. They learn by rote when they must, but learn by rule when they can. More than that, they often resist learning by rote when they must— that is, they try to apply rules to irregular, nonrule-governed forms in the language.

Young children's deep-seated and abiding penchant for finding order in language—even when there is not any—is nowhere more striking than in the acquisition of inflections (e.g., Ervin, 1964; Kuczaj, 1977). For instance, the child may begin by using the irregular plural form "feet" as a rote-learned vocabulary item. Then, having discovered the plural "-s" rule and using it to make "dogs," "boys," and so on, she may start alternating "foots" or even "feets" with "feet." Later, having learned the likes of "kisses" and "horses," she may even try "footses" for a while before finally reinstating "feet" as the only plural of "foot." Another developmental sequence that makes the same point is first "went," then "goed," and finally "went" again.

It is obvious that these strange forms could not possibly be rote parrotings of adult utterances. What adult ever said "footses" to a child? Rather, they are reasonable—creative, actually—overgeneralizations of grammatical rules that are in process of acquisition. Such overgeneralizations are not limited to young learners of English. Children the world over exhibit the same predilection for hypothesis testing and rule discovery in their grammatical acquisition. Indeed, overgeneralizations may be even more common in languages that are more highly inflected than English (Slobin, 1985). And, as indicated earlier, the search for systematicity is not limited to grammar. In the area of semantic development, for instance, children may invent "tomorrow day" and "yesternight" in analogy with "tomorrow night" and "yesterday" (Maratsos, 1976).

NEGATION AND QUESTIONS. Other grammatical acquisitions may also proceed according to a fixed and sensible-looking sequence of developmental steps (e.g., Ingram, 1989; Tager-Flusberg, 1989). For example, children usually begin to express negation by simply attaching "no" or "not" to whatever utterance they want to negate—"No mitten," "No I go," and so forth. This primitive syntactic rule of merely attaching a negative marker to an entire sentence is also an initial developmental step in languages in which the full negation system differs appreciably from that of English. Perhaps it is a common first step because its cognitive processing demands are so low. It is not a very satisfactory system, however, because of its imprecision and potential ambiguity. As Bloom (1970) pointed out, the "No" in "No mitten" can convey any of three meanings: nonexistence ("There's no mitten"), rejection ("No, I won't wear a mitten"), and denial ("That's not a mitten"). Progress toward a better system occurs when the child begins to insert the negative word inside the sentence, in front of the word it negates. "No I go" now gives way to "I no go" or "I not go." Finally, as the child gradually learns how to use auxiliary verbs correctly (a complicated enterprise in English), grammatically correct negative sentences like "I won't go" and "Mary isn't coming" become more frequent. However, the more subtle and tricky aspects of negation in English may continue to give children trouble for some time, resulting in sentences like "No one didn't come in" and "I didn't see something."

The mastery of the syntax of questions shows a somewhat similar developmental sequence. Again, children the world over hit upon a simple starting point: a rise in intonation at the end of the sentence to convey that a question is being asked. Thus "No more milk?" from a thirsty toddler staring at an empty container carries a different message than does "No more milk!" from an inveterate milk-hater. As with negations, the eventual mastery of the adult system is a gradual process. The parallels are well illustrated in the development of so-called *wh* questions—those beginning with "where," "what," "why," and so on. At first, the question word is simply tacked onto the front end of an unmodified affirmative, as in early negations. One hears "What Mommy doing?" and later, when auxiliary verbs are used, "What Mommy is doing?" Still later, the child correctly inverts subject and auxiliary verb to produce "What is Mommy doing?"; "Where are we going?"; and so on. However, more complicated interrogatives still present difficulties. When asking negative questions, for instance, the child may fail to invert subject and auxiliary and thus produce questions like "Why you aren't going?"

OTHER SYNTACTIC ACQUISITIONS. Needless to say, children acquire a functional command of many other syntactic rules during the early- and middle-childhood years. For example, they learn how to relate sentences and clauses to one another to form more intricate sentences, just as they earlier learned how to relate individual words to one another to make simple sentences. They become able to coordinate two sentences or sentence parts and embed one within another. Following are some examples, with one of the two related sentence parts italicized: "Billy ran *and so did I*." "If you hit me *I'll hit you back*." "The man *who fixed the fence* went home." "I don't want *you to use my bike*." "I asked him *what to do*." In fact, the whole foregoing sentence itself represents an extremely complex case in point. If you tried to write a system of rules of sentence production that would always generate grammatically correct English sentences of these complicated types and never generate any grammatically incorrect ones, you would better appreciate what a prodigious, almost unbelievable cognitive accomplishment the child's acquisition of grammar is. Those who try to do it for their living tend to be downright awestruck when they contemplate human grammatical development (see the later section "Explaining Language Development").

Semantics

Children's semantic development proceeds along two general fronts as they move beyond the two-word phase. One sort of development, labeled *propositional semantics* by Ingram (1989), has to do with the ability to convey meaning by combining words in sentences. The various semantic relations identified by Roger Brown (1973)—agent-action, action-object, and so on—become more unequivocally evident in the child's speech. Rather than occurring only in isolation, these relations begin to be combined into larger units; "Mommy drive the big car," for example, encompasses agent-action, action-object, and entity-attribute. Meanings that were not evident at the two-word stage emerge—the indirect object, for example ("Give me the book"), and the instrumental ("Sweep with the broom"). Finally, the child's mastery of inflections permits the encoding of a range of new meanings, such as plurality and present or past tense.

The second sort of development concerns the acquisition of word meanings, or what Ingram (1989) labels *lexical semantics*. Children learn an amazing number of words amazingly quickly (one estimate puts the average 6-year-old's vocabulary size at 14,000—Templin, 1957); they also adjust and refine the meanings of words that are already part of their vocabularies. The goal of research on this aspect of semantics has been to uncover general principles that might account for what children do and do not understand about word meanings. We consider one small part of this very large literature here; we pick up on another aspect of it in our later "Explaining" section.

Much research attention has focused on children's understanding of *relational words*—that is, words that do not carry an absolute meaning but whose meaning depends on some sort of comparison or relation. Some examples are quantifying adjectives such as "big"-"little," "tall"-"short," and "more"-"less," and spatial or temporal prepositions such as "before"-"after" and "in front of"-"in back of." Such terms have been of interest for several reasons. One reason is precisely that they *are* relational and hence would seem to pose problems of understanding not found with words (e.g., "red," "cat," "run") whose meanings are more fixed and "point-at-able." The same quantity that is "big" in one context (e.g., when pouring a drink of water) may be "little" in another (e.g., when filling a bathtub). Such words also embody a number of linguistic and conceptual distinctions that might be expected to affect their difficulty. "Big" and "little," for example, are maximally general quantitative terms, and as such might be expected to emerge earlier than more precise designations such as "tall"-"short" and "wide"-"narrow." Furthermore, within such contrasting pairs one member is the positive or "unmarked" term, in the sense that it is the label for the entire dimension. Thus we ask how big, tall, or wide something is but not (under ordinary circumstances) how small, short, or narrow it is. This distinction has led to the prediction that unmarked terms should be learned earlier than marked ones. Finally, relational words would seem to have obvious ties to the child's cognitive development, and hence the learning of such words has been seen as a prime area in which to look for links between cognition and language. Piaget's work, in particular, offers a host of claims about children's mastery of relevant quantitative, temporal, and spatial knowledge.

Studies of children's understanding of relational words indicate that all of these proposed contributors can in fact be important (Blewitt, 1982; Ingram, 1989; Johnston, 1985). At the same time, there are exceptions and qualifications to any conclusion that might be offered—precisely because many factors can play a role, no single factor consistently accounts for how children interpret relational words. In general, however, children do seem to learn general terms, such as "big"-"little," before more specific terms, such as "tall"-"short" (Bartlett, 1976). Children also usually (although here there are definitely exceptions) find the unmarked or positive member of a pair easier than the marked member—thus "tall" before "short," "deep" before "shallow," and so on (Donaldson & Wales, 1970). It used to be believed that children's difficulty with the marked term extended to confusing it with its opposite (believing, for example, that "less" means the same thing as "more"); this idea, however, has not held up well (Carey, 1977). The child's grasp of the relevant cognitive distinctions can clearly affect when words are acquired and how they are understood. Children's mastery of spatial prepositions, for example ("in," "on," "over," "under," etc.), shows a fairly good fit with the Piagetian account of when various kinds of spatial understanding develop (Johnston, 1985). More prosaic, real-world knowledge can also be important; an example here is the fact that children's knowledge of the sizes of things contributes to their ability to use adjectives such as "big" and "little" appropriately (Sera & Connolly, 1990). More generally, children utilize a variety of cues and recruit a variety of kinds of knowledge for the task of making sense of words, both relational and otherwise. Each of the theories that has been proposed to explain children's understanding of words appears to capture part of the process (Anglin, 1977; E. V. Clark, 1973; Nelson, 1974). No theory, however, provides a complete explanation.

Communicative Development

COMMUNICATION SKILLS. As their cognitive and linguistic development progress, children acquire a wealth of knowledge and skill in the social-communicative uses of language (e.g., Dickson, 1981; Feagans et al., 1984; Shatz, 1983; Warren-Leubecker & Bohannon, 1989). They learn how to converse as well as to talk—that is, how to maintain focus on a single topic during an extended verbal interchange with another person. They gradually become able to go beyond the here, the now, and the real in what they converse about. They gain command of new and cognitively more advanced types of speech acts. For instance, they eventually find out that language can be used not only to assert, request, and question, but also to express psychological states ("I'm sorry"), to commit oneself to future actions ("I promise I'll come"), and even to bring about new states of affairs by verbal declarations ("I quit").

Children learn that what is really meant by an utterance often goes beyond or even differs from what is literally said. They become able to infer what is implied and presupposed but not stated explicitly, an absolutely essential skill for comprehending ordinary discourse. For example, they learn that a statement such as "That's not a cat" does more than explicitly deny that some creature is a feline; it also implicitly presupposes that someone thought or said it *was* a cat. One does not normally deny what nobody has asserted. Similarly, they discover that an utterance that sounds like one kind of speech act may really be another in disguise. For instance, children early discover that the assertion "My, it is noisy in here" and the question "Why are we so noisy today?" are really adult euphemisms for the request "Please be quieter."

Children also learn to adapt their speech production and comprehension to numerous properties of the speakers, the listeners, and the social settings in which the speech occurs. Lakoff (1977) has suggested that such adaptations by adult speakers are in the service of two general goals: be polite and be clear. Children become progressively more skilled both at producing polite utterances and at recognizing politeness (or its absence) in others (Baroni & Axia, 1989; Becker, 1986; Garton & Pratt, 1990). They learn, for example, how to produce requests of different forms, and how to alter their speech as a function of the familiarity or the status (e.g., adult vs. peer) of the listener. For many children, injunctions from parents ("What do you say?" "What's the magic word?") are a definite part of this learning process (Becker, 1988). We will see shortly that there is little evidence that parents intentionally teach grammar to their children. Instruction in etiquette, in contrast, is a common occurrence in many households.

For years, thinking about children's ability to achieve the second of the general goals—be clear—was dominated by Piaget's assertions about the young child's egocentrism. Young children were believed to communicate in an egocentric fashion, without adapting or tailoring their speech to the communication-relevant properties of the listener. There is certainly some truth to this Piagetian picture; young children *are* more "at risk" for egocentric speech than are older children or adults (see Chapter 5). Nevertheless, more recent developmental research in this and other areas of cognitive functioning indicates that we had underestimated the young child's capacity for nonegocentric thinking (e.g., R. Gelman, 1978). In the communication area, there have been a number of impressive demonstrations of nonegocentric-looking adaptations of young children's speech to listener characteristics and needs. Here we offer just a sampling.

When a 4-year-old tells a 2-year-old rather than a peer or an adult about a toy, he or she is likely to "talk down" to the younger listener—for example, use shorter utterances (Shatz & Gelman, 1973). Similarly, when the listener indicates comprehension failure, preschoolers adjust their message in one way for an adult listener and in a different, simpler way for a child listener (Warren-Leubecker & Bohannon, 1983). Even 2-year-olds show some ability to adjust to different listeners; they talk differently to an infant sibling than to a parent (Dunn & Kendrick, 1982b) and differently to a doll than to an adult (Sachs & Devin, 1976). Two-year-olds also can converse quite effectively with each other, assuming that the referents are simple and the context familiar (Wellman & Lempers, 1977). Familiarity is also an important variable for older children; preschoolers show better adjustments to the listener in natural settings than on laboratory tasks (Warren-Leubecker & Bohannon, 1989), and their conversations are most successful when the content is scripted knowledge familiar to both children, such as grocery shopping or eating at McDonald's (L. N. Furman & Walden, 1990). Finally, preschoolers can adjust not only to general status differences among listeners (e.g., younger vs. older) but also to momentary variations in what the listener does or does not know. A study by Menig-Peterson (1975) provides a nice example. Adult A and a preschooler are in room X. Adult A "accidentally" spills a cup of juice on a tablecloth. The two discuss how best to clean it up and eventually do so. A week later the preschooler returns to room X with either adult A or supposedly naive adult B. The empty cup is present and the adult asks, "I wonder what that cup is doing there" and similar queries (if adult B), or "Look at that cup. Do you remember what happened when we were here before?" (if adult A). Menig-Peterson (1975) found that her preschool subjects appropriately—and nonegocentrically—varied their recounting of the spilling incident as a function of which adult was the listener (see also Perner & Leekam, 1986).

METACOMMUNICATION. On the other hand, a number of studies have turned up some unexpected and even startling shortcomings in young children's thought and behavior in communication situations (Asher, 1979; Baker & Brown, 1984; Beal & Belgrad, 1990; Bonitatibus, 1988a; Dickson, 1981; Flavell, 1981a; Flavell, Speer, Green, & August, 1981; Markman, 1981a; Robinson & Robinson, 1981). Most of these studies bear on the child's knowledge and cognitive actions concerning communications—thus, on a type of metacognition or cognition-about-cognition sometimes referred to as *metacommunication* (Flavell, 1976).

Researchers have frequently used variations of the referential-communication task developed by Glucksberg and Krauss (Glucksberg, Krauss, & Higgins, 1975). In one version of this task, the speaker and the listener cannot see one another but both know they have identical sets of objects in front of them (see Figure 7–1). The speaker's task is to describe one of his objects specifically enough for his listener to identify its duplicate in her own set. Many of the young child's metacommunicative problems can be illustrated using this simple task situation.

Suppose the speaker's message is referentially ambiguous. For instance, suppose he says "Pick the red block" but there are two red blocks, one square and one

FIGURE 7–1 Experimental arrangement for one version of the Glucksberg and Krauss communication task. From "The Development of Communication: Competence as a Function of Age" by R. M. Krauss and S. Glucksberg, 1969, *Child Development, 40,* p. 259. Copyright © 1969 by the Society for Research in Child Development. Reprinted by permission.

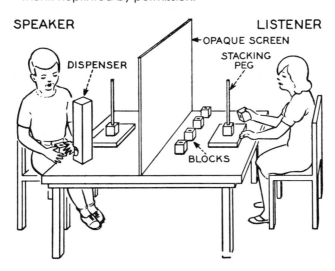

round, in each person's set of objects. The research evidence suggests that a young child listener—age 5, say—would be less likely than an older one to show even minimal signs of detecting the ambiguity. She would be more apt than an older child to listen to the message, focus her attention on only one of the red blocks in front of her, and unhesitatingly pick that block. She should feel that she does not know which red block he means, one would think, but she does not appear to. Instead, young children turn out to be surprisingly poor monitors of their own comprehension. They do not understand something but are often not aware that they do not understand it.

Other metacommunicative immaturities may become apparent even if the young child does notice that two objects fit the speaker's description. If she does notice it, we may see her look properly uncertain and hesitant before settling on one of the two red blocks. However, this feeling of uncertainty is likely not to have the same meaning, importance, and implications for her that it would for an older child or adult. Thus, she probably will not ask the speaker to be more specific, even though she knows she may ask him questions at any time. Also, if asked if she is sure the block she chose is identical to the one the speaker had in mind, she is apt to say that she is sure it is. And finally, if asked whether the speaker or the speaker's message did a good or a poor job of telling her exactly which block to pick, she is very likely to say he or it did a good job (Beal & Flavell, 1982; Flavell, Speer, Green, et al., 1981).

Suppose it then becomes evident that the listener chose a different block than the speaker did; the child sees that the task outcome is a communication failure. Who is responsible? The Robinsons found that older children correctly blame the speaker and his inadequate message, whereas younger ones are likely to blame the listener and her incorrect block selection (e.g., Robinson & Robinson, 1981). Moreover, they are about equally likely to blame the listener no matter who is playing the listener role—for example, a doll or the experimenter rather than them. Moreover, children who blame the listener in this situation are less clear than children who blame the speaker about how to deliberately make the communicative quality of a message better or worse (Robinson, 1981). They also are likelier to accept a disambiguated description of the block they have chosen (e.g., "Pick the red *square* block") as being what the speaker had actually said, when what he actually had said was "Pick the red block" (Robinson, 1981).

We should add some qualifications to this bleak picture of the young child's metacommunicative abilities. As is true for performance in the speaker's role, children's ability to function as effective listeners does vary across settings and across different types of message. Once again, performance tends to be more impressive in natural settings than on somewhat artificial laboratory tasks, such as the Glucksburg and Krauss paradigm (McDevitt & Ford, 1987; Revelle, Wellman, & Karabenick, 1985). Listener skills are also more evident when the focus is on children's ability to respond appropriately in an ongoing dialogue, as opposed to making an abstract judgment of message adequacy (Revelle et al., 1985). These findings make sense: If children's performance as listeners were always as poor as the preceding paragraphs suggest, they could hardly have the success as conversationalists that we have seen they have. Aspects of the speaker or message can also affect children's apparent metacommunicative competence. Children are more likely to spot message inadequacy from a dishonest speaker than from a merely incompetent one (Bonitatibus, 1988b). They are more likely to recognize inadequacy in written than in spoken messages, presumably because the written format emphasizes the literal words of the message and provides an enduring record that can be rechecked (Bonitatibus & Flavell, 1985). And they are more likely to recognize the inadequacy of a message that is incorrect or impossible to follow (e.g., "Pick the red one" when there are no red ones present) than of a message that is ambiguous (e.g., "Pick the red one" when there are two red ones present—Flavell, Speer, Green, et al., 1981). Unlike the patently incorrect message, the ambiguous message at least offers the child a basis, albeit an insufficient one, for making a response.

Despite their occasional successes, children do often show the various meta-communicative deficits and confusions that we have described. Why do they respond in these curious ways? Here are some possible reasons (see also Beal, 1988; Flavell, 1976, 1990; Flavell, Speer, Green, et al., 1981; Mitchell, Munno, & Russell, 1991; Robinson, 1981). The most general reason may be that they are just not much given to thinking about and critically analyzing such intangible mental products as spoken messages. In this area as in others, the development of metacognitive dispositions and skills is simply not very far advanced. As a corollary, young children tend not to understand as clearly as older children the seemingly obvious fact that the quality of a message affects communicative success. The listener's incorrect choice is a salient and recent event that the child may easily interpret as the cause of a communication failure; in contrast, the speaker's inadequate message may be generally less salient for young children, and is also more temporally distant from the outcome. As noted, ambiguous, insufficiently specific messages may be particularly hard for young children to evaluate accurately. They may have learned that a speaker's message should refer to whatever the speaker has in mind, but may not have also learned that the message should refer to that *alone*—in other words, that it should not be referentially ambiguous. In general, young children seem to have difficulty focusing on the literal words of a message—on what was actually said—as opposed to whatever they may already know or believe on other bases. They have special difficulty, therefore, in detecting message inadequacy in cases in which they already know the speaker's intended referent (Beal & Belgrad, 1990; Beal & Flavell, 1984). And they tend to equate performance with intention, judging a message in terms of what they believe the speaker meant to convey, rather than what the speaker's words actually do convey (Bonitatibus, 1988a, 1988b).

Communication involves the creation of mental states in others, and children's beliefs about communication are therefore necessarily linked to their more general theory of mind—in particular, their beliefs about the sources of knowledge. By age 4, children have acquired the important understanding that communication, and not just direct perception, can be a source of knowledge (Wimmer, Hogrefe, & Perner, 1988). They may also understand that a false communication can be the source of a false belief (Perner & Davies, 1988). For the most part, however, young children seem to operate on a one-to-one principle, in which access to information of any sort is assumed to lead automatically to knowledge. Thus unclear or ambiguous messages are assumed to produce knowledge in their listeners, just as an unclear perceptual experience is assumed to be interpretable and informative (Chandler & Helm, 1984; M. Taylor, 1988). It is only at age 6 or so that children come to the realization—a very important realization for their performance as both speakers and listeners—that the informativeness of a message depends on its quality (Sodian, 1988, 1990).

Are there specific, experiential contributors to improvements in children's communicative and metacommunicative skills, in addition to the general cognitive changes that are identified in the work on theory of mind? The answer is undoubt-edly yes, but we still know little about what these experiences are. Piaget (1932) long ago suggested one class of experiences that almost certainly plays a role: the give-and-take of peer interaction in which the child is forced, as both speaker and listener, to come to understand that some sorts of messages simply do not work as well as others. There is also suggestive, although limited, evidence that the feedback that parents provide in response to their children's unclear communications may aid in the development of better message-producing skills (Robinson & Robinson, 1981). Finally, various writers have suggested that experiences associated with for-mal schooling may help children learn about the nature and management of commu-nicative enterprises (Flavell, Speer, Green, et al., 1981; D. R. Olson & Hildyard, 1983). In school, children may encounter more frequent and explicit demands to communicate clearly to others and to monitor the clarity and comprehensibility of the communications they receive. Experience in reading and writing may facilitate the development of metacommunication; unlike evanescent spoken messages, writ-ten ones "stay put" and remain accessible to the recipient for critical evaluation. And, of course, a primary goal of literacy is the ability both to communicate one's ideas clearly to others and to understand the vast array of messages that the written word makes available.

EXPLAINING LANGUAGE DEVELOPMENT

Describing the interesting phenomena of development is one of the tasks for the developmental psychologist; explaining how those phenomena come about is the other task. We have seen throughout this book that our ability to describe often outstrips our ability to explain, and such is certainly the case in the study of chil-dren's language. Nevertheless, some intriguing and no doubt partially correct explanations have been proposed, and these are the subject of the current section. We begin with semantics.

Semantics

At first glance, learning the meanings of new words might seem a simple task, at least in comparison to the obvious complexities involved in mastering the syntax of the language. Presumably, what the young word learner must do is to come to associate particular sounds with particular concepts—thus "milk" means that good-tasting liquid I like when I'm thirsty, "cat" means those small, furry, pet-able animals, and so forth. In fact, the task is enormously more complicated than this simple description suggests. The following passage from Markman (1989), based on an argument by the philosopher Quine (1960), summarizes some of the complexities. The example concerns a young child, ignorant as yet of the word "rabbit," who sees a rabbit nearby.

> Someone points in some direction and utters a word. On what grounds is the child to conclude that a new unfamiliar word—say, "rabbit"—refers to rabbits? What is to prevent the child from concluding that "Rabbit" is a proper name for that particular rabbit, or that "rabbit" means "furry" or "white" or any number of other characteris-tics that rabbits have? Finally, what prevents the child from concluding that "rabbit" means something like "the rabbit and its carrot" or "the rabbit next to the tree" or "mother petting the rabbit"? (Markman, 1989, p. 20)

The point that both Quine and Markman make is that there are always an indefinite number of logically possible meanings for any word—that is, meanings that are compatible with the evidence available to the child. Some possibilities, to be sure, can be ruled out as more evidence becomes available ("the rabbit and its carrot" can be rejected if "rabbit" is used in the absence of a carrot), but others will always remain (the rabbit's ears plus its tail, the rabbit that is not floating in space, etc.). How, out of this wealth of possibilities, does the child ever figure out that "rabbit" means rabbit? And note that we have not even mentioned a prior problem: How does the child hear "rabbit" in the first place—that is, how does he or she parse the continuous speech stream ("Lookattheprettyrabbitnearthetree") into the individual words?

FAST MAPPING. Perhaps the most obvious implication of the Quinean argument is that word learning should be a slow, laborious process, as the child encounters a particular word in enough different contexts to rule out many possible meanings and to zero in on the correct meaning. Yet if there is one thing that we know about word learning it is that the process often appears far from slow; it has been estimated that children acquire an average of nine new words a day in the years between 2 and 6 (Carey, 1978). Any theory of word learning must somehow account for the rapidity with which at least some words are acquired.

An often-cited experiment by Carey and Bartlett (1978) attempted to identify some of the conditions under which rapid learning occurs. These investigators presented 3- and 4-year-olds with a new color term, "chromium," which was used to refer to the color olive. The term was introduced in a natural, nondidactic manner: In the course of the nursery-school day, the teacher told the child, "Bring me the chromium tray, not the blue one, the chromium one." Note that this instruction contains some potentially quite useful information; "chromium" does not mean blue, and it probably does mean some other color. Carey and Bartlett found that most of their young subjects did learn, from this single exposure, that "chromium" was the label for a color, and some of them learned something about the particular color as well. The learning, to be sure, was partial, for most did not come, even with further exposures, to associate "chromium" solely with the color olive. Nevertheless, the children had learned a fair amount about a new word from a single, naturally presented instance. Such a rapid acquisition of at least part of a word's meaning from one or a few exposures is referred to as *fast mapping*.

Since the Carey and Bartlett (1978) report, a number of other studies have verified that fast mapping occurs (Au & Markman, 1987; Dickinson, 1984; Dollaghan, 1985; Heilbeck & Markman, 1987; Rice & Woodsmall, 1988). Fast mapping has been demonstrated in children as young as 2 and as old as 11. It has been shown for nouns as well as for adjectives, and for terms having to do with shape or texture as well as for color terms. It has been shown when a number of new words are introduced at the same time, as opposed to the one-word-at-a-time method of Carey and Bartlett. And it has even been shown for words presented on TV.

Children make use of a number of kinds of information when they engage in fast mapping. Explicit linguistic contrast of the sort presented by Carey and Bartlett ("the chromium, not the blue") can clearly be helpful. On the other hand, explicit contrast is not necessary, for fast mapping can occur even in its absence. Doubtless in many cases the contrast is implicit rather than explicit; if the child hears "the chromium tray" in the presence of two trays that differ only in color, it is a reasonable inference that "chromium" is a label for the less familiar of the two colors. More generally, children use contextual cues and real-world knowledge to arrive at plausible interpretations of new words. They also use syntactic cues; the placement of "chromium" between "the" and "tray" suggests an adjective, just as the placement of "koop" in "find the red koop" suggests a noun (Landau & Gleitman, 1985; Waxman, 1990). Parents' labeling practice may be helpful; parents tend to talk about things to which their children are already paying attention, and to do so in ways that correspond to the child's interests and understanding (A. Adams & Bullock, 1986; Callanan, 1985; Tomasello & Farrar, 1986). Even when a parent's focus and the child's focus are initially discrepant, children can use the parent's direction of gaze to zero in on the intended referent (Baldwin, 1991). Finally, children's existing conceptual and lexical knowledge can be an important determinant of their ability to make sense of a new word. Learning of a new color term, for example, occurs much more readily if the child already knows a few color words than if the child does not (Carey, 1982; Rice, 1978). Apparently, a critical step that the child must make involves the realization that there *are* color words; once color has become a category in the lexicon, new terms can be added and existing terms reorganized relatively easily.

Although fast mapping permits a quick initial grasp of a word's meaning, it is important to stress that this understanding *is* initial and partial. Children typically refine and perfect their understanding of a word for many months after the word's first appearance. Thus word learning is both fast and slow—fast in its initial phase, slow in the movement to completion. Carey (1978) provides a good summary of the process.

> Suppose that, on the average, six months is required for the full acquisition of a new word (surely an underestimate, as we will see). If the child is learning nine new words a day, then he is working out the meanings of over 1,600 words at a time. This fact is a clue to the real significance of the fast mapping. What is included in that initial mapping—that the new word is a word along with some of its syntactic and semantic properties—must allow the child to hold onto that fragile new entry in his lexicon and keep it separate from hundreds of other fragile new entries, and it must guide his further hypotheses about the word's meaning. (pp. 274–275)

CONSTRAINTS. We began our discussion of word learning with the Quinean puzzle: How does the child narrow down the many logically possible meanings of a word to the one actual meaning? The work on fast mapping suggests that children have a variety of kinds of information—contextual, lexical, syntactic—available to them for this task, and that even so, full mastery of a word may be an extended process. Nevertheless, this work also shows that children somehow hit upon the basic, core nature of a word—this is a color term, this is the name of an animal, and so on—quite quickly and accurately. Studies of fast mapping document this phenomenon, but it is not clear that they have fully explained it. Instead, there still seems to be a leap on the child's part—some going beyond the evidence to arrive at a solution that was not guaranteed by the data.

In recent years a number of researchers have suggested that such leaps may be possible because children's word learning is guided by a set of *constraints* concerning the possible meanings that words might have. Waxman (1989) provides a capsule summary of what is meant by the notion of constraints: "The essential idea in a constraints approach is that the child brings to the task of learning and development tacit biases or tendencies that lead her to favor some interpretations of events and objects over others" (p. 13). As applied to the task of word learning, the central claim of the constraints approach is that the child encountering a new word is constrained to consider only a small number of the many logically possible interpretations of what that word might mean. In the case of "rabbit," for example, it simply never occurs to the child that the reference might be to some subset of the animal's parts, or to the animal and some nearby object, or to the animal in some particular spatial location. Because all these possibilities are ruled out from the start, the task of figuring out what the word actually does mean is enormously simplified.

What sorts of constraints might guide children's word learning? A variety have been proposed (Behrend, 1990; Carey, in press; Clark, 1987, 1988; Golinkoff, Bailey, Wenger, & Hirsh-Pasek, 1989; Markman, 1990, 1991; Merriman & Bowman, 1989; Mervis, 1989; Waxman, 1989). Here we concentrate on three (drawing on Golinkoff and co-workers' overview—terminology and distinctions vary some across authors). One very basic constraint is Object Scope: the assumption that words label whole objects and not the parts or attributes of objects. This constraint implies that a child who hears "rabbit" in the presence of a furry, hopping animal should assume that the label applies to the animal as a whole, and not to a part such as the tail or an attribute such as the color.

A second, closely related, constraint is the Taxonomic Assumption (Markman, 1991). The principle of Object Scope provides a good start toward word learning, but this principle alone leaves unclear how a word is to be extended—to what other objects, besides the specific labeled example, should "rabbit" apply? Conceivably, the other objects could be ones that enter into some sort of thematic relationship with the rabbit—the rabbit's food, the rabbit's dwelling place, and so on. In fact, children's extensions seem to follow the Taxonomic Assumption: the belief that words label categories of like objects—objects from the same taxonomic category. Thus "rabbit" will be extended not to carrots but to other furry, hopping animals. Note that the extensions need not be at first correct—the child may call a squirrel "rabbit"—but at least they will be to the right *kind* of thing.

Finally, the constraint of Mutual Exclusivity (Markman, 1991) refers to the belief that each object has only one label—that the referents for different words are mutually exclusive. This constraint applies most obviously to situations in which the child already knows some of the relevant words. Suppose that the child hears "rabbit" while watching a dog chase a rabbit. Since the child already knows the label "dog," he or she will reject the possibility that "rabbit" refers to dogs, thus increasing the chances of attaching the word to the correct referent. We saw that this sort of learning by contrast plays an important role in many instances of fast mapping.

As the "rabbit" example suggests, various constraints may often work together. Indeed, constraints *have* to work together for mature word learning to be possible. Consider the Object Scope constraint. This constraint may be very useful for early word learning, but eventually it must be overcome; after all, not all words refer to whole objects. Markman (1991; Markman & Wachtel, 1988) has argued that Mutual Exclusivity may help children to overcome the limits of Object Scope. Suppose that mother says "Feel the soft fur" while petting a rabbit. The child who already knows the label "rabbit" should, following Mutual Exclusivity, reject the possibility that "fur" is also a label for rabbit. Once the whole object has been ruled out, the child can concentrate on the particular aspect on which the mother is concentrating. It is in this way that children learn that words can apply to parts and attributes and not simply whole objects. They also may learn that a particular object can be labeled at several levels of abstraction: basic (e.g., "dog," "car"), superordinate (e.g., "animal," "vehicle"), and subordinate (e.g., "collie," "Chevy"). The child who hears either "animal" or "collie" applied to an object that he or she knows to be "dog" should assume, following Mutual Exclusivity (and also Clark's Principle of Contrast—see Clark, 1987, 1988), that some difference in meaning is being signalled—that "animal" is not simply another label for "dog." Waxman (1990) has shown that the particular alternative labels that are supplied can help children to form both superordinate and subordinate categories.

Constraints hypotheses are currently the most popular approach to explaining semantic development. Such arguments have not won over every student of early word learning, however (Gathercole, 1987, 1989; MacWhinney, 1991; K. Nelson, 1988, 1990). Critics of constraints theorizing point to both weaknesses in the evidence offered in support of constraints and a certain fuzziness in the theories themselves. Empirically, both naturalistic and experimental studies verify that children often do honor all of the various constraints that have been proposed (Merriman & Bowman, 1989; Woodward & Markman, 1991). Such studies also make clear, however, that constraints are sometimes more honored in the breach than in the observance, for exceptions and violations are not hard to find. It is true, of course, that we would expect the child eventually to violate constraints, since no constraint is invariably applicable (recall our discussion of Object Scope). It is true also that some violations may occur because it takes a while for constraints to develop; proponents of constraints are still not agreed as to whether constraints are present from the start of word learning or somehow emerge with development (Merriman & Bowman, 1989; Mervis, 1987; Woodward & Markman, 1991). Nevertheless, children's adherence to such principles as Object Scope or Mutual Exclusivity does not have the predictability and uniformity that the term "constraints" would seem to imply. Some softer term—"bias," "tendency," "strategy"—may be a more accurate depiction of what is going on.

The origin of such biases or tendencies is also an unresolved issue at present. Another common implication of "constraint" is that of a biological basis—that development is constrained by biological forces to follow a certain course. Such a nativistic emphasis is evident in discussions of constraints for cognitive development in general (e.g., Keil, 1981), as well as in the use of constraints to explain aspects of syntactic development (e.g., Chomsky, 1981)—indeed, the application of the notion of constraints to syntax predated and has clearly influenced the recent work in semantics. Various features of semantic development, however, have been cited as evidence against a really strong biological determination of semantic constraints—the fact that constraints can be so readily violated, for example, or the fact that some seem to emerge with development rather than being always present (K. Nelson, 1988). It is true, as constraints theorists have replied, that such characteristics need not rule out an important biological contribution ("innate" need not mean present at birth, for example); it is also true that most such theorists have not committed themselves to a nativistic position but rather have remained open on the innate versus acquired issue (Woodward & Markman, 1991). Nevertheless, there may be something to Katherine Nelson's (1988) point about the consequent blurring between description and explanation: "Labelling certain behaviors...'constrained' adds nothing to the description of those behaviors themselves.... The term constraint only appears to be explanatory because it appears to invoke an innate mechanism" (p. 239). At the least, we clearly need to know more about where constraints come from. For an interesting recent treatment of this whole issue, see Markman (in press).

We also need to know more about a final (and related) issue: the specificity versus generality of semantic constraints. Are constraints such as Object Scope or Mutual Exclusivity limited to the task of learning words, or do they reflect something more general about the child's cognitive system? Intriguing suggestions have been proposed for more general links (Markman, 1991). Object Scope, for example, may relate to the special status that objects seem to have for children from early in life; recall Spelke's (1988b, 1990) demonstrations of the infant's interest in and ability to apprehend whole objects (Chapter 2). Mutual Exclusivity may relate to the difficulty that young children have in realizing that the same object can be represented in more than one way (Flavell, 1988); recall our discussion of representations and theory of mind in Chapter 3. The specific difficulty in the case of Mutual Exclusivity would lie in realizing that the same object can receive more than one label. Hypotheses such as these—as well as the more general issue of how and why proposed constraints from various domains relate—are currently the subject of much attention (R. Gelman, 1990; Keil, 1990). We return to these issues in Chapter 8.

Syntax

Despite the recent surge of interest in semantics, it is syntactic development that language researchers have been most obsessed with explaining. If a Nobel Prize could be given in the field—only one, and only once—many developmental psycholinguists would want to save it for the genius who finally succeeds in explaining syntactic development. Why the great interest? If you know something about the work of another genius, Noam Chomsky (e.g., 1972), you may already know the answer. Chomsky showed that to "know" a language as an adult native speaker does is to have a functional command of an exceedingly rich and intricate system of grammatical categories and rules. If our grammatical knowledge were a very simple, impoverished system, clearly evident in the speech we hear, then explaining its acquisition would not present much of a problem. However, almost everyone in the field today agrees with Chomsky's claim that the system is in fact incredibly vast and complex. Many also agree that clues to the underlying syntactic structure of sentences are often not present in the surface structure or external form of these sentences. These facts make the task of explaining syntactic development more intriguing—and much more difficult. Useful sources on this topic include Bohannon and Warren-Leubecker (1989), Golinkoff and Hirsh-Pasek (1990), Ingram (1989), MacWhinney (1987b), Maratsos (1983), and Wanner and Gleitman (1982).

The Role of the Environment

Let us first examine possible roles of the external environment, especially of what other people do and say. We can immediately reject the extreme—and absurd—possibility that the external environment plays no role whatever. For example, although all normal children are obviously capable of acquiring as a native language any human language to which they are exposed—witness the many, many different languages in the world—they just as obviously have to be exposed to that one to learn it. But what sorts of experiences, beyond mere exposure, might play a role in this learning?

IMITATION AND REINFORCEMENT. A traditional view emphasizes the processes of imitation and reinforcement. By this view, children learn to speak like adults because their caregivers model syntactically correct sentences in their speech; children then imitate these sentences, and the caregivers selectively reinforce both these imitations and children's spontaneous utterances, responding more positively to grammatical than to ungrammatical productions. Plausible though this account may seem—and helpful though such a state of affairs would no doubt be—the available evidence goes strongly against it. We mainly just list the objections; details and supporting evidence can be found in the previously mentioned sources.

First, the evidence clearly shows that a great deal of syntactic learning can and does go on without benefit of sentence imitation. Some children hardly ever imitate adult sentences. Most children rarely imitate adult sentences after the early phases of grammatical acquisition, although of course they still continue to acquire new rules. When children do imitate, their imitations are typically no more advanced than their spontaneous productions, a finding that suggests that imitations reflect already acquired knowledge rather than mediate the acquisition of new knowledge. Children typically comprehend new syntactic forms before they produce them in their own speech—again, syntactic acquisition without benefit of imitation. The ultimate case of comprehension preceding production, and thus of imitationless acquisition, was an otherwise normal boy who was physically incapable of producing speech (Lenneberg, 1962). Even though he could never have imitated a single English sentence, this boy achieved a good receptive command of English grammatical structure. Finally, whatever contribution imitation may sometimes make, children quickly transcend any dependence on literal imitation, for their sentences are creative constructions from early in life. We gave some examples of such creative, clearly not imitated productions earlier; here are a few more: "I'm magic, amn't I?" "Why not me can't dance?" "Did I didn't mean to?" "He was disingappeared."

What about reinforcement? The available evidence (more limited than in the case of imitation) suggests that selective reinforcement of grammatical versus ungrammatical utterances is not a necessary or even an important shaper of syntactic development. It certainly did not shape that of Lenneberg's (1962) speechless boy. Even in normal children, parents tend to reinforce and correct on the basis of the truth value rather than the grammatical quality of their children's utterances. A mother who is curling her child's hair responds "That's right" to the child's ungrammatical "Her curling my hair." However, the grammatical but factually incorrect sentence "There's the animal farmhouse" gets a "No, that's *not* the animal farmhouse" (R. Brown & Hanlon, 1970). Note R. Brown, Cazden, and Bellugi's wry comment on this rather surprising finding, "Which renders mildly paradoxical the fact that the usual product of such a training schedule is an adult whose speech is highly grammatical but not notably truthful" (1969, p. 71).

Imitation and reinforcement, then, do not seem to do the job. What other sorts of assistance might the environment in general, and parents in particular, provide? In recent years attention has focused on three potentially helpful practices in which at least some parents engage while interacting and conversing with their young children.

PREVERBAL INTERCHANGES. Some researchers have stressed the fact that the process of language learning gets started well before the first words appear at a year or so of age (Bruner, 1975; Messer, 1983; Schaffer, 1977). We saw earlier that communications on the infant's part are certainly evident long before the first words are heard. Our focus now is on the parent's part in these early interchanges. Parents have been observed to do a variety of things that might help their infants begin to learn about the nature of language. Most generally, they engage in "dialogues" with their babies, producing some appropriately babyish utterance, waiting for a response from the baby (a smile, coo, babble, or whatever), responding in turn to this infant response, waiting for the baby to behave again, and so on. As the infant grows older, parents "up the ante": Their own messages become more complex and language-like, and their criteria for accepting an infant response as appropriate also grow more stringent—where once mere eye contact would do, now a vocalization is required, and where once a burp or gurgle would suffice, now a babble or even a word may be demanded. In this way, parents help their infants learn how to engage in conversational interchanges (the necessity of turn taking, the appropriateness of certain responses) well before the infants are capable of genuine language. They also help the baby learn how to perform basic speech acts, such as questioning and requesting.

Preverbal interchanges of the sort just described seem a sensible way to initiate the process of language learning. At best, however, such experiences are a start, and much still remains to be explained. There is, clearly, an enormous leap from an exchange of babbles in infancy to the complex syntax of a passive sentence or negative question (R. Gelman, 1983). Furthermore, it seems clear that not all infants experience these sorts of interchanges with their parents, yet all infants eventually learn language. The verdict with respect to the role of preverbal interchanges must therefore be a cautious one: probably helpful, but very probably not necessary, and in any case far from sufficient. This is a conclusion that we will see applies to other parental practices as well.

MOTHERESE. Speech directed to young children tends to differ in various ways from speech directed to adults (Snow & Ferguson, 1977). As we discussed earlier, such speech is simplified phonologically, with slow pacing and exaggerated intonation and stress. It also is simplified syntactically and semantically: Sentences tend to be short, simple, and grammatical, and the focus is on present objects and events. Although "motherese" is the usual label for such speech, mothers are not its only practitioners; fathers and adults in general also simplify their speech to young children. Children do too: As indicated earlier, even 4-year-olds will "talk down" when speaking to 2-year-olds (Shatz & Gelman, 1973). In fact—and happily—it seems virtually impossible to talk to a young child without some such adaptation.

Are such adaptations helpful? We noted two benefits earlier in the chapter: Motherese enhances infants' interest in speech (Fernald, 1985), and motherese helps infants to make phonological distinctions (Karzon, 1985). Kemler Nelson and colleagues report a third benefit: Infants are most successful at segmenting speech at the boundaries between clauses—an important skill with respect to the acquisition of syntax—when the speech is motherese (Kemler Nelson, Hirsh-Pasek, Jusczyk, & Cassidy, 1989). All of these findings suggest that the distinctive sound of motherese does in fact help infants to process and make sense of speech. There also is some correlational evidence in support of the benefits of motherese. A relatively high use of motherese by mothers during infancy and toddlerhood has been found to relate to relatively rapid language gains during early childhood (Furrow, Nelson, & Benedict, 1979).

Just how beneficial motherese is, however, remains controversial (Bohannon & Warren-Leubecker, 1989, in press). The reasons for caution are both empirical and logical. Empirically, the data from correlational studies turn out to be only partially supportive; not all studies report positive relations between motherese and language gains, and when relations do emerge they are generally small. Furthermore, cross-cultural work indicates that motherese is not universal (Schieffelin & Ochs, 1983), yet all children (to repeat a point made earlier) somehow learn language. Theoretically, some linguists have questioned whether motherese is really simplified syntactically; questions and imperatives, for example, are common in motherese, yet in most syntactic analyses such forms are more complex than active declarative sentences (Newport, Gleitman, & Gleitman, 1977). And even if motherese *is* simplified, it is debatable how much such input should really aid language learning; after all, the restriction of forms means that the child is receiving less rather than more information about the structure of language (Wexler, 1982). We therefore repeat our earlier conclusion: probably helpful, but neither necessary nor sufficient.

RESPONSE TO CHILD SPEECH. The work of R. Brown and Hanlon (1970) demonstrated that parents do not typically provide explicit corrections of their children's grammar. Perhaps, however, parents furnish more subtle cues about the structure of language. Parents sometimes expand their children's incomplete utterances into some fully formed adult equivalent. For example, the child's "Throw Daddy" might be reworked into "Throw it to Daddy." Parents also recast their children's utterances into semantically similar expressions that add new information. Thus, "He's going home" might be recast as "He is going home, isn't he?" or "Is that where he's going?" Parents do other things as well, such as prompts, follow-up questions ("You're going where?"), and full or partial repetitions of their own or their children's utterances. There is some evidence, moreover, that parents do these things differentially—that is, that they respond differently to utterances containing grammatical errors than they do to correct utterances (Bohannon & Stanowicz, 1988). For instance, when parents repeat their children's utterances, they tend to leave grammatically correct sentences unchanged but to expand or recast sentences with grammatical flaws. Thus children may receive information both about what is incorrect in their speech and about how to correct it. There is also evidence that children can benefit from such parental practices (Farrar, 1990, 1992).

The data on how parents respond to child speech are relevant to the issue of whether children receive "negative evidence" about the nature of language (Bohannon, MacWhinney, & Snow, 1990; Bohannon & Stanowicz, 1988; Farrar, 1992; P. Gordon, 1990; Pinker, 1989). Children clearly receive "positive evidence" about language—that is, examples (many thousands of examples) of correct linguistic forms. Negative evidence would consist of information about what is *not* correct, about what is *not* a part of language. Parental correction of grammatical errors would fall under the heading of negative evidence. The point of the debate about negative evidence is that how readily language can be learned—and in particular how much innate knowledge must be assumed to make learning possible—depends on whether children have negative as well as positive evidence to work with as they try to make sense of language (M. E. Gold, 1967; Wexler & Culicover, 1980). Our own position on the issue of available evidence is somewhere in between the extremes in either direction. The research of recent years makes clear that children (or, again, *some* children) do receive helpful-looking input—certainly more helpful-looking than nativistically oriented theorists used to claim (Farrar, 1992; Hoff-Ginsberg, 1990; K. E. Nelson, Denniger, Bonvillian, Kaplan, & Baker, 1984; Tomasello, 1992). Helpful is merely helpful, however, and it is still up to the child to perform the task—a very large task by anyone's theory—of transforming this input into knowledge about language. The remainder of this section considers two somewhat different approaches to accounting for the child's contribution to language learning.

The Role of Cognition

Some researchers have attempted to embed language learning within cognitive development in general. By such views, language is but one of many aspects of the world that children come to understand, and the principles that account for cognitive mastery in general should therefore be useful when we attempt to explain the mastery of language in particular. Within this general framework a number of specific positions have been proposed. Here we briefly touch on three.

PIAGET AND LANGUAGE. Piaget's theory offers a number of claims about the cognitive bases for language acquisition (Bates & Snyder, 1985; Piatelli-Palmarini, 1980). Two of these claims are relatively noncontroversial. One concerns the most general cognitive prerequisite for language: the symbolic or semiotic function, that is, the ability to use one thing to refer to something else. As we saw in Chapter 2, Piaget argued that the capacity for representation is not inborn but rather is a developmental achievement of infancy, and that its emergence makes possible not only the use of words but a number of other phenomena of late infancy (object permanence, deferred imitation, symbolic play). The other claim concerns the cognitive bases for the semantics of children's early language. The argument is a straightforward one: Children talk about what they know about, and what they know is what they have mastered during 2 years of sensorimotor development. Gopnik and Meltzoff (1986a, 1986b; Gopnik, 1984, 1988) have demonstrated a number of such cognitive-linguistic links during the one-word stage of language production. They have shown, for example, that words referring to disappearance, such as "gone," emerge at the time that the child is in the process of mastering the most advanced forms of object permanence. Similarly, words denoting the success or failure of actions, such as "there" and "uh-oh," are related to means-ends sorts of achievements in the more general cognitive realm. Roger Brown (1973) has offered a similar analysis with regard to the set of core meanings (agent-action, action-object, etc.) that we saw characterize children's earliest sentences. Brown argues that these characteristic early meanings reflect the cognitive achievements of the sensorimotor period—knowledge about objects and the effects of actions on objects, about spatial and causal relations, about self and world.

The Piagetian approach is strongest with respect to the questions of how children can use words at all (symbolic ability makes it possible) and why they use the particular words and convey the particular meanings that they do. It is weakest with respect to the specific topic of the current section: how children master syntactic rules. Despite efforts by workers in the Piagetian tradition (see, in particular, Bates & Snyder, 1985), no plausible Piagetian account of the acquisition of syntax has ever been forthcoming. A major obstacle to constructing such an account has always been that the prime period for language growth—the years between 2 and 4—is characterized in such negative, can't-yet-do terms in Piagetian theory. As earlier chapters make clear, our views of the "preoperational" child have grown progressively more positive in recent years, and it may be that newer models of preschoolers' abilities can provide a better explanation for language than does Piaget. Thus far, however, there still seems to be a gap:

Nothing that 2- or 3-year-olds have been shown to do in the general cognitive realm seems very close to their extraordinary facility at mastering syntax.

INFORMATION PROCESSING. At present, the most influential attempt to explain language development from the point of view of information-processing theory is the MacWhinney and Bates Competition Model (Bates & MacWhinney, 1987; MacWhinney, 1987a, 1989). Several emphases characterize the Competition Model. One is an emphasis on the functional aspect of language. Language evolved to serve a variety of pragmatic purposes, and the structure that it eventually attained (e.g., the form of syntactic rules) is assumed to reflect these functional origins. Similarly, children's language serves a variety of pragmatic goals (asserting, denying, requesting, sharing information, bonding with others, etc.) from the start, and children learn forms that help them to achieve these goals. An emphasis on the functional nature of language is decidely *not* a characteristic of the more nativistic approaches that we consider in the final section of the chapter.

A second emphasis of the Competition Model is on the variety of kinds of information that must be simultaneously processed and represented for language to perform the functions that it does. Even to produce a simple sentence like "Doggie runned," the child must deal simultaneously with lexical information that governs the choice of words to convey actor and action, phonological information that determines how these words will be pronounced, and syntactic information that determines the way in which the words will be ordered and the selection of the past-tense ending. An emphasis on the multiplicity of processes that underlie cognitive activity, as well as the simultaneous execution ("parallel processing") of many of these processes, is a general characteristic of the information-processing approach.

A final emphasis concerns the "competition" part of the Competition Model. Execution of the numerous processes that underlie language use is complicated by the fact that there are always multiple alternatives at every point in the decision process. "Doggie," for example, may have to compete with "kitty" and other labels for similar-appearing animals, and the "-ed" ending on "run" may have to compete with the frequently heard "ran." The child's past experience will have given these different possibilities different activation strengths in any particular context, and the alternative selected will be the one with the greatest immediate strength. Development occurs as the child's experience in hearing and producing language leads to changes in activation strength. Eventually, for example, "kitty" will become a very low-probability response in the presence of a dog; at the same time, the childish "doggie" will be supplanted by "dog," and more specific labels ("spaniel," "Spot," etc.) will come to the fore in particular contexts. A variety of aspects of the speech input can be important in directing such change, including the availability of a cue (frequently available cues, such as the "-ed" ending, will be more influential than less frequent cues), the detectability of the cue (the more detectable, the more influential), and the reliability of the cue in signaling the linguistic form of interest (the more reliable, the more influential). This analysis can explain why it is, for example, that children's mastery of the past tense typically begins with a few directly learned irregular forms (such as "ran"), then moves to a phase of overgeneralization once the regular form has been learned (thus "runned"), and ends finally with the correct division into regular and irregular forms.

Several features of the information-processing approach are evident in the Competition Model. We have already mentioned the emphasis on multiple underlying processes, all being executed in parallel. The computer simulation methodology is represented; much of the evidence for the model comes from demonstrations that computers can be programmed to operate on the sorts of input available to children and form the same sorts of rules that children form. The Competition Model has a quantitative bent that is characteristic of information processing in general; rather than focusing on mastery of qualitatively distinct, present or absent rules, the theory stresses the gradual adjustment of response strength among multiply available possibilities. Most generally, the theory represents an attempt to embed language learning within information processing as a whole: to explain the acquisition of language through the application of general (and very powerful) information-processing mechanisms to the linguistic input available to any child.

The Competition Model is a relatively new entry in the language acquisition field, and its testing and evaluation are therefore still in the future (for discussions of possible limitations, see Bohannon & Warren-Leubecker, 1989, and Bowerman, 1987). As we will see in the concluding section of the chapter, there is good reason to believe that very strong and specific forms of biological pretuning underlie the development of language, and therefore also good reason to be dubious about any theory, such as the Competition Model, that takes a primarily empiricist, general-learning-mechanisms approach to the problem. Nevertheless, the theory represents an interesting attempt to probe the extent to which such mechanisms really can account for language acquisition.

SEMANTIC BOOTSTRAPPING. One of the mysteries of language development is how children acquire abstract syntactic knowledge that does not seem to have a clear basis in either the linguistic input available to them or general cognitive development. Semantic acquisitions, in contrast, seem relatively easy to explain. Such acquisitions can be tied to experiences that are common to all infants (such as acting upon objects), and the form of early semantic knowledge seems clearly related to the form of early intelligence. Furthermore, the evidence that children are working with semantic categories and relations in the earliest phases of sentence production is stronger than the evidence that they are working with syntactic categories and relations. Perhaps, some researchers have argued, syntactic understanding builds upon earlier-developing semantic understanding. Perhaps, to use a bit of computer terminology, it is semantics that "boots" the syntactic system into operation.

Pinker (1984, 1987) is the theorist who has developed this position most fully. A simplified version of his argument is the following. Children can learn the meanings of individual words prior to mastering much if any of the syntactic system of their language. They can then use these meanings, along with contextual information, to arrive at a semantic interpretation of many sentences, again without knowing much if any syntax. Once certain basic semantic categories and relations have been worked out, the child can exploit the correlations that exist in every language between semantic concepts and syntactic concepts. Names of objects or people, for example, are universally nouns; thus the child who has noted how names are used in sentences can use this information to begin to figure out how nouns in general are used. Similarly, agents of transitive action verbs are invariably the subjects of sentences; thus the young child who has mastered agent-action-object relations (and recall that all young children do master such relations) can begin to identify the syntactic subject. It is through noting such associations that children gradually extract syntactic knowledge from their previously developed conceptual and semantic knowledge.

The gist of the bootstrapping approach is that semantics provides a starting point for syntax. It is important to add, however, that semantics is only a starting point. As we noted earlier, the correlation between semantics and syntax is an imperfect one; not all nouns are names of objects, for example, just as not all subjects are agents. To master fully an abstract category such as noun, the child must go beyond the initial dependence on meaning and begin to utilize purely syntactic-distributional information (he or she might note, for example, that "truth" and "beauty" can appear in the same slots within sentences as "dog" and "car"). Furthermore, there is no assumption in such an approach that the combination of linguistic input and general cognitive development is sufficient to explain the acquisition of syntax. Just the opposite, in fact. Semantic bootstrapping is assumed to work in conjunction with powerful innate constraints concerning the form that syntax can take (knowledge that there is such a category as nouns, for example) and the ways in which semantics and syntax can relate. Semantics may "boot" the syntactic system into operation, but syntax is by no means reducible to semantics. Our final section deals more generally with the idea that syntactic development simply cannot be explained without the assumption of a strong innate contribution.

The Role of Biology

Evidence and arguments of a variety of sorts converge on the conclusion that language acquisition has a strong biological-maturational component (Newport, 1990; Pinker, 1989). Such arguments do not deny a role for experience or for cognitive abilities, but they do maintain that such explanations are far from sufficient.

BIOLOGICAL PRETUNING. We seem to be biologically constructed to learn and use oral language of the human type. The human brain and articulatory apparatus are specialized for producing rapid and extended streams of human speech sounds. There is also some left-hemisphere specialization in the brain for the analysis of language-like input, specialization that may be evident as early as birth (Prescott & DeCasper, 1990). We are also biologically programmed to attend to and analyze the speech sounds we hear. We seem biologically prepared for language learning in rather the same way we are biologically prepared for perceptual and motor-skill learning. We are strongly disposed to do all three and are born with powerful, specialized tools for doing them. That is, evolution has provided us with an indispensable head start or leg up for such learning.

MATURATION. Language development has properties that suggest the workings of an endogenous, maturation-like process. Children the world over go through roughly the same major stages of language acquisition, in the same order, and at approximately the same ages. They do not, to be sure, do so in completely identical fashion, as our earlier discussions of individual differences indicated (and some contemporary workers would emphasize these differences more than we have done). Nevertheless, there appears to be a core of fundamental similarity within which the variations occur.

The similarities are even more remarkable when they occur despite obvious differences in experience. Goldin-Meadow and her co-workers (Goldin-Meadow, 1979) observed six young deaf children whose parents had normal hearing and did not know the sign-language system used by the deaf. Thus, these children did not receive input from any complex linguistic system, oral or manual, and consequently had no opportunity even to learn what human language systems are like. But biology was not to be denied in this instance: These children nevertheless proceeded to develop their own gestural sign language, and in the normal human sequence—first one-sign utterances, then two-sign ones, then longer ones. Moreover, their multisign utterances made use of sign order to specify meaning, a very common device in human languages. For example, the children would consistently produce the sign for the recipient of an object after the sign for the object received, analogous to "book Mother," when the book was to be given to Mother. The children did not demonstrate all the syntactic devices that are common in oral language, for some aspects of syntax seem to be more dependent on specific input—less "resilient," in Goldin-Meadow's terms—than others (Goldin-Meadow, 1982). Nevertheless, it is hard to disagree with Goldin-Meadow's (1979) conclusions that "Even under adverse circumstances, the human child has the natural inclination and the capacity to develop a structured communication system" (p. 186), and that "It may not be unreasonable to suppose that the child, hearing or deaf, brings to the language learning situation certain predispositions which narrow down the field of potential languages to be acquired" (p. 186).

Evidence for such maturationally given predispositions comes as well from studies of the optimal age period for learning language. Most things, of course, are learned better by older children than by younger ones, and better by adults than by children. Not so language. Johnson and Newport (1989) examined the English facility of 46 Chinese and Korean speakers who had emigrated to the United States and learned English as a second language. Age of arrival in the United States, and thus time of first exposure to English, ranged from 3 to 39 years. Johnson and Newport found a strong linear relation between age of exposure and mastery of syntax—that is, the earlier the learning of English began, the fuller the eventual mastery proved to be. This relation held even when other potentially important factors, such as total amount of exposure, were controlled. It held, however, only up until puberty; the limited learning shown by adult immigrants was unrelated to age. Johnson and Newport summarize this surprising pattern of results as follows: "It appears as if language learning ability slowly declines as the human matures, and plateaus at a low level after puberty" (p. 90). It is important to add that greater childhood facility is not limited to second-language learning but applies to first-language acquisition as well. It has been shown, for example, for deaf individuals who are first exposed to American Sign Language at varying points in life (Newport & Supalla, 1990); that is, those who learn it earliest learn it best.

The age-dependent nature of language learning is also evident in case-history reports of individuals who were deprived of normal linguistic input during childhood. For example, Curtiss (1988) reports the case of Chelsea, a deaf woman who—because of her deafness and her family's isolation—grew up without any exposure to a formal language system, either oral or gestural. Chelsea was finally provided with hearing aids when she was 32 years old, at which time intensive language training was begun. Despite much effort across many years, Chelsea's mastery of language remains well short of that routinely achieved in a much briefer time span by any child.

Why should the younger, less mature brain be better at learning language than the older and generally more powerful brain? No one knows for sure, but Newport (1988, 1990) suggests an intriguing hypothesis. The gist of her proposal is that developmental improvements in cognitive ability actually work *against* language learning. They work against language learning because the mature cognitive system, in effect, takes in and retains too much information. Acquisition of syntax requires the ability to analyze the speech stream into the components (morphemes, inflections, clauses, etc.) that convey meaning—requires the ability to deal with pieces and not just unanalyzed wholes. Children—or so Newport argues—are in a favorable position to identify components because pieces are often all they can take in; their limited information-processing abilities save them from the overly inclusive, unanalyzed-wholes sorts of processing that impede language learning in adults. This provocative explanation for childhood superiority is aptly named the "Less is More" hypothesis.

INDEPENDENCE OF LANGUAGE AND INTELLIGENCE. If language is a reflection of cognition in general, then we would expect to find a close relation between linguistic ability and general intellectual ability. In particular, we would expect to find that problems in one domain are paralleled by problems in the other—for example, that general mental retardation is accompanied by greatly lowered linguistic abilities. Such, to be sure, is often the case. But it is by no means always the case—language development sometimes proceeds remarkably well in the face of severe intellectual problems; conversely, in some clinical syndromes language is greatly impaired yet general intelligence remains intact. Either sort of disassociation provides evidence that language is not reducible to cognition in general but rather has its own special, perhaps modular, status.

Recent work on Williams syndrome provides an example (Pinker, 1991; Reilly, Klima, & Bellugi, 1990). Williams syndrome is a rare metabolic neurodevelopmental disorder that results in mental retardation. Individuals with Williams syndrome typically perform poorly on a wide range of cognitive tasks, including measures of linguistic competence that appear dependent on general intellectual ability (e.g., memorization of irregular past tense verbs). Yet their mastery of other aspects of language, including basic syntactic rules, is typically at normal or close-to-normal levels, as is their ability to use language for communicative and affective purposes. In this respect, they show an interesting contrast not only with other categories of retardation (e.g., Down syndrome) but also with autistic children. As we saw in the discussion of theory of mind in Chapter 3, autistic children have a very specific, almost certainly biologically based, deficit in certain areas of social understanding and social interaction. With Williams syndrome, social/affective and linguistic processes remain intact, yet many other aspects of cognitive functioning are impaired. In both cases, the pattern of outcomes suggests a mind composed of many separate, biologically prepared abilities, rather than a single, all-purpose cognitive automaton.

UNIVERSALITY. Just as there are similarities among children the world over as they go about the task of learning language, so are there similarities among the many different languages that are so learned. The most basic similarity is the existence of a rich, grammatically complex language in every human society. Human language is species-wide or universal. Human language is also species-specific; although other species have systems of communication, some quite intricate, none of them closely resembles human language. Of particular relevance to the present argument is the fact that none has a rule-governed, productive syntax of the type found in all human natural languages. There are, moreover, important properties that all of the world's many languages have in common (Clark & Clark, 1977; Slobin, 1985). All, for example, draw from the same pool of possible sounds when forming words, and all show similar restrictions with respect to which types of syntactic rules are or are not possible. The existence of such common properties, or "linguistic universals," is, in fact, a necessary prediction of any biologically oriented account of language development. No one believes that children are prepared by evolution to learn English or Japanese; whatever biological pretuning there may be must work for any language that the child happens to encounter—which means that all languages must be alike in certain fundamental ways. The evidence suggests that all languages *are* alike in fundamental ways.

NATIVISTIC THEORY. The general theoretical tradition within which biologically oriented approaches fall is labeled *nativism*, and the theorist most associated with the nativistic view of language is Noam Chomsky (e.g., 1972, 1981). A rough and simplified version of Chomsky's argument is the following:

1. The grammatical structure of any human language is extremely complex.
2. Clear clues to this complex structure are surprisingly lacking in the utterances children hear. In consequence, an infinite number of different grammars could be induced or inferred from these utterances by a grammar-learning device that was not specifically designed by nature to look for only certain kinds—namely, those found in human languages.
3. Since children do succeed in acquiring the correct grammar in a few short years, they must have such specific design features. They must bring to their learning task the functional equivalent of specific, innately given ideas and expectations about the general kinds of grammatical rules and structures they will find.

The idea that evolution has provided us with language-learning equipment *that* powerful and specific seemed highly implausible to most of us when Chomsky first proposed it, and it still seems farfetched to many. Various alternative positions, however, also tend to seem implausible, or at least incomplete, when examined carefully; certainly no one has yet demonstrated that language acquisition can be explained without positing an important biological contribution. It seems to us, in fact (although others might disagree), that nativistic thinking is gradually inching its way back into favor, after a decade or so of attempts to explain language learning in other ways. Certainly, nativistic approaches to general cognitive development (modularity, constraints, etc.) are more common than was true 15 to 20 years ago.

In any case, it is one thing to favor Chomsky's or some other general stance on the issue and quite another to formulate a detailed and specific theory of language acquisition. One criticism of the nativistic approach has always concerned its lack of specificity: No theorist has explained how—through what experiences and what processes—children transform their innately given knowledge about the universal features of language into specific knowledge about the particular language they are acquiring. Fortunately, such efforts are beginning to appear (Hyams, 1986; Pinker, 1984, 1989; R. Stevenson, 1988; Wexler, 1982). The work on semantic bootstrapping, for example, represents one attempt to capture the interplay of innate knowledge about the possible forms that language can take and more language-specific experiences and acquisitions. There is also interesting work (too complex, alas, for us to do more than mention) that falls under the heading of "learnability": mathematical analyses of the extent to which language is learnable, given assumptions about the input available to the child (it is here that the issue of negative evidence becomes relevant) and the nature of the language being learned (Wexler, 1982; Wexler & Manzini, 1987). One outcome of such analyses is a specification of which aspects of language are not learnable on the basis of the available evidence and hence must be innate.

Efforts such as these represent a promising start. They are, however, just a start, and much remains to be learned. The manner in which young children acquire language is still, to borrow from Winston Churchill, "a riddle wrapped in a mystery inside an enigma."

SUMMARY

Thanks to the work of Chomsky and others, we now recognize that the native speaker of any human language commands astonishingly rich systems of knowledge and skills. Our picture of the childhood acquisition of these systems is also becoming correspondingly rich, and the field of language development is currently one of the most exciting areas in developmental psychology.

The developmental story begins before the advent of language. Phonological and communicative acquisitions during infancy precede and prepare the way for the acquisition of language. Human babies appear to be biologically primed to respond to human speech. Babies are interested in and responsive to speech from early in life, especially speech from familiar speakers (such as the mother) and especially speech that takes the highly intonated form known as *motherese*. Infants are also skilled at making discriminations among different speech sounds. Unlike the perception of most things, perception of speech sounds in adults is discontinuous or *categorical* rather than continuous. Studies have shown that infants as young as 1 month also perceive sounds categorically, an innately given capability that should aid greatly in learning language. Biological-maturational factors also contribute to the infant's ability to produce speech sounds—in particular, to the onset and developmental course of prelinguistic *babbling*. Although the issue is still not resolved, recent evidence suggests that babbling may play a functional role with respect to later language development. Continuity has been more clearly established in the realm of communication, where various acquisitions of infancy prefigure eventual linguistic communication. Such prelinguistic communication achievements include the ability to direct and "read" another person's attention, to produce preverbal forms of *speech acts* such as requests and assertions, and to take turns in nonverbal "conversations."

Children usually begin to produce recognizable words sometime around their first birthday. Children's first words typically refer to salient and familiar objects and events, and they tend to be at an intermediate, so-called basic, level of generality (e.g., "dog" rather than "spaniel" or "animal"). When first learning a new word, children may attach a somewhat different meaning to it than do adults. *Overextensions* (e.g., the use of "dog" to refer to all animals) are common, although less so in comprehension (which is generally more advanced) than in production. *Underextensions* (e.g., "dog" refers only to the family dog) and *complexive* (unstable, shifting) word meanings are also found, as are original coinages, in which the child invents a word to fill a lexical gap. Although children in this period may well be trying to express more meaning than their single-word utterances suggest, it is debatable whether these utterances should be thought of as one-word "sentences."

Among the functions served by language is expression of emotion. Evidence indicates that language and emotion may at first compete for resources in the young child, and that it is only gradually that children come to be able to integrate production of speech with expression of emotion.

Two-word utterances often begin to appear at about 18 months of age. These telegram-like expressions ("more milk," "Mommy kiss," etc.) are remarkably similar in form and meaning the world over. The occurrence of novel utterances (e.g., "Allgone sticky") tells us that even children's earliest sentences are creative, rule-based constructions. Nonetheless, questions remain as to how much and what kind of *semantic* (linguistic meaning) and *syntactic* (grammatical structure) knowledge we should attribute to the child in this period.

Important advances in both syntax and semantics are made subsequent to this period. Children develop *grammatical morphemes* (function words like "in," *inflections* like the past-tense "-ed" ending on verb stems) in a systematic order that is probably determined by their cognitive-processing complexity. Children's acquisition of inflections illustrates their active propensity for testing hypotheses and searching for rules when learning language. For example, we may see developmental sequences such as irregular "feet" alone, followed by regular, rule-governed "foots" alternating with "feet," followed by "feet" alone again. Other grammatical acquisitions concern negations, *wh* questions, and methods of combining simple sentences to make more complicated ones. Semantic advances beyond the two-word period include both improvements in the ability to convey meanings through the combination of words and refinements in the meanings of individual words. A discussion of children's mastery of relational words illustrates the fact that word learning is a multidetermined—and still far from perfectly understood—process.

Children's communication abilities also show dramatic improvements across childhood. Communication skills that develop during the preschool years include the ability to sustain a conversation on a single topic, to discuss the nonpresent and non-real, to infer what is presupposed and implied from what is explicitly said, and to adapt one's speech production and comprehension to numerous properties of speakers, listeners, and social settings. Impressive as these skills are, however, research on *metacommunication* (knowledge and cognition concerning communications) suggests that children of kindergarten age and older still have some important communicative development ahead of them. They need to learn to monitor their own comprehension and to recognize the meaning and implications of feelings of uncertainty or lack of understanding. They need to learn that the communicative quality of a message affects its communicative success, and that referentially ambiguous messages are in many situations communicatively inadequate. Such metacommunicative knowledge and skill relate to general changes in children's understanding of mental states or theory of mind. They may also be helped along by particular experiences, such as peer interaction, parental tuition, and school instruction.

A full account of children's language must include not only a description of important developmental changes but also an explanation for those changes. Attempts to explain the acquisition of word meaning have had to confront the Quinean puzzle: There are always an indefinite number of logically possible meanings for a word, yet children somehow focus quickly on the one actual meaning. Studies of *fast mapping* confirm that discovery of a word's core nature (if not its full meaning) is often a rapid process, and that children exploit a variety of cues when they infer meaning. Many researchers believe that word learning is guided by a set of *constraints* concerning what are and what are not possible meanings for words. Among the constraints that have been proposed are Object Scope (words label whole objects), the Taxonomic Assumption (words label objects from the same taxonomic category), and Mutual Exclusivity (each object has only one label). Although children's adherence to such principles is not as rigid as the term "constraint" might imply, they do seem to use tacit beliefs of various sorts to guide their hypotheses about word meaning.

Explaining the acquisition of syntax has been the primary theoretical goal of most researchers of language development. The role of the environment in grammatical acquisition does not seem to be as direct and specific as was once believed. Children do not appear to master syntax by imitating others, by being reinforced for correct speech, or by a combination of imitation and reinforcement. Other sorts of environmental assistance may play a role; among the parental practices that have been examined are preverbal dialogues in infancy, the use of motherese when talking to the child, and provision of feedback in the form of expansions and recasts. Evidence suggests, however, that such practices are at best helpful; they have not been shown to be either necessary for learning to occur or sufficient to explain how the child acquires so much syntactic knowledge so quickly.

Whatever help the environment may provide, the role of the child in his or her own syntactic development must be an extremely active and powerful one. Some theorists have attempted to embed the mastery of syntax within more general cognitive development. Piagetian-oriented approaches are most persuasive in their discussions of symbolic ability as a prerequisite for the use of words and of sensorimotor achievements as an explanation for the meanings expressed in early speech. Such approaches are least successful in their attempts to explain syntax, for they have not yet resolved the evident gap between the limited cognitive abilities of the young child and the very powerful language-learning capacities of that same child. A more influential cognitive approach at present is the MacWhinney and Bates Competition Model, the grounding for which is in information-processing theory and research. In the Competition Model, the activation strengths of competing linguistic forms (e.g., different forms of the past tense) are gradually adjusted over time through the application of general information-processing mechanisms to the available linguistic input. Another approach to cognition-language links is found in work on *semantic bootstrapping*, the basic idea of which is that young children use their already-developed semantic knowledge as a guide to the syntactic structure of the language they are learning.

Although the bootstrapping approach implicates general cognitive understanding, it also includes a role for innately given knowledge about the possible structure of language. More generally, a variety of considerations, both theoretical and empirical, converge on the conclusion that language acquisition has a substantial innate basis. Human children appear to be biologically equipped to acquire language of the human type; they encounter languages of rich and complex (and in part similar) grammatical structure in every human society; and they acquire such languages in an inexorable, age- and stage-related fashion that does not appear—given our current, admittedly imperfect understanding—to be explicable on experiential bases but rather looks to be strongly maturational.

Questions
and Problems

Most textbooks fail to give the reader an insider's view of the field they cover. A field looks very different to an insider—a "pro"—than it does to an outsider. Insiders continually live with its numerous questions, problems, ambiguities, and uncertainties. They become used to, although never unconcerned about, its untidy, open-ended, no-problem-ever-seems-to-get-solved character. They know how incredibly difficult it is even to think up a research study that will tell us something we really want to know. Most therefore have a healthy modesty with regard to their own such efforts, as well as a healthy skepticism with regard to the claims of others. More positively, they also have a genuine appreciation for work that manages to surmount the problems and tell us things that are really worth knowing.

The aim of this chapter is to present some of the questions and problems you would live with if you were an insider in the field of cognitive growth. By implication, the aim is also to make you feel more insecure and skeptical about everything you have read in previous chapters. We can imagine two reactions that different readers might have to the content of this chapter, depending upon their backgrounds and interests. One is that finally, at long last, we are getting into the *real* issues. The authors have finished describing all the different ways that kids get smarter as they grow older and will now get into more substantive matters. As the section headings indicate, they now talk about how to assess or diagnose the child's cognitive level, about the sorts of systematic patterns (sequences, stages) it exhibits, and about how cognitive growth may be explained rather than just described. They, in short, are trying to tie it all together, provide an overview and perspective, show us What It All Means. The other reaction is that things have suddenly gotten very abstract and hard to follow. The child's cognitive development is now populated with false positives, underlying processes, cognitive entities, structures, concurrences, qualitative changes, and other intangibles. Where did the child go?

Both reactions are perfectly understandable and reasonable. To those who have the first reaction, we would suggest only that even the purely descriptive aspects of cognitive development are scientifically important, and also that—the insider's plight once again—those real issues and substantive matters are going to look very messy, very far from being resolved. To those with the second reaction, we would suggest that you either skip this chapter altogether (if that option is open to you) or else read it in a special way. The special way is to let it wash over you, trying only to get the main points. Above all, try to get a sense or feeling for how cognitive growth might proceed—or more accurately, for the *alternative* conceptions of how cognitive growth might proceed. Try, in other words, to get some sort of wide-angle view of the cognitive-developmental panorama, including the outstanding questions and problems concerning it. Regardless of which of the two reactions you may have, if either, providing you with such a view is one of the main objectives of this chapter.

DIAGNOSIS

What problems and issues do psychologists face in trying to diagnose or analyze children's developing knowledge and abilities? They are many, varied, and very, very troublesome. Discussions of these problems and issues can be found in, for example, A. L. Brown (1983), Chandler and Chapman (1991), Fischer and Bidell (1991), Flavell (1971c), Flavell and Wohlwill (1969), R. Gold (1987), S. A. Miller (1976), and Smedslund (1969).

What is involved in cognitive-developmental diagnosis can best be communicated with reference to a specific example. Transitive inference is a concrete-operational acquisition within Piaget's theoretical system. As mentioned in Chapter 4 ("Improvement in Existing Competencies" section), one form of it is conceived by Piaget as consisting of this type of reasoning process: If A > B (e.g., A is longer than B) and B > C, then it has to be true that A > C—no measurement is necessary. Developmental psychologists may ask two sorts of questions about this or any other cognitive acquisition. They both involve "diagnosis," but in somewhat different senses. One has to do with our *conceptualization* of the acquisition itself, the other with its *assessment* in children.

Conceptualization questions ask what this ability or behavior we call transitive inference consists of, in psychological terms. What are the cognitive processes that actually underlie or comprise acts of so-called transitive inference? What, exactly, happens inside the individual's head when, given A > B, B > C, and A ? C, he or she responds A > C? In short, *what* develops when transitive inference develops?

Assessment questions apply once we have decided on a tentative answer to the conceptualization question. Suppose we provisionally accept someone's (e.g., Piaget's) characterization of what transitive inference is. The question that then arises is how can we determine (assess) whether a given child has or has not acquired transitive inference. This question *is* a question because there are always numerous possible ways of assessing any cognitive target of interest. Clearly our answer to the conceptualization question will guide selection among these possibilities, but there will still be much to decide. In the case of transitivity, the researcher would have to decide (among other decisions) what sorts of stimuli to use, which particular comparisons to present, how to word the transitivity question, and whether to require a logical explanation as well as a correct answer before crediting the child with an understanding of the concept. Other cognitive acquisitions offer a similar range of assessment options.

If children were perfectly consistent in their response to different assessment techniques, then the choice of technique would not really matter—our conclusions would be the same whatever approach we took. They are not, however. Consider the transitivity example again. If children were perfectly consistent in their performance on transitivity problems, then we would find two patterns of response. Some children would succeed on every version of the transitivity task that we might present, and other children would fail on every version. The first group of children would clearly "have" transitivity, and the second group would very probably "not have" it ("very probably" rather than "clearly" because it is always possible that some understanding exists but that it is too underdeveloped to be expressed on even the simplest-seeming task that we have yet been able to devise). In fact, however, in addition to these two extreme types we find all sorts of in-between patterns of performance: children who succeed on some versions of the task but not cn others, and who thus seem sometimes to "have" the concept and other times to "not have" it. We find such heterogeneity, moreover, not just for transitivity but for all sorts of other Piagetian and non-Piagetian cognitive achievements.

What theoretical sense can we make of this untidy state of affairs? Will we need to distinguish several, or even many, different kinds or degrees of "having transitive inference"? If so, how should such distinctions be drawn? Perhaps the several or many we distinguish will line up nicely to form an orderly developmental sequence or progression. That is, we might theoretically define a "beginning" kind (degree? amount?) of capability for transitive inference, followed by a "more advanced" one (in what way?), and so on, until a "completely mature" (in what sense?) capability is achieved. But if we think of transitive inference as more like a developmental succession of different things than like a unitary, present or absent cognitive entity, we find ourselves confronting the conceptualization form of the diagnosis question once again. The conceptualization question, you will recall, asks what cognitive processes actually make up or underlie transitive inferences. However, if transitive inference changes with age, then those cognitive processes must also change with age.

To recapitulate, we begin with a preliminary, working notion of what transitive inference is (conceptualization questions). We then try to find ways to diagnose accurately its presence/absence in the child's task performance (assessment questions). The best available diagnostic procedures suggest that, for many children, it is present sometimes and absent sometimes, depending upon the specifics of the task situation and perhaps other factors. Then we try to make developmental sense out of this lack of consistency, perhaps by hypothesizing an ontogenetic progression of different forms (degrees, or whatever) of transitive-inference-related capabilities. The existence of such a progression implies that these capabilities must change in some way from one point in that progression to another, and, therefore, so also must the nature and/or organization of the cognitive processes underlying them (back to conceptualization problems again). Let us now examine this diagnostic cycle in more detail, beginning with questions of assessment.

Assessment Questions

We begin with the simplifying assumption that a child either does or does not possess the ability to make a transitive inference—with no gradations in between—and that our diagnostic goal is to find out which is the case for an individual child. There are two ways in which our diagnostic efforts might go astray. One possibility is that the child really does possess the ability but gives no evidence of it in his or her performance on the particular measure we have selected. An underestimation error of this sort is labeled a *false-negative* diagnostic error. Alternatively, the child may not really understand transitive inference, but the testing procedures may lead to the false conclusion that he or she does. An overestimation error of this sort would be a *false-positive* diagnostic error.

False-negative errors can occur for a number of reasons. The child might fail to understand the task instructions, fail to attend to or comprehend the premises of the inference (i.e., the fact that A > B and B > C), or forget either the instructions or the premises at the moment when the inference normally would be made. Such failures of attention or memory may be especially likely if the information-processing demands of the task challenge the child's limited resources, hence making execution of the full problem-solving sequence effortful. The task may for some reason elicit from the child a problem-solving approach or strategy that is incompatible with transitive inference. For instance, having just learned through perception rather than inference that A > B and B > C, the child may assume that A ? C must also be solved by perception rather than inference. The child's true ability can also be masked by motivational and emotional factors, such as lack of interest in the "game," or apprehension about the experimenter as an adult stranger. Some cognitive tasks require the child to generate a complex verbal response (e.g., an explanation) so as to demonstrate the cognitive ability in which the examiner is interested; the child may be incapable of generating the verbal response and yet possess the cognitive ability. Every task demands from the child knowledge and skills other than, and in addition to, the target concept or ability it was designed to tap. If the child does not or cannot meet any of these additional, nontarget demands, a false-negative diagnostic error can result.

False-positive diagnostic errors can also stem from several causes. Under certain task conditions, the child may get the right answer by guessing, by direct perception of A > C, or by using some irrelevant (i.e., nontransitive-inference) solution strategy that happens to yield the A > C conclusion. One such strategy that has been identified stems from the young child's frequent tendency to think in absolute (e.g., "A is *long*") rather than relative or comparative terms (e.g., "A is *longer than* B"). The child may code the premises A > B and B > C as something like "A is long, B isn't," and "B is long, C isn't," respectively. Since in this coding, A has been thought of as "long" once but C never has, for this reason the child may tend to choose A when asked which is "longer." The answer is, of course, correct, but it was not generated by transitive inference.

Researchers have thought of various ways to reduce the likelihood of false-positive errors. In the case of transitivity, it is possible to minimize perceptually based solutions by disguising the A-C relation—for example, by showing sticks A and C on a background of Müller-Lyer arrows, which creates the illusion that C is longer than A rather than vice versa. The possibility of absolute ("A is long") solutions can be ruled out by increasing the number of stimuli and comparisons. Suppose we give the child this transitive-inference problem: Given that A > B, B > C, C > D, D > E, what is the length relation between B and D? Since both B and D have been shown to be longer than one thing and shorter than another in this problem, the child cannot get the answer right by using the strategy of coding relative terms as absolutes; both B and D have had a chance to be coded as "long." Also, we can reduce markedly the chances of making a false-positive diagnostic error by requiring the child to explain or justify his or her A > C conclusion. An answer such as "A *has* to be longer than C because it is longer than B, and even B is longer than C" could hardly emanate from a child who had no understanding of the transitivity rule. The requirement of a logical explanation is a criterion that has long been used to reduce false positives not just on transitivity but on a wide range of tasks.

But the reduction of false positives is very likely to result in an increase in false negatives. It is not hard to conceive of a child who would not fare at all well on these more stringent tests, while yet possessing at least some genuine capability for transitive inference. And indeed, we know that such across-task variability in performance in fact obtains: We often find an extended period in the development of a concept during which children succeed on simplified measures of the concept but fail on more rigorous measures. Some of this variability no doubt reflects diagnostic error in one direction or the other: overestimation of ability from the use of simplified tasks that fail to tap the target concept; underestimation of ability from the use of complex tasks that obscure genuine knowledge. We suspect, however, that much of the variability reflects not diagnostic error but the nature of development, and the fact—contra the simplifying assumption with which we began this section—that for many concepts there are a number of intermediate levels of understanding between total absence and full mastery. And so our assessment efforts, which began with some conceptualization of the underlying target, lead back to issues of conceptualization. How should we conceptualize these different levels of understanding?

Conceptualization Questions

The following is one way to think about the different possible meanings and manners of "having" a concept like transitive inference (see also Chapter 4, "Improvement in Existing Competencies" section). Further discussion can be found in A. L. Brown (1983), A. L. Brown et al. (1983), Flavell (1971c), Greeno et al. (1984), and various chapters in Chandler and Chapman (1991).

Let us imagine two children—A and B—both of whom have some understanding of transitive inference. There are various (no doubt related) ways in which A's understanding might be more advanced than B's. The knowledge may be more available to A than to B—that is, more readily called into play in situations that require transitive inference. In this case the knowledge is "in there somewhere" for both children, but B is less likely to evoke it when appropriate than is A. We discussed various reasons in the "Assessment" section above that children might fail to reveal knowledge they possess, and there are doubtless many others as well, especially for recently acquired and hence still fragile competencies. Even if transitive inference *is* evoked, B may be less able to execute a chain of inferential reasoning than is A. Knowing what *should* be done and attempting to do it is no guarantee that the attempt will be successful, again especially in the case of newly acquired abilities. We have seen numerous examples throughout this text of divergence between attempt and outcome in children's cognitive performance (e.g., knowledge of counting principles and actual counting behavior, evocation of an appropriate mnemonic strategy and execution of that strategy).

Child A and child B may also differ in the range of situations in which their knowledge can be applied. There may be expertise-related domain differences, with each child demonstrating the knowledge only in situations in which he or she has sufficient experience. Or there may be more general differences in range of applicability. B may be capable of transitive inference in only one or a few specific situations or types of problem, whereas A's knowledge might be applicable to any transitivity problem that comes along. Undoubtedly an important contributor to range of application is the dimension of problem complexity. Although the argument is sometimes hard to formulate in noncircular terms, it seems reasonable to believe that competencies are first expressed in relatively simple situations and only gradually extended to more complex ones. In the case of transitivity, successful solution might be limited at first to three-term problems with consistent relations (e.g., all "equals" or all "greater thans") and no countervailing perceptual illusions. Ability to solve problems without these simplifying features would come only later. Again, we have seen a number of examples of such a simple-to-complex progression. For example, children's counting skills may be limited at first to small sets of objects, with ability to handle larger sets coming some time later. Similarly, children's ability to conserve number may at first be limited to small sets.

Children may also differ in response to social support—for instance, help from a parent or teacher. B may be less advanced than A in the sense of being more dependent on such support; B may require some degree of assistance to accomplish what A can do on his own. Or A and B may differ in their ability to profit from social support; perhaps A can use such support to go well beyond his independent efforts, whereas B is unable to gain much at all from instruction. Recall that this ability to profit from instruction is at the core of Vygotsky's notion of the zone of proximal development. If we add social context to our assessment efforts, we undoubtedly will pick up differences in children's abilities that are not evident from independent problem-solving alone.

Still further differences between A and B might concern the status that the concept of transitive inference holds in the child's thinking. For child B the knowledge of transitivity might be completely implicit—a kind of procedural knowledge that guides response in certain situations but of which the child is quite unaware. For child A, in contrast, the knowledge may have become explicit—something that can be thought about, verbally justified, shared with others. This sort of implicit to explicit progression may well characterize the developmental course of a number of cognitive acquisitions. Similarly, for child B the A > C conclusion given A > B and B > C may be simply a best guess, something that is seen as probably but by no means definitely true. Child A may realize that the A > C judgment can be offered with certainty; indeed, he may even understand that A > C is a logically necessary conclusion given the particular premises. As we saw in Chapters 3 and 4, there is some evidence that an appreciation of the logical necessity of certain outcomes increases with development.

Suppose that cognitive capacities like transitive inference do in fact show the sort of developmental course just sketched. What more would we want to know? A great deal, actually, because we have not yet discovered what transitive inference really is. We would have some idea of the sorts of changes that transitive inference undergoes with development, but we would still need to specify exactly what it is that is changing. Is transitive inference a single cognitive entity that remains basically the same once it has entered the repertoire, albeit increasing in evocability, utilizability, and generality? Or are there perhaps different kinds of transitive inference, such that the most advanced form is a basically different kind of knowledge from the earliest, fledgling form? And whether we posit one ability or several, what exactly goes on inside the subject's head when he or she engages in a transitive inference? What cognitive processes intervene between the initial representation of the problem and the final generation of a response? Why are these particular processes selected, and how are they integrated and sequenced in the course of problem solution? Questions such as these are at the heart of the conceptualization part of cognitive diagnosis.

Unfortunately, we possess little certain knowledge about the actual processes underlying transitive inference, or any other interesting cognitive acquisition, for that matter. It is not that we necessarily lack theories; Piaget's theory of concrete operations, for example, provides a model of how not only transitivity but also a wide range of other problems are solved. But it has proved very difficult to obtain evidence that can tell us whether the processes proposed by theorists are those that actually characterize children's thinking. Here, we briefly consider one approach to this problem, some research by Trabasso and colleagues (Bryant & Trabasso, 1971; Trabasso, 1975, 1977). This research suggests some surprising conclusions about how transitivity problems are solved. It will also serve to give us an example of an important information-processing methodology.

Subjects in the Trabasso studies (both children and adults) were repeatedly shown the adjacent pairs of a series of different-length sticks, A > B, B > C, C > D, D > E, each stick identifiable by its color. This initial phase continued until the subject had clearly memorized the relative lengths of each adjacent pair. A test phase followed, during which the subject was asked to predict the relative lengths of *all* the possible A through E pairs, not just those that had been directly presented. Measures were taken not only of the solution offered but also of the time taken to reach a solution. According to the standard view of how transitive inferences are made, subjects arrive at an answer by logically combining the relevant premises at the time of solution. By this view, B versus E, which requires the addition of three premises (B > C, C > D, D > E), should take longer to solve than B versus D, which requires the addition of only two premises, and both should take longer than any directly learned pair, such as A versus B or C versus D. In fact, just the opposite proved to be true: the farther apart the two sticks in the A...E series, the shorter the solution time when comparing them. Thus, subjects were actually faster on B versus E, which they had never seen together during training, than B versus C, which they had seen together repeatedly. Trabasso's explanation for the response-time data focuses on the way in which subjects represent the information while learning the adjacent pairs. Rather than storing information about individual pairs (A > B, B > C, etc.), subjects are hypothesized to construct an internal, image-like representation of the entire ordered array: A > B > C > D > E. Once this representation is constructed, subjects can solve any problem by simply "reading off" the length comparison, much as though the five sticks were all lined up in order of length before their eyes. Because B and E are farther apart and more different in length than B and D, B versus E is solved more quickly than B versus D. In contrast to the logical reasoning processes stressed in Piaget's theory, transitivity by this view is a matter more of constructive memory combined with mental imagery.

Trabasso has not shown that people never use inferential rather than quasi-perceptual processes when dealing with transitivity problems, or that older children do not know anything about transitive inference that younger ones do not. Indeed, we doubt that his model applies to every act of transitive inference at every developmental level. Nevertheless, his results furnish some striking, and unexpected, evidence of how certain kinds of transitivity problems are solved. And his research provides both specific testimony to the value of response-time data (a favorite information-processing methodology) and a general model of how theories of underlying process can be evaluated empirically.

Some Conclusions Regarding Diagnosis

We have said that the objectives of cognitive diagnosis include: (1) determining the psychological nature of the acquisition in question; (2) determining its typical developmental course, including sequential changes in its psychological nature, its evocability, and its utilizability; and (3) devising assessment procedures that can tell us what a particular child "has," or where he or she stands developmentally, with respect to (1) and (2). Successful achievement of all three diagnostic objectives is crucially important for several reasons.

One reason is that we cannot determine how various cognitive entities are related without accurate diagnosis. As we discuss more fully in the next section, one major goal of cognitive-developmental research is to identify the interrelations or patterns that hold among the numerous acquisitions that constitute childhood cognitive development. One pattern of interest is that of invariant sequence: the possibility that X always emerges in development before Y, and perhaps that X and Y always emerge before Z. Another pattern of interest—one that is central to the claims of stage theories—is that of concurrence: the possibility that X, Y, and Z all emerge at the same time in development. Whether the focus is on sequences or concurrences, the conclusions that we draw are completely dependent on the accuracy of our diagnoses. If our tests for X, Y, and Z are differentially sensitive—more prone to either false-negative errors or false-positive errors in some cases than in others—then we are quite likely to misjudge the true temporal relation among the acquisitions. In addition, a better analysis of the processes that underlie X, Y, and Z—that is, a revised answer to the conceptualization question—might reveal that the relations among the various acquisitions could not be what we at first thought they were. We might decide, for example, that Y is an entirely different kind of cognitive creature than we had believed, making it quite implausible that it could be either a descendant of X or an ancestor of Z.

Questions of diagnosis are also central to another major goal of cognitive-developmental research: explaining how cognitive change comes about. When we study children's cognitive development, we hope not only to describe the various states through which the cognitive system moves but also to explain how one state changes into another. But clearly we can do so only if we have accurately diagnosed what the various states are. If our conceptualizations of what is developing are faulty or our assessments of various knowledge states are in error, then our explanations of cognitive change are unlikely to be correct.

Finally, diagnosis is central to all psychological study, cognitive developmental or other. In the case of cognitive development, we absolutely must somehow penetrate to the processual heart of the acquisitions we call "transitive inference," the concept of "false belief," and so on, and we must also be able to assess with precision where individual children stand in relation to these acquisitions. Everything that we conclude about cognitive development—our very picture of what that development "is"—depends ultimately on diagnosis.

Because diagnosis is so central to everything that we do, an attempt to review diagnostic innovations and what they have told us would be essentially a review of this entire book. Nevertheless, we would like to offer a few reminders of what seem to us some especially important messages that emerge from recent attempts at cognitive diagnosis.

One message is that for a number of years our assessment techniques led us to underestimate what children were capable of. As newer and more sensitive techniques have been devised, our picture of childhood competence has grown more positive. This revised picture is most evident with regard to infant development. The main innovation here has been the invention and clever exploitation of techniques (such as habituation-dishabituation) that minimize motoric and other extraneous response demands on the young infant, thus yielding a clearer picture of what babies really know. Our view of the preschool child—the poor, failure-prone "preoperational" subject of Piagetian theory—has also grown more positive. Reduction of the verbal demands that characterized many assessments has been important here, as has been a general simplification, stripping down, and movement toward child-friendly and child-natural methods of assessment (see Wellman & Gelman, 1992).

A second message is that it is important not to overstate the implications of these findings of earlier-than-expected competence. Some competence is not full competence, and at any point in development we need a clear model not only of what children can do but also of what still remains to be developed (for discussions of this point with regard to recent claims about infant competence, see Fischer & Bidell, 1991, and Montangero, 1991). A 3-year-old may be more competent in a variety of domains than we used to believe, but his or her competence is seldom fully equivalent to that of a 12-year-old. Specifying the different senses and levels of "having" a concept is, as we saw, a central challenge for cognitive diagnosis. The point for now is simply that it is important not to confuse "first has" with "fully has" (see also Chandler, 1991, and L. Smith, 1991).

A final point concerns the conceptualization aspect of diagnosis—that is, the characterization of the psychological processes that underlie the overt performances that our assessment instruments reveal. Despite some recent advances, it should be clear that we still have much to learn here. It is possible that some relatively new approaches to assessment will provide insights that have not been forthcoming from traditional approaches. For example, contextual theorists emphasize the social origins of individual thought, and the assessment methods that they have devised correspondingly focus not on the child in isolation but on the child in interaction with some more mature, and helpful, other. To the extent that thought really is created in the context of such interactions, these "dynamic" methods of assessment reveal something about how cognitive processes are assembled and organized (but see Paris and Cross, 1988, for a thoughtful critique of this approach to diagnosis). As we saw in Chapter 1, a major goal of the information-processing approach has always been to devise methodologies that can take us beyond surface performance to get at underlying process. The response-time technique utilized by Trabasso in the research discussed earlier in this section is one example of such a method; the Siegler rule-assessment approach discussed in Chapter 4 is another example. Undoubtedly a main reason for the current popularity of the information-processing approach is the promise that it seems to hold of finally providing some answers to questions of underlying process.

PATTERNS

A number of cognitive-developmental entities (concepts, skills, etc.) emerge during an individual's childhood. How might these entities be related to one another in ontogenetic time? What patterns might be discernible in the developmental mosaic?

One possibility is that one entity regularly develops prior to another—that is, a pattern of invariant *sequence*. The temporal relation in this case is one of systematic asynchrony: One thing always emerges before another. A second possibility is that the relation is one of synchrony rather than asynchrony: Two or more entities emerge at the same time in development. The pattern in this case is one of *concurrence*. Finally, it is possible that during certain periods of childhood a whole group of similar or related entities emerge synchronously or concurrently. Such an ensemble of concurrent, tightly knit developments might be referred to as a major *stage* of cognitive growth. A stage would constitute a very important type of developmental pattern.

Sequences

The following discussion of cognitive-developmental sequences is largely based on Flavell (1972, 1982b). Other useful sources include Fischer (1980), Kingma and Van Den Bos (1988), Siegler (1981), and Wohlwill (1973).

Challenges of two sorts confront us when we attempt to determine whether two cognitive entities, X and Y, really develop in the sequence X-Y. One sort of challenge is diagnostic. As indicated earlier in this chapter, determining when and in what sense a child "has" a particular ability is an extremely difficult enterprise; answering the "has" question in comparable fashion for two or more different abilities is even more difficult. Suppose, in the case of X and Y, that, without our knowing it, our test *x* for development X had extraneous but very taxing performance demands not present in our test *y* for development Y. That is, test *x* is harder and less sensitive than test *y* because of heavy information-processing requirements or other task factors that have nothing intrinsically to do with the cognitive acquisition the test was designed to measure. Accordingly, test *x* will underestimate the child's level of development of X much more than *y* will with respect to Y, since it will yield more false-negative type misdiagnoses. This difference in the sensitivities of the two tests could cause developments X and Y to look concurrent when X actually occurs earlier in ontogenesis than Y; it might even create the impression that Y emerges earlier than X. In either case, the diagnostic uncertainties would cause us to misjudge the relation between X and Y.

The second challenge in studying sequences is a theoretical one: explaining any X-Y patterns that we may have identified. Sequences are interesting to us only if we can posit some important way in which X and Y might be related to one another. For instance, the fact that sensorimotor means-end behavior (X) always develops before concrete-operational weight conservation (Y) is not very interesting, because we cannot imagine how the former could figure directly and importantly in the ontogenesis of the latter. Suppose, however, that we could be sure that X and Y usually do or always do emerge in the sequence X-Y and can also imagine an interesting developmental relationship between the two. What might that relationship be? Drawing on Flavell (1972), we suggest that there are five major types or categories of such relationships: *addition, substitution, modification, inclusion*, and *mediation.*

ADDITION.   In most addition sequences, X and Y are alternative cognitive means to the same goal. Y does not replace X once it develops; it is simply added to the active repertoire of routes to that goal. For example (Chapter 6), children learn to use simple rehearsal strategies (X) before acquiring organizational ones (Y) in memory situations, but the former continue to be used in many of these situations after the latter are developed. Similarly (Chapter 3), Wellman (1990) has suggested that children first acquire some understanding of people's desires (a "desire psychology") and only later add to it some understanding of beliefs (a "belief-desire psychology"). The understanding of beliefs does not supplant the ability to reason on the basis of desires; it simply adds to it to provide a fuller theory of mind.

SUBSTITUTION.   X and Y again represent possible alternatives, but here Y more or less completely replaces or substitutes for X once it is acquired. Younger children respond to number-conservation problems by comparing row lengths and concluding that the longer row has more. When they get older they will abandon that strategy completely, substituting for it an inferential approach that will yield a conservation conclusion. Similarly, the strategy of counting up from one when adding will eventually be replaced by more effective strategies, such as the min strategy or memorization of the correct response (Chapters 1 and 3). Recall an interesting point from this research that may apply to a number of other substitution sequences as well: Early responses do not necessarily disappear immediately when more mature ones emerge; rather, various strategies may coexist for some time.

MODIFICATION. In addition and substitution sequences, X and Y are clearly two different cognitive entities. In modification, as the name suggests, there is instead some sort of developmentally progressive modification of a single entity. Y is clearly continuous with and derived from X, as woman from girl or man from boy. Three types of modifications are distinguished: *differentiation, generalization,* and *stabilization.* Initially, a child may rehearse items to be remembered in only one way, for example, but in subsequent years the child may differentiate several different rehearsal patterns. Likewise, any given way of rehearsing may with development become progressively generalized to more and more different memory problems. Finally, as any rehearsal pattern continues to be practiced, it stabilizes as a skill—becomes more readily initiated in appropriate circumstances, more skillfully and effortlessly carried out, and so on. As an additional example, sensorimotor schemes differentiate, generalize, and stabilize during infancy.

INCLUSION. At some point in X's development, X becomes interconnected or coordinated with one or more other cognitive entities to form part of (become included in) a larger cognitive unit Y. For example, the progressive coordination of two sensorimotor schemes to form a means-end whole constitutes an inclusion sequence: Two initially separate Xs are combined to form a larger and more complex Y. In the area of memory development, the earlier-developing ability to name objects becomes integrated into a later-developing rehearsal strategy.

MEDIATION. In these sequences, X serves as a bridge, facilitator, or mediator with respect to the subsequent development of Y. Unlike inclusion sequences, however, X does not become an actual part or component of Y; once developed with the help of (mediation by) X, Y functions independently of X. The inversion and compensation forms of concrete-operational reversible thinking (Chapter 4, "Irreversibility versus Reversibility" section) could conceivably help the child achieve conservation solutions to various conservation problems. These forms of thinking do not become integral parts of conservation concepts as, say, a means scheme becomes an integral part of a means-end whole. If we present an adult with a liquid-quantity conservation problem, the individual surely does not need to go through a whole train of reasoning about how height changes might compensate for width changes in order to reach a conservation conclusion.

Each of these five types of sequences illustrates something about how cognitive growth occurs. The cognitive repertoire is enriched by addition sequences: The child used to have only one approach (X) to a problem but now has two (X and Y). Substitution sequences serve to replace less (X) with more (Y) mature cognitive approaches to problems. A cognitive entity (X) develops to a higher, more mature level (Y) via a modification sequence. Inclusion sequences illustrate that developmental change often occurs neither by modifying old cognitive entities nor by adding or substituting new ones, but by coordinating or integrating existing ones to form larger wholes. Finally, mediation sequences show that the development of one cognitive entity can substantially assist the development of another distinct and independent entity.

Concurrences

The same diagnostic uncertainties that complicate the study of sequences apply as well to any attempt to identify concurrences in development. Again, the difficulties in determining whether and exactly how a child "has" X and Y may cause us to miss a true concurrence or to claim a concurrence when none in fact exists.

As with sequences, concurrences are of interest because they tell us something about the nature and the origin of the cognitive entities that we are studying. In the case of concurrences the relationship of interest is one of common underlying basis: X and Y emerge together because they emanate from the same more general cognitive advance, are reflections of the same underlying rule or structure or process, are in some important sense the "same thing."

Recent work on theory of mind (Chapter 3) provides some examples. Recall our discussion of Postulate 4: the knowledge that the mind can represent objects and events accurately or inaccurately. A number of specific developments can be plausibly linked to this very general realization: Level 2 perspective taking, understanding of false belief, understanding of representational change, and mastery of the appearance-reality distinction, among others. As we saw in Chapter 3, these competencies tend to emerge at about the same time—namely, somewhere around age 4. Furthermore, they are substantially correlated within children—that is, if we assess several of the abilities in the same sample we find that children tend to be consistent in their performance, either passing all or failing all (Flavell et al., 1990; Gopnik & Astington, 1988). The correlations are not perfect, but then we would not expect them to be; the various competencies are only in part the "same thing," and in any case the diagnostic complexities that we have been stressing keep us from expecting a perfect relation between any two assessments. Nevertheless, it is an important task for further work—not only on theory of mind but with regard to other purported concurrences—to determine just how close is close enough when we attempt to decide whether two abilities really emerge at the same time. Most concurrences seem to be of the loose, at-about-the-same-time sort rather than tight, can't-have-one-without-the-other synchrony.

Another important question concerns the breadth or scope of concurrences in development. Few psychologists doubt that certain closely related abilities may emerge in at least rough synchrony. The claims of stage theories, however, are much stronger than this: very many interrelated abilities, all emerging at about the same time because they are all reflections of the same general stage of cognitive development. It is to the notion of stage that we turn next.

Stages

There is no shortage of discussions of stages and of issues related to stages. Among the useful sources are Carey (1987), Case (1985, 1986, 1992), Ceci (1989), Chapman (1988), Demetriou and Efklides (in press), Fischer (1980), Fischer and Silvern (1985), Flavell (1971c, 1982a, 1982b, in press), Flavell and Wohlwill (1969), Keil (1986), Levin (1986), P. H. Miller (in press), Pinard and Laurendeau (1969), Sternberg (1989a), and Wohlwill (1973).

It is useful to focus on Piaget's stage of concrete operations when discussing this topic, since it has been the subject of more theoretical and experimental attention than any other. Our tentative conclusions about stages extend beyond that particular one, however. Indeed, these conclusions extend beyond debates about whether development is or is not stage-like, since the issues involved are central ones in any conception of how development comes about. Most of what needs discussing in this area falls under the headings of *structures*, *qualitative change*, *abruptness*, and—once again and above all—*concurrence*.

STRUCTURES. Piaget argued that what we actually acquire when we acquire, say, concrete operations is a unified set of cognitive *structures*, not just an accumulation of mutually isolated and independent, psychologically unconnected cognitive entities. In fact, the presence of such unified structures—*structures d'ensemble* he called them—was one of Piaget's major criteria for asserting that a given set of developments constitutes a stage.

We can ask two questions concerning cognitive-developmental structures. First, when a given body of knowledge, cognitive skills, and so on has been acquired, might cognitive structures of any sort have been acquired? Do at least some of the products of cognitive growth become interrelated in our heads, get linked into organized functional wholes, or do they tend to remain unorganized, unintegrated, and unconnected? There are good reasons to think that they do become interrelated, both in the area of concrete-operational thinking and elsewhere. We doubt if a serious case could be made that the various processes and concepts inhabiting our cognitive systems do not interact with or otherwise link up with one another—do not exhibit "structure" (Flavell, 1971c, 1982b).

Piaget did not just assert that concrete-operational thinking is structured. Rather, he argued that it possesses a definite, specific type of structure or organization. In fact, he proposed quite detailed logical-mathematical models of how cognition is structured at both the concrete-operational and formal-operational stages. We did not present these models in Chapter 4, for two reasons: Their complexity defies any brief description, and they have in any case not fared well in recent years. Piaget's structural models have been the subject of intense critical scrutiny, the consensus from which seems to be that they are in varying degrees unclear, incorrect, and incomplete as theoretical descriptions of underlying mental processes. Indeed, Piaget himself eventually grew dissatisfied with these models and explored other structural descriptions in his last writings (e.g., Piaget, 1985). It seems reasonable, then, to conclude that, in fact, there is considerable mental organization in the area of concrete-operational thinking, as there undoubtedly is in other areas, but that the specific formal structures Piaget proposed may not capture it very well (Flavell, 1982a, 1982b).

QUALITATIVE CHANGE. One is not tempted to talk about developmental stages in the case of age changes that are purely quantitative in nature. Consider the digit-span memory test mentioned in Chapter 4. It would sound silly to say that Mary was in the "three-digit stage" last year but has now entered the "four-digit stage." A stage-type characterization perhaps would not sound so silly if she had used a rehearsal strategy to memorize things last year but then switched over to a wholly different strategy this year—for example, elaboration. A quantitative change from little apples to big apples is never called a stage change; a qualitative change from apples to oranges might be. If there were no qualitative changes in cognitive development, there could be no "stages" of cognitive development in any meaningful sense.

Are there any such qualitative changes? The answer depends on what one means by "qualitative" and on one's level of analysis or universe of discourse. We personally find it easy to think of the substitution of one memory strategy for another, or a switch from a perceptually based nonconservation answer to a conceptually based conservation one, as qualitative developmental changes; they seem like apples-to-oranges-type transformations. On the other hand, the developmental processes—whatever they are—that underlie these behavioral changes may not exhibit any real qualitative transformations, any significant discontinuities. What looks like a qualitative change at one level of analysis may not at another.

ABRUPTNESS. Cognitive development would look very stage-like if the transition from one cognitive level to another were abrupt rather than gradual. Consider as an example conservation of weight, a concrete-operational acquisition. Suppose that acquisition typically occurred very abruptly. One day, the child shows no signs of weight conservation. The next day, it is present in fully mature form: The child can adequately explain her conservation judgment, the experimenter cannot extinguish it by rigging the scale balance, and so on. If the emergence of weight conservation and other concrete-operational accomplishments occurred in such an abrupt, metamorphosis-like fashion, it would seem wholly natural to speak of stages. Indeed, even that abrupt a *quantitative* change would seem somewhat stage-like.

The truth of the matter, however, is that most important cognitive developments appear to proceed slowly and gradually rather than abruptly (Flavell, 1971c). As indicated in Chapter 4 ("Improvement in Existing Competencies" section), conservation of weight may continue to mature, in the sense of becoming further consolidated and solidified, well after the end of the concrete-operational period. Once again, there are more and less mature ways of "having" weight conservation and other cognitive-developmental products. Research evidence suggests that the period in the child's life between initial, minimal possession and fully mature, maximal command of many of these products can be a matter of years.

Such evidence changes the meaning of "stage" in an interesting way. For a major stage like concrete operations, we might have expected a very brief period of change and transition, during which concrete operations emerge and mature, followed by several years of relative stasis and quiescence, during which children are more or less stably and unchangeably concrete-operational in their thinking. If, instead, children actually continue to perfect, generalize, and solidify their grasp of weight conservation throughout most of middle childhood and perhaps also well into adolescence, the stage of concrete operations is all change and transition, with little or no stasis and stability. Thus, the stage itself, and not the transition to it, becomes the period of continuous growth and change. Because of this continuous growth and change, one cannot predict children's responses to concrete-operational tasks merely from the knowledge that they are in the concrete-operational stage, as one could have if being in that stage meant continuing to have essentially the same mental structure for a period of years. This loss of predictability reduces the scientific value of the stage concept, but we do not think it makes it valueless. Suppose that all concrete-operational skills developed concurrently in an interdependent, mutually facilitative fashion. The fact that all these synchronous, closely interacting developments took a long rather than a short time to be completed would not mean that the term "stage" could not be applied meaningfully and usefully to this developmental pattern. We would simple have a more dynamic concept of stage, one that refers to an extended process of concurrent, interdependent developmental changes.

CONCURRENCE. In fact, most developmental psychologists believe that just this kind of tightly interlocked, concurrent growth must obtain in an area of cognitive development if the term "stage" is to be usefully applied to that area. If concrete-operational entities do not really develop concurrently, for instance, they would say that the concept "concrete-operational stage" is theoretically vacuous. (For a dissenting view on this point, however, see Wohlwill, 1973, chap. 9, and for a somewhat different interpretation of what Piaget's theory predicts, see Chapman, 1988). The general reason for expecting concurrence is the same as that discussed with respect to pairs of abilities: Competencies that emanate from the same underlying cognitive basis should emerge at about the same time in development. In this case, however, the posited underlying basis is quite broad in scope—namely, a general stage of cognitive functioning—and hence the expected concurrence is also quite broad. The prediction—to state the case in terms used earlier in the book—is thus of a considerable degree of domain generality in children's cognitive functioning.

We have discussed both the complexities of diagnosing cognitive entities in isolation and the compounding of the difficulty when two entities must be assessed in comparable fashion simultaneously, as is the case with either an X-before-Y sequence or an X-and-Y-together concurrence. When concurrences of the general-stage sort are at issue, X and Y are joined by U, V, W..., and the problems of matching test sensitivity grow correspondingly greater. Although some researchers appear to have been quite skillful in equating the sensitivity of their tests, there really is no way one can be sure that this goal has been achieved, and therefore no way to be absolutely sure that the concurrence hypothesis is receiving a valid assessment. Despite these problems, we think it is possible to make an educated guess about concurrence-nonconcurrence. Our guess is that nonconcurrence is the rule and concurrence the exception. Two types of relationship among concrete-operational entities are perhaps most commonly seen (albeit through a murky diagnostic lens). In one type, one entity regularly develops prior to another in most or all individuals tested. The pattern, therefore, is not the stage-consistent one of synchrony but rather one of systematic asynchrony, or invariant sequence. Although sequences (as we have just been stressing) may be interesting in themselves, they do not provide support for the usual interpretation of stage. In the other type of relationship, a pair of entities may develop at roughly the same age, on the average, but their levels of development are not highly correlated with one another within individuals. One entity may be developmentally more advanced than the other in this child; the opposite may be true in that child. Whatever concurrence there may be is therefore of the rough, group-average sort. There is little evidence that the developments are interdependent or mutually facilitative in the way that a stage characterization would suggest.

CONCLUSIONS ABOUT STAGES. As noted in Chapter 4, developmental psychologists have become increasingly skeptical in recent years about the theoretical utility of the construct of "cognitive-developmental stage." In particular, Piaget's concrete-operational and formal-operational "stages" have been sharply criticized. The structures used to model concrete- and formal-operational thinking appear inadequate; the stage-to-stage developmental changes are not quite so exclusively qualitative if you look at underlying processes; the within-stage changes are more gradual, important, and extended in time than originally believed; and the same-stage developments are less concurrent than Piagetian theory seemed to require. Furthermore, interesting alternatives to the general-stage view of development have arisen. The development-as-theory-change position (Chapters 1 and 3) appears to capture many of the attractive aspects of stage models (a focus on the coherence of mental processes, the possibility of qualitative changes with development) without some of the more questionable features. Work on expertise (Chapter 4) speaks directly to the domain-specific nature of many cognitive achievements, the attempt being to explain variations in level of performance in terms of differences in experience across different content areas. The notion of biological constraints or innate modules (Chapters 1, 3, and 7) provides a quite different explanation for certain kinds of domain specificity. According to this view, we are predisposed as members of a biological species to process information and acquire knowledge especially readily in certain natural domains (e.g., language, number). Each of these positions explicitly disavows the kind of transdomain generality that has proved to be the most problematic prediction of general-stage theories.

Does all of this mean that the concept of stage will no longer figure importantly in scientific work on cognitive growth in decades to come? Although we raised this question at various points in Chapter 4, you may have noticed that we avoided giving a definite answer to it. There was good reason for such waffling. Despite the problems just discussed, stage theories continue to have able advocates. Neo-Piagetian theorists, in particular, continue to develop stage models that attempt to retain the insights of Piaget's work while at the same time jettisoning some of its less promising features (such as the logical-mathematical structures) and incorporating modern emphases not considered by Piaget (such as changes in information-processing capacity). Important examples of such attempts include Case (1985, 1987, 1992), Demetriou and Efklides (in press), Fischer (1980), Fischer and Farrar (1987), Halford (1982, in press), and Pascual-Leone (1987). How successful such theories will prove to be is still an open question. But to many of us it is hard to believe that cognitive development does not possess *some* general-stage properties—*some* features that are mind-in-general and not just individual "mindlets" in isolation. And so the search for stages or at least stage-like properties seems likely to continue.

COGNITIVE CHANGE

How is cognitive growth accomplished? What factors or variables play what roles in influencing the nature, rate of growth, and ultimate adult level of various forms of knowledge and cognitive ability? How, in short, can we *explain* the various changes we may have *diagnosed*?

Not surprisingly, accounting for cognitive growth is at least as problematic as diagnosing forms of knowledge and identifying patterns among them. It is difficult to be sure even what is meant when we speak of "explaining" cognitive change or of specifying "causes" of development. What is it that makes some factor an explanation and not merely a further description of change? It is difficult as well to know whether different would-be explanations are really referring to distinct contributors, or whether they are perhaps simply different labels for the same idea. It is difficult to know how to go about studying the issue—how to gather evidence that would allow us to test the validity of any proposed explanation. Finally, questions of diagnosis once again loom large, just as they do for any research enterprise. We cannot provide a satisfactory account of change unless we have a clear idea of where the system starts, what intermediate states it moves through, and where it ends up—in short, unless we know what it is that we are attempting to explain.

Our overview of theories in Chapter 1 stressed some of the ideas about change that are found in the major contemporary theoretical positions, and the examinations of particular topics in the ensuing chapters included some further discussions of sources and mechanisms of change. The goals of the present section are both to bring together some of this earlier material and to consider further some of the complexities and uncertainties that are involved in the study of change. We do so under three general headings: biological contributors to cognitive growth; experiential contributors and sources of influence, both social and nonsocial; and developmental principles, processes, or mechanisms that may operate to produce change. Useful further sources on this topic include Butterworth and Bryant (1990), Carey and Gelman (1991), de Ribaupierre (1989), Okagaki and Sternberg (1991), Siegler (1989c), Sternberg (1984), and Wohlwill (1973). Accounts of Piaget's revised equilibration theory (his conception of how children make cognitive-developmental progress) can be found in Furth (1981), Chapman (1988), and Piaget (1985).

Biological Contributors to Cognitive Development

The idea that biological-maturational factors play a central role in shaping the nature, the timing, and the direction of cognitive development is a much more frequently discussed and seriously entertained proposition than was the case even 6 or 8 years ago. Chapters developing specific aspects of this general proposition can be found in edited volumes by Carey and Gelman (1991), Diamond (1990a), and K. R. Gibson and Petersen (1991). The general position is well summarized by Fischer and Bidell (1991, p. 200):

> The behavioral abilities with which human beings are genetically endowed are far richer and more complex than traditional accounts of cognitive development imply. New research seems to have revealed rich sets of perceptual and cognitive abilities in infants and young children. A key neo-nativist argument appears to be that these early abilities show the starting points from which cognitive development must emerge. As starting points, they set limits or constraints on what is possible and thereby help to channel the direction of development.

. As the passage from Fischer and Bidell suggests, it is findings with regard to infant precocity that have been most responsible for the surge of nativistic theorizing in recent years. Infants have turned out to be more competent than we used to believe, and many of the competencies are evident at such early ages that it is impossible to see how they could be instilled by the environment. Furthermore, the kinds of precocious competence that have been identified in recent research appear to correspond to biologically natural, species-typical domains of knowledge—that is, to precisely the sorts of knowledge that we would expect our evolutionary history to have prepared us to acquire quickly and easily. Language is the most long-recognized and perhaps least-disputed of these natural domains. Among the other domains for which innate structuring and innately given principles appear to be important are perception of objects (Chapter 2), perception of causality (Chapters 2 and 3), recognition of the animate-inanimate distinction (Chapter 3), and abstraction of number (Chapter 3).

Demonstrations of earlier-than-expected competence are not the only respect in which recent work departs from what had been established wisdom. Also unexpected has been the highly domain-specific nature of many of these early developments. We seem to be biologically prepared to do very specific kinds of information processing and very specific kinds of learning, with no apparent links between one set of processing mechanisms (e.g., those for discriminating speech sounds) and another (e.g., those for extracting numerical information). Different theorists talk about these highly specialized capacities in different ways—as encapsulated modules, as constraints that channel information processing in adaptive directions, as skeletal principles upon which further developments build. Common to the various conceptions, however, is an emphasis on domain specificity—these are processes that perform very specific tasks, not all-purpose learning mechanisms. It is possible, of course, that some common elements and some trans-domain links will become evident in future work; indeed, this possibility becomes more plausible as the list of early competencies grows and as any particular competency thereby becomes less unique-looking— less out of keeping with anything else that the child is doing. As we saw in the chapter on language, there have recently been attempts to relate some of the constraints that guide language acquisition to more general aspects of early cognitive development. Thus far, however, the emphasis has been more on separation than on connection.

This is not to say that all biological contributors to cognitive growth are of the domain-specific sort. Development includes trans-domain as well as within-domain processes and abilities, and biology undoubtedly contributes to the former as well as to the latter. Scarr (1983) provides some interesting speculations with regard to the biological underpinnings for a set of achievements with a good deal of generality: namely, Piagetian sensorimotor development. A specialist in behavior genetics and human development, Scarr approaches this problem from an unusual point of view—that of evolutionary theory. As is not true of later cognitive acquisitions, Scarr notes, normal human beings everywhere are virtually certain to complete Piagetian sensorimotor development. As she puts it: "Do you know anyone who didn't make it to preoperational thought" (p. 211)? She speculates that the sensorimotor ontogenetic pattern evolved earlier in our primate past than those that follow it in childhood cognitive development—for example, concrete-operational thought.

The evolutionary selection pressures that led to the establishment of sensorimotor development ensured its species-wide universality in two ways: They acted on the infant and they acted on his environment, including the behavior of his caretakers. On the infant's side, selection pressures are hypothesized to have produced an organism genetically predisposed or "canalized" toward the sequential acquisition of Piagetian sensorimotor schemes rather than other imaginable cognitive attainments. This organism's evolutionary history has powerfully biased it to develop in that direction, and we would presumably have to rear it in a highly deviant, "nonhuman" way to prevent that development or deflect its basic course.

On the environmental side, evolutionary selection pressures have produced a species-typical, characteristically "human" rearing environment for this genetically specialized organism. Moreover, it is just the sort of environment needed to promote sensorimotor development in this particular organism. Naturally, human environments differ in many ways, and these differences undeniably contribute to individual differences in cognition, especially in later childhood and adulthood. There are also some basic commonalities across human environments, however, and these are believed to constitute the essential psychological nutriments for the acquisition of sensorimotor intelligence. Despite their diversity within and between cultures, infant worlds are "functionally equivalent," as Scarr puts it, in their capacities to support this particular process of acquisition.

They all provide social and nonsocial objects, events, and experiential opportunities of the kinds needed to allow a properly designed organism to develop sensorimotor cognitive structures.

Notice that this view in no way denies the vital role of environment and experience in the process of cognitive growth. Environmental elements do not become any less essential to a particular form of development just because they are virtually certain to be available for its use. Their near-universality may make it difficult for us to detect them, but they are no less indispensable because of their low visibility. Similarly, the modules-constraints-skeletal principles positions discussed earlier do not deny a role for experience; indeed, exactly the opposite is explicitly the case for many of the proponents of such positions. What biology provides is not the end point of development but rather the capacities that allow us to utilize experience to reach that end point. (For elaborations of this argument, as well as some cautions against interpreting early competence in too strongly nativistic terms, see Fischer and Bidell, 1991, and Karmiloff-Smith, 1991).

So far we have said quite a bit about biological contributors to development without once going beneath the skin to talk about the physiological substrates and physiological processes (neurons, dendrites, synapses, parts of the brain, etc.) that underlie these contributions. There was good reason for such reticence, for our knowledge of such matters is still quite limited. Nevertheless, some progress has been made in recent years. Here we briefly consider two lines of argument concerning possible physiological bases for cognitive change, one of which was touched on earlier in the text and one of which will be new.

As we saw in Chapter 2, Adele Diamond (1990b, 1991a, 1991b; see also Goldman-Rakic, 1987) has argued that many of the cognitive advances of infancy are made possible by maturational changes in the infant's brain. The changes that Diamond especially emphasizes involve the frontal cortex: changes in the supplementary motor area, in dorsolateral prefrontal cortex, and in connections and communication among regions of the cortex. For our purposes, the specific biological bases are less important than the chain of reasoning and evidence that leads to the conclusion that a particular maturational change underlies a particular behavioral development. Consider Piagetian object permanence. Successful response to object permanence tasks requires not only the knowledge that hidden objects still exist (Piaget's interest) but also the ability to organize behaviors into search sequences and to inhibit prepotent but nonoptimal responses (such as the reach for A in an A-not-B paradigm). It is these latter developments, Diamond believes, that must wait upon frontal lobe development in the last half of the first year—which is why infants' ability to act adaptively in hidden-object situations lags so far beyond their first demonstrations of knowledge.

Several kinds of evidence converge on this conclusion. There is, to begin with, an impressive degree of temporal synchrony between developments in the behavioral and biological realms; maturational changes in frontal cortex coincide nicely with the emerging achievements that such changes are meant to explain. In itself, of course, such synchrony is a necessary but far from sufficient basis for inferring a causal relation, since many things are undergoing more or less simultaneous change at any point in a child's development. The synchrony argument gains strength, however, from the fact that similar biology-behavior parallels can be identified in other species at times that correspond to major maturational changes for the species in question. In rhesus monkeys, for example, changes in frontal cortex occur several months earlier than in human infants, and improvements on search and delayed-response tasks are also evident several months earlier. Research with other species, moreover, offers kinds of evidence not available with humans. Experimental interruption of normal frontal lobe functioning—either permanently through surgical lesions or temporarily through techniques such as drug administration—produces deficits in the ability to inhibit behavior and to solve search and delayed-response tasks. The effects, moreover, are quite specific—not across-the-board deficits but impairment of precisely those functions that are thought to be governed by the brain areas in question. In intact and normally functioning brains, increases in both electrical and metabolic activity are evident in the frontal lobe regions when search and delayed-response tasks are performed. Finally, adult humans who have sustained lesions to the frontal lobes show behavioral deficits that are in some ways parallel to those of young infants. They have difficulty, for example, in inhibiting dominant responses and in maintaining memory for objects or locations over time.

The second posited neurological basis for cognitive change involves a process called *synaptogenesis*. Synapses are junctions between neurons across which information can be transmitted, and synaptogenesis is the process by which such connections are established. The growth of synapses shows an interesting developmental course: The number of synapses in many regions of the brain peaks during infancy and then gradually declines across early childhood. Much of development, then, seems to consist of a pruning back of synapses following an initial phase of overproduction. Greenough, Black, and Wallace (1987) have argued that experience plays an important role in determining which synapses survive and which are pruned back. They present various types of evidence indicating that neural connections are most likely to survive if experience gives them a chance to be utilized; conversely, in the absence of relevant experience, connections may wither away. This sort of selective survival of synapses is seen as being especially important for what Greenough and co-workers label *experience-expectant* processes. The term experience-expectant refers to developments that are essentially species-wide because the necessary experiences are available in any normal, expectable environment that a member of the species might encounter (in contrast, *experience-dependent* processes depend on individual learning and the formation of new synaptic connections rather than the survival of preexisting ones). For example, early visual input of various sorts is necessary for normal visual development in a variety of species; such input, however, is ensured in any normal, species-typical environment. Because the necessary experience is available, the synaptic connections that are activated by such input will be maintained and development of the visual system will proceed normally. Note the similarity between this position and Scarr's (1983) more macrolevel discussion of the evolutionary basis for sensorimotor development. In both cases biology and experience are assumed to act together to produce the normal course of development for the species. And in both cases experience does not create or strongly mold this developmental course; rather, we develop as we do because we are biologically predisposed to utilize any reasonably normal set of experiences in species-typical and adaptive ways.

The previous edition of this book contained the following sentence: "We currently know nothing about the physiological events and processes underlying cognitive development." The present summary can be a bit more positive. Although much remains to be learned (always a safe conclusion), we do know *some* things, and more is being learned all the time.

Environmental-Experiential Contributors
to Cognitive Development

There are many ways to conceptualize and to cut up the environmental sources for cognitive growth. Perhaps the most general cut is the division between social and nonsocial: what children acquire from their interactions with other people versus what they acquire from their dealings with the inanimate physical world. Within the realm of social experience we can draw a distinction among different social agents: parents, teachers, siblings, peers. Social experiences can also be divided into those that are explicitly instructional (such as schooling) and those whose cognitive benefits are more incidental and happenstantial. Whether the experience is social or nonsocial, we can ask about the child's own contribution; to what extent is development a matter of self-generated discovery or construction, as opposed to a direct taking in of information from the environment? We can ask about specific modalities and specific types of experiences—what do we acquire from vision, hearing, touch, movement, language? Many theorists have addressed a number of these dimensions, and the field as a whole offers a variety of ideas with respect to each of them.

Suppose that we have identified a putative environmental contributor to cognitive growth—some factor A that we believe helps to engender development X. How can we determine whether A does in fact play a role in the development of X? Two common strategies are to see how X fares in children who have been experimentally provided with A, and to study the development of X in children who for some reason have gone without A. Such investigations are often called *enrichment* and *deprivation* studies, respectively. Piagetian training studies are enrichment studies; see Beilin (1978), D. Field (1987), Halford (1982), and Kuhn (1974) for more information on this extensive body of research. An investigator interested in explaining Piagetian acquisitions might hypothesize that a certain A is the usual developmental bridge to a certain X in everyday human ontogenesis. This investigator might believe, for example, that children gradually acquire conservation of number in the natural environment by gradually learning, through practice coupled with informational feedback, to attend to number-relevant information and disregard number-irrelevant information, such as length of row. The investigator then does a training study to test the hypothesis. Children who do not yet conserve number are provided with such practice and feedback to see whether it leads them to give conservation instead of nonconservation responses. In effect, the investigator attempts to simulate or mimic development in the laboratory to explain how it proceeds in everyday life, much as other psychologists try to simulate human problem solving on the computer in hope of explaining how it proceeds in human minds.

In neither case, however, is it possible for the researcher to conclude that nature has been faithfully imitated—that what happened in the training experience or in the computer is the same as what normally happens in real-life conservation development or problem solving. The same outcomes may have been achieved in both nature and its attempted simulation (although it is sometimes hard to be sure even of this). This is no guarantee, however, that the same processes were responsible for those outcomes. In the developmental case, it is unfortunately true that enrichment studies are just logically incapable of proving that a certain kind of experiential or milieu factor is a *necessary* contributor to any development. In real life, some or all children may acquire conservation of number with the aid of a wholly different factor, via some entirely different "developmental route." The investigator's enrichment study cannot rule out this possibility, no matter how effective his or her training regimen proved to be in that study. At most, such studies can suggest how the development of something *could* proceed; they do not tell us how it actually *does* proceed.

What about deprivation studies? Unlike the case with enrichment experiments, it would be highly unethical to do a deprivation experiment on children. One can, however, study the effects of deprivations that occur naturally. But there are also problems in interpreting deprivation studies. In particular, it may be difficult to determine precisely of what the child in question has and has not been deprived. Deprivation studies can nevertheless be very useful in determining whether particular kinds of experience are really necessary for particular sorts of development.

In a general sense, the message that emerges from deprivation studies is the same as the message suggested by Piagetian training studies. Both kinds of study suggest that human beings are flexible and versatile learners who can utilize a variety of experiences and follow a number of developmental routes in moving toward the same eventual end point. In the case of training studies, an astonishing diversity of experimentally provided experiences have proved to be beneficial in helping children to master conservation and other concrete-operational concepts. If we assume that laboratory demonstrations of this sort have any real-life applicability, the conclusion must be that no single kind of experience underlies such acquisitions for all children; rather, children are capable of extracting the same knowledge from a diverse range of inputs. In the case of deprivation studies, cognitive growth has often been found to proceed remarkably well despite major limitations in the ability to utilize certain types of experience.

For example, research by Furth (1971) and others on deaf children has shown that many aspects of cognitive development are surprisingly similar in deaf and hearing children, despite the fact that the former group are deprived of auditory input in general and (in the case of many deaf children) linguistic input in particular. Research by Landau, Spelke, and Gleitman (1984) has demonstrated an impressive degree of spatial knowledge in a 2-year-old girl who had been blind since birth, and hence lacking in the most obvious channel for information about the spatial world. And several case-study reports (Décarie, 1969; Jordan, 1972; Kopp & Shaperman, 1973) of subjects with severe motoric handicaps (e.g., children born with defects of the limbs because their mothers had taken the drug thalidomide during pregnancy) suggest that the ability to manipulate objects with hands or feet is not a necessary condition for normal cognitive development. This latter group of studies is of special relevance for Piaget's theory of sensorimotor development because such children are largely lacking the motor half of the kinds of sensorimotor experiences that Piaget believed to be crucial in the development of infant intelligence. Of course, a demonstration that development can proceed in the absence of some factor does not mean that the factor is unimportant in the normal, nondeprived case. But it does mean that children are adaptive creatures who can often make do with whatever acquisitional machinery they possess and with whatever environmental content comes their way. If the usual, typical developmental route is blocked, children may find an unusual, atypical one that somehow gets them to at least approximately the same cognitive destination.

We should add some qualifications to these optimistic, Rousseauesque notions of developmental versatility and resiliency. Even if adult-level competence is eventually attained, the rate of development toward this competence may be slowed, and slower-than-average development can pose a number of problems for both child and parent. Furthermore, children do not always prove versatile and resilient in the face of organismic or environmental handicaps. As we saw in Chapter 7 (the case study of Chelsea), even a strongly "biological" development such as the acquisition of grammar may be impaired if the necessary experiences are not available at the necessary time in development. Other aspects of intellectual development show marked individual differences in the quality of children's performance, and limitations in relevant experience are undoubtedly one reason that some children do relatively poorly. Many writers of books on cognitive growth would emphasize both individual differences and their origins more than we have done. Nevertheless, our knowledge on this important issue is still rather limited: We have much to learn about exactly what sorts of experience at what points in development for what sorts of children nurture what kinds of cognitive acquisitions. The importance of this last variable is sometimes overlooked. Some kinds of development appear to be much more dependent on specific and variably available experiences—more "experience-dependent" in the words of Greenough and colleagues (1987)—than do others. The ability to read and write and the ability to speak and understand oral language are both enormously significant cognitive accomplishments. The development of the latter seems much more "biological-evolutionary" than the former, however, and is much more certain to result from exposure to a normal human environment. Some forms of cognitive development clearly exhibit much more versatility and resiliency than others.

Many of the points made in this section can be illustrated through a brief consideration of a popular current approach to studying the experiential bases for cognitive change: the Vygotsky-inspired contextual approach. More than is true for most approaches to the study of cognitive development, issues of change are central to the contextual approach. This centrality is evident in the guiding metaphor for the approach: the child as apprentice (Rogoff, 1990). According to the contextualists, children are embedded in a social context from birth, and cognitive growth occurs through a process of guided participation in which others, especially parents, provide various kinds of help tailored to the child's current level of ability (thus working within Vygotsky's "zone of proximal development"). Cognitive development is therefore not an individual but a joint construction, in which children are guided toward culturally embedded skills and bodies of knowledge, rather than having somehow to discover such knowledge on their own.

Undoubtedly part of the reason for the popularity of the contextual approach lies in the fact that it seems to redress limitations in some of the other major approaches to children's thinking. Although Piagetian theory does talk about the contribution of social experience, the dominant image that one takes away from Piaget's writings is of the autonomous child who self-constructs knowledge through his or her own active commerce with the environment. A focus on the child in isolation could also be argued to be characteristic of much of what is said in both the information-processing and IQ or psychometric perspectives on intelligence. The contextualist's child, in contrast, is rooted in a social world from birth. Furthermore, contextualist theorists have offered a number of interesting ideas about what kinds of social experiences are important at what points in development; they have thus at least begun to address the need for specificity with regard to environmental influences that we stressed earlier. And although theorizing so far outstrips research, workers in this tradition have provided some compelling demonstrations of how social interaction can mediate individual development. A good idea of the achievements of the contextualist approach to date can be gained from books by Gellatly, Rogers, and Sloboda (1989), Resnick et al. (1991), and Rogoff (1990).

What about possible cautions? Is cognitive development really as intrinsically social, as culturally embedded, and as dependent on guidance from others as contextual theorists maintain? It may be, but this claim is a long way from established fact. Our own guess is that some aspects of cognitive functioning are in fact socially created in the ways that contextualists emphasize, but that others are not—or at least not as strongly or as uniformly as some proponents of the approach seem to imply. This guess reflects a theme of this section: Different kinds of knowledge have different kinds of dependence on environmental input. Some forms of knowledge may be dependent on specific sorts of experience, may be in a real sense created by that experience, and may vary across children because the relevant experiences vary across children. Other forms of knowledge may have a much stronger biological basis, may require only very general experience to "prime" their development, and may be common across children because the necessary experiences are common across all human environments. It is true that one of the common elements across "expectable" human environments is the presence of other people and of certain kinds of interaction between children and the more mature members of the culture. Social experience may be involved in a very general sense in any human cognitive acquisition. Nevertheless, we are doubtful that the apprentice model will prove to be the best way to explain (to give a partial list) the infant's understanding of objects, the toddler's mastery of syntactic rules, the preschooler's appreciation of the appearance-reality distinction, or the grade schooler's mastery of Piagetian concepts.

Processes or Mechanisms of Cognitive Development

One approach to the problem of explaining cognitive development is to identify processes or mechanisms that seem to be operative in many or all cases in which cognitive growth occurs (Flavell, 1984; Siegler, 1989c; Sternberg, 1984). Many such mechanisms have been proposed; Siegler (1991a) lists 20 processes that have been put forth as explanations for cognitive change, and this list is undoubtedly far from exhaustive. Clearly, one challenge here is to get clear about similarities and overlap among various proposed mechanisms. Another, once again, is to figure out how to study the question—how to obtain evidence that would tell us whether a proposed mechanism is really operating when cognitive change occurs. Enrichment or training studies are again one possible source of evidence. Just as we can attempt to simulate some environmental contributor experimentally, so can we attempt to create a learning situation in which some mechanism of change will be revealed. Another possible approach is Siegler's *microgenetic method* (Siegler & Crowley, 1991; Siegler & Jenkins, 1989). In a micrognetic study, the researcher records children's behavior as they work repeatedly and intensively within some problem domain—perhaps dozens of hours of observation spread across several weeks. The attempt is to capsulize the time frame for cognitive change—to observe within a relatively short period processes that might ordinarily be spread across a much longer time frame. In contrast to a training study, the typical microgenetic study is relatively nondirective; the researcher's goal is not to teach new knowledge but rather to create situations in which natural processes of knowledge acquisition can be observed. The microgenetic method was the source for many of Siegler's conclusions concerning children's arithmetical strategies that we discussed earlier in the book.

A rough distinction can be drawn between two general categories of change mechanisms. Some proposed mechanisms concern what we might call the on-line processing of information—that is, the processes that operate when children take in information and adapt to environmental challenges. Piaget's assimilation-accommodation model falls in this category. Another example is the construct of encoding that is stressed in some of Siegler's balance-scale research (e.g., Siegler, 1976). As Siegler uses the term, encoding refers to identifying the features of objects and events and using the features to form internal representations. As we saw in Chapter 4, encoding proved to be important in children's response to the balance scale. It was only when Rule I users began to encode information about distance from the fulcrum that they were able to benefit from feedback concerning the effects of distance and begin to formulate rules that took both of the relevant dimensions into account.

Other change mechanisms have to do less with the immediate processing of information than with changes in the general characteristics of the cognitive system that make developmental advances possible. Here, too, we have seen a number of examples. One such mechanism that is stressed in both information-processing and neo-Piagetian theories is increased information-processing capacity. As children develop, the amount of information that they can hold in working memory increases, and this increase permits forms of mental activity that were not possible as long as the system was more limited. Increased capacity is especially important in Case's (1985, 1992) neo-Piagetian theory, in which stage-to-stage changes are explained largely in terms of the new operations that increased capacity allows. A closely related mechanism is increased processing speed. Research by Hale (1990) and by Kail (1991a, 1991b) has shown that the speed with which information is processed increases steadily across childhood. An increase in speed is of obvious benefit—more can be taken in and more can be done within any period of time. In addition, the increase in speed is one basis for the increase in capacity. Finally, the ability to inhibit prepotent responses may be a third general mechanism of this sort. Our discussions in Chapter 2 and earlier in this chapter emphasized the role of inhibition in infant development—in particular, Diamond's (1991a, 1991b) work on object concept. The same general argument, however, has been advanced for older children as well (Dempster, 1992, in press; Harnishfeger & Bjorklund, in press): Mature problem solving often depends on the capacity to inhibit dominant but less mature responses, and as children develop they become more and more capable of such inhibition.

Two points can be made about the change mechanisms just discussed. First, these are factors that have their own developmental histories. That is, capacity, speed, and inhibition all contribute to developmental change, but they are also all processes that undergo development themselves: Older children are better at all of these things than are younger children. This sort of dual role as outcome and as determinant—as both the "what" and the "how" of development—may be true of a number of mechanisms of change (Flavell, 1984). It applies, for example, to encoding: Encoding previously unnoticed information helps children to form new concepts and to solve new problems, but skill at encoding information itself improves as children develop. Similarly, the ability to manipulate symbols is an important outcome of infant development, but once present, symbolic ability contributes enormously to future cognitive change. Many other processes that have been proposed as mechanisms of change (e.g., strategy construction, reasoning by analogy, generalization) show this same dual character: As they develop themselves, they contribute to other developments.

The second point concerns why it is that mechanisms of change undergo change themselves. The reasons are almost certainly both biological and environmental. In the case of processing speed, considerable evidence suggests that some sort of "hard wired" maturational change underlies the general increase in speed that comes with development. Similarly, improvements in inhibition during infancy have been linked to maturational changes in areas of the frontal cortex. Yet it is also clear that experience can contribute to such changes. Practice in executing an operation, for example, can lead to greater efficiency, which in turn can mean both greater speed and more capacity left over for other operations. Practice can also affect the ability to inhibit. A conclusion that nature and nurture are both important is generally a safe one, and such a conclusion is certainly valid here.

Our discussion to this point may have given the impression that there are many different mechanisms that contribute to cognitive growth. If so, this impression was intended: There *do* seem to be multiple bases for cognitive change. Some of these bases are of the on-line processing sort; others of the general-system sort. Some may be highly domain-specific (e.g., techniques for extracting information about language); others may be more domain-general. Some may have both domain-specific and domain-general aspects. For example, the increase in information-processing capacity with age is a quite general change that cuts across a number of aspects of children's development. Yet content-specific expertise can also affect capacity, and children may have greater functional capacity for some domains than for others.

Despite the apparent plethora of change mechanisms, it is still reasonable to ask about possible commonalities. Perhaps the various mechanisms are not really as distinct as they at first seem. Perhaps instead they are specific manifestations of some more general principle—some overarching process of development that subsumes the individual mechanisms and serves as the ultimate explanation for why development proceeds as it does.

The best-known general principle of this sort is Piaget's construct of equilibration. For Piaget, equilibration—or the biological tendency of self-regulation—performed exactly this sort of role as general coordinator and director of development. A very brief synopsis of this complicated notion is as follows (again, see Chapman, 1988, for more details, including a description of how Piaget's thinking about equilibration changed over time). The natural direction of development, according to Piaget, is toward states of equilibrium—that is, states of balance among different elements of the cognitive system, balance between the processes of assimilation and accommodation, and balance between the cognitive system and the outer world. A state of equilibrium implies a synchronized, smoothly running, "comfortable" cognitive system, one that yields ready and consistent answers to the problems with which it is faced.

In contrast, a state of disequilibrium, or cognitive conflict, implies some imbalance, some lack of fit, some uncertainty in the solutions that the cognitive structures yield. Such states are assumed to be motivating; the child will attempt to resolve the disequilibrium and to arrive at a better level of understanding (recall our discussion of Cognitive Motivation in Chapter 2). The conservation of number problem (Chapter 3) provides an example. Initially, the nonconserver tends to focus only on the length of the row of objects, a strategy that yields the conclusion that the longer row contains more. The child's thinking about the problem is in equilibrium, albeit at an immature, nonconservation level. Eventually, however, the child begins to notice that the longer row has also become less dense, a fact that by itself would incline the child to conclude that this row contains fewer objects. If the child finds both of these opposing conclusions plausible at the same psychological moment, then his or her cognitive system has moved from a state of equilibrium to one of disequilibrium for this particular problem. The child can resolve the disequilibrium and achieve a new, more intellectually advanced equilibrium state by considering the length and density changes simultaneously and recognizing that one change compensates for or cancels out the other, hence leaving the number unchanged. A developmental advance has been made by means of a process of equilibration composed of these major steps: (1) cognitive equilibrium at a lower developmental level; (2) cognitive disequilibrium or conflict, induced by awareness of contradictory, discrepant, "nonassimilable" data not previously attended to; (3) cognitive equilibration (or reequilibration) at a higher developmental level, caused by reconceptualizing the problem in such a way as to harmonize what had earlier been seen as conflicting. Piaget argues that all significant cognitive-developmental advances are made through this kind of equilibration process. Notice that this process is an elaboration of the one described in Chapter 1 ("Assimilation-Accommodation as a Model of Cognitive Development" section).

Piaget's equilibration model has been subject to a number of criticisms (Bryant, 1990; Chapman, 1990; Flavell, 1971a; Zimmerman & Blom, 1983). Even if the model makes sense for some cognitive acquisitions, it is by no means clear that every cognitive advance can be explained in terms of a cognitive conflict-reequilibration sequence. Nor is it clear, even if we grant that equilibration is occurring, that we have really fully explained everything. Rather, parts of the equilibration process (How does the child come to perceive a conflict? Why does he resolve it in the way that he does?) could be argued to be themselves in need of explanation. At the least, the model seems incomplete; it provides a general framework for conceptualizing cognitive change, but it leaves much still to be accounted for.

Is there then no single principle of development that applies to every instance of cognitive change? In a recent review of change mechanisms, Siegler (1989c) makes an intriguing suggestion with regard to a possible common element. This common element is competition. As he points out, a number of change mechanisms seem to involve selection among competing possibilities, with more adaptive approaches gradually winning out over less adaptive ones. Such a competition model applies, for example, to his own work on strategy choice in the domain of arithmetical problem solving. It applies to MacWhinney's (1987a) Competition Model of language acquisition (see Chapter 7). It applies, at a neurological level, to synaptogenesis and the selective survival of only some synapses. And it can even be argued to apply to Piaget's equilibration theory, in which the cognitive conflict engendered by competing ways of thinking forces a reworking of the cognitive system. Elsewhere, Siegler (1991a) notes the analogy with evolution. Just as evolution involves a survival of the fittest among species, so may cognitive development involve a survival of the fittest among cognitive processes.

SUMMARY

Psychologists who work in the area of cognitive development see it as replete with difficult questions and problems. Many of these can be subsumed under the headings of *diagnosis*, *patterns*, and *cognitive change*.

Questions and problems in the area of diagnosis can be grouped into two closely related types: those concerned with our *conceptualization* of the underlying nature of the cognitive abilities that we study, and those concerned with our *assessment* of those abilities in children. A useful cognitive-developmental acquisition to illustrate these points is transitive inference concerning length relations—for example, if A > B and B > C, then A > C can be inferred.

Assessments of transitive inference or any other cognitive acquisition can err in two ways. A *false-negative* error consists of erroneously concluding that a particular child has not yet acquired a capacity. Even though the child does really possess this capacity, he or she fails to show it in test performance because of information-processing, linguistic, motivational, emotional, or other problems. All tasks demand more from the child than the target cognitive entity the experimenter is interested in assessing. If the child fails to respond appropriately to any of these nontarget demands, a false-negative diagnostic error can result. Conversely, a false-positive error consists in erroneously concluding that a child does possess the target capacity. For example, the child may conclude that A > C simply because A had been called "longer than" something else (i.e., B) whereas C had not; the child therefore reaches the correct conclusion, but not by means of transitive inference. It is often possible to design a cognitive task in such a way that the probability of making a false-positive diagnostic error is reduced. Unfortunately, these very same changes may increase the risk of false-negative errors.

Such facts suggest that there may be developmental changes in how the child "has" cognitive entities like transitive reasoning, and this possibility leads us to questions of conceptualization. How can we characterize the difference in the way that two children "have" transitive inference? A variety of possibilities were suggested. One child may have a more advanced grasp of the concept in the sense of being able to evoke the knowledge more readily in appropriate situations. Given that the knowledge has been evoked, one child may be able to execute the problem-solving strategy more effectively than another. The range of situations in which the knowledge can be applied may increase with development, expanding from simple and limited to maximally general. Finally, with development the knowledge may change from implicit to explicit, and may come to be held not just as probably true but as certainly and maybe even necessarily true.

Delineation of these various possibilities still leaves some basic questions of conceptualization unanswered. Is transitive inference a single ability that varies along dimensions such as evocability and utilizability, or are there different kinds of transitive inference at different developmental levels? And what exactly takes place in the child's head—what cognitive processes are activated in what order—when the child solves a transitive-inference problem? Some research by Trabasso was described both as an example of how to study these questions and as an illustration that these processes may be quite different from those previously assumed.

Good diagnosis is essential for determining the patterns that hold among cognitive entities, as well as for studying processes of cognitive change. More basically, diagnosis is ultimately at the root of all psychological research and hence of any conclusions that we might draw about children's cognitive development. One conclusion that emerges from a consideration of recent diagnostic innovations is that traditional assessment techniques have often led us to underestimate children's abilities, especially during the infant and preschool periods. The caution is added, however, that these early competencies are typically not full competencies, and that it remains important to trace changes in knowledge beyond its first emergence.

The patterns that hold among cognitive-developmental entities are of interest because they tell us something about the causal-functional relations among those entities. Three possible types of patterns are *sequences, concurrences,* and *stages.* Five types of X-Y developmental sequences can be distinguished, where X and Y represent cognitive entities: Y develops after X and constitutes an additional, alternative cognitive means to the same goal (*addition* sequence). Later-developing Y replaces earlier-developing X as an approach to a given problem (*substitution*). Y is derived from X by *differentiation, generalization,* or *stabilization* (*modification*). X becomes a component part of a larger cognitive unit Y (*inclusion*). X serves as a developmental facilitator of, or bridge to, Y (*mediation*).

The relation of interest in the study of developmental concurrences is one of common origin: X and Y emerge at the same time because they stem from the same underlying cognitive advance. For example, a number of contemporaneous achievements in the domain of theory of mind can be linked to a general understanding of the mental representational process. Here and in general, however, concurrences are typically loose rather than tight.

One implication of the notion of stage is that many related abilities emerge more or less in concurrence. Other concepts relevant to an evaluation of stage theories are *structures, qualitative change,* and *abruptness.* Tentative conclusions were offered with regard to each of these criteria. Cognitive structures develop, but Piaget's structural models may not accurately characterize them. Many of the major cognitive-developmental changes appear to be qualitative rather than quantitative, at least at some level of analysis. Cognitive growth is gradual—perhaps very gradual—rather than abrupt. Although diagnostic problems make it difficult to tell for sure, it does not appear that cognitive acquisitions normally develop in the tightly knit, concurrent fashion that Piaget's theory seems to predict. Thus the existing evidence suggests that cognitive growth is not as strongly and clearly a stage-like process as Piaget's theory claims it is. It should be added, however, that a number of developmental psychologists, especially neo-Piagetians, still advocate some form of stage theory of cognitive development.

How is cognitive growth to be explained? Not entirely by environmental factors, according to much recent research and theorizing directed to the biological bases of cognitive development. Common to much of this work is an emphasis on infant precocity: on skills that are present so early that it is difficult to see how they could be acquired from experience. Many of these early competencies appear to be domain-specific and to correspond to biologically natural, evolutionary prepared domains of development (e.g., language). Scarr has proposed a more domain-general form of evolutionary shaping; she suggests that the human infant is strongly predisposed to acquire sensorimotor intelligence, and that the normal human caretaking environment has evolved to support exactly this sort of development. Although most such proposals have not attempted to specify physiological bases, some progress in this area has been made recently. Two examples were discussed: studies of frontal lobe maturation as a basis for the ability to inhibit dominant responses that interfere with mature problem solving (e.g., on object permanence tasks), and the selective survival of synaptic connections as a function of the availability of relevant experience.

Various sources of environmental influence may contribute to children's cognitive development. Results of *enrichment* and *deprivation* studies are often used to make inferences about environmental-experiential contributions. Piagetian training experiments are instances of enrichment studies, whereas investigations of individuals born with sensory or motor handicaps, or reared in psychologically impoverished circumstances, would be examples of deprivation studies. An enrichment study can show that experience A is capable of facilitating the development of cognitive skill X, but it cannot show that A is necessary to X's acquisition, nor even that it normally plays a formative role in the real-world, extralaboratory ontogenesis of X. In contrast, a deprivation study is potentially capable of showing that A is or is not necessary to X's real-world ontogenesis. Several deprivation studies illustrate how *versatile* and *resilient* a developing child can be; both these studies and Piagetian training studies suggest that there may be multiple routes to the same developmental end point. Developmental versatility is not always in evidence, however, and the extent to which it is found may vary across different sorts of development. Some developments may be more dependent on specific kinds of experience, and hence more variable across environments and across children, than are others. It is suggested that this point may be important in evaluating claims from the contextual approach regarding the role of social experience in cognitive development.

One way to explain cognitive growth is to specify the processes or mechanisms that are operative when growth occurs. Two general categories of such explanations can be identified. Some proposed mechanisms focus on how information is processed and incorporated into the cognitive system; Piaget's assimilation-accommodation model is an example in this category. Other mechanisms concern changes in general characteristics of the cognitive system that facilitate cognitive growth. Examples in this category include increases in information-processing capacity, speed of processing, and the ability to inhibit responses. Mechanisms of this sort undergo development themselves at the same time they affect other developments—something that is probably true of change mechanisms in general. Both biological and environmental factors contribute to these changes.

Current evidence suggests that a variety of mechanisms operate to produce cognitive growth. Nevertheless, the search for a single, overarching principle continues. The best-known such principle is Piaget's construct of *equilibration*. According to the equilibration model, development takes place in three basic steps. Initially, the child's cognitive system with respect to some problem is in equilibrium at a lower developmental level. Subsequently, the child detects something that conflicts with his or her present system, something that the system cannot assimilate or accommodate to, and therefore something which puts it in a state of disequilibrium. Finally, equilibrium is reestablished at a higher developmental level by modifying the cognitive system so that what was formerly perceived as discordant is now readily assimilable. Two criticisms of this model were offered: (1) It may not apply to every instance of cognitive change and (2) it is not sufficiently specific to provide a complete explanation of how change occurs. A recently proposed alternative is Siegler's competition model: the proposal that development occurs through a process of competition among cognitive processes (strategies, rules, etc.) and the selective survival of only the most adaptive processes.

References

ABRAHAMS, B. A. (1979). *An integrative approach to the study of the development of perspective-taking abilities*. Unpublished doctoral dissertation, Stanford University.

ABRAMOVITCH, R., & FREEDMAN, J. L. (1981). Actor-observer differences in children's attributions. *Merrill-Palmer Quarterly, 27,* 53–59.

ACKERMAN, B. P., SPIKER, K., & BAILEY, K. (1989). The relation between resource limitations and optional conceptual processing by children and adults. *Child Development, 60,* 1200–1211.

ACREDELO, C. (1982). Conservation/nonconservation: Alternative explanations. In C. J. Brainerd (Ed.), *Progress in cognitive development* (Vol. 1). New York: Springer-Verlag.

ACREDOLO, C. (1989). Assessing children's understanding of time, speed and distance interrelations. In I. Levin & D. Zakay (Eds.), *Time and human cognition: A lifespan perspective*. Amsterdam: Elsevier.

ACREDOLO, C., & O'CONNOR, J. (1991). On the difficulty of detecting cognitive uncertainty. *Human Development, 34,* 204–224.

ACREDOLO, L. P. (1979). Laboratory versus home: The effect of environment on the 9-month-old infant's choice of spatial reference system. *Developmental Psychology, 15,* 666–667.

ACREDOLO, L. P. (1990). Behavioral approaches to spatial orientation, representation, and mapping. In A. Diamond (Ed.), *The development and neural bases of higher cognitive functions*. New York: The New York Academy of Sciences.

ACREDOLO, L. P., & GOODWYN, S. (1988). Symbolic gesturing in normal infants. *Child Development, 59,* 450–466.

ACREDOLO, L. P., & GOODWYN, S. (1990). Development of communicative gesturing. In R. Vasta (Ed.), *Annals of child development* (Vol. 7). Greenwich, CT: JAI Press.

ADAMS, A., & BULLOCK, D. (1986). Apprenticeship in word use: Social convergence processes in learning categorically related nouns. In S. Kuczaj II & M. Barrett (Eds.), *The development of word meaning*. New York: Springer-Verlag.

ADAMS, R. J. (1989). Newborns' discrimination among mid- and long-wavelength stimuli. *Journal of Experimental Child Psychology, 47,* 130–141.

ADAMS, R. J., & MAURER, D. (1984). Detection of contrast by the newborn and 2-month-old infant. *Infant Behavior and Development, 7,* 415–422.

ADAMS, R. J., MAURER, D., & DAVIS, M. (1986). Newborns' discrimination of chromatic from achromatic stimuli. *Journal of Experimental Child Psychology, 41,* 267–281.

ADLAM-HILL, S., & HARRIS, P. L. (1988). *Understanding of display rules for emotion by normal and maladjusted children.* Unpublished paper, University of Oxford.

ALOISE, P. A. (1991, April). *The development of self-presentation.* Paper presented at the meeting of the Society for Research in Child Development, Seattle, WA.

ALOISE, P. A., & MILLER, P. H. (1991). Discounting in preschoolers: Effects of type of reward agent. *Journal of Experimental Child Psychology, 57,* 70–86.

ANDERSON, J. R. (1980). *Cognitive psychology and its implications.* San Francisco: W. H. Freeman.

ANGLIN, J. M. (1977). *Word, object, and conceptual development.* New York: W. W. Norton.

ANISFELD, M. (1991). Neonatal imitation. *Developmental Review, 11,* 60–97.

ANTELL, S. E., & KEATING, D. P. (1983). Perception of numerical invariance in neonates. *Child Development, 54,* 695–701.

ASHER, S. R. (1979). Referential communication. In G. J. Whitehurst & B. J. Zimmerman (Eds.), *The functions of language and communication.* New York: Academic Press.

ASHER, S. R., & COIE, J. D. (Eds.). (1990). *Peer rejection in childhood.* Cambridge: Cambridge University Press.

ASHMEAD, D. H., & PERLMUTTER, M. (1980). Infant memory in everyday life. In M. Perlmutter (Ed.), *New directions for child development: No. 10. Children's memory.* San Francisco: Jossey-Bass.

ASLIN, R. N. (1987a). Motor aspects of visual development in infancy. In P. Salapatek & L. Cohen (Eds.), *Handbook of infant perception: Vol. 1. From sensation to perception.* Orlando, FL: Academic Press.

ASLIN, R. N. (1987b). Visual and auditory development in infancy. In J. D. Osofsky (Ed.), *Handbook of infant development* (2nd ed.). New York: John Wiley.

ASLIN, R. N. (1988). Anatomical constraints on oculomotor development: Implications for infant perception. In A. Yonas (Ed.), *Minnesota symposia on child psychology: Vol. 20. Perceptual development in infancy.* Hillsdale, NJ: Erlbaum.

ASLIN, R. N., PISONI, D. P., & JUSCZYK, P. W. (1983). Auditory development and speech perception in infancy. In M. M. Haith & J. J. Campos (Eds.), P. H. Mussen (Series Ed.), *Handbook of child psychology: Vol. 2. Infancy and developmental psychobiology.* New York: John Wiley.

ASTINGTON, J. W. (1991). Intention in the child's theory of mind. In D. Frye & C. Moore (Eds.), *Children's theories of mind.* Hillsdale, NJ: Erlbaum.

ASTINGTON, J. W., & GOPNIK, A. (1991). Theoretical explanations of children's understanding of the mind. *British Journal of Developmental Psychology, 9,* 7–32.

ASTINGTON, J. W., HARRIS, P. L., & OLSON, D. (Eds.). (1988). *Developing theories of mind.* Cambridge: Cambridge University Press.

ATKINSON, R. C., & SHIFFRIN, R. M. (1968). Human memory: A proposed system and its control processes. In K. W. Spence & J. T. Spence (Eds.), *The psychology of learning and motivation* (Vol. 2). New York: Academic Press.

AU, T. K., & MARKMAN, E. M. (1987). Acquiring word meanings via linguistic contrast. *Cognitive Development, 2,* 217–236.

AVIS, J., & HARRIS, P. L. (1991). Belief-desire reasoning among Baka children: Evidence for a universal conception of mind. *Child Development, 62,* 460–467.

BAILLARGEON, R. (1986). Representing the existence and the location of hidden objects: Object permanence in 6- and 8-month-old infants. *Cognition, 23,* 21–41.

BAILLARGEON, R. (1987a). Object permanence in 3.5- and 4.5-month-old infants. *Developmental Psychology, 23,* 655–664.

BAILLARGEON, R. (1987b). Young infants' reasoning about the physical and spatial properties of a hidden object. *Cognitive Development, 2,* 179–200.

BAILLARGEON, R. (1990, August). *Young infants' physical knowledge.* Paper presented at the meeting of the American Psychological Association, Boston.

BAILLARGEON, R. (1991, April). *Infants' reasoning about collision events.* Paper presented at the meeting of the Society for Research in Child Development, Seattle, WA.

BAILLARGEON, R. (in press). The object concept revisited: New directions in the investigation of infants' physical knowledge. In C. E. Granrud (Ed.), *Visual perception and cognition in infancy.* Hillsdale, NJ: Erlbaum.

BAILLARGEON, R., DEVOS, J., & GRABER, M. (1989). Location memory in 8-month-old infants in a non-search AB̄ task: Further evidence. *Cognitive Development, 4,* 345–367.

BAILLARGEON, R., & GRABER, M. (1988). Evidence of location memory in 8-month-old infants in a non-search AB task. *Developmental Psychology, 24,* 502–511.

BAILLARGEON, R., & HANKO-SUMMERS, S. (1990). Is the top object adequately supported by the bottom object? Young infants' understanding of support relations. *Cognitive Development, 5,* 29–53.

BAKER, L. (1982). An evaluation of the role of metacognitive deficits in learning disabilities. *Topics in Learning and Learning Disabilities, 2,* 27–35.

BAKER, L., & BROWN, A. L. (1984). Metacognition and the reading process. In P. D. Pearson (Ed.), *A handbook of reading research.* New York: Longman.

BAKER-WARD, L., & ORNSTEIN, P. A. (1988). Age differences in visual-spatial memory performance: Do children really out-perform adults when playing Concentration? *Bulletin of the Psychonomic Society, 26,* 331–332.

BAKER-WARD, L., ORNSTEIN, P. A., & HOLDEN, D. J. (1984). The expression of memorization in early childhood. *Journal of Experimental Child Psychology, 37,* 555–575.

BALDWIN, D. A. (1991). Infants' contribution to the achievement of joint reference. *Child Development, 62,* 875–890.

BANERJEE, M., & WELLMAN, H. M. (1990, May). *Children's understanding of emotions: A belief-desire perspective.* Paper presented at the meeting of the Jean Piaget Society, Philadelphia.

BANERJEE, M., & WELLMAN, H. M. (1991, April). *Preschoolers' use of emotion contrastives: Evidence for a mentalistic understanding of emotions.* Paper presented at the meeting of the Society for Research in Child Development, Seattle, WA.

BANKS, M. S., & GINSBURG, A. P. (1985). Infant visual preferences: A review and new theoretical treatment. In H. W. Reese (Ed.), *Advances in child development and behavior* (Vol. 19). Orlando, FL: Academic Press.

BANKS, M. S., & SALAPATEK, P. (1981). Infant pattern vision: A new approach based on the contrast sensitivity function. *Journal of Experimental Child Psychology, 31,* 1–45.

BANKS, M. S., & SALAPATEK, P. (1983). Infant visual perception. In M. M. Haith & J. J. Campos (Eds.), P. H. Mussen (Series Ed.), *Handbook of child psychology: Vol. 2. Infancy and developmental psychobiology.* New York: John Wiley.

BARENBOIM, C. (1977). Developmental changes in the interpersonal cognitive system from middle childhood to adolescence. *Child Development, 48,* 1467–1474.

BARENBOIM, C. (1978). Development of recursive and nonrecursive thinking about persons. *Developmental Psychology, 14,* 419–420.

BARENBOIM, C. (1981). The development of person perception in childhood and adolescence: From behavioral comparisons to psychological constructs to psychological comparisons. *Child Development, 52,* 129–144.

BARON-COHEN, S. (1991a). Do people with autism understand what causes emotion? *Child Development, 62,* 385–396.

BARON-COHEN, S. (1991b). The theory of mind deficit in autism: How specific is it? *British Journal of Developmental Psychology, 9,* 301–314.

BARON-COHEN, S., LESLIE, A. M., & FRITH, U. (1986). Mechanical behavioral and intentional understanding of picture stories in autistic children. *British Journal of Developmental Psychology, 4,* 113–125.

BARONI, M. R., & AXIA, G. (1989). Children's meta-pragmatic abilities and the identification of polite and impolite requests. *First Language, 9,* 285–297.

BARRERA, M. E., & MAURER, D. (1981). Recognition of mother's photographed face by the three-month-old infant. *Child Development, 52,* 714–716.

BARRETT, M. (1982). The holophrastic hypothesis: Conceptual and empirical issues. *Cognition, 11,* 47–76.

BARTLETT, E. J. (1976). Sizing things up: The acquisition of the meaning of dimensional adjectives. *Journal of Child Language, 3,* 205–219.

BARTSCH, K. (1990, May). *Children's talk about beliefs and desires: Evidence of a developing theory of mind.* Paper presented at the Symposium of the Jean Piaget Society, Philadelphia.

BATES, E. (1976). *Language and context: The acquisition of pragmatics.* New York: Academic Press.

BATES, E., BRETHERTON, I., & SNYDER, L. (1988). *From first words to grammar: Individual differences and dissociable mechanisms.* Cambridge: Cambridge University Press.

BATES, E., CARLSON-LUDEN, V., & BRETHERTON, I. (1980). Perceptual aspects of tool using in infancy. *Infant Behavior and Development, 3,* 127–140.

BATES, E., & ELMAN, J. L. (1992). *Connectionism and the study of change* (Tech. Rep. No. 9202). San Diego: University of California, Center for Research in Language.

BATES, E., & MACWHINNEY, B. (1987). Competition, variation, and language learning. In B. MacWhinney (Ed.), *Mechanisms of language acquisition.* Hillsdale, NJ: Erlbaum.

BATES, E., & SNYDER, L. (1985). The cognitive hypothesis in language development. In I. Uzgiris & J. McV. Hunt (Eds.), *Research with scales of psychological development in infancy.* Champaign-Urbana: University of Illinois Press.

BAUER, P. J., & MANDLER, J. M. (1989). One thing follows another: Effects of temporal structure on 1- to 2-year-olds' recall of events. *Developmental Psychology, 25,* 197–206.

BAUER, P. J., & MANDLER, J. M. (1990). Remembering what happened next: Very young children's recall of event sequences. In R. Fivush & J. A. Hudson (Eds.), *Knowing and remembering in young children*. Cambridge: Cambridge University Press.

BAUER, P. J., & SHORE, C. M. (1987). Making a memorable event: Effects of familiarity and organization on young children's recall of action sequences. *Cognitive Development, 2,* 327–338.

BAUER, P. J., & THAL, D. J. (1990). Scripts or scraps: Reconsidering the development of sequential understanding. *Journal of Experimental Child Psychology, 50,* 287–304.

BEAL, C. R. (1983). *The development of knowledge about cognitive cueing.* Unpublished doctoral dissertation, Stanford University.

BEAL, C. R. (1985). Development of knowledge about the use of cues to aid prospective retrieval. *Child Development, 56,* 631–642.

BEAL, C. R. (1988). Children's knowledge about representations of intended meaning. In J. W. Astington, P. L. Harris, & D. R. Olson (Eds.), *Developing theories of mind.* Cambridge: Cambridge University Press.

BEAL, C. R., & BELGRAD, S. L. (1990). The development of message evaluation skills in young children. *Child Development, 61,* 705–712.

BEAL, C. R., & FLAVELL, J. H. (1982). The effect of increasing the salience of message ambiguities on kindergartners' evaluations of communicative success and message adequacy. *Developmental Psychology, 18,* 43–48.

BEAL, C. R., & FLAVELL, J. H. (1984). Development of the ability to distinguish communicative intention and literal message meaning. *Child Development, 55,* 920–928.

BEARISON, D. J. (1969). Role of measurement operations in the acquisition of conservation. *Developmental Psychology, 1,* 653–660.

BECKER, J. A. (1986). Bossy and nice requests: Children's production and interpretation. *Merrill-Palmer Quarterly, 32,* 393–413.

BECKER, J. A. (1988). The success of parents' indirect techniques for teaching their preschoolers pragmatic skills. *First Language, 8,* 173–182.

BECKER, J. A. (1992, April). *"Sneak-shoes," "sworders," and "nose-beards": A case study of lexical innovation.* Paper presented at the meeting of the Conference on Human Development, Atlanta.

BEEGHLY, M., BRETHERTON, I., & MERVIS, C. B. (1986). Mothers' internal state language to toddlers. *British Journal of Developmental Psychology, 4,* 247–261.

BEHREND, D. A. (1990). Constraints and development: A reply to Nelson. *Cognitive Development, 5,* 313–330.

BEILIN, H. (1978). Inducing conservation through training. In G. Steiner (Ed.), *Psychology of the 20th century: Vol.7. Piaget and beyond.* Zurich: Kindler.

BEILIN, H. (1989). Piagetian theory. In R. Vasta (Ed.), *Annals of child development: Vol. 6. Six theories of child development: Revised formulations and current issues.* Greenwich, CT: JAI Press.

BEILIN, H. (1992). Piaget's enduring contribution to developmental psychology. *Developmental Psychology, 28,* 191–204.

BEM, S. (1970). The role of comprehension in children's problem-solving. *Developmental Psychology, 2,* 351–358.

BERG, W. K., & BERG, K. M. (1987). Psychophysiological development in infancy: State, startle, and attention. In J. S. Osofsky (Ed.), *Handbook of infant development* (2nd ed.). New York: John Wiley.

BERKO, J. (1958). The child's learning of English morphology. *Word, 14,* 150–177.

BERNDT, T. J. (1988). The nature and significance of children's friendships. In R. Vasta (Ed.), *Annals of child development* (Vol. 5). Greenwich, CT: JAI Press.

BERNDT, T. J., & HELLER, K. (1985). Predictions of future behavior, trait ratings, and responses to open-ended questions as measures of children's personality attributions. In S. R. Yussen (Ed.), *The growth of reflection.* New York: Academic Press.

BERTENTHAL, B. I., & CAMPOS, J. J. (1990). A systems approach to the organizing effects of self-produced locomotion during infancy. In C. Rovee-Collier & L. P. Lipsitt (Eds.), *Advances in infancy research* (Vol. 6). Norwood, NJ: Ablex.

BERTENTHAL, B. I., CAMPOS, J. J., & BARRETT, K. C. (1984). Self-produced locomotions: An organizer of emotional, cognitive, and social development in infancy. In R. Emde & R. Harmon (Eds.), *Continuities and discontinuities in development.* New York: Plenum Press.

BERTENTHAL, B. I., PROFFITT, D. R., & CUTTING, J. E. (1984). Infant sensitivity to figural coherence in biomechanical motions. *Journal of Experimental Child Psychology, 37,* 213–220.

BEST, C. (1988). The emergence of cerebral asymmetries in early human development: A literature review and a neuroembryological model. In S. Segalowitz & D. Molfese (Eds.), *Brain lateralization in children: Developmental implications.* New York: Guilford Press.

BEST, D. L., & ORNSTEIN, P. A. (1986). Children's generation and communication of mnemonic organizational strategies. *Developmental Psychology, 22,* 845–853.

BEUHRING, T., & KEE, D. W. (1987). Developmental relationships among metamemory, elaborative strategy use, and associative memory. *Journal of Experimental Child Psychology, 44*, 377–400.

BEVER, T. G. (Ed.). (1982). *Regressions in mental development: Basic phenomena and theories.* Hillsdale, NJ: Erlbaum.

BIERNAT, M. (1991). Gender stereotypes and the relationship between masculinity and femininity: A developmental analysis. *Journal of Personality and Social Psychology, 61*, 351–365.

BIGLER, R. S., & LIBEN, L. S. (1989, April). *Racial stereotyping and constructive memory in children.* Paper presented at the meeting of the Society for Research in Child Development, Kansas City, MO.

BIGLER, R. S., & LIBEN, L. S. (in press). Cognitive mechanisms in children's gender stereotyping: Theoretical and educational implications of a cognitive-based intervention. *Child Development.*

BIRNHOLZ, J. C., & BENACERRAF, B. R. (1983). The development of human fetal hearing. *Science, 222*, 516–518.

BJORKLUND, D. F. (1987a). A note on neonatal imitation. *Developmental Review, 7*, 86–92.

BJORKLUND, D. F. (1987b). How age changes in knowledge base contribute to the development of children's memory: An interpretive review. *Developmental Review, 7*, 93–130.

BJORKLUND, D. F. (1989). *Children's thinking: Developmental function and individual differences.* Pacific Grove, CA: Brooks/Cole.

BJORKLUND, D. F., & BERNHOLTZ, J. E. (1986). The role of knowledge base in the memory performance of good and poor readers. *Journal of Experimental Child Psychology, 41*, 367–393.

BJORKLUND, D. F., & GREEN, B. L. (1992). The adaptive nature of cognitive immaturity. *American Psychologist, 47*, 46–54.

BJORKLUND, D. F., & HARNISHFEGER, K. K. (1987). Developmental differences in the mental effort requirements for the use of an organizational strategy in free recall. *Journal of Experimental Child Psychology, 44*, 109–125.

BJORKLUND, D. F., & HARNISHFEGER, K. K. (1990). Children's strategies: Their definition and origins. In D. F. Bjorklund (Ed.), *Children's strategies: Contemporary views of cognitive development.* Hillsdale, NJ: Erlbaum.

BJORKLUND, D. F., MUIR-BROADDUS, J. E., & SCHNEIDER, W. (1990). The role of knowledge in the development of children's strategies. In D. F. Bjorklund (Ed.), *Children's strategies: Contemporary views of cognitive development.* Hillsdale, NJ: Erlbaum.

BJORKLUND, D. F., & ZEMAN, B. R. (1982). Children's organization and metamemory awareness in their recall of familiar information. *Child Development, 53*, 799–810.

BLAKE, J., & FINK, R. (1987). Sound-meaning correspondences in babbling. *Journal of Child Language, 14*, 229–253.

BLEWITT, P. (1982). Word meaning acquisition in young children. A review of theory and research. In H. W. Reese (Ed.), *Advances in child development and behavior* (Vol. 17). New York: Academic Press.

BLEWITT, P. (Ed.). (1989). Acquiring knowledge of hierarchies. *The Genetic Epistemologist, 17*, 1–39.

BLOOM, L. (1970). *Language development: Form and function in emerging grammars.* Cambridge, MA: MIT Press.

BLOOM, L. (1973). *One word at a time: The use of single word utterances before syntax.* The Hague: Mouton.

BLOOM, L., & BECKWITH, R. (1988). *Intentionality and language development.* Manuscript submitted for publication.

BLOOM, L., & BECKWITH, R. (1989). Talking with feeling: Integrating affective and linguistic expression in early language development. *Cognition and Emotion, 3*, 313–342.

BLOOM, L., & CAPATIDES, J. (1987a). Expression of affect and the emergence of language. *Child Development, 58*, 1513–1522.

BLOOM, L., & CAPATIDES, J. B. (1987b). Sources of meaning in the acquisition of complex syntax: The sample case of causality. *Journal of Experimental Child Psychology, 43*, 112–128.

BLOOM, L., LIFTER, K., & BROUGHTON, J. (1985). The convergence of early cognition and language in the second year of life: Problems in conceptualization and measurement. In M. Barrett (Ed.), *Children's single-word speech.* New York: John Wiley.

BOHANNON, J. N., MACWHINNEY, B., & SNOW, C. (1990). No negative evidence revisited: Beyond learnability or who has to prove what to whom. *Developmental Psychology, 26*, 221–226.

BOHANNON, J. N., & STANOWICZ, L. (1988). The issue of negative evidence: Adult responses to children's language errors. *Developmental Psychology, 24*, 684–689.

BOHANNON, J. N., & WARREN-LEUBECKER, A. (1989). Theoretical approaches to language acquisition. In J. B. Gleason (Ed.), *The development of language* (2nd ed.). Columbus, OH: Chas. E. Merrill.

BOHANNON, J. N., & WARREN-LEUBECKER, A. (in press). Recent developments in child-directed speech: You've come a long way, baby-talk. *Language Sciences.*

BONITATIBUS, G. (1988a). Comprehension monitoring and the apprehension of literal meaning. *Child Development, 59*, 60–70.

BONITATIBUS, G. (1988b). What is said and what is meant in referential communication. In J. W. Astington, P. L. Harris, & D. R. Olson (Eds.), *Developing theories of mind.* Cambridge: Cambridge University Press.

BONITATIBUS, G., & FLAVELL, J. H. (1985). The effect of presenting a message in written form on young children's ability to evaluate its communication accuracy. *Developmental Psychology, 21,* 455–461.

BORKOWSKI, J. G., LEVERS, S., & GRUENEN-FELDER, T. M. (1976). Transfer of mediational strategies in children: The role of activity and awareness during strategy acquisition. *Child Development, 47,* 779–786.

BORKOWSKI, J. G., MILSTEAD, M., & HALE, C. (1988). Components of children's metamemory: Implications for strategy generalization. In F. E. Weinert & M. Perlmutter (Eds.), *Memory development: Universal changes and individual differences.* Hillsdale, NJ: Erlbaum.

BORKOWSKI, J. G., & TURNER, L. A. (1990). Transituational characteristics of metacognition. In W. Schneider & F. E. Weinert (Eds.), *Interactions among aptitude, strategies, and knowledge in cognitive performance.* Hillsdale, NJ: Erlbaum.

BORNSTEIN, M. H. (1981). Psychological studies of color perception in human infants: Habituation, discrimination and categorization, recognition, and conceptualization. In L. P. Lipsitt (Ed.), *Advances in infancy research* (Vol. 1). Norwood, NJ: Ablex.

BORNSTEIN, M. H., & SIGMAN, M. D. (1986). Continuity in mental development from infancy. *Child Development, 57,* 251–274.

BOWER, T. G. R. (1966). The visual world of infants. *Scientific American, 215,* 90–92.

BOWER, T. G. R. (1974). *Development in infancy.* San Francisco: W. H. Freeman.

BOWER, T. G. R. (1982). *Development in infancy* (2nd ed.). San Francisco: W. H. Freeman.

BOWER, T. G. R., & WISHART, J. G. (1972). The effects of motor skill on object permanence. *Cognition, 1,* 165–172.

BOWERMAN, M. (1978). The acquisition of word meaning: An investigation into some current conflicts. In N. Waterson & C. Snow (Eds.), *The development of communication.* New York: John Wiley.

BOWERMAN, M. (1987). Commentary: Mechanisms of language acquisition. In B. MacWhinney (Ed.), *Mechanisms of language acquisition.* Hillsdale, NJ: Erlbaum.

BOWLBY, J. (1969). *Attachment and loss: Vol. 1. Attachment.* New York: Basic Books.

BOYSSON-BARDIES, B., HALLE, P., SAGART, L., & DURAND, C. (1989). A crosslinguistic investigation of vowel formants in babbling. *Journal of Child Language, 16,* 1–17.

BRAINE, M. D. S. (1976). Children's first word combinations. *Monographs of the Society for Research in Child Development, 40* (1, Serial No. 164).

BRAINE, M. D. S., & RUMAIN, B. (1983). Logical reasoning. In J. H. Flavell & E. M. Markman (Eds.), P. H. Mussen (Series Ed.), *Handbook of child psychology: Vol. 3. Cognitive development.* New York: John Wiley.

BRAINERD, C. J. (1978a). *Piaget's theory of intelligence.* Englewood Cliffs, NJ: Prentice-Hall.

BRAINERD, C. J. (1978b). The stage question in cognitive-developmental theory. *Behavioral and Brain Sciences, 2,* 173–213.

BRAINERD, C. J., & REYNA, V. F. (1988). Generic resources, reconstructive processing, and children's mental arithmetic. *Developmental Psychology, 24,* 324–334.

BRAINERD, C. J., & REYNA, V. F. (1989). Output-interference theory of dual-task deficits in memory development. *Journal of Experimental Child Psychology, 47,* 1–18.

BRANDT, M. M. (1978). Relations between cognitive role-taking performance and age, task presentation, and response requirements. *Developmental Psychology, 14,* 206–213.

BRANSFORD, J. D., & FRANKS, J. J. (1971). The abstraction of linguistic ideas. *Cognitive Psychology, 2,* 331–350.

BRETHERTON, I. (Ed.). (1984). *Symbolic play.* New York: Academic Press.

BRETHERTON, I. (1988). How to do things with one word: The ontogenesis of intentional message making in infancy. In M. D. Smith & J. L. Locke (Eds.), *The emergent lexicon: The child's development of a linguistic vocabulary.* San Diego: Academic Press.

BRETHERTON, I. (1989). Pretense: The form and function of make-believe play. *Developmental Review, 9,* 383–401.

BRETHERTON, I. (1990). Open communication and internal working models: Their role in the development of attachment relationships. In R. A. Thompson (Ed.), *Nebraska symposium on motivation: Vol. 38. Socioemotional development.* Lincoln: University of Nebraska Press.

BRETHERTON, I. (1991). Pouring new wine into old bottles: The social self as internal working model. In M. R. Gunnar & L. A. Sroufe (Eds.), *Minnesota symposia on child psychology: Vol. 23. Self processes and development.* Hillsdale, NJ: Erlbaum.

BRETHERTON, I., & BEEGHLY, M. (1982). Talking about internal states: The acquisition of an explicit theory of mind. *Developmental Psychology, 18,* 906–921.

BRETHERTON, I., & BEEGHLY, M. (1989). Pretense: Acting "as if." In J. L. Lockman & N. L. Hazen (Eds.), *Action in social context.* New York: Plenum Press.

BRETHERTON, I., MCNEW, S., & BEEGHLY-SMITH, M. (1981). Early person knowledge as expressed in gestural and verbal communication: When do infants acquire a "theory of mind"? In M. Lamb & L. Sherrod (Eds.), *Social cognition in infancy*. Hillsdale, NJ: Erlbaum.

BRIARS, D., & SIEGLER, R. S. (1984). A featural analysis of preschoolers' counting knowledge. *Developmental Psychology, 20*, 607–618.

BRIGGS, J. L. (1970). *Never in anger: Portrait of an Eskimo family*. Cambridge, MA: Harvard University Press.

BRONFENBRENNER, U. (1979). *The ecology of human development: Experiments by nature and design*. Cambridge, MA: Harvard University Press.

BRONFENBRENNER, U. (1989). Ecological systems theory. In R. Vasta (Ed.), *Annals of child development: Vol. 6. Six theories of child development: Revised formulations and current issues*. Greenwich, CT: JAI Press.

BRONSON, W. A. (1971). The growth of competence: Issues of conceptualization and measurement. In H. R. Shaffer (Ed.), *The origins of human social relations*. New York: Academic Press.

BROOKS-GUNN, J., & LEWIS, M. (1984). The development of early visual self-recognition. *Developmental Review, 4*, 215–239.

BROWN, A. L. (1983). *Cognitive development*. Bethesda, MD. Unpublished paper written for the National Institute of Child Health and Human Development.

BROWN, A. L. (1989). Analogical learning and transfer: What develops? In S. Vosniadou & A. Ortony (Eds.), *Similarity and analogical reasoning*. Cambridge: Cambridge University Press.

BROWN, A. L., BRANSFORD, J. D., FERRARA, R. A., & CAMPIONE, J. C. (1983). Learning, remembering, and understanding. In J. H. Flavell & E. M. Markman (Eds.), P. H. Mussen (Series Ed.), *Handbook of child psychology: Vol. 3. Cognitive development*. New York: John Wiley.

BROWN, A. L., & CAMPIONE, J. C. (1990). Communities of learning and thinking, or a context by any other name. In D. Kuhn (Ed.), *Developmental perspectives on teaching and learning thinking skills*. Basel: Karger.

BROWN, A. L., & DELOACHE, J. S. (1978). Skills, plans, and self-regulation. In R. S. Siegler (Ed.), *Children's thinking: What develops?* Hillsdale, NJ: Erlbaum.

BROWN, A. L., & PALINCSAR, A. S. (1985). *Reciprocal teaching of comprehension strategies: A natural history of a program for enhancing learning* (Tech. Rep. No. 334). Urbana: University of Illinois, Center for the Study of Reading.

BROWN, A. L., SMILEY, S. S., & LAWTON, S. Q. C. (1978). The effects of experience on the selection of suitable retrieval cues for studying texts. *Child Development, 49*, 829–835.

BROWN, J. R., & DUNN, T. (1991). 'You can cry, mum': The social and developmental implications of talk about internal states. *British Journal of Developmental Psychology, 9*, 237–256.

BROWN, K. W., & GOTTFRIED, A. W. (1986). Development of cross-modal transfer in early infancy. In L. P. Lipsitt & C. K. Rovee-Collier (Eds.), *Advances in infancy research* (Vol. 4). Norwood, NJ: Ablex.

BROWN, R. (1958). How shall a thing be called? *Psychological Review, 65*, 14–21.

BROWN, R. (1973). *A first language: The early stages*. Cambridge, MA: Harvard University Press.

BROWN, R., CAZDEN, C. B., & BELLUGI, U. (1969). The child's grammar from I to III. In J. P. Hill (Ed.), *Minnesota symposia on child psychology* (Vol. 2). Minneapolis: University of Minnesota Press.

BROWN, R., & HANLON, C. (1970). Derivational complexity and order of acquisition. In J. R. Hayes (Ed.), *Cognition and the development of language*. New York: John Wiley.

BROWNELL, C. A. (1986). Convergent developments: Cognitive-developmental correlates of growth in infant/toddler peer skills. *Child Development, 57*, 275–286.

BROWNELL, C. A., & KOPP, C. B. (1991). Common threads, diverse solutions: Concluding commentary. *Developmental Review, 11*, 288–303.

BRUNER, J. S. (1975). The ontogeny of speech acts. *Journal of Child Language, 2*, 1–19.

BRUNER, J. S. (1990). *Acts of meaning*. Cambridge, MA: Harvard University Press.

BRYANT, P. E. (1990). Empirical evidence for causes of development. In G. Butterworth & P. E. Bryant (Eds.), *Causes of development*. Hillsdale, NJ: Erlbaum.

BRYANT, P. E., & KOPYTYNSKA, H. (1976). Spontaneous measurement by young children. *Nature, 260*, 773.

BRYANT, P. E., & TRABASSO, T. (1971). Transitive inferences and memory in young children. *Nature, 232*, 456–458.

BULLOCK, M., & GELMAN, R. (1979). Preschool children's assumptions about cause and effect: Temporal ordering. *Child Development, 50*, 89–96.

BULLOCK, M., GELMAN, R., & BAILLARGEON, R. (1982). The development of causal reasoning. In W. Friedman (Ed.), *The developmental psychology of time*. New York: Academic Press.

BULLOCK, M., & LÜTKENHAUS, P. (1990). Who am I? Self-understanding in toddlers. *Merrill-Palmer Quarterly, 36*, 217–238.

BURNHAM, D. K., EARNSHAW, L. J., & QUINN, M. C. (1987). The development of the categorical identification of speech. In B. E. McKenzie & R. H. Day (Eds.), *Perceptual development in early infancy: Problems and issues.* Hillsdale, NJ: Erlbaum.

BUTTERWORTH, G. (1977). Object disappearance and error in Piaget's Stage IV task. *Journal of Experimental Child Psychology, 23,* 391–401.

BUTTERWORTH, G. (1982). A brief account of the conflict between the individual and the social in models of cognitive growth. In G. Butterworth & P. Light (Eds.), *Social cognition: Studies of the development of social understanding.* Chicago: University of Chicago Press.

BUTTERWORTH, G., & BRYANT, P. E. (Eds.). (1990). *Causes of development.* Hillsdale, NJ: Erlbaum.

BUTTERWORTH, G., HARRIS, P., LESLIE, A., & WELLMAN, H. W. (Eds.). (1991). Perspectives on the child's theory of mind [Special issues]. *British Journal of Developmental Psychology, 9,* (1, 2).

BYRNE, R. W., & WHITEN, A. (1988). Toward the next generation in data quality: A new survey of primate tactical deception. *Behavioral and Brain Science, 11,* 267–283.

BYRNE, R. W., & WHITEN, A. (1991). Computation and mindreading in primate tactical deception. In A. Whiten (Ed.), *Natural theories of mind: Evolution, development and simulation of everyday mindreading .* Oxford: Basil Blackwell.

BYRNES, J. P. (1988a). Formal operations: A systematic reformulation. *Developmental Review, 8,* 1–22.

BYRNES, J. P. (1988b). What's left is closer to right. A response to Keating. *Developmental Review, 8,* 385–392.

BYRNES, J. P., & BEILIN, H. (1991). The cognitive basis of uncertainty. *Human Development, 34,* 189–203.

CALLANAN, M. A. (1985). How parents label objects for young children: The role of input in the acquisition of category hierarchies. *Child Development, 56,* 508–523.

CAMPIONE, J. C. (1987). Metacognitive components of instructional research with problem learners. In F. E. Weinert & R. H. Kluwe (Eds.), *Metacognition, motivation, and understanding.* Hillsdale, NJ: Erlbaum.

CAMPOS, J. J., & BERTENTHAL, B. I. (1989). Locomotion and psychological development in infancy. In F. J. Morrison, C. Lord, & D. P. Keating (Eds.), *Applied developmental psychology* (Vol. 3). New York: Academic Press.

CAMPOS, J. J., HIATT, S., RAMSAY, D., HENDERSON, C., & SVEJDA, M. (1978). The emergence of fear on the visual cliff. In M. Lewis & L. A. Rosenblum (Eds.), *The origins of affect.* New York: Plenum Press.

CAMPOS, J. J., & STENBERG, C. R. (1981). Perception, appraisal and emotion: The onset of social referencing. In M. E. Lamb, & L. R. Sherrod (Eds.), *Infant social cognition: Empirical and theoretical considerations.* Hillsdale, NJ: Erlbaum.

CAPLOVITZ, K. S., & CAMPOS, J. J. (1983, April). *Wariness of heights: An outcome of locomotor experience or age?* Paper presented at the meeting of the Society for Research in Child Development, Detroit.

CAREY, S. (1977). Less may never mean more. In R. Campbell & P. Smith (Eds.), *Recent advances in the psychology of language.* New York: Plenum Press.

CAREY, S. (1978). The child as word learner. In M. Halle, J. Bresnan, & G. A. Miller (Eds.), *Linguistic theory and psychological reality.* Cambridge, MA: MIT Press.

CAREY, S. (1982). Semantic development: The state of the art. In E. Wanner & L. R. Gleitman (Eds.), *Language acquisition: The state of the art.* Cambridge: Cambridge University Press.

CAREY, S. (1985a). *Conceptual change in childhood.* Cambridge, MA: MIT Press.

CAREY, S. (1985b). Are children fundamentally different thinkers and learners than adults? In S. F. Chipman, J. W. Segal, & R. Glaser (Eds.), *Thinking and learning skills* (Vol. 2). Hillsdale, NJ: Erlbaum.

CAREY, S. (1987). Theory change in childhood. In B. Inhelder, D. de Caprona, & A. Cornu-Wells (Eds.), *Piaget today.* Hillsdale, NJ: Erlbaum.

CAREY, S. (1991). Knowledge acquisition: Enrichment or conceptual change? In S. Carey & R. Gelman (Eds.), *The epigenesis of mind: Essays on biology and cognition.* Hillsdale, NJ: Erlbaum.

CAREY, S. (in press). Procedures toddlers use to constrain word meanings—speculations and a little data. In E. Dromi (Ed.), *Cognition and language: Early childhood years.* Norwood, NJ: Ablex.

CAREY, S., & BARTLETT, E. (1978). Acquiring a single new word. *Papers and reports on child language development* (Department of Linguistics, Stanford University), *15,* 17–29.

CAREY, S., & GELMAN, R. (Eds.). (1991). *The epigenesis of mind: Essays on biology and cognition.* Hillsdale, NJ: Erlbaum.

CARIGLIA-BULL, T., & PRESSLEY, M. (1990). Short-term memory differences between children predict imagery effects when sentences are read. *Journal of Experimental Child Psychology, 49,* 384–398.

CARR, M., KURTZ, B. E., SCHNEIDER, W., TURNER, L. A., & BORKOWSKI, J. G. (1989). Strategy acquisition and transfer among American and German children: Environmental influences on metacognitive development. *Developmental Psychology, 25,* 765–771.

CASE, R. (1985). *Intellectual development: Birth to adulthood.* New York: Academic Press.

CASE, R. (1986). The new stage theories in intellectual development: Why we need them; what they assert. In M. Perlmutter (Ed.), *Minnesota symposia on child psychology: Vol. 19. Perspectives on intellectual development.* Hillsdale, NJ: Erlbaum.

CASE, R. (1987). The structure and process of intellectual development. *International Journal of Psychology, 22,* 571–607.

CASE, R. (1992). *The mind's staircase: Exploring the conceptual underpinnings of children's thought and knowledge.* Hillsdale, NJ: Erlbaum.

CASE, R., HAYWARD, S., LEWIS, M., & HURST, P. (1988). Toward a neo-Piagetian theory of cognitive and emotional development. *Developmental Review, 8,* 1–51.

CASE, R., KURLAND, D. M., & GOLDBERG, J. (1982). Operational efficiency and the growth of short-term memory span. *Journal of Experimental Child Psychology, 33,* 386–404.

CASE, R., MARINI, Z., MCKEOUGH, A., DENNIS, S., & GOLDBERG, J. (1986). Horizontal structure in middle childhood: Cross domain parallels in the course of cognitive growth. In I. Levin (Ed.), *Stage and structure: Reopening the debate.* Norwood, NJ: Ablex.

CECI, S. J. (1989). On domain specificity...More or less general and specific constraints on cognitive development. *Merrill-Palmer Quarterly, 35,* 131–142.

CECI, S. J., ROSS, D. F., & TOGLIA, M. P. (1987). Age differences in suggestibility: Narrowing the uncertainties. In S. J. Ceci, M. P. Toglia, & D. F. Ross (Eds.), *Children's eyewitness memory.* New York: Springer-Verlag.

CECI, S. J., ROSS, D. F., & TOGLIA, M. P. (Eds.). (1989). *Perspectives on children's testimony.* New York: Springer-Verlag.

CECI, S. J., TOGLIA, M. P., & ROSS, D. F. (Eds.). (1987). *Children's eyewitness memory.* New York: Springer-Verlag.

CHANDLER, M. (1988). Doubt and developing theories of the mind. In J. W. Astington, P. L. Harris, & D. R. Olson (Eds.), *Developing theories of mind.* Cambridge: Cambridge University Press.

CHANDLER, M. (1991). Alternative readings of the competence-performance relation. In M. Chandler, & M. Chapman (Eds.), *Criteria for competence: Controversies in the conceptualization and assessment of children's abilities.* Hillsdale, NJ: Erlbaum.

CHANDLER, M., & BOYES, M. (1982). Social-cognitive development. In B. Wolman (Ed.), *Handbook of developmental psychology.* Englewood Cliffs, NJ: Prentice-Hall.

CHANDLER, M., & CHAPMAN, M. (Eds.). (1991). *Criteria for competence: Controversies in the conceptualization and assessment of children's abilities.* Hillsdale, NJ: Erlbaum.

CHANDLER, M., FRITZ, A. S., & HALA, S. M. (1989). Small scale deceit: Deception as a marker of two-, three-, and four-year-olds' early theories of mind. *Child Development, 60,* 1263–1277.

CHANDLER, M., & HELM, D. (1984). Developmental changes in the contributions of shared experience to social role-taking competence. *International Journal of Behavioral Development, 7,* 145–156.

CHANDLER, M., LALONDE, C., FRITZ, A., & HALA, S. (1991, April). Children's theories of mental life and social practices. In C. Brownell (Chair), *Early understanding of others manifested in action and social behavior.* Symposium conducted at the meeting of the Society for Research in Child Development, Seattle, WA.

CHANDLER, M., PAGET, K. F., & KOCH, D. A. (1978). The child's demystification of psychological defense mechanisms: A structural and developmental analysis. *Developmental Psychology, 14,* 197–205.

CHAPMAN, M. (1987). Piaget, attentional capacity, and the functional implications of formal structure. In H. W. Reese (Ed.), *Advances in child development and behavior* (Vol. 20). Orlando, FL: Academic Press.

CHAPMAN, M. (1988). *Constructive evolution: Origins and development of Piaget's thought.* Cambridge: Cambridge University Press.

CHAPMAN, M. (1990, May). *Equilibration and the dialectics of organization.* Paper presented at the meeting of the Jean Piaget Society, Philadelphia.

CHARLESWORTH, W. R. (1966, September). *Development of the object concept: A methodological study.* Paper presented at the meeting of the American Psychological Association, New York.

CHASE, W. G., & SIMON, H. A. (1973). Perception in chess. *Cognitive Psychology, 4,* 55–81.

CHI, M. T. H. (1978). Knowledge structures and memory development. In R. S. Siegler (Ed.), *Children's thinking: What develops?* Hillsdale, NJ: Erlbaum.

CHI, M. T. H. (1985). Interactive roles of knowledge and strategies in the development of organized sorting and recall. In S. F. Chipman, J. W. Segal, & R. Glaser (Eds.), *Thinking and learning skills: Vol. 2. Research and open questions*. Hillsdale, NJ: Erlbaum.

CHI, M. T. H. (1987). Representing knowledge and metaknowledge: Implications for interpreting metamemory research. In F. E. Weinert & R. H. Kluwe (Eds.), *Metacognition, motivation, and understanding*. Hillsdale, NJ: Erlbaum.

CHI, M. T. H. (1992). Conceptual change within and across ontological categories: Examples from learning and discovery in science. In R. Giere (Ed.), *Cognitive models of science: Minnesota studies in the philosophy of science*. Minneapolis: University of Minnesota Press.

CHI, M. T. H., & GLASER, R. (1980). The measurement of expertise: Analysis of the development of knowledge and skill as a basis for assessing achievement. In E. L. Baker & E. S. Quellmalz (Eds.), *Educational testing and evaluation: Design, analysis and policy*. Beverly Hills, CA: Sage Publications.

CHI, M. T. H., GLASER, R., & FARR, M. J. (Eds.). (1988). *The nature of expertise*. Hillsdale, NJ: Erlbaum.

CHI, M. T. H., HUTCHINSON, J. E., & ROBIN, A. F. (1989). How inferences about novel domain-related concepts can be constrained by structured knowledge. *Merrill-Palmer Quarterly, 35*, 27–62.

CHI, M. T. H., & KOESKE, R. D. (1983). Network representation of a child's dinosaur knowledge. *Developmental Psychology, 19*, 29–39.

CHI, M. T. H., & REES, E. T. (1983). A learning framework for development. In M. T. H. Chi (Ed.), *Trends in memory development*. Basel: Karger.

CHILDREN'S COGNITIVE AND SOCIAL-COGNITIVE DEVELOPMENT: DOMAIN SPECIFICITY AND GENERALITY [SPECIAL ISSUE]. (1989). *Merrill-Palmer Quarterly, 35*(1).

CHOMSKY, N. (1972). *Language and mind* (enlarged ed.). San Diego: Harcourt Brace Jovanovich.

CHOMSKY, N. (1981). *Lectures on government and binding*. Dordrecht, Netherlands: Foris.

CHURCHLAND, P. M. (1984). *Matter and consciousness*. Cambridge, MA: MIT Press.

CICCHETTI, D., & BEEGHLY, M. (1990). *The self in transition: Infancy to childhood*. Chicago: University of Chicago Press.

CLARK, E. V. (1973). What's in a word? On the child's acquisition of semantics in his first language. In T. E. Moore (Ed.), *Cognitive development and the acquisition of language*. New York: Academic Press.

CLARK, E. V. (1982). The young word-maker: A case study of innovation in the child's lex-

icon. In E. Wanner & L. R. Gleitman (Eds.), *Language acquisition: The state of the art*. Cambridge: Cambridge University Press.

CLARK, E. V. (1983). Meanings and concepts. In J. H. Flavell & E. M. Markman (Eds.), P. H. Mussen (Series Ed.), *Handbook of child psychology: Vol. 3. Cognitive development*. New York: John Wiley.

CLARK, E. V. (1987). The principle of contrast: A constraint on language acquisition. In B. MacWhinney (Ed.), *Mechanisms of language acquisition*. Hillsdale, NJ: Erlbaum.

CLARK, E. V. (1988). On the logic of contrast. *Journal of Child Language, 15*, 317–335.

CLARK, H. H., & CLARK, E. V. (1977). *Psychology and language: An introduction to psycholinguistics*. San Diego: Harcourt Brace Jovanovich.

COHEN, L., & STRAUSS, M. S. (1979). Concept acquisition in the human infant. *Child Development, 50*, 419–424.

COHEN, R., & SIEGEL, A. W. (Eds.). (1991). *Context and development*. Hillsdale, NJ: Erlbaum.

COLE, M. (1988). Cross-cultural research in the socio-historical tradition. *Human Development, 31*, 137–157.

COLE, M. (in press). Culture in development. In M. Bornstein & M. Lamb (Eds.), *Developmental psychology: An advanced textbook* (3rd ed.). Hillsdale, NJ: Erlbaum.

COLE, M., & COLE, S. (1989). *The development of children*. New York: W. H. Freeman.

COLE, M., & SCRIBNER, S. (1977). Cross-cultural studies of memory and cognition. In R. V. Kail & J. W. Hagen (Eds.), *Perspectives on the development of memory and cognition*. Hillsdale, NJ: Erlbaum.

COLE, P. M. (1986) Children's spontaneous control of facial expression. *Child Development, 57*, 1309–1321.

COLLINS, A., & SMITH, E. E. (1982). Teaching the process of reading comprehension. In D. K. Detterman & R. J. Sternberg (Eds.), *How and how much can intelligence be raised?* Norwood, N.J.: Ablex.

CONNOLLY, K., & DAGLEISH, M. (1989). The emergence of a tool-using skill in infancy. *Developmental Psychology, 25*, 894–912.

COOPER, R. G. (1984). Early number development: Discovering number space with addition and subtraction. In C. Sophian (Ed.), *Origins of cognitive skills*. Hillsdale, NJ: Erlbaum.

COOPER, R. P., & ASLIN, R. N. (1989). The language environment of the young infant: Implications for early perceptual development. *Canadian Journal of Psychology, 43*, 247–265.

COOPER, R. P., & ASLIN, R. N. (1990). Preference for infant-directed speech in the first month after birth. *Child Development, 61*, 1584–1595.

COOPER, R. P., & PISTON, J. (1991, April). *Young infants' processing of prosodic contours in infant-directed speech.* Paper presented at the meeting of the Society for Research in Child Development, Seattle, WA.

CRAIK, F. J. M., & LOCKHART, R. S. (1972). Levels of processing: A framework for memory research. *Journal of Verbal Learning and Verbal Behavior, 11,* 671–684.

CULTICE, J. C., SOMERVILLE, S. C., & WELLMAN, H. M. (1983). Preschooler's memory monitoring: Feeling-of-knowing judgments. *Child Development, 54,* 1480–1486.

CUNNINGHAM, J. G., & WEAVER, S. L. (1989). Young children's knowledge of their memory span: Effects of task and experience. *Journal of Experimental Child Psychology, 48,* 32–44.

CURTIS, R. C., & SCHILDHAUS, J. (1980). Children's attribution to self and situation. *Journal of Social Psychology, 110,* 109–114.

CURTISS, S. (1988). *The case of Chelsea: A new test case of the critical period for language acquisition.* Unpublished manuscript, University of California, Los Angeles.

CUVO, A. J. (1975). Developmental differences in rehearsal and free recall. *Journal of Experimental Child Psychology, 19,* 265–278.

D'ANDRADE, R. (1987). A folk model of the mind. In D. Holland & N. Quinn (Eds.), *Cultural models in language and thought.* Cambridge: Cambridge University Press.

DAMON, W. (1977). *The social world of the child.* San Francisco: Jossey-Bass.

DAMON, W. (1981). Exploring children's social cognition on two fronts. In J.H. Flavell & L. Ross (Eds.), *Social cognitive development: Frontiers and possible futures.* Cambridge: Cambridge University Press.

DAMON, W. (1988). *The moral child: Nurturing children's natural moral growth.* New York: Free Press.

DAMON, W., & HART, D. (1988). *Self understanding in childhood and adolescence.* Cambridge: Cambridge University Press.

DANNEMILLER, J. L., & STEPHENS, B. R. (1988). A critical test of infant pattern preference models. *Child Development, 59,* 210–216.

DANNER, F. (1989). Cognitive development through adolescence. In J. Worell & F. Danner (Eds.), *The adolescent as decision maker.* San Diego: Academic Press.

DAVIDSON, R., & FOX, N. (1982). Asymmetrical brain activity discriminates between positive and negative affective stimuli in human infants. *Science, 218,* 1235–1237.

DAVIS, T. (1992, April). *Sex differences in masking negative emotions: Ability or motivation?* Paper presented at the Conference on Human Development, Atlanta.

DAY, R. H. (1987). Visual size constancy in infancy. In B. E. McKenzie & R. H. Day (Eds.), *Perceptual development in early infancy: Problems and issues.* Hillsdale, NJ: Erlbaum.

DÉCARIE, T. G. (1969). A study of the mental and emotional development of the thalidomide child. In B. M. Foss (Ed.), *Determinants of infant behavior* (Vol. 4). London: Methuen.

DeCASPER, A. J., & FIFER, W. P. (1980). Of human bonding: Newborns prefer their mother's voice. *Science, 208,* 1174–1176.

DeCASPER, A. J., & SPENCE, M. J. (1986). Prenatal maternal speech influences newborn's perception of speech sounds. *Infant Behavior and Development, 9,* 133–150.

DeLOACHE, J. S. (1987). Rapid change in the symbolic functioning of very young children. *Science, 238,* 1556–1557.

DeLOACHE, J. S. (1991a). Symbolic functioning in very young children: Understanding of pictures and models. *Child Development, 62,* 736–752.

DeLOACHE, J. S. (1991b). Young children's understanding of scale models. In R. Fivush & J. Hudson (Eds.), *Knowing and remembering in young children.* New York: Cambridge University Press.

DeLOACHE, J. S., & BROWN, A. L. (1984). Where do I go next? Intelligent searching by very young children. *Developmental Psychology, 20,* 37–44.

DeLOACHE, J. S., CASSIDY, D. J., & BROWN, A. L. (1985). Precursors of mnemonic strategies in very young children's memory. *Child Development, 56,* 125–137.

DeLOACHE, J. S., STRAUSS, M. S., & MAYNARD, J. (1979). Picture perception in infancy. *Infant Behavior and Development, 2,* 77–89.

DeLOACHE, J. S., & TODD, C. M. (1988). Young children's use of spatial categorization as a mnemonic strategy. *Journal of Experimental Child Psychology, 46,* 1–20.

DeMARIE-DREBLOW, D. (1991). Relation between knowledge and memory: A reminder that correlation does not imply causality. *Child Development, 62,* 484–498.

DeMARIE-DREBLOW, D., & MILLER, P. H. (1988). The development of children's strategies for selective attention: Evidence for a transitional period. *Child Development, 59,* 1504–1513.

DEMETRIOU, A., & EFKLIDES, A. (1987). Experiential structuralism and neo-Piagetian theories: Toward an integrated model. *International Journal of Psychology, 22,* 679–728.

DEMETRIOU, A., & EFKLIDES, A. (in press). Experiential structuralism: A frame for unifying cognitive developmental theories. *Monographs of the Society for Research in Child Development.*

DEMPSTER, F. N. (1981). Memory span: Sources of individual and developmental differences. *Psychological Bulletin, 89,* 63–100.

DEMPSTER, F. N. (1985). Short-term memory development in childhood and adolescence. In C. J. Brainerd & M. Pressley (Eds.), *Basic processes in memory development: Progress in cognitive development research.* New York: Springer-Verlag.

DEMPSTER, F. N. (1992). The rise and fall of the inhibitory mechanism: Toward a unified theory of cognitive development and aging. *Developmental Review, 12,* 45–75.

DEMPSTER, F. N. (in press). Resistance to interference: Developmental changes in a basic processing mechanism. In M. L. Howe & R. Pasnak (Eds.), *Emerging themes in cognitive development: Vol. 1. Foundations.* New York: Springer-Verlag.

DENHAM, S. A., & ZOLLER, D. (1990, March). *"When Mommy's angry, I feel sad": Preschoolers' causal understanding of emotion and its socialization.* Paper presented at the Conference on Human Development, Richmond, VA.

DE RIBAUPIERRE, A. (Ed.). (1989). *Transition mechanisms in child development: The longitudinal perspective.* Cambridge: Cambridge University Press.

DE VILLIERS, J. G., & DE VILLIERS, P. A. (1973). A cross-sectional study of the acquisition of grammatical morphemes. *Journal of Psycholinguistic Research, 2,* 267–278.

DE VILLIERS, P. A., & DE VILLIERS, J. G. (1978). *Language acquisition.* Cambridge, MA: Harvard University Press.

DE VILLIERS, P. A., & DE VILLIERS, J. G. (1979). *Early language.* Cambridge, MA: Harvard University Press.

DIAMOND, A. (1985). Development of the ability to use recall to guide action, as indicated by infants' performance on A$\overline{B}$. *Child Development, 56,* 868–883.

DIAMOND, A. (Ed.). (1990a). The development and neural bases of higher cognitive functions. New York: The New York Academy of Sciences.

DIAMOND, A. (1990b). The development and neural bases of memory functions as indexed by the A$\overline{B}$ and delayed response tasks in human infants and infant monkeys. In A. Diamond (Ed.), *The development and neural bases of higher cognitive functions.* New York: The New York Academy of Sciences.

DIAMOND, A. (1991a). Frontal lobe involvement in cognitive changes during the first year of life. In K. R. Gibson & A. C. Petersen (Eds.), *Brain maturation and cognitive development: Comparative and cross-cultural perspectives.* New York, NY: Aldine de Gruyter.

DIAMOND, A. (1991b). Neuropsychological insights into the meaning of object concept development. In S. Carey & R. Gelman (Eds.), *The epigenesis of mind: Essays on biology and cognition.* Hillsdale, NJ: Erlbaum.

DICKINSON, D. K. (1984). First impressions: Children's knowledge of words gained from a single exposure. *Applied Psycholinguistics, 5,* 359–373.

DICKSON, W. P. (Ed.). (1981). *Children's oral communication skills.* New York: Academic Press.

DILALLA, L. F., & WATSON, M. W. (1988). Differentiation of fantasy and reality: Preschoolers' reactions to interruptions in their play. *Developmental Psychology, 24,* 286–291.

DOBSON, V., & TELLER, D. Y. (1978). Visual acuity in human infants: A review and comparison of behavioral and electrophysiological studies. *Vision Research, 18,* 1469–1483.

DODGE, K. A. (1986). A social information processing model of social competence in children. In M. Perlmutter (Ed.), *Minnesota symposia on child psychology: Vol. 18. Cognitive perspectives on children's social and behavioral development.* Hillsdale, NJ: Erlbaum.

DODGE, K. A. (1991). Emotion and social information processing. In J. Garber & K. A. Dodge (Eds.), *The development of emotion regulation and dysregulation.* Cambridge: Cambridge University Press.

DODGE, K. A., & FELDMAN, E. (1990). Issues in social cognition and sociometric status. In S. R. Asher & J. D. Coie (Eds.), *Peer rejection in childhood.* Cambridge: Cambridge University Press.

DODGE, K. A., MURPHY, R. M., & BUCHSBAUM, K. (1984). The assessment of intention-cue discrimination cues in children: Implications for developmental psychopathology. *Child Development, 55,* 163–173.

DODWELL, P. C., HUMPHREY, G. K., & MUIR, D. W. (1987). Shape and pattern perception. In P. Salapatek & L. Cohen (Eds.), *Handbook of infant perception: Vol. 2. From perception to cognition.* Orlando, FL: Academic Press.

DOLLAGHAN, C. (1985). Child meets word: "Fast mapping" in preschool children. *Journal of Speech and Hearing Research, 28,* 449–454.

DONALDSON, M. (1978). *Children's minds.* New York: W. W. Norton.

DONALDSON, M., & WALES, R. J. (1970). On the acquisition of some relational terms. In J. R. Hayes (Ed.), *Cognition and the development of language.* New York: John Wiley.

DORIS, J. (Ed.). (1991). *The suggestibility of children's recollections: Implications for eyewitness testimony.* Washington, DC: American Psychological Association.

DROMI, E. (1987). *Early lexical development.* Cambridge: Cambridge University Press.

DUBE, E. F. (1982). Literacy, cultural familiarity, and "intelligence" as determinants of story recall. In U. Neisser (Ed.), *Memory observed: Remembering in natural contexts.* San Francisco: W. H. Freeman.

DUFRESNE, A., & KOBASIGAWA, A. (1989). Children's spontaneous allocation of study time: Differential and sufficient aspects. *Journal of Experimental Child Psychology, 47,* 274–296.

DUNBAR, K., & KLAHR, D. (1989). Developmental differences in scientific discovery processes. In D. Klahr & K. Kotovsky (Eds.), *Complex information processing: The impact of Herbert A. Simon.* Hillsdale, NJ: Erlbaum.

DUNCAN, E. M., WHITNEY, P., & KUNEN, S. (1982). Integration of visual and verbal information in children's memory. *Child Development, 53,* 1215–1223.

DUNN, J. (1988). *The beginnings of social understanding.* Oxford: Basil Blackwell.

DUNN, J. (1991). Young children's understanding of other people: Evidence from observations within the family. In D. Frye & C. Moore (Eds.), *Children's theories of mind.* Hillsdale, NJ: Erlbaum.

DUNN, J., BRETHERTON, I., & MUNN, P. (1987). Conversations about feeling states between mothers and their young children. *Developmental Psychology, 23,* 132–139.

DUNN, J., BROWN, J., & BEARDSALL, L. (1991). Family talk about feeling states and children's later understanding of others' emotions. *Developmental Psychology, 27,* 448–455.

DUNN, J., BROWN, J., SLOMKOWSKI, C., TESLA, C., & YOUNGBLADE, L. (1991). Young children's understanding of other people's feelings and beliefs: Individual differences and their antecedents. *Child Development, 62,* 1352–1366.

DUNN, J., & DALE, N. (1984). I a daddy: 2-year-olds' collaboration in joint pretend with sibling and with mother. In I. Bretherton (Ed.), *Symbolic play: The development of social understanding.* Orlando, FL: Academic Press.

DUNN, J., & KENDRICK, C. (1982a). *Siblings: Love, envy, and understanding.* Cambridge, MA: Harvard University Press.

DUNN, J., & KENDRICK, C. (1982b). The speech of two- and three-year-olds to infant siblings: "Baby talk" and the context of communication. *Journal of Child Language, 9,* 579–595.

DUNN, J., & MUNN, P. (1985). Becoming a family member: Family conflict and the development of social understanding in the second year. *Child Development, 56,* 480–492.

DWECK, C. S. (1975). The role of expectations and attributions in the alleviation of learned helplessness. *Journal of Personality and Social Psychology, 31,* 674–685.

DWECK, C. S., & REPPUCCI, N. D. (1973). Learned helplessness and reinforcement responsibility in children. *Journal of Personality and Social Psychology, 25,* 109–116.

EDER, R. A. (1989). The emergent personologist: The structure and content of $3\frac{1}{2}$, $5\frac{1}{2}$, and $7\frac{1}{2}$-year-olds' concepts of themselves and other persons. *Child Development, 60,* 1218–1228.

EDER, R. A. (1990). Uncovering young children's psychological selves: Individual and developmental differences. *Child Development, 61,* 849–863.

EDER, R. A., GERLACH, S. G., & PERLMUTTER, M. (1987). In search of children's selves: Development of the specific and general components of the self concept. *Child Development, 58,* 1044–1050.

EILERS, R. E., & OLLER, D. K. (1988). Precursors to speech: What is innate and what is acquired? In R. Vasta (Ed.), *Annals of child development* (Vol. 5). Greenwich, CT: JAI Press.

EIMAS, P. D., MILLER, J. L., & JUSCZYK, P. (1987). On infant speech perception and the acquisition of language. In S. Harnad (Ed.), *Categorical perception.* Cambridge: Cambridge University Press.

EIMAS, P. D., SIQUELAND, E. R., JUSCZYK, P., & VIGORITO, J. (1971). Speech perception in infants. *Science, 171,* 303–306.

ELDER, J. L., & PEDERSON, D. R. (1978). Preschool children's use of objects in symbolic play. *Child Development, 49,* 500–504.

ELKIND, D. (1967). Egocentrism in adolescence. *Child Development, 38,* 1025–1034.

ERVIN, S. M. (1964). Imitation and structural change in children's language. In E. H. Lenneberg (Ed.), *New directions in the study of language.* Cambridge, MA: MIT Press.

FABRICIUS, W. V., & CAVALIER, L. (1989). The role of causal theories about memory in young children's memory strategy choice. *Child Development, 60,* 298–308.

FABRICIUS, W. V., & HAGEN, J. W. (1984). The use of causal attributions about recall performance to assess metamemory and predict strategic memory behavior in young children. *Developmental Psychology, 20,* 975–987.

FABRICIUS, W. V., SCHWANENFLUGEL, P. J., KYLLONEN, P. C., BARCLAY, C. R., & DENTON, S. M. (1989). Developing theories of the mind: Children's and adults' concepts of mental activities. *Child Development, 60,* 1278–1290.

FABRICIUS, W. V., & WELLMAN, H. M. (1983). Children's understanding of retrieval cue utilization. *Developmental Psychology, 19,* 15–21.

FAGAN, J. F., III (1973). Infants' delayed recognition, memory, and forgetting. *Journal of Experimental Child Psychology, 16,* 424–450.

FAGAN, J. F., III (1976). Infants' recognition of invariant features of faces. *Child Development, 47,* 627–638.

FAGAN, J. F., III, SHEPHERD, P. A., & KNEVEL, C. R. (1991, April). *Predictive validity of the Fagan Test of Infant Intelligence.* Paper presented at the meeting of the Society for Research in Child Development, Seattle, WA.

FANTZ, R. L. (1961). The origin of form perception. *Scientific American, 204,* 66–72.

FARRAR, M. J. (1990). Discourse and the acquisition of grammatical morphemes. *Journal of Child Language, 17,* 607–624.

FARRAR, M. J. (1992). Negative evidence and grammatical morpheme acquisition. *Developmental Psychology, 28,* 90–98.

FARRAR, M. J., & BOYER, M. E. (1991). *Knowledge, property type and children's inferences for natural kinds.* Manuscript submitted for publication.

FARRAR, M. J., & GOODMAN, G. S. (1990). Developmental differences in the relation between scripts and episodic memory: Do they exist? In R. Fivush & J. Hudson (Eds.), *Knowing and remembering in young children.* Cambridge: Cambridge University Press.

FARRAR, M. J., & GOODMAN, G. S. (1992). Developmental changes in event memory. *Child Development, 63,* 173–187.

FARRAR, M. J., RANEY, G. B., & BOYER, M. E. (in press). Knowledge, concepts and inferences in childhood. *Child Development.*

FEAGANS, L., GARVEY, C., & GOLINKOFF, R. (Eds.). (1984). *The origins and growth of communication.* Norwood, NJ: Ablex.

FEIN, G. G. (1975). A transformational analysis of pretending. *Developmental Psychology, 11,* 291–296.

FEIN, G. G. (1979a). Play and the acquisition of symbols. In L. Katz (Ed.), *Current topics in early childhood education.* Norwood, NJ: Ablex.

FEIN, G. G. (1979b). Pretend play: New perspectives. *Young Children, 34,* 61–66.

FELDMAN, C. F. (1988). Early forms of thought about thoughts: Some simple linguistic expressions of mental state. In J. W. Astington, P. L. Harris, & D. R. Olson (Eds.), *Developing theories of mind.* Cambridge: Cambridge University Press.

FELDMAN, N. S., & RUBLE, D. N. (1988). The effect of personal relevance on psychological inference: A developmental analysis. *Child Development, 59,* 1339–1352.

FERNALD, A. (1985). Four-month-old infants prefer to listen to "motherese." *Infant Behavior and Development, 8,* 181–195.

FERNALD, A., & KUHL, P. (1987). Acoustic determinants of infant preference for motherese speech. *Infant Behavior and Development, 10,* 279–293.

FERNALD, A., & SIMON, T. (1984). Expanded imitation contours in mothers' speech to newborns. *Developmental Psychology, 20,* 104–113.

FERRETTI, R. P., & BUTTERFIELD, E. C. (1986). Are children's rule-assessment classifications invariant across instances of problem types? *Child Development, 57,* 1419–1428.

FIELD, D. (1987). A review of preschool conservation training: An analysis of analyses. *Developmental Review, 7,* 210–241.

FIELD, J. (1977). Coordination of vision and prehension in young infants. *Child Development, 48,* 97–103.

FIELD, T., HEALY, B., GOLDSTEIN, S., & GUTHERTZ, M. (1990). Behavior-state matching and synchrony in mother-infant interactions of nondepressed versus depressed dyads. *Developmental Psychology, 26,* 7–14.

FISCHER, K. W. (1980). A theory of cognitive development: The control and construction of hierarchies of skills. *Psychological Review, 87,* 477–531.

FISCHER, K. W. (1987). Relations between brain and cognitive development. *Child Development, 58,* 623–632.

FISCHER, K. W., & BIDELL, T. (1991). Constraining nativist inferences about cognitive capacities. In S. Carey & R. Gelman (Eds.), *The epigenesis of mind: Essays on biology and cognition.* Hillsdale, NJ: Erlbaum.

FISCHER, K. W., & FARRAR, M. J. (1987). Generalizations about generalization: How a theory of skill development explains both generality and specificity. *International Journal of Psychology, 22,* 643–677.

FISCHER, K. W., SHAVER, P. R., & CARNOCHAN, P. (1989). A skill approach to emotional development: From basic- to subordinate-category emotions. In W. Damon (Ed.), *Child development today and tomorrow.* San Francisco: Jossey-Bass.

FISCHER, K. W., & SILVERN, L. (1985). Stages and individual differences in cognitive development. In M. R. Rosenzweig & L. W. Porter (Eds.), *Annual review of psychology* (Vol. 36). Palo Alto, CA: Annual Reviews, Inc.

FISCHER, K. W., & WATSON, M. W. (1981). Explaining the Oedipal conflict. In K. W.

Fischer (Ed.), *New directions for child development: No. 12. Cognitive development.* San Francisco: Jossey-Bass.

FIVUSH, R. (1990, August). *Self, gender, and emotion in parent-child conversations about the past.* Paper presented at the meeting of the American Psychological Association, Boston.

FIVUSH, R. (in press). Developmental perspectives on autobiographical recall. In G. S. Goodman & B. L. Bottoms (Eds.), *Understanding and improving children's testimony.* New York: Guilford Press.

FIVUSH, R., & HAMOND, N. R. (1989). Time and again: Effects of repetition and retention interval on 2-year-olds' event recall. *Journal of Experimental Child Psychology, 47,* 259–273.

FIVUSH, R., & HAMOND, N. R. (1990). Autobiographical memory across the preschool years: Toward reconceptualizing childhood amnesia. In R. Fivush & J. A. Hudson (Eds.). *Knowing and remembering in young children.* Cambridge: Cambridge University Press.

FIVUSH, R., & HUDSON, J. A. (Eds.). (1990). *Knowing and remembering in young children.* Cambridge: Cambridge University Press.

FIVUSH, R., & SLACKMAN, E. A. (1986). The acquisition and development of scripts. In K. Nelson (Ed.), *Event knowledge.* Hillsdale, NJ: Erlbaum.

FLAMMER, A., & LUTHI, R. (1988). Strategies in selective recall. In F. E. Weinert & M. Perlmutter (Eds.), *Memory development: Universal changes and individual differences.* Hillsdale, NJ: Erlbaum.

FLAPAN, D. (1968). *Children's understanding of social interaction.* New York: Teachers College Press.

FLAVELL, J. H. (1963). *The developmental psychology of Jean Piaget.* Princeton, NJ: D. Van Nostrand.

FLAVELL, J. H. (1970a). Concept development. In P. H. Mussen (Ed.), *Carmichael's manual of child psychology* (3rd ed., Vol. 1). New York: John Wiley.

FLAVELL, J. H. (1970b). Developmental studies of mediated memory. In H. W. Reese & L. P. Lipsitt (Eds.), *Advances in child development and behavior* (Vol. 5). New York: Academic Press.

FLAVELL, J. H. (1971a). Comments on Beilin's "The development of physical concepts." In T. Mischel (Ed.), *Cognitive development and epistemology.* New York: Academic Press.

FLAVELL, J. H. (1971b). First discussant's comments: What is memory development the development of? *Human Development, 14,* 272–278.

FLAVELL, J. H. (1971c). Stage-related properties of cognitive development. *Cognitive Psychology, 2,* 421–453.

FLAVELL, J. H. (1972). An analysis of cognitive-developmental sequences. *Genetic Psychology Monographs, 86,* 279–350.

FLAVELL, J. H. (1974). The development of inferences about others. In T. Mischel (Ed.), *Understanding other persons.* Oxford: Blackwell, Basil, and Mott.

FLAVELL, J. H. (1976, July). *The development of metacommunication.* Paper presented at the Twenty-First Annual Congress of Psychology, Paris.

FLAVELL, J. H. (1977). *Cognitive development* (1st ed.). Englewood Cliffs, NJ: Prentice-Hall.

FLAVELL, J. H. (1978a). The development of knowledge about visual perception. In C. B. Keasey (Ed.), *Nebraska symposium on motivation* (Vol. 25). Lincoln: University of Nebraska Press.

FLAVELL, J. H. (1978b). Metacognitive development. In J. M. Scandura & C. J. Brainerd (Eds.), *Structural/process theories of complex human behavior.* Alphen a. d. Rijn, The Netherlands: Sijthoff and Noordhoff.

FLAVELL, J. H. (1981a). Cognitive monitoring. In W. P. Dickson (Ed.), *Children's oral communication skills.* New York: Academic Press.

FLAVELL, J. H. (1981b). Monitoring social cognitive enterprises: Something else that may develop in the area of social cognition. In J. H. Flavell & L. Ross (Eds.), *Social cognitive development: Frontiers and possible futures.* Cambridge: Cambridge University Press.

FLAVELL, J. H. (1982a). On cognitive development. *Child Development, 53,* 1–10.

FLAVELL, J. H. (1982b). Structures, stages, and sequences in cognitive development. In W. A. Collins (Ed.), *Minnesota symposia on child psychology* (Vol. 15). Hillside, NJ: Erlbaum.

FLAVELL, J. H. (1984). Discussion. In R. J. Sternberg (Ed.), *Mechanisms of cognitive development.* New York: W. H. Freeman.

FLAVELL, J. H. (1986). The development of children's knowledge about the appearance-reality distinction. *American Psychologist, 41,* 418–425.

FLAVELL, J. H. (1987). Speculations about the nature and development of metacognition. In F. E. Weinert & R. H. Kluwe (Eds.), *Metacognition, motivation and understanding.* Hillsdale, NJ: Erlbaum.

FLAVELL, J. H. (1988). The development of children's knowledge about the mind: From cognitive connections to mental representations. In J. W. Astington, P. L. Harris, & D. R. Olson (Eds.), *Developing theories of mind.* Cambridge: Cambridge University Press.

FLAVELL, J. H. (1990, June). *Perspectives on perspective-taking*. Paper presented at the meeting of the Jean Piaget Society, Philadelphia.

FLAVELL, J. H. (1992). Unpublished raw data.

FLAVELL, J. H. (in press). Cognitive development. *Developmental Psychology*.

FLAVELL, J. H., BEACH, D. H., & CHINSKY, J. M. (1966). Spontaneous verbal rehearsal in a memory task as a function of age. *Child Development, 37*, 283–299.

FLAVELL, J. H., BOTKIN, P. T., FRY, C. L., WRIGHT, J. W., & JARVIS, P. E. (1968). *The development of role-taking and communication skills in children*. New York: John Wiley. (Reprinted by Robert E. Krieger Publishing Company, Huntington, NY, 1975)

FLAVELL, J. H., EVERETT, B. A., CROFT, K., & FLAVELL, E. R. (1981). Young children's knowledge about visual perception: Further evidence for the Level 1–Level 2 distinction. *Developmental Psychology, 17*, 99–103.

FLAVELL, J. H., FLAVELL, E. R., & GREEN, F. L. (1983). Development of the appearance-reality distinction. *Cognitive Psychology, 15*, 95–120.

FLAVELL, J. H., FLAVELL, E. R., GREEN, F. L., & KORFMACHER, J. E. (1990). Do young children think of television images as pictures or real objects? *Journal of Broadcasting and Electronic Media, 34*, 399–417.

FLAVELL, J. H., FLAVELL, E. R., GREEN, F. L., & MOSES, L. J. (1990). Young children's understanding of fact beliefs versus value beliefs. *Child Development, 61*, 915–928.

FLAVELL, J. H., FRIEDRICHS, A. G., & HOYT, J. D. (1970). Developmental changes in memorization processes. *Cognitive Psychology, 1*, 324–340.

FLAVELL, J. H., GREEN, F. L., & FLAVELL, E. R. (1986). Development of knowledge about the appearance-reality distinction. *Monographs of the Society for Research in Child Development, 51* (1, Serial No. 212).

FLAVELL, J. H., GREEN, F. L., & FLAVELL, E. R. (1989). Young children's ability to differentiate appearance-reality and level 2 perspectives in the tactile modality. *Child Development, 60*, 201–213.

FLAVELL, J. H., GREEN, F. L., & FLAVELL, E. R. (1990). Developmental changes in young children's knowledge about the mind. *Cognitive Development, 5*, 1–27.

FLAVELL, J. H., GREEN, F. L., HERRERA, C., & FLAVELL, E. R. (1991). Young children's knowledge about visual perception: Lines of sight must be straight. *British Journal of Developmental Psychology, 9*, 73–87.

FLAVELL, J. H., GREEN, F. L., WAHL, K. E., & FLAVELL, E. R. (1987). The effects of question clarification and memory aids on young children's performance on appearance-reality tasks. *Cognitive Development, 2*, 127–144.

FLAVELL, J. H., LINDBERG, N. A., GREEN, F. L., & FLAVELL, E. R. (in press). The development of children's understanding of the appearance-reality distinction between how people look and what they are really like. *Merrill-Palmer Quarterly*.

FLAVELL, J. H., MUMME, D. L., GREEN, F. L., & FLAVELL, E. R. (in press). Young children's understanding of moral and other beliefs. *Child Development*.

FLAVELL, J. H., OMANSON, R. C., & LATHAM, C. (1978). Solving spatial perspective-taking problems by rule versus computation: A developmental study. *Developmental Psychology, 14*, 462–473.

FLAVELL, J. H., & ROSS, L. (1981). Concluding remarks. In J. H. Flavell & L. Ross (Eds.), *Social cognitive development: Frontiers and possible futures*. Cambridge: Cambridge University Press.

FLAVELL, J. H., SHIPSTEAD, S. G., & CROFT, K. (1978). Young children's knowledge about visual perception: Hiding objects from others. *Child Development, 49*, 1208–1211.

FLAVELL, J. H., SPEER, J. R., GREEN, F. L., & AUGUST, D. L. (1981). The development of comprehension monitoring and knowledge about communication. *Monographs of the Society for Research in Child Development, 46* (Serial No. 192).

FLAVELL, J. H., & WELLMAN, H. M. (1977). Metamemory. In R. V. Kail & J. W. Hagen (Eds.), *Perspectives on the development of memory and cognition*. Hillsdale, NJ: Erlbaum.

FLAVELL, J. H., & WOHLWILL, J. F. (1969). Formal and functional aspects of cognitive development. In D. Elkind & J. H. Flavell (Eds.), *Studies in cognitive development: Essays in honor of Jean Piaget*. New York: Oxford University Press.

FLAVELL, J. H., ZHANG, X-D., ZOU, H., DONG, Q., & QI, S. (1983). A comparison between the development of the appearance-reality distinction in the People's Republic of China and the United States. *Cognitive Psychology, 15*, 459–466.

FODOR, J. A. (1983). *The modularity of mind*. Cambridge, MA: MIT Press.

FOLDS, T. H., FOOTO, M., GUTTENTAG, R. E., & ORNSTEIN, P. A. (1990). When children mean to remember: Issues of context specificity, strategy effectiveness, and intentionality in the development of memory. In D. F. Bjorklund (Ed.), *Children's strategies: Contemporary views of cognitive development*. Hillsdale, NJ: Erlbaum.

FORGUSON, L. (1989). *Common sense*. London: Routledge.

FORREST, D. L., & WALLER, T. G. (1979, March). *Cognitive and metacognitive aspects of reading*. Paper presented at the meeting of the Society for Research in Child Development, San Francisco.

FORREST-PRESSLEY, D. L., MACKINNON, G. E., & WALLER, T. G. (1985). *Metacognition, cognition, and human performance* (Vols. 1 & 2). New York: Academic Press.

FOX, N. A., & FITZGERALD, H. E. (1990). Autonomic function in infancy. *Merrill-Palmer Quarterly, 36*, 27–52.

FOX, R., & MCDANIEL, C. (1982). The perception of biological motion by human infants. *Science, 218*, 486–487.

FRANCIS, D. (1978). *Trial run*. New York: Harper & Row.

FREEMAN, N. H. (1980). *Strategies of representation in children: Analysis of spatial skills and drawing processes*. London: Academic Press.

FREUD, S. (1953). Three essays on the theory of sexuality. In J. Strachey (Ed. and Trans.), *The standard edition of the complete psychological works of Sigmund Freud* (Vol. 7). London: Hogarth Press. (Original work published 1905)

FREUND, L. S. (1990). Maternal regulation of children's problem-solving behavior and its impact on children's performance. *Child Development, 61*, 113–126.

FRIEND, M. J., & DAVIS, T. L. (1991, April). *Children's understanding of physical and affective appearance-reality distinctions*. Paper presented at the meeting of the Society for Research in Child Development, Seattle, WA.

FRYE, D., BRAISBY, N., LOWE, J., MAROUDAS, C., & NICHOLLS, J. (1989). Young children's understanding of counting and cardinality. *Child Development, 60*, 1158–1178.

FRYE, D., & MOORE, C. (Eds.). (1991). *Children's theories of mind: Mental states and social understanding*. Hillsdale, NJ: Erlbaum.

FUKUHARA, H., SHIMURA, Y., & YAMANOUCHI, I. (1988, November). *The transmission of ambient noise and self-produced sound into the human body*. Poster presented at the Second Joint Meeting of the Acoustical Society of America and the Acoustical Society of Japan, Honolulu.

FURMAN, L. N., & WALDEN, T. A. (1990). Effect of script knowledge on preschool children's communicative interactions. *Developmental Psychology, 26*, 227–233.

FURMAN, W., & BIERMAN, K. L. (1983). Developmental changes in young children's conceptions of friendship. *Child Development, 54*, 549–556.

FURROW, D., NELSON, K., & BENEDICT, H. (1979). Mothers' speech to children and syntactic development: Some simple relationships. *Journal of Child Language, 6*, 423–442.

FURTH, H. G. (1971). Linguistic deficiency and thinking: Research with deaf subjects 1964–1969. *Psychological Bulletin, 76*, 58–72.

FURTH, H. G. (1981). *Piaget and knowledge: Theoretical foundations* (2nd ed.). Chicago: University of Chicago Press.

FUSON, K. C. (1988). *Children's counting and concepts of number*. New York: Springer-Verlag.

FUSON, K. C., & HALL, J. W. (1983). The acquisition of early number word meanings: A conceptual analysis and review. In H. P. Ginsburg (Ed.), *The development of mathematical thinking*. New York: Academic Press.

GALLUP, G. G. (1977). Self-recognition in primates: A comparative approach to the bidirectional properties of consciousness. *American Psychologist, 32*, 329–338.

GARDNER, H. (1973). *The arts and human development*. New York: John Wiley.

GARNER, R. (1990). Children's use of strategies in reading. In D. F. Bjorklund (Ed.), *Children's strategies: Contemporary views of cognitive development*. Hillsdale, NJ: Erlbaum.

GARTON, A. F., & PRATT, C. (1990). Children's pragmatic judgements of direct and indirect requests. *First Language, 10*, 51–59.

GARVEY, C. (1990). *Play* (rev. ed.). Cambridge, MA: Harvard University Press.

GATHERCOLE, V. C. (1987). The contrastive hypothesis for the acquisition of word meaning: A reconsideration of the theory. *Journal of Child Language, 14*, 493–531.

GATHERCOLE, V. C. (1989). Contrast: A semantic constraint? *Journal of Child Language, 16*, 685–702.

GAUVAIN, M., & GREENE, J. K. (1991, April). *The emergence of children's ability to distinguish appearance from reality*. Paper presented at the meeting of the Society for Research in Child Development, Seattle, WA.

GELLATLY, A., ROGERS, D., & SLOBODA, J. A. (Eds.). (1989). *Cognition and social worlds*. Oxford: Clarendon Press.

GELMAN, R. (1972). Logical capacity of very young children: Number invariance rules. *Child Development, 43*, 75–90.

GELMAN, R. (1978). Cognitive development. In M. R. Rosenzweig & L. W. Porter (Eds.), *Annual review of psychology* (Vol. 29). Palo Alto, CA: Annual Reviews, Inc.

GELMAN, R. (1982). Basic numerical abilities. In R. J. Sternberg (Ed.), *Advances in the psychology of human intelligence* (Vol. 1). Hillsdale, NJ: Erlbaum.

GELMAN, R. (1983). Reconsidering the transition from prelinguistic to linguistic communication. In R. M. Golinkoff (Ed.), *The transition from prelinguistic to linguistic communication*. Hillsdale, NJ: Erlbaum.

GELMAN, R. (1990). First principles organize attention to and learning about relevant data: Number and the animate-inanimate distinction. *Cognitive Science, 14,* 79–106.

GELMAN, R. (1991). Epigenetic foundations of knowledge structures: Initial and transcendent constructions. In S. Carey & R. Gelman (Eds.), *The epigenesis of mind: Essays on biology and cognition*. Hillsdale, NJ: Erlbaum.

GELMAN, R., & BAILLARGEON, R. (1983). A review of Piagetian concepts. In J. H. Flavell & E. M. Markman (Eds.), P. H. Mussen (Series Ed.), *Handbook of child psychology: Vol. 3. Cognitive development*. New York: John Wiley.

GELMAN, R., & GALLISTEL, C. R. (1978). *The child's understanding of number*. Cambridge, MA: Harvard University Press.

GELMAN, R., & MECK, E. (in press). Early principles aid early but not later conceptions of number. In J. Bideaud & C. Meljae (Eds.), *Les chemins du nombre*. Paris: Les Presses Universitaires De Lille.

GELMAN, R., MECK, E., & MERKIN, S. (1986). Young children's numerical competence. *Cognitive Development, 1,* 1–29.

GELMAN, R., & SPELKE, E. (1981). The development of thoughts about animate and inanimate objects: Implications for research on social cognition. In J. H. Flavell & L. Ross (Eds.), *Social cognitive development: Frontiers and possible futures*. New York: Cambridge University Press.

GELMAN, R., SPELKE, E. S., & MECK, E. (1983). What preschoolers know about animate and inanimate objects. In D. R. Rogers & J. A. Sloboda (Eds.), *The acquisition of symbolic skills*. New York: Plenum Press.

GELMAN, R., & WEINBERG, D. H. (1972). The relationship between liquid conservation and compensation. *Child Development, 43,* 371–383.

GELMAN, S. A. (1988). The development of induction within natural kind and artifact categories. *Cognitive Psychology, 20,* 65–95.

GELMAN, S. A., & COLEY, J. D. (1990). The importance of knowing a dodo is a bird: Categories and inferences in 2½-year-old children. *Developmental Psychology, 26,* 796–804.

GELMAN, S. A., & KREMER, K. E. (1991). Understanding natural cause: Children's explanations of how objects and their properties originate. *Child Development, 62,* 396–414.

GELMAN, S. A., & MARKMAN, E. M. (1986). Categories and induction in young children. *Cognition, 23,* 183–209.

GELMAN, S. A., & MARKMAN, E. M. (1987). Young children's inductions from natural kinds: The role of categories and appearances. *Child Development, 58,* 1532–1541.

GELMAN, S. A., & O'REILLY, A. W. (1988). Children's inductive inferences within superordinate categories: The role of language and category structure. *Child Development, 59,* 876–887.

GELMAN, S. A., & WELLMAN, H. M. (1991). Insides and essences: Early understandings of the non-obvious. *Cognition, 38,* 213–244.

GERBER, E. (1975). *The cultural patterning of emotions in Samoa*. Unpublished doctoral dissertation, University of California, San Diego.

GERBER, M., & KAUFFMAN, J. M. (1981). Peer tutoring in academic settings. In P. S. Strain (Ed.), *The utilization of classroom peers as behavior change agents*. New York: Plenum Press.

GHATALA, E. S. (1984). Developmental changes in incidental memory as a function of meaningfulness and encoding condition. *Developmental Psychology, 20,* 208–211.

GHATALA, E. S., LEVIN, J. R., PRESSLEY, M., & GOODWIN, D. (1986). A componential analysis of the effects of derived and supplied strategy-utility information on children's strategy selection. *Journal of Experimental Child Psychology, 41,* 76–92.

GIBSON, E. J. (1969). *Principles of perceptual learning and development*. New York: Appleton-Century-Crofts.

GIBSON, E. J. (1988). Levels of description and constraints on perceptual development. In A. Yonas (Ed.), *Minnesota symposia on child psychology: Vol. 20. Perceptual development in infancy*. Hillsdale, NJ: Erlbaum.

GIBSON, E. J., OWSLEY, C. J., & JOHNSTON, J. (1978). Perception of invariants by five-month-old infants: Differentiation of two types of motion. *Developmental Psychology, 14,* 407–415.

GIBSON, E. J., OWSLEY, C. J., WALKER, A., & MEGAW-NYCE, J. (1979). Development of the perception of invariants: Substance and shape. *Perception, 8,* 609–619.

GIBSON, E. J., & SPELKE, E. S. (1983). The development of perception. In J. H. Flavell & E. M. Markman (Eds.), P. H. Mussen (Series Ed.), *Handbook of child psychology: Vol. 3. Cognitive development*. New York: John Wiley.

GIBSON, E. J., & WALK, R. D. (1960). The "visual cliff." *Scientific American, 202,* 64–71.

GIBSON, E. J., & WALKER, A. S. (1984). Development of knowledge of visual-tactual affordances of substance. *Child Development, 55,* 453–460.

GIBSON, K. R., & PETERSEN, A. C. (Eds.). (1991). *Brain maturation and cognitive development.* New York: Aldine de Gruyter.

GILLIGAN, C. (1982). *In a different voice: Psychological theory and women's development.* Cambridge, MA: Harvard University Press.

GILLIGAN, C., LYONS, N. P., & HANMER, T. J. (Eds.). (1989). *Making connections: Interpreting the interpersonal world of adolescent girls at Emma Willard School.* Cambridge, MA: Harvard University Press.

GINSBURG, H., & OPPER, S. (1988). *Piaget's theory of intellectual development: An introduction* (3rd ed.). Englewood Cliffs, NJ: Prentice-Hall.

GLASER, R., & CHI, M. T. H. (1988). Overview. In M. T. H. Chi, R. Glaser, & M. J. Farr (Eds.), *The nature of expertise.* Hillsdale, NJ: Erlbaum.

GLEASON, J. B. (1989). Studying language development. In J. B. Gleason (Ed.), *The development of language* (2nd ed.). Columbus, OH: Chas. E. Merrill.

GLEITMAN, L. R., & WANNER, E. (1988). Current issues in language learning. In M. H. Bornstein & M. E. Lamb (Eds.), *Developmental psychology: An advanced textbook.* Hillsdale, NJ: Erlbaum.

GLUCKSBERG, S., KRAUSS, R. M., & HIGGINS, E. T. (1975). The development of communication skills in children. In F. Horowitz (Ed.), *Review of child development research* (Vol. 4). Chicago: University of Chicago Press.

GNEPP, J. (1989). Children's use of personal information to understand other people's feelings. In C. Saarni & P. L. Harris (Eds.), *Children's understanding of emotion.* Cambridge: Cambridge University Press.

GNEPP, J., & CHILAMKURTI, C. (1988). Children's use of personality attributions to predict other people's emotional and behavioral reactions. *Child Development, 59,* 743–754.

GNEPP, J., & GOULD, M. E. (1985). The development of personalized inferences: Understanding other people's emotional reactions in light of their prior experiences. *Child Development, 56,* 1455–1464.

GNEPP, J., & HESS, D. L. R. (1986). Children's understanding of verbal and facial display rules. *Developmental Psychology, 22,* 103–108.

GOBBO, C., & CHI, M. T. H. (1986). How knowledge is structured and used by expert and novice children. *Cognitive Development, 1,* 221–237.

GOLD, M. E. (1967). Language identification in the limit. *Information and Control, 10,* 447–474.

GOLD, R. (1987). *The description of cognitive development: Three Piagetian themes.* Oxford: Clarendon Press.

GOLDBERG, S., PERLMUTTER, M., & MYERS, N. (1974). Recall of related and unrelated lists by 2-year-olds. *Journal of Experimental Child Psychology, 18,* 1–8.

GOLDFIELD, B. A., & SNOW, C. E. (1989). Individual differences in language acquisition. In J. B. Gleason (Ed.), *The development of language* (2nd ed.). Columbus, OH: Chas. E. Merrill.

GOLDIN-MEADOW, S. (1979). Structure in a manual communication system developed without a conventional language model: Language without a helping hand. In H. Whitaker & H. A. Whitaker (Eds.), *Studies in neurolinguistics* (Vol. 4). New York: Academic Press.

GOLDIN-MEADOW, S. (1982). The resilience of recursion: A study of a communication system developed without a conventional language model. In E. Wanner & L. R. Gleitman (Eds.), *Language acquisition: The state of the art.* Cambridge: Cambridge University Press.

GOLDMAN-RAKIC, P. S. (1987). Development of cortical circuitry and cognitive function. *Child Development, 58,* 601–622.

GOLINKOFF, R. M. (1983a). The preverbal negotiation of failed messages: Insights into the transition period. In R. M. Golinkoff (Ed.), *The transition from prelinguistic to linguistic communication.* Hillsdale, NJ: Erlbaum.

GOLINKOFF, R. M. (Ed.). (1983b). *The transition from prelinguistic to linguistic communication.* Hillsdale, NJ: Erlbaum.

GOLINKOFF, R. M., BAILEY, L., WENGER, N., & HIRSH-PASEK, K. (1989, April). *Conceptualizing constraints: Why and how many?* Paper presented at the Meeting of the Society for Research in Child Development, Kansas City, MO.

GOLINKOFF, R. M., & HIRSH-PASEK, K. (1990). Let the mute speak: What infants can tell us about language acquisition. *Merrill-Palmer Quarterly, 36,* 67–91.

GOLINKOFF, R. M., HIRSH-PASEK, K., CAULEY, K., & GORDON, L. (1987). The eyes have it: Lexical and syntactic comprehension in a new paradigm. *Journal of Child Language, 14,* 23–45.

GÖNCÜ, A. (Ed.). (1989). Understanding play [Special issue]. *Developmental Review, 9*(4).

GOODMAN, G. S. (1984). Children's testimony in historical perspective. *Journal of Social Issues, 40,* 9–31.

GOODMAN, G. S., & AMAN, C. (1990). Children's use of anatomically detailed dolls to recount an event. *Child Development, 61*, 1859–1871.

GOODMAN, G. S., AMAN, C., & HIRSCHMAN, J. (1987). Child sexual and physical abuse: Children's testimony. In S. J. Ceci, M. P. Toglia, & D. F. Ross (Eds.), *Children's eyewitness memory*. New York: Springer-Verlag.

GOODMAN, G. S., GOLDING, J. M., & HAITH, M. M. (1984). Jurors' reactions to child witnesses. *Journal of Social Issues, 40*, 139–156.

GOODMAN, G. S., RUDY, L., BOTTOMS, B. L., & AMAN, C. (1990). Children's concerns and memory: Issues of ecological validity in the study of children's eyewitness testimony. In R. Fivush & J. A. Hudson (Eds.), *Knowing and remembering in young children*. Cambridge: Cambridge University Press.

GOODNOW, J. J., & COLLINS, W. A. (1990). *Development according to parents: The nature, sources, and consequences of parents' ideas*. Hove & London: Erlbaum.

GOPNIK, A. (1984). The acquisition of *gone* and the development of the object concept. *Journal of Child Language, 11*, 273–292.

GOPNIK, A. (1988). Three types of early word: The emergence of social words, names and cognitive-relational words in the one-word stage and their relation to cognitive development. *First Language, 8*, 49–70.

GOPNIK, A., & ASTINGTON, J. W. (1988). Children's understanding of representational change and its relation to the understanding of false belief and the appearance-reality distinction. *Child Development, 59*, 26–37.

GOPNIK, A., & GRAF, P. (1988). Knowing how you know: Young children's ability to identify and remember the sources of their beliefs. *Child Development, 59*, 1366–1371.

GOPNIK, A., & MELTZOFF, A. N. (1986a). Relations between semantic and cognitive development in the one-word stage: The specificity hypothesis. *Child Development, 57*, 1040–1053.

GOPNIK, A., & MELTZOFF, A. N. (1986b). Words, plans, things, and locations: Interactions between semantic and cognitive development in the one-word stage. In S. A. Kuczaj II & M. D. Barrett (Eds.), *The development of word meaning: Progress in cognitive development research*. New York: Springer-Verlag.

GORDON, F. R., & FLAVELL, J. H. (1977). The development of intuitions about cognitive cueing. *Child Development, 48*, 1027–1033.

GORDON, P. (1990). Learnability and feedback. *Developmental Psychology, 26*, 217–220.

GOTTLIEB, G., & KRASNEGOR, N. A. (Eds.). (1985). *Measurement of audition and vision in the first year of postnatal life*. Norwood, NJ: Ablex.

GOVE, F. L., & KEATING, D. P. (1979). Empathic role-taking precursors. *Developmental Psychology, 15*, 594–600.

GRAHAM, S., & HARRIS, K. R. (1989). Components analysis of cognitive strategy instruction: Effects on learning disabled students' compositions and self-efficacy. *Journal of Educational Psychology, 81*, 353–361.

GRANOTT, N. (1991, May). *From macro to micro and back: On the analysis of microdevelopment*. Paper presented at the meeting of the Jean Piaget Society, Philadelphia.

GRANRUD, C. E. (Ed.). (in press). *Visual perception and cognition in infants*. Hillsdale, NJ: Erlbaum.

GRATCH, G. (1972). A study of the relative dominance of vision and touch in six-month-old infants. *Child Development, 43*, 615–623.

GRATCH, G., & LANDERS, W. F. (1971). Stage iV of Piaget's theory of infants' object concepts: A longitudinal study. *Child Development, 42*, 359–372.

GRAY, W. M. (1990). Formal operational thought. In W. F. Overton (Ed.), *Reasoning, necessity, and logic: Developmental perspectives*. Hillsdale, NJ: Erlbaum.

GREENFIELD, P. M. (in press). Representational competence in shared symbol systems: Electronic media from radio to video games. In R. R. Cocking & K. A. Renninger (Eds.), *The development and meaning of psychological distance*. Hillsdale, NJ: Erlbaum.

GREENFIELD, P. M., & CHILDS, C. P. (1991). Developmental continuity in bio-cultural context. In R. Cohen & A. W. Siegel (Eds.), *Context and development*. Hillsdale, NJ: Erlbaum.

GREENFIELD, P. M., & LAVE, J. (1982). Cognitive aspects of informal education. In D. A. Wagner & H. W. Stevenson (Eds.), *Cultural perspectives on child development*. San Francisco: W. H. Freeman.

GREENO, J. G., RILEY, M. S., & GELMAN, R. (1984). Conceptual competence and children's counting. *Cognitive Psychology, 16*, 94–134.

GREENOUGH, W. T., BLACK, J. E., & WALLACE, C. S. (1987). Experience and brain development. *Child Development, 58*, 539–559.

GRIESER, D. L., & KUHL, P. K. (1988). Maternal speech to infants in a tonal language: Support for universal prosodic features in motherese. *Developmental Psychology, 24*, 14–20.

GROSS, A. L., & BALLIF, B. (1991). Children's understanding of emotion from facial expressions and situations: A review. *Developmental Review, 11*, 368–398.

GRUELICH, E. D., & BAKER-WARD, L. (1989, April). *The effects of strategic and metamemorial training on kindergarten children's memory and metamemory ability.* Paper presented at the meeting of the Society for Research in Child Development, Kansas City, MO.

GUERRA, N. G., & SLABY, R. G. (1990). Cognitive mediators of aggression in adolescent offenders: 2. Intervention. *Developmental Psychology, 26,* 269–277.

GUNNAR, M. R., & SROUFE, L. A. (Eds.). (1991). *Minnesota symposia on child psychology: Vol. 23. Self processes and development.* Hillsdale, NJ: Erlbaum.

GUTTENTAG, R. E. (1984). The mental effort requirement of cumulative rehearsal: A developmental study. *Journal of Experimental Child Psychology, 37,* 92–106.

GUTTENTAG, R. E., ORNSTEIN, P. A., & SIEMENS, L. (1987). Children's spontaneous rehearsal: Transitions in strategy acquisition. *Cognitive Development, 2,* 307–326.

HAAKE, R. J., SOMERVILLE, S. C., & WELLMAN, H. M. (1980). Logical ability of young children in searching a large-scale environment. *Child Development, 51,* 1299–1302.

HADWIN, J., & PERNER, J. (1991). Pleased and surprised: Children's cognitive theory of emotion. *British Journal of Developmental Psychology, 9,* 215–234.

HAGEN, J. W., JONGEWARD, R. H., & KAIL, R. V. (1975). Cognitive perspectives on the development of memory. In H. W. Reese (Ed.), *Advances in child development and behavior* (Vol. 10). New York: Academic Press.

HAITH, M. M. (1980). *Rules that babies look by.* Hillsdale, NJ: Erlbaum.

HAITH, M. M. (1990). Progress in the understanding of sensory and perceptual processes in early infancy. *Merrill-Palmer Quarterly, 36,* 1–26.

HALA, S., CHANDLER, M. J, & FRITZ, A. S. (1991). Fledgling theories of mind: Deception as a marker of three-year-olds' understanding of false belief. *Child Development, 62,* 83–97.

HALE, S. (1990). A global developmental trend in cognitive processing speed. *Child Development, 61,* 653–663.

HALFORD, G. S. (1982). *The development of thought.* Hillsdale, NJ: Erlbaum.

HALFORD, G. S. (1989). Reflections on 25 years of Piagetian cognitive developmental psychology, 1963–1988. *Human Development, 32,* 325–357.

HALFORD, G. S. (in press). *Children's understanding: The development of mental models.* Hillsdale, NJ: Erlbaum.

HALFORD, G. S., & LEITCH, E. (1989). Processing load constraints: A structure-mapping approach. In M. A. Luszcz & T. Nettelbeck (Eds.), *Psychological development: Perspectives across the lifespan.* Amsterdam: Elsevier.

HALFORD, G. S., MAYBERY, M. T., & BAIN, J. D. (1988). Set-size effects in primary memory: An age-related capacity limitation? *Memory and Cognition, 16,* 480–487.

HARDING, C. (1984). Acting with intention: A framework for examining the development of the intention to communicate. In L. Feagans, C. Garvey, & R. Golinkoff (Eds.), *The origins and growth of communication.* Norwood, NJ: Ablex.

HARNISHFEGER, K. K., & BJORKLUND, D. F. (in press). The ontogeny of inhibition mechanisms: A renewed approach to cognitive development. In M. L. Howe & M. R. Pasnak (Eds.), *Emerging themes in cognitive development: Vol. 1. Foundations.* New York: Springer-Verlag.

HARRIS, J. F., DURSO, F. T., MERGLER, N. L., & JONES, S. K. (1990). Knowledge base influences judgments of frequency of occurrence. *Cognitive Development, 5,* 223–233.

HARRIS, P. L. (1983). Infant cognition. In M. M. Haith & J. J. Campos (Eds.), P. H. Mussen (Series Ed.), *Handbook of child psychology: Vol. 2. Infancy and developmental psychobiology.* New York: John Wiley.

HARRIS, P. L. (1989a). *Children and emotion.* Oxford: Basil Blackwell.

HARRIS, P. L. (1989b). Object permanence in infancy. In A. Slater & G. Bremner (Eds.), *Infant development.* Hillsdale, NJ: Erlbaum.

HARRIS, P. L., BROWN, E., MARRIOTT, C., WHITTALL, S., & HARMER, S. (1991). Monsters, ghosts and witches: Testing the limits of the fantasy-reality distinction in young children. *British Journal of Developmental Psychology, 9,* 105–123.

HARRIS, P. L., DONNELLY, K., GUZ, G. R., & PITT-WATSON, R. (1986). Children's understanding of the distinction between real and apparent emotion. *Child Development, 57,* 895–909.

HARRIS, P. L., & GUZ, G. R. (1986). *Models of emotion: How boys report their emotional reactions upon entering an English boarding school.* Unpublished manuscript, University of Oxford.

HARRIS, P. L., & LIPIAN, M. S. (1985, April). *Distress and the loss of insight into emotion.* Paper presented at the meeting of the Society for Research in Child Development, Toronto.

HARRIS, P. L., & LIPIAN, M. S. (1989). Understanding emotion and experiencing emotion. In C. Saarni & P. L. Harris (Eds.), *Children's understanding of emotions.* Cambridge: Cambridge University Press.

References

HARRIS, P. L., & OLTHOF, T. (1982). The child's conception of emotion. In A. Butterworth & P. Light (Eds.), *Social cognition: Studies of the development of understanding.* Chicago: University of Chicago Press.

HARRIS, P. L., OLTHOF, T., MEERUM TERWOGT, M. & HARDMAN, C. E. (1987). Children's knowledge of the situations that provoke emotion. *International Journal of Behavioral Development, 10,* 319–344.

HARTER, S. (1982). Children's understanding of multiple emotions: A cognitive-developmental approach. In W. F. Overton, (Ed.), *The relationship between social and cognitive development.* Hillsdale, NJ: Erlbaum.

HARTER, S. (1988). Developmental processes in the construction of the self. In T. D. Yawkey & J. E. Johnson (Eds.), *Integrative processes and socialization: Early to middle childhood.* Hillsdale, NJ: Erlbaum.

HARTER, S., & BUDDIN, B. (1987). Children's understanding of the simultaneity of two emotions: A five-stage developmental acquisition sequence. *Developmental Psychology, 23,* 388–399.

HAYES, C. (1951). *The ape in our house.* New York: Harper.

HAYNES, V. F., & MILLER, P. H. (1987). The relationship between cognitive style, memory, and attention in preschoolers. *Child Study Journal, 17,* 21–33.

HEILBECK, T. H., & MARKMAN, E. M. (1987). Word learning in children: An examination of fast mapping. *Child Development, 58,* 1021–1034.

HELLER, K. A., & BERNDT, T. J. (1981). Developmental changes in the formation and organization of personality attributions. *Child Development, 52,* 683–691.

HENRY, L. A., & MILLAR, S. (1991). Memory span increase with age: A test of two hypotheses. *Journal of Experimental Child Psychology, 51,* 459–484.

HICKEY, F. L., & PEDUZZI, J. D. (1987). Structure and development of the visual system. In P. Salapatek & L. Cohen (Eds.), *Handbook of infant perception: Vol. 1. From sensation to perception.* Orlando, FL: Academic Press.

HIGGINS, E. T. (1981). Role taking and social judgment: Alternative developmental perspectives and processes. In J. H. Flavell & L. Ross (Eds.), *Social cognitive development: Frontiers and possible futures.* Cambridge: Cambridge University Press.

HIGGINS, E. T., & BRYANT, S. L. (1982). Consensus information and the fundamental attribution error: The role of development and in-group versus out-group knowledge. *Journal of Personality and Social Psychology, 43,* 889–900.

HILL, J. P., & PALMQUIST, W. J. (1978). Social cognition and social relations in early adolescence. *International Journal of Behavioral Development, 1,* 1–36.

HITCH, G. J., HALLIDAY, M. S., & LITTLER, J. E. (1989). Item identification time and rehearsal as predictors of memory span in children. *Quarterly Journal of Experimental Psychology, 41A,* 321–327.

HOBSON, R. P. (1991). Against the theory of "theory of mind." *British Journal of Developmental Psychology, 9,* 33–51.

HOCHBERG, J. E. (1962). Nativism and empiricism in perception. In L. Postman (Ed.), *Psychology in the making.* New York: Knopf.

HOEK, D., INGRAM, D., & GIBSON, D. (1986). An examination of the possible causes of children's early word extensions. *Journal of Child Language, 13,* 477–494.

HOFF-GINSBERG, E. (1990). Maternal speech and the child's development of syntax: A further look. *Journal of Child Language, 17,* 85–99.

HOFFMAN, M. L. (1978). Empathy: Its developmental and prosocial implications. In C. B. Keasey (Ed.), *Nebraska symposium on motivation* (Vol. 25). Lincoln: University of Nebraska Press.

HOFFMAN, M. L. (1981). Perspectives on the difference between understanding people and understanding things. The role of affect. In J. H. Flavell & L. Ross (Eds.), *Social cognitive development: Frontiers and possible futures.* Cambridge: Cambridge University Press.

HOFFMAN, M. L. (1989). Moral development. In M. H. Bornstein & M. E. Lamb (Eds.), *Developmental psychology: An advanced textbook* (2nd ed.). Hillsdale, NJ: Erlbaum.

HOFSTEN, C. VON., & SPELKE, E. S. (1985). Object perception and object-directed reaching in infancy. *Journal of Experimental Psychology: General, 114,* 198–212.

HOOD, B., & WILLATTS, P. (1986). Reaching in the dark to an object's remembered position: Evidence for object permanence in 5-month-old infants. *British Journal of Developmental Psychology, 4,* 57–65.

HOOD, L., & BLOOM, L. (1979). What, when, and how about why: A longitudinal study of early expressions of causality. *Monographs of the Society for Research in Child Development, 44* (6, Serial No. 181).

HOWE, C. J. (1976). The meanings of two-word utterances in the speech of young children. *Journal of Child Language, 3,* 29–47.

HOWE, M. L., & O'SULLIVAN, J. T. (1990). The development of strategic memory: Coordinating knowledge, metamemory, and resources. In D. F. Bjorklund (Ed.), *Children's strategies: Contemporary views of cognitive development.* Hillsdale, NJ: Erlbaum.

Howe, M. L., & Rabinowitz, F. M. (1989). On the uninterpretability of dual-task performance. *Journal of Experimental Child Psychology, 47,* 32–38.

Hudson, J. A. (1986). Memories are made of this: General event knowledge and development of autobiographic memory. In K. Nelson (Ed.), *Event knowledge: Structure and function in development.* Hillsdale, NJ: Erlbaum.

Hudson, J. A. (1990). The emergence of autobiographical memory in mother-child conversations. In R. Fivush & J. A. Hudson (Eds.), *Knowing and remembering in young children.* New York: Cambridge University Press.

Hudson, J. A., & Fivush, R. (1990). Introduction: What young children remember and why. In R. Fivush & J. A. Hudson (Eds.), *Knowing and remembering in young children.* Cambridge: Cambridge University Press.

Hudson, J. A., & Fivush, R. (1991). As time goes by: Sixth grade children recall a kindergarten experience. *Applied Cognitive Psychology, 5,* 346–360.

Hudson, J. A., & Shapiro, L. R. (1991). From knowing to telling: The development of children's scripts, stories, and personal narratives. In A. McCabe & C. Peterson (Eds.), *New directions in narrative structure.* Hillsdale, NJ: Erlbaum.

Hughes, M., & Donaldson, M. (1979). The use of hiding games for studying the coordination of viewpoints. *Educational Review, 31,* 133–140.

Hughes, R., Tingle, B. A., & Sawin, D. B. (1981). Development of empathic understanding in children. *Child Development, 52,* 122–128.

Hunt, J. McV. (1969). The impact and limitations of a giant of developmental psychology. In D. Elkind & J. H. Flavell (Eds.), *Studies in cognitive development: Essays in honor of Jean Piaget.* New York: Oxford University Press.

Huttenlocher, J., & Smiley, P. (1990). Emerging notions of persons. In N.L. Stein, B. Leventhal, & T. Trabasso (Eds.), *Psychological and biological approaches to emotions.* Hillsdale, NJ: Erlbaum.

Hyams, N. M. (1986). *Language acquisition and the theory of parameters.* Dordrecht, Holland: D. Reidel Publishing Co.

Inagaki, K., & Hatano, G. (1987). Young children's spontaneous personification as analogy. *Child Development, 58,* 1013–1020.

Inagaki, K., & Sugiyama, K. (1988). Attributing human characteristics: Developmental changes in over- and underattribution. *Cognitive Development, 3,* 55–70.

Ingram, D. (1989). *First language acquisition.* Cambridge: Cambridge University Press.

Inhelder, B., & Piaget, J. (1958). *The growth of logical thinking from childhood to adolescence.* New York: Basic Books.

Inhelder, B., & Piaget, J. (1964). *The early growth of logic in the child.* New York: Harper & Row.

Jackowitz, E. R., & Watson, M. W. (1980). Development of object transformations in early pretend play. *Developmental Psychology, 16,* 543–549.

Johannson, G. (1973). Visual perception of biological motion and a model for its analysis. *Perception and Psychophysics, 14,* 201–211.

Johnson, C. N. (1988). Theory of mind and the structure of conscious experience. In J. W. Astington, P. L. Harris, & D. R. Olson (Eds.), *Developing theories of mind.* Cambridge: Cambridge University Press.

Johnson, C. N. (1990). If you had my brain, where would I be? Children's understanding of the brain and identity. *Child Development, 61,* 962–972.

Johnson, J., & Newport, E. (1989). Critical period effects in second language learning: The influence of maturational state on the acquisition of English as a second language. *Cognitive Psychology, 21,* 60–99.

Johnson, M. H., & Morton, J. (1992). *Biology and cognitive development: The case of face recognition.* Cambridge, MA: Blackwell Publishers.

Johnston, J. R. (1985). Cognitive prerequisites: The evidence from children learning English. In D. I. Slobin (Ed.), *The crosslinguistic study of language acquisition: Vol. 2. Theoretical issues.* Hillsdale, NJ: Erlbaum.

Jones, E. E. (1990). *Interpersonal perception.* New York: W. H. Freeman.

Jones, G. E., & Dembo, M. H. (1989). Age and sex role differences in intimate friendships during childhood and adolescence. *Merrill-Palmer Quarterly, 35,* 445–462.

Jordan, N. (1972). Is there an Achilles heel in Piaget's theorizing? *Human Development, 15,* 379–382.

Justice, E. M. (1989). Preschoolers' knowledge and use of behaviors varying in strategic effectiveness. *Merrill-Palmer Quarterly, 35,* 363–377.

Kagan, J. (1981). *The second year.* Cambridge, MA: Harvard University Press.

Kahan, L. D., & Richards, D. D. (1986). The effects of context on children's referential communication strategies. *Child Development, 57,* 1130–1141.

KAIL, R. (1986). ⋅ Sources of age differences in speed of processing. *Child Development, 57,* 969–987.

KAIL, R. (1989). *The development of memory in children* (3rd ed.). New York: W. H. Freeman.

KAIL, R. (1991a). Development of processing speed in childhood and adolescence. In H. W. Reese (Ed.), *Advances in child development and behavior* (Vol. 23). San Diego: Academic Press.

KAIL, R. (1991b). Developmental changes in speed of processing during childhood and adolescence. *Psychological Bulletin, 109,* 490–501.

KAIL, R. (1991c). Processing time declines exponentially during childhood and adolescence. *Developmental Psychology, 27,* 259–266.

KAISER, M. K., McCLOSKEY, M., & PROFFITT, D. R. (1986). Development of intuitive theories of motion: Curvilinear motion in the absence of external forces. *Developmental Psychology, 22,* 67–71.

KAISER, M. K., PROFFITT, D. R., & McCLOSKEY, M. (1985). The development of beliefs about falling objects. *Perception and Psychophysics, 38,* 533–539.

KALISH, C. W., & GELMAN, S. A. (1991). *On wooden pillows: Young children's understanding of category implications.* Unpublished manuscript.

KARMILOFF-SMITH, A. (1988). The child is a theoretician, not an inductivist. *Mind and Language, 3,* 1–13.

KARMILOFF-SMITH, A. (1991). Beyond modularity: Innate constraints and developmental change. In S. Carey & R. Gelman (Eds.), *The epigenesis of mind: Essays on biology and cognition.* Hillsdale, NJ: Erlbaum.

KARNIOL, R. (1978). Children's use of intention cues in evaluating behavior. *Psychological Bulletin, 85,* 76–85.

KARNIOL, R., & ROSS, M. (1976). The development of causal attributions in social perception. *Journal of Personality and Social Psychology, 34,* 455–464.

KARNIOL, R., & ROSS, M. (1979). Children's use of a causal attribution schema and the inference of manipulative intentions. *Child Development, 50,* 463–468.

KARZON, R. G. (1985). Discrimination of polysyllabic sequences by one- to four-month-old infants. *Journal of Experimental Child Psychology, 39,* 326–342.

KATZ, P. A. (1982). Development of children's racial awareness of intergroup attitudes. In L. G. Katz, C. H. Watkins, M. J. Spencer, & P. J. Wagemaker (Eds.), *Current topics in early childhood education* (Vol. 4). Norwood, NJ: Ablex.

KAY, D. A., & ANGLIN, J. (1982). Overextension and underextension in the child's expressive and receptive speech. *Journal of Child Language, 9,* 83–98.

KEARINS, J. M. (1981). Visual spatial memory in Australian aboriginal children of desert regions. *Cognitive Psychology, 13,* 434–460.

KEATING, D. P. (1988). Byrnes' reformulation of Piaget's formal operations: Is what's left what's right? Commentary. *Developmental Review, 8,* 376–384.

KEATING, D. P. (1990). Adolescent thinking. In S. S. Feldman & G. R. Elliot (Eds.), *At the threshold: The developing adolescent.* Cambridge, MA: Harvard University Press.

KEE, D. W., & DAVIES, L. (1988). Mental effort and elaboration: A developmental analysis. *Contemporary Educational Psychology, 13,* 221–228.

KEE, D. W., & HOWELL, S. (1988, April). *Mental effort and memory development.* Paper presented at the meeting of the American Educational Research Association, New Orleans.

KEENEY, T. J., CANNIZZO, S. R., & FLAVELL, J. H. (1967). Spontaneous and induced verbal rehearsal in a recall task. *Child Development, 38,* 953–966.

KEIL, F. C. (1979). *Semantic and conceptual development.* Cambridge, MA: Harvard University Press.

KEIL, F. C. (1981). Constraints on knowledge and cognitive development. *Psychological Review, 88,* 197–227.

KEIL, F. C. (1986). On the structure-dependent nature of stages of cognitive development. In I. Levin (Ed.), *Stage and structure: Reopening the debate.* Norwood, NJ: Ablex.

KEIL, F. C. (1989). *Concepts, kinds, and cognitive development.* Cambridge, MA: MIT Press.

KEIL, F. C. (1990). Constraints on constraints: Surveying the epigenetic landscape. *Cognitive Science, 14,* 135–168.

KEIL, F. C. (1991). The emergence of theoretical beliefs as constraints on concepts. In S. Carey & R. Gelman (Eds.), *The epigenesis of mind: Essays on biology and cognition.* Hillsdale, NJ: Erlbaum.

KEIL, F. C., & BATTERMAN, N. (1984). A characteristic-to-defining shift in the development of word meaning. *Journal of Verbal Learning and Verbal Behavior, 23,* 221–236.

KELLMAN, P. J., & SPELKE, E. S. (1983). Perception of partly occluded objects in infancy. *Cognitive Psychology, 15,* 483–524.

KELLMAN, P. J., SPELKE, E. S., & SHORT, K. R. (1986). Infant perception of object unity from translatory motion in depth and vertical translation. *Child Development, 57,* 72–86.

KEMLER NELSON, D. G., HIRSH-PASEK, K., JUSCZYK, P., & CASSIDY, K. W. (1989). How the prosodic cues in motherese might assist language learning. *Journal of Child Language, 16,* 55–68.

KENISTON, A. H., & FLAVELL, J. H. (1979). A developmental study of intelligent retrieval. *Child Development, 50,* 1144–1152.

KERKMAN, D. D., & WRIGHT, J. C. (1988). An exegesis of two theories of compensation development: Sequential decision theory and information integration theory. *Developmental Review, 8,* 323–360.

KESTENBAUM, R., TERMINE, N., & SPELKE, E. S. (1987). Perception of objects and object boundaries by three-month-old infants. *British Journal of Developmental Psychology, 5,* 367–383.

KINGMA, J., & VAN DEN BOS, K. P. (1988). Unidimensional scales: New methods to analyze the sequences in concept development. *Genetic, Social, and General Psychology Monographs, 114,* 479–508.

KINSBOURNE, M. (1988). A model of adaptive behavior related to cerebral participation in emotional control. In G. Gainotti (Ed.), *Emotions and the dual brain.* New York: Springer-Verlag.

KLAHR, D. (1989). Information-processing approaches. In R. Vasta (Ed.), *Annals of child development: Vol. 6. Six theories of child development: Revised formulations and current issues.* Greenwich, CT: JAI Press.

KLAHR, D. (In press). Information-processing approaches to cognitive development. In M. H. Bornstein & M. E. Lamb (Ed.), *Developmental psychology: An advanced textbook* (3rd ed.). Hillsdale, NJ: Erlbaum.

KLAHR, D., & DUNBAR, K. (1988). Dual space search during scientific reasoning. *Cognitive Science, 12,* 1–48.

KLAHR, D., LANGLEY, P., & NECHES, R. (Eds.). (1987). *Production system models of learning and development.* Cambridge, MA: MIT Press.

KLAHR, D., & SIEGLER, R. S. (1978). The representation of children's knowledge. In H. W. Reese & L. P. Lipsitt (Eds.), *Advances in child development and behavior* (Vol. 12). New York: Academic Press.

KLAHR, D., & WALLACE, J. G. (1976). *Cognitive development: An information-processing view.* Hillsdale, NJ: Erlbaum.

KLINNERT, M. D., CAMPOS, J. J., SORCE, J. F., EMDE, R., & SVEJDA, M. (1983). Emotions as behavior regulators: Social referencing in infancy. In R. Plutchik & H. Kellerman (Eds.), *Emotions in early development* (Vol. 2). New York: Academic Press.

KLUWE, R. H. (1987). Executive decisions and regulation of problem solving behavior. In F. E. Weinert & R. H. Kluwe (Eds.), *Metacognition, motivation, and understanding.* Hillsdale, NJ: Erlbaum.

KOBASIGAWA, A. (1977). Retrieval strategies in the development of memory. In R. V. Kail & J. W. Hagen (Eds.), *Perspectives on the development of memory and cognition.* Hillsdale, N. J.: Erlbaum.

KOHLBERG, L. (1966). Cognitive stages and preschool education. *Human Development, 9,* 5–17.

KOHLBERG, L. (1969). Stage and sequence: The cognitive-developmental approach to socialization. In A. A. Goslin (Ed.), *Handbook of socialization theory and research.* Skokie, IL: Rand McNally.

KOPP, C. B., & BROWNELL, C. A. (Eds.). (1991). The development of self: The first 3 years [Special issue]. *Developmental Review, 11*(3).

KOPP, C. B., & SHAPERMAN, J. (1973). Cognitive development in the absence of object manipulation during infancy. *Developmental Psychology, 9,* 430.

KRAUSS, R. M., & GLUCKSBERG, S. (1969). The development of communication: Competence as a function of age. *Child Development, 40,* 255–266.

KREITLER, S., & KREITLER, H. (1989). Horizontal décalage: A problem and its solution. *Cognitive Development, 4,* 89–119.

KREUTZER, M. A., LEONARD, C., & FLAVELL, J. H. (1975). An interview study of children's knowledge about memory. *Monographs of the Society for Research in Child Development, 40* (1, Serial No. 159).

KUCZAJ, S. A., II. (1977). The acquisition of regular and irregular past tense forms. *Journal of Verbal Learning and Verbal Behavior, 16,* 589–600.

KUCZAJ, S. A., II. (1981). Factors influencing children's hypothetical reference. *Journal of Child Language, 8,* 131–137.

KUHL, P. K. (1987). Perception of speech and sound in early infancy. In P. Salapatek & L. Cohen (Eds.), *Handbook of infant perception: Vol. 2. From perception to cognition.* Orlando, FL: Academic Press.

KUHL, P. K., & MELTZOFF, A. N. (1982). The bimodal perception of speech in infancy. *Science, 218,* 1138–1141.

KUHL, P. K., & MELTZOFF, A. N. (1984). The intermodal representation of speech in infants. *Infant Behavior and Development, 7,* 361–381.

KUHL, P. K., & MELTZOFF, A. N. (1988). Speech as an intermodal object of perception. In A. Yonas (Ed.), *Minnesota symposia on child psychology: Vol. 20. Perceptual development in infancy.* Hillsdale, NJ: Erlbaum.

KUHL, P. K., & MILLER, J. D. (1975). Speech perception by the chinchilla: Voiced-voiceless distinction in alveolar plosive consonants. *Science, 190,* 69–72.

KUHL, P. K., & PADDEN, D. M. (1983). Enhanced discriminability at the phonetic boundaries for the place features in macaques. *Journal of the Acoustical Society of America, 73,* 1003–1010.

KUHN, D. (1974). Inducing development experimentally: Comments on a research paradigm. *Developmental Psychology, 10,* 590–600.

KUHN, D. (Ed.). (1979). *New directions in child development: No. 5. Intellectual development beyond childhood.* San Francisco: Jossey-Bass.

KUHN, D. (1989). Children and adults as intuitive scientists. *Psychological Review, 96,* 674–689.

KUHN, D. (1990). *Thinking as argument.* Unpublished manuscript, Columbia University.

KUHN, D., AMSEL, E., & O'LOUGHLIN, M. (1988). *The development of scientific thinking skills.* San Diego: Academic Press.

KURLAND, D. M. (1981). *The effect of massive practive on children's operational efficiency and short-term memory.* Unpublished doctoral dissertation, University of Toronto.

KURTINES, W. M., & GEWIRTZ, J. (Eds.). (1989). *Moral behavior and development: Advances in theory, research, and application* (Vol. 1). Hillsdale, NJ: Erlbaum.

KURTZ, B. E. (1990). Cultural influences on children's cognitive and metacognitive development. In W. Schneider & F. E. Weinert (Eds.), *Interactions among aptitude, strategies, and knowledge in cognitive performance.* Hillsdale, NJ: Erlbaum.

KURTZ, B. E., & BORKOWSKI, J. G. (1984). Children's metacognition: Exploring relations among knowledge, process, and motivational variables. *Journal of Experimental Child Psychology, 37,* 335–354.

KURTZ, B. E., & WEINERT, F. E. (1989). Metamemory, memory performance, and causal attributions in gifted and average children. *Journal of Experimental Child Psychology, 48,* 45–61.

LACHMAN, R., LACHMAN, J. L., & BUTTERFIELD, E. C. (1979). *Cognitive psychology and information processing: An introduction.* Hillsdale, NJ: Erlbaum.

LAKOFF, R. (1977). What you can do with words: Politeness, pragmatics, and performatives. In A. Rogers, B. Wall, & J. Murphy (Eds.), *Proceedings of the Texas conference on performatives, presuppositions, and inplicatures.* Arlington, VA: Center for Applied Linguistics.

LANCY, D. F., & STRATHERN, A. J. (1981). "Making two's": Pairing as an alternative to the taxonomic mode of representation. *American Anthropologist, 83,* 773–795.

LANDAU, B., & GLEITMAN, L. R. (1985). *Language and experience: Evidence from the blind child.* Cambridge, MA: Harvard University Press.

LANDAU, B., SPELKE, E. S., & GLEITMAN, H. (1984). Spatial knowledge in a young blind child. *Cognition, 16,* 225–260.

LANDRY, M. O., & LYONS-RUTH, K. (1980). Recursive structure in cognitive perspective taking. *Child Development, 51,* 386–394.

LANE, D. M. (1979). Developmental changes in attention-deployment skills. *Journal of Experimental Child Psychology, 28,* 16–29.

LANGE, G. (1978). Organization-related processes in children's recall. In P. A. Ornstein (Ed.), *Memory development in children.* Hillsdale, NJ: Erlbaum.

LANGE, G., GUTTENTAG, R. E., & NIDA, R. E. (1990). Relationships between study organization, retrieval organization, and general and strategy-specific memory knowledge in young children. *Journal of Experimental Child Psychology, 49,* 126–146.

LANGE, G., MACKINNON, C. E., & NIDA, R. E. (1989). Knowledge, strategy, and motivational contributions to preschool children's object recall. *Developmental Psychology, 25,* 772–779.

LANGE, G., PIERCE, S., & SCHEDLER, J. (1989, April). *Memory-strategy generalization in preschool children.* Paper presented at the meeting of the Society for Research in Child Development, Kansas City, MO.

LANGLOIS, J. H., RITTER, J. M., ROGGMANN, L. A., & VAUGHN, L. S. (1991). Facial diversity and infant preferences for attractive faces. *Developmental Psychology, 27,* 79–84.

LAPSLEY, D. K., & QUINTANA, S. M. (1989). Mental capacity and role taking: A structural equations approach. *Merrill-Palmer Quarterly, 35,* 143–163.

LARKIN, J. H. (1979). Processing information for effective problem solving. *Engineering Education, 70*(3), 285–288.

LEMPERS, J. D., FLAVELL, E. R., & FLAVELL, J. H. (1977). The development in very young children of tacit knowledge concerning visual perception. *Genetic Psychology Monographs, 95,* 3–53.

LENNEBERG, E. H. (1962). Understanding language without ability to speak: A case report. *Journal of Abnormal and Social Psychology, 65,* 419–425.

LENNEBERG, E. H. (1967). *Biological foundations of language.* New York: John Wiley.

LENNEBERG, E. H., REBELSKY, F. G., & NICHOLS, I. A. (1965). The vocalization of infants born to deaf and hearing parents. *Human Development, 8,* 23–37.

LESLIE, A. M. (1984). Spatiotemporal continuity and the perception of causality in infants. *Perception, 13*, 287–305.

LESLIE, A. M. (1986). Getting development off the ground: Modularity and the infant's perception of causality. In P. van Geert (Ed.), *Theory building in developmental psychology*. Amsterdam: Elsevier Science Publishers.

LESLIE, A. M. (1987). Pretense and representation: The origins of "theory of mind." *Psychological Review, 94*, 412–426.

LESLIE, A. M. (1988a). The necessity of illusion: Perception and thought in infancy. In L. Weiskrantz (Ed.), *Thought without language*. Oxford: Clarendon Press.

LESLIE, A. M. (1988b). Some implications for mechanisms underlying the child's theory of mind. In J. Astington, P. Harris, & D. Olson (Eds.), *Developing theories of mind*. Cambridge: Cambridge University Press.

LESLIE, A. M. (1991, April). Information processing and conceptual development: The theory of TOMM. In A. Gopnik (Chair), *Developmental processes underlying the acquisition of concepts of the mind*. Symposium conducted at the meeting of the Society for Research in Child Development, Seattle, WA.

LESLIE, A. M., & FRITH, U. (1988). Autistic children's understanding of seeing, knowing, and believing. *British Journal of Developmental Psychology, 6*, 315–324.

LESLIE, A. M., & KEEBLE, S. (1987). Do six-month-old infants perceive causality? *Cognition, 25*, 265–288.

LEVIN, I. (Ed.). (1986). *Stage and structure: Reopening the debate*. Norwood, NJ: Ablex.

LEVIN, I. (1989). Principles underlying time measurement: The development of children's constraints in counting time. In I. Levin & D. Zakay (Eds.), *Time and human cognition: A life-span perspective*. Amsterdam: Elsevier.

LEVIN, I., SIEGLER, R. S., & DRUYAN, S. (1990). Misconceptions about motion: Development and training effects. *Child Development, 61*, 1544–1557.

LEWIS, C., & OSBORNE, A. (1990). Three-year-olds' problems with false belief: Conceptual deficit or linguistic artifact, *Child Development, 61*, 1514–1519.

LEWIS, M. (1989). Cultural differences in children's knowledge of emotional scripts. In C. Saarni & P. L. Harris (Eds.), *Children's understanding of emotion*. Cambridge: Cambridge University Press.

LEWIS, M., & BROOKS-GUNN, J. (1979). *Social cognition and the acquisition of self*. New York: Plenum Press.

LEWIS, M., SULLIVAN, M. W., STANGER, C., & WEISS, M. (1989). Self development and self-conscious emotions. *Child Development, 60*, 146–156.

LILLARD, A. S. (1991). *Young children's conceptualization of pretend*. Unpublished doctoral dissertation, Stanford University.

LILLARD, A. S., & CHO, V. Y. (1991, August). *Young children's understanding of representations*. Paper presented at the meeting of the American Psychological Association, San Francisco.

LILLARD, A. S., & FLAVELL, J. H. (1990). Young children's preference for mental state versus behavioral descriptions of human action. *Child Development, 61*, 731–741.

LILLARD, A. S., & FLAVELL, J. H. (1992). Young children's understanding of different mental states. *Developmental Psychology, 28*, 626–634.

LINDBERG, M. A. (1980). Is knowledge base development a necessary and sufficient condition for memory development? *Journal of Experimental Child Psychology, 30*, 401–410.

LIPIAN, M. S. (1985). *Ill-conceived feelings: Developing concepts of the emotions associated with illness in healthy and acutely ill children*. Unpublished doctoral dissertation, Yale University.

LIVESLEY, W. J., & BROMLEY, D. B. (1973). *Person perception in childhood and adolescence*. London: John Wiley.

LLAMAS, C., & DIAMOND, A. (1991, April). *Development of frontal cortex abilities in children between 3–8 years of age*. Paper presented at the meeting of the Society for Research in Child Development, Seattle, WA.

LOCKE, J. L. (1983). *Phonological acquisition and change*. New York: Academic Press.

LOCKE, J. L. (1989). Babbling and early speech: Continuity and individual differences. *First Language, 9*, 191–206.

LOCKE, J. L., & PEARSON, D. M. (1990). Linguistic significance of babbling: Evidence from a tracheostomized infant. *Journal of Child Language, 17*, 1–16.

LODICO, M. G., GHATALA, E. S., LEVIN, J. R., PRESSLEY, M., & BELL, J. A. (1983). The effects of strategy-monitoring training on children's selection of effective memory strategies. *Journal of Experimental Child Psychology, 35*, 263–277.

LOVETT, S. B., & FLAVELL, J. H. (1990). Understanding and remembering: Children's knowledge about the differential effects of strategy and task variables on comprehension and memorization. *Child Development, 61*, 1842–1858.

LUCARIELLO, J., & NELSON, K. (1985). Slot-filler categories as memory organizers for young children. *Developmental Psychology, 21*, 272–282.

LUDEMANN, P. M., & NELSON, C. A. (1988). Categorical representation of facial expression by 7-month-old infants. *Developmental Psychology, 24*, 492–501.

LUTZ, C. (1983). Parental goals, ethnopsychology, and the development of emotional meaning. *Ethos, 11*, 246–262.

MACWHINNEY, B. (1987a). The competition model. In B. MacWhinney (Ed.), *Mechanisms of language acquisition*. Hillsdale, NJ: Erlbaum.

MACWHINNEY, B. (Ed.). (1987b). *Mechanisms of language acquisition*. Hillsdale, NJ: Erlbaum.

MACWHINNEY, B. (1989). Competition and connectionism. In B. MacWhinney & E. Bates (Eds.), *The crosslinguistic study of sentence processing*. Cambridge: Cambridge University Press.

MACWHINNEY, B. (1991). A reply to Woodward and Markman. *Developmental Review, 11*, 192–194.

MANDLER, J. M. (1983). Representation. In J. H. Flavell & E. M. Markman (Eds.), P. H. Mussen (Series Ed.), *Handbook of child psychology: Vol. 3. Cognitive development*. New York: John Wiley.

MANDLER, J. M. (1988). How to build a baby: On the development of an accessible representational system. *Cognitive Development, 3*, 113–136.

MANDLER, J. M. (1990). Recall of events by preverbal children. In A. Diamond (Ed.), *The development and neural bases of higher cognitive functions*. New York: The New York Academy of Sciences.

MANDLER, J. M. (1991). *How to build a baby: II. Conceptual primitives*. Manuscript submitted for publication.

MANDLER, J. M. (in press). Prelinguistic primitives. In C. Johnson, R. Shields, & L. A. Sutton (Eds.), *Proceedings of the 17th annual meeting of the Berkeley Linguistics Society*. Berkeley, CA: Berkeley Linguistics Society.

MANDLER, J. M., & BAUER, P. J. (1988). The cradle of categorization: Is the basic-level basic? *Cognitive Development, 3*, 247–264.

MANDLER, J. M., BAUER, P. J., & MCDONOUGH, L. (1991). Separating the sheep from the goats: Differentiating global categories. *Cognitive Psychology, 23*, 263–298.

MARATSOS, M. P. (1976). *Language development: The acquisition of language structure*. Morristown, NJ: General Learning Press.

MARATSOS, M. P. (1983). Some current issues in the study of the acquisition of grammar. In J. H. Flavell & E. M. Markman (Eds.), P. H. Mussen (Series Ed.), *Handbook of child psychology: Vol. 3. Cognitive development*. New York: John Wiley.

MARINI, Z. (1992). Synchrony and asynchrony in the development of children's scientific reasoning. In R. Case (Ed.), *The mind's staircase: Exploring the structural underpinnings of human thought and knowledge*. Hillsdale, NJ: Erlbaum.

MARINI, Z., & CASE, R. (1989). Parallels in the development of preschoolers' knowledge about their physical and social worlds. *Merrill-Palmer Quarterly, 35*, 63–88.

MARKMAN, E. M. (1978). Empirical versus logical solutions to part-whole comparison problems concerning classes and collections. *Child Development, 49*, 168–177.

MARKMAN, E. M. (1979). Review of Siegler's *Children's thinking: What develops?* *Contemporary Psychology, 24*, 963–964.

MARKMAN, E. M. (1981a). Comprehension monitoring. In W. P. Dickson (Ed.), *Children's oral communication skills*. New York: Academic Press.

MARKMAN, E. M. (1981b). Two different principles of conceptual organization. In M. L. Lamb & A. L. Brown (Eds.), *Advances in developmental psychology* (Vol. 1). Hillsdale, NJ: Erlbaum.

MARKMAN, E. M. (1989). *Categorization and naming in children: Problems of induction*. Cambridge, MA: MIT Press.

MARKMAN, E. M. (1990). Constraints children place on word meanings. *Cognitive Science, 14*, 57–87.

MARKMAN, E. M. (1991). The whole object, taxonomic, and mutual exclusivity assumptions as initial constraints on word meanings. In J. P. Byrnes & S. A. Gelman (Eds.), *Perspectives on language and cognition: Interrelations in development*. Cambridge: Cambridge University Press.

MARKMAN, E. M. (in press). Constraints on word learning: Speculations about their nature, origins, and domain specificity. In M. R. Gunnar & M. P. Maratsos (Eds.), *Minnesota symposia on child psychology* (Vol. 25). Hillsdale, NJ: Erlbaum.

MARKMAN, E. M., & CALLANAN, M. A. (1983). An analysis of hierarchical classification. In R. J. Sternberg (Ed.), *Advances in the psychology of human intelligence* (Vol. 2). Hillsdale, NJ: Erlbaum.

MARKMAN, E. M., & WACHTEL, G. F. (1988). Children's use of mutual exclusivity to constrain the meanings of words. *Cognitive Psychology, 20*, 121–157.

MARKUS, H. R., & KITAYAMA, S. (1991). Culture and the self: Implications for cognition, emotion, and motivation. *Psychological Review, 98*, 224–253.

MASANGKAY, Z. S., MCCLUSKEY, K. A., MCINTYRE, C. W., SIMS-KNIGHT, J., VAUGHN, B. E., & FLAVELL, J. H. (1974). The early development of inferences about the visual percepts of others. *Child Development, 45,* 237–246.

MASSEY, C. M., & GELMAN, R. (1988). Preschooler's ability to decide whether a photographed unfamiliar object can move itself. *Developmental Psychology, 24,* 307–317.

MASUR, E. F., MCINTYRE, C. W., & FLAVELL, J. H. (1973). Developmental changes in apportionment of study time among items in a multitrial free recall test. *Journal of Experimental Child Psychology, 15,* 237–246.

MCCABE, A. E. (1989). Differential language learning styles in young children: The importance of context. *Developmental Review, 9,* 1–20.

MCCALL, R. B. (1990). Infancy research: Individual differences. *Merrill-Palmer Quarterly, 16,* 141–157.

MCCLELLAND, J. L. (1989). Parallel distributed processing: Implications for cognition and development. In R. G. M. Morris (Ed.), *Parallel distributed processing: Implications for psychology and neurobiology.* Oxford: Clarendon Press.

MCDEVITT, T., & FORD, M. (1987). Processes in young children's communicative functioning and development. In M. E. Ford & D. H. Ford (Eds.), *Humans as self-constructing living systems: Putting the framework to work.* Hillsdale, NJ: Erlbaum.

MCDONOUGH, L., & MANDLER, J. M. (1989, April). *Immediate and deferred imitation with 11-month-olds: A comparison between familiar and novel actions.* Paper presented at the meeting of the Society for Research in Child Development, Kansas City, MO.

MCGILLY, K., & SIEGLER, R. S. (1989). How children choose among serial recall strategies. *Child Development, 55,* 172–182.

MCKENZIE, B. E. (1987). The development of spatial orientation in human infancy: What develops? In B. E. McKenzie & R. H. Day (Eds.), *Perceptual development in early infancy: Problems and issues.* Hillsdale, NJ: Erlbaum.

MCKENZIE, B. E., TOOTELL, H. E., & DAY, R. H. (1980). Development of visual size constancy during the 1st year of human infancy. *Developmental Psychology, 16,* 163–174.

MCLAUGHLIN, G. H. (1963). Psycho-logic: A possible alternative to Piaget's formulation. *British Journal of Educational Psychology, 33,* 61–67.

MCMANIS, M., & MILLER, P. H. (1992, April). *Temperament predicts children's use of a selective strategy.* Paper presented at the Conference on Human Development, Atlanta.

MCPHERSON, S. L., & THOMAS, J. R. (1989). Relation of knowledge and performance in boys' tennis: Age and expertise. *Journal of Experimental Child Psychology, 48,* 190–211.

MEDIN, D. L. (1989). Concepts and conceptual structure. *American Psychologist, 44,* 1469–1481.

MEHLER, J., BERTONCINI, J., BARRIERE, M., & JASSIK-GERSCHENFELD, D. (1978). Infant recognition of mother's voice. *Perception, 7,* 491–497.

MEIER, R. P., & NEWPORT, E. L. (1990). Out of the hands of babes: On a possible sign advantage in language acquisition. *Language, 66,* 1–23.

MELTZOFF, A. N. (1988a). Infant imitation after a 1-week delay: Long-term memory for novel and multiple stimuli. *Developmental Psychology, 24,* 470–476.

MELTZOFF, A. N. (1988b). Infant imitation and memory: Nine-month-old infants in immediate and deferred tests. *Child Development, 59,* 217–225.

MELTZOFF, A. N. (1990a). Foundations for developing a concept of self: The role of imitation in relating self to other and the value of social mirroring, social modeling, and self-practice in infancy. In D. Cicchetti & M. Beeghly (Eds.), *The self in transition: Infancy to childhood.* Chicago: University of Chicago Press.

MELTZOFF, A. N. (1990b). Towards a developmental cognitive science: The implications of cross-modal matching and imitation for the development of representation and memory in infancy. In A. Diamond (Ed.), *The development and neural bases of higher cognitive functions.* New York: The New York Academy of Sciences.

MELTZOFF, A. N., & BORTON, R. W. (1979). Intermodal matching by human neonates. *Nature, 282,* 403–404.

MELTZOFF, A. N., & MOORE, M. K. (1977). Imitation of facial and manual gestures by human neonates. *Science, 198,* 75–78.

MELTZOFF, A. N., & MOORE, M. K. (1983a). Newborn infants imitate adult facial gestures. *Child Development, 54,* 702–709.

MELTZOFF, A. N., & MOORE, M. K. (1983b). The origins of imitation in infancy: Paradigm, phenomena, and theories. In L. P. Lipsitt & C. Rovee-Collier (Eds.), *Advances in infancy research* (Vol. 2). Norwood, NJ: Ablex.

MELTZOFF, A. N., & MOORE, M. K. (1989). Imitation in newborn infants: Exploring the range of gestures imitated and the underlying mechanisms. *Developmental Psychology, 25,* 954–962.

MENIG-PETERSON, C. L. (1975). The modification of communicative behavior in preschool-aged children as a function of the listener's perspective. *Child Development, 46*, 1015–1018.

MERRIMAN, W. E., & BOWMAN, L. L. (1989). The mutual exclusivity bias in children's word learning. *Monographs of the Society for Research in Child Development, 54* (Serial No. 220).

MERVIS, C. B. (1987). Child-basic object categories and early lexical development. In U. Neisser (Ed.), *Concepts and conceptual development: Ecological and intellectual bases of categorizations.* Cambridge: Cambridge University Press.

MERVIS, C. B. (1989, April). *Operating principles and early lexical development.* Paper presented at the meeting of the Society for Research in Child Development, Kansas City, MO.

MERVIS, C. B., & MERVIS, C. A. (1982). Leopards are kitty-cats: Object labeling by mothers for their thirteen-month-olds. *Child Development, 53*, 267–273.

MERVIS, C. B., & ROSCH, E. (1981). Categorization of natural objects. In M. R. Rosenzweig & L. W. Porter (Eds.), *Annual review of psychology* (Vol. 32). Palo Alto, CA: Annual Reviews, Inc.

MESSER, D. J. (1983). The redundancy between adult speech and nonverbal interaction: A contribution to acquisition? In R. M. Golinkoff (Ed.), *The transition from prelinguistic to linguistic communication.* Hillsdale, NJ: Erlbaum.

MESSICK, C. K. (1984). *Phonetic and contextual aspects of the transition in early words.* Unpublished doctoral dissertation, Purdue University.

MILLER, D. J., COHEN, L. B., & HILL, K. T. (1970). A methodological investigation of Piaget's theory of object concept development in the sensory-motor period. *Journal of Experimental Child Psychology, 9*, 59–85.

MILLER, G. A., & CANTOR, N. (1982). Review of R. Nisbett and L. Ross. Human inference: Strategies and shortcomings of social judgment. *Social Cognition, 1*, 83–93.

MILLER, J. G. (1984). Culture and the development of everyday social explanation. *Journal of Personality and Social Psychology, 46*, 961–978.

MILLER, J. G. (1986). Early cross-cultural commonalities in social explanation. *Developmental Psychology, 22*, 514–520.

MILLER, J. G. (1987). Cultural influences on the development of conceptual differentiation in person description. *British Journal of Developmental Psychology, 5*, 309–319.

MILLER, K. F. (1989). Measurement as a tool for thought: The role of measuring procedures in children's understanding of quantitative invariance. *Developmental Psychology, 25*, 589–600.

MILLER, K. F., & STIGLER, J. W. (1987). Counting in Chinese: Cultural variation in a basic cognitive skill. *Cognitive Development, 2*, 279–305.

MILLER, P. H. (1985). Children's reasoning about the causes of human behavior. *Journal of Experimental Child Psychology, 39*, 343–362.

MILLER, P. H. (1990). The development of strategies of selective attention. In D. F. Bjorklund (Ed.), *Children's strategies: Contemporary views of cognitive development.* Hillsdale, NJ: Erlbaum.

MILLER, P. H. (in press). *Theories of developmental psychology* (3rd ed.). New York: W.H. Freeman.

MILLER, P. H., & ALOISE, P. A. (1989). Young children's understanding of the psychological causes of behavior: A review. *Child Development, 60*, 257–285.

MILLER, P. H., & ALOISE, P. A. (1990). Discounting in children: The role of social knowledge. *Developmental Review, 10*, 266–298.

MILLER, P. H., & BIGI, L. (1977). Children's understanding of how stimulus dimensions affect performance. *Child Development, 48*, 1712–1715.

MILLER, P. H., & BIGI, L. (1979). The development of children's understanding of attention. *Merrill-Palmer Quarterly, 25*, 235–250.

MILLER, P. H., & DeMARIE-DREBLOW, D. (1990). Social-cognitive correlates of children's understanding of displaced aggression. *Journal of Experimental Child Psychology, 49*, 488–504.

MILLER, P. H., & HARRIS, Y. R. (1988). Preschoolers' strategies of attention on a same-different task. *Developmental Psychology, 24*, 628–633.

MILLER, P. H., HAYNES, V. F., DeMARIE-DREBLOW, D., & WOODY-RAMSEY, J. (1986). Children's strategies for gathering information in three tasks. *Child Development, 57*, 1429–1439.

MILLER, P. H., & JORDAN, R. (1982). Attentional strategies, attention, and metacognition in Puerto Rican children. *Developmental Psychology, 18*, 133–139.

MILLER, P. H., KESSEL, F. S., & FLAVELL, J. H. (1970). Thinking about people thinking about people thinking about.... A study of social cognitive development. *Child Development, 41*, 613–623.

MILLER, P. H., SEIER, W. S., PROBERT, J. S., & ALOISE, P. A. (1991). Age differences in the capacity demands of a strategy among spontaneously strategic children. *Journal of*

Experimental Child Psychology, 52, 149–164.

MILLER, P. H., & SHANNON, K. (1984). Young children's understanding of the effect of noise and interest level on learning. *Genetic Psychology Monographs, 110,* 71–90.

MILLER, P. H., & WEISS, M. C. (1981). Children's attention allocation, understanding of attention, and performance on the incidental learning task. *Child Development, 57,* 1183–1190.

MILLER, P. H., WOODY-RAMSEY, J., & ALOISE, P. A. (1991). The role of strategy effortfulness in strategy effectiveness. *Developmental Psychology, 27,* 738–745.

MILLER, P. H., & ZALENSKI, R. (1982). Preschoolers' knowledge about attention. *Developmental Psychology, 18,* 871–875.

MILLER, S. A. (1973). Contradiction, surprise, and cognitive change: The effects of disconfirmation of belief on conservers and nonconservers. *Journal of Experimental Child Psychology, 15,* 47–62.

MILLER, S. A. (1976). Nonverbal assessment of Piagetian concepts. *Psychological Bulletin, 83,* 405–430.

MILLER, S. A. (1986a). Certainty and necessity in the understanding of Piagetian concepts. *Developmental Psychology, 22,* 3–18.

MILLER, S. A. (1986b). Parents' beliefs about their children's cognitive abilities. *Developmental Psychology, 22,* 276–284.

MILLER, S. A. (1988). Parents' beliefs about children's cognitive development. *Child Development, 59,* 259–285.

MILLER, S. A., & DAVIS, T. L. (in press). Beliefs about children: A comparative study of mothers, teachers, peers, and self. *Child Development.*

MILLER, S. A., & LIPPS, L. (1973). Extinction of conservation and transitivity of weight. *Journal of Experimental Child Psychology, 16,* 388–402.

MILLER, S. A., SCHWARTZ, L. C., & STEWART, C. (1973). An attempt to extinguish conservation of weight in college students. *Developmental Psychology, 8,* 316.

MISCHEL, H. N., & MISCHEL, W. (1983). The development of children's knowledge of self-control strategies. *Child Development, 54,* 603–619.

MISCHEL, W. (1973). Toward a cognitive social learning reconceptualization of personality. *Psychological Review, 80,* 252–283.

MISCHEL, W., & PEAKE, P. K. (1982). Beyond *deja vu* in the search for cross-situational consistency. *Psychological Review, 89,* 730–755.

MISTRY, J. J., & LANGE, G. W. (1985). Children's organization and recall of information in scripted narratives. *Child Development, 56,* 953–961.

MITCHELL, P., MUNNO, A., & RUSSELL, J. (1991). Children's understanding of the communicative value of discrepant verbal messages. *Cognitive Development, 6,* 279–299.

MODGIL, S., & MODGIL, C. (1976). *Piagetian research: Compilation and commentary* (Vol. 2). Windsor, UK: NFER Publishing Co.

MOELY, B. E., OLSON, F. A., HALWES, T. G., & FLAVELL, J. H. (1969). Production deficiency in young children's clustered recall. *Developmental Psychology, 1,* 26–34.

MONTANGERO, J. (1991). A constructivist framework for understanding early and late-developing psychology competencies. In M. Chandler & M. Chapman (Eds.), *Criteria for competence: Controversies in the conceptualization and assessment of children's abilities.* Hillsdale, NJ: Erlbaum.

MONTGOMERY, D. E. (1991, April). *Young children's understanding of interpretational diversity between different-aged listeners.* Paper presented at the meeting of the Society for Research in Child Development, Seattle, WA.

MONTGOMERY, D. E. (in press). Young children's theory of knowing: The development of a folk epistemology. *Developmental Review.*

MOORE, C., PURE, K., & FURROW, D. (1990). Children's understanding of the modal expression of speaker certainty and uncertainty and its relation to the development of a representational theory of mind. *Child Development, 61,* 722–730.

MORRISON, F. (1987, November). *Making the cut: Contrasting developmental and learning influences on cognitive growth.* Paper presented at the meeting of the Psychonomics Society, Seattle, WA.

MORRONGIELLO, B. A. (1988). Infants' localization of sounds along two spatial dimensions: Horizontal and vertical axes. *Infant Behavior and Development, 11,* 127–143.

MORRONGIELLO, B. A., FENWICK, K. D., & CHANCE, G. (1990). Sound localization acuity in very young infants: An observer-based testing procedure. *Developmental Psychology, 26,* 75–84.

MOSCOVITCH, M. (Ed.). (1984). *Infant memory.* New York: Plenum Press.

MOSES, L. J., & FLAVELL, J. H. (1990). Inferring false beliefs from actions and reactions. *Child Development, 61,* 929–945.

MOSHMAN, D. (1979). To really get ahead, get a metatheory. In W. Damon (Series Ed.), D. Kuhn (Ed.), *New directions in child development: No. 5. Intellectual development beyond childhood.* San Francisco: Jossey-Bass.

MOSHMAN, D. (1990). The development of metalogical understanding. In W. F. Overton

(Ed.), *Reasoning, necessity, and logic: Developmental perspectives*. Hillsdale, NJ: Erlbaum.

MOSHMAN, D., & FRANKS, B. A. (1986). Development of the concept of inferential validity. *Child Development, 57,* 153–165.

MOSHMAN, D., & FRANKS, B. A. (1989). Intellectual development: Formal operations and reflective judgment. In E. P. Maimon, B. F. Nodine, & F. W. O'Conner (Eds.), *Thinking, reasoning and writing.* New York: Longman.

MOSSLER, D. G., MARVIN, R. S., & GREENBERG, M. T. (1976). Conceptual perspective taking in 2- to 6-year-old children. *Developmental Psychology, 12,* 85–86.

MUIR, D., & CLIFTON, R. K. (1985). Infants' orientation to the location of sound sources. In G. Gottlieb & N. A. Krasnegor (Eds.), *Measurement of audition and vision in the first year of postnatal life.* Norwood, NJ: Albex.

MURPHY, C., & MESSER, D. (1977). Mothers, infants, and pointing: A study of gesture. In H. R. Schaffer (Ed.), *Studies in mother-infant interaction.* London: Academic Press.

MYERS, M., & PARIS, S. G. (1978). Children's metacognitive knowledge about reading. *Journal of Educational Psychology, 70,* 680–690.

MYERS, N. A., & PERLMUTTER, M. (1978). Memory in the years from two to five. In P. A. Ornstein (Ed.), *Memory development in children.* Hillsdale, NJ: Erlbaum.

NAUS, M. J., & ORNSTEIN, P. A. (1983). Development of memory strategies: Analysis, questions, and issues. In M. T. H. Chi (Ed.), *Trends in memory development research.* Basel: Karger.

NEIMARK, E. D., SLOTNICK, N. S., & ULRICH, T. (1971). Development of memorization strategies. *Developmental Psychology, 5,* 427–432.

NEISSER, U. (Ed.). (1982). *Memory observed: Remembering in natural contexts.* San Francisco: W. H. Freeman.

NEISSER, U. (Ed.). (1987). *Concepts and conceptual development: Ecological and intellectual bases of categorization.* Cambridge: Cambridge University Press.

NELSON, C. A. (1987). The recognition of facial expressions in the first two years of life: Mechanisms of development. *Child Development, 58,* 889–909.

NELSON, K. (1973). Structure and strategy in learning to talk. *Monographs of the Society for Research in Child Development, 38* (Serial No. 149).

NELSON, K. (1974). Concept, word and sentence: Interrelations in acquisition and development. *Psychological Review, 81,* 267–285.

NELSON, K. (1981). Individual differences in language development: Implications for development and language. *Developmental Psychology, 17,* 170–187.

NELSON, K. (1986). *Event knowledge: Structure and function in development.* Hillsdale, NJ: Erlbaum.

NELSON, K. (1988). Constraints on word learning? *Cognitive Development, 3,* 221–246.

NELSON, K. (1990). Comment on Behrend's "Constraints and Cognitive Development." *Cognitive Development, 5,* 331–339.

NELSON, K., & HUDSON, J. (1988). Scripts and memory: Functional relationships in development. In F. E. Weinert & M. Perlmutter (Eds.), *Memory development: Universal changes and individual differences.* Hillsdale, NJ: Erlbaum.

NELSON, K. E. (1971). Accommodation of visual tracking patterns in human infants to object movement patterns. *Journal of Experimental Child Psychology, 12,* 182–196.

NELSON, K. E., DENNINGER, M. S., BONVILLIAN, J. D., KAPLAN, B. J., & BAKER, N. D. (1984). Maternal input adjustment and non-adjustment as related to children's linguistic advances and to language acquisition theories. In A. D. Pellegrini & T. D. Yawkey (Eds.), *The development of oral and written language in social contexts.* Norwood, NJ: Ablex.

NEWCOMB, N. (1989). The development of spatial perspective taking. In H. W. Reese (Ed.), *Advances in child development and behavior* (Vol. 22). San Diego: Academic Press.

NEWPORT, E. (1988). Constraints on learning and their role in language acquisition: Studies of the acquisition of American Sign Language. *Language Sciences, 10,* 147–172.

NEWPORT, E. (1990). Maturational constraints on language learning. *Cognitive Science, 14,* 11–28.

NEWPORT, E., GLEITMAN, L., & GLEITMAN, H. (1977). Mother I'd rather do it myself: Some effects and non-effects of motherese. In C. E. Snow & C. Ferguson (Eds.), *Talking to children: Language input and acquisition.* Cambridge: Cambridge University Press.

NEWPORT, E., & SUPALLA, T. (1990). *A critical period effect in the acquisition of a primary language.* Unpublished manuscript, University of Rochester, Rochester, NY.

NICOLICH, L. M. (1977). Beyond sensorimotor intelligence: Assessment of symbolic maturity through analysis of pretend play. *Merrill-Palmer Quarterly, 23,* 89–99.

NINIO, A. (1988). On formal grammatical categories in early child language. In Y. Levy, I. M. Schlesinger, & M. D. S. Braine (Eds.), *Categories and processes in language acquisition.* Hillsdale, NJ: Erlbaum.

References   381

NISBETT, R. E., CAPUTO, C., LEGANT, P., & MARCEK, J. (1973). Behavior as seen by the actor and as seen by the observer. *Journal of Personality and Social Psychology*, 27, 154–165.

NISBETT, R. E., & ROSS, L. (1980). *Human inference: Strategies and shortcomings of social judgment*. Englewood Cliffs, NJ: Prentice-Hall.

OAKES, L. M., & COHEN, L. B. (1990). Infant perception of a causal event. *Cognitive Development, 5*, 193–207.

O'BRYAN, K. G., & BOERSMA, F. J. (1971). Eye movements, perceptual activity, and conservation development. *Journal of Experimental Child Psychology, 12*, 157–169.

ODEN, S., & ASHER, S. R. (1977). Coaching children in social skills for friendship making. *Child Development, 48*, 495–506.

OKAGAKI, L., & STERNBERG, R. J. (Eds.). (1991). *Directors of development: Influences on the development of children's thinking*. Hillsdale, NJ: Erlbaum.

OLLER, D. K., & EILERS, R. E. (1988). The role of audition in infant babbling. *Child Development, 59*, 441–449.

OLLER, D. K., EILERS, R. E., BULL, D. H., & CARNEY, A. E. (1985). Prespeech vocalizations of a deaf infant: A comparison with normal metaphonological development. *Journal of Speech and Hearing Research, 28*, 47–63.

OLSHO, L. W., SCHOON, C., SAKAI, R., TURPIN, R., & SPERDUTO, V. (1982). Auditory frequency discrimination in infancy. *Developmental Psychology, 18*, 721–726.

OLSON, D. R., & HILDYARD, A. (1983). Literacy and the comprehension and expression of literal meaning. In F. Coulmas & K. Ehlich (Eds.), *Writing in focus*. New York: Mouton.

OLSON, G. M., & SHERMAN, T. (1983). Attention, learning, and memory. In M. M. Haith & J. J. Campos (Eds.), P. H. Mussen (Series Ed.), *Handbook of child psychology: Vol. 2. Infancy and developmental psychobiology*. New York: John Wiley.

O'NEILL, D. K., ASTINGTON, J., & FLAVELL, J. H. (1992). Young children's understanding of the role that sensory experiences play in knowledge acquisition. *Child Development, 63*, 474–490.

O'NEILL, D. K., & GOPNIK, A. (1991). Young children's ability to identify the sources of their beliefs. *Developmental Psychology, 27*, 390–397.

OPPENHEIMER, L. (1986). Development of recursive thinking: Procedural variations. *International Journal of Behavioral Development, 9*, 401–411.

ORNSTEIN, P. A., LARUS, D. M, & CLUBB, P. A. (in press). Understanding children's testimony: Implications of research on the development of memory. In R. Vasta (Ed.), *Annals of child development* (Vol. 8). Orlando, FL: Academic Press.

ORNSTEIN, P. A., & NAUS, M. J. (1985). Effects of the knowledge base on children's memory strategies. In H. W. Reese (Ed.), *Advances in child development and behavior* (Vol. 19). New York: Academic Press.

ORNSTEIN, P. A., NAUS, M. J., & LIBERTY, C. (1975). Rehearsal and organizational processes in children's memory. *Child Development, 46*, 818–830.

OSHERSON, D. N., & MARKMAN, E. M. (1975). Language and the ability to evaluate contradictions and tautologies. *Cognition, 2*, 213–226.

OVERTON, W. F. (Ed.). (1990). *Reasoning, necessity, and logic: Developmental perspectives*. Hillsdale, NJ: Erlbaum.

OVERTON, W. F., & JACKSON, J. P. (1973). The representation of imagined objects in action sequences: A developmental study. *Child Development, 44*, 309–314.

PALEY, V. G. (1984). *Boys and girls*. Chicago: University of Chicago Press.

PARIS, S. G. (1975). Integration and inference in children's comprehension and memory. In F. Restle, R. Shiffrin, J. Castellan, H. Lindman, & D. Pisoni (Eds.), *Cognitive theory* (Vol. 1). Hillsdale, NJ: Erlbaum.

PARIS, S. G. (1978). Coordination of means and goals in the development of mnemonic skills. In P. A. Ornstein (Ed.), *Memory development in children*. Hillsdale, NJ: Erlbaum.

PARIS, S. G. (1988). Models and metaphors of learning strategies. In C. E. Weinstein, E. T. Goetz, & P. A. Alexander (Eds.), *Learning and study strategies: Issues in assessment, instruction, and evaluation*. San Diego: Academic Press.

PARIS, S. G., & CROSS, D. R. (1988). The zone of proximal development: Virtues and pitfalls of a metaphorical representation of children's learning. *The Genetic Epistemologist, 16*, 27–37.

PARIS, S. G., & LINDAUER, B. K. (1977). Constructive processes in children's comprehension and memory. In R. V. Kail & J. W. Hagen (Eds.), *Perspectives on the development of memory and cognition*. Hillsdale, NJ: Erlbaum.

PARIS, S. G., & MAHONEY, G. J. (1974). Cognitive integration in children's memory for sentences and pictures. *Child Development, 45*, 633–642.

PARIS, S. G., NEWMAN, R. S., & MCVEY, K. A. (1982). Learning the functional significance of mnemonic actions: A microgenetic study of strategy acquisition. *Journal of Experimental Child Psychology, 34,* 490–509.

PARMELEE, A. H., & SIGMAN, M. D. (1983). Perinatal brain development and behavior. In M. M. Haith & J. J. Campos (Eds.), P. H. Mussen (Series Ed.), *Handbook of child psychology: Vol. 2. Infancy and developmental psychobiology.* New York: John Wiley.

PASCUAL-LEONE, J. (1970). A mathematical model for the transition rule in Piaget's developmental stages. *Acta Psychologica, 32,* 301–345.

PASCUAL-LEONE, J. (1987). Organismic processes for neo-Piagetian theories: A dialectical causal account of cognitive development. *International Journal of Psychology, 22,* 531–570.

PATTERSON, F. C. P. (1979). *Linguistic capabilities of a lowland gorilla.* Unpublished doctoral dissertation, Stanford University.

PECHEUX, M., LEPECQ, J., & SALZARULO, P. (1988). Oral activity and exploration in 1–2-month-old infants. *British Journal of Developmental Psychology, 6,* 245–256.

PEEVERS, B. H., & SECORD, P. F. (1973). Developmental changes in attribution of descriptive concepts to persons. *Journal of Personality and Social Psychology, 27,* 120–128.

PERNER, J. (1991). *Understanding the representational mind.* Cambridge, MA: MIT Press.

PERNER, J., & DAVIES, G. (1988). *Young children's conception of mind as an active information processor.* Unpublished manuscript, University of Sussex, Brighton, UK.

PERNER, J., & LEEKAM, S. R. (1986). Belief and quantity: Three-year-olds' adaptation to listener's knowledge. *Journal of Child Language, 13,* 305–315.

PERNER, J., & WIMMER, H. (1985). "John *thinks* that Mary *thinks* that..." Attribution of second-order beliefs by 5- to 10-year-old children. *Journal of Experimental Child Psychology, 39,* 437–471.

PERRIS, E. E., MYERS, N. A., & CLIFTON, R. K. (1990). Long-term memory for a single infancy experience. *Child Development, 61,* 1796–1807.

PIAGET, J. (1929). *The child's conception of the world.* New York: Harcourt, Brace.

PIAGET, J. (1932). *The moral judgment of the child.* New York: Harcourt Brace.

PIAGET, J. (1952). *The origins of intelligence in children.* New York: International Universities Press.

PIAGET, J. (1954). *The construction of reality in the child.* New York: Basic Books.

PIAGET, J. (1962). *Play, dreams, and imitation in childhood.* New York: W. W. Norton.

PIAGET, J. (1970a). Piaget's theory. In P. H. Mussen (Ed.), *Carmichael's Manual of Child Psychology* (Vol. 1). New York: John Wiley.

PIAGET, J. (1970b). *Genetic epistemology.* New York: Columbia University Press.

PIAGET, J. (1985). *The equilibration of cognitive structures.* Chicago: University of Chicago Press.

PIAGET, J., & SZEMINSKA, A. (1952). *The child's conception of number.* New York: Humanities Press.

PIATELLI-PALMARINI, M. (Ed.). (1980). *Learning and language.* Cambridge, MA: Harvard University Press.

PILLEMER, D. B., & WHITE, S. H. (1989). Childhood events recalled by children and adults. In H. W. Reese (Ed.), *Advances in child development and behavior* (Vol. 21). New York: Academic Press.

PILLOW, B. H. (1988a). The development of children's beliefs about the mental world. *Merrill-Palmer Quarterly, 34,* 1–32.

PILLOW, B. H. (1988b). Young children's understanding of attentional limits. *Child Development, 59,* 38–46.

PILLOW, B. H. (1989). The development of beliefs about selective attention. *Merrill-Palmer Quarterly, 35,* 421–443.

PILLOW, B. H. (1991). Children's understanding of biased social cognition. *Developmental Psychology, 27,* 539–551.

PINARD, A., & LAURENDEAU, M. (1969). "Stage" in Piaget's cognitive-developmental theory: Exegesis of a concept. In D. Elkind & J. H. Flavell (Eds.), *Studies in cognitive development: Essays in honor of Jean Piaget.* New York: Oxford University Press.

PINKER, S. (1984). *Language learnability and language development.* Cambridge, MA: Harvard University Press.

PINKER, S. (1987). The bootstrapping problem in language acquisition. In B. MacWhinney (Ed.), *Mechanisms of language acquisition.* Hillsdale, NJ: Erlbaum.

PINKER, S. (1989). *Learnability and cognition: The acquisition of argument structure.* Cambridge, MA: MIT Press.

PINKER, S. (1991). Rules of language. *Science, 253,* 530–535.

POULIN-DUBOIS, D., & SHULTZ, T. R. (1988). The development of the understanding of human behavior: From agency to intentionality. In J. W. Astington, P. L. Harris, & D. R. Olson (Eds.), *Developing theories of mind.* Cambridge: Cambridge University Press.

POULSON, C. L., NUNES, L. R. D., & WARREN, S. F. (1989). Imitation in infancy: A critical review. In H. W. Reese (Ed.), *Advances in child development and behavior* (Vol. 22). San Diego: Academic Press.

POVINELLI, D. J., & DEBLOIS, S. (in press). Young children's (*Homo sapiens*) understanding of knowledge formation in themselves and others. *Journal of Comparative Psychology.*

PRATHER, P., & SPELKE, E. S. (1982, April). *Three-month-old infants' perception of adjacent and partly occluded objects.* Paper presented at the International Conference on Infant Studies, Austin, TX.

PRATT, C., & BRYANT, P. (1990). Young children understand that looking leads to knowing (so long as they are looking in a single barrel). *Child Development, 61*, 973–982.

PREMACK, D. (1976). *Intelligence in ape and man.* Hillsdale, NJ: Erlbaum.

PREMACK, D. (1990). The infant's theory of self-propelled objects. *Cognition, 36*, 1–16.

PREMACK, D., & WOODRUFF, G. (1978). Does the chimpanzee have a theory of mind? *Behavioral and Brain Sciences, 1*, 515–526.

PRESCOTT, P., & DECASPER, A. J. (1990). *Human perception of speech and nonspeech is functionally lateralized at birth.* Manuscript submitted for publication.

PRESSLEY, M. (1982). Elaboration and memory development. *Child Development, 53*, 296–309.

PRESSLEY, M., BORKOWSKI, J. G., & O'SULLIVAN, J. T. (1984). Memory strategy instruction is made of this: Metamemory and durable strategy use. *Educational Psychology, 19*, 94–107.

PRESSLEY, M., BORKOWSKI, J. J., & SCHNEIDER, W. (1987). Cognitive strategies: Good strategy users coordinate metacognition and knowledge. In R. Vasta & G. Whitehurst (Eds.), *Annals of child development* (Vol. 5). Greenwich, CT: JAI Press.

PRESSLEY, M., CARIGLIA-BULL, T., DEANE, S., & Schneider, W. (1987). Short-term memory, verbal competence, and age as predictors of imagery instructional effectiveness. *Journal of Experimental Child Psychology, 43*, 194–211.

PRESSLEY, M., & DENNIS-ROUNDS, J. (1980). Transfer of a mnemonic keyword strategy at two age levels. *Journal of Educational Psychology, 72*, 575–582.

PRESSLEY, M., FORREST-PRESSLEY, D., & ELLIOTT-FAUST, D. J. (1988). What is strategy instructional enrichment and how to study it: Illustrations from research on children's prose memory and comprehension. In F. E. Weinert & M. Perlmutter (Eds.), *Memory development: Universal changes and individual differences.* Hillsdale, NJ: Erlbaum.

PRESSLEY, M., FORREST-PRESSLEY, D. J., ELIOTT-FAUST, D. J., & MILLER, G. E. (1985). Children's use of cognitive strategies, how to teach strategies, and what to do if they can't be taught. In M. Pressley & C. J. Brainerd (Eds.), *Cognitive learning and memory in children.* New York: Springer-Verlag.

PRESSLEY, M., LEVIN, J. R., & BRYANT, S. L. (1983). Memory strategy instruction during adolescence: When is explicit instruction needed? In M. Pressley & J. R. Levin (Eds.), *Cognitive strategy research: Psychological foundations.* New York: Springer-Verlag.

PRESSLEY, M., & MACFADYEN, J. (1983). Mnemonic mediator retrieval at testing by preschool and kindergarten children. *Child Development, 54*, 474–479.

PRICE, D. W. W., & GOODMAN, G. S. (1990). Visiting the wizard: Children's memory for a recurring event. *Child Development, 61*, 664–680.

PRIEL, B., & DE SCHONEN, S. (1986). Self-recognition: A study of a population without mirrors. *Journal of Experimental Child Psychology, 41*, 237–250.

PRYOR, J. B., & DAY, J. D. (Eds.). (1985). *The development of social cognition.* New York: Springer-Verlag.

QUINE, W. V. O. (1960). *Word and object.* Cambridge, MA: MIT Press.

RABINOWITZ, F. M., HOWE, M. L., & LAWRENCE, J. A. (1989). Class inclusion and working memory. *Journal of Experimental Child Psychology, 48*, 379–409.

RADER, N., BAUSANO, M., & RICHARDS, J. E. (1980). On the nature of the visual-cliff avoidance response in human infants. *Child Development, 51*, 61–68.

RATNER, H. H., & MYERS, N. A. (1981). Long-term memory and retrieval at ages 2, 3, 4. *Journal of Experimental Child Psychology, 31*, 365–386.

RECHT, D. R., & LESLIE, L. (1988). Effect of prior knowledge on good and poor readers' memory for text. *Journal of Educational Psychology, 80*, 16–20.

REDDY, V. (1991). Playing with others' expectations: Teasing and mucking about in the first year. In A. Whiten (Ed.), *Natural theories of mind: Evolution, development and simulation of everyday mindreading.* Oxford: Basil Blackwell.

REILLY, J., KLIMA, E. S., & BELLUGI, U. (1990). Once more with feeling: Affect and language in atypical populations. *Development and Psychopathology, 2*, 367–391.

REISSLAND, N. (1988). Neonatal imitation in the first hour of life: Observation in rural Nepal. *Developmental Psychology, 24*, 464–469.

RESCORLA, L. (1980). Overextension in early language development. *Journal of Child Language, 7*, 321–336.

RESNICK, L. B., LEVINE, J. M., & TEASLEY, S. D. (Eds.). (1991). *Perspectives on socially shared cognition.* Washington, DC: American Psychological Association.

REVELLE, G. L., WELLMAN, H. M., & KARABENICK, J. D. (1985). Comprehension monitoring in preschool children. *Child Development, 56,* 654–663.

RHOLES, W. S., NEWMAN, L. S., & RUBLE, D. N. (1990). Understanding self and others: Developmental and motivational aspects of perceiving persons in terms of invariant dispositions. In E. Higgins & R. Sorrentino (Eds.), *Handbook of motivation and cognition: Foundations of social behavior* (Vol. 2). New York: Guilford Press.

RHOLES, W. S., & RUBLE, D. N. (1984). Children's understanding of dispositional characteristics of others. *Child Development, 33,* 550–560.

RICE, M. L. (1978). *The effect of children's prior nonverbal color concepts on the learning of color words.* Unpublished doctoral dissertation, University of Kansas.

RICE, M. L., & WOODSMALL, L. (1988). Lessons from television: Children's word learning when viewing. *Child Development, 59,* 420–429.

RICHARDS, J. E., & RADER, N. (1981). Crawling-onset age predicts visual cliff avoidance in infants. *Journal of Experimental Psychology: Human Perception and Performance, 7,* 382–387.

RICHARDS, J. E., & RADER, N. (1983). Affective, behavioral, and avoidance responses on the visual cliff: Effect of crawling onset age, crawling experience, and testing age. *Psychophysiology, 20,* 633–642.

RIDGEWAY, D., WATERS, E., & KUCZAJ, S. A. (1985). The acquisition of emotion descriptive language: Receptive and productive vocabulary norms for 18 months to six years. *Developmental Psychology, 21,* 901–908.

RIEDER, C., & CICCHETTI, D. (1989). An organizational perspective on cognitive control functioning and cognitive-affective balance in maltreated children. *Developmental Psychology, 25,* 382–393.

RIESS, J. A., & CUNNINGHAM, J. G. (1989, April). *From three to five: Understanding infant facial expressions and multiple emotions in events.* Paper presented at the meeting of the Society for Research in Child Development, Kansas City, MO.

RITTER, K. (1978). The development of knowledge of an external retrieval cue strategy. *Child Development, 49,* 1227–1230.

ROBINSON, E. J. (1981). Conversational tactics and the advancement of the child's understanding about referential communication. In W. P. Robinson (Ed.), *Communication in development.* London: Academic Press.

ROBINSON, E. J., & ROBINSON, W. P. (1981). Egocentrism in verbal referential communication. In M. Cox (Ed.), *Are young children egocentric?* London: Concord Books.

ROGOFF, B. (1990). *Apprenticeship in thinking.* New York: Oxford University Press.

ROGOFF, B., & MISTRY, J. (1990). The social and functional context of children's remembering. In R. Fivush & J. A. Hudson (Eds.), *Knowing and remembering in young children.* Cambridge: Cambridge University Press.

ROHWER, W. D. (1973). Elaboration and learning in childhood and adolescence. In H. W. Reese (Ed.), *Advances in child development and behavior* (Vol. 8). New York: Academic Press.

ROSCH, E., MERVIS, C. B., GRAY, W. D., JOHNSON, D. M., & BOYES-BRAEM, P. (1976). Basic objects in natural categories. *Cognitive Psychology, 8,* 382–439.

ROSE, S. A. (1990). Cross-modal transfer in human infants: What is being transferred? In A. Diamond (Ed.), *The development and neural bases of higher cognitive functions.* New York: The New York Academy of Sciences.

ROSE, S. A., & RUFF, H. A. (1987). Cross-modal abilities in human infants. In J. S. Osofsky (Ed.), *Handbook of infant development* (2nd ed.). New York: John Wiley.

ROSENBACH, D., CROCKETT, W. H., & WAPNER, S. (1973). Developmental level, emotional involvement, and the resolution of inconsistency in impression formation. *Developmental Psychology, 8,* 120–130.

ROSENGREN, K. S., GELMAN, S. A., KALISH, C. W., & McCORMICK, M. (1991). As time goes by: Children's early understanding of growth in animals. *Child Development, 62,* 1302–1320.

ROSS, G. S. (1980). Categorization in 1- to 2-year-olds. *Developmental Psychology, 16,* 391–396.

ROTHENBERG, B. B. (1970). Children's social sensitivity and the relationship to interpersonal competence, intrapersonal comfort, and intellectual level. *Developmental Psychology, 3,* 335–350.

ROVEE-COLLIER, C. K. (1987). Learning and memory in infancy. In J. D. Osofsky (Ed.), *Handbook of infant development* (2nd ed.). New York: John Wiley.

ROVEE-COLLIER, C. K. (1990). The "memory system" of prelinguistic infants. In A Diamond (Ed.), *The development and neural bases of higher cognitive functions.* New York: The New York Academy of Sciences.

ROVEE-COLLIER, C. K., & HAYNE, H. (1987). Reactivation of infant memory: Implications for cognitive development. In H. W. Reese

(Ed.), *Advances in child development and behavior* (Vol. 20). New York: Academic Press.

ROVEE-COLLIER, C. K., SULLIVAN, M. W., ENRIGHT, M., LUCAS, D., & FAGEN, J. W. (1980). Reactivation of infant memory. *Science, 208*, 1159–1161.

RUBIN, K. H., & KRASNOR, L. R. (1986). Social-cognitive and social behavioral perspectives on problem solving. In M. Perlmutter (Ed.), *Minnesota symposia on child psychology: Vol. 19. Cognitive perspectives on children's social and behavioral development.* Hillsdale, NJ: Erlbaum.

RUBIN, Z. (1980). *Children's friendships.* Cambridge, MA: Harvard University Press.

RUBLE, D. N. (1987). The acquisition of social knowledge: A self-socialization perspective. In N. Eisenberg (Ed.), *Contemporary topics in developmental psychology.* New York: John Wiley.

RUBLE, D. N., NEWMAN, L. S., RHOLES, W. S., & ALTSHULER, J. (1988). Children's "naive psychology": The use of behavioral and situational information for the prediction of behavior. *Cognitive Development, 3*, 89–112.

RUBLE, D. N., & STANGOR, C. (1986). Stalking the elusive schema: Insights from developmental and social-psychological analyses of gender schemas. *Social Cognition, 4*, 227–261.

RUDY, L., & GOODMAN, G. S. (1991). Effects of participation on children's reports: Implications for eyewitness testimony. *Developmental Psychology, 27*, 527–538.

RUFFMAN, T. K., & KEENAN, T. R. (1991). *Children's understanding of belief-based emotions: The case for a lag in understanding relative to false belief.* Unpublished manuscript, University of Sussex and University of Toronto.

RUFFMAN, T. K., & OLSON, D. R. (1989). Children's ascriptions of knowledge to others. *Developmental Psychology, 25*, 601–606.

RUFFMAN, T. K., OLSON, D. R., & ASTINGTON, J. W. (1991). Children's understanding of visual ambiguity. *British Journal of Developmental Psychology, 9*, 89–103.

RUSSELL, J. A. (1989). Culture, scripts, and children's understanding of emotions. In C. Saarni & P. L. Harris (Eds.), *Children's understanding of emotion.* Cambridge: Cambridge University Press.

RUSSELL, J. A., & HAWORTH, H. M. (1987). Perceiving the logical status of sentences. *Cognition, 27*, 73–96.

RYAN, E. B., LEDGER, G. W., & WEED, K. A. (1987). Acquisition and transfer of an integrative imagery strategy by young children. *Child Development, 58*, 443–452.

SAARNI, C. (1984). An observational study of children's attempts to monitor their expressive behavior. *Child Development, 55*, 1504–1513.

SAARNI, C. (1988). Children's understanding of the interpersonal consequences of dissemblances of nonverbal emotional-expressive behavior. *Journal of Nonverbal Behavior, 12*, 275–294.

SAARNI, C. (1989, April). Cognitive capabilities involved in the socialization of emotion: Development in middle childhood. In T. Trabasso (Chair), *The social-cognitive basis of emotional understanding.* Symposium conducted at the meeting of the Society for Research in Child Development, Kansas City, MO.

SAARNI, C., & HARRIS, P. L. (Eds.). (1989). *Children's understanding of emotion.* Cambridge: Cambridge University Press.

SAARNIO, D. (1986). *Knowing, remembering, and developing: What are the relationships?* Unpublished manuscript, Northern Illinois University, DeKalb, IL.

SACHS, J. (1989). Communication development in infancy. In J. B. Gleason (Ed.), *The development of language* (2nd ed.). Columbus, OH: Chas. E. Merrill.

SACHS, J., & DEVIN, J. (1976). Young children's use of age appropriate speech styles in social interaction and role-playing. *Journal of Child Language, 3*, 81–98.

SACKS, O. (1985). *The man who mistook his wife for a hat.* New York: Summit Books.

SALAPATEK, P., & COHEN, L. (Eds.). (1987). *Handbook of infant perception.* Orlando, FL: Academic Press.

SALATAS, H., & FLAVELL, J. H. (1976). Retrieval of recently learned information: Development of strategies and control skills. *Child Development, 47*, 941–948.

SALTZ, E., & MEDOW, M. L. (1971). Concept conservation in children: The dependence of belief systems on semantic representation. *Child Development, 42*, 1533–1542.

SAVAGE-RUMBAUGH, E. S., & McDONALD, K. (1988). Deception and social manipulation in symbol-using apes. In R. W. Byrne & A. Whiten (Eds.), *Machiavellian intelligence: Social expertise and the evolution of intellect in monkeys, apes, and humans.* Oxford: Oxford University Press.

SAVITSKY, J. C., & IZARD, C. E. (1970). Development changes in the use of emotion cues in a concept-formation task. *Developmental Psychology, 3*, 350–357.

SAXE, G. B. (1981). Body parts as numerals: A developmental analysis of numeration among the Oksapmin in Papua New Guinea. *Child Development, 52*, 306–316.

SAXE, G. B. (1982). Developing forms of arithmetical thought among the Oksapmin of

Papua New Guinea. *Developmental Psychology, 18,* 583–594.

SAXE, G. B. (1988). The mathematics of child street vendors. *Child Development, 59,* 1415–1425.

SAXE, G. B. (1991). *Culture and cognitive development: Studies in mathematical understanding.* Hillsdale, NJ: Erlbaum.

SAXE, G. B., GUBERMAN, S. R., & GEARHART, M. (1987). Social processes in early number development. *Monographs of the Society for Research in Child Development, 52* (Serial No. 216).

SCAIFE, M., & BRUNER, J. (1975). The capacity for joint visual attention in the infant. *Nature, 253,* 265–266.

SCARR, S. (1983). An evolutionary perspective on infant intelligence: Species patterns and individual variations. In M. Lewis (Ed.), *Origins of intelligence: Infancy and early childhood* (3rd ed.). New York: Plenum Press.

SCHACTER, D. L., MOSCOVITCH, M., TULVING, E., McLACHLAN, D. R., & FREEDMAN, M. (1986). Mnemonic precedence in amnesic patients: An analogue of the AB̄ error in infants? *Child Development, 57,* 816–823.

SCHAFFER, H. R. (1977). *Mothering.* London: Open Books.

SCHAUBLE, L. (1991). Belief revision in children: The role of prior knowledge and strategies for generating evidence. *Journal of Experimental Child Psychology, 49,* 31–57.

SCHIEFFELIN, B., & OCHS, E. (1983). A cultural perspective on the transition from prelinguistic to linguistic communication. In R. M. Golinkoff (Ed.), *The transition from prelinguistic to linguistic communication.* Hillsdale, NJ: Erlbaum.

SCHNEIDER, D. J., HASTORF, A. H., & ELLSWORTH, P. C. (1979). *Person perception* (2nd ed.). Reading, MA: Addison-Wesley.

SCHNEIDER, W. (1985). Developmental trends in the metamemory-memory behavior relationship: An integrative review. In. D. L. Forrest-Pressley, G. E. MacKinnon, & T. G. Waller (Eds.), *Cognition, metacognition, and performance,* (Vol. 1). New York: Academic Press.

SCHNEIDER, W., BORKOWSKI, J. G., KURTZ, B. E., & KERWIN, K. (1986). Metamemory and motivation: A comparison of strategy use and performance in German and American children. *Journal of Cross-Cultural Psychology, 17,* 315–336.

SCHNEIDER, W., KORKEL, J., & WEINERT, F. E. (1987). The effects of intelligence, self-concept, and attributional style on metamemory and memory behavior. *International Journal of Behavioral Development, 10,* 281–299.

SCHNEIDER, W., KORKEL, J., & WEINERT, F. E. (1989). Domain-specific knowledge and memory performance: A comparison of high- and low-aptitude children. *Journal of Educational Psychology, 81,* 306–312.

SCHNEIDER, W., & PRESSLEY, M. (1989). *Memory development between 2 and 20.* New York: Springer-Verlag.

SCHNEIDER, W., & SODIAN, B. (1988). Metamemory-memory relationships in preschool children: Evidence from a memory-for-location task. *Journal of Experimental Child Psychology, 45,* 209–233.

SCHNEIDER, W., & WEINERT, F. E. (1989). Memory development: Universal changes and individual differences. In A. de Ribaupierre (Ed.), *Transition mechanisms in child development: The longitudinal perspective.* Cambridge: Cambridge University Press.

SCHNEIDER, W., & WEINERT, F. E. (Eds.). (1990). *Interactions among aptitudes, strategies, and knowledge in cognitive performance.* New York: Springer-Verlag.

SCHOLNICK, E. K., & WING, C. S. (1988). Knowing when you don't know: Developmental and situational considerations. *Developmental Psychology, 24,* 190–196.

SCHRADER, D. (Ed.). (1990). *The legacy of Lawrence Kohlberg.* San Francisco: Jossey-Bass.

SCHWANENFLUGEL, P. J., FABRICIUS, W. V., & ALEXANDER, J. P. (1991, April). *Theories of mind: Developing concepts of mental activities.* Paper presented at the meeting of the Society for Research in Child Development, Seattle, WA.

SCHWANENFLUGEL, P. J., FABRICIUS, W. V., & ALEXANDER, J. P. (1992, April). *The organization of mental concepts in comprehension monitors and nonmonitors.* Paper presented at meeting of the Southeastern Psychological Association, Knoxville, TN.

SCHWARTZ, S. R. (Ed.). (1977). *Naming, necessity, and natural kinds.* Ithaca, NY: Cornell University Press.

SCOLLON, R. (1976). *Conversations with a one year old.* Honolulu: University Press of Hawaii.

SCOVILLE, R. (1984). Development of the intention to communicate: The eye of the beholder. In L. Feagans, C. Garvey, & R. Golinkoff (Eds.), *The origins and growth of communication).* Norwood, NJ: Ablex.

SECHENOV, I. M. (1935). Elements of thought. In *Selected works.* Moscow/Leningrad: Izd. Akad. Nauk SSSR.

SELMAN, R. L. (1980). *The growth of interpersonal understanding.* New York: Academic Press.

SELMAN, R. L. (1981). The child as friendship philosopher. In S. R. Asher & J. M. Gottman

(Eds.), *The development of children's friendships*. Cambridge: Cambridge University Press.

SELMAN, R. L., & SCHULTZ, L. H. (1990). *Making a friend in youth*. Chicago: University of Chicago Press.

SERA, M. D., & CONNOLLY, L. M. (1990). *Low planes, big worms, and other pairs of terms*. Manuscript submitted for publication.

SHAKLEE, H. (1979). Bounded rationality and cognitive development: Upper limits on growth? *Cognitive Psychology, 11*, 327–345.

SHANTZ, C. U. (1975). The development of social cognition. In E. M. Hetherington (Ed.), *Review of child development research* (Vol. 5). Chicago: University of Chicago Press.

SHANTZ, C. U. (1983). Social cognition. In J. H. Flavell & E. M. Markman (Eds.), P. H. Mussen (Series Ed.), *Handbook of child psychology: Vol. 3. Cognitive development*. New York: John Wiley.

SHATZ, M. (1983). Communication. In J. H. Flavell & E. M. Markman (Eds.), P. H. Mussen (Series Ed.), *Handbook of child psychology: Vol. 3. Cognitive development*. New York: John Wiley.

SHATZ, M., & GELMAN, R. (1973). The development of communication skills: Modifications in the speech of young children as a function of listener. *Monographs of the Society for Research in Child Development, 38*, (5, Serial No. 152).

SHATZ, M., WELLMAN, H. M., & SILBER, S. (1983). The acquisition of mental verbs: A systematic investigation of the first reference to mental state. *Cognition, 14*, 301–321.

SHIMOJO, S., BAUER, J., JR., O'CONNELL, K. M., & HELD, R. (1986). Pre-stereoptic binocular vision in infants. *Vision Research, 26*, 501–510.

SHULTZ, T. R. (1980). Development of the concept of intention. In W. A. Collins (Ed.), *Minnesota symposia on child psychology: Vol. 13. Development of cognition, affect, and social relations*. Hillsdale, NJ: Erlbaum.

SHULTZ, T. R. (1982). Causal reasoning in the social and nonsocial realms. *Canadian Journal of Behaviorial Sciences, 14*, 307–322.

SHULTZ, T. R. (1991). Modelling embedded intention. In D. Frye & C. Moore (Eds.), *Children's theories of mind*. Hillsdale, NJ: Erlbaum.

SHULTZ, T. R., FISHER, G. W., PRATT, C. C, & RULF, S. (1986). Selection of causal rules. *Child Development, 57*, 143–152.

SHULTZ, T. R., & WELLS, D. (1985). Judging the intentionality of action-outcomes. *Developmental Psychology, 21*, 83–89.

SHWEDER, R. A. (1980). Scientific thought and social cognition. In W. A. Collins (Ed.),

Minnesota symposia on child psychology (Vol. 15). Hillsdale, NJ: Erlbaum.

SHWEDER, R. A., MAHAPAHTRA, M., & MILLER, J. G. (1987). Cultural and moral development in India and the United States. In J. Kagan & S. Lamb (Eds.), *The emergence of morality in young children*. Chicago: University of Chicago Press.

SIEGAL, M., & BEATTIE, K. (1991). Where to look first for children's knowledge of false beliefs? *Cognition, 38*, 1–12.

SIEGLER, R. S. (1976). Three aspects of cognitive development. *Cognitive Psychology, 8*, 481–520.

SIEGLER, R. S. (1978). The origins of scientific reasoning. In R. S. Siegler (Ed.), *Children's thinking: What develops?* Hillsdale, NJ: Erlbaum.

SIEGLER, R. S. (1981). Developmental sequences within and between concepts. *Monographs of the Society for Research in Child Development, 46* (2, Serial No. 189).

SIEGLER, R. S. (1983a). Five generalizations about cognitive development. *American Psychologist, 38*, 263–277.

SIEGLER, R. S. (1983b). Information processing approaches to cognitive development. In W. Kessen (Ed.), P. H. Mussen (Series Ed.), *Handbook of child psychology: Vol. 1. History, theory, and methods*. New York: John Wiley.

SIEGLER, R. S. (1988). Individual differences in strategy choices: Good students, not-so-good students, and perfectionists. *Child Development, 59*, 833–851.

SIEGLER, R. S. (1989a). Commentary. *Human Development, 32*, 104–109.

SIEGLER, R. S. (1989b). How domain-general and domain-specific knowledge interact to produce strategy choices. *Merrill-Palmer Quarterly, 35*, 1–26.

SIEGLER, R. S. (1989c). Mechanisms of cognitive development. In M. R. Rosenzweig & L. W. Porter (Eds.), *Annual review of psychology* (Vol. 40). Palo Alto, CA: Annual Reviews, Inc.

SIEGLER, R. S. (1991a). *Children's thinking* (2nd ed.). Englewood Cliffs, NJ: Prentice-Hall.

SIEGLER, R. S. (1991b). In young children's counting, procedures precede principles. *Educational Psychology Review, 3*, 127–135.

SIEGLER, R. S., & CAMPBELL, J. I. D. (1989). Diagnosing individual differences in strategy choice procedures. In N. Fredriksen (Ed.), *Diagnostic monitoring of skill and knowledge acquisition*. Hillsdale, NJ: Erlbaum.

SIEGLER, R. S., & CROWLEY, K. (1991). The microgenetic method: A direct means for studying cognitive development. *American Psychologist, 46*, 606–620.

SIEGLER, R. S., & JENKINS, E. (1989). *How children discover new strategies.* Hillsdale, NJ: Erlbaum.

SIEGLER, R. S., & SHIPLEY, C. (in press). A new model of strategy choice. In G. Halford & P. Simon (Eds.), *Developing cognitive competence: New approaches to process modeling.* Hillsdale, NJ: Erlbaum.

SIGNORELLA, M. L., & LIBEN, L. S. (1984). Recall and reconstruction of gender-related pictures: Effects of attitude, task difficulty, and age. *Child Development, 55,* 393–405.

SIMMONS, W. (1985). A cultural practice theory in domestic sub-cultural research. In S. Chipman, J. Segal, & R. Glaser (Eds.), *Thinking and learning skills* (Vol. 2). Hillsdale, NJ: Erlbaum.

SKEEN, J. A., & ROGOFF, B. (1987). Children's difficulties in deliberate memory for spatial relationships: Misapplications of verbal menmonic strategies? *Cognitive Development, 2,* 1–19.

SKINNER, E. A. (1990). Age differences in the dimensions of perceived control during middle childhood: Implications for developmental conceptualizations and research. *Child Development, 61,* 1882–1890.

SKINNER, E. A. (1991). Development and perceived control: A dynamic model of action in context. In M. R. Gunnar & L. A. Sroufe (Eds.), *Minnesota symposia on child psychology: Vol. 23. Self processes and development.* Hillsdale, NJ: Erlbaum.

SKOWRONSKI, J. J., & CARLSTON, P. E. (1989). Negativity and extremity biases in impression formation: A review of explanations. *Psychological Bulletin, 105,* 131–142.

SLATER, A. (1991). *Visual perception in the newborn baby.* Paper presented at the meeting of the Society for Research in Child Development, Seattle, WA.

SLATER, A., MATTOCK, A., & BROWN, E. (1990). Size constancy at birth: Newborn infants' responses to retinal and real size. *Journal of Experimental Child Psychology, 49,* 314–322.

SLATER, A., MORISON, V., SOMERS, M., MATTOCK, A., BROWN, B., & TAYLOR, D. (1990). Newborn and older infants' perception of partly occluded objects. *Infant Behavior and Development, 13,* 33–49.

SLATER, A., ROSE, D., & MORISON, V. (1984). Newborn infants' perception of similarities and differences between two- and three-dimensional stimuli. *British Journal of Developmental Psychology, 2,* 287–294.

SLOBIN, D. I. (1970). Universals of grammatical development in children. In G. B. Flores d'Arcais & W. J. M. Levelt (Eds.), *Advances in psycholinguistics.* Amsterdam: North-Holland.

SLOBIN, D. I. (Ed.). (1985). *The crosslinguistic study of language acquisition: Vol. 2. Theoretical issues.* Hillsdale, NJ: Erlbaum.

SMEDSLUND, J. (1969). Psychological diagnostics. *Psychological Bulletin, 71,* 237–248.

SMILEY, P., & HUTTENLOCHER, J. (1989). Young children's acquisition of emotion concepts. In C. Saarni & P. L. Harris (Eds.), *Children's understanding of emotion.* Cambridge: Cambridge University Press.

SMITH, C. L. (1979). Children's understanding of natural language hierarchies. *Journal of Experimental Child Psychology, 27,* 437–458.

SMITH, L. (1991). Age, ability, and intellectual development. In M. Chandler & M. Chapman (Eds.), *Criteria for competence: Controversies in the conceptualization and assessment of children's abilities.* Hillsdale, NJ: Erlbaum.

SMITH, L. K. (1989, March). *The influence of education on memory development.* Paper presented at the meeting of the American Educational Research Association, San Francisco.

SMITH, M. C. (1978). Cognizing the behavior stream. *Child Development, 48,* 736–743.

SMITH, M. D. (1988). The meaning of reference in emergent lexicons. In M. D. Smith & J. L. Locke (Eds.), *The emergent lexicon: The child's development of a linguistic vocabulary.* San Diego: Academic Press.

SNOW, C. E., & FERGUSON, C. A. (Eds.). (1977). *Talking to children: Language input and acquisition.* Cambridge: Cambridge University Press.

SODIAN, B. (1988). Children's attributions of knowledge to the listener in a referential communication task. *Child Development, 59,* 378–385.

SODIAN, B. (1990). Understanding verbal communication: Children's ability to deliberately manipulate ambiguity in referential messages. *Cognitive Development, 5,* 209–222.

SODIAN, B., TAYLOR, C., HARRIS, P. L., & PERNER, J. (1991). Early deception and the child's theory of mind: False trails and genuine markers. *Child Development, 62,* 753–766.

SODIAN, B., ZAITCHIK, D., & CAREY, S. (1991). Young children's differentiation of hypothetical beliefs from evidence. *Child Development, 62,* 753–766.

SOMERVILLE, S. C., & HAAKE, R. J. (1985). The logical search skills of infants and young children. In H. M. Wellman (Ed.), *Children's searching.* Hillsdale, NJ: Erlbaum.

SOPHIAN, C. (1988a). Early developments in children's understanding of number: Inferences about numerosity and one-to-one correspondence. *Child Development, 59,* 1397–1414.

SOPHIAN, C. (1988b). Limitations on preschool children's knowledge about counting: Using counting to compare two sets. *Child Development, 24,* 634–640.

SOPHIAN, C., & SOMERVILLE, S. C. (1988). Early developments in logical reasoning: Considering alternative possibilities. *Cognitive Development, 3,* 183–222.

SPEER, J. R., & FLAVELL, J. H. (1979). Young children's knowledge of the relative difficulty of recognition and recall memory tasks. *Developmental Psychology, 15,* 214–217.

SPELKE, E. S. (1976). Infants' intermodal perception of events. *Cognitive Psychology, 8,* 533–560.

SPELKE, E. S. (1979). Perceiving bimodally specified events in infancy. *Developmental Psychology, 15,* 626–636.

SPELKE, E. S. (1982). Perceptual knowledge of objects in infancy. In J. Mehler, E. C. F. Walker, & M. Garrett (Eds.), *Perspectives on mental representation.* Hillsdale, NJ: Erlbaum.

SPELKE, E. S. (1985). Perception of unity, persistence, and identity: Thoughts on infants' conceptions of objects. In J. Mehler & R. Fox (Eds.), *Neonate cognition.* Hillsdale, NJ: Erlbaum.

SPELKE, E. S. (1987). The development of intermodal perception. In P. Salapatek & L. Cohen (Eds.), *Handbook of infant perception: Vol. 2. From perception to cognition.* Orlando, FL: Academic Press.

SPELKE, E. S. (1988a). The origins of physical knowledge. In L. Weiskrantz (Ed.), *Thought without language.* Oxford: Clarendon Press.

SPELKE, E. S. (1988b). Where perceiving ends and thinking begins: The apprehension of objects in infancy. In A. Yonas (Ed.), *Minnesota symposia on child psychology: Vol. 20. Perceptual development in infancy.* Hillsdale, NJ: Erlbaum.

SPELKE, E. S. (1990). Principles of object perception. *Cognitive Science, 14,* 29–56.

SPELKE, E. S. (1991). Physical knowledge in infancy: Reflections on Piaget's theory. In S. Carey & R. Gelman (Eds.), *The epigenesis of mind: Essays in biology and cognition.* Hillsdale, NJ: Erlbaum.

SPELKE, E. S., BORN, W. S., & CHU, F. (1983). Perception of moving, sounding objects in infancy. *Perception, 12,* 719–732.

SPELKE, E. S., BREINLINGER, K., MACOMBER, J., TURNER, A. S., & KELLER, M. (1990). *Infant conceptions of object motion.* Manuscript submitted for publication.

SPELKE, E. S., & CORTELYOU, A. (1981). Perceptual aspects of social learning: Looking and listening in infancy. In M. E. Lamb & L. R. Sherrod (Eds.), *Infant social cognition: Empirical and theoretical considerations.* Hillsdale, NJ: Erlbaum.

SPELKE, E. S., HOFSTEN, C. VON, & KESTENBAUM, R. (1989). Object perception in infancy: Interaction of spatial and kinetic information for object boundaries. *Developmental Psychology, 25,* 185–196.

SPELKE, E. S., & OWSLEY, C. J. (1979). Intermodal exploration and knowledge in infancy. *Infant Behavior and Development, 2,* 13–24.

SPRINGER, K., & KEIL, F. C. (1989). On the development of biologically specific beliefs: The case of inheritance. *Child Development, 60,* 637–648.

SPRINGER, K., & KEIL, F. C. (1991). Early differentiation of causal mechanisms appropriate to biological and nonbiological kinds. *Child Development, 62,* 767–781.

STARKEY, P., SPELKE, E. S., & GELMAN, R. (1980, April). *Number competence in infants: Sensitivity to numeric invariance and numeric change.* Paper presented at the meeting of the International Conference on Infant Studies, New Haven, CT.

STARKEY, P., SPELKE, E. S., & GELMAN, R. (1983). Detection of intermodal numerical correspondence by human infants. *Science, 222,* 179–181.

STARKEY, P., SPELKE, E. S., & GELMAN, R. (1990). Numerical abstraction by human infants. *Cognition, 36,* 97–127.

STEIN, N. L., & JEWETT, J. (1987). A conceptual analysis of the meaning of basic negative emotions: Implications for a theory of development. In C. Izard & P. Read (Eds.), *Measurement of emotion in infants and children* (Vol. 2). New York: Cambridge University Press.

STEIN, N. L., & LEVINE, L. J. (1989). The causal organization of emotional knowledge: A developmental study. *Cognition and Emotion, 3,* 343–378.

STEIN, N. L., & TRABASSO, T. (1989). Children's understanding of changing emotional states. In C. Saarni & P. L. Harris (Eds.), *Children's understanding of emotion.* Cambridge: Cambridge University Press.

STERN, D. (1985). *The interpersonal world of the infant.* New York: Basic Books.

STERNBERG, R. J. (Ed.). (1984). *Mechanisms of cognitive development.* New York: W. H. Freeman.

STERNBERG, R. J. (1985). *Beyond IQ: A triarchic theory of human intelligence.* Cambridge: Cambridge University Press.

STERNBERG, R. J. (1989a). Domain-generality versus domain-specificity: The life and impending death of a false dichotomy. *Merrill-Palmer Quarterly, 35,* 115–130.

STERNBERG, R. J. (1989b). Intellectual development: Psychometric and information-processing approaches. In M. H. Bornstein &

M. E. Lamb (Eds.), *Developmental psychology: An advanced text* (2nd ed.). Hillsdale, NJ: Erlbaum.

STERNBERG, R. J., & NIGRO, G. (1980). Developmental patterns in the solution of verbal analogies. *Child Development, 51,* 27–38.

STERNBERG, R. J., & POWELL, J. S. (1983). The development of intelligence. In J. H. Flavell & E. M. Markman (Eds.), P. H. Mussen (Series Ed.), *Handbook of child psychology: Vol. 3. Cognitive development.* New York: John Wiley.

STEVENSON, H., LEE, S., & STIGLER, J. (1986). Achievement in mathematics. In H. Stevenson, H. Azuma, & K. Hakuta (Eds.), *Child development and education in Japan.* New York: W. H. Freeman.

STEVENSON, R. (1988). *Models of language development.* Philadelphia: Open University Press.

STIPEK, D. J., & DANIELS, D. H. (1990). Children's use of dispositional attributions in predicting the performance and behavior of classmates. *Journal of Applied Developmental Psychology, 11,* 13–18.

STIPEK, D. J., & MACIVER, D. (1989). Developmental change in children's assessment of intellectual competence. *Child Development, 60,* 521–538.

STRAUSS, M. S., & CURTIS, L. E. (1981). Infant perception of numerosity. *Child Development, 52,* 1146–1152.

STRAUSS, S., & LEVIN, I. (1981). Commentary on Siegler's "Developmental sequences within and between concepts." *Monographs of the Society for Research in Child Development, 46,* (2, Serial No. 189).

STRERI, A., & SPELKE, E. S. (1988). Haptic perception of objects in infancy. *Cognitive Psychology, 20,* 1–23.

STRERI, A., & SPELKE, E. S. (1989). Effects of motion and figural goodness on haptic object perception in infancy. *Child Development, 60,* 1111–1125.

SVEJDA, M., & SCHMID, D. (1979, March). *The role of self-produced locomotion on the onset of fear of heights on the visual cliff.* Paper presented at the meeting of the Society for Research in Child Development, San Francisco.

TAGER-FLUSBERG, H. (1989). Putting words together: Morphology and syntax in the preschool years. In J. B. Gleason (Ed.), *The development of language* (2nd ed.). Columbus, OH: Chas. E. Merrill.

TAYLOR, D. A., & HARRIS, P. L. (1984). Knowledge of the link between emotion and memory among normal and maladjusted boys. *Developmental Psychology, 19,* 982–988.

TAYLOR, M. (1988). The development of children's ability to distinguish what they know from what they see. *Child Development, 59,* 703–718.

TAYLOR, M., CARTWRIGHT, B. S., & BOWDEN, T. (1991). Perspective taking and theory of mind: Do children predict interpretive diversity as a function of differences in observers' knowledge? *Child Development, 62,* 1334–1351.

TAYLOR, M., & HORT, B. C. (1990). Can children be trained to make the appearance-reality distinction? *Cognitive Development, 5,* 89–99.

TAYLOR, S. E. (1989). *Positive illusions.* New York: Basic Books.

TEES, R. C., & WERKER, J. F. (1984). Perceptual flexibility: Maintenance or recovery of the ability to discriminate non-native speech sounds. *Canadian Journal of Psychology, 34,* 579–590.

TELLER, D. Y., & BORNSTEIN, M. H. (1987). Infant color vision and color perception. In P. Salapatek & L. Cohen (Eds.), *Handbook of infant perception: Vol. 1. From sensation to perception.* Orlando, FL: Academic Press.

TEMPLIN, M. (1957). Certain language skills in children: Their development and interrelationships. *University of Minnesota Institute of Child Welfare Monograph, 26.*

TENNEY, Y. J. (1975). The child's conception of organization and recall. *Journal of Experimental Child Psychology, 19,* 100–114.

THOMPSON, J. R., & CHAPMAN, R. (1977). Who is "Daddy" revisited: The status of two-year-olds' over-extended words in use and comprehension. *Journal of Child Language, 4,* 359–375.

TOMASELLO, M. (1992). The social bases of language acquisition. *Social Development, 1,* 67–87.

TOMASELLO, M., & FARRAR, M. J. (1986). Joint attention and early language. *Child Development, 57,* 1454–1463.

TRABASSO, T. (1975). Representation, memory, and reasoning: How do we make transitive inferences? In A. D. Pick (Ed.), *Minnesota symposia on child psychology* (Vol. 9). Minneapolis: University of Minnesota Press.

TRABASSO, T. (1977). The role of memory as a system in making transitive inferences. In R. V. Kail & J. W. Hagen (Eds.), *Perspectives on the development of memory and cognition.* Hillsdale, NJ: Erlbaum.

TREHUB, S. E. (1976). The discrimination of foreign speech contrasts by infants and adults. *Child Development, 47,* 466–572.

TREHUB, S. E., & SCHNEIDER, B. A. (1983). Recent advances in the behavioral study of infant audition. In S. E. Gerber & G. T. Mencher (Eds.), *Development of auditory behavior.* New York: Grune & Stratton.

TREHUB, S. E., THORPE, L. A., & COHEN, A. J. (1991, April). *Infants' auditory processing of numerical information.* Paper presented at the meeting of the Society for Research in Child Development, Seattle, WA.

TREIBER, F., & WILCOX, S. (1984). Discrimination of number by infants. *Infant Behavior and Development, 7,* 93–100.

TVERSKY, A., & KAHNEMAN, D. (1973). Availability: A heuristic for judging frequency and probability. *Cognitive Psychology, 5,* 207–232.

TVERSKY, B. (1985). Development of taxonomic organization of named and pictured categories. *Developmental Psychology, 21,* 1111–1119.

UNGERER, J. A., ZELAZO, P. R., KEARSLEY, R. B., & O'LEARY, K. (1981). Developmental changes in the representation of objects in symbolic play from 18 to 34 months of age. *Child Development, 52,* 186–195.

UZGIRIS, I. C., & HUNT, J. McV. (1975). *Assessment in infancy: Ordinal scales of psychological development.* Champaign: University of Illinois Press.

UZGIRIS, I. C., & HUNT, J. McV. (1987). *Infant performance and experience: New findings with the ordinal scales.* Champaign: University of Illinois Press.

VAN LOOSBROEK, E., & SMITSMAN, A. W. (1990). Visual perception of numerosity in infancy. *Developmental Psychology, 26,* 916–922.

VASTA, R. (Ed.). (1989). *Annals of child development: Vol. 6. Six theories of child development: Revised formulations and current issues.* Greenwich, CT: JAI Press.

VERDONIK, F. (1988). Reconsidering the context of rememberings: The need for a social description of memory processes and their development. In F. E. Weinert & M. Perlmutter (Eds.), *Memory development: Universal changes and individual differences.* Hillsdale, NJ: Erlbaum.

VIHMAN, M. M., & MILLER, R. (1988). Words and babble at the threshold of language acquisition. In M. D. Smith & J. L. Locke (Eds.), *The emergent lexicon: The child's development of a linguistic vocabulary.* San Diego: Academic Press.

VURPILLOT, E. (1968). The development of scanning strategies and their relation to visual differentiation. *Journal of Experimental Child Psychology, 6,* 632–650.

VYGOTSKY, L. (1978). *Mind in society.* Cambridge, MA: Harvard University Press.

WAGNER, D. A. (1978). Memories of Morocco: The influence of age, schooling, and environment on memory. *Cognitive Psychology, 10,* 1–28.

WAGNER, D. A. (1981). Culture and memory development. In H. C. Triandis & A. Heron (Eds.), *Handbook of cross-cultural psychology: Developmental psychology* (Vol. 4). Boston: Allyn & Bacon.

WALKER, A. S. (1982). Intermodal perception of expressive behaviors by human infants. *Journal of Experimental Child Psychology, 33,* 514–535.

WALKER, L. J. (1988). Development of moral reasoning. In R. Vasta (Ed.), *Annals of child development* (Vol. 5). Greenwich, CT: JAI Press.

WALKER-ANDREWS, A. S., BAHRICK, L. E., RAGLIONI, S. S., & DIAZ, I. (1991). Infants' bimodal perception of gender. *Ecological Psychology, 3,* 55–75.

WALLACE, I., KLAHR, D., & BLUFF, K. (1987). A self-modifying production system model of cognitive development. In D. Klahr, P. Langley, & R. Neches (Eds.), *Production system models of learning and development.* Cambridge, MA: MIT Press.

WANNER, E., & GLEITMAN, L. R. (Eds.). (1982). *Language acquisition: The state of the art.* Cambridge: Cambridge University Press.

WARREN-LEUBECKER, A., & BOHANNON, J. N. (1983). The effects of verbal feedback and listener type on the speech of preschool children. *Journal of Experimental Child Psychology, 35,* 540–548.

WARREN-LEUBECKER, A., & BOHANNON, J. N. (1989). Pragmatics: Language in social contexts. In J. B. Gleason (Ed.), *The development of language* (2nd ed.). Columbus, OH: Chas. E. Merrill.

WATSON, M. W., & FISCHER, K. W. (1977). A developmental sequence of agent use in late infancy. *Child Development, 48,* 828–836.

WAXMAN, S. R. (1989). Linking language and conceptual development: Linguistic cues and the construction of conceptual hierarchies. *Genetic Epistemology, 17,* 13–20.

WAXMAN, S. R. (1990). Linguistic biases and the establishment of conceptual hierarchies: Evidence from preschool children. *Cognitive Development, 5,* 123–150.

WEINERT, F. E., & KLUWE, R. H. (Eds.). (1987). *Metacognition, motivation, and understanding.* Hillsdale, NJ: Erlbaum.

WEINERT, F. E., & PERLMUTTER, M. (1989). *Memory development: Universal changes and individual differences.* Hillsdale, NJ: Erlbaum.

WEINERT, F. E., SCHNEIDER, W., & KNOPF, M. (1988). Individual differences in memory development across the life-span. In P. B. Baltes, D. L. Featherman, & R. M. Lerner (Eds.), *Life-span development and behavior* (Vol. 9). Hillsdale, NJ: Erlbaum.

WEISS, M. G., & MILLER, P. H. (1983). Young children's understanding of displaced aggression. *Journal of Experimental Child Psychology, 35,* 529–539.

WELLMAN, H. M. (1977). Preschoolers' understanding of memory-relevant variables: A developmental study of metamemory. *Developmental Psychology, 14,* 24–29.

WELLMAN, H. M. (1979). *A child's theory of mind.* Unpublished manuscript, University of Michigan.

WELLMAN, H. M. (1982). The study of preschoolers' cognition. *Newsletter of the American Psychological Association Division on Developmental Psychology.* Spring issue, 13–19.

WELLMAN, H. M. (1983). Metamemory revisited. In M. T. H. Chi (Ed.), *Trends in memory development research.* Basel: Karger.

WELLMAN, H. M. (1985a). *Children's searching.* Hillsdale, NJ: Erlbaum.

WELLMAN, H. M. (1985b). The origins of metacognition. In D. Forrest, G. MacKinnon, & T. Walker (Eds.), *Metacognition, cognition, and human performance.* New York: Academic Press.

WELLMAN, H. M. (1988). First steps in the child's theorizing about the mind. In J. W. Astington, P. L. Harris, & D. R. Olson (Eds.), *Developing theories of mind.* Cambridge: Cambridge University Press.

WELLMAN, H. M. (1989). The early development of memory strategies. In F. W. Weinert & M. Perlmutter (Eds.), *Memory development: Universal changes and individual differences.* Hillsdale, NJ: Erlbaum.

WELLMAN, H. M. (1990). *The child's theory of mind.* Cambridge, MA: Bradford Books/MIT Press.

WELLMAN, H. M. (in press). Early understanding of mind: The normal case. In S. Baron-Cohen, H. Tager-Flusberg, & D. Cohen (Eds.), *Understanding other minds: Perspectives from autism.* Oxford: Oxford University Press.

WELLMAN, H. M., & BARTSCH, K. (1988). Young children's reasoning about beliefs. *Cognition, 30,* 239–277.

WELLMAN, H. M., CROSS, D., & BARTSCH, K. (1986). Infant search and object permanence: A meta-analysis of the A-not-B error. *Monographs of the Society for Research in Child Development, 51* (3, Serial No. 214).

WELLMAN, H. M., & ESTES, D. (1986). Early understanding of mental entities: A reexamination of childhood realism. *Child Development, 57,* 910–923.

WELLMAN, H. M., & GELMAN, S. A. (1988). Children's understanding of the nonobvious. In R. J. Sternberg (Ed.), *Advances in the psy-chology of human intelligence* (Vol. 4). Hillsdale, NJ: Erlbaum.

WELLMAN, H. M., & GELMAN, S. A. (1992). Cognitive development: Foundational theories of core domains. In M. R. Rosenzweig & L. W. Porter (Eds.), *Annual review of psychology* (Vol. 43). Palo Alto, CA: Annual Reviews, Inc.

WELLMAN, H. M., & LEMPERS, J. D. (1977). The naturalistic communication abilities of two-year-olds. *Child Development, 48,* 1052–1057.

WELLMAN, H. M., & WOOLLEY, J. D. (1990). From simple desires to ordinary beliefs: The early development of everyday psychology. *Cognition, 35,* 245–275.

WERKER, J. F. (1989). Becoming a native listener. *American Scientist, 77,* 54–59.

WERKER, J. F., & MCLEOD, P. J. (1989). Infant preference for both male and female infant-directed talk: A developmental study of attentional and affective responsiveness. *Canadian Journal of Psychology, 43,* 230–246.

WERKER, J. F., & PEGG, J. E. (in press). Infant speech perception and phonological acquisition. In C. Ferguson, L. Mann, & C. Stoel-Gammon (Eds.), *Phonological development: Models, research, and implications.* Parkton, MD: York Press.

WERKER, J. F., & TEES, R. C. (1983). Developmental changes across childhood in the perception of non-native speech sounds. *Canadian Journal of Psychology, 37,* 278–286.

WERNER, H., & KAPLAN, B. (1963). *Symbol formation: An organismic developmental approach to language and the expression of thought.* New York: John Wiley.

WERTHEIMER, M. (1961). Psychomotor coordination of auditory-visual space at birth. *Science, 134,* 1692.

WERTSCH, J. V. (1991). *Voices of the mind: A sociocultural approach to mediated action.* Cambridge, MA: Harvard University Press.

WETHERBY, A. M., & PRIZANT, B. M. (1989). The expression of communicative intent: Assessment guidelines. *Seminars in Speech and Language, 10,* 77–91.

WEXLER, K. (1982). A principle theory for language acquisition. In E. Wanner & L. R. Gleitman (Eds.), *Language acquisition: The state of the art.* Cambridge: Cambridge University Press.

WEXLER, K., & CULICOVER, P. (1980). *Formal principles of language acquisition.* Cambridge, MA: MIT Press.

WEXLER, K., & MANZINI, M. R. (1987). Parameters and learnability in binding theory. In T. Roeper & E. Williams (Eds.), *Parameter setting.* Dordrecht, Netherlands: D. Reidel.

WHITE, P. A. (1988). Causal processing: Origins and development. *Psychological Bulletin, 104*, 36–52.

WHITEMAN, M. (1967). Children's conceptions of psychological causality. *Child Development, 38*, 143–156.

WILKENING, F., & ANDERSON, N. H. (1982). Comparisons of two rule assessment methodologies for studying cognitive development and knowledge structure. *Psychological Bulletin, 92*, 215–237.

WILLATTS, P. (1989). Development of problem-solving in infancy. In A. Slater & G. Bremner (Eds.), *Infant development*. Hillsdale, NJ: Erlbaum.

WILLATTS, P. (in press). *Cognitive development in infancy*. Oxford: Basil Blackwell.

WILLIAMS, M. D., & HOLLAN, J. D. (1981). The process of retrieval from very long-term memory. *Cognitive Science, 5*, 87–119.

WIMMER, H., HOGREFE, A., & PERNER, J. (1988). Children's understanding of informational access as source of knowledge. *Child Development, 59*, 386–396.

WIMMER, H., & PERNER, J. (1983). Beliefs about beliefs: Representation and constraining function of wrong beliefs in young children's understanding of deception. *Cognition, 13*, 103–128.

WINER, G. A. (1980). Class-inclusion reasoning in children: A review of the empirical literature. *Child Development, 51*, 309–328.

WINER, G. A., & COTTRELL, J. E. (1991, August). *Developmental changes in understanding perception*. Paper presented at the meeting of the American Psychological Association, San Francisco.

WINER, G. A., HEMPHILL, J., & CRAIG, R. K. (1988). The effect of misleading questions in promoting nonconservation responses in children and adults. *Developmental Psychology, 24*, 197–202.

WOHLWILL, J. F. (1973). *The study of behavioral development*. New York: Academic Press.

WOLF, D. (1982). Understanding others: A longitudinal case study of the concept of independent agency. In G. E. Forman (Ed.), *Action and thought*, New York: Academic Press.

WOOD, D. (1980). Teaching the young child: Some relationships between social interaction, language, and thought. In D. Olson (Ed.), *The social foundations of language and thought*. New York: W. W. Norton.

WOODWARD, A. L., & MARKMAN, E. M. (1991). Constraints on learning as default assumptions: Comments on Merriman and Bowman's "The mutual exclusivity bias in children's word learning." *Developmental Review, 11*, 137–163.

WOODY-RAMSEY, J. (1989, April). *Children's production and utilization of a selective attention strategy: Effects of memory capacity*. Paper presented at the meeting of the Society for Research in Child Development, Kansas City, MO.

WOODY-RAMSEY, J., & MILLER, P. H. (1988). The facilitation of selective attention in preschoolers. *Child Development, 59*, 1497–1503.

WOOLLEY, J. D. (1991, April). *Origin and truth: Young children's understanding of the relation between mental states and the physical world*. Paper presented at the meeting of the Society for Research in Child Development, Seattle, WA.

WOOLLEY, J. D., & WELLMAN, H. M. (1990). Young children's understanding of realities, nonrealities, and appearances. *Child Development, 61*, 946–961.

WORDEN, P. E., & SLADEWSKI-AWIG, L. J. (1982). Children's awareness of memorability. *Journal of Educational Psychology, 74*, 341–350.

WYNN, K. (1990). Children's understanding of counting. *Cognition, 36*, 155–193.

YANIV, I., & SHATZ, M. (1990). Heuristics of reasoning and analogy in children's visual perspective taking. *Child Development, 61*, 1491–1501.

YARROW, L. J., & PEDERSON, F. A. (1972). Attachment: Its origins and course. In W. W. Hartup (Ed.), *The young child: Reviews of research* (Vol. 2). Washington, DC: National Association for the Education of Young Children.

YONAS, A. (1981). Infants' responses to optical information for collision. In R. N. Aslin, J. R. Alberts, & M. R. Peterson (Eds.), *Development of perception: Psychobiological perspectives: Vol. 2. The visual system*. New York: Academic Press.

YONAS, A. (Ed.). (1988). *Minnesota symposia on child psychology: Vol. 20. Perceptual development in infancy*. Hillsdale, NJ: Erlbaum.

YONAS, A., & GRANRUD, C. E. (1985). Development of visual space perception in young infants. In J. Mehler & R. Fox (Eds.), *Neonate cognition*. Hillsdale, NJ: Erlbaum.

YONAS, A., & OWSLEY, C. (1987). Development of visual space perception. In P. Salapatek & L. Cohen (Eds.), *Handbook of infant perception: Vol. 2. From perception to cognition*. Orlando, FL: Academic Press.

YOUNGER, B. (1990). Infants' detection of correlations among feature categories. *Child Development, 61*, 614–620.

YUILL, N. (in press). Children's conception of personality traits: A critical review and analysis. *Human Development*.

YUSSEN, S. R. (Ed.). (1985). *The growth of reflection*. New York: Academic Press.

YUSSEN, S. R., & BIRD, J. E. (1979). The development of metacognitive awareness in memory, communication, and attention. *Journal of Experimental Child Psychology, 28*, 300–313.

ZAITCHIK, D. (1990). When representations conflict with reality: The preschooler's problem with false beliefs and "false" photographs. *Cognition, 35*, 41–68.

ZAITCHIK, D. (1991). Is only seeing really believing?: Sources of the true belief in the false belief task. *Cognitive Development, 6*, 91–103.

ZARAGOZA, M. S. (1987). Memory, suggestibility, and eyewitness testimony in children and adults. In S. J. Ceci, M. P. Toglia, & D. F. Ross (Eds.), *Children's eyewitness memory*. New York: Springer-Verlag.

ZARAGOZA, M. S., & WILSON, M. (1989, April). Suggestibility in the child witness. In G. S. Goodman (Chair), *Do children provide accurate eyewitness reports?: Research and social policy implications*. Symposium conducted at the meeting of the Society for Research in Child Development, Kansas City, MO.

ZELAZO, P. D., & SHULTZ, T. R. (1989). Concepts of potency and resistance in causal prediction. *Child Development, 60*, 1307–1315.

ZIMMERMAN, B. J., & BLOM, D. E. (1983). Toward an empirical test of cognitive conflict in learning. *Developmental Review, 3*, 18–38.

ZUKOW, P. G., REILLY, J., & GREENFIELD, P. M. (1982). Making the absent present: Facilitating the transition from sensorimotor to linguistic communications. In K. E. Nelson (Ed.), *Children's language* (Vol. 3). Hillsdale, NJ: Erlbaum.

Name Index

Somerville, S. C., 246, 247, 260
Sophian, C., 119, 246
Sorce, J. F., 185
Speer, J. R., 246, 297, 298, 299, 300
Spelke, E. S., 17, 24, 32–35, 40–42, 43, 62, 65, 67, 70, 71, 72, 97, 100, 122–123, 160, 179, 305, 341
Spence, M. J., 277
Sperduto, V., 27
Spiker, K., 231
Springer, K., 96
Sroufe, L. A., 204
Stangor, C., 204, 205
Stanowicz, L., 308
Starkey, P., 122–123
Stein, N. L., 190, 193, 288
Stenberg, C. R., 188
Stephens, B. R., 36
Stern, D., 187
Sternberg, R. J., 8, 9, 10, 146, 150, 331, 336, 343
Stevenson, H. W., 16
Stevenson, R., 315
Stewart, C., 158
Stigler, J., 16, 126
Stipek, D. J., 206, 212, 213
Strathern, A. J., 250
Strauss, M. S., 36, 79, 123
Strauss, S., 168
Streri, A., 43
Sugiyama, K., 96
Sullivan, M. W., 205, 232
Supalla, T., 313
Svejda, M., 38, 185
Szeminska, A., 117

Tager-Flusberg, H., 290, 292, 293
Tarkin, B., 251
Taylor, C., 108
Taylor, D., 35
Taylor, D. A., 192
Taylor, M., 110, 112, 299
Taylor, S. E., 206

Teasley, S. D., 15
Tees, R. C., 280
Teller, D. Y., 29, 30
Templin, M., 294
Tenney, Y. J., 257
Termine, N., 33
Tesla, C., 115
Thal, D. J., 85
Thomas, J. R., 144
Thompson, J. R., 287
Thorpe, L. A., 123
Tingle, B. A., 193
Todd, C. M., 236–237
Toglia, M. P., 268, 269
Tomasello, M., 302, 308
Tootell, H. E., 36
Trabasso, T., 193, 325–326, 328, 347
Trehub, S. E., 27, 123, 280
Treiber, F., 123
Tulving, E., 64
Turner, A. S., 62
Turner, L. A., 150, 259, 266
Turpin, R., 27
Tversky, A., 181
Tversky, B., 89

Ulrich, T., 242
Ungerer, J. A., 83
Uzgiris, I. C., 59, 68

Van Den Bos, K. P., 328
van Loosbroek, E., 123
Vasta, R., 3
Vaughn, B. E., 197
Vaughn, L. S., 36
Verdonik, F., 259
Vigorito, J., 279
Vihman, M. M., 282
Vogel, K., 267
Vurpillot, E., 156
Vygotsky, L., 15, 16, 21, 82, 124–125, 132, 342

Wachtel, G. F., 303
Wagner, D. A., 241, 266

Wahl, K. E., 109
Walden, T. A., 296
Wales, R. J., 295
Walk, R. D., 38
Walker, A. S., 35, 41, 42, 43
Walker, L. J., 223
Walker-Andrews, A. S., 41
Wallace, C. S., 339
Wallace, J. G., 9
Waller, T. G., 150, 155, 255
Wanner, E., 288, 305
Wapner, S., 202
Warren, S. F., 44
Warren-Leubecker, A., 295, 296, 305, 307, 311
Waters, E., 189
Watson, M. W., 13, 83, 105
Waxman, S. R., 302, 303
Weaver, S. L., 256
Weed, K. A., 244
Weinberg, D. H., 137
Weinert, F. E., 150, 230, 250, 255, 261, 267
Weiss, M., 205
Weiss, M. G., 212, 244
Wellman, H. M., 17, 18, 63, 64, 65, 81, 90, 91, 96, 100, 101, 103, 104–105, 107, 112, 114, 116, 124, 150, 157, 160, 181, 190, 235, 236, 245, 246, 255, 256, 257, 260, 296, 298, 327, 329
Wells, D., 209
Wenger, N., 303
Werker, J. F., 277, 280, 282
Werner, H., 83, 132
Wertheimer, M., 28
Wertsch, J. V., 15
Wetherby, A. M., 283
Wetzel, M., 267
Wexler, K., 308, 315
White, P. A., 87
White, S. H., 268
Whiteman, M., 212

Whiten, A., 82, 116
Whitney, P., 269
Whittall, S., 105
Wilcox, S., 123
Wilkening, F., 168
Willatts, P., 63, 67–68, 70
Williams, M. D., 247
Wilson, M., 269
Wimmer, H., 103, 106, 218, 299
Winer, G. A., 94, 156, 160, 164
Wing, C. S., 162
Wishart, J. G., 57
Wohlwill, J. F., 320, 328, 331, 333, 336
Wolf, D., 196
Wood, D., 125
Woodruff, G., 100
Woodsmall, L., 301
Woodward, A. L., 304
Woody-Ramsey, J., 240, 244, 264
Woolley, J. D., 81, 103, 104, 106
Worden, P. E., 257
Wright, J. C., 168
Wright, J. W., 176
Wynn, K., 119

Yamanouchi, I., 27
Yarrow, L. J., 187
Yonas, A., 24, 28, 33, 37, 38
Youngblade, L., 115
Younger, B., 90
Yuill, N., 116, 213
Yussen, S. R., 150, 153, 257

Zaitchik, D., 79, 108, 162
Zalenski, R., 201
Zaragoza, M. S., 269
Zelazo, P. R., 83, 167
Zeman, B. R., 250
Zhang, X-D., 110, 115
Zimmerman, B. J., 346
Zoller, D., 194
Zou, H., 110, 115
Zukow, P. G., 283

Subject Index

About the Authors

John H. Flavell is Professor of Psychology at Stanford University. He received his B.A. from Northeastern University and his M.A. and Ph.D. degrees from Clark University. Before coming to Stanford University he taught at the University of Rochester and the University of Minnesota. He has done research on developmental aspects of memory, communication, social cognition, and other processes. He has written or co-edited six books, including *The Developmental Psychology of Jean Piaget*. He is past president of the Society for Research in Child Development and the Developmental Division (Division 7) of the American Psychological Association. He is the recipient of the American Psychological Association Distinguished Scientific Contribution Award and Honorary Degrees from the University of Paris and the University of Rochester.

Patricia H. Miller is Professor of Psychology at the University of Florida. She received her B.A. from the University of Kansas and her Ph.D. degree from the University of Minnesota. Prior to coming to the University of Florida she taught at the University of Michigan. Her research has involved the development of attention, memory, strategies, metacognition, and social cognition. She is the author of *Theories of Developmental Psychology* and serves on the editorial board of *Child Development* and the board of directors of the Jean Piaget Society.

Scott A. Miller is Professor of Psychology at the University of Florida. He received his B.A. from Stanford University and his Ph.D. degree from the University of Minnesota. Prior to coming to the University of Florida he taught at the University of Michigan. His research has been in the area of cognitive development, focusing on Piaget's work, children's understanding of logical necessity, and parents' beliefs about their children's cognitive abilities. He is the author of *Developmental Research Methods* and the co-author (with Ross Vasta and Marshall Haith) of *Child Psychology: The Modern Science*. He is on the editorial board of *Child Development*.